A COMMENTARY

ON

The Gospel According to Matthew

BY

H. LEO BOLES

IN ONE VOLUME

Gospel Advocate Co.
Nashville, Tenn. 37202
1989

COPYRIGHT BY
GOSPEL ADVOCATE COMPANY
NASHVILLE, TENNESSEE

Complete Set ISBN 0-89225-000-3
This Volume ISBN 0-89225-001-1

PREFACE

No apology is offered for presenting another "Commentary on Matthew." Every effort that helps people to come into a fuller knowledge of the truth of God, enables them to see the Christ more clearly as he is presented in the inspired records, and encourages them to love and serve the Christ more faithfully is to be commended. There are good reasons for believing that this volume will fill an important place in religious literature. Only one commentary on Matthew has been written by those who claim to worship God according to "the ancient order of things" within the last century; this one was written by the scholarly J. W. McGarvey, and published in 1875. In some respects this volume is unique, stands alone.

No effort is made to display any deep piety or rare learning; the book is written in a style that meets the popular demand. Those who may claim a high degree of erudition may read it with profit, yet those who may be among the "common people" who heard Jesus gladly will find that it is easily understood and may be comprehended without any great effort. The Greek words which are used are translated into English and explained so that the full meaning may be gathered without reference to a Greek lexicon. The sentence construction is brief and simple; the English words which are used are found in the everyday vocabulary of the average person. The full meaning of the text is thus expressed so that the divine thought may be easily gathered and appreciated.

The plan of the book is also simple. The American Revised Version is used; all the comments are based upon this text; all quotations are taken from it. The book of Matthew is first outlined and then divided into sections; these sections are subdivided and these divisions numbered; the subdivisions are further broken up into paragraphs so that the thought may be analyzed and easily understood. The chapter divisions of the book of Matthew are disregarded where the continuity of thought or historical narratives are broken by the traditional division of chapters and verses. Traditional comments are omitted, and the obvious meaning of the text is expressed; no speculative ideas of comments are offered. The reader will find that the comments develop and enlarge the thought in the text.

This volume is intended to be a companion to the commentaries on the epistles written by David Lipscomb, with supplementary notes by J. W. Shepherd. Hence, quotations of comments made by David Lipscomb are given from the *Gospel Advocate;* the files of the *Gospel Advocate* have been compiled and read to get the comments made by David Lipscomb on Matthew. These comments are gathered from articles written by him and published in the *Gospel Advocate.* The excerpts from his articles are not placed in quotation marks, but are enclosed in brackets [ ]. These quotations are placed at the close of the paragraph.

Due acknowledgement is here made for the very valuable assistance and encouragement rendered the author by J. W. Shepherd and C. E. W. Dorris.

H. LEO BOLES.

CONTENTS

	Page
Introduction	ix
Outline of the Gospel According to Matthew	xiv
The Title	15

SECTION ONE: Human Ancestry, Birth, Childhood, and Youth of Jesus (1: 1 to 2: 23) 16
1. The Genealogy of Jesus (1: 1-17) 16
2. Mary and Joseph (1: 18-25) 23
3. The Birth of Jesus (2: 1-12) 34
4. The Flight into Egypt (2: 13-15) 50
5. A Massacre of the Innocents (2: 16-18) 55
6. The Return to Nazareth (2: 19-23) 58

SECTION TWO: John the Baptist; Baptism and Temptation of Jesus (3: 1 to 4: 11) 64
1. The Mission and Work of John (3: 1-12) 64
2. The Baptism of Jesus (3: 13-17) 88
3. The Temptation of Jesus (4: 1-11) 95

SECTION THREE: Beginning of Jesus' Galilean Ministry; the Principles of the Kingdom of Heaven (4: 12 to 7: 29) 108
1. Jesus Retires to Galilee (4: 12-17) 108
2. Call of Peter and Andrew, James and John (4: 18-22) 112
3. The Theme of His Preaching: Gospel of the Kingdom (4: 23-25) 116
4. The Beatitudes (5: 1-12) 119
5. The Disciples Compared to Salt and Light (5: 13-16) 127
6. Jesus' Relation to the Law of Moses (5: 17-20) 130
7. Teachings Against Murder (5: 21-26) 134
8. Teachings Against Adultery and Divorce (5: 27-32) 139
9. Teachings Against Oaths and Retaliation (5: 33-42) 144
10. The Principle of Love (5: 43-48) 150

CONTENTS

Page

11. Teachings Against Hypocrisy in Almsgiving, Prayer, and Fasting (6: 1-18) 154

12. Teachings Against Riches and the Care of the Necessities of Life (6: 19-34) 164

13. Teachings Against Judging Others (7: 1-5) 172

14. A Caution; Prayer Encouraged; the Golden Rule; the Two Ways (7: 6-14) 175

15. Solemn Warnings (7: 15-29) 179

SECTION FOUR: The Galilean Ministry (8: 1 to 18: 35) 186

1. Group of Miracles Proving Jesus' Divinity and Illustrating His Teaching (8: 1 to 9: 34) 186

2. The Need of More Laborers (9: 35-38) 217

3. Apostles Chosen; Commissioned; Sent Forth (10: 1-33) 220

4. The Cost of Discipleship; Its Rewards (10: 34-42) 234

5. Messengers from John the Baptist; Jesus' Estimate of John (11: 1-19) 240

6. Certain Cities Condemned; a Prayer of Thanksgiving (11: 20-30) 248

7. Opposition Developed (12: 1-21) 255

8. Disputations with the Pharisees (12: 22-45) 265

9. Spiritual Relationships (12: 46-50) 281

10. Group of Parables (13: 1-52) 284

11. Jesus Rejected at Nazareth (13: 53-58) 305

12. John the Baptist Beheaded (14: 1-12) 308

13. Feeding the Five Thousand and Walking on the Water (14: 13-33) 314

14. Jesus in Gennesaret (14: 34-36) 322

15. Opposition of Scribes and Pharisees (15: 1-20) 323

16. The Canaanitish Woman (15: 21-28) 331

17. The Feeding of Four Thousand (15: 29-39) 335

18. Pharisees and Sadducees Unite Against Jesus (16: 1-12) 337

19. The Confession at Caesarea (16: 13-20) 341

20. The Cross Foretold (16: 21-28) 348

21. The Transfiguration (17: 1-13) 353

CONTENTS vii

Page

22. The Epileptic Cured, Power of Faith, and Temple Tax (17: 14-27) 359
23. Warnings Against Giving Offense (18: 1-14) 366
24. How Offenders Are to Be Treated (18: 15-35) 375

SECTION FIVE: The Perean Ministry (10: 1 to 20: 34) 384

1. From Galilee to Perea; Teachings Concerning Divorce (19: 1-12) 384
2. Jesus and Children; Rich Young Ruler; Perils of Riches; and Rewards of Self-Sacrifice (19: 13-30) 390
3. Laborers in the Vineyard; Foretells Again His Death; Rebukes Selfish Ambition of James and John (20: 1-28) 397
4. Two Blind Men Healed at Jericho (20: 29-34) 406

SECTION SIX: Last Days of Jesus' Public Ministry (21: 1 to 26: 46) 409

1. Triumphal Entry into Jerusalem; Second Cleansing of the Temple (21: 1-17) 409
2. Barren Fig Tree Cursed; His Authority Questioned; Parable of the Two Sons (21: 18-32) 416
3. Parable of the Wicked Husbandmen (21: 33-46) 422
4. Parable of the Marriage Feast; Paying Tribute to Caesar (22: 1-22) 427
5. Sadducees and the Resurrection; Opposition of Pharisees (22: 23-46) 434
6. Scribes and Pharisees Exposed; Seven Woes Pronounced (23: 1-39) 441
7. Destruction of the Temple Foretold; Signs of His Second Coming (24: 1-31) 457
8. Lesson from the Fig Tree; Faithful and Unfaithful Servants (24: 32-51) 471
9. The Ten Virgins; Parable of the Talents; the Judgment (25: 1-46) 476
10. Prediction of His Crucifixion; Feast in Simon's House (26: 1-13) 492
11. Bargain of Judas; the Last Supper (26: 14-25) 497

Page

12. Lord's Supper: Peter's Denial Foretold; Gethsemane (26: 26-46) 503

SECTION SEVEN: Arrest, Trial, Crucifixion, Burial, and Resurrection of Jesus; the Commission (26: 47 to 28: 20) 511

1. Betrayal and Arrest (26: 47-56) 511
2. Trial Before Caiaphas and Sanhedrin (26: 57-68) 515
3. Peter's Three Denials; Jesus Before Pilate; the Death of Judas (26: 69 to 27: 10) 521
4. Jesus Before Pilate (27: 11-26) 529
5. Roman Soldiers Mock Jesus; the Crucifixion (27: 27-44) 536
6. Death and Burial of Jesus (27: 45-61) 543
7. Guard Placed Around the Tomb; Resurrection of Jesus (27: 62 to 28: 10) 549
8. Sanhedrin's Falsehood; the Commission (28: 11-20) 559

BIBLIOGRAPHY 567

INDEX 571

INTRODUCTION

I. THE AUTHOR

Matthew the evangelist and apostle was a Galilean Jew; we know very little of his early life, and nothing about him after Pentecost. He comes into view in the divine history at his call by Jesus to discipleship and apostleship. Before his call, Matthew was employed in collecting toll or custom in Capernaum by the Sea of Galilee. (Matt. 9: 9.) He is the same as "Levi the son of Alphaeus," whom, according to Luke 5: 27, 29 and Mark 2: 14, Jesus called from the receipt of custom. He is usually designated as "Matthew the publican." He was the only one of the group of apostles who had formerly been a publican. The change of name from "Levi" to "Matthew" cannot be termed as significant, since he may have worn both names all his life. However, many think that after his call his name was changed to Matthew, and that Levi was his first and birth name. We know that Simon's name was changed to Peter and Saul's to Paul; so many regard Matthew as his name after conversion. Matthew means "the gift of God"; some think that it means "manly." Levi was a common Jewish name and belonged to the third son of Jacob by Leah. Matthew should no tbe confused with the name "Matthias"; the different formations of the words point to a different derivation.

Matthew resided in Capernaum; this was a very large city on the northwest coast of the Sea of Galilee. The highway or great thoroughfare from Damascus and Babylon which connected the southern part of Palestine passed through Capernaum; Capernaum also had a good harbor for ships. A customhouse for the collection of duties upon the commodities of the traffic which passed over this thoroughfare was located by the Roman government at Capernaum. Matthew was one who was selected as the tax collector. He was a Jew, but he had great influence with the Roman officials; they had confidence in him; he was trustworthy, competent, and efficient. Apparently, he conducted his business, unpopular as it was to his nation, and full of temptations, in an honest, upright manner; for there is no suggestion, as in the case of Zacchaeus, of restoring dishonest gains (Luke 19: 8); yet he seems to have been so successful in business as to amass some degree of wealth; he made a feast or entertainment for Jesus at which several publicans ate with Jesus. (Matt. 9: 10; Luke 5: 29.)

His name is found in all of the lists of the apostles. After the ascension of our Lord, we have no certain data with respect to his work; the New Testament furnishes no details of his activities as an apostle after the day of Pentecost. The last mention that we have of him in the New Testament is found in Acts 1: 13. According to Eusebius (Hist. Eccles. 3: 24), Matthew proclaimed the gospel first to the Hebrews, and then went to other nations, after having "committed his gospel to writing in his native language, the Hebrew." Later historians report that he had gone to Ethiopia and there preached the gospel. (Socrates, Hist. Eccles. 1: 19.) According to the earlier statements of Clement of Alexandria, he died a natural death, but other writers speak of his martyrdom. Isidore of Seville represents him as laboring in Macedonia, Syria, Persia, and other places. There has been no dispute about his writing the book that bears his name. From the very earliest history that we have, the first of the books of the New Testament was written by Matthew.

II. DATE OF WRITING

There is a great difference of opinion among scholars as to the date of the writing of the gospel according to Matthew. It is generally thought that he wrote his record before Mark, Luke, and John wrote their records of the life of Christ; however, some think that the gospel according to Mark was written first; the place assigned to Matthew in the New Testament literature favors the opinion that Matthew wrote first. Irenæus reports that it was written when Peter and Paul were preaching in Rome; however, it is not clear that Peter ever visited Rome. Eusebius states that it was written when Matthew left Palestine to preach in other countries. Clement of Alexandria is responsible for the statement that the elders who succeeded each other from the beginning declared that "the gospels containing the genealogies" (Matthew and Luke) were written first. This position is fatal to the current theory that Matthew and others depended on Mark for information. Some have placed the date as early as A.D. 38; others as late as A.D. 70; many fix the date as A.D. 40. However, it is now too late in the world's history, and we have not sufficient evidence for us to settle questions as obscure and indefinite as this. It is enough for all practical purposes for us to believe that it was written between A.D. 38 and A.D. 70, before the destruction of Jerusalem. Professor Sanday, in his article in the new "Hastings' Dictionary of the Bible," expresses the conviction that continued investigation will confirm the fact that the great mass of the "synoptic gospels" had assumed its permanent shape not later than the decade A.D. 60 to 70.

III. CHARACTER AND PURPOSE

The most ancient and trustworthy authorities state that Matthew wrote his gospel in Hebrew; probably the other books of the New Testament were written in Greek. The testimonies confirming the facts about Matthew begin with Papias of Hierapolis, at the beginning of the second century, who evidently refers to the written gospel by Matthew. His statement was confirmed by almost all the older fathers, such as Irenæus, Origen, Eusebius, Jerome and Epiphanius. In character, Matthew's gospel, like those of the other evangelists, is only a chrestomathy, a selection from the great mass of oral tradition concerning the doings and sayings of Jesus which were current in apostolic and early Christian circles, chosen for the special purpose by the guidance of the Holy Spirit which Matthew had in view. He was guided by the Holy Spirit in compiling and selecting such material as would serve the purpose. There is much in common with Mark and Luke, although not a little of this material is also individualistic in character and of such a nature as to perplex the harmonies, such as Matthew's account of the temptation, of the demoniacs at Gadara, of the blind men at Jericho. (Matt. 4: 1-11; 8: 28-34; 20: 29-34.) There is much in Matthew that is peculiar to that book, such as the following: chapters 1, 2; 9: 27-36; 10: 15, 37-40; 11: 28-30; 12: 11, 12, 15-21, 33-38; 13: 24-30; 36-52; 14: 28-31; 16: 17-19; 17: 24-27; 28: 15-35; 19: 10-12; 20: 1-16; 21: 10-16, 28-32; 22: 1-14; 23: 8-22; 24: 42-51; 25: 1-46; 27: 3-10, 62-66; 28: 11-15.

Matthew does not attempt to arrange the events of his record in chronological order. The addresses and parables of Jesus are reported consecutively, although they may have been spoken at different times, and materials scattered in the other records—especially in Luke—are found combined in Matthew. The special purpose which Matthew had in view in his gospel is nowhere expressly stated as it is done by John. (John 20: 30, 31.) The purpose can readily be gleaned from the general contents of the book, as also from specific passages. The traditional view that Matthew wrote primarily to prove that in Jesus of Nazareth is to be found the fulfillment and realization of the Messianic predictions of the Old Testament prophets is beyond doubt correct. There are about forty proof passages in Matthew from the Old Testament in connection with even the minor details of Christ's career, such as his return from Egypt (Matt. 2: 15); this is ample evidence of the fact, although the proof manner and proof value of some of these passages are exegetical, and indeed is the whole way in which the Old Testament is cited in the New Testament.

The question as to whether Matthew wrote for Jewish Christians or for unconverted Jews is of less importance; there is not sufficient evidence to justify this claim beyond all dispute. Matthew emphasizes the kingly feature of Jesus; the character and teachings of Jesus throughout Matthew are regal in character and royal in dignity. Jesus is not only the Messiah of Old Testament prophecy, but he is the King who came through the royal line of David to sit upon his throne forever. Nearly every chapter in Matthew has quotations from the Old Testament; this shows that Matthew was not only a Jew, but that he was familiar with the Old Testament scriptures. Truly he views everything through the eyes of a Jew and keeps his own people in mind as his readers.

Matthew frequently translates into Greek Hebrew words for the benefit of the Greek-speaking Jews. (Matt. 1: 23; 27: 33, 46.) He omits explanations of Jewish customs and local references which Gentile readers would naturally expect (Mark 7: 3, 4; 13: 3); yet he devotes more attention than do all the others to the fulfillment of prophecy. Matthew is the only one that gives the line of ancestry by which Jesus was heir to the throne of David. Matthew wrote as an eyewitness and from the stand point of an intelligent but plain man of business. His language is easily understood. He presents Jesus as the offspring of David, the fulfillment of the prophecies. Viewed in the light of Matthew's gospel, Jesus is the fulfillment of the old covenant, of its laws, of its priesthood, of its sacrifices, and of its prophecies. Matthew presents him in genealogy, history, prophecy, and character as the Son of God; the gospel of Jesus is the gospel of the promised and accomplished atonement, of the predicted and achieved triumph. Jesus died according to the scriptures and became the atoning sacrifice for the world; it is through him that man is reconciled to God, and this reconciliation constitutes the basis of his kngdom.

OUTLINE OF THE GOSPEL ACCORDING TO MATTHEW

SECTION ONE.
1: 1 to 2: 23.

Human Ancestry, Birth, Childhood, and Youth of Jesus.

SECTION TWO.
3: 1 to 4: 11.

John the Baptist; Baptism and Temptation of Jesus.

SECTION THREE.
4: 12 to 7: 29.

Beginning of Jesus' Galilean Ministry; the Principles of the Kingdom of Heaven.

SECTION FOUR.
8: 1 to 18: 35.

The Galilean Ministry.

SECTION FIVE.
19: 1 to 20: 34.

The Perean Ministry.

SECTION SIX.
21: 1 to 26: 46.

Last Days of Jesus' Public Ministry.

SECTION SEVEN.
26: 47 to 28: 20.

Arrest, Trial, Crucifixion, Burial, and Resurrection of Jesus; the Commission.

A COMMENTARY ON THE GOSPEL ACCORDING TO MATTHEW
THE TITLE

The title of the first book of the New Testament is "The Gospel According to Matthew" and not "The Gospel of Matthew." Gospel is a translation of the Greek "euangelion," which means "good message" or "good news." The gospel "according to Matthew" simply means *the good tidings of the kingdom, as delivered or written by Matthew*. "Euangelion" originally signified a *present given in return for joyful news;* later it came to mean *the good news itself*. It is used in this latter sense here. The Holy Spirit guided Matthew in writing this record; he probably wrote it in Hebrew or Aramaic; his manuscript was translated into the Greek at a very early date, and the English text as we now have it was translated from the Greek. Matthew was the writer or editor of this book; he was not the originator of it. "Gospel of Matthew" would signify that Matthew was the originator of it, while "the gospel according to Matthew" means the gospel history as Matthew wrote it; he did not write the gospel as he understood it, but he wrote it as he was guided by the Holy Spirit; this makes God, Christ, and the Holy Spirit the originators of this book. This is the narrative of the great facts pertaining to Jesus which have been grouped into a life history by Matthew, guided by the Holy Spirit, as distinguished from other similar histories by Mark, Luke, and John. The names Matthew and Levi denote the same person (Matt. 9: 9; Mark 2: 14; Luke 5: 27); however, the name Levi does not appear in any list of the apostles found in the New Testament.

SECTION ONE

HUMAN ANCESTRY, BIRTH, CHILDHOOD, AND YOUTH OF JESUS
1: 1 to 2: 23

1. THE GENEALOGY OF JESUS
1: 1-17

1 [1]The book of the [2]generation of Jesus Christ, the son of David, the son of Abraham.

---

[1]Or, *The genealogy of Jesus Christ*
[2]Or, *birth:* as in ver. 18.

---

1 The book of the generation of Jesus Christ,—"The book of the generation" signifies book of nativity, book of origin; it also means genealogy, pedigree, genealogical table; also the book upon the birth of Jesus; it is the record of his genealogy. The word "book" here is not to be understood as Matthew's entire history, but only the particular table of the ancestry of Jesus. "Book of the generation" is frequently used in the Jewish writings: "This is the book of the generations of Adam" (Gen. 5: 1); again, "These are the generations of Jacob" (Gen. 37: 2); and again, "These are the generations of Aaron and Moses" (Num. 3: 1). These show that the phrase has direct reference to the descendants and not to the history that follows the expression. Some have thought that it may signify the entire history of Jesus as given by Matthew. It may not always be used of the pedigree, but the context shows how the expression is to be understood. Here it appears that it refers exclusively to the genealogy of "Jesus Christ."

Jesus is another form of Joshua; it is the same name as Joshua, the former leader and deliverer of Israel; it means God is helper, deliverer, or savior; it is our Lord's private and common name; it is interpreted also to mean "Jehovah is salvation." Christ is the official name of our Lord; it is the Greek form of the Hebrew term Messiah; it signifies "anointed." Messiah was used of kings, priests, and prophets; it is here used in that sense in which it becomes affixed to Jesus as the name of our Lord. It denotes the promised Messiah or anointed one; sometimes it is translated with the

2 Abraham begat Isaac; and Isaac begat Jacob; and Jacob begat Judah

article as "the Christ." Under the law, kings, priests, and prophets were anointed. Jesus Christ is the Lord's anointed and fills the threefold function of king, priest, and prophet. The law, psalms, and the prophets looked forward to the salvation in and through a personal Messiah; Matthew now declares Jesus Christ to be that one.

The son of David, the son of Abraham.—"The son of David" and "the son of Abraham" both refer to our Lord. Son of David was a title frequently used of the Messiah; son of Abraham was too solemn a subject of prophecy and history to be omitted here. These phrases show the character of the gospel according to Matthew. Jesus was of the royal line of David, hence the son of David; his pedigree is to be traced through David the king. Matthew is supposed to have written especially for the Jews, and he placed the emphasis on the kingship of Jesus, hence he was "the son of David." In like manner he is the son of Abraham; he came as the seed of Abraham; his genealogy is traced from Abraham to Joseph and Mary. Being the son of David and the son of Abraham simply means that these two patriarchs are in the fleshly line of the genealogy of Jesus. God had promised Abraham that he would bless the world through Abraham's seed; this promise was repeated to David. Matthew, in giving the genealogy of Jesus, shows that this promise made to Abraham and repeated to David was fulfilled in Jesus Christ.

2-5 **Abraham begat Isaac.**—In the genealogy of Jesus, Matthew starts with Abraham; only those who, among the ancestors of Christ, form a direct line are mentioned. Abraham is father of the Jewish race; everything began and ended with Father Abraham to the Jew. Matthew sees the source of the Jewish race in Abraham and begins to trace the line of descent from him. If one is not a descendant of Abraham, he is not to be dealt with as an heir of the rich blessings of Jehovah according to Jewish attitudes. Jesus is the end of the Old Testament genealogy reaching from Abraham down through David to Joseph and Mary; he is the head of the New

and his brethren; 3 and Judah begat Perez and Zerah of Tamar; and Perez begat Hezron; and Hezron begat ³Ram; 4 and ³Ram begat Amminadab; and Amminadab begat Nahshon; and Nahshon begat Salmon; 5 and Salmon begat Boaz of Rahab; and Boaz begat Obed of Ruth; and Obed begat Jesse; 6 and Jesse begat David the king.
And David begat Solomon of her *that had been the wife* of Uriah; 7 and

---

³Gr. *Aram.*

Testament kingdom because he came through the royal line of David. He came through Isaac, not through Ishmael or Midian or any of the other sons of Abraham. Isaac was the son of promise.

Isaac begat Jacob, and Jacob begat Judah and his brethren. —Jesus came of the tribe of Judah. (Heb. 7: 14.) Jacob had twelve sons, but the pre-eminence was given to Judah and the promise was made to Judah that through him the Messiah should come. The other sons of Jacob are not mentioned because Jesus was not the descendant through any other than the tribe of Judah. Matthew mentions a list of fourteen men from Abraham to David. This is the first step in the human ancestry of Jesus from Abraham. Tamar is mentioned in this connection because of the peculiar circumstances by which she became the mother or Judah's son. (Gen. 38: 12-26.) Rahab is also mentioned in this group of the genealogy because she was brought into the nation of Israel from a depraved and degraded life through her faith in Jehovah. (Josh. 2: 8-11; Heb. 11: 31.) Ruth, the Moabitess and great grandmother of David, is brought into the genealogy because of her faith in Jehovah and her loyalty to him. The blood of all races flowed in the fleshly line of the genealogy of Jesus.

6-11 **David begat Solomon.**—Matthew names fourteen generations from Abraham to David. David stands out prominently in this line; it is "David the king"; there were other kings, but none so prominent and important as David. He attained to such dignity and prominence among the Jews as to be honored in this genealogy; the promise of the Messiah was repeated to David. Jehovah said that one should sit on his throne forever; Matthew shows that Jesus Christ is that one; hence the importance of the genealogy of Jesus through David. Matthew traces this line of descent through Solomon.

Solomon begat Rehoboam; and Rehoboam begat Abijah; and Abijah begat ⁴Asa; 8 and ⁴Asa begat Jehoshaphat; and Jehoshapat begat Joram; and Joram begat Uzziah; 9 and zziah begat Jotham; and Jotham begat Ahaz; and Ahaz begat Hezekiah; 10 and Hezekiah begat Manasseh; and Manasseh begat ⁵Amon; and ⁵Amon begat Josiah; 11 and Josiah begat Jechoniah and his brethren, at the time of the ⁶carrying away to Babylon.
12 And after the ⁶carrying away to Babylon, Jechoniah begat ⁷Shealtiel;

⁴Gr. *Asaph.*
⁵Gr. *Amos.*
⁶Or, *removal to Babylon*
⁷Gr. *Salathiel.*

Another woman is brought into the genealogy because she is a wife of David and the mother of Solomon. David had other wives and other children, but Bathsheba, the wife of Uriah the Hittite, became the wife of David, and so the genealogy of Jesus includes her. David had another son named Nathan; he was also a son of Bathsheba. (1 Chron. 3: 5.) Matthew traces the genealogy of Jesus from David through Solomon to Zerubbabel, fourteen generations or names; Luke traces the genealogy of Jesus from Zerubbabel to David through Nathan; this accounts for some of the differences between the genealogy as given by Matthew and that given by Luke. Matthew names the line of kings from David through Solomon to the captivity of the kingdom of Judah; these were the kings of Judah. The dynasty of the kingdom of Judah did not change; one of David's descendants occupied the throne until Judah was carried into Babylonian captivity.

Matthew omits three kings of Judah between Joram and Uzziah; they are Ahaziah, Joash, and Amaziah. (2 Kings 8: 24; 1 Chron. 3: 11; 2 Chron. 22: 1, 11; 24: 27.) No reason is given for the omission of these names; some think that it was done to preserve symmetry by bringing the number of names in each list to fourteen. (See verse 17.) These names may have been selected for omission because they were immediate descendants of Ahab and Jezebel. Such omissions were common in giving long genealogical tables.

12 After the carrying away to Babylon, Jechoniah begat Shealtiel.—Jechoniah was king of Judah at the time the kingdom of Judah was destroyed and the people carried away into captivity. Jeremiah had predicted Jechoniah's captivity; he said: "Write ye this man childless, a man that shall not pros-

and ⁷Shealtiel begat Zerubbabel; 13 and Zerubbabel begat Abiud; and Abiud begat Eliakim; and Eliakim begat Azor; 14 and Azor begat Sadoc; and Sadoc begat Achim; and Achim begat Eliud; 15 and Eliud begat Eleazar; and Eleazar begat Matthan; and Matthan begat Jacob; 16 and Jacob begat

per in his days; for no more shall a man of his seed prosper, sitting upon the throne of David, and ruling in Judah." (Jer. 22: 30; see also Jer. 36: 30.) Some have pointed out a contradiction between Jeremiah and Matthew; no contradiction here, as Jeremiah and Matthew wrote by the same spirit. Jeremiah does not say Jechoniah should be literally childless, but he does say, "Write ye this man childless," and then explains his statement by these words, "for no more shall a man of his seed prosper, sitting upon the throne of David, and ruling in Judah." Jechoniah was to be childless only in the sense that he would have no son to succeed him on the throne. The author of Chronicles (1 Chron. 3: 17) records Jechoniah as having a son and names him Shealtiel. Matthew records Shealtiel as the son of Jechoniah. After the captivity of the kingdom of Judah, the family of David occupied a humble position, but after the exile, the preservation and restoration of the genealogies became a subject of national concern; this was especially true with respect to the priests.

13-15 Shealtiel begat Zerubbabel; and Zerubbabel begat Abiud.—In 1 Chron. 3: 19 Zerubbabel is represented as the son of Pedaiah, and not of Shealtiel, as Matthew here has it. Ezra and Nehemiah both agree with Matthew; their statements occur in historical passages which are not so liable to corruption through mistakes of transcribers as were the genealogical tables like those in Chronicles. (See Ezra 3: 2; Neh. 12: 1.) Luke also follows the genealogy as given by Ezra and Nehemiah. (Luke 3: 27.) In some way the account in Chronicles has been modifed in the hands of transcribers, and Pedaiah should be written as Shealtiel; for these two names represent the same person. The nine names from Abiud to Jacob (verse 15) are not elsewhere mentioned; they belonged to the period subsequent to the close of the Old Testament record.

Joseph the husband of Mary, of whom was born Jesus, who is called Christ.

16 Jacob begat Joseph the husband of Mary.—Matthew does not connect Joseph and Jesus as father and son. He departs from the usual phraseology of the genealogy and says, "Jacob begat Joseph the husband of Mary, of whom was born Jesus, who is called Christ." This signifies the peculiarity of the birth of Jesus. The name Jesus, or Joshua, was common among the Jews (Col. 4: 11; Acts 13: 6); hence Matthew here explains which Jesus by saying, "Who is called Christ." Matthew differs from Luke again here; Luke says that Joseph was the son of Heli. (Luke 3: 24.) A difficulty is seen here; some have assumed Heli to be the father of Mary and only the father-in-law of Joseph; the record does not say this, and the original does not permit such a translation.

[The difficulty here is that Matthew says Joseph was the son of Jacob, and Luke says he was the son of Heli. How do we know that Jacob and Heli were not the same? In these genealogies and histories of the Old Testament we find that the same person is often called by different names. Gideon was called "Jerubbaal"; Solomon was called "Jedidiah" (2 Sam. 12: 25); Esther was named "Hadassah"; Peter was known as "Simon" and "Cephas." Why may not this "Jacob" and "Heli" be names of the same person? The reason of different names was that there were so many different dialects, or languages, and a person had a different name in each dialect. It was "Saul" among the Jews; it was "Paul" among the Romans. This is given as a possible case to show how little we know on these points. The above may not be the true explanation of the seeming difficulty, but it is a possible one.

One explanation given of it is that one writer follows the genealogy of Joseph; the other, that of Mary. Mary's genealogy is attributed to Joseph, because when there was a daughter, but no son, in a family, she was to marry a near kinsman, and he was to come into the family of his wife and be enumerated as of that family, instead of the wife's being enumerated in his family. Another explanation is that frequently one is called a "son" of a grandfather, or even a remote ancestor, and

17 So all the generations from Abraham unto David are fourteen genera-

not always of his immediate father. We cannot with certainty tell what is the explanation. This is true: the apparent discrepancy gave no trouble to those living at that time, who doubtless understood the matter. We have accounts of various attacks on the Bible in the early age on different grounds, but none for this discrepancy. There are some things which we will have to receive in faith without understanding them, and this is one of them. Let us say that we do not understand it, not that there is a contradiction.]

Scholars are loathe to leave the matter without a better explanation; it is not pleasant to leave so grave a difficulty unsolved; but the honest way is to admit that no solution entirely satisfactory appears, and that the data for one are manifestly inadequate. Fortunately, no important results are affected by these imperfections in the Jewish genealogical records. Both Matthew and Luke's accounts are correct; we simply do not see how to harmonize them.

[Matthew gives the number of generations from Abraham to Christ as forty-two; Luke mentions fifty-five; the same lines of descent are not followed in both cases, and neither of them is full in the sense that every generation in the descent is given. Sometimes two or three generations at a time are omitted for some reason. A grandson or a great-grandson, or even one of lower descent, is called a "son." Jesus is called the "son of David." It does not mean that he was the immediate son, but a descendant of David. Jesus calls Zacchaeus "a son of Abraham" (Luke 19: 9); this means that he was a descendant of Abraham and an heir of the promise made to Abraham. These show that descendants were called "sons." In giving the line of descent, neither Matthew nor Luke gives all the names of those in the line, and one gives more than the other. It is not known why this is done.]

17 **All the generations from Abraham unto David are fourteen generations.**—Matthew's arrangement of fourteen generations is an easy way of remembering the genealogy. The first group is from Abraham to David; the second is from

tions; and from David unto the ⁶carrying away to Babylon fourteen generations; and from the ⁶carrying away to Babylon unto the Christ fourteen generations.

David to the captivity; and the last is from the captivity to Jesus Christ. This is a technical way or method of summing up the generations. The names in the first group, from Abraham to David, were patriarchs, David being the first in the line who was both a patriarch and a king. (Acts 2: 29.) The second list of names were all kings and successors of David, Jechoniah being the last king of Judah in the direct line of descent from David, although his brother Zedekiah reigned eleven years after he and the chief part of the royal family had been carried into captivity. (2 Kings 24: 15-18.) The names of the third group were all heirs of David's throne, but none of them reigned except Jesus, who now sits on David's throne according to the promise. (Acts 2: 29-35; 15: 15-17.) By actual count, Matthew gives fourteen names in the first group, the second group contains fourteen by omitting four names, and the third group contains only thirteen new names, but it is made to count fourteen by repeating the name of Jechoniah, which was the last name of the second division.

2. MARY AND JOSEPH
1: 18-25

18 Now the ⁸birth of ⁹Jesus Christ was on this wise: When his mother Mary had been betrothed to Joseph, before they came together she was

⁸Or, *generation*: as in ver. 1.
⁹Some ancient authorities read *of the Christ*.

---

18 His mother Mary had been betrothed to Joseph.—Matthew, having traced the genealogy of Jesus from Abraham to Mary and Joseph, now begins his narrative at the period when Mary's pregnancy had become a matter of certainty, which was about the time of her return from visiting Elisabeth. She "had been betrothed to Joseph"; the interval between betrothal and the consummation of marriage was sometimes considerable; the betrothed remained in the house of her father till the bridegroom came after her. (Deut. 20: 7.) Matthew does not record the angel's visit to Mary, neither

found with child of the Holy Spirit. 19 And Joseph her husband, being a

does he record the account of her immediate departure out of Galilee into Judea, where she remained with Elisabeth about three months. (Luke 1: 26-56.) Soon after her return from this visit into Galilee her pregnancy was discovered by relatives, and Joseph learned of it. Matthew is clear and definite in stating that "she was found with child" before "they came together"; this excludes Joseph from any connection with her state of pregnancy. It seems that Mary's conception was not until after her betrothal; it took place between the time of her betrothal and the consummation of the marriage. We are not told who discovered that she was with child; we need not suppose that she published the fact, neither need we suppose that the Holy Spirit had made her pregnancy known to anyone. Mary's situation was humiliating; her consciousness of her own integrity and virginity and her strong faith in God supported her under such trying circumstances; her reputation, her honor, and even her life were at stake. If the law of Moses be carried out under such conditions, she should be put to death.

Matthew states clearly that she was "found with child of the Holy Spirit." Her friends and relatives did not know that she was with child by the Holy Spirit; probably they would not have believed her had she told them it was the Holy Spirit; it was a delicate situation for her, and the records are silent as to what Mary had to say about her condition, if she said anything. Luke is more explicit on this point; he says that the angel Gabriel said to Mary, "Thou shalt conceive in thy womb, and bring forth a son, and shalt call his name Jesus. . . . The Holy Spirit shall come upon thee, and the power of the Most High shall overshadow thee: wherefore also the holy thing which is begotten shall be called the Son of God." (Luke 1: 31-35.) The Holy Spirit is that which produced the human existence of Christ, through whose action, which so appeared only in this, the only case of its kind, the origin of the embryo in the womb of Mary was casually produced in opposition to human generation, so that the latter is thereby excluded; Jesus was truly "the seed of the woman."

righteous man, and not willing to make her a public example, was minded to put her away privily. 20 But when he thought on these things, behold, an

"Jesus was as human as his mother Mary, and as divine as his father God." This record testifies that Mary was a virgin; even after she is found to be with child, she is still a virgin. (Verse 23.)

19 **Joseph her husband.**—From the moment of her betrothal a woman was treated as if actually married; the betrothal could be dissolved only by regular divorce. When she became "engaged," she was considered as if "married." Breach of faithfulness was regarded as adultery and was punishable with death. (Deut. 22: 23, 24.) Hence, Joseph is spoken of as "her husband." Joseph was a righteous man; he was righteous according to the standard of the law under which he lived; he was placed in a dilemma. Being a righteous man, he must expose Mary and insist that the law be enforced, which meant she should be put to death; or he must give up his affection for her and abide by consequent circumstances. He was "not willing to make her a public example"; he decided upon hearing of her condition "to put her away privily." Joseph did not wish or desire to make a public example of her; the word here in the Greek means to exhibit, display, point out; Joseph decided not to expose Mary to public shame. Being a righteous man, he was also a merciful man; he determined to put her away or divorce her privately and not assign any cause for the divorce, that her life might be saved. As the offense that she was supposed to have committed was against Joseph, he had a right to pass it by if he chose to do so. Joseph was convinced that Mary had committed adultery, and he at once resolved to put her away, but he hesitated as to how he would dispose of the matter. The law required that he make a public example of her, but his righteousness and his mercy and his affection for Mary caused him to seek another course, and that was to "put her away privily."

20 **An angel of the Lord appeared unto him in a dream.**—The angel that appeared to him in a vision while he was sleeping was "an angel of the Lord." This expression has been used

angel of the Lord appeared unto him in a dream, saying, Joseph, thou son of David, fear not to take unto thee Mary thy wife: for that which is [10]conceived in her is of the Holy Spirit. 21 And she shall bring forth a son;

[10]Gr. *begotten.*

frequently in the Old Testament. (See Gen. 16: 7, 9; Ex. 32: 34; 33: 14; Isa. 63: 9; Mal. 3: 1.) It may have been the angel Gabriel, as this angel delivered the message relating to the birth of Jesus; Gabriel may also be designated as the "angel of the Lord." (Dan. 8: 16; 9: 21.) The angel of the incarnation must be distinguished from later angelic apparitions. Joseph, the husband of Mary, like Joseph of the Old Testament, had a father named Jacob; again Joseph of the New Testament is like Joseph of the Old Testament in that he received his revelations in dreams. This particular form of revelation may have been chosen because of his simplicity and sincerity of heart. It may be that the statement of the angel to Joseph in a dream confirmed what Mary had already related to Joseph; Joseph may have regarded her statement as incredible; so the angel would confirm Mary's statement.

Fear not to take unto thee Mary thy wife.—Here Mary is called his "wife," though they had not been married; this is similar to Joseph's being called "her husband." This emphasizes the fact that during the period of time between the espousal and the consummation of marriage both parties were considered as though they were actually married. The angel addressed Joseph in the dream as "thou son of David." This would remind Joseph of the promised seed and the expectation of the Messiah to come through the lineage of David; it would also stamp the message on Joseph's mind as the announcement of the birth of the Messiah. Since Mary was also of the lineage of David, she could be called "a daughter of David." He is reminded that "Mary thy wife" was the subject of whom the angel was about to speak; this would call to his attention his affection for Mary, his betrothed wife. Joseph was in a state of undecided attitude as to the course he should follow; the angel assures him that he should "take" "Mary thy wife," for she was innocent of any crime. The explanation followed that "that which is conceived in her is of

and thou shalt call his name JESUS; for it is he that shall save his people from their sins. 22 Now all this is come to pass, that it might be fulfilled

the Holy Spirit." If Mary had related her experience and conversation with the angel Gabriel, this would be a confirmation of her statements, and clear her of any taint or guilt of adultery. Matthew records these incidents in such a way, both to Mary and to Joseph, that the child was of miraculous conception. The promise of the Messiah, his mission, and his descent were revealed long before his appearance on earth; his conception, his birth, his name, and his work were equally from the Holy Spirit. We are to understand from the announcement of the angel to Mary and now from the statement of the angel to Joseph that the human nature of Jesus Christ was a real creation in the womb of the virgin by the power of the Holy Spirit.

21 **She shall bring forth a son.**—The angel decided the matter for Joseph; his perplexity was removed, and he was encouraged to consummate his marriage with Mary. Joseph is assured that Mary is with child by the Holy Spirit; he is to understand that the child has no earthly or fleshly father; he is also assured that the child should be a son; he is even instructed as to the name that he should give Mary's son. "Thou shalt call his name Jesus." This name means the same as Joshua, deliverer, savior. Both Mary and Joseph now have instructions from an angel with respect to the course they should follow.

Shall save his people from their sins.—This expresses briefly the mission of Jesus; the great task before him is to "save his people from their sins"; hence he is to be a Savior. He is to save "his people" from the bondage of sin; he is not to establish an earthly kingdom; not to deliver Israel from Roman bondage; he is not even to re-establish the old kingdom of Israel; *he is to save the people from their sins*. His name carries in itself no promise to save those who refuse to become his people; neither is he to save all men irrespective of character and of their relations to him; he is to be the Savior of his believing, penitent, obedient people. No one is encouraged to hope for forgiveness of sins without voluntary

which was spoken by the Lord through the prophet, saying,
23 ¹¹Behold, the virgin shall be with child, and shall bring forth a son,

---

¹¹Is. vii. 14.

---

ceasing from sins. Jesus came to make atonement for the sins of man; he became a sin offering for the world. Joseph may not have understood the full import of this language. Thus early in the history, in the midst of pedigrees, and the disturbances of thrones by the supposed temporal king of the Jews, we have so clear a statement of the spiritual mission of Jesus and the nature of the office of Christ. No indication is here given that he would save his people from *the punishment of their sins,* but it is the *sin itself* from which he will save his people. Jesus did not come as the Jews commonly supposed that he would, simply to save his people from the dominion of foreigners. Here is also indicated the fact that his people would constitute a "spiritual Israel."

22, 23 The virgin shall be with child, and shall bring forth a son.—This is a quotation from Isaiah. (Isa. 7: 14.) It was spoken probably seven hundred years before its fulfillment; the angel tells Joseph in this dream that the condition of Mary is the beginning of the fulfillment of his prophecy. Joseph believed the prophet Isaiah; he is now to believe this statement of the prophet is to be fulfilled and the long-expected Messiah is soon to appear. This is the first great prophecy which the birth of Jesus fulfilled; special emphasis is laid here upon the point of Mary's virginity; she is to become a maiden-mother; this means a deviation from the regular course of nature, and such a deviation was involves special divine power; therefore "the holy thing which is begotten shall be called the Son of God." (Luke 1: 35.) By quoting this prophecy to Joseph the angel proves the fulfillment of it in Mary. "Virgin" as used here means that she had not known man; this fully agrees with Luke's account (Luke 1: 34), and is also in perfect agreement with the promise made to Eve when it was said, "I will put enmity between thee and the woman, and between thy seed and her seed: he shall bruise they head, and thou shalt bruise his heel." (Gen. 3: 15.) Isaiah spoke these words to King Ahaz concerning a threatened invasion of his

And they shall call his name [12]Immanuel; which is, being interpreted, God with us. 24 And Joseph arose from his sleep, and did as the angel of the Lord commanded him, and took unto him

[12]Gr. *Emmanuel.*

territory by the kings of Israel and Syria. (Isa. 7: 10-16; 8: 1-4.) A part of Isaiah's prophecy was fulfilled within a few years after it was spoken; in fact, all except that a virgin should conceive and bring forth a son. When the people of Isaiah's time saw the fulfillment of part of his prophecy, they should have looked forward with stronger confidence to the fulfillment of the remainder. If they had done this, they would have been ready to believe the account of the birth of Jesus.

They shall call his name Immanuel.—There are two spellings of this word, "Immanuel" and "Emmanuel"; it means "God with us," or "God in the flesh." God was with Israel in delivering his people from their enemies at the time of Isaiah, but in a special way he is to be with them in saving them from their sins. This name is only a description of the character and position of Jesus; he was not to be called by this name as he was by the name "Jesus" or "Christ." In what sense is Jesus "God with us" or "Immanuel"? Jesus is called Immanuel, or "God with us," in his incarnation; he is God united to our nature; God with man; God in man; God with us. Jesus is the beginning of "God with us" in a very definite and peculiar way. God is with us in his word, in prayer, and our obedience to him; he comforts, instructs, blesses, and save us. God is with us in a peculiar way since Jesus was born of Mary.

24 **Did as the angel of the Lord commanded him.**—Verses twenty to twenty-three record the speech the angel made to Joseph in a dream; Joseph obeyed the command of the angel. He was conscientious in all that he did; he was conscientious in his intended course to put Mary away privately; the angel had now convinced him of his duty, and he is ready to take her as his wife; he is ready to obey the divine command; he now sees that Mary's condition was not of her choice only, but was imposed by divine injunction; she had no other

his wife; 25 and knew her not till she had brought forth a son: and he called his name JESUS.

---

choice in being faithful to God than to accept conception by the Holy Spirit. Joseph now is convinced that she is faithful to Jehovah in becoming the mother of the Son of God; he must be as faithful to Jehovah in taking her now as his wife. Joseph did not delay, but "arose from his sleep, and did as the angel of the Lord commanded him, and took unto him his wife."

25 **Knew her not till she had brought forth a son.**—Joseph delayed not to take Mary home as his wife; he provided for her reputation and comfort in her present circumstances as far as was within his power; he had no conjugal intercourse with her "till she had brought forth a son." The statement that Joseph knew not Mary (sexually) until she brought forth a son implies that he did know her after this. This explodes the assumption by the Roman Catholics that Mary always remained a virgin; such an assumption is inconsistent with what is here stated and is unsupported by any other passage of scripture; it never would have been advanced except to force it into accordance with a preconceived notion of the perpetual virginity of Mary. It will be noticed that the American Revised Version omits "her firstborn," and gives instead just "a son," but in Luke's record the phrase, "her firstborn son," is found in the American Revised Version. This implies that Mary had other children. Authorities differ as to whether Mary had other children. The following scriptures are relied upon to prove that she had other children: Matt. 13: 55; Mark 6; 3.

The virgin birth.—"The virgin birth" is the correct and only correct term to use with respect to the birth of Jesus as contained in Matthew and Luke. "Immaculate conception" is too confused to be of much value; "supernatural or miraculous birth" is not clear as to the process of the birth; "supernatural or miraculous conception" is equally unsatisfactory. The only statement or term that is sufficiently definite and clear is "virgin birth." The accounts of the virgin birth as given by Matthew and Luke are given with inspired delicacy and reserve, yet with such definiteness and clearness as to leave no doubt as to the facts recorded. The genealogy of Jesus reveals him to be the son of David; the virgin birth reveals him as Son of God. The records as given by Matthew and Luke are either true or false; there is no middle ground. The accounts are true records of the facts, or they are purely a story of invention. Believers in the divinity of Jesus believe the accounts to be true; those who do not believe in the virgin birth do not believe the records given by inspiration. If the virgin birth is not true, then Jesus was born as ordinary children are born, and Jesus was just an ordinary man; so much depends on the virgin birth that to reject it is to reject the divinity of Jesus and therefore the power to save.

One objection urged against the virgin birth is that *it is against the laws of nature.* This objection has but little weight; how do we know that it was against the law of nature? True it did not follow the ordinary line of nature, but that does not prove that it was "against the laws of nature." May it not have been the only way for *divinity* to become *humanity?* No event like this had ever occurred *before* this, and no event like it has occurred *since;* how do we know but that it was the *natural* way for divinity to become humanity? No one can answer this; therefore, no one can determine that the virgin birth was *against* the laws of nature.

Another objection to it is made in these words: One human parent does not guarantee against sinlessness. This objection, if it has any weight, admits only one human parent, but claims that this would not guarantee a perfect sinless character. It is claimed that Jesus could contract from one parent as well as from two parents. Sin is not inherited; sinful nature is not inherited; sins are not transmitted from parent to child. God has repeatedly declared that sin is not inherited, neither is it transmitted from parent to child. (See Deut. 24: 16; 2 Kings 14: 6; Ezek. 18: 2-4.) Jesus did not contract sin from Mary, hence the objection to the virgin birth on this point fails to have any force.

Another argument against the virgin birth is that the New Testament is silent on it except the records of Matthew and Luke. This is the famous argument "ex silentio." It is true that Matthew and Luke are the only writers of the New Testament that give an account of the infancy of Jesus, but the accounts given by Matthew and Luke agree. Many events which are generally accepted are recorded by only one or two writers of the New Testament. A criminal could find one hundred to one who did not see him commit the crime; but the failure of many to see the crime committed does not prove the falsity of the one who did see it committed. This argument proves too much. However, there are other references to the virgin birth recorded in the New Testament. (See Rom. 8: 3; Gal. 4: 4; Phil. 2: 5-8.) Only one writer records this statement of Jesus: "It is more blessed to give than to receive." (Acts 20: 35.) Luke only records this statement, and it is generally accepted; there are many other events and statements recorded by one or two writers of the New Testament; these are not rejected because every writer of the New Testament did not record them; neither should the virgin birth be rejected simply because two and only two writers record it.

Again the objectors to the virgin birth have contended that the whole story has been invented by the disciples of Jesus. Either it is true or it was invented; there is no other alternative; but did the disciples of Jesus invent this story? It was prophesied long before the disciples of Jesus lived. (See Isa. 7: 14.) If the account was invented, it was not invented by the disciples of Jesus; it was invented by the prophets long before the days of the disciples. This clears the disciples of any accusation of inventing the story; so this objection also falls.

Another objection to the virgin birth is that Joseph and Mary are called the parents of Jesus. It is cited that four times the record speaks of Joseph and Mary as his parents. (See Luke 2: 27, 33, 41, 43.) One time the record gives Mary as referring to Joseph as the father of Jesus. (Luke 2: 48.) In reply to this, it is contended that Jesus corrected her for this error in Luke 2: 49. However, if Jesus had called Mary and Joseph his parents, it would have showed (a) respect to Joseph as the husband of Mary, (b) proper respect to his mother, (c) and that Joseph was his legal parent.

It is further urged as an objection to the virgin birth that the *early church did not accept it*. This is an assertion; there is no proof that the early church did not accept the accounts as given by Matthew and Luke. The writings of Ignatius and Justin Martyr show that the church did accept the entire record as given by Matthew and Luke. Not until the eighteenth century was it denied, and then by Voltaire and Tom Paine. In the nineteenth century Strauss and Renan denied the virgin birth; others have followed their example.

Again it is urged that *modern scholarship rejects the virgin birth*. Some modern scholars may reject it, but *all* moderns do not reject it; Christian scholarship accepts it as it is recorded by Matthew and Luke. Suppose modern scholarship did reject it, what would that prove? Scholarship cannot save any one. The world by its wisdom does not know God, and cannot know him. (Matt. 11: 25-27; 1 Cor. 1: 20-25.)

The reasons for accepting the virgin birth far outweigh any of the objections that may be urged against it. The record of it is a part of the New Testament; it has always been a part of it; not a single complete manuscript of the New Testament omits the account of the virgin birth. Some parts of the New Testament (Mark 16: 12-20; John 8: 1-11; Acts 8: 37) have been disputed, but the records of Matthew and Luke on the virgin birth have not been disputed. We accept the testimony of Matthew and Luke on other things, why not on this? When Matthew says that the birth of Jesus was "on this wise" (Matthew 1: 18), it seems that he means to record the facts of a birth that was different from other births in the genealogy. The date of Jesus' birth, Herod's reign, the public census and taxation, which are mentioned in connection with the virgin birth, are admitted. Why admit some of the facts of the account and not all of the facts?

The sinlessness of Jesus implies the virgin birth. If he had been born in the ordinary way, we would not expect him to be sinless; "that which is born of the flesh is flesh" (John 3: 6); if an ordinary birth was that of Jesus, then he was subject to sin and death as others of the human race. He gave his life up for the sins of the world, not that he had to die.

An absolutely holy human being in the midst of sinful humanity seems to have been impossible.

The deity of Jesus is involved in the virgin birth. A denial of it robs Jesus of his divinity. Luke declares that he should be called "the Son of God." (Luke 1: 35.) This marks him as a divine product; "Son of God," and "the Son of the Highest" are titles of relationship to the Father in a unique way. If the virgin birth is denied, Jesus is reduced to the low level of an ordinary man.

3. THE BIRTH OF JESUS
2: 1-12

1 Now when Jesus was born in Bethlehem of Judaea in the days of

1 Jesus was born in Bethlehem of Judaea.—"Bethlehem" means "house of bread"; probably so named from the fertility of the surrounding territory. He was born in "Bethlehem of Judæa." This distinguishes the place of his birth from the Bethlehem in the tribe of Zebulun. (Josh. 19: 15.) Bethlehem Ephrath (Gen. 35: 16, 19) was located in the tribe of Judah (Judges 17: 9; 19: 1; 1 Sam. 17: 12). Ephrath or Ephratah was the earliest name of Bethlehem; it was situated about six Roman miles to the south of Jerusalem, or it was about two hours' walk from Jerusalem. This small town was the ancestral seat of the house of David. (Ruth 1: 1, 2.) It was strongly fortified by Rehoboam (2 Chron. 11: 17), but it remained a place of no importance (Mic. 5: 2), and is not mentioned among the towns of Judah in Joshua or in Neh. 11: 25. Luke records the fact that Joseph and Mary had resided in Nazareth of Galilee previous to the birth of Jesus, but that a decree of Augustus Caesar concerning the enrollment or taxation brought them to Bethlehem. (Luke 1: 26, 27; 2: 1-4.) Matthew omits these events and begins his account as if Bethlehem were the home of Joseph and Mary. Bethlehem, or "house of bread," was the birthplace of him who called himself "the bread of life." (John 6: 35.) This connects the history of Jesus with the ancestry through Ruth, who became the wife of Boaz, and who was in the line of genealogy of David. Bethlehem is called the city of David because David

Herod the king, behold, ¹Wise-men from the east came to Jerusalem saying,

---
¹Gr. *Magi.* Compare Esther 1. 13; Dan. 2. 12; Acts 13. 6, 8.

---

was born there, and he was anointed king over Israel by Samuel there.

In the days of Herod the king.—This is Matthew's nearest approach to giving the date of the birth of Jesus. Herod is called "the king." This is the first mention that we have of Herod in the New Testament. He was an Idumean by birth; that is, he was a descendant of the family of Esau. The Edomites were also called Idumeans. This was Herod the Great; he was a son of Antipater, whom Caesar had appointed as procurator of Judea. Herod was talented, unscrupulous, energetic; he managed to ingratiate himself into the favor of Augustus and came into possession of a kingdom which included Judea, Samaria, Galilee, and Perea, east of the Jordan, as well as Idumea. He became by profession a Jew in religion, although he was in no sense a Jew at heart. He hated the Jews and sought every opportunity to destroy them; he made and unmade priests according to his own whim; to please the Jews and to gain honor for himself, he rebuilt the temple. His list of heartless murders includes Hyrcanus, the venerable grandfather of his wife, Mariamne; he also murdered his oldest son; he invited a number of Jewish nobles into his palace and gave secret orders that upon his decease they should be put to death, that the people, who might otherwise rejoice at his death, should have at least some occasion for general mourning. He took possession of his kingdom 40 or 37 B.C. The Idumeans, the race of Herod the Great, had been for more than one hundred years Jewish in religion; the Maccabee Hyrcanus had compelled them to submit to circumcision.

An error in time.—It is well to note here the error that has crept into our calendar and has been perpetuated. The Christian era should properly begin with the year Jesus was born; by the "Christian Era" is meant the system upon which calendars are constructed, and by which historical events are now dated in practically all the civilized world. The intention of the one who originated the system was to have it begin with the year of the birth of Jesus. The originator of our present system made an error as to the year in which Jesus was born. He fixed the year A.D. 1 *four years too late;* in other words, Jesus was four years old in the year A.D. 1.

This error was made by Dionysius Exiguus. The scheme of beginning dates with the birth of Jesus was not invented until A.D. 532; the inventor, Dionysius Exiguus, was a monk. At that time the system of dates in common use began from the era of the emperor Diocletian, A.D. 284. Dionysius Exiguus was not willing to connect his system of dates with the name of that infamous tyrant and persecutor; so he conceived the idea of connecting his sytem with, and dating all its events from, the birth of Jesus. He wrote to Bishop Petronius the following: "To the end that the commencement of our hope might be better known to us, and that the cause of man's restoration, namely, our Redeemer's passion, might appear with clearer evidence." In this way he expressed his wish to change the system of reckoning dates.

In order to carry out his plan, it was necessary to fix the date of the birth of Jesus in the terms of the chronological system than in use. The Romans dated the beginning of their history from the supposed date of the founding of the city of Rome. Dionysius Exiguus calculated that the year of Jesus' birth was 753 from the founding of Rome. He made his equivalence of dates from Luke 3: 1, "Now in the fifteenth year of the reign of Tiberius Caesar." At this time Jesus was thirty years of age according to Luke 3: 23; but it was ascertained later that a mistake of four years had been made; for it clearly appeared from Matthew's record that Jesus was born *before the death of Herod,* who died in the year 849 from the founding of Rome. Tiberius succeeded Augustus August 19, in the year 767 from the founding of Rome; hence, his fifteenth year would be 779 from the founding of Rome; and from those facts Dionysius Exiguus was right in his calculation. However, it was discovered in later years that Tiberius began to reign as colleague with Augustus *four years before the latter died;* hence, the fifteenth year mentioned by Luke was four years earlier than was supposed by Dionysius Exiguus, and consequently the birth of Jesus was that many years *earlier than the date selected by Dionysius Exiguus.* After the error was discovered, no correction was made in Dionysius Exiguus' scheme, and the error has been perpetuated in our calendar. This must be considered in any computation of dates which involves events which happened before the birth of Jesus, and also in the dates of events which have occurred since the birth of Jesus.

Wise-men from the east came to Jerusalem.—Much has been written about the "wise-men from the east"; it is not necessary to detail here all the conjectures which have been made in answer to this question. "The east" may mean either Arabia, Persia, Chaldea, or Parthia and the provinces adjacent to Palestine. It seems clear from verse two that it was some land not very near Judea. They are also called Magi; there is no ground for supposing the Magi to have been *three* in number; there is no way to determine how many "Wise-men from the east" came at this time. There was a priestly caste among the Persians and Medes, which occupied itself principally with the secrets of nature, astrology, and medicine. Daniel was made president of this order in Babylon. (Dan. 2: 48.) Jeremiah spoke of this class among the Babylonians. (Jer. 39: 3.) The name Magi became familiar to people of that age, and it was transferred, without distinction of country, to all those who had devoted themselves to the study of medicine, astrology, and the secrets of nature. There was an indefinite reference to "eastern lands." (Matt. 8: 11; 24: 27; Luke 13: 29; Rev. 21: 13.) Some have thought that these Magi were kings and that there were three of them to represent the three families of Shem, Ham, and Japheth, but this assumption is to be disregarded with all the other traditions and guesses that have been made. There was a sect of philosophers and religionists who wore the name Magi; some think that these men were from a caste of religion; at least, they were men of some eminence and learning; these sages, or wise men, had learned of this event and were looking out for some intimations of its taking place.

These wise men came to Jerusalem; this was the capital of the country, and these inquirers would naturally come to Jerusalem as they could most readily obtain information con-

2 ᵃWhere is he that is born King of the Jews? for we saw his star in the east,

_{ᵃOr, *Where is the King of the Jews that is born?*}

cerning the newborn king here. The temple of Jerusalem was known all over the east; the Jews at this time had already spread over the known world, and they had made some proselytes or converts among the most intellectual and earnest inquirers of all countries. (John 12: 20.) The ten tribes of Israel that were scattered were largely in Parthia, though their ideas and hopes of the promised Messiah were not very clear and as well defined as those of their brethren in Palestine. Jerusalem was the center of the Jewish religion and the political center for that province. It is natural that these wise men would come to Jerusalem for further information.

2. **Where is he that is born King of the Jews?**—The wise men from the east came to Jerusalem to inquire *where* the lately-born King of the Jews might be. How they had learned that Jesus was "King of the Jews" we are not told; neither are we told to whom in particular they addressed their inquiry. It may be they assumed that all men intelligent in religious matters among the Jews must know; especially in Jerusalem the intelligent worshipers according to the law ought to have been well acquainted with the event and able to direct these inquirers to the place of him who was "born" to be "King of the Jews." When Pilate later asked Jesus while he was on trial "Art thou a king then?" Jesus promptly answered Pilate, "To this end have I been born, and to this end am I come into the world, that I should bear witness unto the truth." (John 18: 37.) Jesus was to be a King; Matthew throughout his record of the life of Jesus puts emphasis on the kingly feature of Jesus. He came to earth to establish a kingdom and to reign over that kingdom as its King.

His star in the east.—Much speculation, guesses, and superstitions have been recorded by man as to the meaning of the "star in the east." It is designated by these wise men as "his star in the east." "The east" literally means "the rising"; some have preferred to translate this "at its rising," or "when it rose." A kindred verb occurs in Matt. 4: 16, which is translated "did light spring up." The same word is translated "dayspring," or "dawn." (Luke 1: 78.) It is a question which has not been settled as to whether the expression of the Magi, "we saw his star," indicates a miraculous appearance or whether it was an ordinary observance in the course of their watching the heavens, and by some means they were informed that a certain star or constellation of stars indicated some great event which had just taken place. Whether some supernatural agency is asserted here by these wise men we shall never be able to determine; there is no use to conjecture on this point. We are honestly endeavoring to ascertain the sense of the record as given by Matthew without regard to any preconceived opinion or system, and fearlessly express this sense in simple terms; hence no conjecture is to be included as a part of the divine will. In some way God had indicated to the Magi through a star that his Son had been born; so we will not conjecture whether God indicated this to them by miraculous agency or by a natural appearance of the star. It is a fact which Matthew records when these men left Jerusalem, that "the star, which they saw in the east, went before them, till it came and stood over where the young child was." (Verse 9.) The question has been raised as to whether this was "a real star"; it is difficult for us to think that a real star moved before these men and stood over a particular house so as to distinguish it from other houses. Did others see this star? Would others follow it? Would not such a miraculous manifestation of a star attract multitudes? This would make the whole affair a stupendous miracle, but this is not necessarily implied, even if the words of the text be taken in their most literal sense. Travel in the east was done largely at night, and especially by such as these wise men. It would not be necessary for a heavenly body which is larger than all Palestine to move forward and guide these men from Jerusalem to Bethlehem and then stand over the particular house where the babe of Bethlehem was; such a heavenly body would be over all the houses in Bethlehem and not over any particular one. Whatever the "star" was, it guided these men and indicated the particular house where they could find the child. The supernatural is admitted here, since there were so many miracles connected with Jesus' birth, and the visit of

and are come to ³worship him. 3. And when Herod the king heard it, he

³The Greek word denotes an act of reverence whether paid to a creature (see ch. 4. 9; 18. 26), or to the Creator (see ch. 4. 10).

the Magi was an event of great spiritual significance, fit to be the occasion of a miracle. If these men were astrologers, it is natural for divine impressions to be made upon them in terms of a "star"; God led the thoughts of these wise men first to notice and to interpret "his star in the east"; next they take this long journey of some months to connect this wondrous birth with the star; then they come to Jerusalem and make inquiry as to the place of his birth.

Come to worship him.—The purpose of the coming of the wise men was to "worship him"; they went to Jerusalem to inquire where he was that they might worship him. They came to do homage or give honor to him. There is no reason expressed by Matthew to believe that they regarded this newborn king as in any sense a divine being, though they apparently expected his reign to influence other nations. The whole scene was a signal honor to the infant King. The word in the Greek from which we translate "worship" means veneration, homage, submission, by prostration of the face to the ground. (Gen. 19: 1; 43: 6.) The word here, however, is to be taken as meaning adoration in the more general sense. Some think that it refers merely to religious, not to political, homage. It is to be noted that Matthew records these Gentiles as the first to know that Jesus was "born King of the Jews." All these events emphasize the fact that Jesus, as "King of the Jews," must have a mission; they originated not with man, but with God. Matthew's record means that God's hand was behind all these movements and that God was responsible for all of the testimony. The visit of the Magi and the similar visit of the shepherds. (Luke 2: 8-20) are utterly incompatible with the theory of the mere humanity of Jesus; they prove his divine Sonship, and admit no other explanation; they honor the infant Jesus, not as one who had name and fame to earn, but as one who brought it with him by his very birth.

was troubled, and all Jerusalem with him. 4 And gathering together all the chief priests and scribes of the people, he inquired of them where the Christ

3 **He was troubled, and all Jerusalem with him.**—When these Magi came to Jerusalem and made inquiry concerning the place of the birth of the "King of the Jews," Herod in some way heard of their inquiry. It may be that someone reported to Herod, as the Magi did not go directly to Herod, for "when Herod the king heard it, he was troubled." He was troubled about the idea of a rival. Herod, as a foreigner and usurper, feared one who was *"born* King of the Jews"; this was near the close of Herod's reign, and naturally he was anxious concerning the succession of one to the throne; he could not hear with any degree of satisfaction that the founder of a rival dynasty had been born or that his successor would be a Jew. He had ambitions that one of his own family would succeed him as ruler. Herod disliked the thought of his throne being overthrown.

Any disturbance with the rulers of Judea would disturb "all Jerusalem with him." All the people would be disturbed at the same time for fear of new tyrannies and cruelties as the effect of Herod's jealous fears. The people were not disturbed so much on account of the times of misfortune which were expected to precede the Messiah, but in keeping with their special circumstances they dreaded the adoption by the tyrant in his maintaining his authority over them. The people had witnessed so many of Herod's cruelties that when a competitor was suspected they seemed to have dreaded new scenes of confusion and bloodshed; they were troubled at that event which should have given them the greatest joy.

4. **And gathering together all the chief priests and scribes of the people.**—When Herod heard of the inquiry of the "Wisemen from the east," he was disturbed; he did not know the prophecies concerning the Messiah, so he quickly assembled "the chief priests and scribes." The Sanhedrin was composed of chief priests, scribes, and elders; it is not known whether this was an assembly of the Sanhedrin or whether it was an extraordinary convocation of all the chief priests and learned

should be born. 5. And they said unto him, In Bethlehem of Judæa: for

men. The "chief priests" were probably the heads of the twenty-four courses or classes; David had divided the priests into twenty-four classes, and had appointed a head of each class; this head was called a "chief priest." (1 Chron. 24: 6; 2 Chron. 36: 14.) Some think that these "chief priests" were not of the twenty-four classes, but were those who had served as high priests. Herod and the Romans had made frequent changes in the high priests; however, this view does not seem to be the correct one; others think that the ex-high priests and the heads of the twenty-four classes are included in "chief priests." The high priest who was in office at the time was probably included in this number.

The "scribes" were learned men; the scribes formed a separate class in the Sanhedrin, though only a portion of them were members of it. These scribes were lawyers and theologians; they obtained their name probably from the work which they originally did; after synagogues were established, copies of the law were required for distribution to the different synagogues; this called for a class of learned men who could transcribe the law. "Scribe" was also applied to one who was well educated; probably not all of the scribes in the days of our Lord were scribes in the sense of copying the law, but were learned men or doctors of the law. (Ezra 7: 6; Matt. 23: 35; Luke 10: 25; Acts 5: 34.) "The elders" are not mentioned here, and some think that this is positive proof that the assembly was not the regular Sanhedrin.

He inquired of them where the Christ should be born.—After assembling those who were supposed to know, Herod made inquiry of them as to "where the Christ should be born." The only point that Herod had in assembling this group of learned men was to make inquiry as to the specific place where the Christ would be born; this was the inquiry that the wise men from the east had made. Their inquiry aroused Herod's interest, and he is now anxious to know just where the scriptures taught that Jesus should be born. Surely if any one among the Jews knew, these men would

thus it is written through the prophet,
6 ⁴'And thou Bethlehem, land of Judah,
Art in no wise least among the princes of Judah:

---

⁴Mic. v. 2.

---

know; Herod summoned together the religious teachers of the nation because the question pertained to religion. These learned men were to tell him what they knew concerning the birthplace of the Messiah; by this question Herod leaves it undetermined whether the birth had already taken place, or was still to come; he is indefinite on this point, but specific in his demand as to the *place* that he should be born.

Here the inquiry is "where the Christ should be born." "Christ" means the anointed one; evidently Herod understood that this newborn King was to be anointed. Herod was very old at this time, and he was much concerned about who should succeed him; he neither understood the spiritual nature of the Messiah's kingdom nor did he consider that a newborn infant was not likely to disturb him. "Christ" is the Greek form of the Hebrew word "Messiah." We are not told whether Herod wanted to use this information in a righteous purpose, but the context clearly shows that he intended to use this information to direct the wise men where to find him, and probably have him put to death.

5, 6 They said unto him, In Bethlehem of Judaea.—Herod became thoroughly aroused when he heard of the inquiry the wise men had made and determined to ascertain the place of the birth of this infant King; he called together the religious leaders of Jerusalem and demanded of them this information. The chief priests and scribes promptly answered and said, "In Bethlehem of Judæa"; it was the Bethlehem that was within the bounds of the tribe of Judah; this distinguished it from the Bethlehem that was in the tribe of Zebulun. (Josh. 19: 15.) They did not hesitate, neither did they have to take time to search; they were familiar with the place where the Messiah should be born. Had they been as definite about other things pertaining to Jesus, they would have appreciated him as a Savior more.

> For out of thee shall come forth a governor,
> Who shall be shepherd of my people Israel.

In support of their answer they quoted from the prophet Micah. They answered Herod, "thus it is written through the prophet"; they had no theory about the place of the birth of Jesus, no assumption was made, no guess was offered, no speculation presented; they answered directly and specifically what the prophet said. They should have been as ready to take what was written concerning him by other prophets as they were to take what Micah said concerning the place. The passage is freely quoted from Micah by Matthew. In Micah the place is called "Bethlehem Ephrathah." Matthew substitutes for "Ephrathah" "land of Judah"; hence, the passage, as these learned men quote it, differs slightly from the Septuagint; yet on the point in question its testimony is very conclusive.

Out of thee shall come forth a governor.—Micah says, "Out of thee shall one come forth unto me that is to be ruler in Israel"; Matthew substitutes "governor" for "ruler." Quoting further from the prophet, this governor is further described as one "who shall be shepherd of my people Israel." The word translated here as "shepherd" is correct; it involves the whole office of the shepherd, as guiding, guarding, folding, and feeding the flock. In ancient Greece the kings were called "the shepherds of the people." The people said to David, "Jehovah said to thee, Thou shalt be shepherd of my people Israel." (2 Sam. 5: 2; Psalm 78: 70-72.) The meaning of Mic. 5: 2 seems to be that, although Bethlehem was the least among the princes of Judah, from it would come the Messiah; though Bethlehem is one of the smallest cities of Judah, it will be one of the greatest in celebrity, as the birthplace of the Messiah; hence, this Messiah should "shepherd" God's people. God is often called a shepherd. (Gen. 48: 15; Psalm 23: 1; 77: 20; 80: 1; Isa. 40: 11; Ezek. 34: 11-31.) Jesus called himself "the good shepherd" (John 10: 11); Peter was commanded to shepherd God's people (John 21: 16); he called Jesus the shepherd of our souls (1 Pet. 2: 25), and the "chief Shepherd" (1 Pet. 5: 4). In Hebrews, Jesus is called "the great shepherd

7 Then Herod privily called the ¹Wise-men, and learned of them exactly

of the sheep." (Heb. 13: 20.) Again Jesus is referred to: "The Lamb that is in the midst of the throne shall be their shepherd." (Rev. 7: 17.) This means that Jesus was the one who would go before, or lead the way for salvation of the human race. "He calleth his own sheep by name, and leadeth them out. . . . He goeth before them, and the sheep follow him." (John 10: 3, 4.) The government of a good king was similar to the care a good shepherd has of his flock, hence both shepherd and king are used here. This would be a wide contrast between the conduct of Herod as ruler and the newborn King.

7 Then Herod privily called the Wise-men.—It is characteristic of Herod to be cunning; he called "the Wise-men" privately. In public Herod doubtless affected unconcern; but he was deeply concerned about this place; if his inquiries should become known, the parties affected might learn of his intention and escape. It was characteristic of Herod's political life to do things in secret; he evidently shared the mistake of the wise men that the birth of the child coincided with the first appearance of the star, and that the child was then in its second year. He artfully called the wise men to his aid and made further inquiry of them "and learned of them exactly what time the star appeared." He was anxious to know the precise time when the star first appeared in order to get his age approximately. Herod wanted to know just when this child who was predicted to be a King was born, which event marked the first appearance of the star. Some think that when these wise men first came he had inquired why they believed the star to signify that a King of the Jews was born; this was important to him in order to carry out his evil intentions. He learned accurately from the chief priests and scribes the place, and now he wants to know definitely the time when this child was born. Of course, he asked them the time of the appearing of the star; how long has it been since you first saw the star in the east? At what time did it appear? These are questions that were in Herod's heart and which he no doubt propounded to the Magi.

⁵what time the star appeared. 8 And he sent them to Bethlehem, and said, Go and search out exactly concerning the young child; and when ye have found *him,* bring me word, that I also may come and ³worship him. 9 And they, having heard the king, went their way; and lo, the star, which they saw in the east, went before them, till it came and stood over where

⁵Or, *the time of the star that appeared*

8 And he sent them to Bethlehem.—After gaining the desired information from the chief priests and elders, and then ascertaining the exact time when the star first appeared to the Magi, he lost no time in sending them to Bethlehem. He said to them, "Go and search out exactly concerning the young child." They were to search diligently until they found the exact location of the child; he now knows the town, but he does not know the exact location of the child. He did not know that the star which had brought them to Jerusalem would also locate specifically the child; he wanted to know the home where the young child was; he wanted to know definitely so that he could carry out his evil intentions.

When ye have found him, bring me word.—Herod gives his command as one in authority; he expects these men to obey him. When they have located the child in Bethlehem, he demands that they return to him and give him the exact location of the child. He gives as his motive for wanting to know the exact location "that I also may come and worship him." This hypocrisy was characteristic of Herod; he had no intention of worshiping the child should he find him. He knew that the wise men had come to worship him, and he identifies his own purpose with theirs; he is not sincere in making his purpose coincide with their purpose. By such treachery Herod hoped to find the child and murder him. Herod's perfidy is manifest; he did not send any of his courtiers with the wise men; this would have excited some suspicion. He wanted the wise men to find Jesus and return to him and make a report, thinking that they would go on to their own country, and he could then carry out his treacherous and diabolical motives. Herod was a man who never left any stone unturned when he wanted to carry out his base intentions.

9, 10 And they, having heard the king, went their way.—They listened attentively and courteously to the demands of

the young child was. 10 And when they saw the star, they rejoiced with exceeding great joy. 11 And they came into the house and saw the young child with Mary his mother; and they fell down and worshipped him;

King Herod; no doubt they intended to obey his command. The Magi were not well acquainted with Herod's character and appear not to have suspected his real design; they left him to carry out his directions. When they left Herod in Jerusalem, "lo, the star, which they saw in the east, went before them, till it came and stood over where the young child was." They rejoiced to see the same star again, and to be guided by it to the very spot where the young child was. God had instructed them by his star that the "King of the Jews" had been born, and now he guides them by the star to the child; the point was too delicate and vital to be left indefinite. There were other children in Bethlehem, and the particular child must be pointed out to them. All liability to mistake must be precluded; nothing indefinite about this affair must occur. The star "went before them," that is, literally, the star led them forward. The star led them to Bethlehem as the place where Jesus was born; hence the star confirmed the prophecy of Micah. Some have conjectured that this all occurred at night, as the star would not have been visible in the daytime; the text as recorded by Matthew lends no encouragement to this; Jehovah could guide them with a star in daylight as well as at night. Some think that this star was a simple luminous meteor in a starlight form, and at a very short distance from the ground, otherwise they could not have ascertained the place where the star lay. It seems that the star which they saw in the east had disappeared before they reached Jerusalem, but now it reappeared and guided them to Bethlehem. This star enabled them to find the child without making inquiries in Bethlehem that would have directed public attention to him and would have interfered with his escape from danger. God in his wisdom and power was protecting the child, and such means are used as will aid him in protecting the child with Joseph and Mary. The Magi rejoiced with exceeding great joy when they saw the star; they could rely now upon Jehovah to lead them to the exact place.

and opening their treasures they offered unto him gifts, gold and frankincense and myrrh. 12 And being warned *of God* in a dream that they

And they fell down and worshipped him.—The wise men had been directed to the very place where the babe was; Joseph and Mary evidently had moved the babe from the stable and manger into some house, probably that of a friend of the family, for "they came into the house and saw the young child with Mary his mother." The Magi did not arrive at Bethlehem until some time after the birth of Jesus; we do not know just how old the babe was at this time. Joseph's name is not mentioned here by Matthew as the Magi "saw the young child with Mary his mother." We are not to think that this house was the place in which the shepherds had found the child on the morning after his birth. (Luke 2: 16.) Very probably it had been some time since the child was born; some think that the visit of the Magi to Bethlehem was after the presentation in the temple of the child, which was forty days after his birth. (Lev. 12: 1-4; Luke 2: 22.) This point is further strengthened by the fact that the flight into Egypt followed immediately after the visit of the Magi. Some even think that there had possibly been a journey to Nazareth (Luke 2: 39), and that Joseph was now making Bethlehem his home.

When the wise men saw the babe and Mary, "they fell down and worshipped him." They did homage to him; we do not know how much they knew about the divinity of Jesus, but we are led to believe that the homage which they paid to the babe was something more than that which is usually paid to royalty; the miraculous manner in which they had been guided to the house must have impressed them that the child was more than the ordinary. These Magi were Gentiles, and they are the first to pay homage to Jesus as King. The worship which they gave to the child expresses their thankfulness for the guidance that they had received in coming to Bethlehem. Their worship is an expression of gratitude to God and homage to the child.

And opening their treasures they offered unto him gifts.— The bags or boxes which contained their treasures had been brought with them to Bethlehem. It was an oriental custom

should not return to Herod, they departed into their own country another way.

---

for one to bring a present or offering when that one entered into the presence of royalty; it is another way of paying homage to the person who is honored. Their gifts were "gold and frankincense and myrrh." Some have interpreted these three gifts as being emblematic of the divinity, regal office, and manhood of Jesus; however, there is nothing in the text to indicate this. The gold which they presented to the child was a providential supply for the expenses to Egypt and to live upon while there. "Frankincense" was a whitish, resinous substance, having an acrid taste and a strong, fragrant odor; it was made from the gum or sap of a tree which grew in Arabia and in India. "Myrrh" was a precious gum, having a strong but not disagreeable odor and a bitter taste; it also was made from a tree which grew in Arabia, Egypt, and Persia; it was much used as a perfume. Frankincense was used chiefly in sacrifices and in the services of the temple. Myrrh was used for fumigation and for improving the taste of wine, and especially as an ingredient for a very precious ointment. These gifts were all in keeping with the oriental custom of paying homage to a notable person.

12 And being warned of God in a dream.—Herod had given specific instructions to the Magi that when they found the babe they should return and inform him of the exact location of the child. Probably they had no other thought in mind but to do as Herod had commanded them; at least, they had no intentions of insulting the king or incurring his displeasure by refusing to obey his orders; but they were "warned of God" not to return to Jerusalem and to Herod. "Of God" is not in the original, though it is implied as in verse twenty-two. We have no indication that they were suspicious of Herod. The fact that God warned them not to return to Herod seems to indicate that it was their intention to return to Herod, or else God would not have gone to the trouble of warning them in a dream not to obey his command. It is probable that the direct way home would have led by Jerusalem. The Greek verb which is translated "warned" means to give a response to one who asks or consults; in the passive voice as used here it means to receive an answer; this would indicate that the wise men had sought counsel of God, and while asleep in a dream God answered them and told them not to return by way of Jerusalem or return to Herod. The Lord took care that these wise men should not become unwittingly a party to the murderous schemes of Herod; hence, God told them to go to their eastern home by another route than through Jerusalem, and leave Herod none the wiser for what they had learned. These wise men were obedient to God as "they departed into their own country another way."

4. THE FLIGHT INTO EGYPT
2: 13-15

13 Now when they were departed, behold, an angel of the Lord appeareth to Joseph in a dream, saying, Arise and take the young child and his mother, and flee into Egypt, and be thou there until I tell thee: for Herod will seek

13 **An angel of the Lord appeareth to Joseph in a dream.**—When the wise men from the east had departed and were returning home, but not by way of Jerusalem as Herod had requested, "an angel of the Lord appeareth to Joseph in a dream." It seems that immediately after the departure of the Magi the angel appeared to Joseph in a dream; though the wise men had withdrawn from the influence of Herod, the child was still in danger. The coming of Jesus into the world was attended by angels; angels sang to the shepherds peace on earth and good will to men when Jesus was born; an angel had announced to Mary that she would have a son; an angel had told Joseph to take Mary to wife; and now an angel is guarding the safety of the child. Herod is fighting against God; he is fighting a losing fight; God will take care of the child that is to be the Savior of the world. It does not mean that Joseph dreamed that an angel appeared to him, but that an angel actually presented himself to Joseph while he was asleep.

Arise and take the young child and his mother, and flee into Egypt.—Joseph is given specific instruction by the angel; God always speaks to man so that man can understand. He is to "take the young child . . . and flee into Egypt"; the mother is to be taken with the child. Mary is as important now in caring for the child Jesus as she was in bringing him into the world; this was a very precious task imposed upon Joseph. The angel gave him a most precious charge when he told him to take care of the child and his mother; he also was exposed to great danger; he was to protect the child and his mother. God's providence is exercised over the child; he would take care of the child, but this does not exclude Joseph; it rather places a responsibility on him, as God is to take care of the child through Joseph.

Egypt was at this time a Roman province and was well governed; its jurisdiction was beyond Herod's authority; the family would be safe from the threatened destruction of Herod. The journey was probably seventy-five miles southwest from Bethlehem to the border, and a hundred miles more would take him into the heart of the country. Egypt was easy of access, and in earlier days it had been a place of refuge for fugitives from Judea. (1 Kings 11: 40; Jer. 43: 7.) There were many Jews in Egypt at this time. Alexander the Great, in building the city of Alexandria, had assigned a place to the Jews, granting them equal privileges with the Macedonians. In Egypt was made the greater part, probably the whole, of the famous translation of the Old Testament from Hebrew into Greek, which we have learned to call the Septuagint. Philo, in a treatise written about A.D. 40, says that the Jews in Egypt numbered about a million. It is probable that the gifts of the Magi aided in the support of Joseph and Mary as they journeyed to Egypt. Joseph received the instructions from the angel; everything was to be done under divine direction, and then it would be done simply and successfully. It was not necessary for Joseph to know the times and seasons, but he should obey God in going into Egypt.

Joseph was to remain in Egypt with the child and his mother until he received further instruction as to what he should do. Joseph is to commit himself and his ways unto God. God will direct him at the appointed time to come out of Egypt. We do not know to what town or village Joseph

the young child to destroy him. 14 And he arose and took the young child and his mother by night, and departed into Egypt; 15 and was there until

went in Egypt; it is not necessary to guess at the town. Some think that he went to Matareeh, a few miles northwest of Cairo. This was about 4 B.C., when Jesus was a few weeks old. Augustus Caesar was emperor of Rome; Herod the Great was king of Judea. Joseph was prompt in obeying God as he departed that night. The arrival of the Magi, their departure, and the flight of Joseph and Mary into Egypt were not known to the people of Bethlehem; all were done under the direction of Jehovah without any publicity. There were different roads that led through the desert into Egypt, but we are not told which route Joseph followed.

For Herod will seek the young child to destroy him.—Joseph was told specifically why he should take the young child and his mother into Egypt; he was under the jurisdiction of Herod while in Bethlehem, and Herod could do what he willed while Joseph was under his authority; so Joseph is to take the child and his mother and get out from under Herod's jurisdiction; this place was Egypt. When we think of the cruelty of Herod and his abominable character, we can realize the danger that Joseph and Mary were in. We read of deaths by strangulation, deaths by burning, deaths by getting cleft asunder, deaths by secret assassination, confessions forced by unutterable torture, acts of insolent and inhuman lust, all these mark the annals of the reign of Herod; we are not surprised that a Jewish writer would say of conditions that "the survivors during his lifetime were even more miserable than the sufferers." Another has written of Herod that "it would be better to be his sow than to be his son." Such presents a vivid picture of the bloodthirsty Herod who sought the life of the young child.

14 He arose and took the young child and his mother by night.—It seems that Joseph left the same night that the angel visited him in a dream; he was prompt and faithful in his obedience, for he trusted fully in God. He probably left the same night, for there was need of great haste; Herod would not delay his vengeance when he learned that the wise

[2:14, 15.]   MATTHEW   53

the death of Herod: that it might be fulfilled which was spoken by the Lord through the prophet, saying, ⁶Out of Egypt did I call my son.

⁶Hos. xi. 1.

---

men had returned another way. Mary and Joseph would not want to wait in the midst of such danger after such a warning. It was customary in the east, when one had to make a long journey, to start early in the morning, hours before daybreak. They could leave suddenly and unexpectedly in the night without danger of Herod's discovering where they had gone, or even the fact of their leaving. Joseph and Mary begin to see that the high honor of being the earthly parent and protector of the child is freighted with great danger; every God-given honor is attended with great responsibility, sacrifice, and sorrow.

And departed into Egypt.—Egypt was an available place of refuge; it was far enough away to be out from under Herod's jurisdiction; it was the nearest place of safe refuge; good roads led through the desert to their destination; they would find other Jews there with whom to associate. This flight to Egypt would have three purposes: the security of the child from his enemies; the showing of divine care and valuation of the holy child; and the making of his childhood's suffering an antitype to the history of chosen Israel. God had imposed upon Mary and Joseph the task of protecting and rearing at all hazards this child; they promptly and cheerfully assumed the task to which God had called them and faithfully fulfilled their mission. Joseph and Mary are now in Egypt where the rage of Herod cannot pursue them.

And was there until the death of Herod.—We do not know how long Joseph and Mary remained in Egypt; it was until after the death of Herod; it is uncertain as to the time that they remained in Egypt. The death of Herod is supposed to have occurred on April 1, 4 B.C.; his death occurred at Jericho; he was nearly seventy years old; it was recorded that he was buried with great pomp at Herodium, which is close to Bethlehem in Judea. Archelaus, his son, was greeted as king, April 2. It is recorded that there was a riot and massacre of the Jews in the temple at the preparation of the Passover on April 10.

Out of Egypt did I call my son.—The prophet Hosea is quoted here, and it is applied by Matthew to Jesus. In Hosea the language is, "When Israel was a child, then I loved him, and called my son out of Egypt." (Hos. 11: 1.) In Joseph's taking Mary and the child into Egypt at the command of God, and in his returning from Egypt at the command of God, this scripture was fulfilled. Joseph did not take the family into Egypt in order to fulfill the prophecy; neither can we say that God sent him into Egypt and called him out in order to fulfill this prophecy; but these incidents which occurred with the child Jesus, Matthew by inspiration says, fulfilled this prophecy. Joseph and the holy family going into Egypt and his returning with the family from Egypt were the antitypes of Israel's entrance into Egypt and the departure from Egyptian bondage. It seems that Hosea referred to Israel's exodus from the bondage of Egypt, not as a prophecy, but as a historical fact that took place many centuries before, and recounted there as proof of God's love for Israel; but the record of Israel's going into Egypt and returning from Egypt became a prophecy concerning the movement of the child Jesus. Both Israel and Joseph with his family went into Egypt at the command of God; both came out of Egypt at the command of God. Israel was figuratively called God's son (Ex. 4: 22), and was considered by the Jews a type of the Messiah. As Israel in the childhood of the nation was called out of Egypt, so was Jesus. We may cite other resemblances in minute detail; his temptation of forty days in the desert resembles Israel's temptation of forty years in the desert, which itself corresponded to the forty days spent by the spies. (Num. 14: 34.) In this way we can see how the historical statement of Hosea concerning Israel may also have been a prediction concerning the Messiah, as Matthew here declares it to be.

5. MASSACRE OF THE INNOCENTS
2: 16-18

16 Then Herod, when he saw that he was mocked of the ¹Wise-men, was exceeding wroth, and sent forth, and slew all the male children that were in Bethlehem, and in all the borders thereof, from two years old and under, according to the time which he had exactly learned of the ¹Wise-men. 17

16 Herod, when he saw that he was mocked of the Wisemen, was exceeding wroth.—The wise men received from Herod the information they needed, and then went back home another way without bringing the information he required of them; they had been warned of God not to return by way of Jerusalem; of course, Herod did not know this. He thought that he had been "mocked" by the Magi; this word in the original means to trifle with, to treat as children treat their fellows. He became very angry; a despotic ruler easily comes to regard the slightest neglect to do his bidding as a gross insult; he had wicked intents to carry out, and was enraged when he thought that others were interfering with his plans; such a neglect or disobedience on the part of the Magi infuriated Herod. If his evil plans were not carried out, or even if they were delayed, he became incensed, and in his blind rage he became more determined to execute his wicked plan. He "was exceeding wroth." He was outwitted, and his rage knew no bounds. While in such a frame of mind, he would naturally magnify the danger which seemed to threaten his dynasty.

And slew all the male children that were in Bethlehem.—Herod was determined not to be outwitted; he did not learn the exact location of the child, so he commanded an act that would include the babe Jesus; he commanded that all the male children "from two years old and under" should be killed. Excessively enraged, he thought still to accomplish his purpose by destroying the male children in Bethlehem within the estimated age of the child Jesus as he inferred it from the wise men. It was not Herod's nature to take the least account of the cruelty or the guilt which his command involved; some translators have put it "all the children," but a better translation is "all the male children," as the original word determines the gender, which is masculine. He did not stop with the destruction of the male children "that were in Bethlehem," but his command included those "in all the borders thereof"; this included the male children in the houses and hamlets which belonged to the territory of Bethlehem. It was a male child that he feared as his rival to his dynasty, hence he was not interested in destroying the female infants. We see a good reason why both the visit of the wise men to Bethlehem and the flight of Joseph and Mary to Egypt had been kept a secret; if these events had been known in Bethlehem, the people could have saved their children by informing Herod that the particular male child that he wanted to destroy had been taken to Egypt.

The New Testament record of this atrocious deed of Herod is the only record that we have of it; for this reason some have doubted the New Testament record. Josephus, a Jewish writer and historian, makes no reference to this foul deed of Herod. It is not known how many children perished; we have no way of determining the population of Bethlehem at that time, neither any way of estimating the number of male children that were there at that time. Commentators have varied in their estimation of the number from one thousand down to twenty; evidently the number could not have been very large. Since no great number of children perished in so small a place as Bethlehem and its neighborhood, it would not make much impression on any historian. Herod had marked the way to his throne with blood; he had murdered his wife and three sons; he had committed many crimes against the Jews; it was likely enough that in his blind fury he would make such a savage law or command as the destruction of the babes in Bethlehem. There is no wonder that the affair is not noticed by Josephus as it was of small importance when compared to the other wicked deeds of Herod. This massacre of the children was not done openly, but was done in a secret at Herod's official act, hence no record of it would be preserved. Herod made sure that he had included the baby Jesus; his plan of destroying all the male children "from two years old and under" gave him a margin on both sides; that is, to include children of such an age that if the star appeared either a

Then was fulfilled that which was spoken through Jeremiah the prophet, saying,
18   ⁷A voice was heard in Ramah,
       Weeping and great mourning,
       Rachel weeping for her children;
       And she would not be comforted, because they are not.

---
⁷Jer. xxxi. 15.

few months after or a few months before the birth of Jesus, he would be included in the number that was slain.

17, 18 Then was fulfilled that which was spoken through Jeremiah the prophet.—"Then was fulfilled" is the way Matthew introduces his quotation from Jeremiah; the prediction is found in Jer. 31: 15. In other places Matthew introduces the prophecy by saying "that it might be fulfilled." This is another fulfillment of a typical prophecy and not a literal prophecy. Jeremiah referred to the deportation of the Jews to Babylon; Rachel, the ancestress of Benjamin, was buried near Bethlehem; she is represented as bewailing from the grave the captivity of her children; the sound of her lamentations reaches northward beyond Jerusalem, and is heard at Ramah, a fortress of Israel on the frontier toward Judah where the captives were collected. It means that the grief caused by the carrying away of the kingdom of Judah into Babylonian captivity caused such lamentation of the female captives that it was heard even by Rachel in her tomb. Jeremiah used figurative language to express the deep sorrow of the exiled mothers of the kingdom of Judah. In the massacre of the infants of Bethlehem the calamity of the mothers of Judah was not only renewed, but its description verified in the fullest and most tragic manner. Rachel represents the mothers of Bethlehem lamenting over their children.

Matthew gives three quotations from the prophets in this chapter. (Verses 6, 15, 18.) These three quotations from the prophets illustrate three different classes of quotations which are found in the New Testament. The first quotation is concerning the birthplace of Jesus, and it is strictly a prediction as it refers directly to that event. The next class refers to the call of Jesus out of Egypt and illustrates **an example of a** prophecy which has a double reference, a primary and a secondary fulfillment; these are sometimes called *typical,* because they are originally spoken concerning a type and find another fulfillment in the antitype. The third class refers to the weeping at Bethlehem by the mothers of the babes that were slain; this is an example in which the event fulfills the meaning of the words used by a prophet, though the words had originally no reference at all to this event; it is a verbal fulfillment, and not a real fulfillment, as is found in the other two classes.

The care that was taken over the infant King helps to establish his later claim as King; God emphasized the prediction that he was to be a king by his miraculously guiding the Magi to him; his protection of him from the slaughter is another proof of the divinity of Jesus. All of the prophecies concerning Jesus up to this point have been fulfilled, and we may expect all others to be as minutely fulfilled as were those pertaining to the birth and infancy of Jesus.

6. THE RETURN TO NAZARETH
2: 19-23

19 But when Herod was dead, behold, an angel of the Lord appeareth in a dream to Joseph in Egypt, saying, 20 Arise and take the young child and

19 But when Herod was dead.—Herod died a few weeks after the flight into Egypt; we have no way of knowing just when Joseph and Mary took the babe to Egypt, hence no way of knowing how long they remained there before the death of Herod. Herod died at Jericho just before the Passover in the year 750 after the building of Rome, four years before the date from which we reckon our time. It has been calculated that the Passover occurred on April 12 that year and that Herod died seven to fourteen days before the Passover. He was buried within the bounds of Bethlehem, where he had murdered the innocent children.

An angel of the Lord appeareth in a dream to Joseph in Egypt.—This is the third time that the angel of the Lord has appeared to Joseph according to Matthew's record; the angel in a dream told him to take Mary to be his wife; the angel

his mother, and go into the land of Israel: for they are dead that sought the young child's life. 21 And he arose and took the young child and his mother, and came into the land of Israel. 22 But when he heard that Arche-

told him to take Mary and the child and flee into Egypt; and now the angel appears again to him and tells him to return from Egypt. Herod had died in his seventieth year, and now the child was safe, hence the angel instructs Joseph to return to his native land. God, ever mindful of his own, now apprizes Joseph by a dream that he may safely return to the land of Israel, for Herod is dead.

20 **Arise and take the young child and his mother.**—This time Joseph is to arise and take the child and his mother and "go"; in going down into Egypt Joseph was told to take the young child and his mother and "flee into Egypt." Joseph patiently and faithfully obeys all orders; he proves himself to be a worthy guardian of the young child and his mother. He is to "go into the land of Israel." This is indefinite as to the exact location; it was definite enough for Joseph while in Egypt; he is to go out of Egypt and go to "the land of Israel."

They are dead that sought the young child's life.—"They" may include Herod and his wicked son Antipater; Antipater was killed five days before his father Herod died; "they" may also include the government officers of Herod who would pass out of office with the death of Herod. We infer from this that there were more than Herod involved in seeking the death of the young child. The angel informed Joseph that all who were seeking the child's life were dead. Some think that only the death of Herod is referred to here; others think that Herod had enlisted the sympathy and services of others in seeking to destroy the young child. If Antipater is included in the statement, we may assume that he had shared his father's hostility to the child.

21 **He arose and took the young child and his mother.**—We are impressed with the promptness with which Joseph obeyed the orders which he had received. God is pleased with such prompt obedience. Joseph is guided by the direction of God in going into Egypt and in returning from Egypt; he is as prompt in his obedience in returning from Egypt, when all

laus was reigning over Judæa in the room of his father Herod, he was

---

dangers have passed, as he was in going down into Egypt when the dangers were numerous; Joseph is an example of prompt obedience to God under all circumstances. Joseph came into the land of Israel and it seems that he intended to return to Bethlehem of Judea. Some think that it was the intention of Joseph to rear the infant King in the city of his birth until the time should come when they would expect him to occupy Jerusalem, "the city of the great King." Joseph would naturally come to Judea first in returning from Egypt as Judea was in the southern part of "the land of Israel."

22 But when he heard that Archelaus was reigning over Judea.—After the death of Herod, his kingdom was divided among his three sons by Augustus Caesar. Archelaus was given Judea, Idumea, and Samaria; Herod Antipas obtained Galilee and Perea; while Philip received Badanea, Trachonitis, and Auranitis. Herod and Philip received the title of "tetrarch, but Archelaus received the title of "ethnarch." The title of king was conferred later on Archelaus. The title of king was to be conferred on Archelaus provided he proved himself worthy; however, nine years after he received his portion he was banished by Augustus Caesar. Upon the death of Herod, Archelaus was proclaimed king by the army, but it was not confirmed by Augustus Caesar. Archelaus was a wicked ruler; his reputation was no better than that of his father.

When Joseph learned that Archelaus was reigning over Judea in Herod's place, "he was afraid to go thither." He probably knew the reputation of Archelaus, and thought that he would take vengeance on him and his family. He knew that Archelaus was wicked enough to destroy the young child, and he did not know but that he had it in mind to do so. Joseph was surprised and disappointed at learning that Archelaus was reigning over Judea. He was afraid to remain in Judea with the holy child. If Joseph went to Bethlehem, that would remind Archelaus of him who was "born King of the

2 : 22, 23.] MATTHEW 61

afraid to go thither; and being warned of *God* in a dream, he withdrew into the parts of Galilee, 23 and came and dwelt in a city called Nazareth; that it

Jews," while if Joseph carried his family to a distance, Archelaus would still imagine that the child was dead.

Being warned of God in a dream, he withdrew into the parts of Galilee.—He turned aside and did not go to his intended destination; it is possible that he took another road when he heard of Archelaus reigning over Judea and went to Galilee. This is the fourth revelation that Joseph has received concerning the child and his care over it; it implies a high tone of spirituality of Joseph. The watchfulness of Joseph for the safety of the child serves as the natural groundwork for divine communication, and the repeated revelations to him in dreams emphasize divine guidance in caring for the child. These four dreams occurred at considerable intervals of time. While Joseph was afraid to dwell in Judea under the authority of Archelaus, he did not make a move until God warned him in another dream to go into Galilee.

Galilee was the northern division or portion of "the land of Israel." At this time Palestine was divided into three divisions—Judea in the southern part, Samaria occupied the central portion, and Galilee composed the northern division. Joseph turned aside "into the parts of Galilee." Archelaus had no authority over Galilee. Herod Antipas was the ruler over this country. He was a different man and governed with more leniency than did his brother Archelaus. Herod Antipas and Archelaus were at enmity with each other at this time; this was a most favorable circumstance for Joseph and his family.

23 And came and dwelt in a city called Nazareth.—Nazareth was Joseph's former home; it was a small town or a large village. It was "called Nazareth"; "Nazareth" means a shoot, or branch, or protectress; it was about twenty miles east of the Mediterranean Sea and sixteen miles west of the Sea of Galilee. And so it came to pass that Jesus was brought up in Nazareth. Nazareth is not mentioned in the Old Testament; very few towns and events are recorded of the northern territory of Palestine. At this time this town had a mean reputa-

might be fulfilled which was spoken through the prophets ¹that he should be called a Nazarene.

¹Isa. xi. 1 in the Heb.?

tion. Later Nathanael asked, "Can any good thing come out of Nazareth?" (John 1: 46.) Nathanael lived in "Cana in Galilee" (John 21: 2), which was only a few miles distance from Nazareth.

Nazareth had no reputation at that time. It was situated about fifty-five miles north of Jerusalem in an elevated basin such as is frequently found in Samaria and Galilee. This basin is about a mile long and is less than a half mile wide; it opens southward by a narrow and winding pass into the great plain of Esdraelon; on the western side of the valley of Nazareth lies the modern town that bears that name. Higher up the slope is a limestone cliff thirty or forty feet high, which may well have been the "brow of the hill whereon their city was built," from which the mob proposed to cast Jesus when they had rejected him as their prophet. (Luke 4: 29.) It was here that the righteous Joseph and the meek Mary lived and where Jesus "advanced in wisdom and stature, and in favor with God and men." (Luke 2: 52.) Here lived the child, the boy, the youth, and the man who was in due time to come forth from this obscure village as the Redeemer and Savior of the world. It was here that Jesus wrought (Mark 6: 3) at the humble calling of the carpenter's trade; it was at Nazareth that he worshiped on the Sabbath in the synagogue of the Jews.

That it might be fulfilled which was spoken through the prophets.—Notice that the plural is used here of "the prophets"; no particular prophet had spoken of Jesus dwelling in Nazareth. It is thought that Matthew quotes the general sentiment of the prophets, that he is giving the equivalent of their language and not their exact language. Many of the prophets had predicted the humble life of Jesus; this is expressed in the proverbial statement that he should be "called a Nazarene." "A Nazarene" is a term of contempt. (John 1: 46; 7: 52.) The very name of Nazareth suggested insignificance; in the Hebrew it meant to sprout or shoot. This name is prophetically given to the Messiah. (Isa. 11: 1.) The figure of the tree is continued by Isaiah and is applied to the Jewish state. As David sprang from the humble family of Jesse, so the Messiah, the second David, shall arise out of great humiliation. The fact that Jesus grew up at Nazareth was sufficient reason for his being despised; he was not a lofty branch on the summit of a stately tree; not a recognized and honored son of the royal house of David, now fallen, but an insignificant "sprout" from the roots of Jesse; a Nazarene, of an insignificant village.

The chronological order of the events as recorded by Matthew seem to be as follows: Soon after the birth of Christ the wise men arrived from the east; their visit was soon followed by the flight into Egypt and the sojourn there for a short time, which must have been very brief, as Herod's death occurred soon afterward; the return from Egypt to the land of Israel, and then to the parts of Galilee and to Nazareth, where Jesus resided for about thirty years. Luke records the presentation in the temple which must have taken place some time before the flight into Egypt. By living in Nazareth Jesus came to be known as the Nazarene, and this name fulfilled the idea expressed by the prophet as belonging to the Messiah. Jesus was "the Branch," "the Shoot," and by his Nazareth name fulfilled the prediction that, though of lowly origin, the small, despised shoot would become a great tree. Some prefer to take the meaning of Nazareth to be one who protects or saves; the name Nazarene then would have reference to Jesus' work as a Savior.

SECTION TWO

JOHN THE BAPTIST; BAPTISM AND TEMPTATION OF JESUS
3:1 to 4:11

1. THE MISSION AND WORK OF JOHN
3: 1-12

1 And in those days cometh John the Baptist, preaching in the wilderness

1 In those days cometh John the Baptist.—There is an interval of about twenty-nine years between the events recorded in the second chapter and those recorded in the third chapter; Jesus spent the time at Nazareth, and Matthew does not record anything that he said or did during these twenty-nine years. Matthew now begins his record of the public work of Jesus. There is a preparation before the public ministry of Jesus; John the Baptist is that prophet who prepares the way for Jesus.

"In those days" means at the close of Jesus' retired life at Nazareth and the beginning of the preparation made by John the Baptist. This is the first mention that Matthew gives of "John the Baptist." John was the son of an aged priest, Zacharias, and Elisabeth; some think that Elisabeth was the cousin of Mary the mother of Jesus; hence, John was the second cousin of Jesus. John was probably born 5 B.C. in an unnamed city in the hill country of Judea; probably he was born at Hebron. He was six months older than Jesus; he was a Nazarite, which means that he was to drink no wine nor strong drink and was to let his hair and beard grow untrimmed, as a sign of consecration to God. (Num. 6.) He was filled with the Holy Spirit from his birth; his early life up to thirty years of age was passed in the solitudes of the wilderness of Judea, where he was prepared for his great mission as the forerunner of the Messiah. He preached for nearly two years; almost a year of his preaching was contemporary with the preaching of Jesus.

The prophets had foretold the coming of John the Baptist. The Old Testament closes with the prophecy of John. (Mal.

of Judea, saying, 2 Repent ye; for the kingdom of heaven is at hand. 3 For

3: 1; 4: 4-6.) His father, Zacharias, was of the tribe of Levi and belonged to the eighth course of priests. (1 Chron. 24: 10; Luke 1: 5.) His mother, Elisabeth, was also of the tribe of Levi and was a descendant of the family of high priests, as she was "of the daughters of Aaron." (Luke 1: 5.) He has been called John, Messenger, Elijah, "the voice of one crying in the wilderness," and "John the Baptist." He has been called "the Baptist" because he baptized. He is also called "John the Baptizer." (Mark 6: 14, 24.) John was the first under the command of God to administer the ordinance of baptism, hence he is given the title of "Baptizer." Some have doubted that John was first to administer baptism; they claim that Jewish proselytes were baptized; however, there is no record of anyone's being directed by Jehovah to administer the ordinance of baptism before John the Baptist. It is true that the law of Moses required the washing of vessels and the bathing of the priests, but such was not called baptism in the sense that John baptized. It has been estimated that there are twenty distinct cases which are specified by the law that required bathing. The writer of the Hebrew letter refers to these as "divers washings." (Heb. 9: 10.) The law of Moses did not require any proselyte to be washed or bathed or baptized.

Preaching in the wilderness of Judaea.—John's special mission was to prepare the way for Jesus, hence no history of Jesus can be complete and omit the history of John, his great forerunner. Matthew introduces John as "preaching in the wilderness." Matthew is definite in his record in telling *what* John was doing, *where* he preached, and *what* he preached. The mission of John was unique and definite; one thing he did, *he preached*. He has been described as a voice, for what there was of him as known to the people of his time was substantially a voice calling on men to do something. He began his work of preaching in the wild uncultivated region of Judea which skirts the western shore of the Dead Sea and is called "the wilderness of Judæa." "The wilderness of Judæa" is for the most part a dreary waste; it stretches west of the Jordan from Jericho to the mountains of Edom; that part of it where John was brought up seems to have been west of the Dead Sea. (Luke 1: 80; 3: 2.) The word "wilderness" or "desert" in the New Testament denotes merely an unenclosed, untilled, and thinly inhabited district. The scene of John's first public appearance was in that part of "the wilderness of Judæa" which is the wild, desolate, district around the mouth of the Jordan. His sojourn was not confined to that locality

2 Saying, Repent ye.—John did not go to Jerusalem to begin his public work of preparing the way for Jesus, but he opened his ministry in the wilderness or in the least populous part of the country; he came "preaching"; his public work was begun by his preaching, proclaiming, announcing publicly; we are not to suppose that John made set speeches or discourses to audiences, but that he traveled the country and heralded his brief messages, first to individuals, families, and small companies wherever he found them, and afterward to crowds who flocked to hear him. John's message was distinct and emphatic; he called upon the people to "repent." The Greek word here is "metanoein," which is a compound of two Greek words, a preposition, "meta," which means after, with, and a Greek verb, "noeo," which means to perceive or to think. The compound word means to "think differently after"; its primary meaning is an afterthought, different from the former thought; a change of mind which issues in regret and in change of conduct. "Repentance" has been rightly defined as "such a virtuous alteration of the mind and purpose as begets a like virtuous change in the life and practice." "Sorrow" is not the primary meaning of the word; Paul distinguished between "sorrow" and "repentance" and put the one as the outcome of the other: "Godly sorrow worketh repentance." (2 Cor. 7: 10.) Repentance signifies to change the thought and so change the opinion or purpose; this is the inward change and naturally leads to a changed outward life, which is usually designated as "a reformation of life." Repentance as used in the New Testament has reference to changing the mind, purpose, from sin to holiness, and no one will do this who does not feel deep sorrow for the sin he has already committed; hence, godly sorrow produces repentance. Sometimes the word translated here as "repentance" is also translated "turn," "be converted."

Matthew briefly expresses the theme of John's praching; it was repentance. This was no new subject; the prophets had called upon the people to "turn" from their wicked ways and serve God. (Joel 2: 12, 13; Isa. 55: 7; Ezek. 33: 11, 15; Zech. 1: 3, 4.) The New Testament meaning of this term is more specific and strictly denotes the inward change, leaving the outward change to result as a consequence. In both the Old Testament and the New Testament exhortation to repent, the element of grief or sorrow for sin is left in the background; neither word directly expressing grief at all, but it is implied in the very nature of the change in mind resulting in a change in life. There is implied further in repentance a return to a former state; after a thing has been done and an error has been noticed, then undo the wrong that has been done.

[Repentance is the determination of the soul to turn away from sin, to cease sin, and, with the help of God, to sin no more. Reformation of life grows out of this repentance, yet it is distinct from it. Repentance is in the heart, the turning from the love of sin. Reformation is the correction of our evil ways. The first has a definite time and is a distinct act of the heart; the latter is a lifework as we from day to day or from year to year see the evil practices into which we have fallen and strive to turn from them and correct all wrongs.]

Repentance should be distinguished, not only from godly sorrow, but also from a mere "quitting of sin"; it is to be distinguished also from sad, gloomy despair; it is also to be distinguished from "forgetting the sin." John the Baptist preached repentance; he knew the difference between mere outward and real repentance, between the passing feeling and the deep change which manifested itself by bearing fruits of righteousness. Repentance according to John's preaching implied an entire renunciation of sin. The repentance that John preached must spring from faith in the prediction regarding the coming Messiah; the repentance that John preached prepared the heart and life for the acceptance of the Messiah who was soon to appear.

For the kingdom of heaven is at hand.—John held out "the kingdom of heaven" as an inducement to people to repent; again "the kingdom of heaven" must be composed of those who have turned their back upon sin. "The kingdom of heaven" is a phrase peculiar to Matthew; the Greek word, "ouranon," as used here for "heaven," is plural; hence, the literal translation would be "the kingdom of the heavens." It is a kingdom of heaven because its origin, its end, its king, its laws, and the character and destiny of its subjects are all heavenly or spiritual.

What is "the kingdom of heaven"? It is the same as "the kingdom of God," "his kingdom," or "kingdom of his dear Son." That which is called by Matthew "his kingdom" (Matt. 16: 28) is called "the kingdom of God" (Mark 9: 1; Luke 9: 27). The same kingdom mentioned in the phrase, "the Son of man coming in his kingdom," is also mentioned in the phrase, "the kingdom of God," for these are two reports of the same speech which Jesus made; the difference in phraseology is due to different writers. This is the same kingdom that is called "the kingdom of heaven" (Matt. 19: 23), "the kingdom of God" (Mark 10: 25), "the kingdom of God is at hand" (Mark 1: 15), and "the kingdom of heaven" as preached here by John. Again Matthew records Jesus as saying, "He that is but little in the kingdom of heaven is greater than he" (Matt. 11: 11), while Luke records the same, "He that is but little in the kingdom of God is greater than he" (Luke 7: 28). These are two records of the same thing, and the same kingdom is meant in both records.

"The kingdom of heaven" which John preached is the same thing as "the kingdom of God." This refers to the same institution that Jesus referred to when he used the phrase, "my church" (Matt. 16: 18), and "the kingdom of heaven" (Matt. 16: 19). On this occasion Jesus, speaking of the same institution, called it "my church" and "kingdom of heaven." The "general assembly and church of the firstborn" and the "kingdom that cannot be shaken" refer to the same institution.

this is he that was spoken of through Isaiah the prophet, saying,
²The voice of one crying in the wilderness,
Make ye ready the way of the Lord,
Make his paths straight.

²Isa. xi. 3.

(Heb. 12: 23, 28.) It is the same institution that is called the "one body" (1 Cor. 12: 13; Eph. 4: 4); all who enter the "one body" are immersed or baptized into it, and all who enter the kingdom are "born anew" (John 3: 3, 5). The same institution is called "the house of God, which is the church of the living God, the pillar and ground of the truth." (1 Tim. 3: 15.) This is the kingdom that John the Baptist preached as "at hand." This kingdom had as yet not come; it was "at hand." The nature of this kingdom was a spiritual institution; John puts this in contrast with the earthly or fleshly kingdom of Israel.

3 **The voice of one crying in the wilderness.**—Again Matthew quotes from the prophets; here he quotes from Isa. 11: 3; this quotation, like the others, is not in the exact words of Isaiah. John is here spoken of by Isaiah as "the voice of one crying in the wilderness." John is the only preacher of whom we read who is called "the voice" and that his work was "in the wilderness." Others of God's prophets went to the towns, villages, and cities, but John began his work in the wilderness. This quotation is made by Matthew and not by John the Baptist; this seems to be another fulfillment of a typical, not a verbal, prophecy. In its primary historical application the quotation contains a summons to prepare the way of Jehovah, who was about to bring back his people from exile. What Isaiah uttered as a typical prophecy became a distinct prediction in Mal. 3: 1; Malachi regarded the mission of John the Baptist as corresponding to Elijah, hence he assigned to him the name of Elijah. (Mal. 4: 5.) Why was John called "the voice"? John's personality is put in the shadow behind Jesus; John was entrusted with a great spiritual mission of introducing Jesus to the Jewish people; he needs to be represented as a mere "voice" crying aloud in the moral wilderness around him; soon he must decrease and Jesus must increase; John is to be removed from the platform and let Jesus occupy the

4 Now John himself had his raiment of camel's hair, and a leathern girdle about his loins; and his food was locusts and wild honey. 5 Then went out

central place; he must fade away, and let Jesus stand out emphatically before the public.

Make ye ready the way of the Lord.—Still quoting from the prophet Isaiah, Matthew uses the figure that Isaiah used with respect to John's work. It was customary for eastern kings, when on an expedition, to send forerunners to prepare the way for the king; the hills were to be leveled, the valleys to be filled, and the road was to be straightened so that the king would have easy access in travel. John came on a similar mission; he was the forerunner of the great King; the preparation for this King was to be made in the hearts and lives of the people. This is another way of expressing "repentance." The people were to prepare themselves for the coming of Jesus; Mark expresses it, "Make ye ready the way of the Lord, make his paths straight," just as Matthew expresses it. (Mark 1: 3.) John prepared the way for Christ by calling upon the people to repent; he prepared the way by removing prejudice and by producing a reformation on the part of the people so that Jesus would have a glad welcome. The law of Moses was to lead the people to Christ; "so that the law is become our tutor to bring us unto Christ." (Gal. 3: 24.) If the Jews had been faithful to the law of Moses, they would have been ready for the coming of Jesus; they were unfaithful, hence the work of John the Baptist. He was "to make ready for the Lord a people prepared for him." (Luke 1: 17.)

4 **Now John himself had his raiment of camel's hair.**—Matthew gives a vivid description of John's dress; it is becoming to the wilderness service that John rendered. "John himself had his raiment of camel's hair"; it seems that John purposely chose such habits of life and such raiment; cloth made of "camel's hair" was a kind of cloth made of the fine hair of the camel, which was coarse and rough; such cloth was manufactured from the long and shaggy hair of camels, which was shed by the animal every year. The raiment of camel's hair was very similar to sackcloth of which we read so much about

in the Bible. (Zech. 13: 4; Rev. 6: 12.) Poor persons and prophets wore such garments in ancient time, and such cloth is still worn in the east by the poor. There is no evidence that the garments made of camel skin like those made of sheepskin and goatskin have been worn by prophets. (Heb. 11: 37.) There is a fine cloth made of camel's hair, which is called camlets, but this is not the dress that John the Baptist wore. Elijah was clothed in a garment of this kind. (2 Kings 1: 8.)

John wore in addition to his "raiment of camel's hair" a "leathern girdle about his loins." A girdle was necessary and almost a universal part of dress for people at that time. (Acts 21: 11.) It was required to bind the long, loose robe in order to do active labor or rapid travel, and it was often a very costly part of the dress (Rev. 1: 13), but John's girdle was made of a cheap rude leather which corresponds to his dress of camel's hair. It is likely that John's girdle was similar to that of Elijah, which was made of undressed skin of animals.

His food was locusts and wild honey.—John's habits of life corresponded to his dress, and his diet corresponded to the simple life that he lived. Locusts were winged insects, closely resembling the grasshopper; they were "clean" and could be used for food among the Jews. (Lev. 11: 22.) They were roasted and sometimes boiled, or salted and preserved, and eaten by the poorer classes of people in all the eastern countries where they were found. Sometimes they were dried in the sun and put away to be used after the locust season had passed. The heads, legs, and wings were removed before they were prepared as food; they were eaten both fresh and dried. They are very different from what we call locusts. There is no evidence that John ate the fruit of the tree which we call locust; in fact, the original forbids such a construction. "Wild honey" may have been the gum which exuded from a tree, but more probably it was the honey of wild bees which had been deposited in trees or in rocks. It was abundant in Palestine; that country has been described as a land "flowing with milk and honey." (Deut. 32: 13; Judges 14: 8; 1 Sam. 14: 25; 26; Psalm 81: 16.)

unto him Jerusalem, and all Judæa, and all the region round about the Jor-

The object of this mode of living is clearly seen when we think of the austere work of John. It was natural and easy under the circumstances in which he lived; it required but little time from John's work to dress and eat as he did; it was befitting to his austere preaching, which was a protest against the luxury of the time and the sins which were ruining the people; it gave John the appearance and the prestige of a pioneer prophet and made him resemble more closely the prophet Elijah, whom he came to represent. We may see in John's dress and food testimony against the Jewish misconception of the Messiah's kingdom; both the man and his message combine their influence to turn the thought of the people toward a spiritual reformation which they needed in order to be prepared for the coming kingdom of the Messiah. Surely no one could see and hear John and believe that he was the forerunner of an earthly king who would establish an earthly kingdom. John was not merely imitating his prototype, Elijah, but everything was in harmony with the work that John was to do and would thus direct the minds of the people to a spiritual renovation.

5 **Then went out unto him Jerusalem, and all Judaea.**—It must be remembered that John did his work in the wilderness; he began his preaching in "the wilderness of Judæa"; he worked among the common people in that sparsely settled country. He began his work in a *quiet* way, but he attracted the *public* attention. "Then went out unto him" the people from the cities; John did not go to them, they came to him; his shrill and earnest cry, "repent ye," was heard by many, and the public went forth to hear him. Not merely persons from Jerusalem and Judea, but such multitudes that it might be said that "all Judæa" was there; great roads from every part of the country passed near by "the wilderness of Judæa," and this gave an accessible way to hear John. What drew these crowds? The wonderful influence which John exercised over them; John's ministry was one of terror; he demanded that they repent or a fearful calamity would befall them. John spoke in earnest, and they could not resist the power which he

exercised in preaching this near approach of "the kingdom of heaven," and the Messiah who was to be King of this kingdom. There was also a deep-felt need of repentance on the part of the people and a rekindling of the hope of salvation. Again there was a general expectation of the promised Messiah; the people felt that it was time for the promises of God to be fulfilled.

And all the region round about the Jordan.—John drew his audiences, not only from Jerusalem and other cities, but from "all the region round about the Jordan." It is likely that the lower part of the river toward the Dead Sea is referred to here. "All" is to be understood as expressing the fact that very many people came forth; it is a hyperbolic expression which abounds in all languages. We learn from John that some came from Galilee, but perhaps at a later period, when John was baptizing higher up the river. (John 1: 35-45; 21: 2.) People from Jerusalem, the country of Judea, and even Galilee were attracted by John's preaching; Jerusalem is first mentioned because of its prominence, and not because it was the first to furnish John an audience; the probable order of places which furnished hearers for John is the district about Jordan, Judea, and Jerusalem.

John began his ministry A.D. 26, which was a Sabbatical year according to some authorities; the people were not occupied in the cultivation of the soil and in the gathering of the grain and gleaning the vineyards; they were in a large measure "resting" or unemployed, hence had sufficient time to listen to the new prophet. Those who strictly observed the law had more than ordinary leisure on this year; it had been centuries since a prophet had appeared. There had been about "four hundred years of silence," which came between the close of the old Testament and the opening of the New Testament. The Jews had often longed for a prophet to guide them; they were sorely oppressed by the Roman authorities. The report spread far and wide, as quickly as the conditions of that country permitted, that at last a prophet had come, who in dress and place of abode resembled the great Elijah; some began to wonder if this prophet was the Messiah. We need not be surprised at such multitudes going out to hear John; the nature

dan; 6 and they were baptized of him in the river Jordan, confessing their

of his announcement and the prevalent expectation of a Messiah were enough to produce the great effect and attract such great multitudes.

6 And they were baptized of him in the river Jordan.— John's baptism was an open confession of repentance for sin; Mark calls it "the baptism of repentance unto remission of sins." (Mark 1: 4.) The Greek word "baptizo" which is used here was very common among Greek-speaking people; it is used in every period of Greek literature and was applied to a great variety of matters, including the most familiar acts of everyday life. Greek speakers and hearers understood the word at the time John was preaching; it had no doubtful meaning. It meant what we express by the Latin word "immerse" and kindred terms; no one could then have thought of attributing to it a different meaning, such as "sprinkle" or "pour." "Bapto" means to dip and had the root "baph," which was akin to "bath" in bathing; bapto is a root form of baptizo. The baptism of John has been erroneously by some regarded as a modified application of the Jewish baptism of proselytes; some deny that the proselyte baptism was in use at the time that John began his ministry; however, John's baptism was not an imitation of any other rite or form; his baptism came from heaven. (Matt. 21: 25; Mark 11: 30; Luke 20: 4.) There is no reason for supposing that John's baptism was a modification of some existing rite, since Jesus distinctly intimated that the baptism of John was "from heaven." John declared that God "sent" him "to baptize in water." (John 1: 33.) The baptism of John is significant and impressive in its simplicity and bears the distinct stamp of divine authority. It is to be understood that John immersed or dipped those who came to him and demanded baptism.

As John was preaching along the banks of the Jordan, his baptism was done "in the river Jordan." This strengthens the proof that the action of baptizing was performed within the limits of the river Jordan. This is the simple meaning of the phrase "in the river Jordan." Some have contended that the Greek preposition "en" means in, within, at, on, with, by, nigh

sins. 7 But when he saw many of the Pharisees and Sadducees coming ³to his baptism, he said unto them, Ye offspring of vipers, who warned you to

³Or, *for baptism*

to, according to the subject, and that in this instance it may mean within the outer bank of the river, which they claim has double banks, or that it was done nigh to the river Jordan. It is denied also that John "immersed" his disciples "in the river Jordan," because there was too large a number for him to immerse; such objection is not only a denial of the plain truth as expressed by Matthew, but is absolutely contrary to the accepted meaning of the word "baptizo." The word "Jordan," always with the article in the Hebrew and the Greek, signifies "the descender" and was so named from its rapid descent in a long and deep valley or fissure; John evidently used one of the fords of the Jordan as a convenient place to baptize; it is not known the exact place of his baptizing.

Confessing their sins.—After hearing John preach repentance the people confessed "their sins"; this was not merely showing a contrite spirit, neither was it merely confessing themselves to be sinners; it was an individual and public confession of their sins. They did not make a private confession of their sins to John, but openly declared their sins and that they were penitent of them. Upon this confession John baptized them. Repentance and confession of sins were prerequisites of their baptism, hence John's baptism was the baptism of repentance, and its object was the remission of sin. The confession would necessarily be brief and emphatic; the original word in the Greek means that the confession was made orally and openly. Their confession was connected with their baptism, and it was an individual confession and perhaps a specific confession of their sins.

7 But when he saw many of the Pharisees and Sadducees coming to his baptism.—These were the two principal parties among the Jews; they were opposed to each other and were opposed later to the work of Jesus. Both of these religious parties originated in the second century before Christ. The Pharisees were the strictest and most popular and most numerous sect of the Jews. They originated in the time of Jonathan the high priest, 159-144 B.C. Some authorities claim that they numbered about six thousand at the death of Herod the Great; they probably derived their name from the Hebrew "pharash," which means "separated"; they separated themselves from other Jews under the pretense of a greater purity and a stricter observance of the law. Whatever they were at their origin, they appear to have been, with some exceptions (John 3: 1; Acts 5: 34), great hypocrites in the name of Jesus, (Matt. 5: 20, 23; Mark 8: 11-15; Luke 11: 52, 18: 9-14). They were the most formidable enemies of Jesus before his crucifixion.

The Sadducees probably derived their name from the Hebrew "zedek," which meant the just; some think that they originated with Zadok, who was president of the Sanhedrin about 260 B.C. They rejected tradition as given by the Pharisees; they denied a future state and the existence of angels and spirits; in this they were opposed to the Pharisees. The Sadducees were not so numerous; they were characterized by worldliness and unbelief, as the Pharisees were by superstition and hypocrisy. Though the Sadducees opposed the Pharisees, yet later they joined them in opposition to Jesus. (Matt. 22: 23-34; Acts 4: 1, 2; 23: 6-8.) The Pharisees and Sadducees were the strongest religious parties that opposed John and Jesus.

John saw representative leaders of the Pharisees and Sadducees "coming to his baptism"; some translate this "coming for his baptism." Why did these come to John? Many think that they came to be baptized of John, while others think that they came either to see or hear what was going on. It seems that they came to be baptized of John; they were interested in the coming Messiah; they would be drawn by the general excitement and interest, as many are now in times of a revival; there may have been a secret and conscious feeling of need of preparation before the advent of the King. If there was a new kingdom coming, and the old was to be destroyed, it would be well for them to escape from the wreck of the old one and be ready for the new kingdom; they did not want to be left out of it; they expected an earthly kingdom.

flee from the wrath to come? 8 Bring forth therefore fruit worthy of ⁴re-

⁴Or, *your repentance*

Ye offspring of vipers, who warned you to flee from the wrath to come?—These two religious sects which were mutually hostile are found frequently in the gospels united in opposition to our Lord; here they are found in opposition to John the Baptist. It seems that they came with others, and because others did come, without any worthy motive, and John discerned their motives and administered this severe rebuke. He called them an "offspring of vipers," a generation of vipers, or brood of vipers. The viper was a venomous serpent; John characterizes them as both deceitful and malicious, and deadly poison to those whom they inoculated with their spirit. They were wicked sons of wicked fathers. John used this phrase of reproach describing these Pharisees and Sadducees as noxious and odious and insidious. It does not appear that John meant to describe these as children of the devil, the old serpent; he meant to describe them as being cunning and deceitful. They have come to be baptized of John, but they were not penitent; they were ready for the new kingdom, as they thought, but they were not ready for a new life. John, it seems was able to read the motives of them and hence he could address them as he did; the smooth, varnished hypocrisy of the Pharisee or Sadducee could not deceive him; his denunciation of them strikes swift and like lightning the deceptive lives of the Pharisees and Sadducees. "Who warned you to flee from the wrath to come?" John asked why they came to him; why have your fears been aroused? Who made you see your danger? The wrath to come means the divine indignation, or the punishment that will come upon the guilty. (Mal. 3: 2; 4: 5.) The reference of John's ministry to this prophecy concerning Elijah would naturally suggest to people the "wrath to come." It was the general expectation of the Jews that perilous times would accompany the appearance of the Messiah. John is here speaking in the true character of a prophet, foretelling the wrath soon to be poured out on the Jewish nation. Though John could rebuke them, yet he was not the man to close against them the door of hope and mercy. John implied

pentance: 9 and think not to say within yourselves, We have Abraham to our father: for I say unto you, that God is able of these stones to raise up

that if they expected to receive mercy from God that they, like all others, must be penitent; they must confess their sins and turn from them, before they are prepared for his baptism.

8 **Bring forth therefore fruit worthy of repentance.**—If they were in earnest, then they would bring forth fruit worthy of their repentance; good fruit comes from good trees; they were to prove their sincerity by a life of righteousness. Their lives must be the exact opposite of what they had been; the good fruits are all forms of righteousness, love to God, mercy, self-control, brotherly love, humility, faith, and every good word and work. They were to bring forth, that is, make "fruit" (singular). As they professed repentance and wished to be baptized, therefore they should produce fruit worthy of their repentance and thus prove that they were sincere. We are not to understand that John refused to baptize them, nor that he asked them to go off and prove their repentance before he could baptize them; he only gave them this instruction. In their impenitent condition they could not escape the wrath of God; they should exhibit that morality of conduct which is appropriate to the change of mind as its result; instead of their unrepentant condition he required genuine repentance. What John here required of the Sadducees and Pharisees he required of all people; this was especially appropriate to the leaders.

9 **We have Abraham to our father.**—John knew what was in the minds of the Pharisees and Sadducees; he knew the answer that they wanted to make; he knew that they would claim to be heirs of the blessings of God because they were the descendants of Abraham; hence, he warned them by saying, "Think not to say within yourselves, We have Abraham to our father." "To say within yourselves" is a common expression in the scripture. (Psalm 10: 6, 11; 14: 1; Eccles. 1: 16; 2: 15.) The Jew boasted of his relation to Abraham; he hoped to enjoy the blessings of the expected Messiah simply on the grounds that he was a descendant of Abraham, and a

children unto Abraham. 10 And even now the axe lieth at the root of the trees: every tree therefore that bringeth not forth good fruit is hewn down,

member of the Jewish race; all Jews claimed to be partakers of the promise given to Abraham; this was one of the mistakes of the Jews. (John 8: 39; Rom. 9: 7.) As the Jews thought that the Messiah's kingdom would be an earthly kingdom and that he would reign over the Jews as a nation, that they would receive the blessings of citizenship in that kingdom as descendants of Abraham; they relied on their relation to Abraham for admittance into the kingdom. Nicodemus made the same mistake and Jesus told him that he must be born again or else he could not enter into the kingdom. (John 3: 3, 5.)

God is able of these stones to raise up children unto Abraham.—John, standing on the bank of the Jordan, could refer to the pebbles as "these stones"; perhaps he may have pointed to the loose stones lying around. The fact is God could with such perfect ease raise up children to Abraham, and so was not dependent on these Pharisees and Sadducees for the continuation of Abraham's posterity in a spiritual sense; this also suggested to them that they might readily be set aside from enjoying the blessings promised to Abraham's descendants. This also implies that the Messianic blessings would not necessarily be enjoyed by all Jews as such (John 1: 29); it may mean too that the Gentiles would form a part of God's people in this coming kingdom which "was at hand." Here John also expresses the omnipotence and independence of God; he can put the Gentiles into the place of the Jews. (Matt. 8: 11, 12; Rom. 4: 1, 2.) John tells these that God is able, notwithstanding their descent from Abraham, to exclude them from the Messiah's kingdom; and, on the other hand, to create and bring forth out of these stones, which lie here around on the bank of the Jordan, such persons as are true children of Abraham. This must have been a surprise to all who heard him.

10 **And even now the axe lieth at the root of the trees.**—John says that the axe is now sharp and ready and is being applied to the tree. He uses the figure that he has introduced, trees; his hearers are compared to the trees in an orchard; an

and cast into the fire. 11 I indeed baptize you [5]in water unto repentance; but he that cometh after me is mightier that I, whose shoes I am not [6]worthy to

[5]Or, *with*
[6]Gr. *sufficient*.

axe is ready to destroy every tree that has not heretofore brought forth good fruit; this tree is about to be cut down and destroyed. In this way John emphasizes personal responsibility without regard to fleshly ancestry. John has already said that the punishment of the unfaithful descendants of Abraham was possible; he now asserts that it was not only possible, but highly probable as the work had already begun. The axe was ready for its destructive work; many of the Jews were unfruitful trees, and even worse, they were bad trees; every tree that brings forth not good fruit is to be cut down. John refers to the unbelieving Jews as those who will be excluded from "the kingdom of heaven." The axe has been brought to the tree and lies ready for use; it will surely be applied if they do not accept the Messiah.

Every tree therefore that bringeth not forth good fruit is hewn down.—The axe is to be applied to "the root of the trees," not to the branches to prune them, but at the root to destroy them. The fruit which the tree is to bring forth is the fruit that God rightly requires of it; the individual who does not bring forth the fruit of the spirit is to be destroyed. God had selected the Jewish race; he had given his law to it; he had sent his prophets to teach and to warn them; these prophets had foretold of the coming of the Messiah; John was his forerunner and came to make ready a people prepared for the Lord; the "kingdom of heaven" was "at hand"; if they failed in their preparation for the Messiah they would be destroyed, there was no salvation for them. There was nothing and no one else upon whom they could rely for salvation. Carrying the figure out, the unprofitable tree was to be cut down "and cast into the fire"; it was to be destroyed. The searching ordeal of moral fruitage was in process; the axe was close at the root of every tree; the barren must go under the axe and into the fire.

11 I indeed baptize you in water unto repentance.—John here emphasizes his mission; he has called upon them to repent; he demanded a complete reformation of life, a radical change in heart which was to result in a change of life. They thought that this was a severe and drastic demand of them, as they were of Abraham's seed; but John now puts in contrast what his preaching demanded of them and what the Messiah would demand of them when he came. John puts in contrast what he is authorized to do for them and what the expected Messiah would do for them. The preparation which John called upon the people to make in order to be ready for the coming kingdom is here put in contrast with the requirements of their entering into the kingdom. These contrasts are introduced by the emphatic word "indeed," which shows the contrast between what he required of them and what the King would require of his subjects.

"Baptize you in water unto repentance." Literally John baptized them in water; he baptized them "in the river Jordan." Some contend that John baptized "with water" and that the act was that of "sprinkling" or "pouring" the water on them. It is claimed that John as well as Matthew uses the phrase "in water" (John 1: 26, 31, 33), but that Luke in a parallel passage uses the phrase "with water" (Luke 3: 16; Acts 1: 5; 11: 16), and that the phrase merely means an instrument by which the water is applied to the subject; it is argued from this that an instrument is always wielded and applied to the object affected by the action, and that "baptize with water" cannot mean immersion. This position is untenable; the water cannot mean an instrument, and the original shows that it is not to be used as an instrument. Luke uses the phrase "in the Holy Spirit" (Luke 3: 16; Acts 1: 5), which is a parallel expression for the phrase "in water," and the Holy Spirit cannot be considered the instrument and applied to the subject by the hand of man.

John's baptism was "unto repentance." What is the meaning of "baptize you in water unto repentance"? Some have interpreted this to mean that the baptism of John brought them to repentance. This cannot be allowed, for John required repentance as a prerequisite to baptism. Others have contended that they were baptized "into repentance"; this is not correct, for, if John's baptism did not bring the one baptized unto repentance, it could not bring them into it. Some have contended that the preposition "eis" should be understood in the sense "because of"; the preposition "eis" is never used to express the idea that one thing is done because of another having been done; hence we are not to understand that John baptized persons "because of" their repentance; it is true that repentance here preceded their baptism, yet it was not because they had repented that they were baptized. The blessing of remission of sins was attached to John's baptism, for it is said by Mark that John "preached the baptism of repentance unto remission of sins." (Mark 1: 4; Luke 3: 3.) The desire to receive the forgiveness of sin would prompt those who had not submitted to John's baptism to repent so that they might be baptized and in so doing receive the remission of sins.

[The context of a scripture is the only safe guide in determining what that scripture means. John tells all Jerusalem and Judea who came out to him and were baptized of him, confessing their sins, that the Messiah and his kingdom would soon appear. He saw among the number many Pharisees and Sadducees coming to his baptism; he especially addressed them as a "generation of vipers"; not that these that came were possibly worse than others, but they were from an evil class. He calls them an offspring of vipers because they belonged to the class of evil ones, but they also were fleeing from the wrath to come. He warned them not to rely upon the Abrahamic family to save them; that every tree, or family, or individual, henceforth would be treated alike, and those who did not bear good fruit would be destroyed. Then, speaking to the same persons, he said: "I indeed baptize you in water unto repentance." If he did what he says he did, he baptized them and all others unto repentance, or to doing work meet for repentance. The works meet for repentance to the different classes are set forth by Luke (Luke 3: 10, 11.) Let him that has two coats give one to him that needeth; publicans, or tax collectors, were warned not to collect more than was right. The soldiers were to do violence to no man in preserving order. Certainly they were not to wait to do all these things before they were baptized unto repentance. In

3: 11.]   MATTHEW   83

bear; he shall baptize you ⁵in the Holy Spirit and *in fire:* 12 whose fan is

Mark 1: 8, John says: "I baptized you in water; but he shall baptize you in the Holy Spirit." There is nothing in the context that intimates that he sent them off to prove their worthiness before he baptized them, and it is contrary to the spirit of God's dealings with man throughout the Old Testament and the New Testament. He did not divide those who came to him into two classes with different laws to each; all were baptized unto repentance and admonished to bear fruit worthy of this repentance.]

He that cometh after me is mightier than I.—Here John institutes a contrast between himself and Jesus. Literally, "he that cometh after me" means "the one coming behind me"; this implies that they had heard of the coming of the Messiah. John means the Messiah of whom he was the forerunner; he here states that he is the forerunner of the Messiah. John describes his personal relationship to the Messiah and draws a sharp contrast between himself and the Messiah. John does not take to himself any honor, but bestows honor upon him whom he came to introduce to the world. He declared that the Messiah who should come after him "is mightier" than he; that is, the Messiah would have power to accomplish that which he could not accomplish; the Messiah would not only be superior in position, but more powerful and able to accomplish that which John could not accomplish. How much "mightier" than John the Messiah would be is immediately pointed out by John.

In contrast the position of John and that of the Messiah and the work of John and that of the Messiah are expressed by John when he says "whose shoes I am not worthy to bear." In his humility John says that he is not worthy to carry the shoes of the Messiah. The word rendered "shoes" signifies what is bound under and denotes the sole of leather, rawhide, or wood which they wore under the foot, and which fastened to the foot by a thong or strap which was run between the toes and bound around the ankle to fasten the sandal to the foot. As stockings were not worn, the feet became soiled, and

in his hand, and he will thoroughly cleanse his threshing-floor; and he will

on entering the house the sandals were taken off and laid away by the lowest servant in the house so that the feet might be washed. The loosing, tying, or carrying the sandal became proverbial to express the humblest service. John means here that he that cometh after him is so much greater in authority and power, and so distinguished, that he was unworthy to do him the humblest service. Mark records this humility of John by saying, "The latchet of whose shoes I am not worthy to stoop down and unloose" (Mark 1: 7); Luke expresses it, "The latchet of whose shoes I am not worthy to unloose" (Luke 3: 16). Matthew records another point of superiority of the Messiah.

He shall baptize you in the Holy Spirit and in fire.—What a baptism! John's baptism was "in water," but the Messiah would baptize "in the Holy Spirit and in fire." The Messiah would entirely immerse the penitent ones "in the Holy Spirit," and those who were impenitent, he would overwhelm with the fire of judgment, and at last in final perdition. This prophecy of John was literally fulfilled on the day of Pentecost (Acts 2: 1-4) and at the house of Cornelius (Acts 10: 44; 11: 15-18) with respect to the baptism "in the Holy Spirit." John does not here state that every subject of the coming kingdom would be immersed in the Holy Spirit. His prediction should be understood in the light of its fulfillment; we have only two records of the fulfillment of the baptism in the Holy Spirit. In the baptism of the Holy Spirit on these two occasions, the Holy Spirit came direct from heaven without any intervention of human agency. The baptism in the Spirit of these two groups of persons has brought blessings to all mankind; the one on Pentecost brought blessings directly to the Jews, and the one at the house of Cornelius brought blessings to the Gentiles; hence the baptism in the Holy Spirit has resulted in blessings to the entire human family.

The baptism "in fire" has been variously interpreted. Some think that it was fulfilled on the day of Pentecost when "tongues parting asunder, like as of fire . . . sat upon each one of them" (Acts 2: 3); but that was not a baptism "in fire," for these "tongues" were not "fire," but only "like as of fire"; again these tongues only sat upon the apostles, but did not immerse them in the tongues "like as of fire." Others have objected to making two baptisms here, one in the Holy Spirit, and the other in fire, because, they say that only one baptism is mentioned here by John; this is an assumption without any proof; John immediately divides people into two classes. He had already divided them into two divisions by his figure of fruitful trees for good people and unfruitful for wicked people. "Fire" is so frequently connected with the final destruction of the wicked. John could only bid people to repent, and could symbolize their purification by his baptism in water, but Jesus would really purify them by forgiveness of sin, and he would finally destroy the impenitent wicked. Mark records John as saying of Jesus that he "shall baptize you in the Holy Spirit" (Mark 1: 8) and omits "in fire." Jesus promised his disciples a baptism in the Holy Spirit (Acts 1: 5), but said nothing about the baptism "in fire" to his disciples. We conclude that the fulfillment of the prediction of the baptism in fire would be realized by the wicked when they are cast into the lake of fire. (Rev. 20: 15.)

12 **Whose fan is in his hand.**—John represents the Messiah as coming with his winnowing fan; "fan" as used here meant a large wooden fork, by which the mass of mingled wheat and chaff is thrown up against the wind, which blows away the chaff, while the heavier grain falls upon the floor. This figure is of the judgment and is a more striking figure than the preceding one of the fruitful trees. In that figure the husbandman removes from his garden all the unfruitful trees as they only cumber the ground; but here at harvesttime there is a separation on the threshing floor of the wheat from the chaff. The fan is in his hand, or the instrument for the separating or purging is with the Messiah. The Jews were familiar with such a figure as John used here. (Psalm 1: 4; Dan. 2: 35; Hos. 13: 3.) The fan or winnowing shovel was "in his hand," which means that already the process of sifting had begun or was ready to begin with the coming of the Messiah.

gather his wheat into the garner, but the chaff he will burn up with unquenchable fire.

He will thoroughly cleanse his threshing floor.—The "threshing floor" was a circular space of beaten earth which had been cleansed so that the grain could be kept clean; the grain was trodden out by oxen; the straw was thrown away with a fork and the mass of grain and chaff was thrown up by the shovel and the grain was left to fall on the clean threshing floor while the chaff was blown away by the wind.

The threshing floor was usually an open hard-trodden space in the middle of the field where the grain could be assembled with the straw. John makes good use of this ancient figure and emphasizes the work that the Messiah would do. After the grain has been separated from the chaff, the threshing floor is cleansed and made ready for another process, or is put in a state of cultivation.

He will gather his wheat into the garner, but the chaff he will burn up with unquenchable fire.—The purpose of the threshing floor was to afford a convenient place for the separation for the wheat and chaff. In verse ten the two classes are represented by the two classes of trees; here the two classes are represented by "his wheat" and "the chaff." The threshing floor is to be thoroughly cleansed and the final separation of the two classes is to be made. The whole figure represents the Messiah as separating the evil from the good, according to the tests of his kingdom and his gospel; the worthy are to be received into his kingdom and given a rich reward, while the unworthy are to be destroyed. There is a sharp contrast not only between the wheat and the chaff, but the destiny of the two classes; the one is to be gathered "into the garner," while "the chaff he will burn up with unquenchable fire." By using the term "unquenchable fire" John extends the meaning of his figure to the eternal destiny.

[The baptism of fire was the destruction that was to come upon the children of disobedience, beginning in this world, ending in the final destruction in everlasting ruin. The destruction of Jerusalem was a type of the everlasting destruction. The baptism by fire was an overwhelming deluge of divine wrath; it ends only with the everlasting destruction of the wicked; there are steps and degrees in this work of destruction on earth, ending in the final ruin forever.

He will gather his wheat into the garner, and will burn the chaff with fire unquenchable. He will bring the good into his kingdom; he will cast the evil into outer darkness, where there is weeping and gnashing of teeth. The salvation of the righteous in his kingdom is typified by the baptism of the Holy Spirit; the destruction of the wicked, by the baptism of fire.

The baptism of the Spirit is the overwhelming of the Spirit so that the spirit of man is brought completely under the influence and control of the Spirit of God. This in the beginning was done miraculously and at once by the pouring out of the Spirit upon the apostles and others who were plenarily inspired. The same end, the bringing of the spirit of man completely under the control and influence of the Spirit of God, is brought about since the days of inspiration through the laws of the Spirit of life in Christ Jesus. This work is gradually accomplished through receiving the law given by the Spirit, and in which he dwells, into the heart and a gradual obedience with its requirements.

A man is baptized when overwhelmed, regardless of the manner in which the overwhelming is accomplished. When the soul of man is completely overwhelmed by the Spirit of God, he is baptized by the Spirit regardless of whether it was done by direct and miraculous outpouring of the Spirit, or by the gradual bringing of the man's spirit under the influence of God's Spirit. The apostles were baptized by the Holy Spirit miraculously on the day of Pentecost, created full-grown men on that day of the descent of the Holy Spirit. Others are begotten of the Spirit, or born as babes into the spiritual kingdom of God, and grow up to manhood in Christ Jesus through the laws for the development of life in Christ Jesus. Whenever these persons are brought fully under the influence of the Spirit, when their spirits are overwhelmed by the Spirit of God, so it rules supremely, they become thus full-grown men in Christ Jesus, and might be said then to be baptized by the Spirit of God. This is not often in the scriptures called a baptism of the Spirit, since it is a gradual growth, and it cannot be said the baptism took place at any certain time.

John the Baptist called the development of the spirit to a full-grown man a baptism of the Spirit. He said of Jesus to the multitudes who came to him: "He [Jesus] shall baptize you in the Holy Spirit and in fire." The context shows plainly that the baptism of fire embraces the punishment of the wicked ending in their final and eternal ruin. The baptism of the Holy Spirit here is promised to the other class and must embrace all the influences of the Spirit, fitting and qualifying them for the blessings of God here and the final salvation in heaven. The spirit of man is fitted for these things only when it is completely under the influence of the Holy Spirit, or when it is baptized by the Spirit of God. This was done miraculously, in a moment of time, on Pentecost; it requires a lifetime to accomplish it under the laws of the Spirit. When it was done miraculously, miracle-working power was present to attest its divine origin; this is not to be expected under the workings of the law of the Spirit.]

2. THE BAPTISM OF JESUS
3: 13-17

13 Then cometh Jesus from Galilee to the Jordan unto John, to be bap-

Then cometh Jesus from Galilee to the Jordan unto John, to be baptized of him.—John had been busy in his ministry for several months; some think that he was just now in the height of his ministry; others think that Jesus came to John near the close of John's ministry. Jesus was now "about thirty years of age" (Luke 3: 23). Some have inferred from Luke 3: 21 that Jesus was the last person that John baptized, that his mission ended with the baptism of Jesus; however, this is not a correct inference. Jesus came "from Galilee to the Jordan" to be baptized. He came from Nazareth in Galilee, where he had spent about thirty years of his life. We do not know the exact place in the Jordan where Jesus was baptized; he came to John who was baptizing in the Jordan. It is generally conceded that Jesus walked from Nazareth to where

tized of him. 14 But John would have hindered him, saying, I have need to be baptized of thee, and comest thou to me? 15 But Jesus answering said

John the baptizing, which was a distance of sixty-five to eighty miles. Not knowing the exact place where John was baptizing, we cannot determine with accuracy the distance that Jesus walked. Some think that John was baptizing at Bethabara (John 1: 28); it is a tradition that this was the place where the Israelites crossed the Jordan into the land of Canaan. This was the beginning of Jesus' public career.

He came to John "to be baptized of him." Why should Jesus, the sinless one, come to John to be baptized? Matthew expresses clearly the purpose of Jesus in coming to John; it was "to be baptized of him"; we know that Jesus did not come to be baptized from a feeling of personal sinfulness, neither because of his personal connection with an impure people, nor for the purpose of showing that there was no incompatibility between his life and the life of others, nor merely to elicit the divine declaration that he was the Son of God, nor to confirm the faith of others in him, neither was it to sanction the baptism of John as having been authorized of God. It was the will of God for him to be baptized, and he came to do the will of God. (Heb. 10: 7.)

14 **But John would have hindered him.**—John at first was opposed to baptizing Jesus; he did not forbid Jesus, but had it in mind to prevent him; the original means that he was for hindering him, or that he "would have hindered him." John was moved to strenuous protest against baptizing Jesus. John felt that it was not in order for him to baptize Jesus; he recognized the superiority of Jesus and his own inferiority, hence he could not understand why the inferior or the less should administer baptism to his superior or the greater. John was conscientious; he was strenuous in his opposition to baptizing Jesus. John knew the purpose of his baptism; he knew that all who had been baptized of him needed to be baptized, but he did not recognize in Jesus anything that would lead him to believe that Jesus needed to be baptized of him.

I have need to be baptized of thee, and comest thou to me? —John, in substance, says that he has far greater need of

unto him, Suffer ⁷*it* now: for thus it becometh us to fulfil all righteousness. Then he suffereth him. 16 And Jesus, when he was baptized, went up

⁷Or, *me*

being baptized of Jesus than Jesus does of being baptized of him. This implies that John had some definite knowledge of the character of Jesus. How did John recognize Jesus as so holy? Their mothers were possibly related; John could not have been brought up in ignorance of some of the circumstances of Jesus' birth; the song of the angels, the visit of the wise men, the song of Mary, and the prophecy of Simeon, all could have been known by John; he may also have had some acquaintance with the pure and sinless life of Jesus at Nazareth; again upon this occasion the Holy Spirit with which John was filled would aid him in recognizing the purity and sinlessness of Jesus. It was on this occasion, after the baptism of Jesus, that John knew with certainty that Jesus was indeed the Messiah. (John 1: 33.) John was looking for the appearing of Jesus and taught others to look forward to his appearing; hence the prophetic anticipation of John, for the appearing of the Messiah helped him to recognize the superiority of Jesus.

15 But Jesus answering said unto him, Suffer it now.—Literally this means permit it now; never mind the contrast between John and Jesus; Jesus asks that John let him take the place of the less or the inferior for the present. The baptism of Jesus was a duty, not only of Jesus, but it was also the duty of John to baptize Jesus; since it was the duty of John to baptize Jesus, Jesus is ready to help John do his duty; there is an implied truth in the objection that John made, but John is to do his duty nevertheless. There are two aspects of baptism; first, it was an act in connection with the remission of sin, and an act of obedience to a positive command of God. Jesus had no sin to be forgiven, but he must obey the command of God; "though he was a Son, yet learned obedience by the things which he suffered" (Heb. 5: 8); Jesus here began to learn obedience to God's will.

For thus it becometh us to fulfil all righteousness.—Jesus said to John that it becometh "us" to fulfill the righteousness

straightway from the water: and lo, the heavens were opened ⁸unto him, and

⁸Some ancient authorities omit *unto him.*

of God. John had a part in the preparation of the people for the coming of Jesus, and also a part in announcing and pointing out Jesus as the Messiah. John thought it would be presumption on his part to baptize Jesus and an unworthy condescension on the part of Jesus to submit to his baptism; but Jesus declares to John that it is befitting in both John and Jesus to perform this act. Nothing must be left undone that would honor God and assist Jesus in beginning and carrying on his ministry. As John's baptism was not "from men" but "from heaven" (Matt. 21: 25; John 1: 33), it became Jesus to receive the baptism of John, and John to administer it. It was fitting that Jesus should fill up the full measure of righteousness in all its forms by accepting the baptism of John. John saw the force of Jesus' words and baptized him. Some think since John baptized Jesus at Jesus' command that Jesus was really the active person in the baptism.

16 And Jesus, when he was baptized, went up straightway from the water.—"Straightway" means immediately; Mark says "straightway coming up out of the water." (Mark 1: 10.) Some think that no other person was baptized at the time Jesus was baptized; others think that there were others who were baptized, but that John detained them in the water until they could make confession of their sins. There is nothing in the text to justify any assumption or speculation on this point; Matthew simply records the fact that Jesus was baptized and "went up straightway from the water." This helps to emphasize the fact that John's baptism was by immersion; Jesus departed "from" the water after he had come out of it.

And lo, the heavens were opened unto him.—Luke says, "Jesus also having been baptized, and praying, the heaven was opened" (Luke 3: 21); hence while Jesus was praying, "the heavens were opened unto him." Some think that the heavens were opened in answer to his prayer, but the record only states that they were "opened" during his prayer; there was an apparent separation or division of the visible expanse,

he saw the Spirit of God descending as a dove, and coming upon him; 17 and lo, a voice out of the heavens, saying, ⁹This is my beloved Son, in whom I am well pleased.

⁹Or, *This is my Son; my beloved in whom I am well pleased.* See ch. 12. 18.

---

as if to afford passage to the form and voice which are mentioned in the next clause. We have similar expressions in the Bible. (Isa. 64: 1; Ezek. 1: 1; John 1: 51; Acts 7: 56.) This signified that Jesus could see into the heavens and hence could communicate with God. The essential idea suggested is that of the removal of every visible thing between him and the father and that the extraordinary gift from heaven could be received by Jesus.

And he saw the Spirit of God descending as a dove, and coming upon him.—Jesus saw the Holy Spirit coming upon him; it seems from the text that the vision was to Jesus alone, but John was also a witness to it (John 1: 32); this was to John the sign by which the Messiah should be recognized. Very likely the multitude did not see this vision, but that it was visible only to Jesus and John; still others think that it was visible to the multitude as Luke affirms that it came "in a bodily form" (Luke 3: 22) like a dove. The form of a dove, and not in the manner of the dove, swiftly and gently as a dove, affirm some. The dove was an ancient symbol of purity and innocence, and was so adopted by Jesus on one occasion. (Matt. 10: 16.) Scholars are divided as to whether the comparison is with the "form" of the dove, or with the "manner of the dove" in descending. Luke says, "descended in a bodily form," which seems to settle the question.

It came upon Jesus; it abode or remained upon him for some time. Some think that this symbolized the great fact that Jesus was henceforth to be permanently in union with the Father and under the influence of the Holy Spirit. Immediately after this we find that Jesus was "led up of the Spirit into the wilderness." (Matt. 4: 1.) The purpose of the visible form or manifestation was to point Jesus out to John; John must bear witness of Jesus; that he is the Messiah; he must have divine authority for this; he receives that authority at this time.

17 and lo, a voice out of the heavens.—This "voice" was the voice of God; it came from the rented heavens; it could have come without the heavens being separated, but the rent in the heavens was the physical manifestation of the supernatural, and this was accompanied with "a voice out of the heavens." This is similar to other expressions. (Comp. Luke 9: 35, 36; Acts 7: 31; 9: 4; 11: 7; Rev. 1: 10; 4: 1; 6: 6.) We have here the three persons of the Godhead, the Father, the Son, and the Holy Spirit; the term "Son" is applied to the Messiah (Psalm 2: 7; Isa. 42: 1), not merely in reference to his official character, but more especially to his divine nature.

Saying, This is my beloved Son, in whom I am well pleased. —The voice from heaven said two things, first, that Jesus was the Son of God; second, that God was well pleased with him. This is the first public acknowledgment that God made of Jesus; it was made at his baptism. The words spoken here are the same that were uttered on the Mount of Transfiguration. (Matt. 17: 5; 2 Pet. 1: 17.) The Greek is emphatic: "This is my Son, the beloved"; the two terms are to a certain extent equivalent; God's Son was his beloved. This voice was specially designed as a revelation to John; it was given him for the purpose of his mission which was to introduce Jesus as the Messiah to the people. However in Mark and Luke there is a more particular reference to Jesus himself as the source of the vision, while John lays special stress upon the part which John the Baptist sustained in the vision. We have recorded three heavenly voices which were heard during Jesus' ministry: (1) at his baptism; (2) at his transfiguration (Mark 9: 7); (3) in the courts of the temple during the last week of Jesus on earth (John 12: 28). The Son is consecrated by the Holy Spirit, and proclaimed by the Father at the baptism of Jesus. This announcement from heaven by the Father at this time was the formal divine authentication of the Messiah's mission; he is now commissioned by the Father and anointed by the Holy Spirit to begin his public ministry for the redemption of man.

[John baptized all who came to him, the vilest wrongdoers as well as others less guilty of sin, until Jesus came to him.

He condemned each for his own sins and directed each to repent of his special sins. John, from the universality of the sinfulness, seems to have caught the idea that baptism was only for the remission of sins until Jesus came. When he came John forbade him saying: "I have need to be baptized of thee." Here the question was before Jesus and John whether baptism is always for, or into, or unto, the remission of sins; and the first revelation he makes from God to man is to baptize and be baptized to fulfill the righteous will of God. All should respect and honor that will by obeying and honoring it. Jesus Christ in this revelation places obeying the will of God as the highest, holiest, best motive that can lead man in the service of God. When this motive leads to obedience, it includes all other motives and blessings and renders the obedience acceptable to God; it embraces and swallows up all other smaller or secondary motives and pleases God best of all. It is the motive that moved Jesus to leave heaven and come to earth to lead man to do what he does because it pleases God. John baptized all who came to him, from Jesus down, to bring them into the fellowship and brotherhood of Christ Jesus, who would bless and save.

Matthew, Mark, Luke, and John make reference to the conception, birth, and childhood of Jesus; these four writers do not give all the points which are recorded of the early life of Jesus; Mark tells all that he gives of the prophecy, descent, and birth of Jesus in nine verses until he comes to his baptism, and then God recognized him as his Son. No account of Jesus being called the Son of God is given by Luke until we come to Luke 3: 21 which records his baptism and voice from heaven owning him as God's Son. John begins his gospel by telling us who and where Jesus as the Word was before the world was made. He tells us that he was made flesh, was born of the virgin Mary, of John's baptizing him, and in John 1: 29 he tells of the baptism of Jesus and that God owned him as his Son; no intimation is given that God acknowledged Jesus to be his Son until he was baptized. John the Baptist said "that he should be made manifest to Israel, for this cause came I baptizing in water" (John 1: 31); that is, God had determined to own him as his Son in his baptism. Therefore,

3. THE TEMPTATION OF JESUS
4: 1-11

1 Then was Jesus led up of the Spirit into the wilderness to be tempted

John came baptizing, that in the baptism God might declare him his Son. This was an example and assurance he owns those who trust him.]

1 Then was Jesus led up of the Spirit into the wilderness to be tempted of the devil.—The temptation of Jesus concludes Matthew's account of events connected with Jesus' entrance upon his public work; that work was now beginning. Modern scholars have speculated on whether the temptation of Jesus was *real* or whether it was only *allegorical,* there is nothing in the record of Matthew, Mark, or Luke that would lead one to think otherwise than that his temptation was as *real* as was his baptism. Immediately after his baptism and after God had publicly acknowledged him as his Son, and at the very beginning of his public work, the temptation of Jesus came. Satan begins his work in an active way as never before so soon as the Son of God begins his active work in the redemption of man.

"Then was Jesus led up of the Spirit"; this shows that Jesus was subjected to temptation according to the will of God; a deliberate purpose of the will of God, and not a purpose of his own, was carried out in his temptation, for he was "led up of the Spirit"; the Spirit carried him away, "the Spirit driveth him forth" (Mark 1: 12), he "was led in the Spirit" (Luke 4: 1); it seems that Jesus was led up from the river Jordan to the mountainous range adjacent. Tradition locates the place as a rugged desolate region between Jerusalem and Jericho, and about four miles from the place of baptism and about twenty miles from Jerusalem; the divine record describes the place as "the wilderness." Jesus was not "driven" against his own will; he voluntarily yielded to the powerful influence of the Spirit as it led him to do the will of God. In order to be the Savior of tempted mankind, it was necessary that he himself should be tempted in all points as we are, yet without sin. (Heb. 4: 15.)

of the devil. 2 And when he had fasted forty days and forty nights, he af-

The express purpose of his being led into the wilderness was "to be tempted of the devil." He was to be tried by the strongest solicitations to sin. "To be tempted" literally means "to be stretched out" or tried to the full strength; "tempt" is from the Latin "tento, tempto" and is an intensive form of "tendo" which means to stretch. Jesus was to be "tempted," enticed to do wrong by the devil, in order that he might be proved and tested for God's work.

It was the will and plan of God for Jesus to be "tempted of the devil." The original Greek for "devil" means "calumniator, slanderer"; it is sometimes applied to men, as to Judas (John 6: 70); in 1 Tim. 3: 11 (slanderers); and in 2 Tim. 3: 3 and Tit. 2: 3 (false accusers). The devil, Satan, the god of this world, is always singular, never plural; it is not the same in the original as "demon," which means an unclean spirit which possessed men and was cast out by Jesus and his apostles. The Greek word for devil conveys the idea of deceiving, accusing, calumniating; the term is never used in the Bible to signify an evil spirit and is never used to personify the evil in man or in the world. The devil is represented in the New Testament as an adversary of human souls, endeavoring by various snares to take us captive, suggesting evil thoughts to our minds, or erasing good impressions which have been produced there, or putting hindrances in the way of good work, or inspiring persecutors of the faithful, and as certain at last to be bound in chains, and finally cast into torment. (Matt. 13: 19; Luke 22: 31; John 13: 2; 2 Cor. 2: 11; 11: 3, 14; Eph. 6: 11; 1 Thess. 2: 18; 2 Tim. 2: 26; 1 Pet. 5: 8, 9; Rev. 2: 10; 12: 9; 20: 1-3, 7-10.) It seems that the devil is a created being of the higher order than man who has fallen from his first estate. (Jude 6.)

2 And when he had fasted forty days and forty nights, he afterward hungered.—We cannot understand the wisdom of God or the deep purposes of God unless he has revealed them to us; it is not recorded why Jesus "fasted forty days and forty nights." He did not fast in the ecclesiastical sense of that word, but in its strictest meaning of abstaining from all

terward hungered. 3 And the tempter came and said unto him, If thou art

food whatsoever; Luke says that "he did eat nothing in those days." (Luke 4: 2.) Moses (Ex. 34: 28 and Elijah (1 Kings 19: 8) fasted the same length of time; such a fast is possible only during intense mental absorption. Moses was a representative of the law and Elijah was a representative of the prophets. Jesus was wholly absorbed by spiritual realities; this was a state which rendered him for a time independent of the common necessaries of life; we are not to understand that he was miraculously sustained during this time.

"He afterward hungered"; this became the occasion for the supreme assault of the tempter; he afterward hungered, or desired food, having eaten nothing during the forty days, his appetite probably being held in abeyance by a spiritual ecstasy, which drew his attention from his physical needs. The records of Mark and Luke lead us to believe that Jesus was tempted during the forty days, while Matthew implies that the temptation came at the close of the forty days; these records all agree, as Mark and Luke refer to the temptation as it began with his fasting, while Matthew describes the supreme effort of Satan at the conclusion of the forty days; Satan at the conclusion of the forty days summoned all of his power and made the final assault on Jesus; it is to this that Matthew directs attention.

3 And the tempter came and said unto him.—The tempter was the devil. Sometimes the temptation of Jesus has been viewed as one temptation with a threefold nature and application; again it has been viewed as *three* different temptations. The purpose of the devil was to get Jesus to obey him, and he makes the appeal to him in his strongest, most alluring, and most enticing way. From the words of both Mark and Luke it appears that Jesus was tempted all the time during the forty days; Mark says that "he was with the wild beasts." The words "the tempter came" need not be understood to mean the *first* approach, but the first *recorded* approach of the tempter, or at a certain time of the temptation. We do not know in what form the devil approached Jesus. He approached Eve in the Garden of Eden in the form of a serpent,

the Son of God, command that these stones become [10]bread. 4 But he answered and said, It is written, [11]Man shall not live by bread alone, but by

[10]Gr. *loaves.*
[11]Dt. viii. 3.

---

and presented the same temptations to her; she yielded to the temptation.

If thou art the Son of God, command that these stones become bread.—Much discussion has been had as to whether the devil meant to cast a doubt on Jesus' being the Son of God; some have understood "if" to have the force of "since"; this would imply no doubt; others have said that there is couched in the form of speech a doubt, and that the devil wished to incite Jesus to prove himself as the Son of God. It is claimed that three things are implied, first, that if the Son of God had come, he must be the expected Messiah; second, that the Messiah could not be any lower personage than the Son of God in a metaphysical use of that term; third, that the greatest miracles might be expected to be wrought by him if he is the Son of God. The Greek is not subjunctive but indicative; therefore the tempter puts the matter in this form and challenges Jesus to prove his claim by a miracle, and intimates that Jesus certainly has the right to do this in order to satisfy his hunger. God's ordinary creatures may suffer, they cannot help it; but if Jesus is the Son of God, he can help it and there is no use in his suffering hunger. Here a good motive is suggested to Jesus and the sinfulness of it is an attempted skillful disguise of the motive.

"Command that these stones become bread"; stones were lying around him in the wilderness and some of them may have had the shape of loaves. This resemblance between a stone and a loaf is noted in Matt. 7: 9. Luke has "stone" in the singular, while Matthew uses the plural, "stones." Since Jesus was the Son of God, it would be easy for him to command the stones to become bread. This first temptation appears to be twofold in its nature; he is tempted to satisfy hunger and to prove himself to be the Son of God. Jesus will not use his divine power to satisfy himself or his bodily appetite, nor to demonstrate to the devil his claim as the Son of God.

every word that proceedeth out of the mouth of God. 5 Then the devil tak-

4 But he answered and said, It is written, Man shall not live by bread alone.—Jesus is ready with the word of God to answer this temptation; "it is written" in Deut. 8: 3; these words, "it is written," are the first upon record that were spoken by our Lord after his entrance into his public ministry; it is significant that the first word spoken by Jesus is a declaration of the authority of the scriptures. Jesus made the word of God his rule of authority; he alleged the scriptures as things undeniable even by the devil himself. It stands written and our Lord met every temptation by a quotation of scripture. The Israelites had lived by the word of God when they subsisted on the manna which was produced by his word. Jesus was hungry, and in a desert; the devil tempts him to work a miracle to supply his wants; Jesus repels the temptation to distrust God by giving the word of God. There are other things which sustain the life than bread; bread will sustain the physical body, but it cannot sustain the spiritual part of man's nature.

But by every word that proceedeth out of the mouth of God.—Jesus does not deny the place and value of "bread" in sustaining physical life; but he emphasizes that there is something else even more important. Man shall not live by ordinary visible food alone; other things are far more necessary to true living. This quotation was originally applied to the Israelites when they had bitterly complained of hunger in the wilderness; even they were taught that there is something more in true living than sustaining the physical part of man. God by his word can supply food out of the ordinary way; he did this in giving Israel manna to eat. God could give Jesus food from heaven; he could turn the stones into bread; but this was not God's will. In sending the manna to the hungry Israelites, God taught them that the true bread was the bread from heaven. (Deut. 8: 2, 3.) Jesus applies this truth to himself; his true bread was to do the will of his Father. To create bread out of stones contrary to God's will and in obedience to Satan would be to die, not to live, and it was for this reason that the devil tempted him to do it; Jesus chose the

eth him into the holy city; and he set him on the [12]pinnacle of the temple, 6 and saith unto him, If thou art the Son of God, cast thyself down: for it is written,

[12]Gr. wing.

---

true life, trusting God to supply his temporal wants; he honored God's word and it sustained him.

5 Then the devil taketh him into the holy city.—Luke puts this temptation last, without saying that it occurred last. "Taketh him" need not be understood that the devil transported Jesus through the air; literally means "takes him with him," or "along with him." We have no means of knowing the manner of going; we are left to suppose that Jesus went as men usually go, and that the devil did likewise. It is a question of no practical value as to how Jesus went from the wilderness to the "holy city," which refers to Jerusalem. Jerusalem is regarded as the holy city because the seat of the temple and its worship were located there.

And he set him on the pinnacle of the temple.—This was probably Herod's royal portico. Jesus did not belong to the Levitical priesthood, and never entered the temple proper; he only entered the court and porches of the temple. There were the long porticoes which were covered and some of these were built up above the wall to a great height; the outer battlement of such a roof, rising above the outer wall, is probably what is here called "the pinnacle of the temple." "The pinnacle" was some very high point of the temple building. The word translated pinnacle means literally a "little wing." The high point was such that a fall from it would be fatal, and especially if one "cast" himself from it.

6 And saith unto him, If thou art the Son of God, cast thyself down.—This temptation also seems to have a twofold meaning, appealing to the natural feeling and to the Messianic aspiration; since Jesus is the Son of God and is now upon the high pinnacle of the temple and can do nothing up there for the salvation of man, he is commanded to cast himself down. The temptation is for him to cast himself down in faith and prove that he was God's Son. Jesus would have full proof of his divine Sonship and others would have the proof of his

> ¹³He shall give his angels charge concerning thee: and,
> On their hands they shall bear thee up,
> Lest haply thou dash thy foot against a stone.
> 7 Jesus said unto him, Again it is written, ¹⁴Thou shalt not make trial of the

---
¹³Ps. xci. 11. 12.
¹⁴Dt. vi. 16.

Messiahship if he would but just spectacularly cast himself from the pinnacle of the temple. Again this was not God's way; although some good might result from this act as it would show how completely he trusted in God and might convince some Jews that he was under special divine protection, yet to leap from the pinnacle would not establish faith in God unless God had commanded it.

For it is written, He shall give his angels charge concerning thee.—This time the devil imitates Jesus and quotes scripture; he quotes Psalm 91: 11. He quoted verbatim from the Septuagint, but perverted the meaning of the scripture. This was written to encourage faith, but not to encourage presumption. The devil plainly makes the inference that this was a promise made to all pious men, and it must apply all the more forcibly to Jesus if he is the Son of God; this application of the promise was false. There is a general watch care of God over his people; but he has not promised to protect them from danger while they are violating his will; neither does this mean that God will put forth any extraordinary means for the protection of those who trust him. It means that man must comply with the will of God and trust in the ordinary means that God has provided for his well-being.

7 Jesus said unto him, Again it is written, Thou shalt not make trial of the Lord thy God.—Jesus did not, as some have, accuse the devil of misquoting the scriptures; neither did he deny the promise referred to in the scripture quoted; he simply replied by giving another quotation. The quotation that Jesus gave did not contradict the quotation the devil gave; all scriptures harmonize. He who quotes scripture must understand that it harmonizes with all other statements of God; and if one quotes scripture as the authority of God, one must obey all scripture, as it represents the authority of God. Jesus quoted "Thou shalt not make trial of the Lord thy God." This

Lord thy God. **8 Again, the devil taketh him unto an exceeding high mountain and showeth him all the kingdoms of the world, and the glory of them;**

was found in Deut. 6: 16; the devil was violating this scripture. It is not pleasing to God to quote one scripture while trying to pervert the meaning of another scripture. A figurative expression must not be construed to mean that which it was not intended to mean; neither should a promise or statement be given an unlimited application, unless the context so justifies. The quotation that Jesus here used qualifies and interprets the one quoted by the devil, but does not refute that quotation of the devil. Jesus meant to say that the quotation of the devil was a scriptural quotation and applicable to himself and would be fulfilled in due time, but to throw oneself into unnecessary danger in order to "tempt" or test God would be a sin, and especially when it was done at the command of the devil.

8 **Again, the devil taketh him unto an exceeding high mountain.**—Again we have the expression "the devil taketh him"; we must understand that Jesus was not forced, but that he submitted to this temptation as it was in God's plan; a better or literal meaning is that he "takes him along with him," or led him up or directed him to this mountain. We do not know what this "high mountain" was; it is impossible for us to determine; some have thought that this was an allegorical expression or at least not a literal mountain; there is nothing in the context to show that it was not literal, neither is there anything to be gained by assuming that it was figurative.

And showeth him all the kingdoms of the world, and the glory of them.—Some think that the devil showed him all the districts of Palestine; there is no authority for rendering "world" to mean the districts of Palestine. The devil may have had supernatural power and presented to Jesus a mental vision of "all the kingdoms of the world, and the glory of them"; again these could have been presented to Jesus by a vivid description of the kingdoms of the world; we cannot tell from the context whether Jesus saw literally the territory of the kingdom of the world or the power, authority, and glory of them; this would have to be done through a vivid imagina-

9 and he said unto him, All these things will I give thee, if thou wilt fall down and ¹worship me. 10 Then saith Jesus unto him, Get thee hence, Satan: for it is written, ²Thou shalt worship the Lord thy God, and him only

¹See marginal note on ch. 2. 2.
²Dt. vi. 13.

tion. It is very likely that Satan described before Jesus the kingdoms of the world and all of their glory, and in this way tempted him. Luke adds that he showed him all of these "in a moment of time" (Luke 4: 5), which strengthens the idea that the vision that Jesus got was that of a supernatural conception of the kingdoms of this world.

9 All these things will I give thee, if thou wilt fall down and worship me.—Luke adds, "For it hath been delivered unto me; and to whomsoever I will I give it." (Luke 4: 6.) Some have argued that the "kingdoms of the world" did not belong to the devil, and that he could not give them to Jesus. Wherein then is the temptation? Surely Jesus knew as much about these as did the devil. This promise of the devil implied that Jesus must unite his own efforts with those of the devil; the devil promises here to relinquish his hold on them, *provided* Jesus would now "fall down and worship" him. The devil is asking Jesus to transfer his allegiance from God to the devil; Jesus must acknowledge the supremacy and sovereignty of the devil. To do this would be to acknowledge a falsehood; the devil was not supreme, neither was he a sovereign; he had only such power as had been granted to him by God. His temptation is for Jesus to make the devil a god. Reward for this is that Jesus will be second or subordinate only to the devil. The real temptation to Jesus is that he can become a king over the kingdoms of the world by falling down and worshiping the devil, whereas, if he carries out God's plan, he must be crucified upon the cross; the way of the cross is the way to the crown with God. Will Jesus accept the proposition? Is there enough in "all the kingdoms of the world, and the glory of them" to entice Jesus to worship the devil? Or will the vision of the cross with its humiliation and suffering with intense agony be sufficient to turn him from God's way to that of the devil?

shalt thou serve. 11 Then the devil leaveth him; and behold, angels came and ministered unto him.

10 Then saith Jesus unto him, Get thee hence, Satan.—Jesus at once repelled Satan; in righteous indignation he denounces Satan with abhorrence as the archenemy of the Father The devil had now thrown off the mask and appeared to Jesus in his real character, so Jesus treated him accordingly. Hitherto Jesus had dealt with him according to his assumed character, although Jesus had understood the motives of the devil. The original for "get thee hence" means "begone, get out of my sight"; "Get thee hence, Satan," is the first exclamation of which we have a record of Jesus uttering.

For it is written, Thou shalt worship the Lord thy God, and him only shalt thou serve.—This quotation is from Deut. 6: 13; the dismissal of Satan the tempter is made with the scripture, "it is written." Jesus puts the emphasis on "only" when he said "and him only shalt thou serve"; Satan had asked Jesus to "fall down and worship" him, and Jesus promptly and emphatically repelled Satan by telling him that there is only one God to be worshiped, and he quotes the scriptures that prove this point. The devil is designated as "Satan" because in this temptation he displayed his real character as the *enemy* of God; he would take the worship and service of God's Son and appropriate them to his own diabolical ends; in revealing himself as the enemy of God, he also reveals himself as the *adversary* of Jesus.

11 Then the devil leaveth him.—Luke adds "he departed from him for a season." (Luke 4: 13.) Jesus had triumphed; later he taught through James "resist the devil, and he will flee from you." (James 4: 7.) It is probable that the temptations were frequently renewed during the ministry of Jesus, and especially when it was about to close. (John 14: 30.) The temptations mentioned here are samples of the whole life of Jesus during his personal ministry; he was subject to temptations as we are during his entire earthly life; "for we have not a high priest that cannot be touched with the feeling of our infirmities; but one that hath been in all points tempted like as we are, yet without sin." (Heb. 4: 15.)

And behold, angels came and ministered unto him.—Some think that angels brought him food; we have no evidence as to the exact nature of their ministration. Elijah was fed by angels and afterward fasted forty days. (1 Kings 19: 5.) The original from which we get "ministered" means "were ministering"; it signifies to attend as a servant, wait on; angels waited on him as human friends might have waited on one whom they found hungry, weary, lonely. Jesus had refused to relieve his hunger by turning stones into bread; he had refused to cast himself down from the pinnacle of the temple with the promise that angels would help him; so with the baffled tempter expelled from his presence, angels ministered to him; he fought the battle with Satan alone.

We can see in these temptations a progressive attack on Jesus by the devil; the tempter appealed to his bodily appetite, to his feeling of security, and to his ambition; these belong entirely to the mind. Next, he proposed a useful miracle, turning stones into bread, and then a useless miracle, that of casting himself down from the pinnacle, and last a gross sin in Jesus' worshiping and serving him. He sought to excite distrust in God, a presumptuous reliance on God, and finally an abandonment of God.

[Someone has affirmed that "the devil is a liar and the truth is not in him; that he did not and does not own a foot of soil"; therefore he did not tell the truth when he stated to Jesus that all the kingdoms of the world belonged to him. The devil is a liar and the father of lies, but he should be accredited with the truth when he speaks the truth, and especially when corroborated by one so truthful as the Son of God. Does the Son of God corroborate the statement that the kingdoms of the world belong to the devil? Matthew says that he was "tempted." Paul says, "For in that he himself hath suffered being tempted, he is able to succor them that are tempted." (Heb. 2: 18.) Now in order to its being a temptation, it must have been a veritable offer of something to the Son of God, which he very intently desired, yet could not take upon the terms offered; it must have been an offer of an object or possession ardently desired, by one having the right or power to bestow it.

Jesus knew the possessor of these kingdoms. It could be no temptation to an individual for me to offer him a title to a tract of land which he knew that I did not have the shadow of a right to do, or the power to obtain that right. In order for the offer to be a temptation to the Son of God, he must have thought the devil had the power to give what he proposed to bestow. Then if the Son of God was tempted by the devil, all the kingdoms of this world were the devil's kingdoms. The object of the mission of the Son of God into this world was to rescue this world from the dominion of the devil and bring it back to a primeval allegiance to his Father. If the kingdoms of this world were not under the dominion of the devil, they could not be rescued from his power. Whatever rule or authority was exercised over the earth was exercised through these kingdoms.

There are but two sources of power in the universe, God and his great enemy, the devil. Every kingdom not originating from God must receive its power and authority from the wicked one. These earthly kingdoms originated in the rebellion of the human family against God, live today by virtue of that rebellion, and must die when that rebellion ceases. Jesus came into this world to strive and wrestle with the devil for the dominion of this world, to rescue and redeem it from the power of the devil. He came as the "sent" of his Father. He came to conquer this world, destroy all dominion and principality, he came to put down *"all* rule and *all* authority and power." When this is accomplished he will deliver up the kingdom to the Father and himself be subject unto the Father. (1 Cor. 15: 24, 28.) He knew that the conquest would cost him suffering, sorrow, maltreatment, indignities, excruciating torments, the very anticipation of which made him draw back with the entreaty, "let this cup pass from me," and brought great drops of blood from his soul of anguish; he knew the strife for the conquest of the world must bring him down to the humiliation of death, the degradation of the grave. The devil, with his subtlety, proposed at the very threshold of his mission, "You are to be a subordinate in this kingdom unto your Father, after all your sorrows and sufferings. Now worship me, or recognize me as head instead of

God, and I will deliver them all into your hand with all their glory, without a struggle, a sorrow, a pang upon your part." There was the point of the temptation, to let him rule the earth through the devil's kingdoms, without suffering, without death, without the grave, instead of through God's will, with all of these.

How came the kingdom or dominion of the earth the devil's? "They were delivered into my hand," says the wicked one. What says the divine record? God made man ruler over the whole undercreation; he was its head; he had the power and authority from God to use and control it as he desired. God having once delegated authority to man never resumed it to himself. Man in refusing to obey God, but rather in following the dictates of the serpent, rebelled against God, and transferred his allegiance to the devil. Man, as the God appointed head and rightful ruler of the world, and the founder of the kingdoms of the world, transferred, with his allegiance, the rule of the world from God to God's greatest enemy, the devil. Jesus came into this world to rescue the world from the dominion of the wicked one, and bring it back to its allegiance to his Father. How will he effect this? He will destroy the kingdoms of the wicked one in the establishing and maintaining in their stead a kingdom of his own. Man has no power to rule himself; all power and rule must come from God or the devil. Every institution on earth, intended to control man, not founded of God, must look back through man, the agent of the wicked one, the prince of the world, as the source from which it sprang. Every institution that exercises authority, rule or power over man is a rival of Christ who claims sole authority over man and all these must be put down. (Dan. 2: 44; 1 Cor. 15: 24, 25.)]

SECTION THREE
BEGINNING OF JESUS' GALILEAN MINISTRY; THE PRINCIPLES OF THE KINGDOM OF HEAVEN
4: 12 to 7: 29

1. JESUS RETIRES TO GALILEE
4: 12-17

12 Now when he heard that John was delivered up, he withdrew into

12 Now when he heard that John was delivered up, he withdrew into Galilee.—Matthew passes over a number of intervening events; he records nothing about another visit of Jesus to Galilee (John 1: 43), the marriage in Cana and the turning of water into wine, the journey to Capernaum in company with his relatives and disciples, and that to Jerusalem to the Passover (John 2), the stay of Jesus at Jerusalem and in the land of Judea previous to the imprisonment of John (John 3), the return of Jesus by way of Samaria, and his stay there (John 4: 1-42.) The occasion of John's imprisonment is stated by Matthew, but not the time. (Matt. 14: 1-13.) Jesus departed into Galilee or "withdrew into Galilee"; he had lived there before his baptism and temptation. As Herod Antipas lived at Machærus in Perea, near the lower Jordan, where John was imprisoned as is supposed, and Nazareth was an obscure town in Galilee, Jesus would be comparatively safe in this retreat. John's reason for Jesus' going to Galilee (John 4: 1-3) harmonizes with Matthew's account. The Pharisees were jealous of Jesus' growing popularity and they would seek occasion to deliver him over to Herod, that he might share the fate of John the Baptist; Jesus prevented this by retiring to Galilee, as his hour was not yet come.

Jesus went up into Galilee when he heard "that John was delivered up"; we need not conclude that the imprisonment of John and the return of Jesus to Galilee occurred immediately after the temptation of Jesus, as other writers of the gospel record numerous events that occurred between these events. It is very likely that all which is recorded in the first three chapters of John, if arranged chronologically, would come between the eleventh and twelfth verses of Matt. 4; perhaps the

Galilee; 13 and leaving Nazareth, he came and dwelt in Capernaum, which is by the sea, in the borders of Zebulun and Naphtali: 14 that it might be fulfilled which was spoken through Isaiah the prophet, saying,

time that elapsed between verses eleven and twelve would be about one year.

13 Leaving Nazareth, he came and dwelt in Capernaum.— This shows that when he returned to Galilee he went to Nazareth his old home; we do not know how long he sojourned there; probably his mother (perhaps a widow) still resided there; she was present at the marriage in Cana which was about nine miles northeast of Nazareth. Some think that this sojourn in Nazareth is identical with that mentioned in Luke 4: 16-30; perhaps Luke records his reason for leaving Nazareth; if this be true, he did not leave Nazareth for some time; he began teaching in Galilee with great acceptance (Luke 4: 15); and then was rejected at Nazareth; he then went to Capernaum.

Capernaum was on the Sea of Galilee "in the borders of Zebulun and Naphtali." It was located on the northwest coast of the Sea of Galilee within the territory of Zebulun, not far from the line of division between Zebulun and Naphtali; the exact location of Capernaum cannot now be identified. Capernaum was afterward called "his own city" (Matt. 9: 1) where he paid taxes (Matt. 17: 24). Capernaum was one of the chief cities of Galilee at that time; it had a synagogue in which Jesus often taught; a Roman garrison and custom station was located there; it was the home of Peter and Andrew and James and John and probably Matthew made his home there. (Matt. 9: 1-9; Mark 1: 21; Luke 5: 27; 7: 1, 8; John 6: 59.) Later Capernaum was denounced by Jesus for its rejection of him. (Matt. 11: 23.)

Matthew very accurately describes the situation at Capernaum, yet it has been destroyed and no trace of it can be found today.

14-16 That it might be fulfilled which was spoken through Isaiah the prophet.—Jesus had a program before him; this he carried out; his earthly life was ordered in such a way as to fulfill the divine will concerning him as was predicted by the

15	³The land of Zebulun and the land of Naphtali, ⁴Toward the sea, beyond the Jordan, Galilee of the ⁵Gentiles,
16	The people that sat in darkness Saw a great light, And to them that sat in the region and shadow of death, To them did light spring up.

³Is. ix. 1, 2.
⁴Gr. *The way of the sea.*
⁵Gr. *nations:* and so elsewhere.

prophet; the prophets merely announced beforehand what would be the program of Jesus. Here is a fulfillment of Isa. 8: 22 and 9: 1, 2; the quotation as recorded by Matthew does not follow literally that which is recorded in Isaiah; in fact, the quotations from the Old Testament in the New are seldom verbally exact.

"The land of Zebulun and the land of Naphtali" refer to the territories which were allotted to these tribes; they embraced the territory west of the Sea of Galilee and constituted one of the most important fields of Jesus' ministry. This territory extended north and east of Asher and west of the Jordan; the land of Zebulun extended along the west side of the Sea of Galilee, while the land of Naphtali extended north of Zebulun to the northern boundary of the land of Canaan. Isaiah did not use the phrase as it was used during the captivity to denote the country west of the Jordan, but east. "Galilee of the Gentiles" included all the northern part of Palestine, lying between the Jordan and the Mediterranean Sea and between Samaria and Phoenicia. Some think that it was called "Galilee of the Gentiles" because so many foreigners from Phoenicia, Arabia, and Egypt had settled there.

The people that sat in darkness saw a great light.—This means the people who abode in the darkness of ignorance and sin and misery; the Galileans who lived far from the temple, and who did not attend temple worship regularly, were considered a benighted as heathens. The language expresses a symbol of hopeless gloom; it signifies more than "walked in darkness"; they "sat in darkness." They "saw a great light"; this light was the gospel which brought to them the joy of salvation. Isaiah had prophesied that this people would see this light and now it is being fulfilled in the teachings and

17 From that time began Jesus to preach, and to say, Repent ye; for the kingdom of heaven is at hand.

work of Jesus. They are represented as those who "sat in the region and shadow of death"; to these "did light spring up." "Shadow of death" is a common figure in the Old Testament. (Job 10: 21; Psalm 23: 4; Jer. 2: 6.) The figure seems to be that of a person who had lost his way in the dense darkness, and upon whom arose the great light of the morning. All the Jews were in spiritual darkness, and the Galileans were inferior in religious privileges to the Judeans and despised by them. (John 7: 41, 49, 52.) The meaning of this prophecy seems to be that the territories of Zebulun and Naphtali, the region about the Sea of Galilee, the country beyond the Jordan, the whole of Galilee, which was contemptuously designated as "Galilee of the Gentiles," whose inhabitants sat in the darkness of ignorance and under the gloom of impending death, from which there was no one to deliver, these should be the first to see the light the Messiah brought to earth. In their simplicity and possibly in their ignorance, they were not blinded by the prejudice of bigoted religious leaders. So Jesus fulfilled the prophecy with this people.

17 From that time began Jesus to preach, and to say, Repent ye.—Jesus began his ministry at Jerusalem by casting out the traders and his conversation with Nicodemus (John 2: 13; 3: 1-8), but as Matthew does not record those events, the account of Matthew begins with his work in Galilee; Matthew was an eyewitness to that which occurred in Galilee, but was not a disciple of Jesus when his work began in Judea. "From that time" means the time from which Matthew proceeds to give a record of the public ministry of Jesus. This is the time that Jesus began to fulfill the prophecy of Isaiah in Galilee; his regular ministry dates from the time of his removal from Nazareth to Capernaum. (Acts 10: 36, 37.)

"Repent ye; for the kingdom of heaven is at hand." The substance of Jesus' preaching was the same as that of John. (See Matt. 3: 1, 2.) Jesus never ceased to preach repentance; he kept before the people the fact that "the kingdom of heaven is at hand"; repentance was necessary to prepare the people for the reception of the kingdom. There was no cessation of Jesus on insisting that people should repent; he kept it before them from the beginning of his public ministry to the time of his death; after his death he incorporated repentance in the world-wide commission that he gave to his disciples. His preaching at first was only the preaching of repentance, like that of John the Baptist, but he grew more explicit in developing the principles and nature of the kingdom of heaven as he advanced in his public ministry. We learn from Mark that along with his exhortation to the people to repent he called upon them to "believe in the gospel." (Mark 1: 15.) The people were not only to repent of their sins as a preparation for their entrance into his kingdom, but they were to have faith in the Messiah and his gospel. Jesus at this time does not designate himself as the Messiah, yet the kingdom which was approaching was the kingdom of the Messiah, and in this indirect way they were to see in him the promised Messiah.

2. CALL OF PETER AND ANDREW, JAMES AND JOHN
4: 18-22

18 And walking by the sea of Galilee, he saw two brethren, Simon who is called Peter, and Andrew his brother, casting a net into the sea; for they

---

18 **And walking by the sea of Galilee, he saw two brethren, Simon who is called Peter, and Andrew his brother.**—The account of Luke is fuller than that of Matthew. (Luke 5: 1-11.) "Walking by the sea of Galilee" does not mean that Jesus was idly strolling along; he is still carrying out his program of ministry and redemption. "Sea of Galilee" is also called Lake of Gennesaret (Luke 5: 1), Sea of Chinnereth (Num. 34: 11), Chinneroth (Josh. 11: 2; 1 Kings 15: 20), and Tiberias (John 6: 1; 21: 1). The most common name of this body of water is here mentioned by Matthew; this body of water is formed by the waters of the Jordan and is about twelve miles long and six miles broad. It is an expanse of the river Jordan; its most remarkable feature is its deep depression, being no less than seven hundred feet below the level of the sea.

were fishers. 19 And he saith unto them, Come ye after me, and I will make you fishers of men. 20 And they straightway left the nets, and followed him.

"Simon who is called Peter" (John 1: 42); Jesus gave him the name of Peter; it is a designation with a historical anticipation; it means "rock" or "stone." Simon is contracted from Simeon and means hearing or favorable hearing. This is the first mention that Matthew makes of this disciple. "Andrew his brother" is mentioned here with Peter. Peter and Andrew, and probably John, had accepted Jesus as the Messiah nearly a year before this event (John 1: 35-42), and had accompanied him to Cana of Galilee (John 2: 2) as his disciple. They did not receive a formal call at that time to leave all and follow Jesus permanently, and probably they had returned for a time to their occupation as fishermen, till they were called expressly to be fishers of men. Peter had another name "Cephas" which means rock or piece of rock. "Andrew" is a Greek word meaning manly; we do not know whether he was older or younger than his brother Simon; they had formerly lived in Bethsaida (John 1: 44), but had afterward gone to Carpernaum to live. (Luke 4: 31, 38.)

These brothers were busy; God or Jesus never called one while that one was in idleness. These brothers were "casting a net into the sea" as they were fishers by occupation. There may be a distinction between "casting a net" and the hauling in of a net; the one is smaller than the other and may be handled by one man. Fishing was a humble but respectable occupation; one who follows that occupation is usually vigorous of body.

19, 20 **And he saith unto them, Come ye after me, and I will make you fishers of men.**—The meaning evidently is that they were to gain souls for the kingdom of heaven from the sea of the world; the figure that Jesus employed connects their former occupation with the work that he now has for them to do. Their secular employment served as an emblem of their spiritual calling; again they are now catching fish merely to feed men, but their occupation is to be that of catching men. This was a glorious work for them and elevated them to the highest calling on earth. In order to do this they were to

21 And going on from thence he saw two other brethren, ᵃJames the *son* of Zebedee, and John his brother, in the boat with Zebedee their father, mending their nets; and he called them. 22 And they straightway left the boat and

ᵃOr, *Jacob*

"come ye after me"; they were to follow Jesus and *he* would make them fishers of men. In their present condition they were not as yet ready for this great work. It is commendable in Peter and Andrew that "they straightway left the nets, and followed him." They immediately, without delay, obeyed his command; they recognized Jesus as the Messiah, and they were willing to follow him; they did not hesitate nor falter in indecision; their minds were made up so soon as the call came. Their nets were the means of their living, but they left these; they were willing to forsake all for the sake of Jesus to follow him wherever he should lead. Their faith in the Messiah and their prompt obedience to his call revealed marks of qualifications for the great work.

21, 22 And going on from thence he saw two other brethren, James the son of Zebedee, and John his brother.—A little time seems to have intervened which Jesus occupied in conversing with Simon and Andrew; the brief words of Matthew's record are an epitome of the conversation that Jesus had with Simon and Andrew. He saw after going further along the coast of the Sea of Galilee "two other brethren"; these also are named as James and John; they were partners of Peter and Andrew in the business of fishing (Luke 5: 10), and probably John was the disciple not named, who accompanied Andrew in his first visit to Jesus on his return from the temptation of Jesus (John 1: 37-40). James and John were sons of Zebedee; their father was with them in the boat at this time. James is probably the elder of the two brothers; his name is the Greek form of the Hebrew name "Jacob"; he is usually called the greater or elder to distinguish him from James the less. He was beheaded by order of Herod Agrippa (Acts 12: 2) about A.D. 44 and was the first martyr among the apostles. John means "the grace of God" he is designated as the disciple "whom Jesus loved." He was the writer of the gospel that bears his name, three epistles, and Revelation. He was among the first

their father, and followed him.

disciples of Jesus, and followed him faithfully through a long life of service and was the last of the apostles to die. He lived nearly seventy years after this call by Jesus. Zebedee means "Jehovah's gift"; he was the husband of Salome, the sister of Mary, the mother of Jesus (John 19: 25); she ministered to Jesus (Matt. 27: 56). James and John were cousins of Jesus. Zebedee is not mentioned among the disciples of Jesus. The mention of hired servants (Mark 1: 20), of the two vessels employed (Luke 5: 7), and the subsequent allusion of John's acquaintance with a person in so high a position as the high priest (John 18: 15) seem to indicate that Zebedee, if not a wealthy man, was at any rate of some position at Capernaum.

And they straightway left the boat and their father, and followed him.—They were mending their nets at the time Jesus came along; the nets were broken by the great draught of fishes. (Luke 5: 6.) Jesus called them to become fishers of men as he had called Peter and Andrew. They immediately "left the boat and their father" and followed Jesus. Some think that they probably got the consent of their father before they accepted the call; they were men and not boys; it is likely that they would make some arrangement with their father about their business before giving up everything and following Jesus. The call of God is above all earthly demands. (Matt. 10: 37.) The hired servants were there with the father, hence he was not left without some provision. God's call does not bid us leave our parents to suffer, but rather to make provision for them. (Mark 7: 10-13.) This call of these disciples was their call to be his disciples or constant companions and not the formal call to be his apostles; this came at a later period. (Luke 6: 12, 13.) These disciples not only left their property and their business, but left their homes and their families in order to follow Jesus.

3. THE THEME OF HIS PREACHING: GOSPEL OF THE KINGDOM
4: 23-25

23 And [7]Jesus went about in all Galilee, teaching in their synagogues, and preaching the [8]gospel of the kingdom, and healing all manner of disease and

---

[7]Some ancient authorities read *he*.
[8]Or, *good tidings:* and so elsewhere.

---

23 And Jesus went about in all Galilee.—Here we have Jesus making a circuit of Galilee; he did this on two other occasions later. (Matt. 9: 35 to 11: 1; Luke 8: 1-3.) Matthew does not give the details of this circuit here but does later. It may be that "Galilee" as used here implied only "Upper Galilee"; some so think; others think that all Galilee was included in this circuit. Galilee formed the northernmost part of Palestine; it was about ten miles long and four to five miles broad, bounded on the west by the Mediterranean Sea and Phoenicia, on the north by Coelesyria, on the east by the Jordan and the Sea of Galilee, and on the south by Samaria. It was considered mountainous and rugged, yet it was the most fertile part of the country, being well adapted to pasturage and agriculture. It is claimed that it contained 404 towns and villages.

Teaching in their synagogues, and preaching the gospel of the kingdom.—Jesus "taught" in the synagogues and "preached" the gospel of the kingdom. Jesus is called the "Great Teacher" because he instructed people who frequented the synagogue; he interpreted the law of Moses to them and gave them information as to the facts of God's word and instructed them with respect to its principles. "Synagogues" were common at that time; much of the teaching of the Jews was received in the synagogue; Jews were commanded to teach their children at home on all occasions (Deut. 6: 4-10), but at this time many homes neglected the teaching and sent their children to the synagogue. The Greek word which is designated by "synagogue" signifies a collection of objects or persons; the synagogue came into use during the Babylonian captivity and became very common by the time of the advent of the Messiah. To preach means to proclaim; not necessarily

all manner of sickness among the people. 24 And the report of him went forth into all Syria: and they brought unto him all that were sick, holden

to proclaim for the first time, but it includes the first proclamation of the gospel.

Much of the Jewish worship was carried on in the synagogue; this gave Jesus an opportunity to preach "the gospel of the kingdom." The "gospel of the kingdom" was the good news of the approaching reign of the Messiah; his kingdom was "at hand," "it drew nigh." The word "gospel" is composed of two words, "god" and "spell," which means good tidings and corresponds to the Greek word which means "good news." The Jews associated the idea of joy with the coming of the Messiah; now Jesus proclaimed "the good news" that the kingdom or the reign of the Messiah was near. The gospel as preached by Jesus here does not have the same content that the word "gospel" later had.

Healing all manner of disease and all manner of sickness among the people.—Jesus confirmed his teaching and his preaching by miracles; the ultimate aim of these miracles was the manifestation of Jesus himself, and of the kingdom of heaven; while the diseased were blessed in that they were healed, yet Jesus had a higher motive than merely curing the ailments of the physical body. Matthew is general in narrating the miracles of Jesus; he healed "all manner of disease" and "all manner of sickness"; the word for "disease" seems to denote infirmity or such diseases as produce feebleness rather than positive suffering, while the word for "sickness" includes those severe, violent, and dangerous ailments. "Disease" expresses something stronger than "sickness." The miracles of Jesus cannot be separated from his teaching and preaching. The spiritual teachings, the perfect character, and the miracles of Jesus all support each other, and together form the foundation of our faith and hope.

24 And the report of him went forth into all Syria.—Such miracles which brought healing to the people naturally would attract the attention; hence the fame of Jesus passed to the north and east, rather than to the south. Galilee was connected by trade with Damascus, rather than with Jerusalem;

with divers diseases and torments, ⁹possessed with demons, and epileptic, and palsied; and he healed them. 25 And there followed him great multitudes from Galilee and Decapolis and Jerusalem and Judæa and *from* beyond the Jordan.

---

⁹Or, *demoniacs*

however "Syria" was a name of variable extent, denoting in general a country east of the Mediterranean, between Asia Minor and Arabia. We are to understand Matthew to mean that the report of Jesus' miracles of healing passed beyond the bounds of Galilee and went far away into the districts northward. Mark says "the report of him went out straightway everywhere into all the region of Galilee round about." (Mark 1:28.)

And they brought unto him all that were sick.—In consequence of what they had heard of his great power to heal, all others who were afflicted were anxious to be healed. Those who could not come of their own strength were brought by relatives and friends. It seems that they had not heard so much of the teachings of Jesus as his power to heal; naturally people would be more interested in the physical comfort and ease than they would in the good news of the approaching kingdom. There were many kinds of diseases then and Jesus healed them; some of these diseases were attended with excruciating pain; others were "possessed with demons" and were healed. It seems that the difference between this and other diseases was in its cause and not its symptoms. We find violent madness (Mark 5:4; Luke 8:29), epilepsy (Mark 9:18; Luke 9:39), dumbness (Matt. 9:32; Luke 11:14), blindness (Matt. 12:22), all ascribed to persons who were possessed with demons. There were diseases among them which were not caused by evil spirits. There seems to have been certain moral and physical conditions in which demons gained possession both of the body and of the mind, bringing disease upon the body, and insanity to the mind. All these were brought to Jesus for his help.

25 And there followed him great multitudes from Galilee and Decapolis and Jerusalem and Judaea and from beyond the Jordan.—Great crowds followed him; possibly a confused crowd or throng of people followed Jesus wherever he went. "Multitudes" means "crowds" without designating the number; this should be understood throughout the record of Matthew. The miracles of Jesus for a season attracted such crowds and excited so many that they saw and heard but little else than the power of Jesus to cure diseases; many did not appreciate his teaching, neither did they look forward with great anxiety to the coming kingdom. The miracles of Jesus, if properly understood, would mean that he who wrought the miracle had the power of God, and if he had the power of God in working miracles, God was with him in his teachings. God was manifested in the teaching and preaching of Jesus as much as he was in the healing of all manner of diseases.

Great crowds came from "Galilee and Decapolis and Jerusalem and Judæa and from beyond the Jordan." It seems that the crowds were drawn first from Galilee, where Jesus was teaching; then the crowds were increased by others coming from Decapolis, which was a section of country with ten cities; these "ten cities" very likely varied at different times; it was a region in the northeastern part of Palestine, on the east and southeast of the Sea of Galilee. The crowds also came from Jerusalem and Judea and "from beyond the Jordan"; this means the other side of the Jordan from Jerusalem, and it was usually called Perea. Syria was north of Galilee, Decapolis southeast of the Sea of Galilee, "beyond the Jordan" or Perea was east of the Jordan and Judea was the southern division of Palestine. Jesus had retired from Judea to Galilee, but many followed him to Galilee.

4. THE BEATITUDES
5: 1-12

1 And seeing the multitudes, he went up into the mountain: and when he

---

1, 2 And seeing the multitudes, he went up into the mountain.—We are not told what mountain this was; tradition has it that it was "a mountain" or hill between Mount Tabor and Tiberias; it has been called the "Mount of Beatitudes" and is visible from the shores of the Sea of Galilee; it rises sixty feet

had sat down, his disciples came unto him: 2 and he opened his mouth and taught them, saying,
3 Blessed are the poor in spirit: for theirs is the kingdom of heaven.

above the ridge and is easily accessible from the lake. When Jesus saw the great multitudes or crowds which thronged about him to hear and to be healed (Matt. 4: 24, 25), he went up from the level place on the mountain (Luke 6: 12, 17), where the people were gathered, to a higher point, from which he could more easily be seen and heard by them. He assumed the posture of Jewish teachers at the time, "when he had sat down"; Jesus frequently saw multitudes around him, but here a peculiar emphasis is laid on that circumstance. "His disciples came unto him"; those who were anxious to learn of him. "Disciple" means a "learner" as opposed to a "teacher," and is used in that sense here. When Jesus took the position of a teacher, than his disciples drew near and assumed the posture and attitude of learners.

When the crowds had assembled and when all had become quiet, Jesus "opened his mouth and taught them." The original will bear the translation of "was teaching" or "went to teaching"; his disciples were close to him and are designated here as distant from the crowds (Luke 6: 20), and are especially addressed in this discourse. It is probable that Jesus repeated often the teachings that he here gave; Matthew records his teaching in this sermon with 107 verses, while Luke gives only thirty verses. The first part of this sermon is called "the beatitudes," from "beatus," the Latin word for "blessed" there are eight in number; some say nine (Luke adds four woes, 6: 24-26); these are promises of blessings which are distinctly promised to the citizen of the kingdom of heaven. In these beatitudes Jesus teaches the characteristics of the citizen of his kingdom; they are the fundamental principles of the Christian character.

3 Blessed are the poor in spirit.—"Blessed" is translated by some as "happy." "The poor in spirit" are those whose minds are suited to the humble station of life; "poor" means destitute of something; poor in spirit means those who are destitute of the proud, haughty, arrogant spirit of the world. The

4 ¹⁰Blessed are they that mourn: for they shall be comforted.
5 Blessed are the meek: for they shall inherit the earth.

¹⁰Some ancient authorities transpose ver. 4 and 5.

Jew looked upon wealth as being one of the chief elements of prosperity which was proof that its possessor was the object of God's special favors; Jesus here contradicts that conception; "the poor in spirit" are those who are destitute of spiritual possessions and who know their true condition and long for a better spiritual state. The poor in spirit are conscious of their need; the poor in spirit are opposite of pride and self-righteousness. It is the same spirit that is required when we are told that we must become as little children, if we would enter the kingdom of heaven. It is the door to the kingdom of heaven; "for theirs is the kingdom of heaven." His spiritual kingdom, begun here, completed hereafter, above; those who are poor in spirit shall enter that kingdom and belong to it. The heavenly riches, honor, glory, and happiness belong to those who are poor in spirit. "The poor in spirit" fitly describes a state of mind lowly and reverent before God; humble, not proud; contrite, not rebellious. This is a fundamental principle of the character and teachings of Jesus.

4 Blessed are they that mourn.—It is a very impressive paradox to say happy are they that grieve, but such is the meaning of this statement of Jesus. Those who mourn for their own sins and over the sins of others are to be blessed; all who enter the kingdom of heaven are brought into the experience of mourning. The mourning referred to springs from sympathy with God, whose will is so grievously disregarded and thwarted by men. Not every sort of mourning can claim this blessing; the sorrows of disappointed ambition, the tears of wounded pride, have no claim on the blessings referred to here. The promise to those who mourn is that "they shall be comforted." "The sorrow of the world worketh death" (2 Cor. 7: 10), but those who mourn as here described are comforted. No mourner as described by Jesus has never missed the blessings of divine consolation.

5 Blessed are the meek.—The primary meaning of "meek" is "mild, gentle"; this is a meaning that Christ gave to this

6 Blessed are they that hunger and thirst after righteousness: for they shall be filled.

word and lifted it to a higher plane than its previous meaning; many today do not give to it its elevated significance. The nicer shades of the meaning of terms descriptive of character are often best shown under the light of their opposites, by the aid of contrast—as the poor in spirit are those who are not proud, so the meek are those who are not harsh and implacable. The meek are those who suffer in love, or love in patience; they are those who in the strength of love, boldly yet meekly, meekly yet boldly, bear injustice, and thereby conquer. Meekness is opposed to arrogance; meekness is a spirit the opposite of the ambitious and self-seeking ones which is characteristic of men of the world. The promise is that the meek "shall inherit the earth." The real enjoyment of earthly blessings belongs not to those who grasp for them and assert and maintain with vehemence and care their right to them, but to those who hold them lightly, and who, ranking them inferior to spiritual blessings, are not burdened by them while they possess them; they are not harassed by the fear of losing earthly possessions. Selfish people may *possess* the earth, but it is the meek alone who inherit the real blessings of this earth and of the spiritual kingdom. The meek will enjoy the temporal blessings more than others and finally will triumph over the earth in the kingdom of God.

6 **Blessed are they that hunger and thirst after righteousness.**—No words could be plainer than these; hunger and thirst are of the best known experiences in human life. The promise is not to those who merely desire righteousness, but those who have an intense desire that must be satisifed. The greatness of the soul is measured by the *number,* the *intensity,* and the *quality* of its desires; this is the highest and best desire, and men are good in proportion to its intensity. These beatitudes treat of personal character, and describe individual characteristics. The promise to those who have such an intense desire for righteousness is that "they shall be filled." A perfect inner and outer life are the results of righteousness; perfect conformity to God's law and nature; righteousness is

> 7 Blessed are the merciful: for they shall obtain mercy.
> 8 Blessed are the pure in heart: for they shall see God.

the beauty of holiness. A citizen of the kingdom of heaven must have a deep longing after goodness, godliness, and the qualities that belong to heaven, and not after wealth, honor, or worldly fame. The promise is that "they shall be filled"; not partly filled, not modified in form, but completely satisfied or filled. Life is a series of desires and their disappointments or fulfillments; to those who hunger and thirst after righteousness in the kingdom of heaven their desires shall be fulfilled.

7 Blessed are the merciful.—"Merciful" includes the idea of compassion, as in Prov. 14: 21; Heb. 2: 17, and implies a desire to remove the evils which excite compassion. The merciful are those who pity, sympathize with, and help to relieve, all misery and suffering; this is the natural outward expression of the inner hungering after righteousness. Mercy is near akin to forgiveness and love; it relieves spiritual want and darkness, as well as temporal. Those who are merciful are not only merciful to the guilty, but extend pity to the suffering and help to the needy. To be merciful is not the ground of receiving mercy from God, but an occasion and condition thereof. The promise to the merciful is that "they shall obtain mercy." They shall obtain it frequently from their fellows, and always from God. (Psalm 41: 1; Prov. 11: 25; James 2: 13.) This beatitude comprises every degree of sympathy and mutual love and help; we may show mercy, not by giving money to help the poor, but by word; if we have no other way, we can show mercy by the sympathizing tear. Showing mercy to others proves that we have a state of heart which makes it safe for God to extend mercy to us; for God to forgive the unmerciful would be to encourage the sin of vengeance; the unforgiving are in every sense unfit to receive forgiveness—the unmerciful, to receive mercy. (Luke 6: 37.)

8 Blessed are the pure in heart.—This is put in contrast with mere external or bodily purification, about which the Jews, and especially the Pharisees, were very scrupulous. (Matt. 23: 25, 28.) The "pure in heart" are those who

9 Blessed are the peacemakers: for they shall be called sons of God.

are pure, sincere, clean in motive and purpose; it is the state of heart which repels, loathes, every vile or sinful thing. Purity of heart is freedom from evil desires and purposes. James says, "Purify your hearts, ye doubleminded." (James 4: 8.) Nothing is said here about how the heart is purified; we learn later that it is purified by faith. (Acts 15: 9; 1 Thess. 5: 23; 1 Tim. 1: 5; 1 Pet. 1: 22.) A heart that does not believe in God or Christ is an impure heart; all worshipers of idols have impure hearts. The precious promise to those who are pure in heart is that "they shall see God." The impure in heart and life cannot see God; they cannot see him in nature, and cannot in grace. To "see God" is to enjoy him, to enjoy his presence. Jesus in conversation with Nicodemus said at one time that if one is not born again, "he cannot see the kingdom of God"; and again expressing the same thought he said to Nicodemus if one is not born of water and the Spirit, he "cannot enter into the kingdom of God." (John 3: 3, 5.) To "see" the kingdom of God was to enjoy it; so to "see God" is to enjoy the presence of God here and hereafter. The pure in heart have intercourse with God and thus enjoy him. Of all our senses that of sight comes nearest perfection—gives us a clearer, fuller knowledge of its objects than any other of the senses. Hence, transferring it from the physical to the mental and spiritual, it should express a better apprehension—a clearer knowledge of God than any other illustration possible from the material world. Not only do the pure in heart see God here, but they shall see him face to face. "We know that, if he shall be manifested, we shall be like him; for we shall see him even as he is." (1 John 3: 2.)

9 **Blessed are the peacemakers.**—This is in wide contrast with the worldly kingdoms; they are maintained by strife and war; the kingdom of God is a peaceful kingdom; its citizens are "peacemakers." They bring about peace between enemies; they make peace with God, with their fellows, and with their own consciences; the peacemaker is one who loves God and man and who utterly detests, abhors, and abominates all strife, wars, and dissensions; the peacemaker includes those

10 Blessed are they that have been persecuted for righteousness' sake: for theirs is the kingdom of heaven. 11 Blessed are ye when *men* shall reproach you, and persecute you, and say all manner of evil against you falsely, for

who, by their presence and disposition, as well as by their conscious acts, carry with them the spirit of peace and quietness; he is one who, like Jesus, seeks to reconcile men to God and to bring divine peace into the lives of men; the peacemaker is subject to the "Prince of Peace" and has the spirit of God. The promise to the peacemakers is that "they shall be called sons of God." Since God is a God of peace, Christ the Prince of Peace, the gospel a gospel of peace, and the kingdom of God a kingdom of peace, all subjects of this kingdom must be peacemakers. Those who are in the kingdom of God are the children of God, hence they are called sons of God.

10, 11 Blessed are they that have been persecuted for righteousness' sake.—One characteristic of a citizen of the kingdom of God is that one must be ready and willing to endure persecution; this follows closely the attribute of the peacemaker. In order to maintain peace many times one must suffer persecution. The work of the peacemaker is not a light and easy work; it often entails the persecution of the world and even those who should be reconciled to God. The blessing is pronounced upon those who are "persecuted for righteousness' sake," and not those who are persecuted for their opinions or their misbehavior. Jesus was already beginning to be bitterly hated and reviled; evil men were seeking his life. (Mark 3: 6; Luke 6: 7, 11.) Persecution can be made in different ways; it can be done by taking one's property, by misrepresenting one, by slandering one's character, or by willfully impugning one's motives. This plainly signifies that "the kingdom of heaven" must encounter opposition; righteousness has its foes in unrighteousness. There is antagonism between good and evil, truth and error, right and wrong, Christ and the devil; the evil forces are at war against the forces of righteousness; those who maintain a firm stand for righteousness may expect to be persecuted. "Yea, and all that would live godly in Christ Jesus shall suffer persecution." (2 Tim. 3: 12.) Those who suffer persecution have the prom-

my sake. **12** Rejoice, and be exceeding glad: for great is your reward in heaven: for so persecuted they the prophets that were before you.

ise of the blessings of "the kingdom of heaven." Persecution for righteousness drives the persecuted closer to God as a refuge; the closer we get to God, the richer and fuller the blessing.

12 Rejoice, and be exceeding glad.—Those who are persecuted for righteousness' sake are to rejoice; they are to rejoice and "be exceeding glad" that they are counted worthy to suffer for the kingdom of heaven. Jesus knew that those who would enter his kingdom and prove faithful would be persecuted; he prepares them for this by foretelling them and then promising to be with them. He reminds them that they would have to suffer greatly as did the prophets of old; "for so persecuted they the prophets that were before you." Jeremiah was scourged (Jer. 20: 2); Zechariah, son of Jehoiada, was stoned (2 Chron. 24: 21); Isaiah, according to Jewish tradition, was sawn asunder by Manasseh. Elijah's life was sought, and many other prophets were persecuted; and within two years Jesus himself was to be persecuted even unto death. To suffer persecution for righteousness puts one in the brotherhood of the faithful of God; it assures one that persecution is no mark of God's disfavor, for God's best beloved ones had suffered and were suffering. The persecution was no proof that their cause would not succeed. Persecution made them, when the time came, partakers of Christ's sufferings, and therefore of his glory. (Rom. 8: 17.) The disciples of Jesus were to rejoice because "great is your reward in heaven." Though the crown of glory will be a free gift to those who have suffered, nevertheless it will be a reward for the suffering. Christians do not receive their reward here; seemingly the more faithful one is to the Lord the more difficult will be the life in the service of God; the more zealous and faithful, the more assurance they have of a rich reward in heaven.

5. THE DISCIPLES COMPARED TO SALT AND LIGHT
5: 13-16

13 Ye are the salt of the earth: but if the salt have lost its savor, wherewith shall it be salted? it is thenceforth good for nothing, but to be cast out

13 Ye are the salt of the earth.—The citizens of this heavenly kingdom that Jesus preached was at hand are to become "the salt of the earth." The citizens of this kingdom are described by the beatitudes, and they are to have a saving influence in the world. Faithful Christians are to the human race what salt is to food—the element which preserves it from corruption and gives savor and relish. How are Christians the salt of the earth? They are present as proof of the success of truth, and are monuments of what the principles of the kingdom will make one; they preserve the life of Christ in the earth; they are the means of spreading the truths of the gospel, and propagating the salvation of Jesus, by which the world is preserved. Salt was used in the Levitical sacrifices. (Lev. 2: 13.) Livy called Greece "the salt of the nations" as they were enlightened by the wisdom of Greece; so Christians are called by Jesus "the salt of the earth," because they are to save the world.

But if the salt have lost its savor.—The salt of the ancient world was not purified as it now is; hence it retained all of the less soluble compounds of lime, iron, and other things which occur in all natural salt water; therefore it contained a large quantity of insoluble substance which remained flavorless after the real salt had been dissolved out of it; the eastern salt was generally somewhat dark and dirty. Jesus said if the salt (or mass of material) has lost its genuine salty quality, it is fit for nothing; it is not only good for nothing itself, but it actually destroys all fertility of soil where it is thrown; this is the reason it is cast into the street where it is "trodden under foot of men." Salt which is pure cannot lose its savor, and is good for its proper uses. So, if the disciples of Jesus have lost their savor, they too are good for nothing but to be cast out. If Christians become untrue to their high calling and degenerate spiritually, they cannot have a good influence on the world.

and trodden under foot of men. 14 Ye are the light of the world. A city set on a hill cannot be hid. 15 Neither do *men* light a lamp, and put it under the bushel, but on the stand; and it shineth unto all that are in the house.

14 Ye are the light of the world.—Salt operates *internally*, in the mass with which it comes in contact; the sunlight operates *externally*, irradiating all that it reaches; hence the disciples of Jesus are "the salt of the earth," with reference to the masses of mankind with whom they are associated; but "the light of the world," with reference to the vast and variegated surface which feels its structifying and gladdening radiance. Light is not only opposed to darkness, but it overcomes it; it dispels darkness; so the truth and holiness possessed by the disciples of Jesus, who is the true light, dispel the world's darkness, by overcoming its ignorance and sin. The world lies in moral darkness; it is enveloped in spiritual chaos; the light of Christ is to shine through his disciples on the world. Such light cannot be hidden, any more than "a city set on a hill"; not only is it not hidden, but it occupies a very prominent place. Possibly Jesus has in mind the comparison between the city on a hill and a group or church of his disciples; their influence cannot be ignored in the world. There is no greater light for God than the church that is filling its mission in a community.

15, 16 Neither do men light a lamp, and put it under the bushel.—The word "bushel" is from the Latin term "modius," which was about equal to a peck; it was used for measuring grain and was a common article. The lamps then were of earthenware or of metal in the shape of a saucer, turned up on one side to hold the wick; olive oil was used to burn in them. The proper place for the lamp was "on the stand" and not "under the bushel." It would be of no service to anyone if put "under the bushel." "The stand" was the place for the lamp to diffuse the light and expel the darkness; if put under a bushel, the darkness is not expelled. The disciples of Jesus should not conceal the light of the knowledge of the gospel; neither should they attempt to live as a hermit; Jesus intended that his disciples live in human society and diffuse their light to those who are in spiritual darkness. A Christian cannot fill his mission by living alone. If the lamp is placed on

16 Even so let your light shine before men; that they may see your good works, and glorify your Father who is in heaven.

the stand, which is its proper place, then "it shineth unto all that are in the house"; it becomes a blessing to all who may come under its influence; so the life that a Christian must live is the life of service to all whose life may be touched by his life.

Even so let your light shine before men.—Jesus draws his own conclusions and makes his own application. He says *"let"* your light shine before men, not *shine* your light before men. Christians should keep their light burning and should let nothing hide the light. The purpose of light is to dispel darkness; if a disciple of Jesus is not dispelling darkness somewhere, his light is under a bushel or has become extinguished. Christians should boldly uphold the truth that others may be blessed by the truth. The purpose of Christians letting their light shine is not for self-glorification, honor, or exaltation, but that other men "may see your good works, and glorify your Father who is in heaven." Jesus gives a little different turn when he refers to their "good work," yet it is by these "good works" that the Christian's light shines before others. There should be no false display of piety or boasts of one's goodness as a member of the church, but the "good works" or the life will proclaim the life of Christ. Others are to be brought to glorify God through the light that shines from Christians.

[Christians shine through their honest lives and upright deportment among men. Those who lack uprightness of character can do nothing to help forward the religion of Jesus Christ. He was holy, harmless, separated from sinners, and became higher than the heavens. Christians, in their anxiety to make money and get rich, go in debt, fail, and bring reproach on themselves and the cause of God. Lying and stealing are closely allied. They are different degrees of the same evil disposition. A lie is dishonesty in word. To steal is a lie developed into action. All lying, prevarication, falsehood, deception are condemned severely by God, and dim the light and life of a disciple of the Lord.]

6. JESUS' RELATION TO THE LAW OF MOSES
5: 17-20

17 Think not that I came to destroy the law or the prophets: I came not

17 Think not that I came to destroy the law or the prophets.—Jesus had been proclaiming a new kingdom of God, and had laid down some of its laws and principles; the Jewish nation had been ordained of God; its laws were given by him. Jesus now explains his relation to the law of the Jewish nation; he is to explain the relation of this new kingdom with its laws and principles to the old kingdom and its laws. The Pharisees had already (Mark 2: 24; John 5: 16, 18) accused Jesus of disregarding the law of Moses. Jesus answers their accusation in attitude if not in words to him for what he was doing and teaching. He did not come "to destroy"; here the word "destroy" means "to loosen down, to dissolve, undo"; he did not come to abrogate or set aside the law and the prophets. "The law or the prophets" here not merely means the Pentateuch or the prophets as listed in the Old Testament scriptures, but all for which the law and the prophets stood. The law included the ritualistic, civil, and moral codes of Israel, while the prophets included the prediction and commands which were given through the prophets.

I came not to destroy, but to fulfil.—"To destroy" is put in contrast with "to fulfil." Jesus, instead of destroying the law, fulfilled it; instead of setting aside the prophets, he fulfilled their predictions. He fulfilled the law theoretically by unfolding its deep spiritual significance; he fulfilled it practically in his holy life; ceremonially, he fulfilled it by becoming the antitype of all its types and shadows. "Not to destroy, but to fulfil" is a general principle which clearly describes Jesus' attitude toward the law. The Jews were to see in Jesus the end of the law. Jesus came to fulfill all of the types of the law and all the unfulfilled predictions of the prophets; Jesus and his kingdom, with all that pertains to them, constitute the object and fulfillment of all the prophets.

18 Till heaven and earth pass away, one jot or one tittle shall in no wise pass away from the law, till all things be ac-

to destroy, but to fulfil. 18 For verily I say unto you, Till heaven and earth pass away, one jot or tittle shall in no wise pass away from the law, till all things be accomplished. 19 Whosoever therefore shall break one of these least commandments, and shall teach men so, shall be called least in the kingdom of heaven: but whosoever shall do and teach them, he shall be

complished.—Here Jesus declares again his attitude toward the law and the prophets. "Till heaven and earth pass away" is another way of saying that "the law or the prophets" shall not pass away until all are fulfilled in the minutest detail. The law shall last till the new order of things is brought into force; the prophets shall stand until their predictions become history. "Jot" is for the Hebrew letter "jod," which is the smallest letter in the Hebrew alphabet. "Tittle" is the little bend or point which serves to distinguish certain Hebrew letters of similar appearance. The Jews were familiar with the expression used by Jesus. Everything else may change, but the word of God expressed by either "the law" or "the prophets" must stand until it has accomplished that which God intended. All shall stand "till all things be accomplished." Some make a distinction between "fulfilled" and "accomplished"; they are not the same words in the original. Jesus meant to say that the law should remain in full force until it shall have accomplished that which God intended it to accomplish. The law seems to have had a twofold termination, a negative and a positive; negatively, it terminated with the old Jewish nation; positively, it is realized in the new and spiritual kingdom, which Jesus inaugurated.

19 Whosoever therefore shall break one of these least commandments.—The Greek word here for "break" is generally translated "loose" and carries with it the idea of freeing from restraints, as in Mark 1:7; Luke 13:15; 19:30, 31; John 11:44; the idea seems to be that anyone who should loosen the authority or obligation of even the "least commandments" should be condemned; not the one who would abrogate or destroy the commandment, but the one who should violate it by loosening its obligations on anyone. The one who should do this should be called "least in the kingdom of heaven." The man who would break what he considered one of the least commandments of God under one dispensation would be

called great in the kingdom of heaven. 20 For I say unto you, that except

proportionately disobedient under another dispensation, and hence would sustain the wrong attitude toward the authority of God. "Least" may refer to the same as "one jot or one tittle" in verse eighteen; it means that no one has authority to violate in the minutest detail any of the commands of God.

But whosoever shall do and teach them, he shall be called great in the kingdom of heaven.—Jesus here puts *doing* before *teaching*; this is the proper order; these are the two great things one can do; he can keep all of God's commandments and teach others to keep them, or he can disobey them himself and encourage others to disobey them. To relax the obligation of law either by precept or example is not the way to attain eminence in piety ourselves, or to promote it in others. It is bad to do wrong, but it is worse if in addition we teach others to do wrong. The one who breaks the commandment of God will be held in contempt by all the loyal subjects of the kingdom of God, but one who obeys the commandments of God shall be held in honor by the ones who are loyal subjects of his kingdom.

[The one who breaks one of the commandments of God is out of harmony with God. Harmony with God is heaven; discord with God is hell. The world was once in harmony with God; it was an outer court of heaven—the home of peace and joy—in which God dwelt and walked in the cool of the day as the companion of man, and in which man was immortal. The devil turned man from obedience to God, breathed into the world the spirit of discord and strife, changed the world into an antechamber of hell, and it became a charnel house of death and ruin. This was brought about by man's breaking the commandments of God.]

[If one sets aside or rejects one of the least commandments of God, and so teaches men, he will be rejected as the least and most unworthy of those in the kingdom, as such will be cast out into outer darkness, where there is weeping and gnashing of teeth; but he who shall do and teach all these commandments shall be great in the kingdom of heaven.

your righteousness shall exceed *the righteousness* of the scribes and Pharisees, ye shall in no wise enter into the kingdom of heaven.

This breaking of the commandment seems to be willful, since connected with it was the teaching of others to set aside the law. It means the same that James meant when he said, "For whosoever shall keep the whole law, and yet stumble in one point, he is become guilty of all." (James 2: 10.) Our fidelity to God is tested as easily in literal things as in great ones; rather, nothing is little where God's authority is at stake.]

20 For I say unto you, that except your righteousness shall exceed the righteousness of the scribes and Pharisees.—Here Jesus puts his authority to the fore and declares that the righteousness of the citizens of his kingdom must exceed even the righteousness that is claimed by the scribes and Pharisees. The scribes were the leaders and teachers of the Pharisaic sect; they were an order known as "scribes," or writers or teachers of the law, who devoted themselves to the study of the law, and became the recognized authorities in all matters connected with the law. The righteousness of "the scribes and Pharisees" was in general artificial, outward, and unreal; they professed to be exceedingly righteous, but were hypocrites. Jesus does not mean to say that they were as righteous as they professed to be; he knew them to be hypocrites.

The disciples of Jesus are to get a high conception of the righteousness that Jesus required of his disciples; their righteousness must "exceed" the professed righteousness of the scribes and Pharisees. The righteousness of the disciples of Jesus must exceed the righteousness of the scribes and Pharisees, because theirs was outward, but the disciples must have spiritual righteousness; it must grow out of love to God and to man and not be a mere boasted self-righteousness; it must be a true moral righteousness and not a ceremonial one.

Ye shall in no wise enter into the kingdom of heaven.—In no sense or by no means can they enter "the kingdom of heaven," if their righteousness does not exceed the professed righteousness of those who had great repute for their sanctity. They are not excluded arbitrarily, but by the very nature of the kingdom and the principles on which it is conducted. The righteousness of the Pharisees, if extended to every person in the world, would not bring the blessings of God upon all or constitute the kingdom of heaven on earth; the righteousness of Jesus is the standard of righteousness for all who enter the kingdom of heaven.

[The fault with the righteousness of the Pharisees was: it was formal, and not from the heart; it consisted in external acts to be seen of men. The Pharisees made long, formal prayers, but would devour widows' houses. The righteousness of Christians must be greater than theirs, in that it must be genuine, from the heart, and must be in secret as well as public.]

7. TEACHINGS AGAINST MURDER
5: 21-26

21 Ye have heard that it was said to them of old time, ¹Thou shalt not

¹Ex. xx. 13; Dt. v. 17.

---

21 Ye have heard that it was said to them of old time, Thou shalt not kill.—Here Jesus alludes to the teaching of the scribes in which they recited passages of the law, and put a corrupt interpretation on it; they had heard in the synagogues the interpretation that the leaders of that day put on the sixth commandment of the Decalogue. Murder was prohibited by this commandment, "Thou shalt not kill." (Ex. 20: 13.) The law when first given to the Jews was followed without any interpretation, but later the scribes and other teachers added their comments to it and it was difficult to get the meaning of the law from the traditions of the Jews. This commandment was simple and clear; it condemned murder, but the teachers had so interpreted it as to let some on certain occasions escape the penalty of the law. They said that those who should kill should "be in danger of the judgment." That is, they should be "liable" to be brought before the tribunal. This is not what the law said, that they should be "in danger of the judgment," but that the penalty for murder was death. (Ex. 21:

kill; and whosoever shall kill shall be in danger of the judgment: 22 but I say unto you, that every one who is angry with his brother ²shall be in danger of the judgment; and whosoever shall say to his brother, ³Raca, shall be in danger of the council; and whosoever shall say, ⁴Thou fool, shall be in

---

²Many ancient authorities insert *without cause.*
³An expression of contempt.
⁴Or, *Moreh,* a Hebrew expression of condemnation.

12.) The Jews had made two points with respect to this commandment: first, that it forbade murder for the intentional taking of human life; second, that it taught that the murderer made himself obnoxious to society and would be in danger of the condemnation of the Sanhedrin.

22 But I say unto you, that every one who is angry with his brother shall be in danger of the judgment.—Jesus sets over against the interpretation of the Jews the true meaning of the law; he gives a deep spiritual meaning to the commandment that the Jews had not seen. Murder is the overt act of a murderous spirit, which accompanies anger; Jesus goes back to the very roots of murder and shows that the true teaching of the law as set forth now by the principles of his kingdom forbids even the thoughts of murder. Every one who "is angry with his brother shall be in danger of the judgment"; many ancient authorities insert "without cause" in this verse, but it is not in the original. The one who has murderous thoughts "shall be in danger of the judgment"; he shall be considered a murderer, who has murderous thoughts in his heart.

Again "whosoever shall say to his brother, Raca, shall be in danger of the council." "Raca" is derived from the Hebrew "rak," which means to be empty or vain; it is an Aramæan term of contempt or reproach; it means a worthless fellow, empty-headed, and was an expression of anger; it was a step further than merely *thinking* murderous thoughts, it was *expressing in words* murderous intentions. The one who went thus far was in danger of "the council." To be "in danger of the judgment" was to be in danger of a sentence from the lower courts, but to be "in danger of the council" was to be in danger of a sentence by the Sanhedrin.

Whosoever shall say, Thou fool, shall be in danger of the hell of fire.—"Fool" is a term which expresses more than want

danger ⁵of the ⁶hell of fire. 23 If I therefore thou art offering thy gift at the

---

⁵Gr. *unto* or *into*.
⁶Gr. *Gehenna of fire*.

---

of wisdom; it means stupid fool, vile apostate; impious wretch; it expresses a stronger degree of reproach and contempt than Raca, and hence an intenser passion and hate which led to its utterance. This word embodies a bitter judgment of one's spiritual state and decrees him to certain destruction. The one who sustains this attitude toward his fellow is "in danger of the hell of fire." Literally this means "the Gehenna of fire." Jesus here makes three grades of crime, rising each above the preceding one; these three corresponding grades of punishment as penalties are also expressed. The sin of murder lies in anger itself; anger, though only a passion of the soul, which has not yet resulted in the overt act of taking life, is really a breach of the commandment, "thou shalt not kill." The second grade of the sin—saying to his brother, Raca—adds to anger *contempt*. This attitude ignores his brother's rights of common humanity and assumes that he has no rights which so great a man as the one who condemns him is bound to respect. The third grade, that of calling him a fool, adds the element of extreme wickedness, holding him to be abandoned of God, outlawed, and a reprobate among men. These are the three grades of crime recognized by Jesus.

The three grades of punishment are denoted by the terms "judgment," "council," and "hell of fire." "Judgment" refers to the lower tribunals which were established in the towns of Palestine; the next higher court was "the council," the Jewish Sanhedrin. The third grade of penalty should be interpreted in harmony with the two preceding ones. The penalty of the "judgment" was death for murder, which was inflicted with the sword; while the penalty of death sentenced by the Sanhedrin was inflicted by stoning; while the third grade of penalty inflicted by the civil law for the crime of murder was inflicted by exposing the dead body to the detestable valley described by "Gehenna"; this penalty made a death odious and revolting in the extreme.

altar, and there rememberest that thy brother hath aught against thee, 24 leave there thy gift before the altar, and go thy way, first be reconciled to thy brother, and then come and offer thy gift. 25 Agree with thine adversary quickly, while thou art with him in the way; lest haply the adversary

23 If therefore thou art offering thy gift at the altar.—Jesus has just taught the danger of anger; "therefore" if one is even making an offering, so soon as one sees the danger and guilt of all anger or wrong feelings, he is to stop at that moment, it matters not what he is doing, even if at the sacred altar, he is to stop and get rid of that state of feeling. To bring a sacrifice to the altar was the Jewish method of public worship. So important is it that one must get rid of anger, which is the root of murder, that the public worship can wait, must wait, until the state of feeling against a brother has been adjusted.

24 Leave there thy gift before the altar.—The worship must stop; reconciliation to a brother takes the right of way; this should be done at once, even if it requires the interruption of sacrifice; it should be done with all earnestness. "First be reconciled to thy brother, and then come and offer thy gift." Remove the offense and make friendly overtures to him and change the attitude from that of anger to that of love, before proceeding with the worship. It is dangerous to let anger harbor in the heart. This throws a new light on the commandment, "Thou shalt not kill"; this interpretation of Jesus would prevent all murder.

25 Agree with thine adversary quickly, while thou art with him in the way.—"Agree with him" literally means "be well disposed toward him," which suggests that one must secure the good will of another by showing good will to that one. "Adversary" means an accuser in a lawsuit; anger and hatred often find expression in suits today. Emphasis is put on agreeing with the adversary "quickly"; the judicious teachings of Jesus here would settle all difficulties. If one will agree quickly, anger will not have time to take deeper roots in the heart. "While thou art with him in the way," that is, while on the road to the court or judge; it is better to settle the matter before it is brought before the judge or court, for

deliver thee to the judge, and the judge [7]deliver thee to the officer, and thou be cast into prison. 26 Verily I say unto thee, Thou shalt by no means come out thence, till thou have paid the last farthing.

[7]Some ancient authorities omit *deliver thee.*

---

then it will be too late and anger can develop into hatred. According to the Roman law, the plaintiff could carry the accused with him before the judge; the defendant might settle the matter on any terms while they were on the way, but after the tribunal was reached the thing must go according to law; the law must take its course after the matter as been brought to the court.

Lest haply the adversary deliver thee to the judge.—The judge was the one whose duty was to hear the matter. The judge, if he thought the cause a worthy one, would deliver the accused over "to the officer." The officer was the same as our sheriff, and could deliver the accused to prison; the judge passed the sentence; the officer executed the sentence by committing the accused to prison. It is far better to agree with the adversary than to suffer the punishment in prison; one in prison would suffer the consequences of the adversary's anger which might have been avoided, had one become reconciled to his brother and thus desoroyed the anger by kind and loving reconciliation to him.

26 **Verily I say unto thee, Thou shalt by no means come out thence.**—When the time of punishment comes, it will be too late for reconciliation. After the sentence of the court has been passed, and after commitment to prison, there is no opportunity for reconciliation. There is an illusion here to imprisonment for debt; if it were not paid, the accused must remain in prison until the time expires for the indebtedness. The disciples of Jesus are taught how to keep from suffering from the anger of others and also how to inhibit their own anger.

[If a man never becomes angry without a just cause, he will not murder or do violence to his fellow man. Human laws and penalties can only affect a commission of the evil deed. God's law goes behind the deed and removes all ground or occasion for excuse for the evil deed. It removes the ground or occasion for an evil deed in the heart of one; it removes the spirit that prompts the evil deed in the inflicter of the wrong. The command to cherish no evil thoughts or angry feelings in the heart, to settle all difficulty and differences with your fellow man quickly and promptly, to return good for evil, comes to a man in his quiet unexcited moments, and he sees that if these directions are followed good will follow evil, and he will conquer difficulties and change enemies into friends and promote his happiness and popularity among men.]

8. TEACHINGS AGAINST ADULTERY AND DIVORCE
5: 27-32

27 Ye have heard that it was said, [8]Thou shalt not commit adultery: 28 but I say unto you, that every one that looketh on a woman to lust after her hath committed adultery with her already in his heart. 29 And if thy right

---
[8]Ex. xx. 14; Dt. v. 18.

27, 28 Ye have heard that it was said, Thou shalt not commit adultery.—This is the seventh commandment of the Decalogue. Ex. 20: 14 and Deut. 5: 18 record this commandment; the punishment fixed by the law of Moses for this crime was the death of both parties by stoning. (Lev. 20: 10; Deut. 22: 22-27.) If the woman were a slave, she was to be whipped, not put to death, and the man was to bring a trespass offering. (Lev. 19: 20-22.) In case of a wife who is suspected of adultery by her husband, a singular ordeal was provided for her trial, the only case of trial by ordeal known to the Jewish law. (Num. 5: 11-31.) The law punished the overt act of sin, and did not reach any further.

But I say unto you, that every one that looketh on a woman to lust after her hath committed adultery with her already in his heart.—Jesus puts emphasis on what he has to say; there is a contrast between what they "have heard" concerning the law and what Jesus says; he declares the sin to be in the heart and not in the external act merely; Jesus goes behind the act and legislates against the thoughts which precede the act. "Every one that looketh on a woman," the one who gazeth on a woman, whether married or single, with impure desire, has committed the sin of adultery; this looking is "to lust after

eye causeth thee to stumble, pluck it out, and cast it from thee: for it is profitable for thee that one of thy members should perish, and not thy whole

her"; it is a gazing with a view to feed a lustful desire; it refers to an intentional and conscious desire to gratify the lust. The lascivious look and the intending or enkindled passion constitute the roots of the sin of adultery; hence the teachings of Jesus plainly forbid such "looking" as enkindles lascivious passion; there the sin begins and takes its root, and it must be resisted at that point and ruled out of the life. The desire must not be developed into overt action. The Jews did not apply the commandment, "Thou shalt not commit adultery," to anything but the overt act; it was not directly against the desire as well as the act. (Ex. 20: 14; Prov. 6: 25; 2 Pet. 2: 14.) The thing which is condemned is not the look of admiration or affection, but the look of lust. As murder begins in the heart, so adultery begins in the heart. Jesus lays down a principle here which may be applied to both sexes.

[Fornication is the lewdness of unmarried persons, adultery of married. The expression "looketh on a woman to lust after her" has the force of a cherished purpose. So the Bible goes behind the overt act, and characterizes the first formation of an evil purpose in the heart as the sin. It thus proposes to stifle the first emotions of sin and check the impulses that lead to it. The same manner of dealing with sin is manifest in the expression, "Whosoever hateth his brother is a murderer." The feeling of hatred in the heart is charged with the full guilt and condemnation of the accomplished sin to which it leads. The knowledge of this truth and the necessity to which it gives rise of repressing the first buddings of the emotion or propensity to sin constitute the only safeguard from sin.]

29, 30 **If thy right eye causeth thee to stumble, pluck it out, and cast it from thee.**—Continuing the thought that sin originates in the heart, Jesus says "if thy right eye" is responsible for a sin, it must be plucked out. The "right eye" is considered more important of the two; it was considered more ser-

body be cast into ⁰hell. 30 And if thy right hand causeth thee to stumble, cut it off, and cast it from thee: for it is profitable for thee that one of thy

---

⁰Gr. *Gehenna*.

---

viceable than the left, particularly in battle; if it is the cause of one's stumbling, it must be destroyed. The orignal from which we get "causeth thee to stumble" carries with it the giving of offense or provoking; it also means a "snare," "a stumblingblock" and the stick in a trap on which the bait is placed, and which springs up and shuts the trap at the touch of an animal. It is better to pluck the eye out and let one member of the body perish than to let that member involve the whole body. It is better for the one member to perish than that the "whole body be cast into hell." "Hell" here means "Gehenna" where the whole body may be consumed. The Jews under the law condemned adultery and some other sins of the flesh by putting to death the guilty parties. At Jerusalem, the guilty party was taken by the chief witness to a spot overhanging Gehenna (valley of Hinnon) and cast down on a rock in the valley; the second witness hurled a great stone on his breast; if he survived this, the spectators stoned him till he died. Sometimes the body was burned to death in Gehenna. The indulgence of a sinful passion may afford temporary gratification, but as it entails the loss of the soul, it is emphatically expedient to forego such indulgence. (Rom. 8: 13; Gal. 5: 24; Col. 3: 5-8.)

If thy right hand causeth thee to stumble, cut it off, and cast it from thee.—The eye and the hand are taken as examples for illustration of the principle which Jesus here teaches; he means that any organ of the body whatever which becomes a snare to sin must be subdued and brought under with unsparing rigor and resolute determination. Any one of the bodily organs, by ensnaring into sin, may work the ruin not of the whole body only, but of the soul as well. Jesus teaches the duty of keeping the whole body under subjection to the law of God and of purity, with special reference to the sin of adultery which he had just before condemned. The eye and

members should perish, and not thy whole body go into ⁹hell. 31 It was said also, ¹⁰Whosoever shall put away his wife, let him give her a writing of divorcement: 32 but I say unto you, that every one that putteth away his wife,

¹⁰Dt. xxiv. 1, 3.

---

the hand are used here by the way of illustration, but the principle is general and may be applied to any member of the body or may be used symbolically. The self-denial and seeming deprivation of enjoyment are really gains, for in the one case only one organ of life is lost for this world, while in the other the whole life is gained.

31, 32 **It was said also, Whosoever shall put away his wife, let him give her a writing of divorcement.**—The commandment, "Thou shalt not commit adultery," is violated in spirit and literally often by the sin of divorce; Jesus here makes application of the principle to those who would violate the spirit of the command by divorcement. The law concerning divorce is found in Deut. 24: 1. Jesus does not here contrast the external law of Moses and the spirit of his teaching, but he gives this as a further illustration of the subject of adultery. The common divorces which existed among the Jews at the time that Jesus was on earth were the occasion, on a large scale, of the sin of adultery. The law of Moses required that if a man determined to put away his wife, he should give her a formal document to that effect. The Jews were divided on the question of divorcement; many of them held that it was lawful for a man to dismiss his wife "for every cause" (Matt. 19: 3), and that there was no restriction at all except that he must give her the required papers; hence divorces were very common with this class; another class of the Jews held that there was but one cause for separation, that being the sin of adultery. At this early stage in his public ministry Jesus deemed it important to declare his teaching on this sharply mooted question. At a later period (Matt. 19: 3-12; Mark 10: 2-12; Luke 16: 18) the question was pressed upon him by unfriendly critics in the hope of involving him in controversy with either one party or the other. The enemies of Jesus hoped to make

saving for the cause of fornication, maketh her an adulteress: and whosoever shall marry her when she is put away committeth adultery.

trouble for him on this point. Jesus teaches clearly on this point; he cannot be misunderstood.

But I say unto you, that every one that putteth away his wife, saving for the cause of fornication, maketh her an adulteress.—It seems that the law of Moses left the party at liberty to determine for himself what was a proper cause of divorce; Jesus does not repeal the law, but he authoritatively restricts its application, and thereby condemns all misapplications of the principle. He is clear on this point; he lays down his teaching here with entire precision; he admits but one valid ground for divorce, namely fornication. Whoever puts away his wife for any other reason than this causes her to commit adultery because he tempts her to marry again; Jesus assumes that the pretended divorce goes for nothing; that she is still his wife, and that marrying again involves adultery. Not only does she become an adulteress, but whoever shall marry her becomes an adulterer. A divorce for reasons other than the only legitimate one involves the sin of adultery in all the parties implicated—in the husband who puts his wife away, and in the wife herself, and in the man who marries her. Under the law of Moses a husband could divorce his wife, but the wife could not divorce the husband; hence Jesus in dealing with this principle uses the masculine gender; but the ethical principle is applicable to both sexes.

[The language of Jesus on the subject of adultery and divorce is plain. I see nothing difficult to understand in it; I cannot write a plainer sentence than the one that says, "That every one that putteth away his wife, saving for the cause of fornication, maketh her an adulteress: and whosoever shall marry her when she is put away committeth adultery." Every man and every woman that has separated from a husband or wife save for the cause of fornication, and is living with another, is living in adultery. The law is positive and clear; and no reasoning of man, whether preacher or not, can change it. I do not see what more can be said on that point.]

9. TEACHINGS AGAINST OATHS AND RETALIATION
5: 33-42

33 Again, ye have heard that it was said to them of old time, [11]Thou shalt not forswear thyself, but shall perform unto the Lord thine oaths: 34 but I say unto you, Swear not at all; neither by the heaven, for it is the throne of

---

[11]Lev. xix. 12; Num. xxx. 2; Dt. xxiii. 21.

---

33 Ye have heard that it was said to them of old time, Thou shalt not forswear thyself.—Again Jesus refers to another part of the law of Moses which the Jews were continually perverting. This refers to the law recorded in Lev. 19: 12; Num. 30: 2; Deut. 23: 21. Jesus frequently refers "to them of old time" or the ancients, when he means to refer to some clause of the law of Moses as frequently referred to by the religious teachers of his day. To "forswear" means to perjure oneself; it means false swearing and a profane use of the name of God; the Hebrew word which answers to "in vain" may be rendered to include "forswear thyself." The Jews held that all oaths were not binding unless the sacred name of God should be invoked at the time that the oath was taken. Some think that Jesus here had reference not to judicial oaths, but to nonjudicial; others think that he had reference to all oaths. To "forswear" is to perjure oneself which stands over against "shall perform unto the Lord thine oaths." Jesus goes further than prohibiting all oaths in ordinary communication. The Pharisees made frivolous and pernicious distinctions between certain oaths. Jesus prohibits making distinction between oaths and states clearly that one is under obligation to perform all of his oaths.

34, 35 But I say unto you, Swear not at all.—The oath authorized by the law of Moses was not taken in the name of God. (Deut. 6: 13.) The Jewish teachers held that no oath had any binding force unless it brought in the name of God; swearing by the heavens, or by the earth, or by the stars went for nothing, because the name of God was not expressed. They thought by this practice to honor the name of God, but by it they really dishonored God. Swearing "by the heaven,"

God; 35 nor by the earth, for it is the footstool of his feet; nor [12]by Jerusalem, for it is the city of the great King. 36 Neither shalt thou swear by thy head, for thou canst not make one hair white or black. 37 [13]But let your speech be, Yea, yea; Nay, nay: and whatsoever is more than these is of [14]the evil *one*.

---

[12]Or, *toward*
[13]Some ancient authorities read *But your speech shall be.*
[14]Or, *evil:* as in ver. 39; vi. 13.

"by the earth," "by Jerusalem," "by thy head" all were not authorized of God; Jesus teaches that such oaths should not be practiced. The Jew claimed that he could swear by these and still not have to perform his oath, but Jesus prohibits this and all other kinds of oaths. Those who have written on this subject vary widely in their comment; some say that one should not swear at all unless it is with due reverence toward God; others say that one should not swear *lightly* in ordinary life; others say that one should not swear after the manner of the Jews; others, it is not applicable to our duty as citizens in the state; still others say that it prohibits at all times and under all circumstances the taking of any oath. Jesus does forbid plainly the swearing as mentioned here.

36, 37 Neither shalt thou swear by thy head.—Jesus has forbidden swearing by heaven as it is the throne of God; he has also prohibited the swearing by the earth as it is "the footstool of his feet"; he has also prohibited the swearing by Jerusalem, "for it is the city of the great King." He now forbids the swearing by one's own head as one cannot "make one hair white or black"; these are all foolish and wicked oaths and the disciples of Jesus cannot indulge in them. Man has not the power to make one hair become white or black; God alone can do that, and since he has absolute proprietorship on us, we have no right to swear by ourselves or by any member of our body; the significance of an oath consists in its calling God to witness the truth of the assertion.

But let your speech be, Yea, yea; Nay, nay.—Instead of an oath for confirmation of what has been said, the disciple of Jesus should be content with the simple affirmation of "Yea, yea," or the simple negation of "Nay, nay." The Christian

38 Ye have heard that it was said, An [15]eye for an eye, and a tooth for a

[15]Ex. xxi. 24; Lev. xxiv. 20; Dt. xix. 21.

must live so that whatever he states will be accepted as the truth; his character and life give affirmation to what he says, and no oath is needed to confirm his statement. James 5: 12 confirms this teaching when he said, "Let your yea be yea, and your nay, nay"; these are to be used only in their simplicity. Jesus adds that "whatsoever is more than these is of the evil one." James adds another reason when he said, "that ye fall not under judgment." (James 5: 12.) Christians should be content with a serious affirmation or denial of any statement and others should be satisfied to take a Christian's statement at face value. What is more than these comest of "the evil one"; this may mean either of the evil that lie latent, or of the evil one (Satan) who fosters all evil, and not least the evil which forever flows from profane swearing.

[Jesus does not here refer to common vulgar profanity; he speaks of performing the oath in contrast with forswearing oneself, which is to swear and not to perform. The oaths of which Jesus spoke here seem to be made to the Lord, and to him they are to be performed. This would indicate vows made to God; yet the language, "swear not at all," seems to prohibit all oaths, either judicial or those made to God. The oath of confirmation is an appeal to God to visit wrath upon one if one does not tell the truth. This seems to violate the divine law. The courts allow an affirmation without calling on the name of God.]

38, 39 **Ye have heard that it was said, An eye for an eye, and a tooth for a tooth.**—Again Jesus quotes from the law of Moses and puts his interpretation over against the traditions of the Jews. Jesus is still teaching against *retaliation;* the Jews had perverted Ex. 21: 23, 24; Lev. 24: 20; Deut. 19: 21. God had never taught the spirit and practice of retaliation as the Jews were teaching and practicing it. It was never the law of God for any one who had lost an eye to knock out the eye of his enemy, or if in personal combat one had lost a

tooth: 39 but I say unto you, Resist not ¹him that is evil: but whosoever smiteth thee on thy right cheek, turn to him the other also. 40 And if any

---

¹Or, *evil*

---

tooth, that he could knock out a tooth of his assailant; no such procedure was permitted without *judicial* process; this was the law that should govern judges and juries in placing the penalty on one who had attacked his fellow; it did not permit personal vengeance, as the Jews were practicing it at that time. They practiced it under their construction of the law, and Jesus opposed their practice; he was not opposed to the law; he came to fulfill the law, but not to disregard it. Some think that the Mosaic law permitted individual retaliation, but did not make it compulsory; however, that which was done by the hand of the magistrate or judge cannot be called individual retaliation. Even in the case of murder the avenger of blood became an officer in executing punishment of the murderer.

But I say unto you, Resist not him that is evil.—Jesus implies here that the malice and wrongdoing of the world to his disciples is the work of the devil. (1 John 2: 13, 14; Rev. 2: 10). All evil originates with the devil; it emanates from him and is inspired by him; those who do evil intentionally are led by his spirit. There is a sense in which we are to resist the evil one; "but resist the devil, and he will flee from you" (James 4: 7); we must resist evil with all of our might in this sense, but as used here we are not to resist "the evil one." In what sense may we not resist? In the sense of doing evil for evil; we are not to oppose violence with violence; we are not to "fight fire with fire"; "be not overcome of evil, but overcome evil with good," is the method that Christians are to use in opposing evil; our warfare is to overcome, not evil with evil, but evil with good. There are those who may overcome evil with evil. (Rom. 13: 1-4.)

But whosoever smiteth thee on thy right cheek, turn to him the other also.—To slap a man in the face was a common mode of insult. (1 Kings 22: 24; Lam. 3: 30; Matt. 26: 67; John 18: 22; 19: 3.) Smiting on the "right cheek" (literally jaw), was both an injury and an insult (2 Cor. 11: 20), and

man would go to law with thee, and take away thy coat, let him have the cloak also. 41 And whosoever shall ²compel thee to go one mile, go with

²Gr. *impress.*

---

yet this was done to Jesus more than once. Jesus here gives the rule of conduct that his disciples should follow. There has been much discussion as to whether these examples cited by Jesus should be taken figuratively or literally; there seems to be no just grounds for taking them other than literally. The principle and spirit that Jesus here gives are against retaliation, and emphasize his statement, "Resist not him that is evil." Jesus' conduct when smitten illustrates his meaning; he turned the other cheek to those who would smite him. Rather than resent the first insult, Jesus teaches that we are to submit to a second; he does not mean that we should invite a repetition of the insult, but that we should meekly endure it and suffer another rather than resist evil with evil.

40, 41 **And if any man would go to law with thee.**—If any one should be disposed to contend and take a matter to law, it is better rather to suffer than to resist or resent by going to law. This is another example or application that Jesus gives against retaliation. If one should go to law and "take away thy coat, let him have thy cloak also." "Coat" as used here means a shirtlike undergarment or tunic; it was the less expensive garment worn. "Cloak" was the outer garment or mantle; it was used as a covering for the night, and therefore was forbidden by the Mosaic law to be retained in pledge overnight. (Ex. 22:26, 27.) To give up the cloak without resistance implied a higher degree of concession.

And whosoever shall compel thee to go one mile, go with him two.—This is the third application that Jesus makes of the principle of submitting rather than retaliating; the first, if smitten on one cheek turn the other; the second, if compelled to give up the inner garment, give the outer garment also; and third, if compelled to go one mile, go two. There was a custom which originated with the Persian government that a man traveling on a mission for the government, if need be, could compel others to assist him in carrying out the demands of the government; the Greeks took up the same custom and

him two. 42 Give to him that asketh thee, and from him that would borrow of thee turn not thou away.

put it into a law; finally the Romans enlarged upon it and incorporated this principle into a law. Unfair advantage was taken of this law; sometimes the Jews were compelled to assist Romans when the official authority had not demanded it. It was a beautiful custom at first, when a man traveling and about to pass a post station, where horses and messengers are kept in order to forward royal messages as quickly as possible, such could be commanded into the service of the government; but to pervert this custom or principle for private gain or advantage was mean; the Jews resented it, but Jesus teaches that it is better to suffer this inconvenience and injury than to retaliate.

42 **Give to him that asketh thee.**—This has its limitations and is still on the teaching against retaliation; the meaning of this can be understood from the conduct of Jesus. He said later, "If ye shall ask anything in my name, that will I do." (John 14: 14.) Jesus did not always give what was asked of him; sometimes God does not give what we ask of him. (2 Cor. 12: 8, 9.) Sometimes we do not receive because we ask amiss. (James 4: 3.) Our beneficence must be regulated by a due regard to those who may ask of us. Those who "would borrow of thee turn not thou away"; those who would borrow because they need should not be rejected; but those who borrow in order to make gain or profit are to be rejected. The spirit of retailation is still before Jesus; if one has injured us, but is in need and should ask, we should not refuse to give that which is needed because the one asking has done us an injury; to withhold from one who asks in need would be to retaliate; this is forbidden. The teaching of Jesus on this was expressed in the law of Moses. (Deut. 15: 8-10.)

[Jesus here gives a positive law of his kingdom; his subjects must not return evil for evil, but they must return good for evil. This is a positive law for the government of every subject of his kingdom. The object as set forth by Jesus is to make us the children of our Father who is in heaven and to perfect us like God our Father. To every one then that has an aspiration to be a child of God, to be made perfect like God, it is necessary to conform to this solemn law. And no man can be a child of God without cultivating and continually practicing this spirit. The whole life and teachings of Jesus were a continued exemplification of this law. He uncomplainingly bore evil, persecution, contumely, and contempt during his life; he endured sorrow and affliction while he lived on earth. His life was falsely sworn away, and he suffered a cruel and ignominious death, as a malefactor, without a word of bitter reproach escaping from him.]

10. THE PRINCIPLE OF LOVE
5: 43-48

43 Ye have heard that it was said, ³Thou shalt love thy neighbor, and

---
³Lev. xix. 18.

43, 44 Ye have heard that it was said, Thou shalt love thy neighbor, and hate thine enemy.—Again Jesus refers to another section of the law of Moses; he does not combat what the law taught, but their interpretation and application of it. The Old Testament in many places did teach abhorrence of heathen character and heathen habits (Deut. 7: 1, 2, 16, 23-26; 12: 27, 32; Josh. 23: 12, 13; Psalm 139: 21, 22); and the law of love as revealed in the Old Testament had an appearance of being confined to the Israelites (Lev. 19: 17, 18; Deut. 23: 3-6); but God has never taught his children to hate each other or to hate any one else. They are taught to hate sin and every evil way, but they are not to hate the sinner. The Jews made no distinction between the sinner and his sin; they interpreted God's abhorrence for idolatry and wicked ways as an abhorrence of the people. Jesus here enlarges upon the principle of love.

"Neighbor" is another word to which the New Testament has given a broader and deeper meaning; literally it means the one *near* (neighbor equals "nigh-bor"), indicating a mere outward nearness of proximity; in this sense a neighbor might be an enemy. The Old Testament meaning covers national or tribal fellowship, and in this sense Jesus gave the quotation here. The Christian sense is expounded by Jesus in the para-

hate thine enemy: 44 but I say unto you, Love your enemies, and pray for them that persecute you; 45 that ye may be sons of your Father who is in heaven: for he maketh his sun to rise on the evil and the good, and sendeth

ble of the Good Samaritan and includes the whole brotherhood of man, as founded in love for man. (Luke 10: 29-37.) The law of Moses taught love for the neighbor, but it did not teach them to hate their enemy, but on the contrary it taught, "Thou shalt not hate thy brother in thy heart . . . Thou shalt not take vengeance, nor bear any grudge against the children of thy people; but thou shalt love thy neighbor as thyself." (Lev. 19: 17, 18.)

But I say unto you, Love your enemies.—Jesus again puts his teaching in contrast with their perverted interpretation and practice of this principle. Jesus emphasizes that love has a much broader application than they were making of it; they "loved their neighbor," but "hated their enemies"; Jesus teaches now that they are to "love your enemies, and pray for them that persecute you." The disciples of Jesus are to love those who personally hate, curse and despise them; they are to do this because it is enjoined by the great principle of love. We are to love with a love of benevolence even our enemies; we may thus love our most deadly foes, those whom we cannot love with any affection of gratitude or esteem. To love is to do good; it is to seek the highest good and welfare of others; in this sense we can love our enemies. Again Jesus' life illustrates the principle of love; he sought the highest good even of his enemies, and prayed for them while they were crucifying him.

45 That ye may be sons of your Father who is in heaven.— The principle of love helps to make the disciples of Jesus lovable; it helps to make them like Jesus; hence it makes them indeed sons of God. God makes no distinction so far as his benevolence is concerned; he "maketh his sun to rise on the evil and the good"; he makes no distinction, for he "sendeth rain on the just and the unjust." As God first created the sun to shine upon the earth, so he still controls it; it shines upon the good and the bad with the same glory and warmth; his rain falls on the just and the unjust with no distinction; if we

rain on the just and the unjust. 46 For if ye love them that love you, what reward have ye? do not even the ⁴publicans the same? 47 And if ye salute your brethren only, what do ye more *than others?* do not even the Gentiles

⁴That is, *collectors or renters of Roman taxes.*

would imitate God, we must bless those that curse us and do good to them that would injure us. To be Godlike is to do as God does, and since he makes no distinction with his material and physical blessings, neither should we when it comes to doing good. God loves all regardless of their attitude toward him; however there is a special sense in which he loves those who adjust their lives to his will. Jesus, here in enforcing the principle of love, refers his disciples to the example of his Father, in order to show the nature and universality of the principle of love.

46 **For if ye love them that love you, what reward have ye?**—What reward have those whose love goes no further than to love those who love them? This would be only a reciprocal love and would be from its very nature selfish; but to extend love to those who do not love us makes us Godlike. "The publicans" love those who love them, and if the disciples of Jesus only love those who love them, they are no better than the publicans. "Publican" is a Latin word and designates those who hired themselves to the Roman government to collect taxes for it. The publican was odious in the sight of the Jew; Jews did not like to pay taxes to the Roman government, and any Jew who would hire himself to the Roman government to collect taxes from Jews was a wicked wretch in the sight of the Jew. With this conception of the publican, Jesus says that if his disciples do not take the general principle of love and let it have it have its broad application, they are no better than the publican.

47 **And if ye salute your brethren only, what do ye more than others?**—The Greek word for "salute" here may mean "embrace," say some; it is a word which expresses a strong degree of kind feelings. Jews did not salute Gentiles as a rule; the oriental custom of salutation or greeting was to lay the right hand on the breast and bow the body low; to persons of great rank they would bow nearly to the ground and

the same? 48 Ye therefore shall be perfect, as your heavenly Father is perfect.

kiss the hem of their garment, and sometimes the feet and the knees. Jews would not salute Gentiles, except occasionally for policy's sake. The principle of love as laid down by Jesus causes one to go beyond merely saluting those who salute them; it forces one to salute every one without prejudice or distinction. It is another way of saying that his disciples must regard the principle of love as being universal. "Gentile" means any one who was not a Jew or a proselyte to the Jewish religion; they were regarded by the Jew as being beneath salutation.

48 **Ye therefore shall be perfect, as your heavenly Father is perfect.**—The "ye" here is emphatic and means the disciples of Jesus in contrast with publicans and Gentiles. "Therefore" introduces the deduction that Jesus himself has made from that which precedes; the universal principle of love only can make one perfect as God is perfect. The term rendered "perfect" is used in a variety of connections, and its precise meaning must always be determined by the context; sometimes it simply means "complete" without any moral element (Heb. 9: 11), and in other instances it means complete in growth of body or mind, "fullgrown" (1 Cor. 14: 20; Eph. 4: 13; Heb. 5: 14, 6; 1). Again it may mean complete morally. (Matt. 19: 21; Col. 1: 28; 4: 12; James 1: 4, 25; 3: 2.) There are scriptures in which it seems to mean complete in both knowledge and moral excellence. (Phil. 3: 15.) "Perfect" does not mean "sinless"; when Christians love their enemies, even those who revile and curse them, it is a long step toward perfection. When God's children love their enemies and bless those who curse them as God does and because he does, they are perfect in their sphere even as their Father is in his, which standard is the highest possible standard of perfection. The meaning that Jesus gives to the principle of love is that his disciples are to let their love be universal, unconfined by partialities, and with respect to its objects as large as God's; not that their love, either to enemies or friends, can be supposed in other respects to be in proportion to the divine love.

[These teachings of Jesus were to make his disciples pure, holy, true, doers of good "that ye may be sons of your Father who is in heaven." What it took to make them good, it takes to make us good. There is no reason we should not be required to seek as high standard of holiness as was required of these early Christians. All effort to set aside one or another moral requirement as not applicable to us is derogatory to the authority and integrity of the Bible.]

11. TEACHINGS AGAINST HYPOCRISY IN ALMSGIVING, PRAYER, AND FASTING
6: 1-18

1 Take heed that ye do not your righteousness before men, to be seen of them: else ye have no reward with your Father who is in heaven.

1 Take heed that ye do not your righteousness before men, to be seen of them.—Jesus now turns to the *motives* for doing things; he has exposed the corruptions or erroneous interpretations of the law; he has taught the right interpretation and application of some common phases of the law, but now turns attention to "righteousness." He has told his disciples that their "righteousness" must "exceed the righteousness of the scribes and Pharisees" or else they would have no place in the kingdom of heaven. In this section he presents the three great forms in which self-righteousness and hypocrisy of the scribes and Pharisees manifested itself; they were "almsgiving," "prayer," and "fasting." These were the three principal manifestations of practical piety among the Jews, and were abused by the Pharisees to exhibit their own superior piety. The Pharisees thought that they had attained the highest eminence in these three phases of their religious life.

Jesus now instructs his disciples to "take heed" that they do not perform any deeds of righteousness to be seen of men. "Righteousness" is a broader term than "alms"; it includes almsgiving, prayer, and fasting. He does not condemn doing works of righteousness; he had just told them to let their lights so shine before men that others may "see your good works, and glorify your Father who is in heaven." (Matt. 5: 16.) We are to live before others so that they may see the

2 When therefore thou doest alms, sound not a trumpet before thee, as the hypocrites do in the synagogues and in the streets, that they may have glory of men. Verily I say unto you, They have received their reward. 3 But when thou doest alms, let not thy left hand know what thy right hand doeth: 4 that thine alms may be in secret: and thy Father who seeth in secret shall recompense thee.

---

beauty of the Christian life; what Jesus condemns here is the motive of doing righteousness to be seen of men. There is always danger in worship and in the religious life of having the wrong motive; man is prone to do things to be seen of others and receive the praise of others. (Ex. 23: 13; Deut. 11: 16; Matt. 26: 41; 1 Cor. 10: 12.) When the righteousness is done just to be seen of men, and men see it, no other reward may be expected; the citizens of the kingdom of heaven must always have the right motive in serving God.

2-4 **When therefore thou doest alms, sound not a trumpet before thee.**—Jesus here takes up one of the elements of "righteousness." He commends doing good and giving to help the distressed; but he condemns sounding a trumpet before doing a good deed and calling attention of men to the deed. Some have taken this literally and said that hypocrites sounded a trumpet before doing a good deed; it was customary to call people together by a trumpet to see a great spectacle (Num. 10: 3; 2 Kings 9: 13; Psalm 81: 3); but others think that these hypocrites did not have literal trumpets, but only called attention to what they were doing; that is a proverbial expression of the habit of self-laudation and display of good works in general. Jesus condemns all ostentation in worship and service and the blowing of trumpets may be taken either literally or figuratively. It was revolting to Jesus to see the display and read the motives of the hypocrites of that day. They were doing this for display "that they may have glory of men"; they had received the praise of men and were not entitled to any other reward.

But when thou doest alms, let not thy left hand know what thy right hand doeth.—Jesus not only condemns unworthy motives in doing things, but he also teaches his disciples how to give alms. It is a pleasing figure or picture that Jesus presents here; it suggests a man passing one who is in need, and

5 And when ye pray, ye shall not be as the hypocrites: for they love to stand and pray in the synagogues and in the corners of the streets, that they may be seen of men. Verily I say unto you, They have received their re-

with his right hand giving alms in so quiet a way that even his own left hand does not know what is going on. The motive should be to help the needy in the name of Christ; the motive should be to glorify God and not to receive glory for self. When one does have the right motive there will be no display, no parade, no self-laudation; but there will be the quietness of spirit and simplicity of purpose to honor and glorify God. God sees such, as there is nothing kept secret from him and "thy Father who seeth in secret shall recompense thee." One may do a good deed in public with the right motive; God looks at the motive and rewards according to the motive. When people do things to be seen of men, they are feeding their own vanity and defeating themselves, as they will receive no reward from God. There is a sense in which good deeds may be published with the right motive; Jesus published the liberality of the poor widow. (Mark 12: 41-44.) The liberality of Barnabas was published (Acts 4: 36, 37), but this is not done to honor and glorify Barnabas, but to encourage others to do good.

5, 6 **And when ye pray, ye shall not be as the hypocrites.**— Jesus now takes up the second element of "righteousness"— prayers. The praying of hypocrites which Jesus here condemns was not the prayer of public worship, but of private devotion; it was not prayer in which the people were expected to unite, but was the personal, individual prayer of the Pharisees. The hypocrites are described as those who "love to stand and pray in the synagogues and in the corners of the streets, that they may be seen of men." The Pharisees used a public place in the synagogue and even at the street corners as places of private devotion; they sought out conspicuous places to pray that they may be seen of men. The Jews frequently stood in prayer (Mark 11: 25), especially in the synagogue and at the crossings of the street, where there was a great crowd of people. Here again Jesus condemns the motives of these hypocrites; they were praying to be seen of men

ward. 6 But thou, when thou prayest enter into thine inner chamber, and having shut thy door, pray to thy Father who is in secret, and thy Father who seeth in secret shall recompense thee. 7 And in praying use not vain repetitions, as the Gentiles do: for they think that they shall be heard for

and they had received their reward. It is said that the Pharisee took care to be at the cross streets and in the public places when the crowd was the largest, in order that he might be seen; he was displaying a false piety; Jesus severely condemns this by telling his disciples that they should "not be as the hypocrites."

But thou, when thou prayest, enter into thine inner chamber.—The contrast that Jesus draws here is very forceful; he puts in contrast the *public* display of the hypocrites and the *private* devotion of his disciples; the difference between the two is the motive; the teachings of Jesus take hold of the heart and would direct the action by controlling the thoughts, motives, aspirations, and purposes. Jesus directs the motives of the heart in praying acceptably to God. Jesus instructs his disciples to go "into thine inner chamber," and after going into the "inner chamber," they are to "shut thy door"; God can see in secret; he sees even the motives of the heart, and will reward according to the motives. The soul must be serious before God; nothing should interfere with the freest outpouring of thought, emotion, desire, of the heart; hence the importance of going into "thine inner chamber." Every child of God has seasons of communing with God in which no other person can be present; there should be seasons when the soul of man is in constant communion with God alone.

7, 8 And in praying use not vain repetitions, as the Gentiles do.—Jesus now corrects certain errors that were common in prayers at that time; they are warned against "vain repetions"; the Gentiles frequently used "vain repetitions"; possibly the emphasis is put on "vain" and not on "repetitions." Jesus repeated the same prayer three times (Matt. 26: 44); hence it is not the mere "repetition" of petitions or words that is condemned here. What makes a prayer vain? or what makes repetition "vain"? The Greek from which we get "vain repetitions" is "battalogein," which means to stammer,

their much speaking. 8 Be not therefore like unto them; for ⁵your Father knoweth what things ye have need of, before ye ask him. 9 After this man-

---

⁵Some ancient authorities read *God your Father*.

---

stutter, then to babble or prate, to repeat the same formula many times as did the worshipers of Baal and Diana of Ephesus. (1 Kings 18: 26; Acts 19: 34.) Literally Jesus tells his disciples not to "battologize" which seems to be an onomatopoetic term, and may have given the name to Battus, the Cyrenian prince, who stammered; to Battus, the silly poet, who made prolific hymns full of tautology. Such vain repetitions impeached the wisdom and goodness of God and was therefore forbidden. The "vain repetitions" and "much speaking" were used by Gentiles in heathen worship and lose sight of the true motive in praying to God; these are condemned. Christians should be careful to restrict the use of their words in prayer and should use great simplicity and not high-sounding phraseology; we are speaking to God in our prayers and should be careful of our speech.

Be not therefore like unto them.—Jesus frequently warns his disciples against being like the Pharisees, hypocrites, and Gentiles. The heathen have not the true motive in prayer, the hypocrite hides his motive in prayer, and the Pharisee is synonymous with the hypocrite; the disciples of Jesus must avoid such chattering, prating, and running off mere words in prayer. The disciples of Jesus are to avoid such folly and sin as belonged to the Pharisees, hypocrites, and heathen. Our Father knows our needs; he is willing to supply them according to his own will, but he wants his children to ask him for them. We feel more keenly our indebtedness to God when he, in answer to our prayers, gives us those things which we need.

[Jesus warns his servants to avoid seeking honor of men in the acts of kindness and favor they do to their fellow men. If we do these works to secure the favor of men, we put their approval in competition with the favor and approval of God, and that which is done to please men is taken from what is due God. God refuses to accept divided service. Christians

ner therefore pray ye: Our Father who art in heaven, Hallowed be thy

---

are not to give alms, pray, fast, or do any other service before men to get honor or glory of men, but they are to perform these services to God. If a man does these things to get glory of men, none will reckon it a glory to him, to God, or to others.]

9 After this manner therefore pray ye.—The Greek shows that the emphasis should be on "ye." Jesus had just warned his disciples about praying as did the hypocrites and Gentiles; he now instructs them *how* they should pray. They are to pray "after this manner," which means that the prayer which followed is a model prayer; this prayer as recorded by Luke was given at the request of his disciples when they said to him, "Lord, teach us to pray, even as John also taught his disciples." (Luke 11: 1.) Others in their prayers used "vain repetitions" and "much speaking," but the disciples of Jesus are to pray according to this pattern or according to these words, "after this manner."

Our Father who art in heaven, Hallowed be thy name.— Here we have the invocation; many prayers of the Bible begin with a very solemn address to God, which we call the "invocation." This was a new form of addressing God; this invocation is calculated to inspire reverence and confidence; God is "our Father." Under the Old Testament God is addressed as the Creator, Almighty God, Jehovah, and the Great God; God's people were recognized under the law as *servants,* but in Christ they are regarded as *children,* hence they can address God as *Father.* "Our Father" is "in heaven"; this shows that the real object of our prayers is a personal God and that he is located in heaven. The Bible recognizes the omnipresence of God, that he is everywhere, but when regarded as Father his personality is located in heaven. "Hallowed be thy name" means that his name is to be treated as holy; it is to be spoken reverently and due respect is to be given unto God as a Father. We can come into the true spirit of prayer only as we hallow the name of God.

name. 10 Thy kingdom come. Thy will be done, as in heaven, so on earth.

10 Thy kingdom come.—While Jesus was on earth, he was preparing material for his kingdom; he preached that the "kingdom of heaven is at hand," that is, it was soon to appear; hence he taught his disciples to look forward to the coming of his kingdom and to pray for its appearance and establishment on earth. Since his kingdom has been established, his children now pray for the "spread of the kingdom." We can pray for the perfect obedience and allegiance of all created beings to the will and word of God, hence that the kingdom come in that sense.

Thy will be done, as in heaven, so on earth.—The disciples of Jesus are to pray that the will of God be done here among men as it is done in heaven among the angels; they are to pray that the will of God be done *everywhere, at all times,* and *by all beings.* In praying that the will of God be done on earth, the disciples of Jesus commit themselves to the doing of his will and to the teaching of his will to others and encouraging them to do it. There is nothing to oppose the will of God in heaven, so there should be nothing to oppose his will on earth; for the will of God to be done there must be perfect obedience to God's law in every realm of life. For the will of God to be done on earth means to expand the kingdom of God on earth and all men to be brought into that kingdom as loyal subjects.

[The Old Testament is the account of the efforts of God to get man to obey and follow him and of the failures of man to do so. The great end of God's creating and dealings with man is to bring him to honor and to obey God, that through this training and obedience man may be made like God and be made a fit companion to dwell with God forever. All the training of the ages was to train and fit the people to obey and honor God. The end of the training was to fit man to follow God, to obey God so faithfully that God's will "be done, as in heaven, so on earth." When God's will is done by men on earth as it is by the angels of God in heaven, men will be equal to the angels of God and the earth will become the dwelling place and the home of God with man.]

11 Give us this day ⁶our daily bread. 12 And forgive us our debts, as we also have forgiven our debtors. 13 And bring us not into temptation, but deliver us from ⁷the evil *one*.⁸ 14 For if ye forgive men their trespasses,

⁶Gr. *our bread for the coming day.* Or, *our needful bread*
⁷Or, *evil*
⁸Many authorities, some ancient, but with variations, add *For thine is the kingdom, and the power, and the glory, for ever. Amen.*

---

11 **Give us this day our daily bread.**—Jesus taught his disciples to pray for their "daily bread." The word translated "daily" has given commentators trouble; it occurs only here and in Luke 11: 3. Some think that it simply means our "necessary sustenance," which includes all of our physical needs, as Paul said to Timothy, "but having food and covering we shall be therewith content." (1 Tim. 6: 7.) This would mean that they were to pray for what was necessary for their physical welfare. Others have given a spiritual meaning to it and hence, they say that his disciples were to pray for all the spiritual needs of this life. It seems evident that only the physical needs are included in this petition. The disciples are to be dependent on God for even the physical food; and surely they are dependent upon him for all spiritual food.

12 **And forgive us our debts.**—In Luke 11: 4 it is "and forgive us our sins"; this is the same in meaning. Obedience is due to God, and by failing in our duty we become indebted to his justice, which demands the execution of the penalty of the law; when we are forgiven our sins that obligation is discharged. The Greek word translated "forgive" is the same translated "left" in Matt. 4: 20, 22, and "left" in Matt. 13: 36, and "leaving" in Mark 4: 36, and "leave" in 1 Cor. 7: 11, 12. It carries the idea of absolute putting away of sins. The condition that God is asked to forgive "us our debts" is that "we also have forgiven our debtors." We have forgiven those who have trespassed against us, and therefore ask God to forgive us. There is implied here that God will not forgive us if we have not forgiven others.

13 **And bring us not into temptation.**—This condition is for God not to bring us into a state of trial and severe testing. It is another way of saying "suffer us not to be led into temptation"; it is a plea for God to shield us from being tempted

your heavenly Father will also forgive you. 15 But if ye forgive not men their trespasses, neither will your Father forgive your trespasses.

above that which we are able to bear. God does not tempt us to do evil (James 1: 13), but he may exercise his care over us in such a way as to lead us into circumstances which become the means of testing us. Rather the disciple of Christ prays to be delivered from the evil one; he prays to be able to escape the severe temptations that the devil may present to him. The petition is not merely to be delivered from evil, either in the moral or physical sense, but to be delivered from the devil who is the author of the temptations.

14, 15 For if ye forgive men their trespasses.—This verse does not belong to the prayer; it is added by Jesus to show why the petition for forgiveness of sins must be conditional. The one who cannot forgive others or who will not forgive others puts himself where he cannot ask God to forgive him. "Trespasses" means offenses, or the sins that our fellows commit against us. Jesus emphasizes the fact that God will forgive the forgiving, but will not forgive the unforgiving. It does not mean that our forgiving others merits God's forgiving us. It does make a forgiving spirit the *condition* of our receiving forgiveness from God. Our *forgiving* spirit towards our fellows stands on the same footing with our *penitent* spirit for our sins toward God.

This has been called "the Lord's prayer" because it is a model prayer which he gave to his disciples; some object to calling it "the Lord's prayer." This prayer embodies the essential desires of a praying heart; it is simple in form and comprehensive in its scope. It is generally arranged or divided into three parts: the *invocation* or preface, the *petitions,* and the *conclusion,* doxology. The *petitions* are naturally divided into two parts: the first, respecting the glory of God; the second, the wants of men; hence "thy" in the first part and "our" in the second. The first part presents a descending scale from God's name to the doing of his will on earth; the second, an ascending scale from "daily bread" to final deliverance in glory. The spirit of the prayer implies obedience, loyalty, dependence, faith, and the spirit of forgiveness. The

16 Moreover when ye fast, be not, as the hypocrites, of a sad countenance: for they disfigure their faces, that they may be seen of men to fast. Verily I say unto you, They have received their reward. 17 But thou, when thou fastest, anoint thy head, and wash thy face; 18 that thou be not seen of men to fast, but of thy Father who is in secret: and thy Father, who seeth in secret, shall recompense thee.

seven petitions imply an obligation to carry out on our part that for which we pray. The "doxology," "for thine is the kingdom, and the power, and the glory, for ever. Amen," is omitted by the best authorities.

16-18 Moreover when ye fast, be not, as the hypocrites.—We now come to the third division of Jesus' teaching here; the other two were almsgiving and prayer. "Fasting" was common as a religious act among the Jews. The word means to abstain totally from food for a given time on a religious account. Fasting among the Jews was both public (Zech. 8: 19) and private (2 Sam. 12: 16, 21.) Jesus neither enjoins fasting nor forbids it, but rather assumes that it will be done sometimes for moral and spiritual purposes. He is warning his disciples against a hypocrisy of the scribes and Pharisees. They fast with the wrong motive; they appear with "a sad countenance"; they assume a gloomy, sad appearance to excite the sympathy and pity of men. Sometimes "they disfigure their faces, that they may be seen of men to fast." Literally they deform their faces by letting the hair go untrimmed, putting ashes on the head, and assuming a woebegone expression; this was all done to be seen of men, to attract attention to their assumed piety. Jesus warns against all deceptive "make-ups" as they have in them the seeds of hypocrisy. These hypocrites were fasting "that they may be seen of men to fast"; "they have received their reward" when seen of men and need not expect to receive a reward from God; their motive for fasting was impure.

But thou, when thou fastest, anoint thy head, and wash thy face.—Jesus not only condemns the impure motive that the hypocrites had, but he teaches the true motive for all service to God. They were to "anoint" their head and "wash" their face; they were to appear as at other times. The Jews anointed and washed regularly, except on days of humiliation.

(Ruth 3: 3; 2 Sam. 12: 20, 21; Eccles. 9: 8; Dan. 10: 3.) Jesus enjoined the usual care of the person so that there should be nothing apparent before men to indicate the fasting; his disciples were to manifest their fasting only to God. He means to say to his disciples that if they have sorrow of heart and desire to fast, they should let no thought of man's presence or eye intrude; their fasting should be known only to their own soul and God. God will reward because he knows the motive and the secrets of the heart.

12. TEACHINGS AGAINST RICHES AND THE CARE OF THE NECESSITIES OF LIFE
6: 19-34

19 Lay not up for yourselves treasures upon the earth, where moth and rust consume, and where thieves ⁹break through and steal: 20 but lay up for yourselves treasures in heaven, where neither moth nor rust doth consume,

⁹Gr. *dig through.*

19, 20 **Lay not up for yourselves treasures upon the earth.** —The "treasures" of the people in the East were of two kinds —the precious metals and clothing; the clothing was better adapted for accumulation then than now, because nothing went out of fashion then; the precious metals might suffer from rust and their clothing from the moth; their best earthly treasures were perishable; their houses were of such material that thieves could easily "break through and steal." Jesus does not prohibit the accumulation of property here, but the prohibition of *hoarding;* the first reason for not laying up our treasures upon earth is that the moth and rust will destroy them; again they are temptations to thieves. One of the most common forms of riches in the East was garments, which were liable to moth (Josh. 7: 21; 2 Kings 5: 22; James 5: 2, 3); the rust would consume the precious metals; and the owner would put his trust in his riches.

But lay up for yourselves treasures in heaven.—This means that we should prefer heavenly treasures to earthly ones; the laying up of treasures in heaven is to be preferred to laying treasures up upon earth; we should make our earthly treasures the means by which we lay up heavenly treasures.

and where thieves do not ᵇbreak through nor steal: 21 for where thy treasure is, there will thy heart be also. 22 The lamp of the body is the eye: if therefore thine eye be single, thy whole body shall be full of light. 23 But if

---

There are many reasons why we should lay up treasures in heaven; they are not subject to moths and rust, neither can thieves "break through nor steal" them. The treasures in heaven are secure; they are put in contrast to earthly treasures. How may we lay up treasures in heaven? We do this by living as God teaches us to live; we go about as did Jesus doing good, and in this way were laying up treasures in heaven.

21 For where thy treasure is, there will thy heart be also.—"Heart" here means the affection and includes the thought and volition; our hearts go with our treasures. The heart is spoken of in the scriptures as the seat of affections; the thoughts, feelings, and will power are all involved in the "heart"; it is the seat and center of man's life, especially the desires and aspirations, out of which are the issues of life. (Prov. 4: 23.) If we lay up our treasures on earth, our desires and aspirations, and our life will be of the earth earthy.

[Laying up treasures in heaven means to live so that God keeps blessings in store in heaven. The same word is here translated "lay up treasures" as is translated "lay by in store" in 1 Cor. 16: 2. It is used in the same way in Luke 12: 21. No investment can be found on earth so safe, so permanent, or that pays so good dividends as laying up treasures in heaven. It is the only investment on earth that will pay dividends in the next world.]

23, 23 The lamp of the body is the eye.—All the light and vision of the body come through the eye; the eye supplies for the whole body the benefits of light and vision. "If therefore thine eye be single" means that the eye does not see double or does not look at two objects at the same time. The picture is that of a piece of cloth or other material neatly folded once, and without a variety of complicated folds; the idea of simplicity or singleness is here expressed; in a spiritual sense the eye is not diseased, is not impure; it is sound and in good condition if it sees single or gives a perfect vision. Since the eye

thine eye be evil, thy whole body shall be full of darkness. If therefore the light that is in thee be darkness, how great is the darkness! 24 No man can serve two masters: for either he will hate the one, and love the other; or else he will hold to one, and despise the other. Ye cannot serve God and

is the only organ to furnish sight and vision to the body, if it be in good condition, then the "whole body shall be full of light."

But if thine eye be evil.—For the eye to be evil is for it to be in a diseased condition so that light and vision are blurred or obscured; in a spiritual sense if the eye be evil the power of distinct and clear vision of spiritual things is lost and the whole body in a spiritual sense is full of darkness. If the spiritual eye is evil, all spiritual vision is distorted and one does not understand; one is in darkness. If the organ which functions for light and vision is impaired, then the whole body will be in darkness, for there is no other organ to furnish light to the body. This figure used by Jesus has direct reference to laying up treasures; he who lays up treasures upon earth has an evil eye, but he who lays up treasures in heaven has a clear vision and the whole body is full of light.

[The organ that carries light to our body is the eye. If the eye be kept single and free, receiving only the word of God, the true light of the world, how well the body is lighted! But if the eye is double, filled with error, how dark does the body become! Wealth and riches cannot bring earthly or spiritual happiness; wealth and earthly honors and fleshly gratifications are short-lived, deceptive, and despoil us of true wisdom and a true goodness. They serve to distract our attention from a higher good and more lasting blessings and leave us to perish forever; this plunges us into total and eternal darkness.]

24 **No man can serve two masters.**—This is a truism; no man can be the servant of, yield full obedience to, two masters, for they demand different and opposite things; the commands of different masters are opposite and no one can obey two contradictory or opposite commands. If a servant obeys one master he must disobey the other; the very act of obedience to one is disobedience to the other. Jesus tells the result

mammon. 25 Therefore I say unto you, Be not anxious for your life, what ye shall eat, or what ye shall drink; nor yet for your body, what ye shall put on. Is not the life more than the food, and the body than the raiment? 26

of attempting to serve two masters; one will hate the one and love the other, or the other way round, "he will hold to one, and despise the other." Jesus makes this more emphatic when he says, "Ye cannot serve God and mammon." This is Jesus' application of the principle. God and mammon are of such opposite natures that it is impossible to love either one supremely without hating the other; that which attracts to one repels from the other. The more one loves God, the more he must hate evil. "Mammon" is a Syriac word which means "riches"; it is riches or wealth personified. "Mammon" means the riches of this world; one cannot trust in wealth and trust in God; one cannot serve God and lay up treasures upon earth. Some claim that "mammon" is a name of an idol worshiped as the God of riches; others dispute this. Jesus does not here condemn riches, but he does condemn becoming a slave to riches. God is a jealous God and will not accept a service that is divided with Satan.

[Two masters, each claiming to rule and guide men, cannot be served by one and the same spirit. All spiritual service must be gladly and cheerfully done. God accepts no service that does not come from the heart. If we seek to serve a different master that divides the feelings, the affections, the service due to God, we deprive God of the service. Mammon is the god of riches, the god which bestows, the worship of whom gives riches and worldly power as its reward and blessing, the god of this world, and stands in antagonism to the worship of God. No one can worship the God of heaven and mammon, the god of this world. To love one is to hate the other.]

25 Therefore I say unto you, Be not anxious for your life. —The service of mammon leads to anxiety and worry, but the service of God leads to peace, joy, and happiness. Jesus here cautions his disciples against being anxious, overcareful for the necessary things of life. He would not have his people worry and be anxious for the things which belong to this

Behold the birds of the heaven, that they sow not, neither do they reap, nor gather into barns; and your heavenly Father feedeth them. Are not ye of much more value than they? 27 And which of you by being anxious can add one cubit unto ¹the measure of his life? 28 And why are ye anxious con-

---

¹Or, *his stature*

---

world. Ordinary thought or care is not forbidden (2 Thess. 3: 10; 1 Tim. 5: 8), but an overanxiety which distracts the mind is forbidden. When thought about temporal things becomes anxiety, it has become distrust of God. Jesus specifies the things about which we should not be anxious; these are food, drink, and raiment; the three essentials for the body are food, clothing, and shelter. Jesus would not have his disciples overanxious about these things. The world gives special emphasis to these three things; in fact, these become the objects of greatest affection and interest. Jesus asks, "Is not the life more than the food, and the body than the raiment?" The argument is, will not God, who has given the greater gifts, the life and the body, also provide the lesser, food and raiment? Since God gave us a body, he will provide in his own way the necessary things of this body.

26 Behold the birds of the heaven.—Jesus had laid down the principle that his disciple should trust in God and not in the uncertainty; that if they would trust in him that he would provide all things necessary for their trusting and serving him. He now illustrates this by "the birds of the heaven." Man is greater than the birds; the birds do not sow, reap, "nor gather into barns," yet God has provided for them; he feeds them. He asks, "Are not ye of much more value than they?" If the birds which neither sow nor reap nor store away are cared for in the way God appoints to them, how much more will he care for his disciples who put their trust in him? Men can sow, reap, and store away, and they should do this, but not with *anxiety*.

27 And which of you by being anxious can add one cubit unto the measure of his life?—A "cubit" was a measure of eighteen to twenty-one inches in length; it was originally the length of a man's arm from the elbow to the end of the middle finger. No man could add anything to his age or to his stature in an arbitrary way by being anxious about them; it is

cerning raiment? Consider the lilies of the field, how they grow; they toil not, neither do they spin: 29 yet I say unto you, that even Solomon in all his glory was not arrayed like one of these. 30 But if God doth so clothe the grass of the field, which to-day is, and to-morrow is cast into the oven, *shall he* not much more *clothe* you, O ye of little faith? 31 Be not therefore anx-

foolish to give anxiety to these things. Nobody thinks of adding a cubit to his height by any amount of attention given to it; Jesus cites this illustration to enforce his principle that man must trust in God and God will take care of him.

28, 29 And why are ye anxious concerning raiment?—This is another example or illustration that Jesus gives to impress the principle of trusting in God. Perhaps more attention is given to raiment than to any of the three necessary things of the physical life; even the disciples of Jesus are too anxious about clothing. All should dress in as neat and attractive way as their circumstances will permit, but to give so much attention to and be anxious for clothing is a violation of the principle that Jesus has laid down. He enforces this principle by calling attention to "the lilies of the field." It is claimed that lilies were common in Palestine and that on every hand they were within sight of his auditors at the time he was speaking; some who have visited Palestine have said that in the spring the hillsides of Galilee are clothed with lilies of all shades and colors; they do not work in man's way for their gorgeous array, yet they are far more beautiful than anyone can make himself by putting on raiment. Jesus cites Solomon and compares the beauty of the lilies which give no attention to their gorgeous array to his studied display of royal splendor: "Solomon in all his glory was not arrayed like one of these." Solomon represented to the Jewish mind the ideal of regal magnificence. (1 Kings 10: 1-29.) Solomon's glory was external, a glory put on, while that of the flower is a part of its nature, being developed from within. God gives the beauty to the flowers, and he will give such adornment to his disciples as may be best for them.

30-32 But if God doth so clothe the grass of the field.—The point here is that God's wonderful providence clothes the lilies with their beauty and even the short-lived grass of the field, so he will take care of his disciples. Every kind of herb

ious, saying, What shall we eat? or, What shall we drink? or, Wherewithal shall we be clothed? 32 For after all these things do the Gentiles seek; for your heavenly Father knoweth that ye have need of all these things. 33 But seek ye first his kingdom, and his righteousness; and all these things shall be

on earth is a product of God's power and care; he gives to them their different shades, tints, and hues of color; these are far inferior to man; will he not care for man who is so superior to these things? "Shall he not much more clothe you, O ye of little faith?" He will provide such raiment as his disciples may need for their service to him. God will care for his people. But how? Does he forbid sowing and reaping? It is by our diligent sowing and careful reaping that he cares for us. "O ye of little faith." We have a God who can supply us with all the necessary things of life, and he has promised to do so; hence we should trust him for these things. It is a lack of faith in God when we are overanxious about these material things. We should not be like the Gentiles who scarcely know God and who are anxious about the material things of this life. We should remember that our heavenly Father knows how great and real are our needs for food, clothing, and shelter, and he is good enough to supply them. We do not expect the Gentiles or heathen to trust God for these material blessings, but we do expect his children to trust him for them. He knows our needs and in his own way will supply them. He is wise enough to know our needs, good enough to supply them, and powerful enough to do so; furthermore, he has promised to do this; hence we can trust him.

33 But seek ye first his kingdom.—"Seek" means to search for, strive for, aim; his kingdom should be the chief aim of all; it should be first in time and first in importance. The kingdom of God, which is the church of God, is of greatest importance and must be so regarded by all who would follow Jesus. We should seek not to accumulate food and raiment, nor to hoard wealth, but the things which belong to the kingdom of God. Our anxiety should not be for material things, but for the kingdom of God. This kingdom of God has its righteousness. To the one in the world the seeking of the kingdom of God should come first, and to those who are in the

added unto you. 34 Be not therefore anxious for the morrow: for the morrow will be anxious for itself. Sufficient unto the day is the evil thereof.

church, they should seek the full and rich righteousness of the kingdom of God. If we put the kingdom of God and its righteousness first, we have the promise that "all these things shall be added" unto us; that is, all material necessities of life will be given to those who earnestly put the kingdom of God and its righteousness first.

34 **Be not therefore anxious for the morrow.**—We should not be troubled, distracted, anxious, about the future; our anxiety should be for the kingdom of God and the righteousness of God. All worldly things are of minor importance, and as God will supply such of them as are needful, we should not be anxious about future supplies of them. The future day by day will bring its own troubles, and we need not be anxious for it. We should let "the morrow" take care of itself; today has its own responsibilities and sorrows, so we need not borrow any from tomorrow; each day has enough of trials and burdens, and if we add more by anxiety about the future, we are adding to the present burdens of life; this is wrong and unfits us for present duties. "Sufficient unto the day is the evil thereof." Each day brings its own responsibilities and evils; and if we add tomorrow's evils to today, we have increased our burdens unnecessarily. We do this when we are anxious about the material things of this life.

[We are not only told to seek the kingdom of God, but we are also told to seek his righteousness—the righteousness of God. This is but another form of expressing the thought: Seek the kingdom of God. The righteousness of God is constituted a feature of the kingdom of God; it is the outgrowth and fruit of seeking the kingdom. "Righteousness" means right doing. The righteousness of God means the right doing of God. Seek the right doing of God; seek to do right as God does right; seek then to make God's ways our ways; this will make his character our character; it will make his standard of right our standard of right. We should make all efforts and labors of life subservient to the higher one of honoring God. This world is a temporary sojourning place in which we may be prepared to live with God in his eternal home. Let us not lose sight of this high end and be turned aside by earthly ends. To do this is to sell the birthright to immortal honors and glories for an earthly mess of pottage "that perishes with the using."]

13. TEACHINGS AGAINST JUDGING OTHERS
7: 1-5

1 Judge not, that ye be not judged. 2 For with what judgment ye judge, ye shall be judged: and with what measure ye mete, it shall be measured

---

1, 2 Judge not, that ye be not judged.—"Judge" carries with it the meaning of "condemn" or harsh, censorious judgment. Jesus here forbids censuring others hastily and uncharitably, for in so doing one invites the severe judgment of others. (Rom. 2: 1; 14: 3, 4, 10, 13; 1 Cor. 4: 3-5; James 4: 11, 12.) The word "judge" here does not mean "form an opinion," for everyone must do this of many persons and things; it means that we should not impute wrong motives, put the worst construction on the words and actions of others; the judgment that we pass on others will be passed on us; hence Jesus says, "For with what judgment ye judge, ye shall be judged." We judge ourselves or condemn ourselves by judging others, when we are guilty of the same sin; again we are judged by our fellow men, for we give occasion and invite severe judgment from others when we pass sentence on others; again God will severely judge us if we harshly judge others. As we censure others they will be very apt to censure us; by the rule with which we deal out censure and judgment to others, by that rule others will mete out to us judgment. Our own standard of judging others will be applied to us. Haman was hanged on the gallows he had prepared for Mordecai (Esth. 7); "he that diggeth a pit shall fall into it" (Eccles. 10: 8).

[The word "judge" means "condemn"—condemn not. Do not cultivate a harsh, bitter, faultfinding spirit that looks on the ill side of persons and actions and that seeks to see evil in others so they can find fault and complain. It is one of the

unto you. 3 And why beholdest thou the mote that is in thy brother's eye, but considerest not the beam that is in thine own eye? 4 Or how wilt thou say to thy brother, Let me cast out the mote out of thine eye; and lo, the

fixed and unchangeable principles of right and justice among men that a man must be judged by the same principles with which he judges others. God so arranges that men will so judge and fix the fate or destiny of each other, paying back each in his own coin, and God will be greatly governed by the same principle. The faultfinding spirit soon runs to the unreasonable and harsh extreme that men with great faith overlook these in finding motes in the walk and character of others.]

3 **And why beholdest thou the mote that is in thy brother's eye?**—The word in the original from which we get "beholdest" means to stare at from without, as one who does not clearly see; it means to observe with scrutiny. 'Mote" is a little speck, chaff, or wood; the figure as used by Jesus here means a small particle of dust, chip, or splinter of the same material with the "beam." A "mote" may be so small that it takes very close staring to see it. Jesus asks why "beholdest" the mote that is in another's eye, "but considerest not the beam that is in thine own eye." A "beam" is a log, joist, rafter; it indicates a great fault. Jesus shows how morally grostesque the conduct of the faultfinder is; it is implied that the censorious judge or faultfinder is, to the eye of the candid onlooker, himself characterized by some greater fault than the person whose fault he is taking such zest in pointing out. Such a faultfinder has always this greatest of all faults, he is destitute of sympathy and love for the other. What a *mote* is to one looking on another is to that other himself a *beam;* the order is reversed in the estimation by each. It is common for us to minimize our own faults and magnify the faults of others; what may seem to be a minor defect of conduct in ourselves becomes a gross fault in others.

4, 5 **Or how wilt thou say to thy brother, Let me cast out the mote out of thine eye?**—How can we have the face to say to the other that he is guilty of a sin, when we are guilty of

beam is in thine own eye? 5 Thou hypocrite, cast out first the beam out of thine own eye; and then shalt thou see clearly to cast out the mote out of thy brother's eye.

the same sin in a magnified form? It is an absurdity for one to attempt to criticize another for the same sin of which he is guilty. It is ridiculous for one who has a large beam in his own eye to offer his services to his brother who has a small speck in his eye; he does not realize that he is blind. One cannot cure his neighbor's faults except in a spirit of humility. (Gal. 6: 1.) Victory over evil in ourselves will give us strength to help our brother; if we clear up our own moral vision, we can then see how to help our brother. Jesus calls the one who attempts to correct the mistakes and sins of another, when he has not corrected his own larger mistakes and blunders, a hypocrite. He tells us to correct our own mistakes and then we can help correct others. The first thing for us to do is to correct our own lives and then encourage others to correct their lives. We should look at the sins of others with undistorted vision because we cannot help them if we do not see properly their faults. One of the causes of judging others harshly is self-conceit; again one recognizes the excuses for his own failure, but will not consider the excuses that the other offers. From this teaching of Jesus we have the proverbs: "He who lives in a glass house should not throw stones"; "the pot should not call the kettle black"; "the kiln calls the oven burnt house" and "Satan rebuking sin."

[No man is permitted by Jesus Christ to hunt motes in his brother's eye, or faults in his brother's walk and character, while his own is full of much greater sins; and no man can look upon the character and work of his brother with a censorious, bitter, faultfinding spirit. If he comes to look on his brother's character or work with a bitter, faultfinding spirit, he should at once be stopped and told to purify his own life. "Thou therefore that teachest another, teachest thou not thyself? thou that preachest a man should not steal, dost thou steal? . . . thou who gloriest in the law, through thy transgression of the law dishonorest thou God?" (Rom. 2: 21-23.)]

14. A CAUTION; PRAYER ENCOURAGED; THE GOLDEN RULE; THE TWO WAYS
7: 6-14

6 Give not that which is holy unto the dogs, neither cast your pearls before the swine, lest haply they trample them under their feet, and turn and rend you.

7 Ask, and it shall be given you; seek and ye shall find; knock, and it shall be opened unto you: 8 for every one that asketh receiveth; and he that

---

6 **Give not that which is holy unto the dogs.**—The meats which were offered on the altar were holy; the holy things prepared for the temple service were to be regarded as holy as they aided men in worshiping God; "whatsoever toucheth the altar shall be holy" (Ex. 29: 37); hence a part of the sacrifice which was placed on the altar was reserved for the priests (Lev. 2: 3), and was regarded among the Jews as peculiarly sacred. This must not be given to "dogs," but must be used as Jehovah directed. Dogs and swine were regarded as unclean animals; they were regarded as scavengers of the city and were fed refuse and other putrefied things. Neither were they to "cast your pearls before the swine"; to give that which was holy to dogs and to cast their pearls to the swine involved the same principle. The swine could not appreciate the pearl and were just as ferocious as ever; they would "trample them under their feet" and devour the ones who gave pearls to them. Swine could not appreciate the beauty of pearls nor understand their value. The meaning of this caution is that the disciples of Jesus must learn the true value of sacred things and must not misuse or abuse them by giving them to those who were incapable of appreciating them. The church and all that belongs to it is sacred and must not be used for an unholy purpose; when the truth is presented and people reject it, then one should not waste time with them any longer; some people are so sensual and their hearts so hard that they will not accept the truth and a persistent presentation of it only provokes their anger; so it is best not to press the truth upon this class.

7, 8 **Ask, and it shall be given you.**—Jesus here uses three words—ask, seek, and knock; these three words imply distinct degrees of intensity. There is the "asking" in the spoken

seeketh findeth; and to him that knocketh it shall be opened. 9 Or what man is there of you, who, if his son shall ask him for a loaf, will give him a

words of prayer, the "seeking" in the efforts and labors which are put forth in carrying out prayer, and the "knocking" at the gate with the urgent importunity which claims admission to the Father's house. Earnest prayer is encouraged here. These three words forbid any ritualistic or formal prayer. Those who so ask and seek and knock are assured that they will receive, "for every one that asketh receiveth; and he that seeketh findeth; and to him that knocketh it shall be opened." Corresponding to the three words—ask, seek, and knock—are the three words—receiveth, findeth, and shall be opened. The climax is reached by "knocking," and this implies an importunity that will not be denied; seeking may be anywhere, but we knock at the door of the one from whom we expect to receive. Prayer must be in faith; God answers prayers in three ways: (1) In the praying itself is an answer as we commune with God; (2) there is the giving of the exact thing for which we as; (3) the prayer is answered in the spirit of our prayer when something else is better than that for which we ask is given. Acceptable prayer must be made in harmony with God's will; we must ask in faith (James 1: 6, 7); we must not ask to gratify our own lust (James 4: 3); and we must ask according to the will of God (1 John 5: 14.)

[God looks with more than an earthly father's love and care upon those who serve him. He is more willing to bestow good things on those who seek his blessing than the best of earthly fathers are upon their children. He requires that they should ask, seek, knock for the good where it is to be found on the conditions he proposes to give. Jesus not only proposes that he will bestow good on those who ask it, but even beyond what they ask or know bounties and blessings shall be bestowed upon the humble and lowly.]

9-11 Or what man is there of you, who, if his son shall ask him for a loaf, will give him a stone?—Jesus here appeals to the affection of an earthly parent to emphasize the great truth of God's willingness to give to those who ask, seek, and knock. No earthly father would mock his child when he

stone; 10 or if he shall ask for a fish, will give him a serpent? 11 If ye then, being evil, know how to give good gifts unto your children, how much more shall your Father who is in heaven give good things to them that ask him? 12 All things therefore whatsoever ye would that men should do unto you, even so do ye also unto them: for this is the law and the prophets.

asked for bread by giving him "a stone." The love of sinful men to their children is here contrasted with that of God. There is implied here that God will answer prayer and give that which is better than that for which we ask; since his love is divine and ours human, and since human love prompts us to give that which is best for our children, so God will give that which is best to those of his children who importune him. If a child asks for a fish, the father will give that which will sustain life and not mock him by giving his child a serpent. God is able to do more for us than we can ask or think; his love for us prompts him to do that which he is able to do for us. Jesus here makes his own application and enforces his own conclusion by saying that if imperfect and sinful beings will do that which is best for their children, how much more will a just, merciful, and loving father "give good things to them that ask him?" God gives "good gifts" unto his children; all that God gives is good, and all that is good comes from God. If God does not answer prayer, and if what he gives us in response to our asking is not the best for us, then God is not as good as an earthly parent; if he does answer prayer, and if he does give unto those who ask him that which is best for them, then his goodness becomes the boon of our lives.

12 **All things therefore whatsoever ye would that men should do unto you, even so do ye also unto them.**—This has universally been called "The Golden Rule." Jesus draws the conclusion as expressed here, not from the preceding paragraph, but from that part of his sermon which precedes this verse. This principle forms the basis of the relationship that God's people should bear to each other and the world; it expresses a fundamental principle of the kingdom of heaven. It is an expression of God's wisdom in guiding us; it is positive, not negative; it was coined by him who wrought as well as

13 Enter ye in by the narrow gate: for wide ²is the gate, and broad is the way, that leadeth to destruction, and many are they that enter in thereby. 14 ³For narrow is the gate, and straitened the way, that leadeth unto life, and few are they that find it.

²Some ancient authorities omit *is the gate.*
³Many ancient authorities read *How narrow is the gate, &c.*

---

taught righteousness. Other teachers had expressed this principle in part in a negative way, but it was left to Jesus to express clearly and fully in a positive way such a simple, and yet profound principle.

[The Golden Rule, properly understood, is a rule for settling all difficulties and matters in the church or out of it, if a Christian can have a difficulty not a matter of church discipline. That law does not require us to do what our fleshly impulses and passions would prompt us to desire one would do to us. It means to do to others as we, enlightened by the word of God, desirous of doing his will, would desire them to do to us. This would lead us to do what would promote the spiritual good of the other. Certainly this is what should be done in discipline.]

13, 14 **Enter ye in by the narrow gate.**—Jesus here presents in a very vivid way the two ways—the narrow way and the broad way. These two ways are brought in contrast by a series of words; narrow is opposed to wide; few, to many; and life, to destruction; the "straitened" way has an entrance of "the narrow gate," and "few" enter the narrow gate and travel the straitened way and find "life"; while the broad way has a "wide" entrance, "many" enter this broad way and travel to "destruction." The narrow way is as broad as the love of God can make it; Jesus did not *make* the way narrow; he only states a *fact;* it is a *necessary* fact. The narrow road cannot be made wider without lessening the good which is to be gained.

[The way to life is entered through a narrow gate. The pathway to life is hedged and hindered by many difficulties and troubles. It must be walked with care and watchfulness, lest the way be missed and evil befall us. The way of life is a plain and simple way; but there are obstacles and difficulties in man's tendencies to go his own way that hinder his walking

15. SOLEMN WARNINGS
7: 15-29

15 Beware of false prophets, who come to you in sheep's clothing, but inwardly are ravening wolves. 16 By their fruits ye shall know them. Do

---

15 Beware of false prophets.—The first of the solemn warnings that Jesus gives here concerns "false prophets." He has just presented the "two ways" and has encouraged them to enter the narrow gate and travel the straitened way, and now he tells them to beware of those who would mislead them. "Prophets" is derived from the Hebrew word which originally signified to boil over, and it embodies the idea of a fountain bursting forth from the heart of man into which God had poured his ideas or words; a "prophet" in the true sense means one who speaks for God; a "false prophet" is a false speaker or teacher; one who claims to speak for God, but God has not put his words into the heart or mouth of the speaker. It may include the Pharisees and religious leaders of that time, but it certainly includes all false teachers. (Matt. 24: 11, 24.) Hence, a false prophet is not merely an erroneous teacher, but a lying teacher, one pretending to be inspired, but who does not have the spirit of God; "false prophets" may include any teacher who deliberately deceives others; it does not signify one deceiving himself; and so unconsciously deceiving others. (2 Tim. 2: 17, 18; 2 Pet. 2: 1; 1 John 4: 1-3.) These false teaches appear to be gentle and meek, interested in the spiritual welfare of others, but they are like wolves which come in "sheep's clothing." The metaphor here is of a wolf putting on the sheep's skin in order to deceive.

16-20 By their fruits ye shall know them.—Jesus now tells how false teachers may be detectsd; it is "by their fruits." The question would naturally arise, how can these false teach-

men gather grapes of thorns, or figs of thistles? 17 Even so every good tree bringeth forth good fruit; but the corrupt tree bringeth forth evil fruit. 18 A good tree cannot bring forth evil fruit, neither can a corrupt tree bring forth good fruit. 19 Every tree that bringeth not forth good fruit is hewn down, and cast into the fire. 20 Therefore by their fruits ye shall know

---

ers to detected? They are disguised in appearance; the answer is, "By their fruits ye shall know them." Jesus here calls to attention the figure of fruit trees; it may be that the trunk, limbs, and foliage of certain trees are very much alike; they may be similar in appearance in many ways, but one definite way of knowing the nature of the tree is by its fruit. The wolf may appear like a sheep; it may for a time act as a sheep, but its nature will be revealed sooner or later. "Fruits" do not necessarily mean the *doctrines* of false teachers, but the entire moral effect of their teaching. The infallible test of all religious teaching is its practical result in the lives of those who receive it. The hypocrisy of all false teachers will be detected by those who closely watch them. The good fruit of a good life cannot be had from false teachings and bad principles; men do not "gather grapes of thorns, or figs of thistles."

Even so every good tree bringeth forth good fruit.—This was a matter of common observation; worthless shrubs do not bring forth good fruit; the good tree does bring forth good fruit, and a bad tree produces bad fruit. The only way to have good fruit in our lives is to have good hearts and righteous principles to guide our conduct. The fruit of a worthless tree is evil—that is, it is good for nothing. All teachings of a religious nature contrary to the teachings of Jesus produce evil fruit; all the teachings of Jesus will produce good fruit. The truth of God yields the peaceable fruit of righteousness. No evil heart can bear good fruit; no good heart can bear evil fruit. Trees in an orchard which do not bear good fruit are "hewn down, and cast into the fire"; they are worthless and should be destroyed; so they are not to be left to take the place of good trees. The destruction of worthless trees indicates the final destruction of false prophets and all who accept their false teaching. The judgment denounced

them. 21 Not every one that saith unto me, Lord, Lord, shall enter into the kingdom of heaven; but he that doeth the will of my Father who is in heaven. 22 Many will say to me in that day, Lord, Lord, did we not prophesy by thy name, and by thy name cast out demons, and by thy name do

against false teachers here should be a warning to all. Verse twenty is a repetition of verse sixteen.

21-23 Not every one that saith unto me, Lord, Lord, shall enter into the kingdom of heaven.—Jesus laid down here the principle in a negative way of entering his kingdom; it is by obedience to the will of God. His warning here is against formal and mere external worship, and includes not only entering the church or kingdom of God on earth, but also of gaining an entrance into the heavenly kingdom; we must do the will of God to enter the church, and we must continue to do the will of God to enter heaven. No mere profession of piety or worship will do; *the will of God must be done* by all who receive the reward of heaven. Not all who profess Christ repeatedly and loudly by saying "Lord, Lord" shall enter the kingdom of heaven; God's real spiritual kingdom, where Christ rules in the heart, must be entered by doing God's will; all who remain as citizens in that kingdom must do his will. False pretenses are of no avail.

Many will say to me in that day, Lord, Lord.—"That day" is the final day, the day toward which all other days look forward, and in which all time merges—the great judgment day. The warning here is against ignorance of God's will; people may live deceived, die deceived, and come before God in judgment deceived. This warning has refence to false teachers; we are not to let them deceive us. We have now the complete will of God expressed to us, and there is no excuse for anyone being deceived or being ignorant of the word of God. The repetition, "Lord, Lord," expresses strong importunity; those who come before God in judgment need not make importunity to God to change his will at the judgment. They will claim that they have prophesied in his name, cast out demons by his name, and done "many mighty works" by the name of Jesus, and plead for mercy on these grounds. Such will have taught some truth of God and taken their place with the people of God; they seemed to have taken a stand at times against the

many ¹mighty works? And then will I profess unto them, I never knew you: depart from me, ye that work iniquity.

¹Gr. *powers.*

devil, the archenemy of Jesus, but they did this with the wrong motive; they even will claim that they have done wonderful things or wonderful works by the name of Jesus, but the decision at that time against them will be, "I never knew you: depart from me, ye that work iniquity." Jesus will say that he did not recognize them as true disciples, for all the time that they were acting Jesus looked into their hearts and saw the wrong motives. As their claim of relationship to Christ is unfounded, he will say "depart from me," that is, he will banish them from him. (2 Thess. 1: 9.) They are called workers of "iniquity"; these false teachers and all who do not follow the will of God are lawless, sinful, and workers of iniquity. We are warned here against deceptive dealings with the teachings of Christ and impure motives of heart.

[Jesus had testified that every tree in his vineyard was to be judged according to the fruit it produced; by this he gave to us the true standard of knowing teachers. He now warns against these false prophets and false motives of heart. Doing the things he has commanded is the test and declaration of our faith in God and willingness to obey him. Faith that does not work is dead. The only test of man's confidence in God is found in his doing what God commands, and doing it because God commands it. A man may do things God commands from other motives than to do God's will and please him. It is not acceptable service to God unless done to obey and please him.

Here Jesus gives us beforehand a conversation at the last judgment. These people were honest at that day and made the claim that they had served the Lord and had done many works in the name of Jesus. They thought they had really done these things or they never could have made this plea at the judgment seat of God. Yet they were deceiving themselves in reference to this service, and so fatally and fearfully

24 Every one therefore that heareth these words of mine, and doeth them, shall be likened unto a wise man, who built his house upon the rock: 25 and the rain descended, and the floods came, and the winds blew, and beat upon that house; and it fell not: for it was founded upon the rock. 26 And every

---

doing it that only the sentence of the Judge, "Depart from me, all ye workers of iniquity," would undeceive them. God regards all service to him, save obedience to his commands, as iniquity and sin. Since this is true, many who claim to be his servants and doing wonders in his name will be driven from the presence of God for doing what they imagine good service to him. We cannot be too cautious in doing his commandments and in rejecting from his service everything not commanded by him. "If a man love me, he will keep my word" (John 14: 23) is the law of God by which man must be judged.]

24, 25 **Every one therefore that heareth these words of mine, and doeth them.**—Growing out of his solemn warning concerning facing God at the judgment, Jesus now presents a picture of two classes of hearers; he has dealt with, by implication, two classes of teachers—false prophets and true prophets—and now gives warning to the two classes of hearers. The picture is not of two men deliberately selecting foundations upon which to build a house, but it contrasts one who carefully chooses and prepares his foundation with the one who builds carelessly. This is more strongly brought out by Luke (6: 48) when he says, "Who digged and went deep, and laid a foundation upon the rock." The one who hears the words of Jesus and obeys them is "likened unto a wise man, who built his house upon the rock"; this means those who do the will of God (verse 21) are like the man who carefully prepared the foundation and built his house. The hills of Palestine were subject to heavy rainstorms at certain seasons of the year, and consequently to floods; water rushing down the ravines would soon undermine the foundation, if the house was not built on a rock. If the house is built on the rock, it is safe; so the one who builds his character by hearing and doing what Jesus teaches will stand approved of God in the day of judgment.

one that heareth these words of mine, and doeth them not, shall be likened unto a foolish man, who built his house upon the sand: 27 and the rain descended, and the floods came, and the winds blew, and smote upon that house; and it fell: and great was the fall thereof.

28 And it came to pass, when Jesus had finished these words, the multitudes were astonished at his teaching: 29 for he taught them as *one* having authority, and not as their scribes.

26, 27 **And every one that heareth these words of mine, and doeth them not.**—The other class of hearers is the one who hears, but *does not do* what God commands. Both classes are alike in that both *hear,* but they are different in that one *does* and the other *does not.* This class of hearers is likened unto a "foolish man, who built his house upon the sand." The points of similarity of the two classes are that both hear, build a house, rain descended upon it, floods came, winds blew and beat upon the house. The differences in the two classes are that one does and the other does not; one is wise, the other foolish; the one built upon a rock, the other upon sand; the one stood, the other fell. It is worse than useless to *hear* and not to *do;* such hearing only aggravates guilt; the more the hearer knows of his duty, the more guilty is he if he obeys it not; such guilt brings down upon his vainly-founded house the torrents of swift, utter retribution and destruction. This illustration of Jesus makes its own impression. He who hears the words of Jesus, and does them, is safe against all the evil influences of the world, safe forever; he who simply hears, and does not do, is doomed to fail of salvation, and be crushed in utter destruction.

28, 29 **And it came to pass, when Jesus had finished these words.**—Jesus concluded this sermon with the simple, yet beautiful, figure of the two classes of hearers; Matthew now adds his comment. The sermon was delivered to "his disciples" (5: 1), but the multitudes were present. Matthew gives no comment as to the effect of this sermon on "his disciples," but confines his remark to the effect that it had upon "the multitudes." The crowds were "astonished at his teaching"; the people were astounded, amazed "at his teaching." The simplicity, the content of the sermon, its profound philosophy of life, and the authority by which Jesus spoke "astonished" "the multitudes." Jesus did not pose as a hero, but the simple gospel historian recorded the effect that it had upon the people. Jesus' manner was not dogmatic, dictatorial, nor with an authoritative air which self-conceited, shallow men are accustomed to assume. His innate dignity of surpassing moral power—a bearing of himself as one who consciously came from God, and therefore could not speak with clear, impressive thought—impressed his hearers as they had never been impressed before. "Their scribes" could not speak with the authority of originality; they could only speak as interpreters of the law of Moses; they could quote what others had commented about the law, but they could not go any further. The scribes made it their business simply to state, to explain, and to apply the teachings of the Old Testament, together with the decisions of Jewish tribunals; they could go no further. Jesus has spoken with authority of God; we have a record of the will of God, we dare not go further; his will as recorded in the New Testament has the same authority that Jesus had in speaking it.

SECTION FOUR

THE GALILEAN MINISTRY
8:1 to 18:35

1. GROUP OF MIRACLES PROVING JESUS' DIVINITY AND ILLUSTRATING HIS TEACHING
8:1 to 9:34

1 And when he was come down from the mountain, great multitudes followed him. 2 And behold, there came to him a leper and ²worshipped him,

---
²See marginal note on ch. 2. 2.

Immediately after stating the principles and the laws of the kingdom of heaven, Matthew records ten miracles which were wrought by Jesus; these did not all occur at this time, but they are recorded here by Matthew in accordance with his general plan of massing his facts. He has just recorded the "Sermon on the Mount" as a specimen of the teachings of Jesus, and now he gives us a group of his miracles; the sermon shows that he *taught* as one having authority, and the miracles show that he *acted* as one having authority. These miracles show not only the authority of Jesus, but they illustrate the truth that he taught.

1, 2 And behold, there came to him a leper and worshipped him.—"When he was come down from the mountain, great multitudes followed him"; they had been attracted and astonished by his teachings. One of the multitude was "a leper"; for thousands of years the lepers in the East had formed a distinct class; they married among themselves, and so perpetuated this fatal disease. Its name is derived from *Lepis,* a scale, because it shows itself in dry, thin scales or scabs, which are white in some instances. (Ex. 4:6; Num. 12:10; 2 Kings 5:27.) There are two kinds of leprosy; one has been considered incurable; the miserable wretches afflicted with this kind of leprosy were clothed in shrouds, as if already dead, while they were separated from other people. Leprosy has been considered a type of sin. This poor leper came to Jesus and "worshipped him, saying, Lord, if thou wilt, thou canst make me clean." This was a sublime expression of faith in the divine power of Jesus; the very act of his coming to

saying, Lord, if thou wilt, thou canst make me clean. 3 And he stretched forth his hand, and touched him, saying, I will; be thou made clean. And straightway his leprosy was cleansed. 4 And Jesus saith unto him, ³See thou tell no man; but go, show thyself to the priest, and offer the gift that Moses commanded, for a testimony unto them.

³Lev. xiii. 49; xiv. 2 ff.

Jesus proved his faith in Jesus. In the case of lepers the word is always "cleansed," not "healed." The cleansing implied a cure, and meant a new life for the afflicted one.

Mark says "kneeling down to him" (Mark 1: 40), while Luke says "he fell on his face" (Luke 5: 12), while Matthew expresses it "worshipped him"; he paid Jesus respect offered to superiors, and perhaps recognized him as a prophet of God. It was a pathetic appeal that he made to Jesus in this prostrated position, "Lord, if thou wilt, thou canst make me clean"; this may have expressed a doubt of Jesus' willingness to cleanse him.

3, 4 **And he stretched forth his hand, and touched him.**—Jesus, moved with compassion for the unfortunate man, put out his hand, and "touched him." None besides Jesus would dare touch a leper; he alone was safe from the pollution of the contact; this "touch" of Jesus strengthened the faith of the man and Jesus accompanied the touch with the words, "I will; be thou made clean." Then a marvelous change came over the man; his body was transformed and he became a cleansed man. It has been a mooted question as to whether all who received bodily healing from Jesus also received spiritual cleansing; in many instances such was not the case, but in others they may have received spiritual blessings. Whether this leper received any spiritual blessing cannot be determined from the context.

And Jesus saith unto him, See thou tell no man; but go, show thyself to the priest.—Jesus laid upon him two commands; first he strictly charged him to "tell no man," and second he should show himself to the priest. His testimony of Jesus' cleansing him was of small value until he had the priest's certificate of cure, as many would not believe his testimony; again his conduct might interfere with Jesus' work. Jesus could not give all of his time to bodily healing; he has a

5 And when he was entered into Capernaum, there came unto him a centurion, beseeching him, 6 and saying, Lord, my ⁴servant lieth in the house

⁴Or, *boy*

greater work to do. He was to show himself to the priest, "and offer the gift that Moses commanded, for a testimony unto them." The law specified "the gift" (Lev. 14: 1-32); Jesus respected the ceremony of the law until it had all been fulfilled (Matt. 5: 17). The testimony would be proof to the priest that God had cured his leprosy; the ceremonial cleansing followed the curative cleansing. (Lev. 14: 3, 4.) This is the first instance that we have recorded that Jesus prohibited anyone from speaking of his power to cleanse; Matthew records frequent prohibitions. Sometimes Jesus reversed this course and commanded men to go and tell what he had done for them. (Mark 5: 19, 20.)

5, 6 **And when he was entered into Capernaum, there came unto him a centurion.**—This miracle is recorded also by Luke. (Luke 8: 1-10.) Jesus came to Capernaum; this was his home city and was located near the Sea of Galilee. "There came unto him a centurion"; he did not come in person, but by friends who brought his message. Luke says, "And when he heard comcerning Jesus, he sent unto him elders of the Jews." (Luke 7: 3.) It was a common way of expressing what one did through another as though that one did it himself. "A centurion" was a Roman military officer, captain of a hundred soldiers; this centurion was probably the chief officer of the Roman forces in Capernaum which was on the great commercial route between Assyria and Egypt.

[We are said to do what we do through others; we frequently say we went to others for help when we only sent to them for help. This is a very common style of speaking. The centurion went to Jesus and besought him through the elders. This shows that each writer told the facts in his own way and style, and that there was no effort at telling the same tale. The apparent diversities add assurance to the statement, for there is real agreement.]

Lord, my servant lieth in the house sick of the palsy.—This seems to have been the centurion's personal servant, a confi-

sick of the palsy, grievously tormented. 7 And he saith unto him, I will come and heal him. 8 And the centurion answered and said, Lord, I am not [5]worthy that thou shouldest come under my roof; but only say [6]the word, and my [4]servant shall be healed. 9 For I also am a man [7]under authority, hav-

---

[5]Gr. *sufficient*.
[6]Gr. *with a word*.
[7]Some ancient authorities insert *set:* as in Lk. 7, 8.

---

dential attendant, like a private secretary. Luke says that he "was dear unto him"; there was a very close relation between the centurion and this servant; he was very much concerned about his servant as he was "sick of the palsy, grievously tormented." "Palsy" is a contraction of paralysis; the term "palsy" or "paralysis" is used by the ancients in a much wider sense than we now use it; the term then included what we now call tetanus, catalepsy, cramps, and other fearful maladies. He was "grievously tormented," which means that he was in that stage of palsy when the patient suffers great agony; Luke says that he was at the point of death.

7-9 He saith unto him, I will come and heal him.—Jesus, at the request of the messengers at once stated that he would heal the centurion's servant; he said, "I will come," with much emphasis on "I." It seems that Jesus started back with the messengers to the House of the afflicted servant, but before he arrived at the house the centurion had learned that Jesus was coming and sent a fresh deputation of "friends" who said, on his behalf, what Matthew here reports as said by himself. He said, "Lord, I am not worthy that thou shouldest come under my roof; but only say the word, and my servant shall be healed." Luke puts it, "Lord, trouble not thyself," for I am not worthy that you should enter my house; he indicated great politeness as well as profound humility; he did not think himself worthy to come to Jesus in person, neither did he think that he was worthy for Jesus to come into his house. This centurion knew the custom or law of the Jews that they would not go into the house of a Gentile, hence this centurion so expressed himself. He did not think it necessary for Jesus to come to his house in order to heal his servant; he thought that Jesus could heal the servant without subjecting himself to the violation of Jewish custom or law.

ing under myself soldiers: and I say to this one, Go, and he goeth; and to another, Come, and he cometh; and to my servant,⁸ Do this, and he doeth it. 10 And when Jesus heard it, he marvelled, and said to them that followed, Verily I say unto you, ⁹I have not found so great faith, no, not in Israel. 11

⁸Gr. *bondservant.*
⁹Many ancient authorities read *With no man in Israel have I found so great faith.*

For I also am a man under authority, having under myself soldiers.—The centurion made a very plausible argument which showed his faith in Jesus. His argument was that he was a man under authority as well as Jesus; the centurion compared Jesus' position with his own. Jesus had authority over disease; the centurion *also* had authority over soldiers. As the centurion had only to say to a soldier "go" and he went, so Jesus had only to say to disease "go" and it would obey him. Some state the argument another way; since the centurion who was under authority to his superior officers could still say to the soldiers under him "go" and "come," so Jesus who was under no authority could command the power of life and death. At any rate, the argument of the centurion evinced strong faith; Jesus recognized this faith.

10 And when Jesus heard it, he marvelled.—The faith of this centurion stood out so clearly amidst the prevailing unbelief of the Jews; only twice do we read that Jesus "marvelled" and this was only over "two things": one at the *unbelief* of his fellow citizens at Nazareth (Mark 6:6) and one at the *faith* of this Roman officer. The centurion's faith was great; it was based on facts that he had learned about Jesus; it overcame great obstacles. It was unselfish; it was a faith that worked; it was faith in God and in his Son. Jesus said to those present, "I have not found so great faith, no, not in Israel." There is a similar case of great faith on the part of the heathen recorded in Matt. 15:22-28. This is a wonderful statement of Jesus; he was greatly impressed with such faith in a Roman centurion, a Gentile, that he declared he had not seen such faith in Israel among the Jews. The place and the people where he had a right to expect great faith, he found only *unbelief,* and where even the Jews did not expect to find anything good, Jesus found "so great faith."

And I say unto you, that many shall come from the east and the west, and shall ¹⁰sit down with Abraham, and Isaac, and Jacob, in the kingdom of heaven: 12 but the sons of the kingdom shall be cast forth into the outer darkness: there shall be the weeping and the gnashing of teeth. 13 And

¹⁰Gr. *recline.*

11, 12 And I say unto you, that many shall come from the east and the west, and shall sit down with Abraham, and Isaac, and Jacob.—The faith of this Gentile officer suggested to him the future calling and conversion of the Gentiles; this was in God's great plan of salvation. In a similar expression Luke adds "and from the north and south." (Luke 13: 29.) The meaning is that Gentiles from all parts of the world shall come and "sit down," that is, shall be placed at a table "with Abraham, and Isaac, and Jacob." This expression is drawn from the custom of the recumbent position in which the orientals ate their meals; it was customary among all nations to represent the joys of heaven under the notion of a banquet or feast. Abraham, Isaac, and Jacob were representative believers of the Jewish race; they were the patriarchs of the Jewish race. "In the kingdom of heaven" we have another repetition made by Jesus to the institution or church which he came to establish. However, some think that here he had reference to the "kingdom of glory" (Matt. 26: 29; Luke 16: 22; Rev. 19: 9); others think that he had reference only to the church.

But the sons of the kingdom shall be cast forth into the outer darkness.—The "sons of the kingdom" were the Jews; they were heirs of the kingdom according to the promise; to them it was first offered, and it was because they rejected it that they were to "be cast forth into the outer darkness." While the Jews rejected Christ as their Messiah, the Gentiles would accept him as their Savior; this prophecy of Jesus has literally been fulfilled. These Jews were "sons of the kingdom" as the wicked are "sons of disobedience" (Eph. 2: 2), and "children of obedience" (1 Pet. 1: 14) and "children of wrath" (Eph. 2: 3.) "Outer darkness" is an expression which denotes "the blackness of darkness." (Jude 13; 2 Pet. 2: 17.) It is described as a place where "there shall be the weeping and the gnashing of teeth," while at the same time others, Gentiles,

Jesus said unto the centurion, Go thy way; as thou hast believed, *so* be it done unto thee. And the ⁴servant was healed in that hour.

shall be enjoying a feast with Abraham, Isaac, and Jacob. "The weeping and the gnashing" represent intense suffering; they shall weep because they have lost their favor with God, and shall gnash their teeth because others have obtained it.

[Jesus came and introduced his mission by declaring, "Blessed are the poor in spirit: for theirs is the kingdom of heaven." All the powers of earth and hell cannot hinder a man that is sensible of his own poverty of spirit, and his need of help from without to preserve his spiritual life, from praying to a spiritual being, real or imaginary, for help. The centurion, an officer in the Roman army, came and pleaded for mercy from Jesus in behalf of his servant sick of the palsy. When Jesus heard his pleading and saw his faith he was constrained to say, "I have not found so great faith, no, not in Israel." He then added that the Gentiles should come in and enjoy the blessings of God with Abraham, Isaac, and Jacob and that the Jews would be cast into outer darkness because of their rejection. The promise was that Jesus came to call and bless the Gentiles, and many of these would hear the call of God, while the Jews would refuse him. He heard of this Gentile and answered his prayer by healing the servant.]

13 **And Jesus said unto the centurion, Go thy way.**—Some think that this indicates that the centurion in person came out to meet Jesus, but this does not prove it. (See 1 Sam. 25: 40, 41.) Jesus added "as thou hast believed, so be it done unto thee." The centurion's faith was great and his blessings should be commensurate with his faith. This centurion believed that Jesus could heal his servant by speaking the word and without going to the servant; as was his faith so was the blessing to him and to his servant. We are to understand from this that Jesus did not go to the house of the servant and that the centurion returned to his house and found that "the servant was healed in that hour." The healing of the servant was instantaneous and perfect; Luke adds that the centurion

14 And when Jesus was come into Peter's house, he saw his wife's mother lying sick of a fever. 15 And he touched her hand, and the fever left her; and she arose, and ministered unto him. 16 And when even was come,

"returning to the house, found the servant whole." (Luke 7: 10.)

14, 15 And when Jesus was come into Peter's house, he saw his wife's mother lying sick of a fever.—This miracle is also recorded by Mark (1: 29-31) and Luke (4: 38, 39); both Mark and Luke give a fuller record than does Matthew. Mark tells us that this was the house of Simon and Andrew, his brother; he also records that James and John, the two sons of Zebedee, were present. This miracle was a domestic scene—a miracle in the very home of his earliest disciples, and in the presence of two more. The original home of Peter was in Bethsaida, which was a suburb of Capernaum; it may have been there that the miracle was performed. (See John 1: 45; Mark 1: 29.) "His wife's mother" shows that Peter was a married man, and that his mother-in-law was living with him; we cannot tell from this whether Peter's wife was living at this time. She was "lying sick of a fever"; she was confined to bed with a fever; Luke says "a great fever" and that her friends "besought him for her." They did this as soon as he entered the house according to Mark.

And he touched her hand, and the fever left her.—Jesus usually made some visible sign suitable to the miracle which he wrought. Luke says, "He stood over her, and rebuked the fever"; Mark says, "He came and took her by the hand, and raised her up"; these were all significant actions. The result was that "the fever left her." She was healed immediately and was able at once to minister unto Jesus. It was evident that the miraculous cure came from Jesus and that it was a complete cure. The proof of the completeness of the cure was that she arose and ministered unto Jesus. Her service probably consisted in supplying food and any other needed attention. A severe fever always leaves a person very weak, but the miraculous healing of Jesus was so complete that the patient was given normal strength at once.

they brought unto him many [11]possessed with demons: and he cast out the spirits with a word, and healed all that were sick: 17 that it might be fulfilled which was spoken through Isaiah the prophet, saying, [12]Himself took our infirmities, and bare our diseases.

[11]Or, *demoniacs*
[12]Is. liii. 4.

16, 17 And when even was come, they brought unto him many possessed with demons.—Jesus had healed Peter's wife's mother on the Sabbath day, but as it was noised abroad, the Jews brought their sick to him "when even was come"; that is, when the Sabbath had ended. The Jewish day was reckoned as beginning and ending at sunset; so they came the moment the Sabbath was past and brought "many possessed with demons." Matthew had already mentioned that Jesus healed all the demoniacs that were brought to him during this circuit of Galilee. (Matt. 4: 24.) Those possessed with demons had evil spirits; the evil spirits had taken possession of them; they were prepared in heart for the reception of the demons; oftentimes they were torn and afflicted because of the demon. Jesus "cast out the spirits with a word"; he commanded and the demons obeyed. The possession of demons in that age was very peculiar; we are not told how wicked spirits gain possession of people, neither are we told the condition of mind or body which exposed one to the possession of demons. One thing we are certain of and that is they obeyed the command of Jesus; they sometimes recognized his authority and feared him. Jesus had power over the unseen realm.

That it might be fulfilled which was spoken through Isaiah. —The quotation from Isaiah is found in Isa. 53: 4. In the events that took place here in casting out the evil spirits and in healing "all that were sick," Jesus fulfilled the prophecy which said, "Himself took our infirmities, and bare our diseases." Jesus took away the infirmities and the diseases by healing them; the context shows that this is the meaning of this prophecy. Isaiah did not merely mean that Jesus cured all of the bodily and mental diseases, but that he finally suffered for the sins of the world. In his miracles of healing, Jesus seems to have participated in the sufferings of the afflicted, bearing a deep sympathy for those who were suffering.

8:18-20.]   MATTHEW   195

18 Now when Jesus saw great multitudes about him, he gave commandment to depart unto the other side. 19 And there came ¹a scribe, and said unto him, Teacher, I will follow thee whithersoever thou goest. 20 And

¹Gr. *one scribe.*

"Infirmities" and "diseases" may mean the same thing; some make "infirmities" refer to chronic disability, while "diseases" include violent disorders of the body. Jesus took upon himself and thus took away from us, all the distresses produced by sin. He bore the sickness of men on his heart and his healing of them with his strong hand fulfilled the prophecy of Isaiah.

18 Now when Jesus saw great multitudes about him.—Matthew does not follow any chronological order. When Jesus saw the great multitude, he gave "commandment to depart unto the other side"; he was on the west side of the Sea of Galilee, but now he gives commandment to go to the east side. It seems that the multitude was too great and he withdrew from it; it was an easy method of escape by going to the east side. The miracles of Jesus had greatly impressed the people; they were astonished more at his miracles than they were at his teachings. The excitement of the hour attracted so many that it was impossible to handle such a multitude and do them good; again Jesus' work could be done more in private than in the midst of an excited multitude. By withdrawing from the multitude, he would have only those present who sought him.

19, 20 And there came a scribe, and said unto him.—"A scribe" was one who copied the law; he was one who was supposed to know the law since he had copied it. There was a class of teachers of the law known as "the scribes"; so one of them either followed Jesus across the Sea of Galilee or came to him after he crossed "unto the other side." Matthew records the interview with this scribe as though most of Jesus' followers were men of private station and men of humble life, but here was one of the teachers, a Rabbi, who had come to him. He expressed a noble desire; he said, "I will follow thee whithersoever thou goest." Disciples usually accompanied their teacher; they followed their teacher about and learned

Jesus saith unto him, The foxes have holes, and the birds of the heaven *have* ²nests; but the Son of man hath not where to lay his head. 21 And another of the disciples said unto him, Lord, suffer me first to go and bury my

---

²Gr. *lodging-places.*

---

from him. Their teaching then was not in houses as are our schools today; the teacher frequently strolled through the country and his disciples "followed him." Some think that this scribe was influenced by a prospect of temporal advantage in Jesus' kingdom; he had witnessed the wonderful miracles that Jesus wrought, and perhaps was attracted more by these than anything else; hence Jesus tested his motives.

Jesus saith unto him, The foxes have holes, and the birds of the heaven have nests.—This was a severe test to the faith of this scribe; the foxes have their dens and the birds have their nests, that is, a place of shelter; "nests" as used here does not mean the place where the birds brood, but a place to roost under some shelter. While the foxes and birds have their homes or places of rest, "the Son of man hath not where to lay his head." That is, Jesus had no place on earth that he could recline his head and call it "his own"; this implied that he had no secure or fixed place of abode; Jesus uses here the title "Son of man"; he frequently referred to himself by this title. It recognized his human birth, and his human nature; but it also implied that he had a dignity exclusively his own. He is *the* distinguished *Son of man* to whom there can be no second of like rank; he became the *Son of man* by being truly *the Son of God.* Jesus here suggested to this scribe that to follow him entailed many hardships and much suffering. We are not told whether this scribe successfully stood the test; some suggest that his motives were impure and therefore he turned back from following Jesus.

21, 22 And another of the disciples said unto him, Lord, suffer me first to go and bury my father.—Some think that this man was one of the twelve; they think that it was James or John and that Zebedee was the father who was to be buried; but this is a mere guess as there is nothing in the context to indicate who this disciple was. Luke does not call him a disciple; he was a disciple only in a large sense of the word,

father. **22** But Jesus saith unto him, Follow me; and leave the dead to bury their own dead.

23 And when he was entered into a boat, his disciples followed him. **24** And behold, there arose a great tempest in the sea, insomuch that the boat

as the scribe may have been. At any rate, he asked that he might be permitted to go and bury his father before following Jesus. It was considered a sacred filial duty to take care of aged parents and to bury them; but the language "first to go and bury my father" intimates, as does the next verse, that the burying was now to be done; whereas Jesus was just leaving that region, and if the disciple accompanied him he could not perform that service, so think some that this is its meaning. It is suggested by some that there is a play on the word "dead"; that the man who was to be buried was physically dead, but those who were to bury him were dead in another sense. At least, Jesus teaches that one must not let anything come between him and following Jesus. We see here extremes meeting in Jesus; he is merciful and sympathetic toward those who are afflicted and at the same time he commands with the authority of an autocrat when he says, "Follow me," and let nothing interfere with your following me. Some observe that this was a critical time of decision for this disciple; he was in actual danger of burying himself while burying his father. Luke records the case of a third who volunteered to accompany Jesus. (Luke 9:61, 62.)

23-27 And when he was entered into a boat, his disciples followed him.—The boat into which he entered was either the boat that had carried him and his disciples to the other side or another boat which was waiting to carry him away. The scene and miracle which is here related is also narrated by Mark (4:35-41), and by Luke (8:22-25); Mark gives a fuller account than Matthew, and Luke's account of it is briefer than Matthew's. Mark connects this miracle chronologically with what had just been recorded before. After a long weary day of varied labors Jesus, followed by his disciples, "entered into a boat"; some think that is possibly belonged to Peter or the sons of Zebedee.

And behold, there arose a great tempest in the sea.—The Greek indicates an "earthquake"; such a commotion of the

was covered with the waves: but he was asleep. 25 And they came to him, and awoke him, saying, Save, Lord; we perish. 26 And he saith unto them, Why are ye fearful, O ye of little faith? Then he arose, and rebuked the

elements described here corresponds to an earthquake. Mark and Luke call it a *furious* storm, a hurricane, the Sea of Galilee is subject to sudden and violent storms. The violent tempests are accounted for by the fact that the Sea of Galilee is about six hundred feet lower than the ocean; the vast and naked plateaus which surround it have ravines and deep gorges converging into the sea; these act like gigantic funnels to draw down the cold wind from the mountains and thus disturb the sea. Jesus soon fell asleep in the boat after it left the shore. The waves of the water were higher than usual as they are described as covering the boat. Matthew brings into wide contrast the tempestuous sea with its wild waves raging around and over the boat and the perfect calmness and serenity of Jesus while asleep. Upon one occasion when David was in great danger he said, "I laid me down and slept; I awaked; for Jehovah sustaineth me." (Psalm 3:5.) The disciples of Jesus learned the lesson of perfect trust in God, for years later Peter, expecting any moment to be brought out for execution, slept in his dungeon so sweetly that the angel had to smite him on the side to awake him. (Acts 12:6, 7.)

And they came to him, and awoke him, saying, Save, Lord; we perish.—In their distress and anxiety for themselves and for Jesus they cry unto Jesus loud enough to wake him from the peaceful slumber into which he had fallen. Mark records their cry as "Teacher, carest thou not that we perish?" and Luke is still more concise in recording their earnest appeal to Jesus for help; his statement is, "Master, master, we perish." It is likely that all of these forms of speech and expressions were used; some would use one expression snd some another. Matthew records the expression used by some of the disciples, while Mark and Luke record expressions used by others.

And he saith unto them, Why are ye fearful, O ye of little faith?—The disciples were with Jesus; why cannot they trust him? "O ye of little faith" is the mild yet firm rebuke that

winds and the sea; and there was a great calm. 27 And the men marvelled, saying, What manner of man is this, that even the winds and the sea obey him?
28 And when he was come to the other side into the country of the Gadarenes, there met him two ³possessed with demons, coming forth out of the tombs, exceeding fierce, so that no man could pass by that way. 29 And

---

³Or. *demoniacs*

Jesus gave them. They had seen that day many manifestations of his power, and yet they were afraid of a storm with Jesus in the boat. They had some faith, but their faith was not strong enough; the miracle which followed was to strengthen their faith in him as their Messiah. Jesus first rebuked his disciples, and then "rebuked the winds and the sea"; the result was "a great calm" immediately came upon the waters. Mark quotes the words of Jesus, "Peace, be still"; the wind ceased; the Greek indicates that it "grew weary, tired, and sank into a restful calm." Another meaning of the Greek word as used by Mark is that he "muzzled" the sea like an ox and it became calm. The effect on his disciples was that they "marvelled"; they asked each other, "What manner of man is this, that even the winds and the sea obey him?" The terrific storm had been brought so suddenly to a calm at the command of Jesus that they were astonished at the wind and the sea obeying him. Jesus had power over the material world as well as over the spiritual world; his power had been manifested over the spiritual realm by casting out demons; it was now manifested by his commanding the tempest and the mighty waters. The inconceivable wonder of arresting a hurricane was a new revelation of Jesus' power even to his disciples, and their faith was strengthened in him.

28 And when he was come to the other side into the country of the Gadarenes.—Matthew is not clear in giving the geography of the tours of Jesus; "the other side" usually means the east side of the Sea of Galilee; probably Jesus was going from Capernaum to "the other side" when the storm arose, and they continued on the journey to the "country of the Gadarenes," arriving there in the early morning. This scene is recorded both by Mark (5: 1-17) and Luke (8: 26-37.) The main difference in these three narratives is that Matthew

behold, they cried out, saying, What have we to do with thee, thou Son of God? art thou come hither to torment us before the time? 30 Now there

speaks of *two* demoniacs, while Mark and Luke speak of but one. There is a similar incident in the account of the healing of the blind near Jericho; Matthew (20: 30-34) speaks of two, while Mark (10: 46-52) and Luke (18: 35-43) speak of but one. No special importance is attached to these differences. The country of the "Gadarenes" was on the east side of the Jordan, and a little to the south; the exact location cannot be determined. Sometimes the historian speaks of the "Gerasenes" and "Gadarenes" and "Gadara." When he arrived in that country, "there met him two possessed with demons"; these came out of the tombs and were very fierce, "so that no man could pass by that way." They were dangerous. Mark and Luke mention but one, and probably the one that they mention was the more ferocious of the two, and they direct attention to the most dangerous one. Some of the ancient tombs were like caves and other places of abode, hence one would be well sheltered in the tombs; this was a very suitable place of resort for demoniacs. The case of these two demoniacs is closely allied to the wild raving insanity known in every insane asylum. It was dangerous for one to come in contact with such characters.

29-34 And behold, they cried out, saying, What have we to do with thee, thou Son of God?—Some think the meaning of the question here is what have we in common? or what have we do do with each other? The evil spirits in these two men recognized Jesus as the "Son of God"; they recognized his authority and power; they feared him. "Thou believest that God is one; thou doest well: the demons also believe, and shudder." (James 2: 19.) The evil spirit in a soothsayer following "after Paul and us cried out, saying, These men are servants of the Most High God, who proclaim unto you the way of salvation." (Acts 16: 17.) The demons in these two men were disturbed over the presence of Jesus and asked, "Art thou come hither to torment us before the time?" Jesus had commanded the unclean spirits to come out of these men. (Mark 5: 8.) They seemed to apprehend that Jesus crossed

was afar off from them a herd of many swine feeding. 31 And the demons besought him, saying, If thou cast us out, send us away into the herd of swine. 32 And he said unto them, Go. And they came out, and went into the swine: and behold, the whole herd rushed down the steep into the sea and perished in the waters. 33 And they that fed them fled, and went away into the city, and told everything, and what was befallen to them that were ³possessed with demons. 34 And behold, all the city came out to meet Jesus: and when they saw him, they besought *him* that he would depart from their borders.

---

the lake for the purpose of afflicting or annoying them by depriving them of their power over their unhappy victims. They asked if Jesus had come to torment them "before the time"; that is, before the day of judgment. (2 Pet. 2: 4; Jude 6.) In Mark we have the record that Jesus asked the man his name and the reply was "Legion; for we are many." A Roman legion numbered 6,000, but it came to mean, as with us, a large number, a host. The demons asked Jesus not to send them out of the country; Luke says, "into the abyss," the place of evil spirits; their request seems to be to send them anywhere, anywhere but to perdition.

Now there was afar off from them a herd of many swine feeding.—Mark says there were at the foot of the mountain a herd of many swine feeding, about two thousand (Mark 5: 13), and when they besought Jesus to send them into the herd of swine, Jesus "said unto them, Go." At the command of Jesus the demons left the men "and went into the swine." "Swine" was considered an unclean animal among the Jews. When the evil spirits entered the swine, "the whole herd rushed down the steep into the sea and perished in the waters." As there was a "legion" of them in one of the men, there were enough to furnish several for every one of the swine, though there were about two thousand of them. The swine "were choked" or suffocated, drowned. How demons could enter into swine we are not told, but it is no more of a mystery than the connections of the demands with the mind and body of a man. Jesus came to save man, not property; hence, he places a higher value upon the men who were saved than he did the herd of swine. The people of that country, instigated by the owners of the herd, besought Jesus to leave the country. Thus the devil played upon the cupidity of these

1 And he entered into a boat, and crossed over, and came into his own city. 2 And behold, they brought to him a man sick of the palsy, lying on a bed: and Jesus seeing their faith said unto the sick of the palsy, ⁴Son, be of

⁴Gr. *Child.*

people to induce them to ask Jesus to leave them forever—and he did. We do not read that Jesus ever returned to that people. Some of the richer citizens were owners of the swine and it is through their influence that the people besought Jesus to leave them. This miracle impressed all with the power of Jesus, even over the spirit world.

9: 1 **And he entered into a boat.**—On leaving the country of the Gadarenes Jesus entered a boat, probably the boat which had carried him to this country, and crossed the Sea of Galilee, "and came into his own city." "His own city" was Capernaum. (Matt. 4: 13; 9: 1.) According to Jewish custom thirty days' residence made a man an inhabitant, and a year's residence, in a city, a citizen thereof. This verse seems to close the narrative which was begun in Matt. 8: 18. When Jesus left the borders of the Gadarenes one of the men asked to go with him, but he was sent back to tell the people what God had done for him. Capernaum is now the home city; truly Bethlehem bore him, Nazareth reared him, Capernaum was his residence.

2 **And behold, they brought to him a man sick of the palsy.** —The series of miracles (8: 1, 18) is now continued by giving the healing of the paralytic; this is also recorded by Mark (2: 1-12) and Luke (5: 17-26). "A man sick of the palsy," a paralytic; he could not walk and was brought on a litter or mattress. The full record is to be found in Mark and Luke; he was brought to the house where Jesus was, but they could not get near Jesus for the crowd, so they went upon the housetop and let the sick man down through the roof of the house into the presence of Jesus. Jesus saw their faith as was evinced by the expedient that they adopted to bring the man to Jesus, so Jesus said to him, "Son, be of good cheer; thy sins are forgiven." It was an encouraging address for Jesus to call him "Son"; "be of good cheer" means that he should take courage; this would give him hope and strengthen his faith. We have

good cheer; thy sins are forgiven. 3 And behold, certain of the scribes said within themselves, This man blasphemeth. 4 And Jesus [5]knowing their thoughts said, Wherefore think ye evil in your hearts? 5 For which is eas-

[5]Many ancient authorities read *seeing*.

only two recorded occasions that Jesus said, "Thy sins are forgiven." The other occasion is recorded in Luke 7: 48; some make the statement of Jesus to the dying robber equivalent to "thy sins are forgiven." (Luke 23: 43.)

3-8 **And behold, certain of the scribes.**—Luke adds that the Pharisees joined with the scribes; these were the religious leaders and they said "within themselves," not aloud; the word in Mark here means "held a dialogue with themselves." They reached the conclusion that Jesus was a blasphemer; they were not courageous enough to accuse him of blasphemy; probably they talked among themselves about Jesus and accused him of blasphemy, but were not bold enough to openly make the accusation. Their argument was, "It is blasphemy for any but God to assume the prerogative of forgiving sins; but this man does so; therefore he blasphemeth." The Jews reasoned in a similar way (John 10: 31-36), when they were ready to stone Jesus; this was the penalty for blasphemy according to the law (Lev. 24: 15, 16.) To blaspheme was to speak profanely, irreverently of God and religion, so as to diminish his influence among men. It is high treason against the kingdom of God to speak blasphemously.

And Jesus knowing their thoughts.—While they did not speak aloud, but only reasoned "within themselves," Jesus knew their thoughts and answered their accusation. They must have been greatly surprised when Jesus said to them, "Wherefore think ye evil in your hearts?" "But Jesus did not trust himself unto them, for that he knew all men, and because he needed not that any one should bear witness concerning man; for he himself knew what was in man." (John 2: 24, 25.) Hence, Jesus asked them why these faults and injurious reasonings concerning his character and claims; when they perceived that Jesus knew their thoughts, they ought to have been prepared to recognize his claims, as the power of reading the heart was one of their criteria of the Messiah.

ier, to say, Thy sins are forgiven; or to say, Arise, and walk? 6 But that ye may know that the Son of man hath authority on earth to forgive sins (then saith he to the sick of the palsy), Arise, and take up thy bed, and go unto thy house. 7 And he arose, and departed to his house. 8 But when the

Jesus now gives the proof that he had power to forgive sin. He said to them, "Which is easier, to say, Thy sins are forgiven; or to say, Arise, and walk?" "Which is easier?" He who can say with effect, arise and walk, can say with effect, thy sins are forgiven; both were possible for God, but impossible for man. In the case of the healing they could test the reality of the power he claimed; they could see whether the paralytic arose and walked; and from this they ought to infer that he possessed the other power also, seeing that he claimed to possess it, and that one who could work a miracle ought to be believed. The scribes could not deny that it was as easy to say with effect to the man, "Thy sins are forgiven," as to say, "Arise, and walk."

But that ye may know that the Son of man hath authority. —"Son of man" is a title that Jesus used in referring to himself and also a title that the Jews used in referring to the Messiah, the ideal man, the head and representative of the new humanity, the Son of God manifested in the flesh. That they might know that he had "authority on earth to forgive sins," he would say, "Arise, and take up thy bed, and go unto thy house." It would be impossible without a miracle for this paralytic to do as Jesus commanded him; that they might know that Jesus had both right and might, authority and power, to forgive sins on earth, he would command the man sick of palsy to arise and take up his bed and walk; if the man obeyed his command, then they would know that he had the power and authority to forgive sins. So Jesus demonstrated his power to forgive sins by commanding the man who was paralyzed to arise from his bed and take it up and go home. The man immediately "arose and departed to his house." He took up his bed in the presence of the assembly (Mark), departed to his house; this was a living unimpeachable witness to Jesus that he was the Messiah, doing precisely what the Messiah naturally would do.

multitudes saw it, they were afraid, and glorified God, who had given such authority unto men.

9 And as Jesus passed by from thence, he saw a man, called Matthew, sitting at the place of toll: and he saith unto him, Follow me. And he arose, and followed him.

But when the multitudes saw it.—The multitudes that saw what was done were afraid and "glorified God"; Luke adds, "they were filled with fear." The miracle awakened a religious awe in the minds of the people such as men ever feel in the presence of a great and mysterious power. They were filled with wonder, reverence, and gratitude when they saw that God had imparted such authority over physical and moral evil; it is probable that they had no knowledge of Jesus' divine nature. We are not told what influence this miracle had on the prejudiced scribes and Pharisees; such men are rarely touched by any possible demonstration of goodness and grace; but the multitude marveled and glorified God. Mark describes the effect on the multitude by recording that they said, "We never saw it on this fashion" (Mark 2: 12); and Luke expresses it, "We have seen strange things to-day" (Luke 5: 26.)

9 **And as Jesus passed by from thence, he saw a man, called Matthew.**—The call of Matthew is recorded by Mark (2: 14-17) and by Luke (5: 27-32). It is impressive to note how Matthew records so briefly his own call. As Jesus went along "he saw a man"; this man was Matthew; he was busy "at the place of toll." Luke calls him Levi; his father's name was Alphaeus; "Matthew" in Hebrew means "the gift of God." This name may have been given at this time as Simon's name was changed to Cephas, Peter. He was a Jew, a publican, that is, a tax collector, or a collector of customs from the commerce that passed through the city on the great road from the east to Egypt. Publicans, especially Jewish publicans, were hated, despised, disreputable men; for the opportunity to grow rich by fraud and extortion was so great that publicans failed to resist the temptation, and this gave a bad name to the whole class. Matthew was "sitting at" the place of toll; literally he was sitting *on* the elevated platform or bench which was the principal feature of the toll office.

10 And it came to pass, as he ⁶sat at meat in the house, behold, many ⁷publicans and sinners came and sat down with Jesus and his disciples. 11 And when the Pharisees saw it, they said unto his disciples, Why eateth

⁶Gr. *reclined:* and so always.
⁷See marginal note on ch. 5. 46.

"Place of toll" was a tollbooth, or toll cabin; this custom office was at Capernaum, the landing place for the many ships which traversed the lake or coasted from town to town. Jesus simply said to him as he passed by, "Follow me"; this was a call to become his disciple; Matthew immediately arose and followed Jesus. Probably Matthew knew of Jesus before this and that this meant that he should be his constant attendant. Jesus saw in Matthew that which would make of him a faithful disciple.

10-13 And it came to pass, as he sat at meat in the house.— We learn from the record of Mark 2: 15 and Luke 5: 29 that this feast was in the house of Matthew; some think that it was a farewell banquet or feast that Matthew gave to his friends; however Jesus was present. "He sat at meat in the house" and many publicans and sinners came to this feast and sat with Jesus. Matthew modestly omits some details which are recorded by Luke, who says it was "a great feast," "a feast for all comers." Matthew gave his friends an opportunity to see and hear Jesus; it seems from the record that the feast was held immediately after the call of Matthew. "Publicans" were tax collectors and "sinners" were notoriously wicked persons; they disregarded the law and the tradition of the elders and were regarded by the Pharisees as unfit for association. It may be that the "sinners" were not as wicked as the Pharisees thought they were. Jesus was in the house of Matthew with other publicans and sinners; this was, to the Pharisees, a ridiculous surrounding for one who claimed to be the Messiah.

And when the Pharisees saw it.—The Pharisees were not present at the feast, but they could pass along the street and observe what was going on in Matthew's house; the self-righteous Pharisee would not pollute himself by going into the house of a publican and making common with sinners. The scribes were associated with the Pharisees. They asked the

your Teacher with the ⁷publican and sinners? 12 But when he heard it, he said, They that are ⁸whole have no need of a physician, but they that are sick. 13 But go ye and learn what *this* meaneth, ⁹I desire mercy, and not sacrifice: for ⁹I came not to call the righteous, but sinners.

⁸Gr. *strong.*
⁹Hos. vi. 6.

---

disciples of Jesus, "Why eateth your Teacher with the publicans and sinners?" Luke records it, "Why do ye eat and drink with the publicans and sinners?" They asked this of the disciples of Jesus after the feast, and the disciples reported it to Jesus. The Pharisees and scribes were astonished at the thought of a "Teacher" of the Jews going into the house of a publican; they thought that a teacher ought carefully to avoid all intercourse with such persons. There was not only the social objection to keeping company with such a low class, but there was the pollution which resulted from contact with those who were ceremonially unclean. Jesus replied, "They that are whole have no need of a physician, but they that are sick." Those who are sound in health do not need a physician; this was a proverbial expression. The application of this proverb is obvious; the physician goes among the sick, and why should not the Teacher of salvation go among sinners? Jesus then added that they should learn a lesson which was, "I desire mercy, and not sacrifice: for I came not to call the righteous, but sinners." Here is a quotation from Hos. 6: 6, "I desire mercy," kindness and sympathy and helpfulness, and "not sacrifice." Jesus does not mean that there are any who do not need a Savior, but there were those who claimed to be righteous, and therefore did not need a Savior. His quotation has an ironical application to the Pharisees, who really needed repentance as much as the publicans.

[Then, as now, there were self-righteous Pharisees and scribes who felt it was contamination to go near these weak, sinful classes, and even refused to countenance Jesus when he was working signs and wonders, because he went among these weak and sinning classes. It was a serious charge they made against him, that "he eateth with publicans and sinners." His response is wisdom and instruction to us if we will hear and be guided by it: "I came not to call the righ-

14 Then come to him the disciples of John, saying, Why do we and the Pharisees fast ¹oft, but thy disciples fast not? 15 And Jesus said unto them, Can the ²sons of the bridechamber mourn, as long as the bridegroom is with them? but the days will come, when the bridegroom shall be taken away

¹Some ancient authorities omit *oft.*
²That is, *companions of the bridegroom.*

---

teous, but sinners to repentance." Jesus did not see the rich or the fashionable, the learned or the elite, but he came to call sinners to repentance. To those who felt and acknowledged themselves to be sinners, and they heard.]

14, 15 Then come to him the disciples of John.—The question of fasting is now brought to the attention of Jesus; it is recorded by Mark (2: 18-22) and by Luke (5: 33-38) with only slight variations from Matthew's record. The disciples of John were the disciples of John the Baptist; Mark adds "and the Pharisees"; so the Pharisees joined the disciples of John in asking the question, "Why do we and the Pharisees fast oft, but thy disciples fast not?" It seems that John's disciples were honest in making the inquiry, and the Pharisees may have been honest, but they are so hypocritical that we never know when they make an honest inquiry. Luke in recording this adds "prayers" to the practice of fasting. The Pharisees fasted regularly every Monday and Thursday, and on many special occasions, as in times of pestilence, famine, war, and droughts. John had taught his disciples to fast and the Pharisees were taught to fast, but "thy disciples fast not" was the accusation that they brought against Jesus. At least, the disciples of Jesus did not fast according to the tradition of the Pharisees. John's disciples did not ask Jesus why they fasted or why the Pharisees fasted; they were satisfied that their practice was correct, but they wanted to know why Jesus did not teach his disciples to fast. The feast at Matthew's house which was on a fast day (see Mark 2: 18) naturally would bring this question up. It is very likely that the Pharisees prompted the disciples of John to ask this question.

Jesus said unto them, Can the sons of the bridechamber mourn, as long as the bridegroom is with them?—The friends, or companions, of the bridegroom were called "sons of the

from them, and then will they fast. 16 And no man putteth a piece of undressed cloth upon an old garment; for that which should fill it up taketh from the garment, and a worse rent is made. 17 Neither do *men* put new wine into old ³wine-skins: else the skins burst, and the wine is spilled, and the skins perish: but they put new wine into fresh wine-skins, and both are preserved.

³That is, *skins used as bottles.*

bridechamber" because they had access to it during the bridal feast. (Judges 14: 10, 11.) The festivities at a marriage were commonly prolonged for a week; the guests invited to a wedding go for joy and to have a good time generally; they go to feast and not to fast. If the bridegroom should be suddenly taken away from them by accident, sickness or death, there would be occasion for fasting; but so long as the bridegroom was present his friends enjoyed the feast with him. Jesus seems to have alluded to the hour when he himself would be taken from his disciples, but so long as Jesus was present with his disciples there was no occasion for mourning.

[There was no occasion for the disciples to fast and sorrow while he was with them to comfort them. But the time would come when he would leave them, then they would fast and mourn. Fasting is usually connected with mourning. The disciples after his departure would have frequent occasion for mourning and sorrow.]

16, 17 **And no man putteth a piece of undressed cloth upon an old garment.**—No one "seweth" a new piece of cloth, rough from the weaver, "undressed," unshrunken, upon an old garment; if it should be done the new would shrink and would rend the garment. The new piece would shrink the first time it got wet and would tear the rent still wider; the same would occur should "new wine" be put into "old wine-skins." The new wine would ferment and expand and would burst the "old wine-skins," which had very little strength and no elasticity. Some think that Jesus here taught by these two illustrations that it would be absurd to patch the old Jewish law with the new gospel of Christ; or that it would not do to put the new gospel into old Jewish law; others think that it was not a question of the proper relation between the gospel and the

18 While he spake these things unto them, behold, there came [4]a ruler, and [5]worshipped him, saying, My daughter is even now dead: but come and lay thy hand upon her, and she shall live. 19 And Jesus arose, and followed

[4]Gr. *one ruler*. Compare Mk. 5. 22.
[5]See marginal note on ch. 2. 2.

Jewish law, but it was the propriety of fasting on certain occasions. The argument seems to be that Jesus showed the absurdity of his disciples fasting, as a sign of mourning, while he was with them; this would vindicate his disciples in not following the custom of the Pharisees to fast and impress the lesson that the value of fasting was only when proper occasions demanded it.

[Skins were used for bottles in the days of Jesus. When they were new, and new wine was put into them, they would stretch when the wine fermented and would not burst. When they became old they would burst from the fermentation of the wine. Jesus evidently intended to teach that his disciples were correct in not following the traditions of the Pharisees in fasting.]

18, 19 **While he spake these things unto them.**—We have here a record of two miracles which interlocked—the second occurring during the stages of the first; they serve to illustrate the great number and frequency of Jesus' miracles. A record of these miracles is found also in Mark (5: 22-43) and in Luke (8: 41-56). The record given by Matthew is most brief, as he omitted many of the incidents recorded by Mark and Luke; Mark's record seems to be the fullest and most in detail. Mark and Luke place the raising of Jairus' daughter immediately after the cure of the Gadarene demoniac; but they do not say that it took place just as Jesus landed on the western side of the Sea of Galilee. Matthew seems to make the miracle occur immediately after the feast in his house. "There came a ruler," Mark and Luke say, "one of the rulers of the synagogue, Jairus by name." This ruler came and "worshipped him"; that is, he bowed down before him as an expression of profound respect; he fell at the feet of Jesus and besought him saying, "My daughter is even now dead: but come and lay thy hand upon her, and she shall live." Mark uses a term which denotes "my dear little daughter," while

9: 20-22.] MATTHEW 211

him, and *so did* his disciples. 20 And behold, a woman, who had an issue of blood twelve years, came behind him, and touched the border of his garment: 21 for she said within herself, If I do but touch his garment, I shall be ⁶made whole. 22 But Jesus turning and seeing her said, Daughter, be of good cheer; thy faith hath ⁷made thee whole. And the woman was ⁶made whole

⁶Or, *saved*
⁷Or, *saved thee*

Luke records it, "for he had an only daughter, about twelve years of age, and she was dying." Matthew omits the message from the house (Luke 8: 49) and states the case briefly: she is just dead; the father had left her dying, and he thought perhaps that she was dead by the time he came to Jesus. At his earnest request Jesus arose and followed him; his disciples accompanied him, but an interference occurred as they were on the way to Jairus' house.

20-22 **And behold, a woman, who had an issue of blood twelve years.**—This interruption naturally delayed the arrival of Jesus at Jairus' house; the woman is described as having "an issue of blood twelve years." We not told any of the particulars of the nature of the hemorrhage, but the obvious supposition is probably correct. (Lev. 15: 19-33.) She had suffered for twelve years and had sought in vain physicians to heal her, but grew worse rather than better. She had faith in Jesus' power to heal her. Jesus and his disciples were following Jairus, and a multitude of people was following them; this poor woman "came behind him, and touched the border of his garment"; literally "border" means a tassel of threads suspended from each of the four corners of the upper garment; it means the fringe worn on the border of the outer garment. (Num. 15: 38.) She had said or reasoned within herself that "if I do but touch his garment, I shall be made whole." Her faith in Jesus' power to heal her was so great that she thought that if she could but just touch his garment or the fringe on his garment she could be made whole. Such a faith moved her to press her way through the crowd to Jesus and stretch forth her hand that she might touch his garment. She had heard of Jesus and believed that she would be cured by touching the border of his garment. She did this. Matthew omits the facts narrated by Mark and Luke that Jesus insisted on being told who had touched him; the disciples taught that it

from that hour. 23 And when Jesus came into the ruler's house, and saw the flute-players, and the crowd making a tumult, 24 he said, Give place: for the damsel is not dead, but sleepeth. And they laughed him to scorn. 25 But when the crowd was put forth, he entered in, and took her by the hand; and the damsel arose. 26 And ⁸the fame hereof went forth into all that land.

⁸Gr. *this fame.*

---

was preposterous to make such inquiry as there was a great multitude thronging about him. Jesus turned and saw the woman and said, "Daughter, be of good cheer; thy faith hath made thee whole." Her faith had brought her to Jesus; it had caused her to press through the thronging multitude to reach him, and now she was blessed by the recognition of her faith and a complete cure of her ailment. Her faith had been rewarded by the restoration of her health. Her faith was not the source of the healing, but it brought her into touch with Jesus who had the power to heal.

23-26 **And when Jesus came into the ruler's house.**—The healing of the woman took place at the time that she touched Jesus and there was a short delay in his journey, but Matthew resumes the narrative without any further interruption. Jesus went into the house of Jairus and "saw the flute-players, and the crowd making a tumult." While Jesus was talking to the woman word had been received that Jairus' daughter was dead, and it was the custom for the relatives and special friends of the dying person to gather round a couch, and the moment the breath ceased they would break out into loud cries, with every exclamation and sign of the most passionate grief.

Frequently the friends and relatives would exhaust themselves and would hire professional mourners, especially women, who would keep up the loud, wailing cry throughout the day and night. (Jer. 9:17; 16:6; Ezek. 24:17; Amos 5: 16.) People of wealth could afford to hire musicians, and Jairus being a ruler of the synagogue, we find that the flute players had already arrived when Jairus and Jesus arrived. Jesus asked that they give him opportunity and space to enter the house or room, and added that "the damsel is not dead, but sleepeth." The figurative language used by Jesus here was not understood by the people; death is frequently spoken of as

27 And as Jesus passed by from thence, two blind men followed him,

a sleep; but these people "laughed him to scorn." They derided him; they knew that she was dead; they did not understand the meaning of Jesus' language. At the command of Jesus the crowd left the room and Jesus in the presence of Peter, James, and John and the father and mother "took her by the hand; and the damsel arose." In the presence of these five persons who could be witnesses to the miracle Jesus brought the damsel to life; the noisy crowd and minstrels were excluded from the presence of so sacred a scene. Jesus did not take her by the hand to raise her up, but accompanied his miracle with some outward act. Peter took Dorcas by the hand to lift her up, but that was after she was restored to life. "The damsel arose" shows that Jesus did not raise her up; according to Mark and Luke, Jesus had said, "Damsel, I say unto thee, Arise," and "Maiden, arise." "Her spirit returned, and she rose up immediately"; Jesus then commanded that food be given her. The fame of Jesus spread abroad in the land because of what he had done.

27 And as Jesus passed by from thence, two blind men followed him.—Matthew is the only one that gives a record of this miracle; the remainder of chapter nine records things peculiar to Matthew. The blind man at Jericho (Matt. 20: 29-34) and the man born blind (John 9) were distinct from this miracle. Probably as Jesus and his disciples left the house of Jairus, these "two blind men followed him." Blindness was common in that eastern country; blindness was one of the very common afflictions of the natives of Palestine; the blear eyes, often crusted round with dried secretion and fly-infested, make some of the most sickening sights that may be seen in a Syrian village today. This common affliction in Palestine was thought to be due to ophthalmia, caused partly by the sun glare and partly by lack of cleanliness. These two blind men cried out as they followed Jesus, saying, "Have mercy on us, thou son of David." They present a contrast between their conduct and Jairus'; he was quiet and reverential, but these two then cried aloud with importunity like Bartimaeus,

crying out, and saying, Have mercy on us, thou son of David. 28 And when he was come into the house, the blind men came to him: and Jesus saith unto them, Believe ye that I am able to do this? They say unto him, Yea, Lord. 29 Then touched he their eyes, saying, According to your faith be it done unto you. 30 And their eyes were opened. And Jesus [9]strictly charged

[9]Or, sternly

"Have mercy on us, thou son of David." "Son of David" was a designation frequently used of the Messiah. (Matt. 12: 23; 15: 22; 20: 31; 21: 9, 15; 22: 44, 45.) Blind men had doubtless heard of the miracles that Jesus had already performed, and may have just learned of his raising Jairus' daughter from the dead. Jesus did not speak of himself as the "son of David."

28, 29 **And when he was come into the house, the blind men came to him.**—"The house" was the house to which he returned from Jairus' house; it may have been Matthew's house or Peter's house, or some other which Jesus made his usual place of abode at Capernaum. It is to be observed that all that Matthew records here occurred at Capernaum. These blind men followed Jesus into the house; the failure to notice them at first was probably designed to strengthen their faith, and to avoid the excitement which another public miracle would produce. Before healing the blind men Jesus asked them, "Believe ye that I am able to do this?" The emphasis here may be placed on "believe," as Jesus wanted to show them his power as proof of his claim to be the Messiah. They had shown faith by following Jesus, but he demanded an expression of their faith, hence the question. Jesus replied, "According to your faith be it done unto you"; that is, let it be done to you according to your faith. He touched "their eyes" as he said this to them. Touching their eyes was a natural and kindly act, like taking the hand of one prostrate with fever. His touch also would show that the miraculous power emanated from him. "According to your faith" is an important expression, which shows the relation of man's faith to God's grace. This is a general principle upon which God bestows his spiritual blessings upon man; we will receive them according to our faith.

30, 31 **And their eyes were opened.**—They received their

them, saying, See that no man know it. 31 But they went forth, and spread abroad his fame in all that land.

sight; Matthew uses a common Hebrew expression here. (2 Kings 6: 17; Isa. 35: 5.) We notice here the ease with which Jesus restored sight to the blind; it was with a mere touch of his infinite power. It was instantaneous; there was no gradual process of healing as is usual in cases of man's healing the afflicted. They received the faculty of sight as proof that they had faith in his ability to help them and that it was not misplaced. We have no means of determining whether this physical blessing was attended with any spiritual blessing. Jesus "strictly charged them, saying, See that no man know it." Some think that "strictly charged" involved the idea of anger or great displeasure in case of disobedience (Mark 1: 43); others say that he "sternly" charged them not to make any report of what he had done for them. We do know that Jesus commanded strict silence on their part as to what he had done for them. He had just given a similar command concerning the daughter of Jairus (Mark 5: 43); he did not want the report of his miracles of healing published so that multitudes would beseech for help and he would not have sufficient time to preach and teach his disciples. His mission to earth was not merely to heal diseases, but to preach the gospel.

But they went forth, and spread abroad his fame in all that land.—It would seem strange that they would be so disobedient to his command; we can hardly believe that they rebelliously disobeyed his command; they probably thought Jesus' command not to tell it was due to his modesty, and that common gratitude on their part demanded that they give credit or honor to whom honor was due. We cannot believe that they were so ungrateful that they would willfully disobey his command, for one who had power to restore sight would have power to punish for disobedience. Jesus was not seeking any notoriety as a "divine healer"; his miracles were to confirm his claim that he was the Messiah. However, their failure to obey his command cannot be put to their credit; good impulses should never be held to justify positive disobedience.

32 And as they went forth, behold, there was brought to him a dumb man possessed with a demon. 33 And when the demon was cast out, the dumb man spake: and the multitudes marvelled, saying, It was never so seen in

32-34 And as they went forth, behold, there was brought to him a dumb man possessed with a demon.—This case is not mentioned by any of the other writers; "and as they went forth," that is, as they "were going" out of the house in which they had been where Jesus healed the two blind men; "they" is slightly emphatic, standing in contrast to the next person who came to be healed. There was "brought to him a dumb man" who was also possessed with a demon. The word for "dumb" in the original also means "deafness" (Matt. 11: 5; Mark 7: 32; Luke 7: 22); it means "dull" or "blunted"; in the New Testament the word is used only of hearing and speaking, the meaning in each case being determined by the context. We are not told who brought this afflicted man to Jesus; in addition to being "dumb" he was "possessed with a demon." It may be that his dumbness was due to the demon which he possessed; those who were possessed of demons were affected in different ways; some were deprived of reason (Mark 5: 15); some were deprived of one or more of the senses. Later Matthew mentions one who was possessed of a demon, and "blind and dumb." (Matt. 12: 22.)

And when the demon was cast out, the dumb man spake.—Jesus never failed; the demon was cast out and the effect was that "the dumb man spake"; the cause being removed, the dumb man spoke again, to the amazement of the people who had never seen such a case; they said, "It was never so seen in Israel." The multitude was amazed because they had never seen such before; Jesus was doing in their midst that which they had never seen before; Jesus was the wonder-working prophet among them and hence many are ready to believe on him as the Messiah. Prophets had miraculously healed the sick and raised the dead, but it was a prerogative of the Messiah to cast out demons; the pretended exorcisms of the Jews had never been followed by such results as they now witnessed.

Israel. 34 But the Pharisees said, [10]By the prince of the demons casteth he out demons.

[10]Or, *In*

But the Pharisees said, By the prince of the demons casteth he out demons.—They could not deny the miracle; it was evidence of superhuman power; there were only two alternatives for these Pharisees to take: either Jesus cast out demons by the power of God, or he did by the power of the devil. If he exercised the power of God, then God was with him and he was true in making his claim in being the Messiah; if the Jews rejected him, they must reject the power by which Jesus cast out demons; they did this by attributing his power to that of the devil. The devil was "the prince of the demons"; the demons were the agents of the devil. These Pharisees rejected Jesus in their unbelief. Faith in Jesus as the Son of God is the noblest possible attitude of the soul; sneering at that faith is the most ignoble attitude of the soul, and leads the soul into the blackest peril. It seems that Jesus made no reply to these Pharisees at this time; the insulting charge was blasphemy against both Jesus and God.

2. THE NEED OF MORE LABORERS
9: 35-38

35 And Jesus went about all the cities and the villages, teaching in their

35 Jesus went about all the cities and the villages, teaching. —This was Jesus' second missionary tour in Galilee; the first Matt. 4: 23. "Cities and the villages" were about the same as in modern times; villages were unincorporated and cities were larger centers of inhabitants. This is identified with the tour recorded by Luke 8: 1; the first tour occurred some six months before this. His work is expressed by "teaching in their synagogues, and preaching the gospel of the kingdom." "Synagogue" was the place of study and worship among the Jews; Jesus visited the synagogue at the hours of worship as a teacher; he had a new message; he both taught and preached; he taught them the will of the Father and proclaimed the glad tidings, or "the gospel of the kingdom."

synagogues, and preaching the [11]gospel of the kingdom, and healing all manner of disease and all manner of sickness. 36 But when he saw the multitudes, he was moved with compassion for them, because they were distressed

[11]See marginal note on ch. 4. 23.

Jesus was doing some preparatory work to sending out his disciples.

In addition to his preaching and teaching he healed "all manner of disease and all manner of sickness." "Disease," a weakness, want of health and vigor; "sickness," positive ailment; he healed their temporary ailments and also their permanent ailments. His chief purpose was to teach and preach, but he healed their diseases. He was a divine healer and by his power to heal their diseases he established his claim as a teacher come from God. Many lost sight of his teaching and were blessed only by his healing.

36 **He was moved with compassion for them.**—The sympathies of Jesus are deeply moved by the sight of great multitudes, hungry for the bread of life, and yet more by their spiritually forlorn condition. This is frequently stated of Jesus (Matt. 14: 14; Mark 1: 41; 6: 34); when he saw the vast multitudes attracted by the fame of his miracles, and heard their cries for mercy, he was moved with pity; this continued throughout his ministry in Galilee. He saw the people not only afflicted with all manner of diseases, but they were as "sheep not having a shepherd." They were scattered abroad. Many of them came from other parts of Galilee and beyond the Jordan and were fatigued with journeying and dispersed about the fields in search of food and the necessary things of life. He saw the people neglected by those who ought to have been teachers; they were ignorant, helpless, hopeless, dying, and unfit to die; the sight moved him to deep pity. The figure of the flock and shepherd was familiar in Palestine. They were in a pitiable condition as they were shepherdless and scattered. He was their true and rightful shepherd; he came to revive them and bring them back to the fold. Those who should have been interested in them were like wolves instead of shepherds; he was deeply moved for the poor misled people whose guilt he merges in their misery, imputing that

and scattered, as sheep not having a shepherd. 37 Then saith he unto his disciples, The harvest indeed is plenteous, but the laborers are few. 38 Pray ye therefore the Lord of the harvest, that he send forth laborers into his harvest.

---

guilt all the more severely to those who had been instead of their shepherds their deceivers.

37, 38 The harvest indeed is plenteous.—Such a scene would call forth this statement. The figure is changed from flock and shepherd to field and harvesters. There was an abundant harvest; so much teaching needed; the people so ignorant and helpless; but the laborers were few. The harvest of souls was ready, but there were but few laborers or those who were interested in the spiritual condition of the people. The harvest is a frequent symbol in the Bible of spiritual work. God is the husbandman (John 15: 1); the world is a field (Matt. 13: 38); faithful disciples are workmen whom the Lord employs (Matt. 20:1); souls are God's husbandry (1 Cor. 3:9); the faithful children of God are separated from sinners by a process of threshing and winnowing (Isa. 21: 10; Matt. 3: 12); the end of the world witnesses the gathering of the grain in the barns and the destruction of tares (Matt. 13: 30). The more bountiful the harvest, the greater number of laborers needed; this was true while Jesus was on earth; it is equally true today.

Pray ye therefore the Lord of the harvest.—The spiritual condition is uppermost in the mind of Jesus; the scribes and Pharisees, the teachers of the people were worse than worthless as shepherds and bishops of human souls; the great mass of people had no religious shepherds and were in an ignorant state concerning the law and the prophets. Jesus exhorts his disciples to "pray" for more laborers. They could not pray for laborers without being impressed that they were to labor themselves. Jesus is about to send his apostles out and this exhortation is a part of their preparation to do faithful work. No one can set limits to the resources of the Lord of the harvest when his sympathizing people cry unto him for help. It is the duty of all Christians to pray that faithful ones may be prepared to go into the harvest to gather souls unto salvation.

In the harvest, when the grain is ripe, men go in with sickles and gather it, bind it into bundles to be kept in the garners, leaving the tares to be burned; so the world at that time was likened to a harvest because men were ripe for knowledge, ready to hear, and in many instances to become disciples of Jesus. Only teachers were wanting to instruct them in "the gospel of the kingdom." Jesus immediately appointed and sent on a short mission the twelve disciples.

3. APOSTLES CHOSEN; COMMISSIONED; SENT FORTH
10: 1-33

1 And he called unto him his twelve disciples, and gave them authority

---

1 He called unto him his twelve disciples.—This follows immediately Jesus' observation of the conditions of the people as represented in the figures of the flock and shepherd, harvest and laborers. There is no break in the context and only the division of chapters marks a wider separation than the context shows. It seems that Jesus had chosen his twelve apostles before this. (Mark 3: 14; Luke 6: 13.) He had made a number of disciples, and from his disciples he now chooses his twelve apostles; they were to be his more intimate friends and witnesses (Acts 1: 21, 22), who were afterwards to become the messengers of the gospel. The name "disciple" means "learner"; Jesus was with them and instructing them. After his ascension they were to be independent teachers of others, and were called "apostles," or those sent, i.e., messengers. There were at first those who had merely followed him because they desired to learn more of him; but now these are directly and specially appointed for a particular work. They were qualified to do that which Jesus sent them to do. He gave them "authority over unclean spirits" and "to heal all manner of disease and all manner of sickness." They had power to work miracles to convince the people that they were sent of God. By working miracles of this kind they would command the attention and respect and confidence of the people; when these were had, they could teach them. God has never called and sent any one to do anything for him but that he has qualified that one to do the work; all whom he has

over unclean spirits, to cast them out, and to heal all manner of disease and all manner of sickness.

2 Now the names of the twelve apostles are these: The first, Simon, who is called Peter, and Andrew his brother; [12]James the *son* of Zebedee, and John his brother; 3 Philip, and Bartholomew; Thomas, and Matthew

---

[12]Or, *Jacob*

---

called have in some measure been qualified to do the work for which they were called to do. We are not told here whether these twelve should use at their own discretion the power given to them or whether it would be used under the special promptings of the Holy Spirit; neither are we informed as to the limitations, if any, of the exercise of this authority; they had full authority to do that which the Lord wanted them do do.

2-4 **Now the names of the twelve apostles are these.**—By a careful comparison of the four different catalogs of the apostles given in the New Testament, we find that they may be divided into three groups, each group being headed by the same name, and each group including the same name, but with the lower names in each group variously arranged.

Matt. 10: 2-4	Mark 3: 16-19	Luke 6: 14-16	Acts 1: 13
Simon Peter	Simon Peter	Simon Peter	Peter
Andrew, his brother	James	Andrew	John
James, son of Zebedee	John	James	James
John, his brother	Andrew	John	Andrew
Philip	Philip	Philip	Philip
Bartholomew	Bartholomew	Bartholomew	Thomas
Thomas	Matthew	Matthew	Bartholomew
Matthew	Thomas	Thomas	Matthew
James, son of Alphæus	James	James	James
Lebbeus, Thaddeus	Thaddeus	Simon Zelotes	Simon Zelotes
Simon, the Canaanite	Simon	Judas, son of James	Judas, son of James
Judas Iscariot	Judas Iscariot	Judas Iscariot	. . . .

Peter was a native of Bethsaida and was placed at the head of the list of apostles and was given the keys of the kingdom of heaven. Andrew was the brother of Peter and was a disciple of John the Baptist. James and John were sons of Zebedee and were grouped with Peter. Peter and Andrew, James and John were two pairs of brothers. Philip was also from Bethsaida; Thomas had two names, the other was Didymus, and signifies twin; he has been called "the doubting apostle,"

the ¹publican; ²James the *son* of Alphæus, and Thaddæus; 4 Simon the ³Canananæan, and Judas Iscariot, who also ⁴betrayed him.
    5 These twelve Jesus sent forth and charged them, saying, Go not into *any* way of the Gentiles, and enter not into any city of the Samaritans: 6 but go rather to the lost sheep of the house of Israel. 7 And as ye go, preach,

¹See marginal note on ch. 5. 46.
²Or, *Jacob*
³Or, *Zealot*. See Lk. 6. 15; Acts 1. 13.
⁴Or, *delivered him up*

---

but this epithet conveys the wrong idea about him. Matthew is always called the publican. James, the son of Alphæus, has been called "James the Less"; it is thought that his mother was Mary, the sister of Mary the mother of Jesus. Lebbeus was surnamed Thaddeus; he is called Thaddeus by Mark and Judas by Luke. Simon the Canaanite is the least known of all the twelve; he is not mentioned in the New Testament other than in the catalog of apostles. Bartholomew is supposed to be identical with Nathanael, mentioned in first chapter of John's gospel. Judas Iscariot is styled by Luke as the traitor; his name is uniformly brought last because he was least respected of the apostles.

5, 6 **These twelve Jesus sent forth.**—Jesus sent these twelve on a limited commission; he gave them the universal commission after his resurrection. He first told them where they should not go; they were forbidden to go to "the Gentiles" and "any city of the Samaritans." We are not told why they were forbidden to go to the Gentiles and Samaritans. One road led through Samaria, and another went around through Perea. At this time they are limited to Palestine and to Israel. Jesus' personal ministry was limited in the same way. The Samaritans had a corrupted form of worship and a traditional copy of the law. At the time Jesus was on earth the Jews had no dealings with the Samaritans. (John 4: 9.)

After telling them where they should not go, Jesus then tells them where they are to go—"to the lost sheep of the house of Israel." "Lost sheep" is a figurative expression that Jesus uses to show the desolate condition of the Israelites; they were like sheep without a shepherd and were wandering from the true fold. They were children of the covenant, yet their leaders had deceived them and they were not disposed to

saying, The kingdom of heaven is at hand. 8 Heal the sick, raise the dead, cleanse the lepers, cast out demons: freely ye received, freely give. 9 Get

obey the voice of the shepherd. "The house of Israel" simply means the Jews of the covenant, or God's people. The time for the Gentiles to hear the gospel would come later, but now it belongs only to the lost sheep of the house of Israel.

7, 8 And as ye go, preach, saying, The kingdom of heaven is at hand.—They were to announce that the kingdom of heaven, the long-looked for Messiah and King, "was at hand." This was a spiritual kingdom, hence it is called the kingdom "of heaven," in contrast to all other kingdoms which were of the earth. Their central theme was the same which John the Baptist had introduced and which Jesus had proclaimed. Under his preaching they had enjoyed ample opportunities to learn what this kingdom meant, what it implies; but as we see later they had misconceptions of its nature which they must correct. When they proclaimed the approach of "the kingdom of heaven," they, of course, implied the coming of the Messiah or its King. The kingdom had not appeared at this time; "at hand" simply means that it drew nigh or approached. (Matt. 21: 1, 34; Mark 11: 1; Luke 15: 25.) In their preaching they did not instruct the people, but simply raised an expectancy of it, and in that way prepared the way for instruction which Jesus afterward gave.

They were not only to preach, but they were to "heal the sick, raise the dead, cleanse the lepers, cast out demons." They were given power to do this. This is the first bestowal of miraculous power on the disciples. Their preaching was to be confirmed by miracles. The four diseases which these miracles removed were sickness, leprosy, death, and demons. They had freely received and they were to give freely; they were to sell no miracles, not to sell the gospel; no bribe could be taken for healing any one. The apostleship, the gospel, and the power were received by them without price and so they are to give without price. This implies that those who were freely blessed would be grateful and would supply such temporary needs of the apostles that would enable them to fill their mission. They were to use freely their great powers

you no gold, nor silver, nor brass in your ⁵purses; 10 no wallet for *your* journey, neither two coats, nor shoes, nor staff: for the laborer is worthy of

---
⁵Gr. *girdles.*

---

without prejudice or favor for the relief of human suffering. This would win the good will of the people, attest their high commission, and would illustrate the blessedness of the gospel of spiritual salvation.

9, 10 Get you no gold, nor silver, nor brass in your purses. —They were to lean on divine care during their brief journey. Here their outfit is expressed in negative terms; they were not to take those things which would burden them on their journey; they were to go with their gospel of salvation and their miracle-working powers, and then throw themselves upon the gratitude and hospitality of the people for their bread and their transient home comforts. Gold, silver, and brass were used as money then; brass was used as money in the smaller coins as we now use copper pennies. Their "purse" was in their loose outer robe which was commonly worn by the Jews and gathered at the waist by a sash or girdle; this was drawn close in labor or traveling to keep the garment away from the feet; the hollow part of the robe over the bosom was used as a pocket to carry valuables or money. They were to take "no wallet" or traveling bag or sack large enough to carry food; it was usually made of leather or coarse cloth, and hung over the shoulders. They were not to take "two coats, nor shoes, nor staff." They were not to provide extra shoes or clothing for comforts, but were to be uncumbered; they were to go as swift messengers to arrest attention by their unusual conduct in passing through the country, so unprepared for a journey, and impress on men the truth of the near-approaching kingdom as much by their manner as their words. They were to take only one staff (Mark 6: 8); this was to aid them in walking and protect them from common dangers; "for the laborer is worthy of his food." This maxim applies always to the work of the Lord. They being workmen for God to build up the people in spiritual things are justly deserving of a temporal support; it is not best for the people to receive such blessings, and not share in the support of

his food. 11 And into whatsoever city or village ye shall enter, search out who in it is worthy; and there abide till ye go forth. 12 And as ye enter into the house, salute it. 13 And if the house be worthy, let your peace come upon it: but if it be not worthy, let your peace return to you. 14 And who-

those who bring the blessings to them; such would cultivate ingratitude on the part of the people and they would soon appreciate less the valuable blessings brought to them. The more favors received and blessings bestowed upon any one the more grateful that one should be; God declares it to be the duty of Christians to give liberally to the help of those whom he has sent to minister (Luke 10: 7; 1 Cor. 9: 7; Gal. 6: 6); they are to be treated with due reverence (John 13: 20; 1 Thess. 4: 8; 5: 12).

11-13 And into whatsoever city or village ye shall enter, search out who in it is worthy.—Jesus had now limited their territory and had given them power to work miracles and had told them what to proclaim, and had in a negative way told them how they should be dressed, and now he tells them about their conduct. They were to inquire for some worthy host, that is, some good and pious Jew, a "son of peace," and hospitable. (Luke 7: 4.) They were not to change their lodging from pride or luxury, nor to go "from house to house"; they were to maintain the dignity of the servants of God and prophets of God; levity and fickleness detract from the dignity of their message. They were on a swift journey through the country, villages, and cities with an important message and were to make inquiry for those citizens who were "worthy" and were to deliver their message to that house and hasten on. They were to remain in this house until they had delivered their message and then hasten on to another. "And as ye enter into the house, salute it"; they were to say, "Peace be to this house." (Luke 10: 5.) It was a Jewish custom, meaning a kindly wish for the prosperity of the family, which is always most surely promoted by peace. If the house be worthy, the blessings should abide upon it; if it were not worthy, their prayers should return to them; the blessings that they had invoked, God would withhold from that house, and give it back to the messengers.

soever shall not receive you, nor hear your words, as ye go forth out of that house or that city, shake off the dust of your feet. 15 Verily I say unto you, It shall be more tolerable for the land of Sodom and Gomorrah in the day of judgment, than for that city.
16 Behold, I send you forth as sheep in the midst of wolves: be ye there-

14, 15 And whosoever shall not receive you.—Jesus tells how they were to salute the house that was worthy, and then tells them how they were to treat that house that was unworthy. The underlying principle is that guilt and condemnation are measured by the light sinned against. The Jews considered the dust of a heathen country polluted (Amos 7: 17) and shook it off them when entering their own land. "Shake off the dust of your feet" was a testimony against the lack of hospitality and the rejection of Jesus' messengers and message. By this symbolical act the apostles renounced all intercourse with the obstinate Jews, and absolved themselves from all responsibility connected with their mission.

Jesus himself passes judgment upon the city that rejected his messengers: "It shall be more tolerable for the land of Sodom and Gomorrah in the day of judgment, than for that city." Sodom in her moral darkness could not incur such fearful guilt as those cities at whose doors messengers of Jesus had knocked in vain. Gen. 19: 1-28 describes the sins of Sodom and Gomorrah and the miraculous destruction of them; Jude informs us that the destruction of these cities was symbolic of the eternal wrath of God. (Verse 7.) The temporal fire is a visible emblem of the invisible fire never to be quenched. "It shall be more tolerable" is a phrase that Jesus uses to express the fearful condemnation that shall come upon the cities that reject him. "Day of judgment"; this is the first mention that we have of this time in the New Testament; the Jews believed in the coming of this day, which they called "the day of Jehovah" or the "great day." (Isa. 13: 6; 34: 8; Zeph. 1: 18; Joel 2: 11.) The punishment here mentioned is in the future and has reference to the day of general judgment. The condemnation may imply a persistent rejection of the blessings of the gospel.

16-18 Behold, I send you forth as sheep in the midst of wolves.—Here Jesus expands his instruction from the view of

fore wise as servants, and ᵉharmless as doves. 17 But beware of men, for they will deliver you up to councils, and in their synagogues they will scourge you; 18 yea and before governors and kings shall ye be brought for my sake, for a testimony to them and to the Gentiles. 19 But when they

---

ᵉOr, *simple*

---

the present limited mission so as to include the warfare and sufferings of their entire service as apostles. He draws a vivid picture of the perils which they must encounter; they are as innocent, helpless sheep "in the midst of wolves." They are innocent, helpless sheep "in the midst of wolves." They are helpless, unarmed, undefended, to all appearances, and doomed to destruction. Their enemies shall be as eager to destroy them as wolves are to destroy sheep; only by their prudence and innocence will they be kept from such enemies; they are to be "wise as serpents, and harmless as doves." The serpent by his cunningness has found a place in the east as an example of wisdom and prudence; only the shrewd wisdom and prudence of the serpent are commended here, not its deceitful cunningness. The dove is a symbol of innocence and purity. His disciples are to be as innocent as sheep and as guileless as doves, yet not stupid and silly as those animals. Their prudence must not degenerate into guile, their simplicity must go hand in hand with the serpentine prudence. The serpent is the bodily emblem of Satan, and the dove is the bodily emblem of the Holy Spirit; Jesus' apostles must be shrewd like Satan, yet pure like the Holy Spirit.

Next, Jesus instructs his apostles about the character of some men; he warns them against such; "for they will deliver you up to councils, and in their synagogues they will scourge you." "Councils" mean the smaller courts in Palestine, yet including the Sanhedrin in Jerusalem. Scourging is mentioned as a punishment in the law. (Deut. 25: 13.) The victim was laid upon the ground and scourged with a whip of three lashes, so that thirteen blows would inflict thirty-nine stripes. This was the forty save one which Paul received. (2 Cor. 11: 24.) The synagogue was the ordinary place of the Jewish courts of justice. (Mark 13: 9; Acts 22: 19.) They should be brought before Roman officials such as Pilate, Felix, Festus, Herod, Agrippa, and the Roman emperor; two classes

deliver you up, be not anxious how or what ye shall speak: for it shall be given you in that hour what ye shall speak. 20 For it is not ye that speak, but the Spirit of your Father that speaketh in you. 21 And brother shall deliver up brother to death, and the father his child: and children shall rise up against parents, and [7]cause them to be put to death. 22 And ye shall be

---

[7]Or, *put them to death*

---

are mentioned here, governors and kings; Paul was brought before both classes as also was Jesus. This would give them the opportunity to testify for Jesus before these Gentile officials. In testifying for Jesus, they testified against those who were persecuting them. To testify in behalf of Jesus before those who are persecuting Jesus is to testify against the persecutors. This intimates that the gospel will be spread to distant lands and to other nations than the Jews.

19, 20 But when they deliver you up, be not anxious how or what ye shall speak.—The apostles would be delivered through treachery and betrayal by their own countrymen to the heathen powers; this would be done suddenly and through treachery; hence they would not have time to prepare their defense, and they need not make any preparation for defense, as it should be given to them "in that hour what ye shall speak." They would use all their natural powers, but were not to depend upon them only as aided and overruled by the Holy Spirit. They were to place themselves in the care of God and depend on divine aid as they were faithfully serving God. Jesus wanted his apostles to know in the outset the worst that would befall them. The Holy Spirit would guide them and aid them to win a way into the hearts of their hearers or defend them against temptations and persecutions which they could not bear. The Holy Spirit would give to them such language as would please God in their defense; they were to rely wholly upon God for his protection; they were to trust him for all things necessary to fill their mission.

21-23 And brother shall deliver up brother to death, and the father his child.—The persecution that should be brought against the apostles would also be waged against the disciples of Jesus; persecutions in which all natural ties should be disregarded were predicted and fulfilled; brother would give information to the magistrate or governor against brother, and

hated of all men for my name's sake: but he that endureth to the end, the same shall be saved. 23 But when they persecute you in this city, flee into the next: for verily I say unto you, Ye shall not have gone through the

---

father against child, and children against parents. This is a frightful description of persecution, when children shall accuse their parents of being Christians and cause them to be put to death. The hatred of the heathen and their persecutions of Christians have made the early accounts of the church one of the darkest pages in human history. It was soon discovered, first by the Pharisees and afterward by the pagan philosophers and rulers, that Christianity was an entirely new element in human society, and must either be crushed or it would triumph over everything else. Hence, the violence, the hostility to it in the minds of the people, the severe laws and persecutions of it by governors and emperors. The strife between truth and error invaded the sacred retreats of home, and everything which is here foretold by Jesus has repeatedly occurred.

And ye shall be hated of all men for my name's sake.—All classes of evil men, Jews, Gentiles, wise and ignorant, rulers and subjects, all have hated Christianity and persecuted those who faithfully lived it. Jesus knew that this would occur; he knew the long and eternal warfare between right and wrong, truth and error, the lovers of God and the lovers of wickedness. Only those who should endure to the end would receive the blessing. The endurance of persecution and the abhorrence of error was neither a fiery fanaticism nor a vain superstition; the early Christians endured this for the sake of Jesus; they suffered for truth, for Christ, and for God. To have once put faith in Christ is not the full condition of salvation; faith and perseverance of faith to the end are the complete conditions. One may renounce the faith as some did in the early days; the Savior once accepted may be afterward rejected; apostasy may forfeit the reward.

But when they persecute you in this city, flee into the next. —The apostles and early Christians were not necessarily cowards; they were obeying the command of Jesus when they fled from persecution. Heroism such as the world admires is not

cities of Israel, till the Son of man be come.
24 A disciple is not above his teacher, nor a ⁸servant above his lord. 25 It is enough for the disciple that he be as his teacher, and the ⁸servant as his lord. If they have called the master of the house, ⁹Beelzebub, how much

⁸Gr. *bondservant*.
⁹Gr. *Beelzebul*.

what Jesus required; his disciples who acted from the spirit of opposition, or the love of glory, were very apt to apostatize in time of danger. The true martyr never sought death, never made a display of heroism, and never failed, when reposing faith in Christ, to meekly suffer for his sake. Jesus says that work of bearing witness for him and suffering for him will not have been finished "till the Son of man be come." It is not clear just what is meant by "till the Son of man be come"; it would take place before all the cities of Israel should be evangelized, hence it would mean the coming of Christ to destroy the Jewish nationality. Commentators differ widely in their interpretation of this expression. It has been referred to the judgment day, or second advent of Christ; it may have a primary fulfillment in the limited mission of the apostles and finally an ultimate fulfillment in the second advent of Christ. Some think that it belongs to the destruction of Jerusalem; the most obvious meaning is that with the speediest circuit the disciples would not have gone over the cities of Israel till the Son of man be *come,* or that he would immediately follow them to those cities.

24, 25 **A disciple is not above his teacher.**—According to many Jewish proverbs, the pupil of the rabbi was far his inferior; if the master undergo indignity, still deeper insult must a servant accept. So if Jesus must suffer persecution and even death, his disciples may not hope to escape great sufferings. The teaching of Jesus here takes a broader range; the circumstances lead him to contemplate the Christian life as to violent persecution. His disciples should bear bravely and joyfully after Jesus had suffered and died. As they abused the master, the enemy would much more seek to intimidate his followers; "if they have called the master of the house Beelzebub, how much more them of his household!" "Beelzebub" is the Greek form of the name "Baal-zebub," the

10:25-28.] MATTHEW 231

more them of his household! 26 Fear them not therefore: for there is nothing covered, that shall not be revealed; and hid, that shall not be known. 27 What I tell you in the darkness, speak ye in the light; and what ye hear in

Philistine god worshiped at Ekron, and signified "the lord of flies" (2 Kings 1: 2); it is claimed that the Jews changed the name into "Beelzeboul," as it is in the Greek New Testament, lord of dung, or of idols, by way of throwing contempt on idolatry; the Jews gave this title to the prince of demons or unclean spirits, as he is the great patron of idolatry. Men have feared names of opprobrium in the mouths of prejudiced persons; such names have the force of condemnation or a curse. We are to fear God and hold to the truth, no matter what harsh names are hurled against us; think of the evil names now in use to impede the truth and persecute the Lord's people! Christians should gird their minds by this instruction of Jesus and do the right though others may hurl epithets against them; they called Jesus "Beelzebub."

26-28 **Fear them not.**—The disciples of Jesus are not to fear any of their enemies; they are not to fear any of the enemies of Jesus. There is no place for a coward in his service; there is nothing that is "covered that shall not be revealed." Persecution manifests itself in different forms, and it was beginning now to work in secret against Jesus; the usual policy of evil is to persecute the exponents of that which is good; evil attempts to make good appear bad; the enemy will not punish men as good men, but will attempt to make it appear that they are bad and deserve punishment; this requires that the reputation be blackened by falsehood; hence, Jesus admonishes that his disciples fear not their calumny, for it shall all be revealed or made clear; the truth will surely come to light, and your commission is to reveal truth. All the words and deeds of darkness and violence will be exposed in the light of God's judgment.

What Jesus taught his disciples privately they were to teach publicly; "and what ye hear in the ear, proclaim upon the house-tops." They were not to allow persecution to suppress the word, but they were to carry it forth from privacy to publicity. The pupil of the rabbi held his ear intent to receive

the ear, proclaim upon the house-tops. 28 And be not afraid of them that kill the body, but are not able to kill the soul: but rather fear him who is able to destroy both soul and body in [10]hell. 29 Are not two sparrows sold for a penny? and not one of them shall fall on the ground without your Father: 30 but the very hairs of your head are all numbered. 31 Fear not

---

[10]Gr. *Gehenna.*

---

the utterance of his master; he is to proclaim to all who will hear that which he learns from his master. We are told that it is still a custom in the East to make public proclamation to the city from a housetop; the public crier ascends the highest roof at hand and lifts up his voice in a long-drawn call. The enemies at their worst could only "kill the body," but could not "kill the soul." The disciples of Jesus were not to fear persecutors, but fear God; the persecutors can only kill the body; they cannot harm the soul. God is able to destroy both body and soul in hell. The destruction which persecutors bring upon the body is of small account when compared with the destruction of the soul; no word can portray the destruction of soul and body in hell. A fear of God's judgment, as well as reference for his majesty is the proper attitude to take toward God; to suffer meekly whatever persecutions may be brought upon Christians is the proper attitude to take toward the enemies of Christ.

29-33 Are not two sparrows sold for a penny?—This is the usual form of a question when an affirmative answer is expected. Sparrows abound in Palestine; they are still sold in the market, and are cheap because of their size and abundance. Luke has five sparrows for two farthings, the price being varied according to the number purchased, or "two pence." (Luke 12: 6.) A sparrow is a small, insignificant bird and is used here to show that God takes notice of them; not even the least thing shall escape the observation of God over his people. God knows all of his preachers and provides for their wants. If the hairs of the head are all numbered, how much more does he know all our thoughts, feelings, and wishes. If a sparrow shall not fall without his notice, how can a Christian be persecuted and die without his seeing it? God cares for the sparrows and has numbered the hairs of the head; surely he will not forget his disciples. He who fills im-

therefore: ye are of more value than many sparrows. 32 Every one therefore who shall confess [11]me before men, [12]him will I also confess before my Father who is in heaven. 33 But whosoever shall deny me before men, him will I also deny before my Father who is in heaven.

---

[11]Gr. *in me.*
[12]Gr. *in him.*

---

mensity with his presence and glory, who built the heavens and holds all the stars in his hand, yet marks every falling sparrow and counts the very hairs of our head will care for his disciples! Are these words very strong? The truth they set forth is yet stronger. If God numbers the hairs of the head, much more does he number the heartthrobs of our pain and measure the nerve twinges of all human suffering; if not a sparrow falls to the earth without him, then never a tear drops from the eye but in his sight; never a hope, dear to our heart, is withered; never a care can burden or a labor can weary us, but it touches the heart of our Father.

Fear not therefore: ye are of more value than many sparrows.—The great number of objects present in no wise forbids a just estimate of their relative worth; the pain of the tiniest sparrow God does not despise, but what can measure the tenderness of sympathy with which he enters into our frailties and griefs and trials? How much comfort and encouragement should the disciples of Jesus gather from these statements! Based on his tender care for his disciples, Jesus gives encouragement to all "who shall confess me before men." The promise is that Jesus will also confess them before the Father who is in heaven. To confess Jesus is to make him the object of our faith and life; it is to own him as a Savior; it is to honor him in the life; it is to espouse his cause and to face opposition and reproach for his sake. Those who do this he will honor as his friends before the Father. Jesus has just described the persecution and sufferings that one must endure in order to be his disciple; hence to confess him means to be willing to suffer for him and rejoice in the suffering. Those who understand the sufferings and refuse to confess Jesus because of persecution and hardships, he will disown them to the Father. It costs something to uphold the life of Jesus in our lives. To deny Jesus is to disown him as a Master for fear of man; he will disown them as his disciples in the judgment, unless, like Peter, one repents of the denial. Jesus represents himself here as the great judge of life and death. All who sincerely profess Christ unto the end he will own before the Father; all who deny him for any cause and continue in this attitude toward him to the end he will deny before the Father. The confession of Jesus which is made at the beginning of the Christian life is not directly alluded to here, but may be included in what is said here.

[There is a confession of Christ taught in the New Testament. (Matt. 10: 32, 33; Luke 12: 8.) This referred to the apostles and those already Christians confessing Christ. The apostles and disciples confessed him unto salvation. Those who refused to confess him did it to their condemnation. Some rulers "did not confess it, lest they should be put out of the synagogue." (John 12: 42.) Thus confession meant an obedience to him in life. All, in the church and out of it, desiring to be saved must confess him by a life of obedience to him. These did not do it because "they loved the glory that is of men more than the glory that is of God." (Verse 43.) Jesus Christ had witnessed this confession before Pontius Pilate. (1 Tim. 6: 13.) This was for faith in Jesus Christ, not a formal question to become a disciple.]

4. THE COST OF DISCIPLESHIP; ITS REWARDS
10: 34-42

34 Think not that I came to ¹⁸send peace on the earth: I came not to

---
¹⁸Gr. *cast.*

34-39 Think not that I came to send peace on the earth.—This paragraph continues Jesus' instruction to his apostles on their limited commission; he here expands more fully the point made in verses twenty-one and twenty-two. Angels announced peace on earth and good will to men at his birth; he is the "Prince of Peace," yet there is a sense in which his mission brought disturbance; from the meekness of his character and the blessings of his teachings one would think that nothing but peace would result; but not so; his mission to earth

¹³send peace, but a sword. 35 For I came to set a man at variance against his father, and the daughter against her mother, and the daughter in law against her mother in law: 36 and a man's foes *shall be* they of his own

was to separate the righteous from the wicked. Jesus' goodness is to attract to itself all the good who have affinity with it; and this affinity of the good for the good, and of evil for the evil, will produce a division, a ferment, a strife, "a sword." When the right goes forth into a world of wrong, there must be war; each principle will rally its own adherents and its own armor under its own banner, and terrible will be the struggle until right or wrong, heaven or hell, attain the victory; the disciples of Jesus believe in the ultimate victory of good, righteousness, peace, and God. Jesus gave spiritual peace which "passeth understanding" in the joys of forgiveness of sin, the hope of holiness, the satisfaction of a true, faithful obedience; but this peace was not given to the world. The Jews expected uninterrupted outward peace in the days of the Messiah, so Jesus corrects that misapprehension. He knew that his mission and truth would provoke persecution. The sword is the symbol of war, the very essence of the vision (Luke 12: 51), civil commotion, and domestic discord (Jer. 14: 13), the opposite of peace and concord.

For I came to set a man at variance against his father.—Though the gospel of Jesus proclaims peace and comes freighted with blessings for man, both individually and socially, yet its incidental results will be violent animosities of its foes against its friends; when God called Abraham he was to separate himself from his idolatrous people. The right, the pure, the good are at variance with the wrong, the defiled, the bad. Light is as much opposed to darkness as darkness is to light; truth would destroy error, and holiness hates sin. The truly converted mother will turn with horror from the impurity of her daughter; the ties of marriage are often dearer than the ties of consanguinity, yet even these must yield to higher claims, and the ties of God and truth are higher than any ties of man to man. So often the dividing principle cuts like a straight sword through the center of the family and divides it; upon either side of that line, born of the same blood, are the

household. 37 He that loveth father or mother more than me is not worthy

opposing adherents of heaven and hell. It was not the express mission of Jesus to so disturb human society, but his teachings have these results.

[Jesus is the "Prince of Peace." His advent was heralded by the angels crying, "Glory to God in the highest, and on earth peace among men." The end of his mission was to spread peace among men and to rule over a kingdom whose principle and rule is peace. This seems to contradict Matt. 10: 34-36, yet they are both true. Jesus means that the end of his mission and work is peace; but the immediate and preparatory influence of his mission will bring division and strife, war and destruction. No one person has ever excited the division, the strife, and destruction among men that the coming of Christ has done. His mission, his teaching, has been a continued cause of division and strife among men from the day of his advent until now, and the promise is yet for division and strife for years to come. Jesus requires his disciples to separate from all sin and evil and to make increasing war on all wrong and all wickedness. This conflict between good and evil begins in the heart of every person; the good and the evil that dwell in each heart are at enmity; they make war upon each other. The enmity is uncompromising and the conflict can end only with the destruction of the one or the other. This enmity and war rage not only in the heart of every man, but they rage between the good and the evil in the family, in the neighborhood, in the country, and among the whole race of mankind. This war can never end between good and evil, virtue and vice, between right and wrong, until one or the other triumphs and the other is brought to destruction. Back of these two principles are God and the devil. God is the author of all good and the guide and director of all the forces working for good in the universe. The devil is the author and guide of all sin and wickedness in the universe, and the guide and promoter of all the influences that work for evil.]

He that loveth father or mother more than me is not worthy of me.—The closest fleshly ties, when they come into

of me; and he that loveth son or daughter more than me is not worthy of me. 38 And he that doth not take his cross and follow after me, is not worthy of me. 39 He that ¹findeth his life shall lose it; and he that ²loseth his life for my sake shall find it.

¹Or, *found*
²Or, *lost*

---

competition with our duties to God, must be disregarded; but only when there is a conflict. Father and mother are here supposed to stand against Christ, and to throw their parental influence against the child's espousing his name. Jesus and his name can be second to none other; we must love him above all others, or not have his love. Truth is more authoritative than a parent. Jesus has done more for us than the nearest relative can possibly do; where the affections for parent would seduce us to sin their power must be rejected; Jesus must have full control of the heart and life. If one lets any earthly tie have precedence over our love for Jesus, we are "not worthy" of him. The condition of heart that lets anything shut out Jesus renders itself unfit for Jesus; he will not dwell in the heart without being supreme.

And he that doth not take his cross and follow after me, is not worthy of me.—Jesus thus early in his ministry intimates his death by crucifixion; the cross is the symbol of death by crucifixion. When a criminal was condemned to crucifixion, a part of his sentence was that he should carry his cross to the place of execution. To "take his cross" means to submit to the fate of trouble and persecution which was to come upon them; it means a willingness to suffer for Christ; he desires that his disciples have courage and faith to trust him in all trials which he may put upon them. This does not mean that one must carry the cross of Jesus, but it means that he must take up his own cross and bear it. Christ bore his own cross to his crucifixion, so his disciples should bear each his own cross to his own crucifixion. So the great crucified leader is to be followed by an endless train of crucified followers; they are crucified symbolically, in all their sufferings of mind or body, in behalf of Christ and truth. Each disciple who has the spirit of the Lord is crucified in fact or in readiness of mind; the spirit of Christ is the spirit of martyrdom. Paul expressed

40 He that receiveth you receiveth me, and he that receiveth me receiveth him that sent me. 41 He that receiveth a prophet in the name of a prophet shall receive a prophet's reward: and he that receiveth a righteous man in the name of a righteous man shall receive a righteous man's reward. 42

this to the Galatians. (Gal. 2: 18-21.) To "follow after me" literally means to attend him (Matt. 4: 25), to follow or imitate, to tread in his steps, imitate his example (Matt. 16: 24). It is not likely that his disciples understood his first prophetic hint of his crucifixion, but it is clear that he did. (John 12: 32, 33.) Jesus mentions two things that render one unworthy to be his disciple—to love father and mother more than him and to fail to bear the cross after him.

He that findeth his life shall lose it.—The one who attempts to find or save his life by avoiding the cross mentioned in the last verse shall lose his life; the word "findeth" is here used in the sense of "saveth" in order to form an antithesis with the word "loseth." If one apostatize and deny Jesus, and so find his life, he shall lose his soul, his hope, and the spirit of God, which is his true life; but he who bravely adheres to Christ and dies for his faith shall find by a short transit a life such as eye hath not seen, or mind conceived. By denying Christ before persecutors in order to escape persecution, one loses his soul; but when one remains faithful to Christ and suffers persecution even unto death, that one finds eternal life. Jesus means simply to say that he who, at the expense of duty and faithfulness, preserves his temporal life shall lose his eternal life; and he who, for the sake of Christ, sacrifices his temporal life shall inherit eternal life. The Greek word "psyche" signifies either "life" or "soul"; it the same word translated "soul" in verse twenty-eight.

40-42 **He that receiveth you receiveth me.**—Here Jesus concludes his instruction to his apostles for their limited commission. His apostles being his servants and going forth among the people represent him; those who receive the apostles and protect them because they are disciples and apostles of Christ and shall receive, if they will have faith, Jesus also. Rahab received the spies as servants of God, lodged them, served them in danger at her own risk, and sent them away, and was

And whosoever shall give to drink unto one of these little ones a cup of cold water only, in the name of a disciple, verily I say unto you he shall in no wise lose his reward.

---

saved and all her house. (Josh. 2: 8-22; Heb. 11: 31.) So did Obadiah in the wicked reign of Jezebel. (1 Kings 18: 3, 4.) To receive Christ is to receive his teachings; no one can reject the teachings of Christ and receive Christ; no one can reject the apostles and receive Christ; those who reject the apostles and their teaching reject Christ and have the condemnation of Christ, while those who accept them have the reward. Jesus expands this truth so that it applies not only to the apostles, but to a prophet or any disciple of Jesus. The apostles represented Christ as Christ represented the Father (John 20: 21; Heb. 3: 1), with this difference his representation was perfect (John 5: 19-37; 14: 9; Heb. 1: 3), while his apostles were imperfect (Gal. 2: 11-14). One who receives "a prophet" in the name of a prophet, that is, with a full recognition of his character and mission, in spite of the persecutions, shall receive a prophet's reward, that is, shall share both in the prophet's faith, his dangers, persecutions, and shall share in his reward.

And whosoever shall give to drink unto one of these little ones a cup of cold water only.—Jesus speaks tenderly of his apostles; calls them "little ones"; they were sheep in the midst of wolves harmless like doves, tender like little ones. "A cup of cold water" represents a very small service. The ones who give this in recognition of their apostleship, and because they were disciples of Jesus, shall receive a reward. Simply Jesus says you are my disciples, my representatives, and those who receive you receive me. Just as those who receive the prophet received a prophet's reward so those who receive you shall share in your reward. Even so small a favor as a cup of cold water, given to a disciple because he is such, evinces love to that disciple, and through him to his Lord. We are encouraged by the fact that the least service done to those who work in the name of Jesus is observed and rewarded of God. No act of service, no matter now small, escapes the observation of God. He observes who is kind to them, as Lydia was to Paul (Acts 16: 15), and those who throw difficulties in their way as did Diotrephes to John (3 John 9). All our daily experiences are recorded and God remembers them and gives due reward for them. The chief butler forgot Joseph when he was restored to his place (Gen. 41: 9), but the Lord never forgets any of his people who serve in his name. He will say to many who little expect it, in the resurrection morning, "I was hungry, and ye gave me to eat; I was thirsty, and ye gave me drink; I was a stranger, and ye took me in; naked, and ye clothed me; I was sick, and ye visited me; I was in prison, and ye came unto me. . . . Inasmuch as ye did it unto one of these my brethren, even these least, ye did it unto me." (Matt. 25: 35-40.)

This closes his instructions to his apostles for their mission. Mark and Luke say that the apostles immediately went out and fulfilled their mission. (Mark 6: 12; Luke 9: 6.)

5. MESSENGERS FROM JOHN THE BAPTIST; JESUS' ESTIMATE OF JOHN
11: 1-19

1 And it came to pass when Jesus had finished commanding his twelve disciples, he departed thence to teach and preach in their cities.

1 **And it came to pass when Jesus had finished commanding.**—The instruction given in chapter ten is here called "commanding"; he had finished his "commanding" them for their limited commission, and some of his teachings were expanded to all his disciples for all time; that is, the principles given by Jesus were universal. After sending "his twelve disciples" away on their hasty mission "he departed thence to teach and preach in their cities." "To teach" means to give instruction; this was done in their synagogue; to "preach" means to proclaim as a herald; this is more general and public than teaching. "Their cities" means the cities of Galilee. This verse could properly belong to the close of chapter ten, as it informs us how Jesus was engaged during the absence of his twelve apostles; while each pair of the apostles took their own way, Jesus himself was active about his Father's business.

2 Now when John heard in the prison the works of the Christ, he sent by his disciples 3 and said unto him, Art thou he that cometh, or look we for

2, 3 **Now when John heard in the prison.**—John had rebuked Herod for his sin and had been cast in prison. (Matt. 14:3.) Luke 7:18 says that "the disciples of John told him of all these things" while he was in prison and John the Baptist sent two disciples to inquire of Jesus whether he was really the Messiah; perhaps John's disciples still thought that the fame of Jesus would eclipse John's (John 3:25). Why did John make this inquiry? Commentators are not agreed as to the answer. Some think that John was despondent, discouraged, and doubted whether Jesus was the long-looked-for Messiah. John knew very well that Jesus was the expected Messiah (John 3:27-36); he had pointed Jesus out to his disciples as the Lamb of God that taketh away the sin of the world (John 1:29). How then could he doubt that Jesus was "he that cometh"? Others think that John made this inquiry for the benefit of his disciples who were mortified at his imprisonment, and disappointed because Jesus did not in so many words assert his Messiahship, and deliver his forerunner from prison. Again others think that John was not skeptical, but anxious; that he doubted not the divinity of Jesus, but wanted to know more about his future course; that John expected a more rapid development of the Messiah's kingship; Jesus claimed to be a prophet, and he could tell what would be John's destiny and the trend of affairs in general. It is useless to speculate as to why John made this inquiry; we accept the facts as stated by Matthew and rest our faith on these facts. John had been in prison about twelve months at Machærus, a point fifteen miles southeast from the northern extremity of the Dead Sea and about seventy miles distant from the cities on the Sea of Galilee; whether John doubted the divinity of Jesus, or whether he wished to suggest the expediency of pushing his claims to the Messiahship more vigorously and openly, or whether he would remind him that he had one faithful friend in hard confinement and great peril, or whether it were rather to satisfy his disciples than himself, must be left to conjecture.

another? 4 And Jesus answered and said unto them, Go and tell John the things which ye hear and see: 5 the blind receive their sight, and the lame walk, the lepers are cleansed, and the deaf hear, and the dead are raised up, and the poor have ³good tidings preached to them. 6 And blessed is he, whosoever shall find no occasion of stumbling in me.

³Or, *the gospel*

4-6 **And Jesus answered and said.**—Jesus' answer was clear but indirect; Jesus bids John's disciples to witness his works and report them faithfully. "Go and tell John the things which ye hear and see." Luke tells us that "in that hour he cured many of diseases and plagues and evil spirits; and on many that were blind he bestowed sight." (Luke 7: 21.) They would remember the words of Isaiah about the nation's Messiah and that the prophet specified these very miracles— opening blind eyes and deaf ears, giving feet to the lame, and songs to the dumb. (Isa. 35: 5, 6; 61: 1.) Most striking of all was that "the dead are raised up, and the poor have good tidings preached to them." No false prophet ever did this; no system of false religion ever made this its distinctive characteristic. The open invitation to see his works, and to tell all that they saw, shows that Jesus adopted none of the arts of an imposter. "The poor have good tidings preached to them"; the promises of the gospel are proclaimed to poor people, who were generally overlooked by religious teachers then and even now. The preaching of the gospel to "the poor" is classed with the miracles that Jesus wrought, and it shows that due consideration for the poor was as extraordinary as the working of miracles. The teachings of Jesus belong to the poor; the poor more readily accept them and are blessed by them. Jesus added a blessing to "whosoever shall find no occasion of stumbling in me." The humble life of Jesus was a stumbling block to many. How could one, of whose coming such great things had been foretold, remain in obscurity by his own choice? The time had not come for Jesus to explain this difficulty, hence he warns them, by a promise of blessing, not to deny him, because this one difficulty was yet unexplained. Jesus might have tacitly suggested that he was *not* disputing the supremacy of Cæsar, neither was he trying to unseat

7 And as these went their way, Jesus began to say unto the multitudes concerning John, What went ye out into the wilderness to behold? a reed shaken with the wind? 8 But what went ye out to see? a man clothed in soft *raiment?* Behold, they that wear soft *raiment* are in kings' houses. 9 [4]But wherefore went ye out? to see a prophet? Yea, I say unto you, and much more than a prophet. 10 This is he, of whom it is written, [5]Behold, I sent my messenger before thy face, Who shall prepare thy way before thee.

---

[4]Many ancient authorities read *But what went ye out to see? a prophet?*
[5]Mal. iii. 1.

---

the Herods or override their judicial authority or send their prisoners home; his work was to restore and lift up crushed men; there may have been a suggestive hint to John in these closing words—"Blessed is he, whosoever shall find no occasion of stumbling in me." John and others were not to stumble at the obscure appearance and the spiritual character of Christ's kingdom. (Matt. 16:23.)

7-10 **And as these went their way, Jesus began to say.**— Here we have Jesus' estimate of John. He did not praise John in the presence of John's disciples, but when they were gone he eulogized him lest the people should go away with an unjust depreciation of John. If John's messengers to Jesus made an unfavorable impression on any one, these words about John should correct it. Every word is in commendation. Some of the hearers had seen and heard John; what kind of a man did they find him? Was he easily shaken like the reed? "A reed shaken with the wind" is symbolic of a timeserver, an unstable person, one easily influenced by outward circumstances. John's fidelity to the truth, and his imprisonment for it, showed that he was not such a weak character. "Reeds" or cane grew profusely along the banks of the Jordan and shivered in every breeze; John was not like these reeds. For emphasis Jesus repeats the question and asks if they went out to see "a man clothed in soft raiment." Were you attracted into the wilderness of Judea to see an effeminate man dressed as a courtier; his raiment of camel's hair and leather girdle, locusts and wild honey, all showed that John did not live in luxury as fawning courtiers do; he was not found in kings' courts (Amos 7:13), though he found his way into a king's prison. The people would not have gone to the wilderness to find

11 Verily I say unto you, Among them that are born of women there hath not arisen a greater than John the Baptist: yet he that is ^obut little

^oGr. *lesser.*

---

such a man dressed in soft raiment, but would have gone to the palace of Herod or some other court.

Jesus further asked, "Wherefore went ye out? to see a prophet?" He then answered his own question and said, "Yea, I say unto you, and much more than a prophet." They went to find something better than kings or courtiers, namely, a prophet of God; Jesus assured them with emphasis that they were not mistaken. They had forgotten John's message. John was "much more than a prophet"; he not only foretold the future, but his own coming was foretold (Mal. 3: 1); he was born in a miraculous manner; he was filled with the Holy Spirit from his mother's womb (Luke 1: 15); he seems to have been a remarkably self-denying and righteous man; he closed the line of prophets, bore direct, open testimony to Jesus, baptized him, and saw the vision of the spirit at his baptism, and was thus the link that joins the old and new covenants. Indeed John was "much more than a prophet"; perhaps John did not surpass other prophets in iron firmness and fortitude, but he was honored with the task of being the forerunner of Christ. He was superior to a prophet in filling the mission that God had for him.

11 **Among them that are born of women.**—This idiom is found in Job 11: 12; 14: 1; 15: 14; 25: 4. It is a form of speech especially applied to the appearance of great persons. "A greater than John the Baptist"; he was spoken of by preceding prophets; he pointed out the fulfillment of their predictions concerning the Messiah, whose successful course he predicted after preparing the way before him. "Yet he that is but little in the kingdom"; John was not a citizen of the kingdom; Jesus had not established his kingdom at this time so John was not in the kingdom. However, the humblest member of the body of Christ or citizen of his kingdom is greater than John, because he is elevated from the position of a servant as under the law to the place of a child in our

in the kingdom of heaven is greater than he. 12 And from the days of John the Baptist until now the kingdom of heaven suffereth violence, and men of violence take it by force. 13 For all the prophets and the law

Father's house. Some apply this only to prophets and teachers in the church, but this seems to be too narrow an application of it; to be "great" in the gospel sense is to be good and humble, and diligent in serving God. Jesus simply says that the least in the kingdom is greater than John, because he is a member of the body of Christ and enjoys fuller and richer blessings.

12-15 **From the days of John the Baptist.**—From the beginning of John's ministry "the kingdom of heaven suffereth violence" "until now." This marks the definite period that Jesus had in mind—from the beginning of John's ministry down to the time that he was speaking; the "kingdom of heaven" suffered violence from the time that its preparatory stage began even unto the present stage of its development. "The kingdom of heaven" is used frequently by Matthew and means the kingdom of God on earth. It is here compared to a city under siege, or rather under assault by storm; it "suffereth violence, and men of violence take it by force." The figure alludes to the vast crowds that were baptized by John who pressed each other in a crowd with eager desire to get the benefits of the kingdom; perhaps they mistook the nature of the kingdom and when John announced it in the popular style of his ministry, they were ready to "rush into" it "and take it as by storm." Men of violence today get control of congregations and handle affairs in a violent way.

For all the prophets and the law prophesied until John.— The parallel in Luke says, "The law and the prophets were until John: from that time the gospel of the kingdom of God is preached, and every man entereth violently into it." (Luke 16: 16.) The idea seems to be that one forces oneself by violence into this stage of the development of the kingdom; it describes the impatience with which men were entering into the kingdom of God with a misunderstanding of its nature. The law contained types and prophecies of the future gospel (Heb. 10: 1); the coming of John was an epoch marking the change

prophesied until John. 14 And if ye are willing to receive ⁷it, this is Elijah, that is to come. 15 He that hath ears ⁸to hear, let him hear. 16 But whereunto shall I liken this generation? It is like unto children

---
⁷Or, *him*
⁸Some ancient authorities omit *to hear*.

---

of conditions pertaining to the kingdom; "the law and the prophets" foretold a future kingdom; John declared that this kingdom was "at hand." The "prophets and the law" had been the working agencies for saving men up to the coming of John; his preaching brought in some fresh elements of power; he was the prophet foretold under the name of "Elijah." (Matt. 4: 5, 6.) "And if ye are willing to receive it, this is Elijah." Jesus implies that they would hardly do so, as they expected Elijah the Tishbite to appear in person; nevertheless Jesus declares that John the Baptist is the "Elijah" which was designated by Mal. 4: 5 whom the Jews fondly expected, and some still expect, as the immediate forerunner of the Messiah; John is the antitype of the Messiah and was prophetically called "Elijah" as he came "in the spirit and power of Elijah." (Luke 1: 17.) They had asked John at one time in the early part of his ministry whether he was Elijah (John 1: 21), and he answered "I am not," meaning that he was not the Elijah in person that they expected to come. Jesus declared that John was the messenger of the Messiah, just before the destruction of the Jewish state, while the second temple was standing as Mal. 3: 1; 4: 5, 6 stated; and since the messenger of the Messiah had already come, they might expect the Messiah; or if Elijah was to herald the Messiah, and John was Elijah, then Jesus was the Messiah, "he that is to come." Jesus frequently used the expression to demand special attention, "he that hath ears to hear, let him hear." (Matt. 13: 9; Mark 4: 9; Luke 8: 8; Rev. 2: 7.)

16-19 But whereunto shall I liken this generation?—With all the impetuous zeal for the kingdom of God that the people had toward John the Baptist and the Messiah, their conduct was childish; hence Jesus represents them as "children sitting in the marketplaces, who call unto their fellows and say, We piped unto you, and ye did not dance." The ancient markets

sitting in the marketplaces, who call unto their fellows 17 and say, We piped unto you, and ye did not dance; we wailed, and ye did not ⁹mourn. 18 For John came neither eating nor drinking, and they say, He hath a demon. 19 The Son of man came eating and drinking, and they say,

⁹Gr. *beat the breast.*

were places in which not only men transacted their business, but children played with each other. The figure not only represents the attitudes of the people as childish, but it represents them as being like crowds of children who are dissatisfied with one another and the games which they are playing; it is like one set wanting this play and another that, one is angry or silent, while the others try to soothe and persuade to join in their sport. They were not pleased with John nor with Jesus; they wanted things their own way, or no way. "We piped unto you," why did you "not dance"? They mimic a wedding procession with singing and dancing, but it did not please them; they next "wailed," but they did "not mourn"; that is, they mimicked a funeral procession without any effect. They then complained against the other that they did not know what to do, when neither laughing nor crying with them in imitation of grown people would please them; so Jesus says that the present generation is obstinate, changeful, and capricious.

For John came neither eating nor drinking, and they say, He hath a demon.—That is, he lived a prophet's life, was ascetic, attended no feast, took no wine, but came exactly as the prophets came before. They could see all the signs of a prophet in John, yet they did not obey him; they called him melancholy, wild, raving, as if he was guided by an evil spirit. Now, "the Son of man came eating and drinking" and they accused him of being "a gluttonous man and a winebibber, a friend of publicans and sinners." That is, Jesus came eating and drinking, living as others, mingling in the common duties and innocent festivities of daily life, found at feasts and weddings, yet they were not satisfied with him. John was a Nazarite (Luke 1: 15), and had to live as he did; a Nazarite had to abstain from all the common gratifications of life. They exaggerated the conduct of Jesus; he was neither "a glutton-

Behold, a gluttonous man and a winebibber, a friend of [10]publicans and sinners! And wisdom [11]is justified by her [12]works.

---
[10]See marginal note on ch. 5. 46.
[11]Or, *was*
[12]Many ancient authorities read *children:* as in Lk. 7. 35.

---

ous man" nor a "winebibber." "Gluttonous" means given to an excessive love of food and good living; "winebibber" was one given to much wine. Those who accused Jesus were sanctimonious hypocrites; they knew that he was neither a glutton nor a drunkard; there is no form of virtue or excellence which wicked men cannot malign and charge with being a vice which bears some analogy to that virtue. No wonder Jesus compares that generation to children who made music as at a wedding, but the others did not respond by dancing; then they sang dirges of wailing, but the others did not beat their breasts or tear their hair in mourning. John lived on a very meager diet and dressed as a prophet, so they said he had a devil and was beside himself; but Jesus ate and drank very much as other men, and this pleased them no better. They accused him of being "a friend of publicans and sinners"; he was a friend to every one; but he did not encourage any one in sin. One can be a friend without encouraging the sinful life of one; this was Jesus' attitude toward "publicans and sinners." "Publicans" were taxgatherers for the Roman government; the Jews hated them and classed them with "sinners," robbers, murderers, and moral degenerates. Jesus added that "wisdom is justified by her works." The works of wisdom are the best evidence of wisdom; the children of wisdom, that is, wise men, justify the conduct of both John and Jesus; those who did not justify the conduct of both put themselves out of the class of the wise.

6. CERTAIN CITIES CONDEMNED; A PRAYER OF THANKSGIVING
11: 20-30

20 Then began he to upbraid the cities wherein most of his [13]mighty

---
[13]Gr. *powers.*

20-24 Then began he to upbraid the cities.—The preceding verses naturally suggest Jesus' condemnation on certain cit-

works were done, because they repented not. 21 Woe unto thee, Chorazin! woe unto thee, Bethsaida! for if the [18]mighty works had been done in Tyre and Sidon which were done in you, they would have repented long ago in

ies; he did not "upbraid" all cities, but he did those "wherein most of his mighty works were done." To "upbraid" means to blame publicly, to denounce the conduct of those cities publicly. He reproached the inhabitants of certain cities; "most of his mighty works were done" in these cities that he publicly condemned. "Mighty works" means works of might or power, miraculous works by divine power; only a few of his "mighty works" are recorded. (Luke 4: 23; John 21: 25.) The principle is that if any one does the work of God by divine aid, he is a messenger from God; when people see such demonstrations, and fail to believe the message that accompanies such mighty works, they are not consistent and justly fall under the condemnation of God.

Next, Jesus specified some of the cities which he condemns. "Woe unto thee, Chorazin! woe unto thee, Bethsaida!" These were small towns on the northern shore of the Sea of Galilee near Capernaum. Jesus had been present in them at different times, and the people there had been able to judge his miracles. Bethsaida was the town of Philip, Andrew, and Peter. (John 1: 44.) The name means a "place of hunting or fishing"; the woe denounced against it was soon fulfilled, it is claimed, and it is now a poor village consisting of a few miserable cottages. Chorazin is thought to have been more on the west side of the sea; its site is not known. Some think that it was located about two miles from Capernaum. We see in the condemnation of these cities a condemnation of all who refuse to accept Jesus on the testimony that has been given. "If the mighty works had been done in Tyre and Sidon" which had been done in Chorazin and Bethsaida, "they would have repented long ago in sackcloth and ashes." The reason the condemnation was pronounced on these cities was "they repented not." "Tyre and Sidon" were cities of the Philistines or Phoenicians, situated on the eastern shore of the Mediterranean. They were heathen cities, famous for great wealth, commerce and luxury, and also great vices. Tyre was about

sackcloth and ashes. 22 But I say unto you, it shall be more tolerable for Tyre and Sidon in the day of judgment, than for you. 23 And thou, Caper-

one hundred miles northwest of Jerusalem and was often mentioned in the Old Testament; it was denounced by the prophets for its pride and wickedness. (Isa. 23: 7-18; Ezek. 26: 14; 27: 1-11; 28: 1-10.) Sidon was twenty miles north of Tyre; it was in the bounds of the tribe of Asher. (Josh. 19: 28.) It waa also a commercial city, and famous for its valuable timber and skillful workmen. These cities were condemned by the prophets; Chorazin and Bethsaida had greater opportunities for repentance than did Tyre and Sidon; the latter had the pronouncement of the prophets, but the former had the testimony of Jesus confirmed by his "mighty works." If Tyre and Sidon had heard and seen what Chorazin and Bethsaida had heard and seen, they would have repented in the long ago "in sackcloth and ashes"; these were marks of contrition and humiliation. (Isa. 58: 5.) "Sackcloth" was the coarsest fabric for garments then known and was used only by the poorest people. When any one or a city desired to express sorrow for sin, and to deprecate the anger of God, they repented in "sackcloth and ashes." (Jonah 3: 5.) They put off their rich and soft garments, threw ashes on their heads, and sat in the dust. (Job 2: 8, 12; Jonah 3: 5.)

But I say unto you, it shall be more tolerable for Tyre and Sidon in the day of judgment, than for you.—For the reasons mentioned above, "it shall be more tolerable" for these cities "in the day of judgment" than for Chorazin and Bethsaida; Tyre and Sidon had fewer opportunities for knowing the truth; some see in this different degrees of retribution for guilt. The clearness of the light against which sin is committed aggravates the guilt. "The day of judgment" seems to point to the general judgment, and at that time a more severe fate will be visited on the inhabitants of Chorazin and Bethsaida, because they sinned against so much more light than did Tyre and Sidon. Some think that "the day of judgment" may have reference to the time when the cities shall be destroyed; there is no good reason assigned for such a view.

naum, shalt thou be exalted unto heaven? thou shalt ¹go down unto Hades: for if the ²mighty works had been done in Sodom which were done in thee, it would have remained until this day. 24 But I say unto you that it shall be more tolerable for the land of Sodom in the day of judgment, than for thee.

¹Many ancient authorities read *be brought down.*
²Gr. *powers.*

And thou, Capernaum, shalt thou be exalted unto heaven?
—Capernaum is "upbraided" with Chorazin and Bethsaida. It is the city to which Peter removed from Bethsaida, and was the dwelling place of Jesus after he left Nazareth. (Matt. 4: 13.) It was located on the seacoast of Galilee and was one of the principal cities on the Sea of Galilee. It boasted of its great fame; it was "exalted unto heaven" in the estimation of its citizens. Not only did Jesus dwell there for a time, but many miracles were performed within its borders; its inhabitants had opportunity to hear much of the teachings of Jesus, yet they had not repented and did not accept Jesus as the Messiah. The inhabitants forfeited their claim to exaltation by their impenitence and because of their impenitence it should be brought "down unto Hades." "Hades" means a vast abyss in the lower parts of the earth opposed to the heavens or the firmament over our heads; it is the opposite of "exalted unto heaven"; Hades means an unseen place, the invisible world; hence it is applied to the state of the dead—the grave, and the unseen world of separate spirits, whether of torment (Luke 16: 23) or in general (Rev. 1: 18). Capernaum has been literally reduced to "Hades," for no one can with certainty now tell where it was located. Jesus further pronounces Capernaum's condemnation by saying, "If the mighty works had been done in Sodom which were done in thee," Sodom "would have remained until this day." (Gen. 19: 24; Ezek. 16: 48, 49.) Carpernaum, like Chorazin and Bethsaida, had better opportunities with more light to turn from wickedness than did Sodom. Sodom was destroyed for its wickedness, but had it had such advantages as Capernaum, it would not have been destroyed, "it would have remained until this day." Jesus pronounces the same condemnation on Capernaum as he did on Chorazin and Bethsaida by saying that "it shall be more tolerable for the land of Sodom in the

25 At that season Jesus answered and said, I ªthank thee, O Father, Lord of heaven and earth, that thou didst hide these things from the wise and understanding, and didst reveal them unto babes: 26 yea, Father, ⁴for so it

---

ªOr, *praise*
⁴Or, *that*

---

day of judgment, than for thee." The climax is here to be observed: Chorazin and Bethsaida are compared to Tyre and Sidon; Capernaum, greater in sin and punishment, is singled out, and compared to Sodom, whose sin and punishment were greater than those of Sidon. (Deut. 32: 32; Isa. 1: 9, 10; Lam. 4: 6; Ezek. 16: 46-57.)

[The surest of temporal punishments had been meted out to Sodom and Gomorrah; but their punishment was temporal. Capernaum had not been guilty of the fleshly depravity which was common to them of Sodom; but great spiritual truths had been presented. Capernaum had rejected these; the punishment is of the spirit and is far-reaching. Capernaum had been the center of the public ministrations, works and teachings of Jesus; she had been exalted to heaven by these privileges; she had rejected them all, and, by her rejection, she brought herself down to hell.]

25-27 At that season Jesus answered and said.—In quick succession the upbraiding of some of the cities of Galilee is followed by a prayer of thanksgiving by Jesus. There is a wide break in the thought here as if it would make a good division between chapters. (See Matt. 12: 1; 14: 1.) He "answered." This word is frequently used where no question is recorded. (Matt. 22: 1; Mark 9: 5, 38; 11: 14; Luke 13: 14.) However there is usually a reference in the mind of the speaker or hearer, and the question is suppressed for brevity or one which might arise from certain actions. Its frequent occurrence indicates the perfection of Jesus' teaching, as he could speak to the unspoken thoughts and feelings as well as to the words and actions of those who waited on his ministry. At this time it seems that he responded to the thoughts and inquiries elicited by his discourse concerning the things which have just been studied. Jesus frequently prayed; so at this time he addressed God as "Father, Lord of heaven and earth."

was well-pleasing in thy sight. 27 All things have been delivered unto me of my Father: and no one knoweth the Son, save the Father; neither doth either know the Father, save the Son, and he to whomsoever the Son willeth to reveal *him*. 28 Come unto me, all ye that labor and are heavy laden, and

This expresses his relation to God as his Son, and therefore, his divinity; it also ascribes to God the Ruler of heaven and earth. The object of his prayer was a thanksgiving because God had hidden "these things from the wise and understanding," and had revealed "them unto babes." Frequently what God permits to be done, it is said that he does, hence having permitted these things to be hidden to the wise, he now reveals them unto children in knowledge. (Ex. 7: 3, 4; 2 Sam. 12: 11, 12; Isa.12: 1; Rom. 6: 17.) Jesus does not so much thank God for concealing the gospel truths from the worldly-minded, as for revealing them to simple believers; these words describe the wisdom of the world which "is foolishness with God." "The wise and understanding" means those who are skilled in abstract questions. The wise men of Athens called Paul "a babbler" because he preached "Jesus and the resurrection." "Babes" means disciples of Christ, unlearned, yet believing men. (1 Cor. 1: 27.) The mysteries of the gospel require faith; we cannot fathom them; we can know them only by faith in the word of God. In speaking of "the wise and understanding" men, Jesus simply called them what they claimed to be, and not simply what they were. It is well-pleasing to God to do this; hence Jesus praises the equity and wisdom of God in this mystery. (Matt. 18: 14; 1 Cor. 1: 21.) There was a perfect mutual understanding between the Father and the Son, and the Son always did that which was well-pleasing in the sight of God. No one knows the Son perfectly but the Father; no one knows the Father but the Son and those to whom the Son reveals him. This implies that the great scheme of God's spiritual kingdom over which Jesus is to reign as king and the administering of which is committed by the Father to the Son is revealed to man only through Jesus the Christ.

28-30 **Come unto me, all ye that labor.**—This is an invitation to all the Jews and to all who labor under burdens of any kind; it is a universal invitation. It is a fitting close for the

I will give you rest. 29 Take my yoke upon you, and learn of me; for I am meek and lowly in heart: and ye shall find rest unto your souls. 30 For my yoke is easy, and my burden is light.

discourse that Jesus has just delivered. It may possibly refer to all who were suffering from any disease and were burdened by moral and mental stresses, but its deeper significance is those who are weary, being heavily burdened with sin and spiritual defects; it would embrace those described in Matt. 23: 4, Acts 15: 10, and Gal. 5: 1, and all others who are burdened in soul. Jesus assures them that he will give them rest; rest from their labors and burdens whatever they may be; if burdened with sin, he will give them remission of sins. This invitation opens the door to the kingdom of heaven and goes into effect when his kingdom is established. All whose souls are sighing for rest and groaning under burdens are to come to him. There is no other source for them, and his assurance is positive, "I will give you rest."

Take my yoke upon you, and learn of me.—The yoke is the emblem of subjection and service, whether oppressive and painful (Deut. 28: 48; Jer. 28: 14; Lam. 1: 14; Gal. 5: 1), or easy and pleasant, as "the law of Christ," whose service is perfect freedom (1 John 5: 3). One must take the yoke of Christ. Some think that this figure means that we are yoked with Christ and are to become colaborers with him; others think that it symbolizes the government of Jesus and that one is to place oneself under the discipline of the principles of Christianity; it may be either. The "yoke is easy"; it is of no great weight, yet it enables one to do much service. To take the yoke of Christ is simply to become his disciple and to keep his commandment. Jesus is "meek and lowly in heart"; he is gentle and condescending as teacher, and is meek and quiet in loving-kindness. (2 Cor. 10: 1; 2 Tim. 2: 24, 25.) "Ye shall find rest unto your souls." "Rest" in verse twenty-eight may be equal to forgiveness of sin, and "rest" in verse twenty-nine may refer to the rest that faithful ones have in heaven. If one comes to Jesus and lives as he teaches that one to live, he shall have rest from all sins and have a home in heaven at last.

7. OPPOSITION DEVELOPED
12: 1-21

1 At that season Jesus went on the sabbath day through the grainfields; and his disciples were hungry and began to pluck ears and to eat. 2 But the

1, 2 At that season Jesus went on the sabbath day.—Matthew, like the other writers of the gospel, does not bring the events in the life of Jesus in chronological order; it is impossible for us to determine the *exact* order in which events in the earthly life of Jesus came; no writer of the gospels claims to record them in *the exact order in which they occurred;* the order of mention is not the order of occurrence. Sometimes an event may be placed in order of occurrence. It is not necessary for us to know the exact order of occurrence. It is thought that Matthew records this event out of its chronological place. The facts recorded here are grouped together in order to show the deepening hostility which Jesus encountered from the Jewish leaders. The first two occurred soon after the first assault on Jesus at the Passover, and were the proper prelude to the later instance to blasphemy. There is a marked increase in the intensity of the Pharisaic hostility. "At that season," just after the second Passover of Jesus' ministry; Luke says that "it came to pass on a sabbath." (Luke 6: 1.) Jesus on this Sabbath went "through the grainfields." Presumably he did not travel that day further than "a sabbath day's journey," which was about two thousand paces, or about six furlongs from the wall of the city, which, in English count, would be little more than one-half of a mile.

And his disciples were hungry and began to pluck ears and to eat.—It is probable that the grain here was barley or wheat, as the fields of barley were usually ripe at the Passover. Such grains they could get out of the husks easily by rubbing the ears in their hands as they walked through the field. Indian corn was not known till the discovery of America and is properly called "maize." "Began to pluck ears and to eat." This action itself was lawful. (Deut. 23: 25.) The Pharisees did not accuse them of taking what was another's, but only for doing manual labor on the Sabbath; they argued that the small labor of plucking and rubbing out the grain

Pharisees, when they saw it, said unto him; Behold, thy disciples do that which it is not lawful to do upon the sabbath. 3 But he said unto them, ⁵Have ye not read what David did, when he was hungry, and they that were

---

⁵¹ S. xii. 6.

---

with their hands was considered as harvesting and grinding, and hence violated the Sabbath. The Pharisees accused Jesus' disciples of doing "that which it is not lawful to do upon the sabbath." They were overstrict and scrupulous about the Sabbath; they had weighted it down with many traditions and laws which were made by their leaders. The Pharisees watched Jesus to do him harm with the people; they were more anxious to condemn Jesus than they were to carry out their laws regarding the Sabbath. The laws of the Jewish Sabbath or seventh day of the week were clear enough. (Ex. 20: 10; 35: 2, 3; Num. 15: 32-36.) The disciples had plucked the grain and had eaten it as they were hungry; paths or roads extended through fields, and the grain grew near enough for them to walk along the path and pluck the grains; this was all that they had done and it is a striking instance in which the Jews had come to bring some accusation against Jesus.

3-5 Have ye not read what David did?—Jesus is not contending for a violation of the law, but for a true construction or interpretation of it. The analogy here between David's fleeing from Saul and Jesus' withdrawing for a while from the enemies who sought his life is very striking. David and his company were hard pressed by King Saul; in great extremity he came to Abimelech, the high priest, to ask for food to save his company from starvation, and found only the showbread in the tabernacle; he asked for it, received it, and he and his companions ate it. (1 Sam. 21: 1-7.) This incident was well known to the Pharisees, and they believed David was a righteous man and a prophet, and in this case justified him. Therefore, in a case of like necessity, to avoid hunger and weariness, the disciples of Jesus were only doing as David had done—keeping the spirit of the law. Necessary labor may always be done on the Sabbath. Since they justified David in what he did, to be consistent, they ought to justify the disciples of Jesus. The showbread was prepared by the

with him; 4 how he entered into the house of God, and ⁶ate the showbread, which it was not lawful for him to eat, neither for them that were with him, but only for the priests? 5 Or have ye not read in the law, ⁷that on the sabbath day the priests in the temple profane the sabbath, and are guiltless?

⁶Some ancient authorities read *they ate.*
⁷Num. xxviii. 9, 10.

---

priests on the Sabbath in twelve loaves and placed on the table of showbread; the old bread was removed on the Sabbath and could be eaten by the priests only. (Lev. 24: 9.) The tabernacle is spoken of here as "the house of God"; the temple was not built until after David's death. David entered only the court of the tabernacle or the room occupied by the priests. (23: 19.)

"Have ye not read in the law?" "The law" here means the law of Moses. (Lev. 24: 5-9; Num. 28: 9, 10; 1 Sam. 21: 6.) This is a stronger case than the historical precedent of David. The law positively orders work to be done by the priests on the Sabbath; the preparation of the showbread, the offering of sacrifices, including the killing, dressing and burning the sacrifice, all were to be done by the priest on the Sabbath so the law of itself made provision for these things to be done on the Sabbath. There is something striking in the remark that Jesus, who was to be king and priest of the new dispensation, draws his justifying example from a king and the priest of the old dispensation. In reality the priest did not "profane the sabbath," but by fair interpretation of the traditions and man-made laws of the Pharisees, the priests did "profane the sabbath, and are guiltless." Since they could do this and be guiltless, why could not his disciples pluck the grain on the Sabbath and eat it to satisfy their hunger without being guilty? They were unable to answer this.

[The Sabbath law is not reenacted in the new covenant, or New Testament. When the disciples plucked the ears of corn and ate them on the Sabbath, the Pharisees remonstrated with the Master for his desecration of the day by his disciples. Jesus answered them that "the Son of man is lord of the sabbath." This shows that Jesus was "lord" or ruler "of the sabbath" and that he had the right to annul its requirements as God did in the two examples noted. Jesus fulfilled the law

6 But I say unto you, that ⁸one greater than the temple is here. 7 But if ye had known what this meaneth, ⁹I desire mercy, and not sacrifice, ye would

⁸Gr. *a greater thing.*
⁹Hos. vi. 6.

---

in his own body, rested in the grave on the Sabbath, took it out of the way, and rose from the dead on the first day of the week and "brought life and immortality to light." He introduced the new and everlasting covenant. This covenant rested on the truth that Jesus is the Christ, the Son of God. He was "declared to be the Son of God with power, . . . by the resurrection from the dead." (Rom. 1: 4.) He was raised from the dead on the first day of the week, and in the new dispensation this was consecrated as the day of all days, the day of perpetual worship. Jesus met with the disciples on the first day of the week, and on the second first day he again met with them, not having met with them during the intervening time. The Holy Spirit descended from heaven to earth to begin his personal ministry on the first day, Pentecost, and on this day took up his abode with the church of God to guide it into the fullness of all truth. (Acts 20: 7; 1 Cor. 16: 1, 2.) The first day of the week was thus sanctified by Christ and the Holy Spirit as the Lord's day, the day for the Lord's worship. From this time forward it is called "the Lord's day." (Rev. 1: 10.)]

6-8 **But I say unto you, that one greater than the temple is here.**—To be greater than the temple, which was honored by the Jews as the most holy place on earth, as the dwelling place of Jehovah himself, was to claim equality with God. Haggai (2: 7-9) in encouraging the Jews under Zerubbabel to finish rebuilding the temple said that the smaller temple which was then being built would exceed the former in glory when "the precious things of all nations shall come." This prophecy was fulfilled when Jesus came and filled "this house with glory," and "the latter glory of this house shall be greater than the former." The glory of Christ who visited the temple was greater than the glory of the former temple. Since this is true, whatever he permitted his disciples to do was in fact a divine permission as much as the labors of the

not have condemned the guiltless. 8 For the Son of man is lord of the sabbath.
9 And he departed thence, and went into their synagogue: 10 and behold,

---

priests in the temple on Mount Zion. Jesus was greater than the temple, as "he that built the house hath more honor than the house" (Heb. 3: 3), so he who is worshiped in the temple is greater than the temple. They should have understood that Jesus was the Messiah and that his claim to the Messiahship was true. If they had known the true meaning, they would have known that God desired mercy, "and not sacrifice," and they would not have condemned Jesus and his disciples. They were cruel in their rigidness, and while they thought they were keeping the Sabbath law, they were destroying themselves by crimes against mercy and truth. God has ever required mercy of men; the sacrifices and ceremonies, when understood, called for mercy and justice.

For the Son of man is lord of the sabbath.—Jesus had just said that he was greater than the temple, and now he affirms himself greater than the statute law of Moses. As the lawgiver is greater than the law, so Christ is greater than the Sabbath. Mark adds here that "the Son of man is lord even of the sabbath." (Mark 2: 28.) Jesus claims to be the divine legislator of the world; he is truly God manifest in the flesh. His declaration of his high dignity should have silenced the murmuring of the Jews. It seems here that he, by being Lord of the Sabbath, indicates that some change would be made in its observance under the new dispensation. Jesus is here asserting his authority to revoke and annul the law pertaining to the Sabbath; he at this time gives a true interpretation of the law and thus condemns the false notions and traditions of the Pharisees. The Sabbath was given for man; that is, the good of man, and was intended to help and not hinder any real good or welfare of man. As the supreme lawgiver he can dispense with the law when the time comes for something better to be given.

9-14 He departed thence, and went into their synagogue.—Mark and Luke record this same incident. (Mark 3: 1-5; Luke 6: 6-10.) Matthew's record seems to make this miracle

a man having a withered hand. And they asked him, saying, Is it lawful to heal on the sabbath day? that they might accuse him. 11 And he said unto them, What man shall there be of you, that shall have one sheep, and if this fall into a pit on the sabbath day, will he not lay hold on it, and lift it out?

follow on the same Sabbath, but Luke records that it was "on another sabbath." This fact is another proof that Matthew did not follow the order of time, but has grouped some events together under the same subject. There was a man present who had "a withered hand"; his hand was dried up and the muscles shrunk; it was paralyzed; it was his right hand, says Luke; "they asked him, saying, Is it lawful to heal on the sabbath day?" They asked him this, not for information, but "that they might accuse him"; they were looking for an occasion to accuse Jesus. The scribes and Pharisees, from this time forward, plot the destruction of Jesus; they watch him in order to find an occasion for bringing accusations against him; they seek to take advantage of the public assembly in the synagogue by asking the question. They cared but little at this time for any knowledge or instruction; they cared but little for this afflicted man; they cared more for an occasion to accuse Jesus than for anything else. Mark records that "when he had looked round about on them with anger, being grieved at the hardening of their heart." This is the only record of an instance where Jesus is said to have been moved "with anger" or rightous indignation. The attitude of the minds of his accusers was peculiar and strange; they did not doubt that he would work a miracle; they expected it; but they are intending to make out that his miracles are contrary to the law of God, and are therefore contrary to the will of God. If they can make out this case, they would then have some ground for saying that he worked miracles by a diabolical power; which charge they did soon begin to make. Jesus pressed upon them an invincible argument, that if they would labor on the Sabbath to save the life of an animal, could not he save life and do good to men? In making the argument Jesus asked, "What man shall there be of you, that shall have one sheep, and if this fall into a pit on the sabbath day, will he not lay hold on it, and lift it out?" Questions of this sort are put in the form of an argument; it constituted an unanswer-

12 How much then is a man of more value than a sheep! Wherefore it is lawful to do good on the sabbath day. 13 Then saith he to the man, Stretch forth thy hand. And he stretched it forth; and it was restored whole, as the other. 14 But the Pharisees went out, and took counsel against him, how they might destroy him.

able "argumentum ad hominem," for they allowed animals to be watered, lifted out of pits and other things on the Sabbath. Jesus then points his argument with this statement, "How much then is a man of more value than a sheep!" By this simple and natural exclamation, which all present, who were perhaps mostly villagers of Galilee, and owned sheep, had often had occasion to consider this doubt in accidents happening among their rocky hills, Jesus settles the question more effectually than volumes of abstract proofs could do. He showed every one of them that it was a law impressed on their very consciences, and practically allowed by them, that it was pleasing to God, to do good at all times, and to place charity above ceremonial observances.

Having now answered his enemies, he does the simple and merciful act of healing the man. He commanded him to "stretch forth thy hand." At this command, "he stretched it forth," and it was healed. When a miracle follows a doctrine as it does in this case, it becomes a proof of what was before said. Jesus did not labor on the Sabbath; it was easy for him to speak the word and restore the withered hand. The Pharisees could not claim that a *word* is unlawful labor; Jesus showed himself to have divine power to sustain his claim to the Lord of the Sabbath. The man to be healed believed that Jesus had power, as he obeyed at once. He did not hesitate and argue, "How can I stretch out my hand? It is withered." He simply obeyed, and that which he could not do, the divine energy acting with his will supplied what was lacking in the place. It would seem from human reason that Jesus had commanded an impossible act, yet the effort to stretch forth his hand was not impossible, and when the will was exerted, power to accomplish was granted. Instead of rejoicing with the man who was healed, "the Pharisees went out, and took counsel against him, how they might destroy him." They were determined not to admit the defense which they could

15 And Jesus perceiving *it* withdrew from thence: and many followed him; and he healed them all, 16 and charged them that they should not make

not refute, and were bent upon using the act to charge Jesus' miracles to the power of Satan. They "took counsel against him"; Mark says that the Pharisees called in the aid of the Herodians, those who were the partisans of Herod, who maintained the rightfulness of the Roman dominion over Judea, and the propriety of introducing Greek and Roman customs among the Jews. We see here these Pharisees, sticklers for the law of Moses, unite with its bold political subverters in order to accomplish their evil designs against Jesus. Malice as well as misery makes "strange bedfellows." (Matt. 22: 16.) These Herodians had greater interest at court and possibly had more influence in court than the Pharisees, so they are brought into the council. Jesus had performed no outward act in healing the man, and they had no legal hold on him for violating the Sabbath, hence they needed somebody to help them make out a case. The absurd doctrine of the Jewish doctors permitted medical treatment of acute diseases on the Sabbath, but forbade it to cases that were chronic. The test cases which Jesus relieved on the Sabbath were chronic; the withered hand had been in this condition for some time.

15-21 And Jesus perceiving it withdrew from thence.—Jesus saw what the Pharisees were about to do; he read their hearts and knew that they were determined to destroy him. His hour had not come, and he "withdrew from thence." Jesus was no coward; he was not fleeing from danger. They could do nothing with him until his hour arrived. Jesus went to the Sea of Galilee and prepared to cross it (Mark 3: 7; 4: 34); as his hour was not yet come, he did not wish to have his work interfered with or reduce himself to the necessity of working miracles to prevent it. Wherever he went he found those who were afflicted; in fact, "many followed him; and he healed them all." He was no respecter of persons; he "healed them all"; there was no exception; he had to make no excuse for any exception as do "modern divine healers." He charged them seriously that they should "not make him known."

him known: 17 that it might be fulfilled which was spoken through Isaiah the prophet, saying,
¹⁰18   Behold, my ¹¹servant whom I have chosen;
          My beloved in whom my soul is well pleased:
          I will put my Spirit upon him,
          And he shall declare judgment to the ¹²Gentiles.
19   He shall not strive, nor cry aloud;
          Neither shall any one hear his voice in the streets.

---

¹⁰Is. xlii. 1 ff.
¹¹See marginal note on Acts 3. 13.
¹²See marginal note on ch. 4. 15.

Jesus did not want to arouse his enemies to greater activities; his deeds of mercy must be kept in secret; at the proper time they would be told or published. Jesus performed his miracles in public and wanted them to be witnesses of his claim, but he did not want the reputation of a mere wonder-worker; his miracles were subordinate to his teachings. Many of those who were healed were not prepared to proclaim publicly Jesus as the Son of God; therefore it is best for them to be quiet and let Jesus publish his own miracles and commission others who were better qualified to do it.

That it might be fulfilled which was spoken through Isaiah the prophet.—In following this course Jesus fulfilled the prophecy of Isaiah which foretold the characteristics that the Messiah should possess. This quotation is from Isa. 42: 1-4, and varies from the original in some points. Jesus as the Messiah fulfilled all the prophecies pertaining to his first advent and executed the will of his Father; this was necessary to accomplish the work of redemption. (Psalm 40: 7; John 9: 4; 17: 4; Phil. 2: 6-8; Heb. 10: 7.) Jesus in quietness fulfilled this prophecy, and Matthew guided by the Holy Spirit quotes the prophecy and applies it to Jesus. These points are predicted of the Messiah, and the description of his character reveals them in him: (1) the Messiah should come from God as his minister and servant; (2) his own personal character should be mild and gentle; (3) he should be tender in his dealings with man; (4) he should give victory to truth and righteousness in the world; (5) not only Jews, but Gentiles should trust in his name. "My beloved," Jesus was the only begotten and beloved Son of God. (Matt. 3: 17; John 3: 16.) It was

20   A bruised reed shall he not break,
     And smoking flax shall he not quench,
     Till he send forth judgment unto victory.
21   And in his name shall the ¹Gentiles hope.
¹See marginal note on ch. 4. 15.

further predicted that he should "declare judgment to the Gentiles," and this was done in his preaching the gospel through his apostles to the Gentiles. "He shall not strive"; he withdrew from his enemies and excited no warfare or strife among the people. Jesus neither shouted for war nor raised an army to wage a war. His work was done in quietness; these three phases of the prophecy were fulfilled in him; he did not strive, nor cry aloud, nor raise his "voice in the streets." He was the prince of peace, gentle, meek, and condescending to heal the wounded. It is this characteristic in Jesus which has separated Christians from carnal warfare. "A bruised reed shall he not break." A reed growing on the watercourses, and bruised or ready to fall and die, Jesus did not finish its destruction. "Smoking flax" he did not quench. The expiring wick of a lamp, for which purpose flax was used by the Jews, Jesus did not extinguish. He would continue his mild and unostentatious career until he had finished his mission and "judgment unto victory" "in his name" shall have come to the Gentiles. The Gentiles have no hope without Christ. (Eph. 2: 12; 1 Thess. 4: 13.) No one has any hope of salvation out of Christ. This quotation from Isaiah is peculiar to Matthew, who taks a special interest in noticing fulfillments of prophecy by Jesus. The plot against the life of Jesus and the great publicity of his numerous and notable miracles induced him to withdraw suddenly from that locality. The case exemplified his quiet, unobtrusive ways, his wonderful gentleness of bearing, and the strong and striking contrast in all these respects between "the Prince of Peace" and the world's proud conquerors and monarchs; yet Jesus was to become the mightiest of earth's conquerors and kings, for under him justice and judgment should become victorious in all the earth, and in his name the nations should put their trust. In this way the prophecy of Isaiah is beautifully and perfectly fulfilled in Jesus.

8. DISPUTATIONS WITH THE PHARISEES
12: 22-45

22 Then was brought unto him ²one possessed with a demon, blind and dumb: and he healed him, insomuch that the dumb man spake and saw. 23 And all the multitudes were amazed, and said, Can this be the son of David? 24 But when the Pharisees heard it, they said, This man doth not cast out demons, but ³by ⁴Beelzebub the prince of the demons. 24 And knowing

---

²Or, *a demoniac*
³Or, *in*
⁴Gr. *Beelzebul.*

22, 23 Then was brought unto him one possessed with a demon.—A record of this miracle is given by Mark 3: 22-27 and Luke 11: 14-28. It follows immediately the prophecy from Isaiah as a sequel of it. This man was doubly cursed by the demon as he was "blind and dumb"; Luke says that the demon "was dumb"; the man's affliction was caused by the demon; diseases and the possession of demons are usually found together. The cure of this poor demoniac man seems to have been a signal instance of power; the man could neither hear nor see. Besides this, scribes had come "down from Jerusalem" (Mark 3: 22), and the miracle was done boldly in their presence and that of a great multitude. The common people asked the question, after seeing and hearing the man who had been healed, "Can this be the son of David?" They meant by this the Messiah. They saw him fulfilling prophecy and were convinced by his teaching and miracle that he fulfilled the words of the prophet. (Isa. 36: 5.) They reasoned that the Messiah could do no greater things than these. (John 7: 31.) Jesus was at this time again in Capernaum. The multitude asked this question in amazement, and could understand him in no other way; he must be "the son of David," and if so, the Messiah; if not the son of David, he must be some other prophet of God; in either case they should hear and heed his teachings.

24 But when the Pharisees heard it.—The Pharisees reacted in the very opposite; the multitude could reach no other conclusion than that he was from God, or the son of David; but the Pharisees said, "This man doth not cast out demons" by the power of God, "but by Beelzebub the prince of the demons." "Beelzebub" was the name taken from an idol of the

their thoughts he said unto them, Every kingdom divided against itself is brought to desolation; and every city or house divided against itself shall not stand: 26 and if Satan casteth out Satan, he is divided against himself; how

Philistines of Ekron. (2 Kings 1:2.) It meant the god of the fly which was worshiped to obtain deliverance from the injuries of that insect; some think that it signified the god of filth; it was a name of bitter contempt in the mouth of the Pharisees. Here is an admission by the Pharisees that Jesus worked miracles; that is, he performed deeds beyond the reach of any unaided human power, but they attribute this power to Beelzebub instead of to God. They did not mean to cast a reflection on God, but on Jesus; they did not understand the close relation between God and Jesus. This miracle was performed in the spiritual realm of Satan, yet they declared that it was done by "the prince of the demons." They should have known better, may have known better; the devil cannot do works of pure goodness. These Pharisees knew that if the teachings of Jesus should prevail their influence was at an end; so the miracle they do not deny, but ascribe it to an infernal power, "Beelzebub the prince of the demons."

25-27 **And knowing their thoughts he said unto them.**—Jesus knew the thoughts of men; he could see into the secret chambers of the heart and read the thoughts of men; "he needed not that any one should bear witness concerning man; for he himself knew what was in man." (John 2: 25.) So Jesus read the hearts of these Pharisees and answered their thoughts before they expressed them. This act of his would be another proof of his divinity as it showed another well-known attribute of God in which it is not known that Satan has any power, or that he could read the hearts of men without the help of their words. (Psalm 44:21; 139:2.) He said, "Every kingdom divided against itself is brought to desolation." If he had cast out the demon by the prince of demons, Satan's kingdom was divided against itself, and would soon come to "desolation." Thus Jesus refuted their false reasoning by a simple and universal fact. A family, state, or kingdom at war with itself will soon be destroyed. If Satan destroys his own work, he destroys at one time what he builds

then shall his kingdom stand? 27 And if I ³by ⁴Beelzebub cast out demons, ³by whom do your sons cast them out? therefore shall they be your judges. 28 But if I ³by the Spirit of God cast out demons, then is the kingdom of

at another; he is not so guilty of folly as to do this, but would be worthy of ridicule by men. So "if Satan casteth out Satan, he is divided against himself"; the Jews were not ready to concede this; again if this be the case with Satan, Jesus puts this question to these Pharisees, "How then shall his kingdom stand?" If their reasoning be correct, they should be able to answer this question. If Jesus used the power of Satan in casting out this demon, Satan's kingdom is divided against itself and will soon fall; if he cast out the demon by the power of God, then the kingdom of God and the kingdom of Satan are in direct conflict with each other, and to cast out Satan is the strongest proof that can be visibly given of hostility to Satan.

And if I by Beelzebub cast out demons, by whom do your sons cast them out?—"Your sons" here means your disciples or followers; Jesus shows them that their cavil against him could be retorted upon them with more truth than they had imagined. His reasoning is that your followers or disciples, against whose actions they had made no objection and had actually taught and encouraged them so to do, pretended to cast out demons in some cases, and they had found no fault with them. These Pharisees claimed that their followers could exercise such power only with the power of God; therefore it is foolish and wicked in you now to urge such a cavil against me for doing the very same thing. Some among the Jews claimed this power of exorcism. (Mark 9: 38; Acts 19: 13, 14.) After making this argument, Jesus then added "therefore shall they be your judges." They will arise in judgment against you to prove that you are actuated by ill will and malice. Jesus literally crushed them with this argument, but they were too obstinate to yield to it.

28, 29 But if I by the Spirit of God cast out demons.—Luke says by "the finger of God"; that is, the power of God. The magicians reported to Pharaoh that the miracles wrought by Moses were done by "the finger of God." (Ex. 8: 19.) This

God come upon you. 29 Or how can one enter into the house of the strong *man*, and spoil his goods, except he first bind the strong *man?* and then he will spoil his house. 30 He that is not with me is against me; and he that gathereth not with me scattereth. 31 Therefore I say unto you, Every sin

was the only conclusion that could be reached, it was done by "the finger of God," or the power of God; and since this was true, "then is the kingdom of God come upon you." The phrase "kingdom of God" is equivalent to saying that the Messiah has come and is in their midst; it is near enough to you to require you to believe and seek it. The kingdom of God is near, and therefore a kingdom of Satan is invaded and weakened. They ought to have rejoiced in the signs of this conquest of good over evil; they should have prepared their hearts to receive a kingdom which had power to perform such works of mercy. But truly they loved darkness rather than light, because their deeds were evil. (John 3: 19.) Again Jesus enforces his argument with an illustration: "How can one enter into the house of the strong man, and spoil his goods, except he first bind the strong man?" If the kingdom of the Messiah has not come near them in the person of Jesus, how can this power be granted unto Jesus? Jesus now pushed them to extremity. They knew that no prophet had ever claimed such power; they knew that the prophets had foretold that this power would belong to the Messiah. (Isa. 49: 25; 53: 12.) Therefore if Jesus is not the Messiah, this power to cast out demons, as he had done, would be impossible according to their own prophets; but if it was possible and the Messiah should have such power, it was manifested in him and they should accept him as the Messiah. He had entered the strong man's house and had cast out a demon, thus manifesting his power to bind the strong man. The argument was unanswerable; but their perverse hearts were invincible.

30 **He that is not with me is against me.**—In the great conflict between life and darkness, good and evil, the kingdom of God and of Satan, there is no middle ground; there is no neutral position; there is no third power to which these miracles can be attributed. These Pharisees were obliged either to join with Christ or be against him; they had to become allies

and blasphemy shall be forgiven unto men; but the blasphemy against the Spirit shall not be forgiven. 32 And whosoever shall speak a word against

with God or coworkers with Satan; there was no other alternative. "No man can serve two masters" at the same time. (Matt. 6: 24.) The teachings of Jesus with his unanswerable arguments forced the conclusion upon these Pharisees, and they must now take sides with Jesus or join issue with him; the choice is theirs; sufficient instruction, evidence, and light have been given them for the choice; hence the responsibility of the choice rests upon them. To make the matter clear and easy for them to see, Jesus presents only two alternatives—if they are not with him, they are against him. Jesus further enforces this point by saying "he that gathereth not with me scattereth." This figure may be taken from the image of war, with two opposing sides, or a harvest field, where the reapers either gather the harvest, or foolishly waste it. Mark 9: 40 reverses these words and says "for he that is not against us is for us"; but his meaning is entirely different. Jesus here speaks of the war on Satan's kingdom, but in Mark he speaks of the charity which his disciples were to show to such as use his name while they were too timid to follow him. The maxim taught by Jesus here is true in every age; people must be for Christ or against him; they are scattering, opposing him, or they are gathering with him.

31, 32 Therefore I say unto you, Every sin and blasphemy.
—This is Jesus' conclusion and application of his teaching. "Blasphemy" is injurious and malicious speaking against God or his attributes; to blaspheme in the scripture sense denotes improper and unworthy speeches against God, his attributes, works, or temple; it means to ascribe to God the weaknesses of men, or to attribute to men the perfections and works of God. Here Jesus fixes a limit of divine mercy. What is "the blasphemy against the Spirit"? Mark 3: 30 tells us that the Pharisees had been guilty of blasphemy "because they said, He hath an unclean spirit." This sin was maliciously ascribing a miracle of divine power to the power of Beelzebub. It is not said here "a sin against," but "blasphemy against," which is explained by "speak against the Holy Spirit." The "blas-

the Son of man, it shall be forgiven him; but whosoever shall speak against the Holy Spirit, it shall not be forgiven him, neither in this ⁵world, nor in

---

⁵Or, *age*

---

phemy against the Spirit shall not be forgiven," but "every sin and blasphemy shall be forgiven unto men" but the one "against the Holy Spirit." Man may speak "a word against the Son of man" and "it shall be forgiven him," but "whosoever shall speak against the Holy Spirit, it shall not be forgiven him, neither in this world, nor in that which is to come." There has been much speculation about "the unpardonable sin" and "the blasphemy against the Holy Spirit." Jesus came in the flesh, dwelt among men, and revealed the will of God to man. God the Father revealed his will to the Jews through Moses, and Jesus revealed the will of God to us. The Holy Spirit was to come in person and complete the work of Jesus. He said, "It is expedient for you that I go away; for if I go not away, the Comforter will not come unto you; but if I go, I will send him unto you. And he, when he is come, will convict the world in respect of sin, and of righteousness, and of judgment." (John 16: 7, 8.) Many misunderstood Jesus, his teachings, and his kingdom while he was on earth, and even denied him as being the Messiah, who afterwards repented and were pardoned, and became Christians. (Acts 2: 37, 38; Acts 9: 1, 17.) Many could and did reject Jesus while he was on earth, but when the Holy Spirit came and testified of him, they accepted Christ. But when the Holy Spirit came and gave the complete will of God, if men rejected this, there was no other evidence to be furnished, no other divine agency to be given, and if they finally rejected the Holy Spirit, there was no forgiveness for them. There was no forgiveness "neither in this world, nor in that which is to come." Mark says "hath never forgiveness, but is guilty of an eternal sin." (Mark 3: 29.) No sin unforgiven here or in this world will be pardoned or forgiven hereafter.

[God bore testimony to men through the Old Testament scriptures; Jesus Christ bore testimony in person, given in the New Testament; and he stated that his testimony was incomplete, and he would send the Holy Spirit to complete or perfect that testimony. (John 16: 7, 8, 13, 14.) (Read also John 14: 14, 20-27; 15: 26; 16: 8.) They all teach that neither the revelations of the Father nor the Son were complete to guide into life eternal, save as people received the teachings of the Holy Spirit. The Spirit would come, perfect the testimony, and guide into all truth. Without this guidance being followed, they could not know the full faith of God. It is in perfect harmony with all these scriptures and with all the facts recorded in the Bible for Jesus, when they charged him with acting by the power of the devil, to warn them that they might do this now to him and find forgiveness; but if they so rejected and treated the Holy Spirit when he came, there would be no forgiveness, for there would be no more testimony and no more opportunity to repent. It refers, of course, to the final rejection of the will of God. To reject the will of God was to sin against God, to reject the words of Jesus was to sin against him, and to reject the teachings of the Holy Spirit was to sin against the Holy Spirit.

To blaspheme is to oppose and speak against. Many construe this to mean that Jesus defined the attributing the works of Jesus to the evil power as the sin against the Holy Spirit; but the Bible does not say so, nor anything that implies this. Read Mark 3: 28-30; Luke 12: 10. All classes and kinds of men, those that maligned, persecuted, and abused Jesus in every form and manner were warned and exhorted by the Holy Spirit to turn to Jesus and live. Paul was a persecutor and blasphemer of the Lord Jesus and sought the destruction of the whole church of God. Jesus did not mean to say that those who blasphemed and rejected Christ Jesus and regarded him as a servant of Satan might not turn to God when the Holy Spirit brought its message of love and power. He only meant to tell them: "You may reject my teachings, malign and abuse me as you are now doing; but when the Holy Spirit is come and bears his testimony, if you reject that, there will be no further offices of love and mercy, either in this world or the world to come." To disobey and reject God was to blaspheme him; to reject and disobey Jesus was to blaspheme him; to reject and disobey the teachings of the Holy Spirit

that which is to come. 33 Either make the tree good, and its fruit good; or make the tree corrupt, and its fruit corrupt: for the tree is known by its fruit. 34 Ye offspring of vipers, how can ye, being evil, speak good things? for out of the abundance of the heart the mouth speaketh. 35 The good man out of his good treasure bringeth forth good things: and the evil man out of

was to blaspheme him; and when the Holy Spirit performed his work to teach and save men, God's provisions of mercy were exhausted.]

33-35 **Either make the tree good, and its fruit good.**—The general principle that a tree is known by its fruits is often applied by Jesus to the proof that a man's actions reveal the character of his life. (Matt. 7: 15-20.) Some think that this explains the preceding verses concerning blasphemy against the Holy Spirit, because it follows immediately those verses. Such malicious language is justly condemned because it proceeds from a corrupted heart. Perhaps it applies and explains a general argument of Jesus that he had worked a miracle by divine power; they could judge Jesus and his character by his teachings and conduct; that is, he said, "Judge of me as you do of trees, by their fruit. Regard me either as good or bad according to my actions. I do works of mercy, and speak reverently of God; these results can come only from a pious heart." (John 9: 25, 30, 33.)

Ye offspring of vipers, how can ye, being evil, speak good things?—A viper is a serpent which was familiar in the east; the poison of its bite caused death with great agonies. John the Baptist had used this expression when many of the Pharisees and Sadducees came to him for baptism; he addressed them, "ye offspring of vipers." At another time Jesus addressed them, "ye serpents, ye offspring of vipers." (Matt. 23: 33.) This was a forceful way of addressing them as they were guileful and hypocritical. As teachable believers and pious persons are likened to doves and lambs, which are innocent and harmless animals, so the malicious and unbelieving are compared to goats, dogs, and vipers, according as they are sensual, foul, or malicious. These Pharisees had shown the hatred and venom of serpents and deserved this epithet. Good works and clear reasoning could not be expected from

his evil treasure bringeth forth evil things. 36 And I say unto you, that every idle word that men shall speak, they shall give account thereof in the

them; they were corrupted; and hence "out of the abundance of the heart the mouth speaketh." Their hearts were not right and the principles of their lives were wrong, therefore the exhibitions of character were only such as could have been expected. This reveals a very depraved condition and shows the dire need of the Savior whom they were rejecting. The other side is illustrated by the "good man out of his good treasure bringeth forth good things." The heart of a good man is a treasure of good things. Divine truths, blessed expressions, holy emotions dwell there richly and abound. Like a wealthy banker, he has only to draw the precious treasure forth as occasions demand. On the other hand, "the evil man out of his evil treasure bringeth forth evil things." From the evil heart comes hostile feelings against truth and goodness, skeptical arguments, malign emotions purposed to prefer self-interest to the right, hatred of God and his truth. All these heaped together make a storehouse of evil works from which the evil man may draw abundantly.

36, 37 **Every idle word that men shall speak.**—"Idle word" does not mean here what is usually termed now as "idle words"; it does not mean careless, innocent talk on subjects secular and social, and opposed to serious conversation. Rather it signifies wicked, malicious, injurious, slandering, impious words. To "give account thereof in the day of judgment" means that we will be held responsible for such wicked and vicious words uttered against God, Christ, and the Holy Spirit. Our social, insignificant words among friends will not be sufficient to condemn us; only such words as manifest the real principle of our actions, whether we love God truly, or love the world and self, will serve to justify or condemn us. It is dangerous for Christians to be always engaged in foolish, unmeaning conversation, and more dangerous still, a profane and unseemly jesting, because such conduct manifests a state of heart which justifies condemnation. This does not mean that a Christian cannot engage in innocent jesting and levity. "A cheerful heart is a good medicine; but a broken spirit

day of judgment. **37 For by thy words thou shalt be justified, and by thy words thou shalt be condemned.
38 Then certain of the scribes and Pharisees answered him, saying,**

drieth up the bones." (Prov. 17: 22.) A genial and pleasant gracefulness of conversation in social relations helps to adorn a Christian. A mother's prattling to her babe may be as innocent and as clearly prove a loving heart as her tears over its grave. So the term "idle word" may mean not merely unimportant or insignificant, but implies that there is some positive evil in the word.

[Idle words and jesting mean those which are vulgar and coarse and corrupt the hearer. Idle words are evil words that excite the lusts and corrupt man. Idle words are compared with speaking against the Son of man and the Holy Spirit. In Eph. 5: 4 jesting is classed with fornication, uncleanness, or covetousness, and in contrast with giving of thanks. The corrupt communication is that which excites the lusts, corrupts and depraves the heart, and in contrast with that which ministers grace to the hearer.]

For by thy words thou shalt be justified.—This explains the preceding verse; by our words, however unimportant, we shall be justified or condemned, according as they are good or evil. If our words are good, we shall "be justified" by them; but if our words be evil, we shall "be condemned." By good words, good thoughts, and good deeds, we will be judged righteous in the final judgment; but by evil words, evil thoughts, and evil deeds we will be condemned. This is the meaning of "justified" here as in James 2: 21-25, not as in Rom. 5: 1, pardoned, which is by faith.

38-40 Then certain of the scribes and Pharisees answered him.—The term "answered" does not mean that Jesus had asked a question; in this instance they made a request of him. They requested to "see a sign" from Jesus; he claimed to be the Son of God; they asked for a sign proving his claim. Luke says that they "sought of him a sign from heaven." (Luke 11: 16.) To ask for this sign was to ignore and count as useless all that he had done; it was to deny that he had

Teacher, we would see a sign from thee. 39 But he answered and said unto them, An evil and adulterous generation seeketh after a sign; and there shall

---

worked any miracles by the power of God; hence they now call on him to show them "a sign from heaven." Paul said the Jews sought after signs and Greeks after wisdom (1 Cor. 1: 22); that is, some particular exhibition of divine power and glory. Satan tempted Jesus to show signs of his authority as a Son of God. (Matt. 4: 6; John 2: 18; 6: 30.) The carnal minds of the Jews prevented them from perceiving the real truth.

Jesus said in reply, "An evil and adulterous generation seeketh after a sign." A wife who leaves her husband and commits sin against the marriage covenant is called an adulterous person; the Jews were bound to the law by a holy covenant, having all the sacredness of the marriage vow (Ezek. 16: 38; Hos. 3: 1) even as Christians now are wedded in the most solemn vows to Christ (Eph. 5: 24, 32). When Israel committed idolatries, or sought help from heathen nations, it received this epithet, "adulterous generation." They merited it because of their unfaithfulness to Jehovah. Jesus called the generation of his day an "adulterous generation" because they had refused him, even after he had given them sufficient evidence of his claim. He told them that no signs should be given "but the sign of Jonah the prophet."

The "sign of Jonah the prophet" was "as Jonah was three days and three nights in the belly of the whale; so shall the Son of man be three days and three nights in the heart of the earth." Ezekiel was a sign to the people (Ezek. 24: 4); Isaiah walked barefoot for a sign (Isa. 20: 3); Jonah was a sign to the Ninevites to foretell their destruction; hence, the Son of man, after his resurrection, would be a sign to prove to the Jews the terrible fate of their unbelief. We have an account of Jonah's experience in Jonah 1: 17 and chapter 2. The word "whale" does not determine the kind of animal which became the typical grave of Jonah. The book of Jonah says, "Jehovah prepared a great fish to swallow up Jonah; and Jonah was in the belly of the fish three days and three nights." (Jonah 1:

no sign be given to it but the sign of Jonah the prophet: 40 for as Jonah was three days and three nights in the belly of the whale;⁶ so shall the Son of man be three days and three nights in the heart of the earth. 41 The men of

⁶Gr. *sea-monster*.

17.) "Three days and three nights"; here we have an expression which has given some trouble to students of the Bible. Jesus was in the grave but two nights and parts of three days, and it is likely that Jonah was in the fish the same length of time. (Luke 24: 6-8.) If we had no knowledge beyond the modern division of time, we would be at a loss to explain the difference between the words of Christ and the actual event. The Jews had no word corresponding to our natural day of twenty-four hours, or from midnight to midnight; their meaning was expressed by a word meaning "a night-day," and to this they added the custom of saying "night and day" for what we mean by a natural day or a revolution of the earth; hence, to express the time of a part of three consecutive days, they were obliged to say three night-days, or three days and three nights. (See Esth. 4: 16 compared with 5: 1 and 1 Sam. 30: 12 compared with verse 13.) Esther said she would not eat for "three days, night or day," yet on the third day she went to the king to ask him to her banquet. The Egyptian whom David found is said to have eaten nothing "three days and three nights," yet again he says it was the "third day" since he fell sick. (See also 2 Chron. 10: 5, 12.) The Jews in reckoning time counted a part of a day as a day, and began their days in the evening. Jesus was crucified on Friday, was in the grave part of Friday, all day Saturday, and rose early on Sunday morning, or the first day of the week, and was, in their language, three days and nights in the earth. "In the heart of the earth"; this means simply the grave, or the interior or "lower parts of the earth." (Psalm 63: 9; Eph. 4: 9.) It is the same as the abyss of which Peter spoke (Acts 2: 27) where Christ "went and preached unto the spirits in prison" (1 Pet. 3: 19). The separate state and place of spirits according to the Jew's conception was "in the region under the earth," hence "the heart of the earth." Some have claimed since Jesus was not buried in the ground, but enclosed in a

Nineveh shall stand up in the judgment with this generation, and shall condemn it: for they repented at the preaching of Jonah; and behold, [7]a greater than Jonah is here. 42 The queen of the south shall rise up in the judgment

[7]Gr. *more than.*

tomb of rock, that it cannot be truthfully said that he was in "the heart of the earth"; but the rock is a part of the earth as much so as the soil, and there is nothing in the cavil.

41, 42 The men of Nineveh shall stand up in the judgment. —Nineveh was the capital of Assyria; it was a large city on the river Tigris, northeast of Babylon, and was built in early times by Asshur. (Gen. 10: 11.) It was about fifty miles in circumference, and surrounded by a wall one hundred feet high with fifteen hundred towers, each two hundred and fifty feet in height. It is estimated that its population was six hundred thousand in the time of Jonah. They were idolaters and very wicked but being warned by Jonah to repent they humbled themselves and repented; God spared them and their city for two hundred years longer. Nahum and Zephaniah also prophesied their destruction. (Nah. 2: 6; Zeph. 2: 13, 15.) Nineveh "shall condemn" "this generation" "in the judgment." The reason assigned for this is that Nineveh "repented at the preaching of Jonah"; but this generation did not repent at the preaching of Jesus who was "a greater than Jonah." Nineveh compared with that generation had acted prudently and piously; she would show by contrast the awful obstinacy and wickedness of the generation which crucified Jesus. The far superior example of the Ninevites shall reflect condemnation on the inhabitants of that generation. Nineveh repented on much less evidence than had been given to Jerusalem and that generation; however, they had rejected the miracles of Jesus, denied his claim, persisted in their sins, and died in impenitence.

The queen of the south shall rise up in the judgment.—"The queen of the south" was the queen of Sheba. (1 Kings 10: 1-13.) She was from the southern part of Arabia which was from its great distance from Jerusalem called "the ends of the earth." If she came from Arabia, she may have been a descendant of Abraham by Keturah, one of whose sons begat

with this generation, and shall condemn it: for she came from the ends of the earth to hear the wisdom of Solomon; and behold, [7]a greater than Solomon is here. 43 But the unclean spirit, when [8]he is gone out of the man, passeth through waterless places, seeking rest, and findeth it not. 44 Then

---

[8]Or, *it*

Shebah. She may have had a traditional knowledge of the true God, and came to hear Solomon "concerning the name of Jehovah." She was deeply affected by the visit to Solomon and gave praise to God; her conduct in going so far to seek for better knowledge of God, her generosity and open confession, will all manifest in a more hateful light the hardness of heart which was shown by those to whom Jesus was speaking. Josephus calls her "queen of Egypt and Ethiopia"; however, the Arabians claim her. "A greater than Solomon is here." The queen of Sheba went a great distance to be instructed by Solomon, yet "a greater than Solomon" was in the very midst of these Jews, and they would not hear him; hence, the example of the queen of Sheba condemned the Jews then and will condemn them "in the judgment." The example of Solomon and the queen of Sheba reinforces the argument that Jesus based on Jonah and the Ninevites.

[In the days of Solomon the highest good man could attain for himself or bestow on others was to be attained by fearing God and keeping his commandments. This was the whole duty of man. When Jesus came he exclaimed, "Behold, a greater than Solomon is here." He showed his superiority by bringing to the world greater and more heavenly laws embodying more of the divine spirit. Still the greatest good possible for man to enjoy or bestow is found in doing the commandments of God. The highest claim of excellence put forth by Jesus Christ was that he did the will of his Father who sent him. Any claim to a higher spirituality than can be attained through the faithful observance of God's laws which were revealed through Christ is blasphemy.]

43-45 But the unclean spirit, when he is gone out of the man.—Jesus warns the Jews that the evil spirits which he had cast out would return, and if they found the man impenitent, they would take possession of his heart with greater malignity

⁸he saith, I will return into my house whence I came out; and when ⁸he is come, ⁸he findeth it empty, swept, and garnished. 45 Then goeth ⁸he, and taketh with ⁹himself seven other spirits more evil than ⁹himself, and they

⁹Or, *itself*

---

than ever and would hasten him on to ruin. The unclean spirit is represented as going "through waterless places, seeking rest, and findeth it not." The Jews, Arabs, Egyptians, and others believed that deserts were the haunts of evil spirits. The words "wild beasts" and "owls" are referred to as inhabiting deserts. (Isa. 34: 14; Jer. 50: 39.) Hence, the evil spirit finds habitation in the desert; it is represented as a man in a fever, who in vain turns to every side for ease, but finds none, or one whose nervous system is disorganized, and cannot remain still, but is driven about by restless madness; so a wicked soul is its own incessant curse; goodness is the soul's health. The demon, driven by divine power from the hearts of men, is pictured by Jesus as going about searching for a fit abode and restless because no human heart is found for residence.

Then he saith, I will return into my house whence I came out.—That is, return to the living human frame, from whence it had been driven out. When it returns it finds the heart better suited for its abode; the impenitent heart is the fit dwelling place of Satan. When he returns "he findeth it empty, swept, and garnished." What a garnishing is that which tempts the wicked one to return! Judas, as an individual, is an example of the truth of this parable; the Jewish nation, after the crucifixion of Jesus, illustrated this in terrific outlines. It is a dark picture of sin to find a heart where the best faculties become only as baits and allurements for the foul spirits to take up their abode. Many attractions and qualities which are valued by men are but parts of this evil adorning. Impenitent wills, mere physical beauty, learned talents are often the vanities which have changed the destiny of the soul and given it up to the powers of evil.

Then goeth he, and taketh with himself seven other spirits more evil than himself.—"Seven" was a favorite number with the Jews, and very often used to denote any finished or com-

enter in and dwell there: and the last state of that man becometh worse than the first. Even so shall it be also unto this evil generation.

plete number, also to signify several persons or things, answering to our word "many." (1 Sam. 2: 5.) The evil spirit will not reenter weak and alone; he will take with him a strong reinforcement so as not again to be ejected. "The last state of that man becometh worse than the first." This seems to indicate that there are different degrees of depravity among demons as well as among men; they are worse after having returned, and the man into whom they reenter is sevenfold worse. "Even so shall it be also unto this evil generation." These words show Jesus' application of the parable; we can now say so it *was* with that generation. The account given by Josephus of the last years of Jerusalem present a picture of infatuation, demoniac madness and crime such as the world has never elsewhere beheld. The parable refers not merely to verses thirty-eight to forty-two, but to the whole narrative (verses 22-42) which was occasioned by the miracle in verse twenty-two.

[There were evil spirits in those days who took possession of men's hearts. When cast out, they were supposed to inhabit dry desert places. One was cast out and he walked through dry places, seeking rest, finding none. He said, "I will return into my house," the heart whence he was cast out. He did so, found it empty, swept, fitted for the abode of a spirit, but none inhabited it. When the evil spirit had been cast out, he did not take it in a good spirit as he should have done. The evil spirit, finding it unoccupied with a good spirit, entered in and took with him seven other spirits more wicked than himself, and the last state of that man is worse than the first. All, too, because he did not fill his heart with good when the evil was cast out. Jesus said it should be so with that evil generation. He had come and by his teaching checked the evil tendency; but as they failed to take him as their guiding spirit it would end in evil. They would be the worse for having known and rejected Jesus. This principle applies to men now. If we know the truth, and fail to practice and obey it, the heart is hardened. We are the worse for having known it. The gospel is a savor of life unto life, or of death unto death.]

9. SPIRITUAL RELATIONSHIPS
12: 46-50

46 While he was yet speaking to the multitudes, behold, his mother and his brethren stood without, seeking to speak to him. 47 [10]And one said unto

[10]Some ancient authorities omit ver. 47.

46, 47 **While he was yet speaking.**—Other records of this may be found in Mark 3: 31-35; Luke 8: 19-21. This occurred in Galilee, but in what house we do not know. Jesus was in the house and was surrounded by a dense multitude; it may have been in a synagogue. Luke places this after the explanation of the parable of the sower, but he does not say "while" as does Matthew, but simply marks a transition without necessarily indicating any chronological connection. While he was crowded in the house "his mother and his brethren stood without, seeking to speak to him." There is no reference to Joseph, Mary's husband; in fact, he does not appear in gospel history after the period of Jesus' childhood (Luke 2); it is likely that Joseph was dead; this is strengthened by the fact that "the carpenter's son" (Matt. 13: 55) is called in the parallel (Mark 6: 3) "the carpenter," as, according to the Jewish custom, he had, in all likelihood, assumed the position of his reputed father on the death of the latter. They desired "to speak to him." We do not know what they desired to discuss with him; it may be that they intended more than a mere conversation, as he had been accused of being "beside himself." (Mark 3: 20, 21.) "His burden"; this means his half brothers; probably the children of Mary or the children of Joseph by a former marriage. We have no way of telling. Some have claimed that these were only cousins of Jesus. Their names are given as James, Joses, Simon, and Judas. He had cousins whose names were the same, but these do not seem to be his cousins. "Brethren of the Lord" is used ten times in the New Testament and they are never called

him, Behold, thy mother and thy brethren stand without, seeking to speak to thee. 48 But he answered and said unto him that told him, Who is my mother? and who are my brethren? 49 And he stretched forth his hand

cousins. It is incredible, therefore, that they should have been other than literal brothers, "half brothers." This supposition is strengthened by the fact that these brothers are mentioned in connection and in company with "his sisters" and his "mother," all of whom collectively are called his "house" or family. If the mother was a literal mother, the sisters must have been literal sisters, and the brethren literal brothers. Mary the mother of Jesus seems to have had a sister by the same name, Mary; she had sons named James, Joses and Jude; it appears also that the brothers of Jesus were also named James, Joses, Jude, and Simon. Some argue that these brothers are the same and are only cousins to Jesus, but it is quite credible that two sisters, themselves of the same name, should purposely give corresponding names to three of their children. One objection to this is that Jesus committed the keeping of his mother not to these brethren, but to the apostle John; they argue that if he had half brothers he would have committed her to them. This inference is not sound; he did not choose his disciples from his own house, but from others. He dealt in sharp words with his brothers. (John 7:7.) His brothers were not found among his believers until after the resurrection, hence Jesus chose to commit his mother unto the beloved disciple rather than to her other sons. This idea refutes the claim that Mary was at once a wife and a nun, and that she should be worshiped. However, many scholars claim that Mary had no children after the miraculous conception.

When it was reported to Jesus that his "mother and his brethren" were without desiring to speak to him, it furnished Jesus the occasion to teach a lesson on spiritual relationships.

48-50 But he answered and said unto him that told him, Who is my mother?—This does not cast any reflection on his mother, neither does it deny his fleshly relation; Jesus simply shows that spiritual ties are far more important, binding and sacred, than fleshly ties. Jesus respected his mother. (Luke 2:51; John 19:25-27.) He did not deify her, but left her to

towards his disciples, and said, Behold, my mother and my brethren 50 For whosoever shall do the will of my Father who is in heaven, he is my brother, and sister, and mother.

remain as other good women. The superstitious worship of Mary and the false conception that she is the fit mediatrix between us and her Son according to the flesh is shown to be false and foolish. Her relationship to Jesus gives her no greater influence with God than other good women. Jesus is the only mediator between God and man, and no priest, pope, or "deified saint" comes between man and God. While this does not imply disrespect toward his mother, neither should we infer from it that she did not believe in him, but it does imply a gentle rebuke of her interference with the movements of her Son, which, of course, he could not allow. He never let anything interfere with his work as the Savior of man.

And he stretched forth his hand towards his disciples, and said, Behold, my mother and my brethren!—It seems that Jesus refused, or at least delayed, to see his relatives long enough to teach an important lesson. There is nothing that is more closely related to Jesus than his disciples; the ties of human relationship are physical and temporal; the ties of Christ are spiritual and eternal. The connection of any saint with Jesus is greater than ties of blood relation. Jesus speaks of mother, brother, and sister; but never of any human father. Jesus includes in the family of God all believers in him; he binds them together with strong ties of love and sympathy. "For whosoever shall do the will of my Father who is in heaven, he is my brother, and sister, and mother." His relation to God was beautifully expressed in a spiritual sense when he throws all earthly relationships into the background and brings to the foreground his spiritual relationships. Obedience to God's will is the spiritual test of our discipleship. He calls those who obey the Father's will by the endearing names of brother and sister and mother. Why? Because he that obeys does all that the will of God requires. He believes, which is the first step and beginning of future obedience; he repents of and confesses his sin; he is baptized into Christ, and grows in grace and in the knowledge of the truth, thus being partakers of the divine nature. Those who obey are members of his body, and members one of another.

[When men deliberately refuse to do the will of God, they are no longer brethren of the Lord. When they cease to be brethren of the Lord, they cease to constitute his church; and it certainly is not right to leave questions involving duty to God to those who deliberately refuse to obey God, that add to and take from his commandments.]

10. GROUP OF PARABLES
13: 1-52

1 On that day went Jesus out of the house, and sat by the sea side. 2 And there were gathered unto him great multitudes, so that he entered into a boat, and sat; and all the multitude stood on the beach. 3 And he spake to

---

1, 2 **On that day went Jesus out of the house.**—We now enter upon a new phase of the teachings of Jesus; here we have the parable of the sower (verses 3-9), reasons for speaking in parables (verses 10-15), the blessedness of hearing such instruction (verses 16, 17), Jesus' explanation of the parable of the sower (verses 18-23), parable of the wheat and tares (verses 24-30), of the mustard seed (verses 31, 32), of the leaven (verse 33), Jesus' use of parables fulfilled prophecy (verses 34, 35), parable of the tares explained (verses 36-43), parable of the hidden treasure (verse 44), of the man seeking pearls (verses 45, 46) of the dragnet (verses 47-52).

The time of this chapter is not definitely known; "on that day" does not fix the events in chronological order in the life of Jesus. Luke tells us that a crowd had come from the cities to the seashore to hear him; the crowd was so great that he entered into a small vessel and moved far enough from the multitude on the water and there taught them as they stood on the shore. Some have fixed the time as the fall of the year just at the time they commenced to sow some of their grain. Surrounded by the beauty of the lake on one side, with multitudes of anxious people standing "on the beach," with the hills of Galilee sloping toward the sea with the fields prepared for the sowing of grain, Jesus spake the parable of the sower with the other parables grouped with this one.

them many things in parables, saying, Behold, the sower went forth to sow;
4 and as he sowed, some *seeds* fell by the way side, and the birds came and

---

3 And he spake to them many things in parables.—A parable is literally "something laid alongside of another thing, to measure, compare, or explain it." The term "parable" is sometimes applied to short, pithy sentences or maxims; but in the New Testament parable means an illustration drawn from natural things to instruct in spiritual things. It is a short narrative of some event or fact in which a continued comparison is carried on frequently between literal and spiritual objects. Some important truths, morals, and doctrines are taught in parables. A parable differs from a fable in that it never represents impossible circumstances, such as trees walking, animals talking, and suchlike. Jesus never violated the reality of things in his parables. There is simplicity, aptness, force, propriety, and pathos in all that Jesus taught. There are many advantages gained by teaching in parables. Parables are easily remembered and yield up the truth to the reverent heart. Not only are parables simple, but they create an interest and thus may be remembered longer. The setting, scenery, incidents, turns of conversation, all are easily remembered until they may be understood. Jesus filed the memory of his hearers with forms of thought which had a spiritual meaning; he drew on the memories of his hearers by these earthly narratives and expressed the great outlines of "the truth" (John 16: 7, 13), the spiritual system of the new covenant. Therefore "without a parable spake he not unto them" (Mark 4: 33, 34).

The sower went forth to sow.—His hearers could see in their imagination the common occurrence of a sower going forth to cast the seed into the ground. Jesus points out the analogy between the sower, the seed, the ground, and the results, and the proclaimer of the gospel, the word of God, the hearer, and the results.

4-9 Some seeds fell by the way side.—The sower would drop the seed by accident along the way to the field, or along

devoured them: 5 and others fell upon the rocky places, where they had not much earth: and straightway they sprang up, because they had no deepness of earth: 6 and when the sun was risen, they were scorched; and because they had no root, they withered away. 7 And others fell upon the thorns; and the thorns grew up and choked them: 8 and others fell upon the good ground, and yielded fruit, some a hundredfold, some sixty, some thirty. 9 He that hath ears,[1] let him hear.

---

[1]Some ancient authorities add here, and in ver. 43, *to hear:* as in Mk. 4. 9; Lk. 8. 8.

---

the hard and trodden path through his field, or where it would not be covered with sufficient soil. Footpaths were frequently made through their fields and these were beaten so hard that grain would remain on the surface and "the birds came and devoured them." The birds of the field were eager to feed upon the seed as it lay exposed on the hard ground.

Others fell upon the rocky places.—These were places where the earth was lodged in the hollow places and basins of rocks, or where the rock was close to the surface with just a very thin layer of dirt over it. In these places the rains and the heat would cause a more rapid growth than in other places. The grass in Palestine grew abundantly for a time during rainy seasons where it had little or no dirt, as for instance on the flat roofs of houses. (Isa. 37:27.) But so soon as the rain ceased, and the hot suns followed, the grass withered immediately.

Others fell upon the thorns.—That is, some seed fell into thorny or briary places; certain brambles and coarse briars in hot climates have a very rapid growth. Their roots occupy the whole earth, take the moisture from everything else, and their matted foliage covers the few plants which may struggle up to the surface, and choke them; they are shut out from the light. These thorns and briars deprive the seed of their share of light, moisture, strength of soil, and air.

And others fell upon the good ground.—This was ground which had been properly prepared, from which the stones and thorns had been removed. Some preparation is necessary for the successful growth of the seed. The good ground yielded abundant harvest; sometimes each seed produced a hundred

10 And the disciples came, and said unto him, Why speakest thou unto them in parables? 11 And he answered and said unto them, Unto you it is given to know the mysteries of the kingdom of heaven, but to them it is not

times, sixty, or thirty times as much, "a hundredfold, some sixty, some thirty." Jesus then added, "He that hath ears, let him hear." This means that those who have faculties are responsible for their proper use; those who have powers of attention should exert them as very important lessons are about to be given.

10-13 **And the disciples came, and said unto him.**—After Jesus had finished the parable, his disciples came to him and asked, "Why speakest thou unto them in parables?" Mark says that they did this "when he was alone." (Mark 4: 10-12; Luke 8: 9, 10.) This was a new phase of teaching and his disciples did not understand why he had at this time made the change, and perhaps they did not understand this new form of teaching. At least they did not understand why Jesus would adopt such a form of teaching as to furnish seven parables in one discourse. Jesus replied and gave the reason for his using parables on this occasion; his reason may justify the use of parables on any and all other occasions.

Unto you it is given to know the mysteries of the kingdom of heaven.—They had been selected to receive the full instruction of the kingdom of heaven; they had been selected as his apostles, and hence they are to understand "the mysteries of the kingdom of heaven." Mysteries to others but plain truths to them; Jesus furnishes them the key to the understanding of his parables. The parbolic form veils the truth from those who do not want it, but unveils the truth to those who are ready for it and will receive it. "The kingdom of heaven" is frequently used by Matthew; all seven of the parables here have for their subject the kingdom of God; its planting principles are given, its developments, and its final victory. This is the kingdom that Jesus came to establish and that had its form of beginning on the first Pentecost after his resurrection, and the kingdom over which Jesus is reigning now as king. "But to them it is not given." It is not given to

given. 12 For whosoever hath, to him shall be given, and he shall have abundance: but whosoever hath not, from him shall be taken away even that which he hath. 13 Therefore speak I to them in parables; because seeing they see not, and hearing they hear not, neither do they understand. 14 And

those who are not willing to receive it. It was given to the disciples, to receive this preparatory teaching, and in some measure to profit by it, because they were obedient and repentive, and were to be the future teachers of the church. (1 Cor. 4: 1.) The others would not receive the teachings of the gospel, even if plainly revealed, and therefore they were not yet disclosed in their fullness.

For whosoever hath, to him shall be given, and he shall have abundance.—The one that has and uses his knowledge wisely will be given more. In the great matter of the offer of free salvation Jesus placed all men on an equality. What then makes the difference? People themselves make the difference. All heard in this great multitude what Jesus taught; but into some hearts which listened with candor and pondered earnestly, it increased to more knowledge; the seed grew. In others it died. Those who received his word were blessed, but those who rejected it and scoffed at it were cursed in that "whosoever hath not, from him shall be taken away even that which he hath." To the multitude Jesus spoke in narrations and parables that they might search into them if they had a desire to do so; to those who did not have the desire to accept and examine his truth, the parables were riddles and the opportunity of understanding them at this time was withdrawn. Jesus lays down a general principle.

Therefore speak I to them in parables; because seeing they see not.—They had ears to hear, but did not hear; they had eyes to see, but did not see; they had faculties of attention and understanding, but did not give attention and did not understand; the responsibility rested upon them. Hence, Jesus says that in order to take from them that which they have, namely, the means of understanding his teachings merely to pervert and abuse them, he spake in parables. They could see and hear the narrative of the parables, but did not understand the truths embodied in them. Mark 4: 12 and Luke 8: 10

unto them is fulfilled the prophecy of Isaiah, which saith,
>²By hearing ye shall hear, and shall in no wise understand;
>And seeing ye shall see, and shall in no wise perceive:
>15 For this people's heart is waxed gross,
>And their ears are dull of hearing.

²Is. vi. 9, 10.

state that "seeing they may not see." This means that the people would not hear and therefore the truth was uttered in a form to leave them free to hear or not; hearing the recitation of the parables was not hearing the truth of them. They had witnessed great miracles, but the sight did them no good; they were as much opposed to Jesus as they were before they witnessed the miracles. They had heard the plainest offers of mercy, but were deaf to them; why then should the more secret truths of the gospel, which were yet incomplete, be exposed to the scorn of unbelievers? God gives light; but if a man blinds himself, God does not force that one to see. There is a penalty for the nonuse of the powers which God has given us; there is a penalty for the nonimprovement of our faculties; there is a condemnation on our failing to see the plain and simple truth of God.

14-16 And unto them is fulfilled the prophecy of Isaiah.— This quotation from Isaiah is found in Isa. 6: 9, 10; Jesus applied it to the people of his day who refused to accept his teaching. Paul made a similar application of it. (Acts 28: 26, 27.) It is true and may be applied in every age. Isaiah asks, "Lord, how long?" And Jesus answered "until cities be waste," that is, he extended Isaiah's prophecy which was fulfilled in his day and extended it into a prediction. It seems that the Jewish nation was ever obstinate and rebellious; their history reveals this fact. The strong inference from the application that Jesus makes of it is that, no matter what he would do or say, they would not obey him or receive what he said. It was like casting the pearls of truth before swine to present his teachings to their sensual and prejudiced minds.

For this people's heart is waxed gross.—This is an ancient figure used by Isaiah; their hearts had become fat, as applied to the body; sensual and stupid as applied to the mind; they

> And their eyes they have closed;
> Lest haply they should perceive with their eyes,
> And hear with their ears,
> And understand with their heart,
> And should turn again,
> And I should heal them.
>
> 16 But blessed are your eyes, for they see; and your ears, for they hear,

were like a man overcome with obesity, too heavy and dull to hear or see, sleepy and brutish. The spiritual spark is buried in a heap of earthly cares and pleasures. (Deut. 32: 15.) There is an analogy between the condition and the diseases of the body and the attitude and sins of the soul. Those whose hearts are surfeited with carnal objects are unwilling to listen to the gospel. Paul described young widows who, "when they have waxed wanton against Christ, they desire to marry . . . because they have rejected their first pledge." (1 Tim. 5: 11.) These people preferred to close their eyes against the truth, "lest haply they should perceive with their eyes, and hear with their ears, and understand with their heart, and should turn again, and I should heal them." These people had hardened their own hearts, had closed their own eyes, had refused to exercise their own powers of understanding, because they did not want to know the truth. The responsibility rested upon them for their present condition; they could not blame the law, God, or any one else; they were wholly responsible. It is the law of God's spiritual kingdom that resistance to truth hardens the heart. To reject the truth and excuse and defend themselves in opposition to it, they armed themselves with countless errors and falsehoods. Their minds get into that state that the truth does not benefit them, but rather injures them and condemns them; it may be then an act of mercy to withhold the truth from such; they may use it to evil purposes, and thereby bring upon themselves greater sin; or they may have so insulted the truth that they have by their own guilt rendered themselves unworthy of it.

But blessed are your eyes, for they see.—The disciples of Jesus had learned to love him as a teacher and had accepted his truth; they saw not only the outside shell of truth, but the inner kernel; they heard not only the literal narrative of the

17 For veritly I say unto you, that many prophets and righteous men desired to see the things which ye see, and saw them not; and to hear the things which

parable, but its secret meaning. That hidden meaning is the very substance of divine wisdom; it revealed the truths of the Messiah's kingdom of grace on earth and of glory in heaven; it opens the truth of the Old Testament to their minds and explains the mysteries dimly sen by the ancient prophets. His apostles had received what was offered, had obeyed the call to follow him, had been able to exercise faith in his miracles and his teachings; they had seen and heard. This faith others seemed to despise. The disciples were blessed, while others were condemned.

17 **Many prophets and righteous men desired to see.**—The disciples were blessed above "many prophets and righteous men," for they were privileged to hear and see things that "holy men of old" "desired to see," but were not permitted to. Though there had been the faithful company of prophets and good men, of whose fame they had heard, yet these disciples were more blessed than the others who had preceded them. The "prophets and righteous men" of the Jewish race looked to the future for the coming of the Messiah; the disciples had seen him, were associated with him daily, and had received a fuller knowledge, greater gifts, and more excellent promises than they had. "Abraham rejoiced to see my day; and he saw it, and was glad." (John 8: 56.) Moses, looking to that future day, chose "rather to share ill treatment with the people of God, than to enjoy the pleasures of sin for a season; accounting the reproach of Christ greater riches than the treasures of Egypt: for he looked unto the recompense of reward." (Heb. 11: 25, 26.) In the patriarchal and Jewish dispensations, good men walked by faith in the future coming of the Messiah; the light of their knowledge increased from age to age, but never equaled the full revelation of the gospel. The disciples of Jesus had come into a full realization of those blessings to which "many prophets and righteous men" had desired to see. The enemies of Jesus rejected him, and thereby rejected those blessings which the "prophets and

ye hear, and heard them not. 18 Hear then ye the parable of the sower. 19 When any one heareth the word of the kingdom, and understandeth it not, *then* cometh the evil *one,* and snatcheth away that which hath been sown in his heart. This is he that was sown by the way side. 20 And he that was sown upon the rocky places, this is he that heareth the word, and straight-

---

righteous men" had foretold and desired to enjoy. No wonder the condemnation was so severe upon them. The times of the Messiah, the character of his kingdom were all a matter of profound interest to the prophets of the Old Testament. All these were now being revealed to the humble and obedient apostles of our Lord; the men of old saw them only by faith in types, shadows, and dim intimations; the Jews rejected them; the leaders among them rejected them; but the simple disciples of Jesus received them and were blessed.

18-23 **Hear then ye the parable of the sower.**—Jesus at the request of his apostles when they were alone explained the parable of the sower; it was given to them "to know the mysteries of the kingdom of heaven" (verse 11) and Jesus now makes clear to them its meaning. First he explains the meaning of the seeds which "fell by the way side." "When any one heareth the word of the kingdom, and understandeth it not, then cometh the evil one, and snatcheth away that which hath been sown in his heart." Jesus does not make distinctions of grace to depend on the intellect merely, but on the use of all our faculties. The one who lays the word to heart and obeys it does all he needs to do to be saved. There are at least three kinds of false hearers described here: (1) Who receive, as if they were not receiving; (2) who receive not into their affections; (3) who receive without expelling their sinful passions. As the grains fell "by the way side" and the birds devoured them, so the word of God, which is the seed of the kingdom, when it falls into the hearts of such hearers, is permitted to be taken out or snatched away by "the evil one" or the devil. The devil knows the power of the word of God and he seeks to remove it before it has had effect on the life. If the devil can fortify the mind in advance with doubtful arguments, he is satisfied. Many hearers come within this class; they let "the evil one" take away and nullify the word of God.

way with joy receiveth it; 21 yet hath he not root in himself, but endureth for a while; and when tribulation or persecution ariseth because of the word, straightway he stumbleth. 22 And he that was sown among the thorns, this is he that heareth the word; and the care of the ³world, and the deceitfulness of riches, choke the word, and he becometh unfruitful. 23 And he that was

---

³Or, *age*

And he that was sown upon the rocky places.—Rocky surfaces were covered with thin soil. The seed fell into this soil and sprang up as though it would grow and bear abundantly; but so soon as the sun came out the plants withered. Jesus says that such hearers are those who "with joy receiveth" the word, "yet hath he not root in himself, but endureth for a while." Hearers of this description were more clearly seen to fall away in times of persecution; they seemed for a while to be very promising and to make faithful members of the church, but "when tribulation or persecution ariseth because of the word, straightway he stumbleth." There are many hearers with a surface soft and yielding, but a nature truly hard at the bottom. In such the shallow emotions are quickly stirred, but their deeper nature remains untouched. The Jews were full of joyous excitement at John's first preaching that "the kingdom of heaven is at hand," but, with many of them, there was only a superficial arousement; the heart was not truly converted. When the Messiah's true nature was disclosed, they soon showed that the subsoil was unchanged rock. Such hearers have always been upon the earth; they make weak, trifling and unstable members of the church, into whose hearts the true principles of piety have no more descended than the fibers of a plant into the flinty rock. (James 1: 23-26.) They conform to the lowest standards of piety if they remain in the church and keep up fellowship with the world.

And he that was sown among the thorns.—This represents "he that heareth the word; and the care of the world, and the deceitfulness of riches, choke the word, and he becometh unfruitful." While the rains lasted, both thorns and the good seed grew; but when they ceased the bad prevailed and the

sown upon the good ground, this is he that heareth the word, and understandeth it; who verily beareth fruit, and bringeth forth, some a hundredfold, some sixty, some thirty.

good was destroyed. Such hearers show many virtues and some graces for a time. The seed is good, the soil is good, the growth is genuine, internally everything is right; but while all is going well within there are difficulties without, which in time prove fatal. What are those enemies without? Jesus says they are "the care of the world, and the deceitfulness of riches." The cares of the world have a powerful effect on the hearts of the disciples of Jesus; there is the constant warfare between the good and the affairs of this world. These affairs are business, pleasure, desire for worldly comfort and splendor, the roots of anger, fierce passions, and ignorance, and suchlike. All these are enemies of the soul. The second thing is "the deceitfulness of riches." Some become rich, others desire to be rich. Wealth is always deceitful because it promises what it never performs; again, it is frequently possessed, hoarded, and employed in a deceitful manner. (Luke 21: 34.) "But they that are minded to be rich fall into a temptation and a snare and many foolish and hurtful lusts, such as drown men in destruction and perdition. For the love of money is a root of all kinds of evil: which some reaching after have been led astray from the faith, and have pierced themselves through with many sorrows." (1 Tim. 6: 9, 10.)

And he that was sown upon the good ground.—Luke says "in an honest and good heart." (Luke 8: 15.) A sincere and honest desire for truth, a candor in hearing it, and a willingness to receive it are necessary to produce an abundant harvest. Nothing that we can do will merit in any degree salvation, but we must still do what God commands in order to receive the blessings of salvation. "This is he that heareth the word, and understandeth it." The good ground of the human heart takes God at his word and without hesitation does what he commands and trusts him implicitly for his blessings. He is willing to be guided by the truth of God and is satisfied

24 Another parable set he before them, saying, The kingdom of heaven is likened unto a man that sowed good seed in his field: 25 but while men slept, his enemy came and sowed [1]tares also among the wheat, and went away. 26 But when the blade sprang up and brought forth fruit, then appeared the tares also. 27 And the [2]servants of the householder came and said unto him, Sir, didst thou not sow good seed in thy field? whence then hath it tares? 28 And he said unto them, [3]An enemy hath done this. And the [2]servants say unto him, Wilt thou then that we go and gather them up? 29 But he saith, Nay; lest haply while ye gather up the tares, ye root up the wheat

[1]Or, *darnel*
[2]Gr. *bondservants*
[3]Gr. *A man* that is *an enemy.*

---

with that truth; such a one bears abundant fruit, "some a hundredfold, some sixty, some thirty."

The parable of the sower divides the hearers of the gospel into four classes. This is Jesus' classification and we must accept it. These classes are as follows: (1) The mere unintelligent hearer, who hears but receives not; (2) the shallow hearer, whose emotions are superficially touched, but whose heart is still hard; (3) the hearer whose heart is fully right, but is at last conquered by outward temptations; (4) the persevering and fruitful receiver of the word; of the four classes, only the last one can be saved.

24-30 Another parable set he before them.—"The kingdom of heaven" is elsewhere in the New Testament "the kingdom of God," "kingdom of the Son of his love," etc. The Jews misunderstood the spirit and nature of this kingdom; even his disciples did not understand it, thinking that it would be an earthly kingdom. This parable of the tares represents another phase. It is likened "unto a man that sowed good seed in his field"; in the dead of night, while the man was asleep, and the soil prepared, his enemy came and maliciously sowed "tares also among the wheat, and went away." "Tares" is better known as "darnel," which is a species of the same family with the wheat, resembling it very closely up to the point of the forming of its head, and is therefore a sore pest and nuisance to the wheatgrower. It was a common practice in the days of Jesus for enemies to do such things. We are told that "darnel" resembles our American "cheat," but the head does not droop like cheat, nor does it branch out like oats.

with them. 30 Let both grow together until the harvest: and in the time of the harvest I will say to the reapers, Gather up first the tares, and bind them in bundles to burn them; but gather the wheat into my barn.
31 Another parable set he before them, saying, The kingdom of heaven is like unto a grain of mustard seed, which a man took, and sowed in his field: 32 which indeed is less than all seeds; but when it is grown, it is greater than the herbs, and becometh a tree, so that the birds of the heaven come and lodge in the branches thereof.

When the "servants of the householder came and said unto him." The servants of the man who sowed the good seed discovered about the time that the wheat began to head that the enemy had sown tares; they did not know what to do about it and asked the master, "Wilt thou then that we go and gather them up?" The master replied that it was best to "let both grow together until the harvest," and that then the reapers would "gather up first the tares, and bind them in bundles to burn them." Too much wheat would be destroyed at that time if the "darnel" was destroyed. The explanation of this parable is found in the comments on verses thirty-six to forty-three.

31, 32 **The kingdom of heaven is like unto a grain of mustard seed.**—Here another phase of the "kingdom of heaven" or earthly kingdom is presented. This time a man took a mustard seed and sowed it in his field; it was "less than all seeds," but it grew and became a tree, "so that the birds of the heaven come and lodge in the branches thereof." The mustard seed is not the smallest seed known, but it was smaller than wheat, rye, barley, and suchlike; it was smaller than any seed commonly planted in gardens; this is the point that Jesus makes. From such a small seed a large shrub grows, and becomes a good illustration of great results from very small apparent causes. The parable means that though the kingdom of heaven may begin with a small group of insignificant men, yet it will grow to enormous proportions. The parable represents the growth of the kingdom from its small beginning on the day of Pentecost to its large borders of the present day; and its growth is not yet attained. It will continue to grow until Christ comes again. Its growth may increase in the heart and life of an individual and it may grow in external proportions.

33 Another parable spake he unto them; The kingdom of heaven is like unto leaven, which a woman took, and hid in three ⁴measures of meal, till it was all leavened.

---

⁴The word in the Greek denotes the Hebrew seah, a measure containing nearly a peck and a half.

This parable is so simple and its meaning so obvious that no explanation of it was asked by the disciples nor offered by Jesus.

33 The kingdom of heaven is like unto leaven.—"Leaven" or yeast is an element used in making bread. The realm of the housewife supplies this parable. The leaven, hid in meal, diffuses itself by its very nature, pressing evermore outward from one particle to another till it permeates the whole mass. The kingdom of heaven in one particular is like this leaven, "which a woman took, and hid in three measures of meal, till it was all leavened." In this parable there is no significance to be given to "a woman" nor to "three measures of meal." The parable is taken from the domain of women and it was their business to do the cooking; "three measures" was the amount usually used for a meal. The parable simply means that the gospel truth when planted in the heart will leaven the life of the individual, and also will permeate and influence human society. The parable seems to be prophetic and is in fulfillment today. It is the nature of the kingdom of God to influence and bless all that may come within reach of it.

[Leaven is an active working principle. It may be an active working principle of good, or it may be an active principle of evil. Place either in an inactive mass, and it will leaven the whole mass into a good or bad working mass. The church of God is intended to be a leaven, an active working leaven of good in the world. If it retains its working principle, it will leaven for good the world around it.

The church itself often becomes an inactive, lifeless mass. A leaven of good or evil working and spreading in the church will work for good or evil and leaven the whole church for good or evil. Lukewarmness is contagious, and from one or two may destroy the whole church. Zeal and devotion, life and activity in a few for good may leaven the whole church

34 All these things spake Jesus in parables unto the multitudes; and without a parable spake he nothing unto them: 35 that it might be fulfilled which was spoken through the prophet, saying,
⁵I will open my mouth in parables;
I will utter things hidden from the foundation ⁶of the world.

⁵Ps. lxxviii. 2.
⁶Many ancient authorities omit *of the world*.

---

for good, and may transform the church into an active, living power for good in the world. God demands his children shall throw off their lukewarmness and indifference and should leaven the whole church into an active, living body, that in turn will leaven the world for much good.

Do we constitute a leaven for good or for evil? If for good, God's blessing will rest upon us that we may be a blessing to others. If we are a leaven of lukewarmness, God will spew us out of his mouth and reject us. We will be a curse to ourselves and to others. Which will we be? Are we helping the church and the world, or are we dead weights to be carried by others?]

34, 35 **All these things spake Jesus in parables.**—These principles or truths pertaining to the kingdom of heaven were spoken in parables to the multitude. At this time he spake nothing to the people concerning his kingdom or church except in parables. On matters of duty and things pertaining to his own Messiahship, Jesus often instructed the multitude by direct teaching, as it is seen in the sermon on the mount; but now, speaking of that which was yet future and concealed, of which they were not able to judge, he taught them by parables "as they were able to hear it." (Mark 4: 33.) So before and after this occasion he taught in literal language. In doing this was fulfilled the scripture. Matthew frequently states that scriptures were fulfilled by the teaching of Jesus and events connected with his earthly ministry; Matthew sometimes expresses it as though Jesus did this *in order to fulfill the scriptures,* whereas in the doing of it the scriptures were fulfilled. This scripture is found in Psalm 78: 2. This psalm is ascribed to Asaph, the chief of the singers in King David's time. (1 Chron. 6: 39.) Matthew quotes the meaning of this song instead of the exact words. The sentiment of

36 Then he left the multitudes, and went into the house: and his disciples came unto him, saying, Explain unto us the parable of the tares of the field. 37 And he answered and said, He that soweth the good seed is the Son of man; 38 and the field is the world; and the good seed, these are the sons of the kingdom; and the tares are the sons of the evil *one;* 39 and the enemy that sowed them is the devil: and the harvest is ⁷the end of the world; and

---

⁷Or, *the consummation of the age*

---

the psalm was exemplified by this mode of Jesus' teaching. "I will utter things hidden from the foundation of the world" means that Jesus was giving for the first time a description of his kingdom and its nature. The secret things contained in Jesus' parables were the mysteries of the gospel, "which for ages hath been hid in God who created all things." (Eph. 3: 9.) So the words of the psalmist were fulfilled in the teachings of Christ by his use of the parables.

36-43 Then he left the multitudes, and went into the house.—Jesus had been teaching the multitudes on the seashore; he now dismissed the congregation and "went into the house." He went into one of the houses near by. After entering the house "his disciples came unto him" and asked him to "explain unto us the parable of the tares of the field." They did not ask for an explanation of the other parables, either because they had understood them, or were not further interested in them. Jesus at once explained to them the parable recorded in verses twenty-four to thirty.

This parable has been misunderstood and erroneous applications of it have been made. Yet, it and the parable of the sower are the only two that Jesus explained. It seems that we might takes Jesus' explanation of it and be satisfied. Some have been eager to find here authority for "church discipline" and "excommunication" which is not found elsewhere in the New Testament. It is a case of fitting the parable to instances of evil practices to justify them. Jesus said that the Son of man sowed the good seed; that "the field is the world," not the church"; "the good seed" "are the sons of the kingdom"; "the tares" "are the sons of the evil one"; "the enemy that sowed them is the devil"; "the harvest is the end of the world"; "and the reapers are angels." These points are clear and emphatic; no one should misunderstand them, as

the reapers are angels. 40 As therefore the tares are gathered up and burned with fire; so shall it be in the ⁷end of the world. 41 The Son of man shall send forth his angels, and they shall gather out of his kingdom all things that cause stumbling, and them that do iniquity, 42 and shall cast them into the furnace of fire; there shall be weeping and the gnashing of

---

Jesus has so plainly listed them. There is no list of laws of discipline of church members here. To suppose that Jesus meant to teach that good and bad men must be permitted to live and work together in the church with no discipline by withdrawal is a perversion of the simple meaning given by Jesus of this parable. He does not say that "the field is the church," but that "the field is the world." There is no hint in the parable that his thought is upon church discipline. The sower is the Redeemer, the field is the world, the good seed are Christians, the tares are the wicked, and their sower is Satan. At the end of the world the angels shall gather out the harvest of wicked men to cast them into the fire of retribution. "The Son of man shall send forth his angels, and they shall gather out of his kingdom all things that cause stumbling, and them that do iniquity, and shall cast them into the furnace of fire." The final separation of the wicked from the righteous, and the destruction of them in fire, seems to be the burden of the parable. It has been disputed as to whether reference is made to all the wicked in the world, or only those in the church. The wicked shall be gathered "out of his kingdom" and destroyed. The term "kingdom" is usually limited to the church, but inasmuch as "all authority hath been given unto me in heaven and on earth" (Matt. 28: 18), his kingdom in reality includes the whole earth, and in one of the parables, that of the pounds (Luke 19: 14, 15, 27), the term is used to include both his willing subjects and those who "will not that this man reign over us." We can only determine by the context the meaning of the term "kingdom of heaven," that is, whether it has a wider application than that of the church. Two reasons force us to conclude that in this parable it has a wider application: (1) The field in which both the good and the bad were sown and the kingdom out of which were gathered are the same; but the field is the world, and therefore the kingdom is the world; (2) the good seed represent "the sons

teeth. 43 Then shall the righteous shine forth as the sun in the kingdom of their Father. He that hath ears⁸, let him hear.

⁸See ver. 9.

of the kingdom," those who accepted and submitted to the reign of Christ over the world. The tares represent all the children of the wicked one within the field, that is, all the wicked in the world.

Then shall the righteous shine forth as the sun in the kingdom of their Father.—The final results are that at the end of the world the wicked shall be destroyed and the righteous shall be gathered into the paradise of purity and bliss to shine forth as the sun in the kingdom of their Father. However hidden before, they shall be manifested then, as the Son reveals himself by his splendor. "In the kingdom of their Father" means the heavenly state. (1 Cor. 15: 24.) We have here a very clear contradiction of the millenarian theory that there are two resurrections, one of the righteous, another of the wicked, a thousand years apart; neither is there any teaching that God will first destroy the wicked and allow the saints to reign on earth a thousand years before the final judgment. In the parable the wicked and the righteous will both continue undestroyed until the final judgment when the separation will take place.

[The parable of the tares teaches that no angel or superhuman being will interfere in the affairs of earth till the end. God created the world, sowed good seed in it, and entrusted it to men to keep and rule. The earth was the kingdom. Men slept, were off guard, and while asleep an enemy, or the enemy, sowed the seeds of sin in it. When the angels saw this, they asked the Master: "Shall we root out these tares which the enemy has sown?" God said: "No, lest in rooting up the evil you root up the good also. Let them remain in the earth until the end of the world, then will I send forth my servants, the angels, and gather the good into my garner and burn up the tares, the wicked." In the parables the angels are his servants. The wheat represents the good people; the tares, the wicked. The servants cannot represent the angels

44 The kingdom of heaven is like unto a treasure hidden in the field; which a man found, and hid; and ⁹in his joy he goeth and selleth all that he hath, and buyeth that field.
45 Again, the kingdom of heaven is like unto a man that is a merchant

---

⁹Or, *for joy thereof*

and the good people both. The parable teaches there will be no interference of the affairs of earth until the judgment.]

44 The kingdom of heaven is like unto a treasure hidden in the field.—No one parable can teach all the truth and develop all points of the kingdom of heaven; hence, Jesus presents another parable. In some particular the kingdom of heaven is like a hidden treasure, "which a man found, and hid" again; then "in his joy he goeth and selleth all that he hath, and buyeth that field." In the east, we are told that it is very common for men to hide their treasures in the ground, either in the ground floor of a house or in the field. Oftentimes the man who has hidden the treasure dies without revealing the place of its concealment. This man found a treasure, but did not take it from the field, but removed it to another spot where he would know its location; he then, knowing the value of it, sold all that he had, and purchased that field. Jesus does not commend the action of the man in taking advantage of the owner of the field; he impresses the man's eagerness to purchase the field. The man is willing to give up everything that he has in order to purchase this field; with like joy, with such supreme endeavor and with similar wisdom of plan should men seek for the kingdom of heaven. When they get only a dim glimpse of the priceless treasure there is in it, they can spare nothing to attain it; it is worthy of such sacrifices and endeavors. The joy of the man at the discovery of the treasure, and the eagerness with which he sold his possessions in order to purchase the field, is the joy and eagerness that one should have in discovering the truth of God.

45, 46 Again, the kingdom of heaven is like unto a man that is a merchant.—As the parable of the hidden treasure illustrates the joy and eagerness which one should manifest in discovering the kingdom of God, so this parable illustrates its

13: 46-50.] MATTHEW 303

seeking goodly pearls: 46 and having found one pearl of great price, he went and sold all that he had, and bought it.

47 Again, the kingdom of heaven is like unto a [10]net, that was cast into the sea, and gathered of every kind: 48 which, when it was filled, they drew up on the beach; and they sat down, and gathered the good into vessels, but the bad they cast away. 49 So shall it be in [7]the end of the world: the angels shall come forth, and sever the wicked from among the righteous, 50 and shall cast them into the furnace of fire: there shall be the weeping and the gnashing of teeth.

[10]Gr. *drag-net*.

---

unsurpassed duty and value. Pearls are gems of great beauty and value. The dealer in pearls finds one of exquisite beauty and rareness; it is unequal to any one that he has ever seen; he loves it; he will own it, if it costs all that he has; it will make him happy to possess it. All else is cheap beside it. So the inheritance of Christ's kingdom is a pearl which any man is wise to sell all he has to buy. One must put this estimate upon the kingdom of God and its truth or else he will never enjoy them. He must forego all else that he holds dear to make sure of the kingdom of God. This parable, like the hidden treasure, shows how truly wise one is who puts Christ before and above all other good—that puts the kingdom of God first.

47-50 **Again, the kingdom of heaven is like unto a net.**—In this parable the kingdom of heaven is like a dragnet which sweeps the bottom of a fishpool; it is extended far into the sea, corked at the upper edge and leaded at the bottom, so as to catch the fish at the entire depth. The ends are then brought together so as to encompass them, and then the net is drawn in. All sorts are brought into it, and they gather the good into vessels, but the bad they cast away. The kingdom of God is like the net in that it gathers both good and bad into it, and in that there will be eventually a separation of the two classes; this is similar to the parable of the tares. Jesus says nothing about the destiny of the good, but draws attention to the destiny of the evil. "The angels shall come forth, and sever the wicked from among the righteous, and shall cast them into the furnace of fire." Fire has been the emblem of

51 Have ye understood all these things? They say unto him, Yea. 52 And he said unto them, Therefore every scribe who hath been made a disciple to the kingdom of heaven is like unto a man that is a householder, who bringeth forth out of his treasure things new and old.

---

the punishment of the wicked all down through God's dealings with man.

Again it is noted that the good and bad are left together until "the angels shall come forth, and sever" them. "The furnace of fire" is the well-known place of woe for the persistent, unrepentant enemies of God; it is the symbol of the eternal destruction of the wicked. The "furnace of fire" mentioned here and in the parable of the tares (verse forty-two) represents the final abode of the wicked, since the wicked are cast into it "in the end of the world." "The weeping and the gnashing of teeth" is a strong figure representing the intense suffering and agony of the doomed and damned.

51, 52 **Have ye understood all these things?**—Jesus was anxious that his disciples understand him; when God speaks to man, he wants man to hear and understand, and he speaks in man's language so that man may understand. He had spoken in parables, and unless they are understood they mean but little. He meant not merely to ask if they understood the narration of the stories, but their second and deeper meanings. They answered "Yea." They said they understood and they thought they did, but they did not understand the full meaning of his teachings.

Therefore every scribe who hath been made a disciple to the kingdom.—A "scribe" originally meant one who by profession was a transcriber of the manuscripts of the law, but ultimately came to be applied to religious instructors. He is likened by our Savior "unto a man that is a householder, who bringeth forth out of his treasure things new and old." They did not have banks then as we have now, but did have treasure houses in which moneys, clothes, and other useful things were stored. "A householder" was one who had charge of a family, whose duty it was to clothe, feed, and govern them. From his storehouse he brought out "things new and old" as any members of his household needed things. The one who learns of the kingdom of God and has his heart filled with the knowledge of the truth or one who lets "the word of Christ dwell" in him "richly" is like this householder. His stores of treasured truth, his illustrations of it, should be so full that in any emergency he can bring forth "things new and old" with wise adaptation to the ever varying need of his household.

Matthew has grouped seven parables in this chapter. There is a natural historical advancement in the seven parables. The first one, the sower, the word of God is sown as seed among the different hearers of men; the second, that of the tares, shows the struggle between good and evil to be permanent to the final separation; the third, the grain of mustard seed, shows the small beginning, but final triumph of the kingdom of God; the fourth, parable of the leaven, shows the progress of the kingdom of God, in the heart of the individual and in society; the fifth, hidden treasure, shows the value of the truth, even in its obscured and hidden state; the sixth, merchants seeking goodly pearls, shows the worthiness of the kingdom of God and its truth to be far above any price; seventh, householder, shows the wealth in the heart of the one who received and retained the words of Jesus. Four of these parables were spoken to the multitudes on the shore of Galilee, and three of them to his disciples in the house, probably his home in Capernaum.

11. JESUS REJECTED AT NAZARETH
13: 53-58

53 And it came to pass, when Jesus had finished these parables, he departed thence.

---

53 When Jesus had finished these parables.—Jesus was in Capernaum and in a few days after this teaching left; it is supposed to be October or November. Some think that he probably went to Jerusalem in December to attend the feast of dedication; however, we do not know, and the Holy Spirit has not recorded in chronological order the events of his life; therefore it is not necessary to attempt to arrange them in

54 And coming into his own country he taught them in their synagogue, insomuch that they were astonished, and said, Whence hath this man this wisdom, and these ¹mighty works? 55 Is not this the carpenter's son? is not his mother called Mary? and his brethren, James, and Joseph, and Simon, and Judas? 56 And his sisters, are they not all with us? Whence then hath this man all these things? 57 And they were ³offended in him. But Jesus

¹Gr. *powers.*
²Or, *Jacob*

---

such order. These events seem to close the second year of his earthly ministry.

54-56 And coming into his own country he taught.—"His own country," that is, Nazareth, which was only a few miles west of Capernaum. "He taught them in their synagogue," which was on the Sabbath. (Mark 6: 1-6.) The questions asked concerning him were asked on the Sabbath, after he had taught the people in their synagogue. It was common for any prophet or good man to address the people in the synagogue; Jesus was busy teaching the people; he never lost an opportunity. His wisdom "astonished" them, and they asked, "Whence hath this man this wisdom, and these mighty works?" Jesus had astonished his home people on a former occasion. (Luke 4: 16-32.) The question that they asked about his wisdom implied contempt as they asked "whence hath this man" such wisdom? So long as they rejected him there was no solution to the question, but if they accepted him as the Messiah, all was clear and simple.

They further asked, "Is not this the carpenter's son?" Mark records it, "Is not this the carpenter?" A carpenter here means one who worked in iron, stone, or wood. The ancient tradition has it that Joseph was a carpenter, and Matthew bears this out. Mark's record shows that Jesus followed the humble occupation of his reputed parent until he began his ministry, and went about his "Father's business." Jesus was a carpenter and his apostles were Galilean fishermen; none of his disciples today should be ashamed of any humble profession. They further asked, "Is not his mother called Mary? and his brethren, James, and Joseph, and Simon, and Judas?" Some have attempted to show that Mary remained a virgin after her miraculous conception and the birth of Jesus;

said unto them, A prophet is not without honor, save in his own country,

---

ᵃGr. *caused to stumble.*

---

hence they have worshiped her as such. They claim that these mentioned here as brothers of Jesus were his cousins. It seems that Mary the mother of Jesus had a sister named Mary and that this sister had sons by the same names; this seems unreasonable, but is an explanation offered by many scholars. The "mother" and "sisters" here seem to be literal mother and sisters, and hence the brethren were literal brothers; probably they were half brothers. At any rate, they are mentioned here to show that Jesus was only an ordinary man; that he was not what he claimed to be. Hence, they contemptuously asked, "Whence then hath this man all these things?" In Matt. 12: 46-50, we have his mother and brethren who came from Nazareth to visit him and probably to persuade him to give up his public work. It may be of little consequence as to whether these mentioned here were only his kinspeople or whether they were members of his immediate family.

57, 58 And they were offended in him.—The jealously, pride, and self-conceit, which go to make up the trait of character here exhibited, must impress us painfully as it did Jesus. He never manifested the slightest qualities of character or spirit to provoke enmity against him; there never was a man more meek, modest, humble, and affectionate; Jesus had every quality that upright souls should love and esteem, yet he could not escape even the jealousy of his own people; neither could he avoid their positive hostility toward him. Hence, Jesus applied to them the common maxim, "A prophet is not without honor, save in his own country, and in his own house." It seems that some slighted Jesus for the lowliness of his parentage, and rejected his teachings from prejudice. The people had often seen the truth of the proverb that Jesus here quoted, and so they should have profited by it, and not again have fulfilled it to their own shame. His people stumbled at his superiority and did not want to acknowledge that he was better than themselves; their stupid pride blinded their hearts

and in his own house. 58 And he did not many ¹mighty works there because of their unbelief.

so that they could not see in his teachings and his mighty works the evidence of his Messiahship.

And he did not many mighty works there because of their unbelief.—Mark adds that he "laid his hands upon a few sick folk, and healed them." (Mark 6: 5.) The reason assigned for the lack of his working miracles among them is "because of their unbelief." Their invincible prejudice against him rendered them inattentive to his doctrine and stirred their prejudice against him. Miracles were wrought as evidence that his teachings were true; he did not wish to work miracles before men who stubbornly refused to see a prophet in their townsmen. These same Nazarenes sought to take his life. (Luke 4: 29.) They blinded their eyes and hardened their hearts; they refused to accept Jesus; hence, it would be a waste of divine power to perform miracles that would be disregarded and condemned. It may be that the people refused to let many of the afflicted come to Jesus for healing. Both morally and physically they rendered the performance of mighty works a thing out of the question. Mark puts it that "he could there do no mighty work." (Mark 6: 5.) Jesus would not do a useless and unsuitable deed. The light that they had and what they might have had became their heaviest curse, so that ultimately Nazareth fell under more fearful woes than did Sodom.

12. JOHN THE BAPTIST BEHEADED
14: 1-12

1 At that season Herod the tetrarch heard the report concerning Jesus,

1, 2 At that season Herod the tetrarch heard the report.—"At that season" does not fix definitely the order of the events. Parallel records of this are found in Mark 6: 14-16; Luke 4: 7-9. Some place this at the time that the apostles were away on their limited commission. "Herod the tetrarch" is Herod Antipas. There are three men of this name, and four of the family mentioned in the New Testament. Herod had died (Matt. 2: 19), while Joseph and Mary, with

2 and said unto his servants, This is John the Baptist; he is risen from the

the child Jesus, were in Egypt; at his death Herod left his kingdom to be divided between his three sons. Archelaus received Judea, Idumea, and Samaria; Herod Philip received Batanea, Trachonitis, and Gallonitis; and Herod Antipas, the tetrarch, notorious for the murder of John the Baptist, received Galilee and Perea. He first married a daughter of Aretas, whom he dismissed for love of Herodias. He was banished by Caligula to Gaul, and the province given to Herod Agrippa. "Tetrarch" is a Greek word signifying a ruler of the fourth part of the kingdom. Under the order of the emperor of Rome, the kingdom of Herod the Great, father of Herod Antipas, was, upon his death, divided into three tetrarchies, and given to Herod's sons. It is not clear why the kingdom was divided into three parts, but a ruler over one part called "tetrarch."

Herod Antipas and Herod Philip were brothers, both being sons of Herod the Great; Herodias, Philip's wife, was their niece, being a daughter of Aristobulus. Herod Philip was living in retirement in Rome when his brother Herod Antipas became his guest. While enjoying his hospitality there, the transfer of Philip's wife Herodias to his brother, Herod Antipas, took place, and in a way which fastened crime upon both parties, and probably not least upon Herodias. Her greater guilt may account for her sharper resentment and more desperate revenge. There was no excuse for the crime, as Herod Antipas' wife was still living, and Herodias' husband still alive. The forsaken wife of Antipas was a daughter of Aretas, king of Arabia, who resented the insult to his family and throne, and marched upon Herod Antipas shortly after this murder of John the Baptist, and routed him with great slaughter.

When Herod "heard the report concerning Jesus," he "said unto his servants, This is John the Baptist." John had been beheaded before this and Herod thought that Jesus was John the Baptist "risen from the dead." This is the reason assigned by Herod for the mighty works which Jesus was

dead; and therefore do these powers work in him. 3 For Herod had laid hold on John, and bound him, and put him in prison for the sake of Hero-

doing. We learn from Luke 8: 3 that among those who administered to Jesus of their substance was Joanna, the wife of Chuzas, Herod's steward. Again in Acts 13: 1 we have "Manaen the foster-brother of Herod the tetrarch" mentioned among other distinguished converts. So at a later period there were saints in Caesar's household as there were believers in the household of Herod. We are not told why Herod thought that Jesus was John the Baptist rather than some other prophet; but the inference is clear that Herod was disturbed by his own guilty conscience, as he had slain John to please a lewd woman against his own convictions. From Mark 6: 15 we learn that this fear had taken fast hold of Herod, and he would not believe those who offered other explanations of the miracles of Jesus; he could only see the consequence of his own crime hanging over him. Herod had heard of the great fame of Jesus and his haunted conscience made him yet more active in seeking an explanation for the miracles of Jesus; he saw John the Baptist whom he had murdered risen from the dead, and therefore clothed with power for such miracles.

3-5 **For Herod had laid hold on John.**—At this point Matthew goes back in time to the occasion and scenes of this murder and relates the details of it. We have no way to determine how long it has been since the crime was committed. Herod had put John in prison where he remained probably a year. John was imprisoned soon after Jesus began his public ministry; John's ministry and Jesus' ministry overlapped about six months. The cause of John's imprisonment as recorded is that John had rebuked Herod and Herodias for their sinful life; he had said, "It is not lawful for thee to have her." Herod claimed to be a believer in the law of Moses, and this law forbade such relations as Herod and Herodias had formed. (Lev. 18: 14-16; 20: 21.) Herod had heard John in his early ministry and may have committed himself to John's preaching. Herodias seems to have been more revengeful

dias, his brother Philip's wife. 4 For John said unto him, It is not lawful for thee to have her. 5 And when he would have put him to death, he feared the multitude, because they counted him as a prophet. 6 But when Herod's birthday came, the daughter of Herodias danced in the midst, and pleased Herod. 7 Whereupon he promised with an oath to give her whatsoever she should ask. 8 And she, being put forward by her mother, saith, Give me

---

than Herod; her husband was living at the time, as was Herod's wife; so they were living in adultery, and as she was the wife of his half brother, it was also incest. It appears from Luke 3: 19, 20 that John had reproved Herod for other crimes. John was the true antitype of Elijah; as Elijah reproved Ahab and Jezebel, so John reproved Herod and Herodias. Herodias' grudge against John was because of his condemnation of her marriage with Herod. (Mark 6: 18, 19.) Herod would have put John to death earlier, but "he feared the multitude, because they counted him as a prophet." Herod was teased and urged by Herodias to put John to death, and would have yielded before he did had he not been afraid of the people, for they considered John a prophet.

6-12 **But when Herod's birthday came.**—The ancients, both Jews and Gentiles, kept their birthdays with great rejoicings. (Gen. 40: 20.) Frequently there would be a number of festivities on such occasions. According to Mark, Herod's birthday festivities were done with great magnificence, as he "made a supper to his lords, and the high captains, and the chief men of Galilee." (Mark 6: 21.) The nobility of Galilee must have come some distance for this occasion. At this time "the daughter of Herodias danced in the midst, and pleased Herod." Female dancers in the east are still a customary part of great entertainments; on this occasion the dancer was of high birth, being no other than the princess Salome, daughter of Herodias. She was the daughter of Philip, Herod's brother, and by his marriage to her mother, she was his stepdaughter. Herodias, herself, was Herod's niece. If this girl's dancing partook of all the lascivious motions of the Greek dancers, she was a fit daughter of such parents. History reveals the corruption that was exhibited in eastern courts; dancers exhibited themselves in immodest attire and aped all of the emotions of sensual carnality. "And pleased Herod."

here on a platter the head of John the Baptist. 9 And the king was grieved; but for the sake of his oaths, and of them that sat at meat with him, he commanded it to be given; 10 and he sent and beheaded John in the prison.

This shows the corruption of the court as such delighted Herod and his associates. He was so pleased that he made a rash promise. He may have been drunken as was the custom at such festivities. He "promised with an oath to give her whatsoever she should ask." This was an extravagant and unguarded promise; it ill befitted a ruler of any people. He not only made the promise, but made it "with an oath." This was a foolish and wicked oath for a ruler to make; the rashness and madness of it could be exceeded only by the horrible purpose to which it was perverted. It is unwise in parents to promise children "anything they want"; again, any one is very foolish to give that which is harmful because one has promised it. Herod promised this dancing girl all she could ask, which meant all that she would be expected to ask in return for such a feat of dancing. He should have refused her bloody request.

The girl was encouraged by her mother to ask for the head of John the Baptist on a platter. Herod was grieved when she made this request, "but for the sake of his oaths, and of them that sat at meat with him, he commanded it to be given." "A platter" is a large deep plate or basin, and is frequently used on such occasions; the Greek word signifies "a flat board," used for any purpose, as for a "writing table or tablet"; it may mean a large dish in which meat or other food is carved or served. It seems that there was no delay and that the plot was doubtless previously laid by Herodias, and that she was just waiting for this occasion. It was customary for kings to grant any petition presented on a festal occasion of this sort. In the east as soon as any one is condemned to death, an officer is called and immediately takes the warrant of death to the person who is to die, lets him read it, puts him to death with the bowstring, cuts off his head, and brings it back to the monarch as a proof that he has done his will. Herodias could not be satisfied until she had seen the ghastly head of her

11 And his head was brought on a platter, and given to the damsel: and she brought it to her mother. 12 And his disciples came, and took up the corpse, and buried him; and they went and told Jesus.

---

enemy; hence, Salome requested that John the Baptist's head be brought in on a platter as evidence that the execution had taken place.

And he sent and beheaded John in the prison.—He had been urged to do this by Herodias previous to this. He made a rash promise, sealed it with oaths in the presence of his company; and now for the sake of his oath, goaded by the friends who sat with him at the feast, and persistently urged by Herodias, John was beheaded. Herod knew that John had done nothing worthy of death; he knew that John was a righteous man, yet through the conspiracy of circumstances he is forced to have him put to death. Herod was afraid to stand by his convictions; afraid to do that which is right marks a man a coward, especially when man knows what is right. It is worthy to note how calmly Matthew relates this event, without one word of anger or resentment; he narrates the story just as it hapepned. His narration gives us confidence in the truthfulness of the historian, who manifests such a regard for truth. The head was brought "on a platter, and given to the damsel," and "she brought it to her mother." John died as a martyr for the truth and exchanged his dungeon for a world where the wicked cease from troubling and the weary are at rest—a world in whose light his rejoicing soul could discover the ways of God. He had finished his work; the speedy end of his ministry served to give glory to God and opportunity for Jesus to finish his work. There was no further work for John to do; he had been in prison for about a year and was sacrificed, it seems, by wicked men. The wrath of man is made to work out the design of God as well as his glory. It is related of Salome that she met a tragic death by her head being severed from her body. We rejoice that John's disciples "came, and took up the corpse, and buried him." It is probable that John's body was cast over the walls of the prison. The Jews paid great respect to the bodies of their deceased friends, and so did the early Christians. (John 19: 38-42; Acts 8: 2.) The disciples of John were taught by him to look unto Jesus as his superior, and now in their bereavement and sorrow they naturally report to Jesus what had been done to John and would receive sympathy and counsel. Doubtless Jesus knew the whole story before they came to tell him.

13. FEEDING THE FIVE THOUSAND AND WALKING ON THE WATER
14: 13-33

13 Now when Jesus heard *it,* he withdrew from thence in a boat, to a desert place apart: and when the multitudes heard *thereof,* they followed him

---

13, 14 **Now when Jesus heard it.**—The death of John occurred while the twelve were absent on their mission as described in chapter ten. Their return and the news of the death of John caused Jesus to withdraw "from thence in a boat, to a desert place apart." Jesus gave his disciples the reason for this; he said, "Come ye yourselves apart into a desert place, and rest a while." (Mark 6: 31.) In relation to his disciples this was a true and tender reason, but with respect to himself and his mission there was a far higher reason. When Jesus, at his early home in Nazareth, heard that John was baptizing in the Jordan, he realized that he was summoned to enter upon the preparation for his ministry. After his baptism, for a while, Jesus stood in the background while John was preparing the way for him. Soon after Jesus began his public ministry and some of his disciples were complaining about the work of Jesus, John said in reply to them of Jesus that "he must increase, but I must decrease." (John 3: 30.) The forerunner and subordinate must gradually retire before the Superior and Messiah. When John was imprisoned (Matt. 4: 12), a period arrived in which our Lord commenced his public ministration. John ceased his labors and has been put to death; now Jesus enters fully into his work. The twelve had been sent out; they had returned; his fame had gone abroad and even filled the halls of Herod Antipas. It is now both a crisis of great danger and time of his broadest en-

on ⁴foot from the cities. 14 And he came forth, and saw a great multitude, and he had compassion on them, and healed their sick. 15 And when even was come, the disciples came to him, saying, The place is desert, and the

---

⁴Or, *by land*

---

largement. To avoid the ruling powers, whose eyes are now in search of him, he departs for northern Galilee, where he spends the remainder of the time during his "Galilean ministry."

It seems that he could get no rest, and that his disciples could have no quietness with him in order to make their report and to receive further instruction from him. "When the multitudes heard thereof, they followed him on foot from the cities." This remarkable passage in the life of Jesus is recorded by the other three writers of the gospel. (Mark 5: 32-44; Luke 9: 10-17; John 6: 1-14.) Mark tells us that at the same time John's disciples came to find Jesus his apostles returned from their mission, and that he went aside to avoid the people who were thronging him constantly. Some think that there was a design on the part of the multitudes to force him to lead them in an insurrection against Herod. This is another instance where the people showed themselves willing to take part with him against his enemies; hence, to prevent this and any collision with Herod, he went across the sea to the other side of Galilee. However, he did not escape the attention of the multitude, for when they saw him on the way they followed him to the "desert place" where "he had compassion on them, and healed their sick." They were left to the misguiding instructors of the Pharisees, and were ruled by such men as Herod. They were as "sheep not having a shepherd." (Mark 6: 34.) The people in such condition touched the heart of Jesus and he had compassion on them.

15-21 And when even was come, the disciples came to him. —The miracle of feeding the five thousand is recorded by the four writers of the gospel. (Mark 6: 34-44; Luke 9: 12-15; John 6: 1-13.) Luke records fewer details, and Mark records more; John records the point that the first suggestion as to feeding the multitudes came from Jesus. The miracle came

time is already past; send the multitudes away, that they may go into the villages, and buy themselves food. 16 But Jesus said unto them, They have no need to go away; give ye them to eat. 17 And they say unto him, We have here but five loaves, and two fishes. 18 And he said, Bring them hither

---

into view in the breaking and distribution of the food; no material agencies whatever were apparent, neither, under the circumstances, possible; it was simply to keep on breaking and distributing.

John records that Jesus asked Philip, "Whence are we to buy bread, that these may eat?" (John 6: 5.) It seems that Jesus asked this question to try his faith or to see if one of his disciples would suggest another alternative. It was plain that they could not do it. Philip answered him that they did not have sufficient means to buy enough for each one to "take a little," to say nothing of each one eating sufficient to satisfy hunger. He even said that "two hundred shillings' worth of bread" was not sufficient to feed such a multitude. "Shilling" here denotes a coin worth about fifteen or seventeen cents in our money; this would amount to about thirty or thirty-four dollars. This was a sum far beyond their means; here we see a strong proof of the poverty of the disciples when so small a sum exceeded their common treasury. Andrew had discovered that there was a lad in the crowd "who hath five barley loaves, and two fishes"; in reporting this he added, "but what are these among so many?" (John 6: 9.) "Barley loaves" was a common cheap food among the Jews; their leaven bread was usually about a half an inch thick; the unleavened bread thinner, and was broken by the hands, and not cut with a knife, as we cut a loaf. Their loaves were like large, thin biscuits. The "two fishes" were very small, and perhaps the "five barley loaves, and two fishes" were enough for one meal or lunch. The multitude was arranged "to sit down on the grass" in an orderly manner. This was done that the disciples might easily serve them, and that the multitude might see the miraculous power manifested on this occasion.

When the multitude was arranged in order, Jesus looked "up to heaven" and "blessed, and brake and gave the loaves to

14: 18-33.] MATTHEW 317

to me. 19 And he commanded the multitudes to ⁵sit down on the grass; and he took the five loaves, and the two fishes, and looking up to heaven, he blessed, and brake and gave the loaves to the disciples, and the disciples to the multitudes. 20 And they all ate, and were filled: and they took up that which remained over of the broken pieces, twelve baskets full. 21 And they that did eat were about five thousand men, besides women and children.

22 And straightway he constrained the disciples to enter into the boat, and to go before him unto the other side, till he should send the multitudes

⁵Gr. *recline.*

---

the disciples, and the disciples to the multitudes." Mark tells us that the people sat "down in ranks, by hundreds, and by fifties." (Mark 6: 40.) This left room for the disciples to walk and the number could be easily counted. Jesus "blessed" or gave thanks (John 6: 11); he gave thanks unto God as the author and giver of every good thing. In this he set an example for his disciples at that time and for all time. His giving thanks to God showed his connection with God as well as his gratitude for the goodness and mercy of God. This was no ordinary meal; the meaning of the miracle was to be seen in Jesus' teaching; it was an acted parable; it typified the spiritual food that Jesus was able to give.

And they all ate, and were filled.—No one had lack of anything; the hunger of all was satisfied. The same power which created the worlds, which increased the widow's cruse of oil (1 Kings 17: 16), at the word of a prophet, is here shown in increasing the substance of bread and fish far beyond all natural powers. That which was before held in the hand, after satisfying an immense crowd, cannot now be restored to its original compass. Jesus further taught the lesson of economy by commanding that they "gather up the broken pieces which remain over, that nothing be lost." (John 6: 12.) Nothing is said about the size of the baskets; twelve in number were gathered full, a basket for each apostle. The multitude numbered five thousand men "besides women and children." The people were astonished at such proof of power and future success; they plotted to make him king (John 6: 15) which caused him again to retire from them.

22-33 And straightway he constrained his disciples to enter into the boat.—It was late in the day, "when even was come,"

away. **23 And after he had sent the multitudes away, he went up into the mountain apart to pray: and when even was come, he was there alone. 24 But the boat ⁶was now in the midst of the sea, distressed by the waves;** for

⁶Some ancient authorities read *was many furlongs distant from the land.*

---

that Jesus fed the multitude of five thousand; this was on the northeastern shore of the Sea of Galilee. After dismissing the multitude he "constrained the disciples to enter into the boat, and to go before him unto the other side, till he should send the multitudes away." His disciples were to go back across the Sea of Galilee to the western coast, while the multitude was to return to their cities around the northern coast of the sea. After sending his disciples away and dismissing the multitude, Jesus "went up into the mountain apart to pray." We now see three companies: the disciples are in the boat struggling for the western shore of the sea, the multitude wending their way homeward and dispersing into small groups and families, and Jesus "alone" up in the mountain praying. Jesus had "constrained the disciples" to leave him; the Greek word for "constrained" is very strong, and this implies that his disciples were reluctant to part from him. It seems that Jesus had a twofold motive in this, namely, to secure for himself a season of retirement and to give his disciples some experience alone on the Sea of Galilee in a storm. It is significant that Jesus wanted to be alone in prayer with his Father when he saw that the people so grossly misunderstood the nature of his kingdom, and would make him a king over a material kingdom. (John 6: 15.) In this retirement Jesus escapes the attention of the multitude and the confusion which had been continued since the disciples of John came to him; he could meditate on the death of John and upon his own death which would, before long, follow; he would have opportunity to pray for the weak disciples and the multitude, that they might hunger more for the spiritual food and understand better the nature of his kingdom.

But the boat was now in the midst of the sea, distressed by the waves.—The storms on the Sea of Galilee often were sudden and frightful. They had sailed "about five and twenty or thirty furlongs"; that is, they had sailed three or four miles,

the wind was contrary. 25 And in the fourth watch of the night he came unto them, walking upon the sea. 26 And when the disciples saw him walking on the sea, they were troubled, saying, It is a ghost; and they cried out for fear. 27 But straightway Jesus spake unto them, saying, Be of good

---

as a furlong was an eighth of a mile or about two hundred yards. They had rowed far enough to be just in the center of the sea, where the current of the Jordan caused the greatest commotion in a storm. The sea, where they were crossing, was about six miles wide. His disciples were in great danger as they were tossed about with the waves. While in this situation "and in the fourth watch of the night he came unto them, walking upon the sea." "The fourth watch of the night" shows that they had been nearly all night on the sea struggling to get to the shore. A "watch" is a period of the night spent by soldiers, in keeping awake, to guard against enemies, or to prevent the escape of prisoners; it means any division of the night. The Jews had, just before Matthew recorded this, changed their own ancient custom of "three watches of the night" to that of the Roman custom of "four watches." The first watch (Lam. 2: 19) was the first division with the Jews, the second (Judges 7: 19) was the middle watch; and the last division was the third division. These watches began, according to Roman usage, to which the Jews had now changed, at six, nine, twelve, and three. (Mark 15: 25.) It was after three in the morning that Jesus came to his disciples; through the early dawn they saw him walking on the sea. When his disciples saw "him walking on the sea, they were troubled" and said "it is a ghost." They were frightened as "they cried out for fear." The Jews believed in spiritual apparitions. (1 Sam. 28: 15.) They supposed the spirit of a dead man in form like a person was manifested. Their belief was similar to the supersitition of some today who believe in "ghosts." To see one was an omen of evil; no wonder the disciples "cried out with fear." They were already in great danger of being destroyed by the storm and had been battling against the waves nearly all night, and now to see some one walking on the water was enough to frighten them. They had been brought to the end of human

cheer; it is I; be not afraid. 28 And Peter answered him and said, Lord, if it be thou, bid me come unto thee upon the waters. 29 And he said, Come. And Peter went down from the boat, and walked upon the waters ¹to come to Jesus. 30 But when he saw the ²wind, he was afraid; and beginning to sink, he cried out, saying, Lord, save me. 31 And immediately Jesus

---

¹Some ancient authorities read *and came.*
²Many ancient authorities add *strong.*

---

protection and were ready to despair. At this time Jesus spoke to them.

Be of good cheer; it is I; be not afraid.—The disciples had asked among themselves what it was that they had seen; they had asked in terror, and Jesus now speaking to them banished their fear; he bade them "be of good cheer" and assured them of his identity. Peter was the spokesman of the group; to assure himself and others that it was truly Jesus he said, "Lord, if it be thou, bid me come unto thee upon the waters." Peter was impetuous and ever ready to venture forward even at the risk of failure. He was a man of undoubted physical courage; this was shown now and when he attacked the mob in Gethsemane. He was now beginning to see that there was a mystery about his Master, which he had not at first seen, that he was "the Son of the living God." Jesus said to him "come." He did not say, "come to me," but "come"; and Peter did "come," but not quite to Jesus, Jesus came to him. Peter "walked upon the waters to come to Jesus." He had asked if it be Jesus that he come to him upon the waters, and Jesus had bidden him to come. Peter performed a miracle in walking upon the water. While he was walking on the waters to come to Jesus "he saw the wind, he was afraid"; he began to sink, and "cried out, saying, Lord save me." Oftentimes Peter has been called rash, headlong, cowardly, and suchlike; but there is no mark of such a character in him; if he were cowardly, we have no record of it in the gospels; he was impetuous. At this time he had too much confidence in himself and not enough faith in our Lord. Later he is to be a partaker "of the divine nature." (1 Pet. 5: 6, 7; 2 Pet. 1: 4.) At this time Peter manifests the characteristics of impulsiveness, promptness, and eagerness to do something. Why could he not walk on the water too? He could, if his Lord would only

stretched forth his hand, and took hold of him, and saith unto him, O thou of little faith, wherefore didst thou doubt? 32 And when they were gone up into the boat, the wind ceased. 33 And they that were in the boat ³worshipped him, saying, Of a truth thou art the Son of God.

³See marginal note on ch. 2. 2.

say, "come"! Jesus had said this and down the ship's side and out upon the billows, off he goes; all is well till his eye drops from the Master to the rising of the tempest and to the more fearful surging of the billows. Then, beginning to go under, he cried, "Lord, save me."

And immediately Jesus stretched forth his hand, and took hold of him.—Jesus was ready to help him; "man's extremity is God's opportunity." Peter had exhausted himself; he is no longer the hero of the group; he is the humble petitioner for help; he is wholly dependent now on Jesus. It is often good for one to be reduced to such circumstances. Why did Peter begin "to sink"? We have the answer in Jesus' statement to him after he was brought up and placed safely in the boat. "O thou of little faith, wherefore didst thou doubt?" Peter was sustained on the water by the strength or power that came through faith in Jesus; for some reason Peter doubted. He had taken hold of the power by faith which Jesus used in walking on the water, and, as doubt is the opposite of faith, he had lost his hold on the power that sustained him, and immediately began to sink. So soon as Peter was safely back in the boat "the wind ceased," and "they that were in the boat worshipped him, saying, Of a truth thou art the Son of God." We have here the narration of a collection of wonders, and may well ponder them to ask why they were done and what lessons do they teach? There were none others in the ship but his apostles. They reverently bowed in worship before him and confessed that he was "the Son of God." This is the confession made soon after in Matt. 16: 16. This scene strengthened the faith that the disciples had, taught them to rely upon Jesus, and assured them that Jesus was willing and able to save to the uttermost all who took him at his word. At the time that Peter was rebuked for the lack of faith, he and the other apostles gathered new faith and strength which was expressed in their confession to Jesus that he was "the Son of God."

14. JESUS IN GENNESARET
14: 34-36

34 And when they had crossed over, they came to the land, unto Gennesaret. 35 And when the men of that place knew him, they sent into all that region round about, and brought unto him all that were sick; 36 and they besought him that they might only touch the border of his garment: and as many as touched were made whole.

34 And when they had crossed over . . . unto Gennesaret. —"Gennesaret" was the region on the west side of the Sea of Galilee, of which Capernaum was the chief town, and from which the lake is sometimes named. The name signifies "garden of the prince." The Sea of Galilee had three other names. It was called the "sea of Tiberias," from the celebrated city of that name. (John 6: 1.) It was called in the Old Testament "the sea of Chinnereth" or "Chinneroth" (Num. 34: 11; Josh. 12: 3), from a town of that name which stood on or near its shore (Josh. 19: 35). At the northwestern angle of the lake was a beautiful and fertile plain called "Gennesaret" and from that the sea derived the name of "lake of Gennesaret" (Luke 5: 1). It is probable that the disciples left the eastern coast of the sea to go to Capernaum om the western coast, but the storm had driven them out of their course and they landed south of Capernaum.

35, 36 And when the men of that place knew him.—Jesus and his disciples had often walked over the beautiful plain of Gennesaret and he had uttered many of his discourses to the people there and drew some of his illustrations from the varied scenes of earth, sea, and sky. So when he arrived at this time, and it was known, "they sent into all that region round about, and brought unto him all that were sick." Messengers were sent abroad over all the country to gather in the poor subjects of distress and infirmities, that they might see this wonder-working man, and be healed by him. The greatest impression that they had received of him was that he was able to heal their diseases; they were looking for temporal blessings and prized them higher than any spiritual blessing that

Jesus had to bestow. They were so eager to be cured that "they besought him that they might only touch the border of his garment." All who touched him "were made whole." There was no exception; his mercy and power were not exhausted and their faith is manifested in their eagerness to touch the border of his garment.

15. OPPOSITION OF SCRIBES AND PHARISEES
15: 1-20

1 Then there come to Jesus from Jerusalem Pharisees and scribes, saying,
2 Why do thy disciples transgress the tradition of the elders? for they wash

---

1-9 Then there come to Jesus from Jerusalem Pharisees and scribes.—Other records of this are found in Mark 7: 1-9 and John 7: 1. The scenes of love and faith closing chapter fourteen are now suddenly reversed. It is generally supposed that Jesus attended the Feast of the Passover at Jerusalem, which was the third Passover of his ministry. This now brings us to the last year of his earthly ministry; at the next Passover, "his hour comes," and he laid his life on the cross. The "scribes" were the teachers of the law; originally they were those who transcribed the law and made copies of it for use in the synagogue, but they came to be the religious teachers of the people. There were two classes of scribes, civil and ecclesiastical. They are also called lawyers or doctors. (Matt. 22: 35; Luke 5: 17.) The "Pharisees" were a sect of the Jews at the time of Jesus; they were a rival sect of the Sadducees; they held strictly to the law of Moses and the traditions that belong to it. The Pharisees are often mentioned in the New Testament and the name signifies "separatists, the pure"; they believed in the existence of spirits and souls and the resurrection of the body. Jesus was probably in Capernaum when the scribes and Pharisees came to him. They were "from Jerusalem"; they may have been sent by the Sanhedrin, or may have come of their own accord.

Why do thy disciples transgress the tradition of the elders?—They did not bring an accusation directly against Jesus; their objection is to his disciples. If they were follow-

not their hands when they eat bread. 3 And he answered and said unto them, Why do ye also transgress the commandment of God because of your tradition? 4 For God said, ⁴'Honor thy father and thy mother: and, ⁵'He that speaketh evil of father or mother, let him ⁶die the death. 5 But ye say,

---

⁴Ex. xx. 12; Dt. v. 16.
⁵Ex. xxi. 17; Lev. xx. 9.
⁶Or, *surely die*

---

ing his teachings, this objection was against him; if the disciples follow the Master, any objection against his disciples is an accusation against the Master. They asked why his disciples "transgressed the tradition of the elders." The traditions of the elders means the comments of the elders. "The elders" were the learned men living in the olden times; they originally meant the rulers of the cities. Their traditions signified the religious customs or precepts which were handed down from generation to generation; the traditions were regarded of equal sacredness with the written law. These traditions were a very important part of the Jewish system. The Pharisees taught that when Moses received the "written law" he was instructed also in another law, which he was not to write down, but to deliver to the elders of the congregation. This oral law, they maintained, was the only authorized interpretation of the written law, so that a Jew could never be certain of the meaning of the written law, until he had inquired of the Pharisees the explanation of the former. These traditions or interpretations of this oral law were enforced on the common people, and punishment for violation of them was as severe as the punishment for the violation of "the written law." They had observed that the disciples of Jesus had not washed their hands when they ate bread. Their tradition said, "He who eats bread with unwashen hands is as bad as if he were to commit fornication." Jesus drew a distinction between "the law of Moses" and "the tradition of the elders." Jesus disregarded their traditions and replied to their question by asking, "Why do ye also transgress the commandment of God because of your tradition?" Jesus shows them that their system of tradition is false. The word of God is to be held sacred above all things; their traditions were the words of men, but the law was the word of God. They had set aside the word of

Whosoever shall say to his father or his mother, That wherewith thou mightest have been profited by me is given *to* God; 6 he shall not honor his father. And ye have made void the ⁸word of God because of your tradition.

⁷Some ancient authorities add *or his mother.*
⁸Some ancient authorities read *law.*

God and had exalted the traditions of men; for this Jesus severely condemned them. Their traditions violated the law of God. Jesus' direct question convicted the scribes and Pharisees publicly. They had come with the secret purpose of prejudicing the people against Jesus, but Jesus publicly condemned them.

Jesus cited an example of the contradiction between "the tradition of the elders" and the law of God. The law had said, "Honor thy father and thy mother" and a further explanation of that was that "he that speaketh evil of father or mother, let him die the death." These were statements of the word of God; they were plain and simple, but the scribes and Pharisees taught, "Whosoever shall say to his father or his mother, That wherewith thy mightest have been profited by me is given to God. Instead of helping their aged parents with the means at their command, they claimed that it had been offered to God. Mark says that they said to their father and mother, "That wherewith thou mightest have been profited by me is Corban, that is to say, Given to God." (Mark 7: 11.) "Corban" means a thing solemnly set apart by a formal vow to the sacred use of the service of God, hence it could not be used by or for any other person. Their traditions had invented a secret reserve beneath this form of words; the Jew said to his parents, either in selfishness or anger, "It is Corban, all that I can give to you." From that time he could not apply any of his property to the support of his parents because, said the Pharisees, he broke a vow to God; but he was not bound nor expected actually to devote it to God; he was only bound by it *not to support his parents. He might use it freely upon himself.* In doing this Jesus accused them of making "void the word of God because of your tradition." In verse three they are charged with transgressing "the commandment of God" and here they are charged with making

7 Ye hypocrites, well did Isaiah prophesy of you, saying,
8 ⁹This people honoreth me with their lips;
But their heart is far from me.
9 But in vain do they worship me,
Teaching as *their* doctrines the precepts of men.

⁹Is. xxix. 13.

"void the word of God" because of their tradition. They were not sincere in doing what they had done; they knew what the law required toward their parents, but avoided doing it under the pretense of obeying the traditions of the elders.

Ye hypocrites, well did Isaiah prophesy of you.—They claimed to believe the prophets; they claimed to follow the prophets, but the prophet Isaiah condemned the very course which they had followed. If Isaiah condemned them, they could not condemn Christ for doing what Isaiah had done without condemning their great Messianic prophet, Isaiah. Here Jesus identifies his teachings with the teachings of Isaiah. To reject his teachings was to reject their prophet Isaiah. To accept the teachings of Isaiah was to accept the teachings of Christ, and to stand as self-confessed hypocrites before the public. Isaiah had described such as honoring God "with their lips," while "their heart is far from me." With their lips they uttered pious "Corban" or consecration to God, but with their hearts they meant to break the commandment of God and rob their parents. This reference is to Isa. 29: 13. Jesus introduced this by saying, "Well did Isaiah prophesy"; "well," rightly, truly, and aptly did Isaiah speak of them. Many today act as hypocritically as these scribes and Pharisees; they honor God with their lips, both in prayer and praise, but their heart is far from him. Further quoting Isaiah, "In vain do they worship me, teaching as their doctrines the precepts of men." They substituted the "precepts of men" for the commandment of God; this made a vain worship. God did not accept it. "In vain" means to no purpose; God sees the heart and knows that it is impure and will not accept such worship. (Prov. 15: 8; John 4: 24.) They taught for "their doctrines the precepts of men." Many today teach as doctrines necessary to salvation the precepts of men; they

10 And he called to him the multitude, and said unto them, Hear, and under-

are under the same condemnation that Jesus passed on these scribes and Pharisees. Every willful addition to the commandments of God, every subtraction from the word of God, and every substitution for his command that requires an act of worship only calls for vain worship, and is condemned before God.

[Washing the hands was harmless and commendable. It interfered, so far as we can see, with obedience to no command of God, yet when added as a religious service it was a sin that calls forth this lesson—that it is presumptuous sin to add anything to the service of God, however harmless or commendable in our eyes. It is infringing upon the legislative prerogatives of God. His prerogative is to give laws; man is to obey. He uses this harmless addition to show that no additions can be made of any kind. We might give other equally strong lessons from Jesus on this point, but his application of the prophecy of Isaiah shows his condemnation of such sins.

The quotation from Isaiah and Jesus' application of it show clearly that to profess to worship God, yet to intermingle in that worship things not commanded by God, is regarded by God as evidence that the heart is not right in the sight of God, that the heart is not loyal and true to him, but it is far from him. Any disposition to add things resting upon the precepts or commandments of man to the service of God is evidence the heart is disloyal to God, is far from him. Anything offered as service to God, even if commanded by God, if done because it appears wise and fitting to men, becomes offensive to God. When we worship God, it must be what he commands; and we must do it to honor and obey him, or he is not pleased with the service. We cannot be too cautious in serving him.]

10, 11 **And he called to him the multitude.**—The scribes and Pharisees had come all the way from Jerusalem to discuss in their fierce style some matters with Jesus; they were answered and fell back out of notice, and Jesus turns to the mul-

stand: 11 Not that which entereth into the mouth defileth the man; but that which proceedeth out of the mouth, this defileth the man. 12 Then came the disciples, and said unto him, Knowest thou that the Pharisees were [10]offended, when they heard this saying? 13 But he answered and said, Every [11]plant which my heavenly Father planted not, shall be rooted up. 14 Let them

[10]Gr. *caused to stumble.*
[11]Gr. *planting.*

---

titude. They were asked if they understood his teaching; the multitude seems more inclined to learn, hence Jesus gives his attention to those who are ready and anxious to learn. "Not that which entereth into the mouth defileth the man." It is not food and drink that defileth the soul. Certain meats were forbidden in the law to school the minds of the Jews and prepare them for the spiritual law of Christ; but they had grossly perverted the law and imagined that they could be spiritually defiled by certain meats; hence, Jesus gives the broad principle that sin does not lie in food or matter, but in the soul. "Sin is lawlessness" (1 John 3: 4), or a transgression of the law. That which people eat or that which goeth into a man is put in contrast to that which goeth "out" of the man; that is, the moral action, that goeth forth from the man's will and intention. A man's intentional thoughts, words, and deeds defile the soul. Jesus teaches that not physical touch but moral action makes a man truly impure before God.

12-14 **Then came the disciples, and said unto him.**—The scribes and Pharisees and the multitude have gone and Jesus further instructs his disciples. They asked Jesus if he knew that "the Pharisees were offended" by his teachings. They were not only offended, but were angry at being exposed before the multitude. They had come to place Jesus in an awkward and inconsistent attitude before the multitude, but Jesus had tactfully exposed and placed them in a ridiculous plight before the multitude; their weapons had been turned against them. Perhaps the disciples of Jesus heard the Pharisees talking and brought what they had heard to Jesus. Jesus made reply to his disciples and said, "Every plant which my heavenly Father planted not, shall be rooted up." Some explain "every plant" to mean "every doctrine" which is probably what is meant. The Jews called a doctrine a seed or

alone: they are blind guides. And if the blind guide the blind, both shall fall into a pit. 15 And Peter answered and said unto him, Declare unto us the

plant. Jesus called "the word of God" seed. (Luke 8: 11.) The traditions of the elders were plants which God had not planted; they were the doctrines of men, and such can never stand before the word of God. Jesus assured his apostles that the truth would ultimately and finally be victorious and that all doctrines of men must fail. The truth shall prevail over all false opinions. The disciples were to see the hatred and prejudice of the enemies of the truth overcome. Some think that "plant" may have reference to the Pharisees as a class of religious teachers, and that the disciples would see them rejected and teachers of Christianity prevail in their stead.

Let them alone.—Perhaps the disciples thought that Jesus had not noticed the anger of the Pharisees; however, it had not escaped his attention as they thought it had. Jesus very tactfully passed it by without calling attention to it or letting anyone know that he had noticed it; this is an example that we might imitate frequently with great profit. They were blind guides or blind travelers; they were deceivers of the deceived; both classes have the common fate or doom, "both shall fall into a pit." Both the seducers and the seduced shall perish. We may learn from this that we should not be deterred from doing our duty and speaking the truth in the face of opposition or popularity; it is the duty of teachers to compare their teaching with the word of God and that Christians must be patient in the face of adversaries. These were "blind guides" or leaders; they did not see the truth because they refused to see it. (John 9: 40.) Jesus uses a very impressive figure when he represents them as blind guides or blind travelers.

15-20 Peter answered and said unto him, Declare unto us the parable.—It seems that his disciples should have understood the parable of Jesus concerning the ceremonial observances with respect to food; it was not hard to be understood, but the entrenched prejudices of the Jews prevented the disciples, in common with other Jews, understanding its meaning.

parable. 16 And he said, Are ye also even yet without understanding? 17 Perceive ye not, that whatsoever goeth into the mouth passeth into the belly, and is cast out into the draught? 18 But the things which proceed out of the mouth come forth out of the heart; and they defile the man. 19 For out of the heart come forth evil thoughts, murders, adulteries, fornications, thefts, false witness, railings: 20 these are the things which defile the man; but to

(Acts 11: 1-18.) Jesus mildly rebuked his disciples by asking them, "Are ye also even yet without understanding?" Writers of the gospel seem to make no distinction between parable, proverb, or other figures of speech. It was difficult for the disciples to understand why the Pharisees should be called blind leaders. Mark says that all of the disciples asked the question which is here attributed to Peter. (Mark 7: 17-20.) Peter may have asked the question for the others and one writer notices the one fact, while the other records another fact, and both are true. Jesus proceeded to further develop the thought expressed in the parable. The difference between what goes into the mouth and what comes "out into the draught" ought to be clear to even the dullest in thought. Jesus speaks of the mouth as the instrument of food and conversation; as an instrument of food that which goes into the mouth passes to the stomach and out as draught, but that which cometh *from* the mouth comes from the heart and it is what comes *from* the mouth that defiles, and not that which goeth *into* the mouth. Our words come from the heart and are spoken by the mouth; they proceed from the inward intentions, and thereby not merely our *words,* but our *actions,* come from the heart. "For out of the heart come forth evil thoughts, murders, adulteries, fornications, thefts, false witness, railings." "Evil thoughts" are placed first, as if to represent the fountain from which the other sins proceed. Thought, deliberation, reasoning, purposes, all precede every responsible act of word and deed. "The heart" means the inward man. (Mark 7: 21; Luke 11: 39; Rom. 2: 29; 7: 22; 2 Cor. 4: 16; 1 Pet. 3: 4.) It will be noticed that the catalog of sins here follows closely the second list of commandments in the Decalogue, beginning with the sixth commandment. Jesus concludes that "these are the things which defile the

15: 20, 21.] MATTHEW 331

eat with unwashen hands defileth not the man.

man" and not merely the eating "with unwashen hands." The Pharisees had failed to make this distinction.

16. THE CANAANITISH WOMAN
15: 21-28

21 And Jesus went out thence, and withdrew into the parts of Tyre and

21 And Jesus went out thence.—Mark 7: 24-30 records this same scene with very little variation. Jesus' reply to the Pharisees and his warnings to the people not to substitute outward for inward purity gave great offense to the Pharisees and alarmed his disciples. To avoid the Pharisees and to be with his disciples to further instruct them, Jesus withdrew "into the parts of Tyre and Sidon." Jesus left the dominion of Herod and went into the region of Tyre and Sidon; these were cities situated on the eastern coast of the Mediterranean Sea. Since the death of John the Baptist, Jesus was the object of notice by Herod Antipas, and as "his hour" had not come, he retires to a country not under the jurisdiction of Herod. This region of country appears to have been the tract in which were situated the cities that Solomon gave to Hiram, and which, because they did not please him, Hiram restored to Solomon, who improved them for his subjects. (Josh. 19: 27; 1 Kings 10: 12, 13; 2 Chron. 8: 2.) Tyre and Sidon were two Phoenician cities situated on the Mediterranean, and the regions to which they belonged adjoined the land of Israel on the south and east; it was allotted originally to the tribe of Asher, but does not appear to have been entirely taken by that tribe (Josh. 19: 24-31), and was embraced in the land promised to Abraham (Gen. 10: 15-19; 15: 18-21). Mark tells us that Jesus desired to enter "into a house, and would have no man know it." (Mark 7: 24.) He was seeking seclusion for meditation and further instruction to his apostles.

22-28 And behold, a Canaanitish woman came.—Jesus did not remain in seclusion as this woman "came out from those borders, and cried, saying, Have mercy on me, O Lord, thou son

Sidon. 22 And behold, a Canaanitish woman came out from those borders, and cried, saying, Have mercy on me, O Lord, thou son of David; my daughter is grievously vexed with a demon. 23 But he answered her not a word. And his disciples came and besought him, saying, Send her away; for

---

of David." Mark calls her "a Greek," a Syrophoenician by race. The two names were given to the same tract of country, "Syria" and "Phœnicia"; it was originally called Canaan, hence "a Canaanitish woman." She was not a Jewess, hence the important fact about the name is that she was a Gentile. So far as we know she was the first of Gentiles to obtain a blessing by faith in Jesus. She lived in that outlying region where the great famine in Ahab's time was, and where Elijah found the poor widow who supplied him food during the famine. We do not know how she learned of Jesus; we only know that she had learned something about him. She calls him "thou son of David"; this confessed him to be the Messiah. It is remarkable that a Gentile woman should have such faith in him upon such meager evidence at her command. She had a daughter who was "grievously vexed with a demon." Mark describes the woman as coming and falling at the feet of Jesus. She came in faith and humility; she pleaded with the earnestness of her soul for help. No one can doubt her faith, her humility, her anxiety, and her persistent earnestness. She besought Jesus to have mercy on her and heal her daughter.

But he answered her not a word.—At first this seems to be a strange attitude toward this poor woman. We may see two plain reasons for Jesus not answering her immediately. They are to try her faith before others; he saw her good faith and developed it to make the blessing more remarkable. The second reason may have been that since she was neither by birth an Israelite nor by profession a worshiper of the God of Israel, she should be put to some previous trial of faith so that she may show herself more worthy of so high a preference in his ministry. At least, Jesus "answered her not a word" for a time. He said no unkind word to her; he did not repel her; he simply kept upon his way to pass her, as though he would not heed her earnest request. The pause or delay was trying

she crieth after us. 24 But he answered and said, I was not sent but unto the lost sheep of the house of Israel. 25 But she came and ¹worshipped him, saying, Lord, help me. 26 And he answered and said, It is not meet to take

¹See marginal note on ch. 2. 2.

and painful to his disciples. So his disciples "besought him, saying, Send her away; for she crieth after us." Some think that the disciples wanted him to dismiss her with his blessings so that she would not annoy him any longer; others think that his disciples wanted him to send her away without the blessing, as she was not entitled to it, being a Gentile. We are not told by either record why they requested her to be sent away; so there is no use in our spending an opinion on it. Such is not germane to the lesson taught in this instance. Jesus answered his disciples that he was "not sent but unto the lost sheep of the house of Israel." The children of Israel or Jews were designated as "the lost sheep of the house of Israel." His mission was primarily to the Jews while he was on earth; he was sent to them, was born among them, lived with them, and died by their hands. He came to save all, to become a ransom for many, but his earthly ministry of his preparatory work for his kingdom was confined to the Jews.

But she came and worshipped him, saying, Lord, help me.—There is an exquisite beauty in the simplicity and brevity of her prayer. She urged no argument, perhaps her voice was choked by her tears; she looked into Jesus' face and saw the mercy that disproves his words, and earnestly pleaded, "Lord, help me." The soul that bows as she did need say no more than "Lord, help me." Jesus further tested and developed her faith by saying, "It is not meet to take the children's bread and cast it to the dogs." The Jews considered themselves as the peculiar favorites of heaven and despised Gentiles; Jesus called out her confession, spake as if he felt as the other Jews, that she was too far inferior to him to receive such a blessing. The same principle is taught is Isa. 54: 7, 8. Jesus here puts her in a most humble place that she may prove that she has an humble heart, though a Gentile. It seems that the poor

the children's ²bread and cast it to the dogs. 27 But she said, Yea, Lord: for even the dogs eat of the crumbs which fall from their masters' table. 28 Then Jesus answered and said unto her, O woman, great is thy faith: be it done unto thee even as thou wilt. And her daughter was healed from that hour.

---

²Or, *loaf*

---

woman comes nearer to Jesus as he talks to her and as she replies to him. She "worshipped" him, that is, continued to worship him by prostrating herself before him and beseeching him to help her. When Jesus replied that it was not fitting to take the bread that belonged to the children and give it to the dogs, she quickly responded with an argument for her case that could not be ignored. She said, "Yea, Lord," that may be true; yet she said, "Even the dogs eat of the crumbs which fall from their masters' table." She was willing to be placed in the humblest position, even as a dog under its master's table; she did not deserve any other place, but she did desire the crumbs which fell from the master's table. She meant, "Dog is it I am? and the Jews my masters? Then, at least, let me have the crumb that mercy does not deny to the very dog." She was willing for Jesus to give the Jews what he would, but she desired that he deny her not this mercy; out of his abundance it was only a crumb; they cannot be the poorer by his giving her this crumb, and she would be immeasurably richer. Jesus never did, and could not from his nature, deny any good thing asked for with such faith, with such humility, with such perseverance.

Then Jesus answered and said unto her, O woman, great is thy faith.—We see now in this Jesus' purpose in delaying the blessing to her; he knew how much trial her faith would bear; he had in view the very result which followed. He has his own way of measuring out tests for our faith and endurance; he knows how much discipline we may need in order to be more worthy of the blessings. Her faith takes her out as an exception to the whole Gentile world and holds her up as an example of faith to the Jewish race. Mark tells us that when she returned home, she "found the child laid upon the bed, and the demon gone out." (Mark 7: 30.) Jesus had told her that it should be "unto thee even as thou wilt."

17. THE FEEDING OF FOUR THOUSAND
15: 29-39

29 And Jesus departed thence, and came nigh unto the sea of Galilee; and he went up into the mountain, and sat there. 30 And there came unto him great multitudes, having with them the lame, blind, dumb, maimed, and many others, and they cast them down at his feet; and he healed them: 31 insomuch that the multitude wondered, when they saw the dumb speaking, the maimed whole, and the lame walking, and the blind seeing: and they glorified the God of Israel.
32 And Jesus called unto him his disciples, and said, I have compassion on the multitude, because they continue with me now three days and have nothing to eat: and I would not send them away fasting, lest haply they faint

---

29-31 And Jesus departed thence.—He departed from the northwest to the northeastern part of Galilee. He may have passed by Capernaum without stopping as he had lately abruptly left there after the altercation with the Pharisees. He went up into the mountain "and there came unto him great multitudes." He went through the region of Decapolis on the east side of the sea. The people of this region took advantage of his visit and brought to him "the lame, blind, dumb, maimed, and many others, and they cast them down at his feet; and he healed them." He had visited this region once before and they knew of him. He healed all manner of diseases. "The maimed" were those who had broken limbs or crippled. (Acts 3: 2.) The people were greatly astonished "when they saw the dumb speaking, the maimed whole, and the lame walking, and the blind seeing." These miracles caused them to glorify "the God of Israel." The people on the east side of the Jordan were Jews, but they had fallen into great errors with respect to the law. The people naturally attributed the power of working these miracles to "the God of Israel"; they attributed the power to the right source, and should have accepted Jesus on his claim to be the Son of God, which many of them did.

32-39 And Jesus called unto him his disciples.—The multitude had witnessed the healing of many of their fellow citi-

on the way. 33 And the disciples say unto him, Whence should we have so many loaves in a desert place as to fill so great a multitude? 34 And Jesus said unto them, How many loaves have ye? And they said, Seven, and a few small fishes. 35 And he commanded the multitude to sit down on the ground; 36 and he took the seven loaves and the fishes; and he gave thanks and brake, and gave to the disciples, and the disciples to the multitudes. 37 And they all ate, and were filled: and they took up that which remained over

zens, and had remained there with him "now three days" and Jesus had "compassion on the multitude" because they had "nothing to eat." He would not send the multitude away without feeding the people "lest hapy they faint on the way." It is not necessary to infer that the multitude had fasted three days, but had been with Jesus three days and had exhausted all their supplies for food and were now suffering from hunger. (Mark 8: 1-10.) The only difference between this miracle and that recorded in Matt. 14: 14-21 is the number fed. The place was the same, the plain near the mount where the beatitudes were spoken, close to the sea; the cause of it the same; the manner the same. The persons receiving support in this miraculous manner were not the same, as those who had been fed with the five thousand came from the western shore, and those of the four thousand came from the region of Decapolis. It is not necessary to infer that these were Gentiles as some have done; they were Jews who lived in that region of country.

And the disciples say unto him, Whence should we have so many loaves in a desert place as to fill so great a multitude? —It seems that his disciples had forgotten that he had power to feed the multitude. It had not been long since the multitude of five thousand men had been fed. Perhaps they believed he had the power to feed the multitude, but they were not sure he would repeat the miracle. They did not have the boldness to ask him to perform a miracle, hence they just asked, "Whence should we have so many loaves in a desert place as to fill so great a multitude?" They then watched every movement that was made. Jesus inquired, "How many loaves have ye?" And he received in reply, "Seven, and a few small fishes." The multitude was commanded to sit down on the ground and Jesus, as on the former occasion, "gave thanks

of the broken pieces, seven baskets full. 38 And they that did eat were four thousand men, besides women and children. 39 And he sent away the multitudes and entered into the boat, and came into the borders of Magadan.

and brake, and gave to the disciples, and the disciples to the multitudes." In like manner he took the "few small fishes" and "blessed" them and had his disciples to serve the multitude. After they had eaten "and were filled" they gathered up "that which remained over of the broken pieces, seven baskets full." There were "four thousand men, besides women and children." Twice in the same general region of country, and under the same general necessity, did Jesus supply "bread in the wilderness" to the needy multitudes who, far from their homes, stayed to listen to his word. This multitude did not think of making him king as did the other multitude that he fed; so he quietly departed with his disciples.

"And he sent away the multitudes" and he with his disciples "entered into the boat, and came into the borders of Magadan." This is the place from which Mary Magdalene received her name. Mark says that Jesus and his disciples left and "came into the parts of Dalmanutha." (Mark 8: 10.) The great moral lessons of the feeding of the five thousand and of the four thousand are the same; the circumstances call for a supply of food by a miracle; the same power here as before was equal to the emergency; the same love and wisdom provided it.

18. PHARISEES AND SADDUCEES UNITE AGAINST JESUS
16: 1-12

1 And the Pharisees and Sadducees came, and trying him asked him to

1 And the Pharisees and Sadducees came.—These two sects were hostile to each other; there were no points in which their doctrines agreed. Enemies to each other as they were, yet they could be friends in order to oppose Jesus; they could unite against Jesus as did Herod and Pilate. (Luke 23: 12.) These two religious sects among the Jews combined their hate and opposition to Jesus and henceforth they seek to destroy

show them a sign from heaven. 2 But he answered and said unto them, ³When it is evening, ye say, *It will be* fair weather: for the heaven is red.

³The following words, to the end of ver. 3, are omitted by some of the most ancient and other important authorities.

---

him. At this time they came "trying him" by asking "him to show them a sign from heaven." They attempted to seduce him with evil motives into sin; they did not really wish to see a sign from heaven, that they might believe in him, or that others might believe in him; but either they wished him to fail to show the sign, or they hoped to prove to the multitude that, by his not producing a sign, he was not the Messiah, and if not the Messiah, he was an impostor and should be put to death. They asked for the "sign from heaven"; they implied that such a sign would prove him to be a prophet. Prophets of old had shown signs; Moses, manna (Ex. 16: 4; John 6: 31); Samuel, thunder (1 Sam. 12: 16-18); Isaiah, a change of the dial (Isa. 38: 8). Jesus had more than equaled those prophets, so these Pharisees and Sadducees had already sufficient signs. The heavens were opened at his baptism; miraculous bread had been eaten by the multitudes after he had blessed it; these were sufficient and it was presumption on their part to ask him to do more.

[The Pharisees and Sadducees with full knowledge of all the miracles wrought by Jesus, came to him, tempting him, and asked that he would show them a sign from heaven. Jesus refused to be put on trial by men; he refused to work a miracle for them, but pointed them forward to his death, burial, and resurrection, the sign of all signs, prefigured in the case of Jonah. This is quoted by the pretenders who have never wrought a sign and point forward to no sign in the future as excuse for their failure to do what they claim.]

2-4 But he answered and said unto them.—Jesus in replying to the Pharisees and Sadducees revealed to them and others that their motives were impure. They could foretell the weather by the clouds and indications peculiar to their climate, and by the very same sign of redness in the sky, at one time say it would be fair weather, again foul weather. The condition of the weather, as they claimed, could be determined

3 And in the morning, *It will be* foul weather to-day: for the heaven is red and lowering. Ye know how to discern the face of the heaven; but ye cannot *discern* the signs of the times. 4 An evil and adulterous generation seeketh after a sign; and there shall no sign be given unto it, but the sign of Jonah. And he left them, and departed.
5 And the disciples came to the other side and forgot to take ⁴bread.

⁴Gr. *loaves.*

---

at different times of the day by the appearances in the heaven. Whether their interpretations were correct and a true forecast of weather conditions is not affirmed nor denied by Jesus; he simply takes them on their own claims and shows their inconsistency. The Jews even at that time published almanacs, prognosticating the rains of the coming year; they did not have the scientific knowledge that "weather forecasters" have today; yet they claimed with equal positiveness to give correct iinterpretations. Jesus simply said to them that they were men of average sagacity in judging the weather signs in the sky, hence they should judge with equal sagacity the signs in the moral heavens—the sign which appeared with respect to his coming. When men ignore such signs as they had done, it was of no use to give them other signs.

An evil and adulterous generation seeketh after a sign.—They were "evil" because they were seeking to destroy him; they were "adulterous" because they had left Jehovah and his prophets and were guided by the traditions of men—they simply had given their love and affection to their own doctrines rather than to the law of God; this made them "adulterous." "There shall no sign be given unto it, but the sign of Jonah." (Matt. 12: 38-40.) Mark says, "He sighed deeply in his spirit." (Mark 8: 12.) He was grieved by their hardness of heart and the certainty of their condemnation. Jesus left them to themselves without further reproof or remonstration. He had briefly referred them to his previous illustration of Jonah.

5-12 **And the disciples came to the other side.**—They came to the northern shore of the Sea of Galilee to the town of Bethsaida. The following conversation occurred in the ship as they were sailing, for they had only "one loaf" of bread

6 And Jesus said unto them, Take heed and beware of the leaven of the Pharisees and Sadducees. 7 And they reasoned among themselves, saying, We took no ⁵bread. 8 And Jesus perceiving it said, O ye of little faith, why reason ye among yourselves, because ye have no ⁵bread? 9 Do ye not yet perceive, neither remember the five loaves of the five thousand, and how many ⁶baskets ye took up? 10 Neither the seven loaves of the four thousand, and how many baskets ye took up? 11 How is it that ye do not perceive that I spake not to you concerning ⁵bread? But beware of the leaven of the Pharisees and Sadducees. 12 Then understood they that he bade them not beware of the leaven of ⁵bread, but of the teaching of the Pharisees and Sadducees.

⁵Or, It is *because we took no bread*
⁶*Basket* in ver. 9 and 10 represents different Greek words.

with them. (Mark 8: 14-21.) They could not get other supply of bread now until they landed; this gave Jesus the opportunity to teach the following lesson: "Take heed and beware of the leaven of the Pharisees and Saducess." His disciples did not understand to what he referreed; so "they reasoned among themselves, saying, We took no bread." His disciples were often brought into contact with the influence and conversations of the Pharisees and the Sadducees when Jesus was not present. (Matt. 15: 12-20.) The disciples were somewhat disconcerted because of their oversight in not taking bread. The Pharisees forbade their disciples buying bread of heathens and Samaritans; Jesus' disciples had not planned to buy bread of the Pharisees and the Sadducees, hence they were confused as to what Jesus meant. Jesus knew their confusion and reasoning in their hearts, and said, "O ye of little faith, why reason ye among yourselves, because ye have no bread?" He did not refer to literal bread as they had understood him; he asked them if they did not remember "the five loaves of the five thousand, and how many baskets" were taken up; again he called their attention to his feeding the four thousand with "the seven loaves." He then declared that they should have understood him when he said, "Beware of the leaven of the Pharisees and Sadducees."

Then understood they that he bade them not beware of the leaven of bread, but of the teaching of the Pharisees and Sadducees.—The evil principle of the Pharisees had changed and corrupted the law of God. The spirit of their teaching is the point warned against. (Luke 12: 1.) "Teaching of the Pharisees and Sadducees" means the body of instruction and discipline of these sects. The system of instruction taught by Jesus is called "his doctrine" and that taught by his apostles is called "the apostles' teaching." (Acts 2: 42.) "Doctrines" (Matt. 15: 9) are the opinions of men taught on special subjects; "doctrines" is the whole system and body of the teaching. The system of the Pharisees was corrupt in the mass, like leaven, it puffed up the heart. The Pharisees and Sadducees had rejected the miracles of Jesus; they had ascribed his mighty power to Satan; their cavilling in demanding a sign from heaven; all these furnished Jesus with the occasion to warn his disciples against "the leaven of the Pharisees and Sadducees." With all Jews, leaven was the symbol of hypocrisy, vanity, and pride; hence, Jesus warns his disciples against the teachings of the Pharisees and Sadducees.

19. THE CONFESSION AT CAESAREA
16: 13-20

13 Now when Jesus came into the parts of Cæsarea Philippi, he asked his disciples, saying, Who do men say ¹that the Son of man is? 14 And they

---

¹Many ancient authorities read *that I the Son of man am.* See Mk. 8. 27; Lk. 9. 18.

---

13 Now when Jesus came into the parts of Caesarea Philippi.—This is the most northern point of which we have any record that Jesus reached during his personal ministry. "Cæsarea Philippi" is to be distinguished from "Cæsarea" which is frequently mentioned in Acts of the apostles as the seat of the Roman government for that region. Cæsarea was about seventy-five miles northwest of Jerusalem on the coast of the Mediterranean Sea. Cæsarea Philippi was situated at the easternmost and most important of the two recognized sources of the Jordan. It is not mentioned in the Old Testament and is mentioned only twice in the New Testament (Matt. 16: 13; Mark 8: 27); these two mentions are with respect to the same transactions. It was named for Herod Philip; his name was added to Cæsarea to distinguish it from the other Cæsarea. Jesus and his disciples were alone and Luke tells us that Jesus was praying. (Luke 9: 18.) Jesus asked his

said, Some *say* John the Baptist; some, Elijah; and others Jeremiah, or one

disciples, "Who do men say that the Son of man is?" By this question he begins to lead to the great confession made by his disciples. We may mark with fairly clear accuracy the development of the faith of his apostles. The first step was their following the call of Jesus; the second was their obedience to the limited commission; and the third stage of development begins with their confession. Jesus' earthly ministry has now about reached its zenith. He has exhibited his character and laid his lessons clearly before his disciples; he has trained them so that they may go into all the world bearing his message. They need their faith strengthened and their convictions deepened. This occasion serves to do these two things. They had returned from their limited commission and had gathered some information as to what the people generally thought of him. "Son of man" was a usual designation that Jesus used with respect to himself. The question simply meant, "Who do men say that I, Jesus, am?"

14 And they said, Some say John the Baptist.—They could have said that some affirmed that he was an agent of Beelzebub; possibly only a few made this affirmation. They further could have reported that he was a prophet as some thought that he was merely another prophet. However the apostles chose to give the most favorable reports that they had heard; this is natural in speaking to or of a friend. So they answered, "John the Baptist." Herod had started this report. (Matt. 14: 1-3.) It was thought that John had been raised from the dead; hence he had supernatural power. In this way they could account, they thought, for the miracles of Jesus without acknowledging him to be the Messiah. However public opinion was not agreed on who he was, as some said that he was "Elijah." Elijah had lived in the days of King Ahab; he had rebuked the wicked king and his queen Jezebel for their sins, and had been taken up to heaven without dying a natural death. (2 Kings 2: 1-12.) The Jews cherished a tradition that this Elijah would come back to earth; they thought that when he did come back he would do mighty

of the prophets. 15 He saith unto them, But who say ye that I am? 16 And Simon Peter answered and said, Thou art the Christ, the Son of the living God. 17 And Jesus answered and said unto him, Blessed art thou, Simon

wonders; they also misunderstood the prophecies which referred to John the Baptist and Jesus as Elijah. This was another way of accounting for the mighty works of Jesus without acknowledging him as a Son of God. Still others claimed that he was "Jeremiah, or one of the prophets." Jeremiah was the prophet of God who lived in the last days of the kingdom of Judah before it was carried into Babylonian captivity. (Jer. 1: 1-3.) He had wept over Israel and had pleaded for Jehovah. Some saw in Jesus a similar work to that of Jeremiah, hence they ascribed to him the works of Jeremiah rather than acknowledge him as the Son of God.

15-17 **But who say ye that I am?**—This question is presented after the preparation made by the answer of the question, "Who do men say that the Son of man is?" This question struck down to the depths of their hearts and called for a confession of their own conviction; it probed to the very depth of their faith and called for a clear and definite expression of their faith. Jesus knew what they believed; he knew the strength and depth of their faith; but for their good he asks for a confession. It is the question that every one ought to ask his own heart. Jesus did not care so much what others thought of him, but he wanted an expression from his disciples as to what they believed about him. In answer to the former question the disciples could relate the various opinions that others had of Jesus, but this question called for a faith, and not an opinion.

Simon Peter answered and said, Thou art the Christ, the Son of the living God.—Simon Peter true to his prompt, decisive nature, always ready to speak out, whether for himself or for his brethren, gave this clear, emphatic, and decisive answer. We have in this chapter the good and the dark side of Peter's character. Peter was possibly the senior apostle and on this occasion represented the entire group. "The Christ" is Greek for "the Messiah"; Messiah is the Hebrew for

Bar-Jonah: for flesh and blood hath not revealed it unto thee, but my Father who is in heaven. 18 And I also say unto thee, that thou art ²Peter, and upon this ³rock I will build my church; and the gates of Hades shall not

---

²Gr. *Petros*.
³Gr. *petra*.

---

anointed, and means the anointed of God as the Redeemer of the world. "The Son of God" is put in contrast with "Son of man"; he is not merely the Son of man, but he is "the Son of the living God." "Living God" is used to distinguish God from the dead idols of the heathen, distinguishes him as the source of all life; he is "the living God," the eternal and everlasting God.

Jesus answered, "Blessed art thou, Simon Bar-Jonah." The word "Bar" is the Syriac for the Hebrew "Ben," both meaning "the son of." Jonah was the father of Peter, hence "Bar-Jonah," son of Jonah. This blessing was pronounced upon him and as he spoke for the group, the blessing belongs to the group. It also belongs to all henceforth who so confess him. The source of evidence had not come from "flesh and blood," but had been revealed by "my Father who is in heaven." Here Jesus claims God as his Father and thus emphasizes the truth confessed by Peter that he is "the Son of the living God." "Flesh and blood" is used in the New Testament simply to represent men. (Gal. 1: 16; Eph. 6: 12; Heb. 2: 14.) Men had not taught the disciples of Jesus this truth; they differed about him and would not believe in him as the Son of God. Jesus' disciples had not been swayed by the prejudices and opinions of those who rejected him. God had revealed this knowledge to them, not by any unusual or extraordinary communication, nor by any partial or arbitrary favor to them, but as a result of their faith and obedience. These disciples had not received their evidence from the scribes or religious teachers of that day. The prophets of the Old Testament were moved by the Holy Spirit, and when Jesus fulfilled these prophecies in the presence of his disciples, God was declaring unto them that Jesus was his Son.

18-20 **Thou art Peter, and upon this rock.**—The name "Peter" here means "a stone" (John 1: 42), and in the Greek

prevail against it. 19 I will give unto thee the keys of the kingdom of

is in the masculine gender. Peter as a rock should be firm, immovable, fixed as to preaching the gospel in the clearest terms, on facts and reasonings which enemies could not successfully deny. Peter's energy and boldness helped to mold the first growths of the early disciples in the form of stern, simple unyielding characters. In the first wave of persecution against the church he was the rock on which the rage of the Jews spent itself. (Acts 4: 8-10; 12: 3, 5.) His inflexible courage defended the flock in the first absence of the chief Shepherd.

Upon this rock.—"Rock" here is feminine and refers to the foundation upon which Jesus built his church. "Petros," which means "a stone," is one thing, and "Petra," which means a ledge of rock, is another. Jesus did not say nor mean to say that his church would be built upon "a stone," but upon a solid "ledge of rock"; a stone might be too small for a foundation, but a ledge of rock furnished sufficient foundation for the greatest superstructure. What was this "petra" upon which the church was to be built? Various answers have been given to this question. Some have said that it was Peter, but this is impossible; others have said that it was Peter's confession"; still others have said that it was the "faith" that Peter confessed; still others have said that it was the "truth" embodied in the divinity of Jesus; and others have said that it was the person of Jesus. It is true that Jesus is referred to as the foundation by Paul in 1 Cor. 3: 11. It seems clear from the context that Jesus by using the term "Petra" referred to the truth that Peter had just confessed, which was the deity of Jesus. The truth that Jesus is the Son of the living God is the most fundamental and basic of all truths pertaining to man's redemption.

I will build my church.—The future tense is here used, which shows that at this time Jesus had not established his church. It was only in a *preparatory* stage, and was yet to be established . This is the first instance of the use of the word "church" in the New Testament. The church as here referred

heaven: and whatsoever thou shalt bind on earth shall be bound in heaven;

to by Jesus as "my church" was not set up during the days of Abraham, neither during the days of John the Baptist, nor during the personal ministry of Jesus up to this point; he simply says now that "I will build my church." What has heretofore been spoken of by Jesus as "the kingdom of heaven," "the kingdom of God," is here spoken of as "my church." "Church" is derived from the Greek "ekklasia" which is composed of the Greek preposition "ek," which means out, and "kaleo," which means to call or summons; hence "ekklasia" means called out or assembly. Here "my church" means the assembly or people who have been called out of the world by the gospel of Christ.

The gates of Hades shall not prevail against it.—Ancient cities were surrounded by walls with gates; these gates were often assaulted in battle, and were guarded by special garrisons. The protection of the city was estimated by the strength of its gates; hence the word "gates" became synonymous with "powers." "The gates of Hades" means "the powers of Hades." "Hades" was originally the name of the god who presided over the realm of the dead; hence the phrase "house of Hades." It designates the place to which all who depart this life descend, without reference to their moral character. In the New Testament, Hades is the realm of the dead; here "Hades" is represented as a mighty city with gates representing its power. Jesus simply meant that though he would be crucified, buried, yet he would arise from the dead and build his church; the powers of death or the unseen world, or "the gates of Hades,' 'would not be able to hold him in the unseen realm and prevent his coming out and building his church. Not only would the church be established in spite of the powers of Hades, but the church would be continued in spite of these powers. The church will never fail, though generation after generation yields to the power of death, yet other generations will perpetuate the church, and it will continue until it has filled its mission on earth.

I will give unto thee the keys of the kingdom of heaven.—This is another way of saying, "I will give unto thee the

and whatsoever thou shalt loose on earth shall be loosed in heaven. 20 Then charged he the disciples that they should tell no man that he was the Christ.

terms or conditions of admitting people into the church." "The keys" is a figure of speech from which its meaning may easily be determined. (Isa. 22: 22; Rev. 3: 7.) This expression occurs also in Luke 11: 52; Rev. 1: 18; 9: 1; 20: 1. In all these references the one who bears the keys is the one who has power over the subjects assigned to him. There is no significance attached to the plurality of "keys" further than it represents the power to admit into the kingdom or church. Peter exercised the authority to announce to the Jewish people on the day of Pentecost the terms of admission into the church. (Acts 2.) He also announced first the terms of admission of the Gentiles into the church. (Acts 10.) The same terms were announced in both cases.

Jesus promised to ratify in heaven just what the apostles preached on earth. They were not left to their own wisdom, but were guided by the Holy Spirit in announcing the terms of admission into the kingdom of God on earth. The terms of admission into the church were the terms of the forgiveness of sins. Those who complied with these terms were forgiven and constituted a part of his church; heaven ratified this. Those who refused to comply with the terms were still held guilty and stood condemned; this condemnation was ratified in heaven. "Then charged he the disciples that they should tell no man that he was the Christ." He strictly forbade his disciples publishing at this time that which they had just confessed, namely, that he was "the Christ, the Son of the living God." Two reasons may be clearly seen for this charge: (1) It would endanger his life and would hinder his work by exciting more prejudice in the minds of his enemies; (2) the disciples were unfit to preach this doctrine; they did not know at this time what rising from the dead meant; they did not understand that Jesus had to die, be buried, and be raised from the dead before he could establish his kingdom. They would preach that he would establish a temporal kingdom, hence it is best for them to remain silent until they had all of the facts necessary and could proclaim them by the guidance of the Holy Spirit.

[Here the church and the kingdom of heaven are used interchangeably to denote the same institution. The statement that "the gates of Hades shall not prevail against it" says, in other words, it "shall never be destroyed," "it shall stand forever."

The church was to be built on the truth confessed by Peter and proved by the resurrection that Jesus is the Son of God. Peter was to bear and use the keys to this kingdom of heaven. This settles beyond the possibility of a doubt that the kingdom was set up in the lifetime of Peter. To use the keys was to open the door or give the terms of entrance into the kingdom of God. Did he give the keys of the kingdom to Peter thousands of years before it was set up? When did Peter open the door of the kingdom of heaven and direct men into it? Persons who followed the direction of Peter when he told them what to do to be saved were introduced into the kingdom of heaven, or Jesus was mistaken.]

20. THE CROSS FORETOLD
16: 21-28

21 From that time began ⁴Jesus to show unto his disciples, that he must go unto Jerusalem, and suffer many things of the elders and chief priests and

⁴Some ancient authorities read *Jesus Christ*.

---

21 From that time began Jesus to show.—After the confession the ministry of sorrow now begins. Jesus began now to disclose to his apostles his approaching death; heretofore they had not sufficient faith to appreciate this teaching, but now they have attained some degree of firmness and faithfulness that Jesus reveals to them further the great sacrifice that he must make. The idea is gradually unfolded to them and yet they did not fully appreciate the tragedy that awaited Jesus. Their faith now is sufficient for him to prepare and fortify their minds for his crucifixion. The language of Jesus is simple enough; they could have understood it had not their conception of an earthly kingdom blinded them to his truth. He

16:21-23.] MATTHEW 349

scribes, and be killed, and the third day be raised up. 22 And Peter took him, and began to rebuke him, saying, ⁵Be it far from thee, Lord: this shall never be unto thee. 23 But he turned, and said unto Peter, Get thee behind me, Satan: thou art a stumbling-block unto me: for thou mindest not the

---

⁵Or, God *have mercy on thee*

---

reveals that he must go to Jerusalem and there "suffer many things of the elders and chief priests and scribes, and be killed, and the third day be raised up." Matthew gives but little of the ministry of Jesus in Jerusalem and Judea; his record is almost exclusively confined to Galilee. Jesus had delayed the prediction of his death until his disciples might be better able to bear it and comprehend its full significance. He knew that their conception of the Messiah gave no place for the cross, but they must be prepared for it.

22, 23 Peter took him, and began to rebuke him.—We are astonished at the boldness of Peter so soon after his confession that Jesus is the "Son of the living God," yet he does not hesitate to "rebuke him." "Peter took him" means that he either took him to one side from the other apostles or that he took him by the hand and expostulated with him. The prediction that Jesus had just given was so foreign to the impetuous Peter's conception of the Messiah that he would not admit that Jesus had spoken the truth. Peter was in earnest; his love for the Master, and his courage and determination, with his misconception of the nature of the kingdom of God, would not let him accept such a program for Jesus. So he bluntly said, "Be it far from thee, Lord: this shall never be unto thee." "Be it far from thee" was an expression used in the Old Testament as a prayer against an evil. (Gen. 18:25.) Jesus had just been talking about a kingdom, and had committed to Peter the keys of the kingdom; now he speaks of death and the cross. Peter would not admit that these things should be.

Get thee behind me, Satan.—This is the reply that Jesus made to Peter's rebuke. The word "Satan" is from the Hebrew, and means an adversary, an offense or impediment, an opposer; because of his prominence in evil this name is applied to the devil. David used the same word with reference

things of God, but the things of men. 24 Then said Jesus unto his disciples, If any man would come after me, let him deny himself, and take up his cross,

to the "sons of Zeruiah." (2 Sam. 19: 22.) Jesus does not call Peter "a devil," or an evil-minded tempter, but simply rebukes his misguided zeal which made it more difficult for Jesus to teach the doctrine of the cross. He added in reply to Peter, "Thou art a stumbling-block unto me." Peter instead of being a help to him was a hindrance. By urging Jesus in this manner he was doing that which he did not know. Jesus came to die for the sins of the world and Peter, if he carried out his wish, would thwart the very purpose for which Jesus came to earth; hence he was a stumbling block to him. Jesus added, "Thou mindest not the things of God, but the things of men." Peter did not understand God's will in the matter; he was following his own judgment and feelings. He was acting and feeling as men do, and not as God wills. Peter did not know just what he was doing; he was deeply agitated, and his words gushed out of a zealous, loving heart, almost without thought.

24-28 If any man would come after me.—A record of this is also found in Mark 8: 24-38 and Luke 9: 23-27. Here Jesus presents the doctrine of the cross; the terms of discipleship are expressed here. If the disciple follows the Master, he must endure what his Master endures; he must travel the same road and bear the same burdens. The cost of discipleship is self-denial. In order to be the disciple of Jesus one must do two things, namely, "deny himself" and "take up his cross" and follow him. The self-denial which one must practice to follow Jesus is to deny oneself of all earthly comforts and conveniences, to quit all temporal interests and enjoyments, even life itself if need be. The disciples of Jesus do not not take up the cross of Jesus, but they must take their own crosses and bear them. As each one must deny himself, so each one must take up his own cross. No one is to make trouble for himself or deny himself of the natural blessings which are his, but one must use these blessings for the good of others. In prosperity a disciple of Jesus must be humble and willing to submit,

and follow me. 25 For whosoever would save his life shall lose it: and whosoever shall lose his life for my sake shall find it. 26 For what shall a man be profited, if he shall gain the whole world, and forfeit his life? or what shall a man give in exchange for his life? 27 For the Son of man shall

praying for strength when the day of trial comes; he must be willing to take the cross that may come his way. With horror Peter had recoiled from the thought that Jesus should make his life a sacrifice for men, but Jesus presses the point further; not only must Jesus die upon the cross, but those who would be his disciples must suffer with him; they must make the sacrifice of self-denial and bear the burdens in order to follow Jesus. We have no expression from Peter as to what he thought of this doctrine.

Whosoever would save his life shall lose it.—These words are taken from the period of bitter persecution, when Christians were brought before cruel pagan governors or mobs, not knowing what fate would befall them. If one, under such circumstances, should deny Jesus, or announce the faith of a Christian, in order to save his life, that one was not worthy of Jesus; he might save his temporal life by so doing, but he would lose spiritual life and life eternal; but the one who in steadfastness of faith remained loyal to Jesus might lose his physical life, but would gain spiritual and eternal life. Jesus then calls to their minds the figure of a balance, or scales, and puts the life or soul on one side and all temporal things on the other; by this figure he shows that the soul of spirit of man is worth more than all things else. This point is put forcibly by the two questions: "What shall a man be profited, if he shall gain the whole world, and forfeit his life? or what shall a man give in exchange for his life?" If Peter and the Jews should gain a temporal kingdom, yet lose their soul, what profit would it be to them? The truth that Jesus had taught said that it would be folly to give the whole world in exchange for a soul; that is, a soul is worth more than all temporal things. Jesus wanted them to so understand him. In John 11: 25, 26 Jesus teaches a similar truth with respect to living and dying. The loss of the present life is temporal death; the loss of the future life is death eternal.

come in the glory of his Father with his angels; and then shall he render unto every man according to his ⁶deeds. 26 Verily I say unto you, There are

⁶Gr. *doing*.

[One who would follow Jesus and so become like him and share his glories must deny himself, his fleshly lusts, and the gratification of his appetites and passions, and bear whatever cross this life of self-denial requires, that he may follow the steps and grow into the likeness of Jesus. In this way he becomes a partaker of the divine nature, and in being a partaker of the divine nature he becomes like Christ. (2 Pet. 1: 3, 4.) Through the lusts of the flesh, its passions, ambitions, and wordly desires, corruption, the desire to do wrong for selfish gratification and gain spreads among men, and it makes us delight in doing the wrong and rebelling against the true and the good. God's nature is free from all desire or sympathy with evil. We can free ourselves from this controlling desire by participating in the divine nature through laying aside the evils and corruptions that come through our lusts. The reign and rule of lust hinders obedience to God and makes it difficult to walk in the way that has been plainly marked out by God for us to purify ourselves and to fit us to live in heaven where no corruption or ill will entice us.]

For the Son of man shall come in the glory of his Father with his angels.—This seems to refer to the second advent of Christ; then he shall come "in the glory of his Father with his angels." The supernatural brightness which surrounds and beams forth from God shall accompany Jesus and the angels when he comes again. This same glory is called the glory of Christ. (Matt. 25: 31; John 17: 5.) Jesus sought to turn their eyes from the earth to heaven, and give them glimpses, as they could bear it, of the glorious doctrine which is now so familiar to us. He is coming again and at that time "shall he render unto every man according to his deeds." He will reward the righteous for their faithful service to him, and punish the wicked, when he comes. For every suffering that his disciples endure there will be a compensation; in view of this reward at the judgment day, his disciples may toil and suffer

some of them that stand here, who shall in no wise taste of death, till they see the Son of man coming in his kingdom.

and rejoice in the suffering. All will be judged according to the works that they have done and by the word of God.

There are some of them that stand here, who shall in no wise taste of death, till they see the Son of man coming in his kingdom.—There seems to be two comings mentioned here. The first coming (verse 27) has reference to the final coming as he will come in the glory of the Father, and with the holy angels, and will reward all according to their works. The coming in verse twenty-eight has reference to his "coming in his kingdom," or when his kingdom was fully established on earth. Though he should suffer and die and be buried, yet he would be raised from the dead and through the Holy Spirit would come on the day of Pentecost and would establish his kingdom. Hence, he would come in his kingdom during the lifetime of some of his apostles. We know that only Judas died before the kingdom was estabished.

21. THE TRANSFIGURATION
17: 1-13

1 And after six days Jesus taketh with him Peter, and [7]James, and John his brother, and bringeth them up into a high mountain apart: 2 and he was

[7]Or, *Jacob*

1, 2 And after six days Jesus taketh with him.—Parallel records of the transfiguration are found in Mark 9: 2-10 and Luke 9: 28-36. Luke says "it came to pass about eight days," while Matthew says "after six days"; Mark says "after six days." According to the Jewish mode of reckoning, by counting the first and last days, six whole days intervening, Luke's words may be naturally reconciled to those of Matthew and Mark. It is thought that the transfiguration occurred exactly one year before our Lord's ascension. Jesus took with him "Peter, and James, and John his brother." These three were the select three on other occasions. Their traits of character and faith rendered them capable of special revelations and

transfigured before them; and his face did shine as the sun, and his garments became white as the light. 3 And behold, there appeared unto them Moses

manifestations. (Mark 5: 37; Matt. 26: 37; Luke 8: 51.) Jesus was not partial to these, but they were better prepared in heart and life for these scenes. Jesus brought them "up into a high mountain apart." The place is of little importance, yet tradition assigns it to Tabor, but many scholars think that it was some peak of Mount Hermon, near which they are known to have been both before and after the transfiguration. As they came down from the mountain, Jesus joined the other disciples, and it seems that he had left them in the region of Caesarea Philippi, so it could not have been Mount Tabor as that mountain was too far away.

He was transfigured before them.—His appearance was changed. The word "transfigured" is used also by Mark (9: 2) and means "transformed" or changed. Jesus was "transfigured" or appeared in his glorified state not veiled by human flesh. "His face did shine as the sun, and his garments became white as the light." Jesus made this change of his human body visible to these three disciples; this was done to teach them the mystery of his nature (John 1: 14), which he should assume after his suffering; again it would show these disciples the cessation of the authority of the law and the prophets. Such earthly splendor and glory as they beheld him suggested the supernal and eternal glory with which he was clothed before the world was, and which should be his habilaments after his ascension to the Father.

3 **There appeared unto them Moses and Elijah.**—The raiment of Jesus was white and glistening, even whiter than snow; in this condition there appeared Moses and Elijah. The disciples were weary and had fallen asleep while Jesus prayed; they did not see the beginning of this vision, nor hear all the conversation. Moses and Elijah were talking with Jesus about "his decease which he was about to accomplish at Jerusalem." (Luke 9: 31.) The conversation must have shown also who they were, as Peter called their names. It is noticeable that there had been for many centuries a mystery

and Elijah talking with him. 4 And Peter answered, and said unto Jesus, Lord, it is good for us to be here: if thou wilt, I will make here three ⁸tabernacles; one for thee, and one for Moses, and one for Elijah. 5 While

⁸Or, *booths*

---

connected with the end of Moses and Elijah. Moses in the full vigor of his strength, was summoned to the top of Mount Nebo, where he died; no human hands buried him or knew where he was buried. (Deut. 34: 6.) The Jews had a tradition that his body was buried by angels, and that evil spirits contended for it. (See Jude 9.) He was the great prophet of the law; a type of the Mediator, the one on whose name and authority the Jews especially depended. Elijah "went up by a whirlwind into heaven." (2 Kings 2: 11-16.) The Jews supposed that he was translated to paradise. He is a representative of the prophets. These two, Moses and Elijah, the representative of the law, and the representative of the prophets, appeared with Jesus and yielded their positions to him.

4, 5 **And Peter answered, and said unto Jesus.**—Peter with James and John had been asleep and being suddenly aroused in the very midst of the vision, as was his nature, spoke to Jesus; he is the spokesman of the apostles and on this occasion said, "It is good for us to be here." It is not definitely known just what Peter meant as he did not know himself what he was saying. Luke tells that he did not know "what he said," and since Peter did not know what he said, he could not know what he meant, and we cannot know what he meant. His suggestion was that "three tabernacles" be made, "one for thee, and one for Moses, and one for Elijah." A tabernacle was a tent. (Num. 24: 5.) The Israelites for a long period dwelt in them. The Jews had a "feast of tabernacles" in memory of their once living in tents. (Lev. 23: 34.) A tabernacle also means a tent pitched for the honor of God, in which the divine glory was present. (Ex. 25: 8, 9.) It seems that Peter suggested an abode or place to worship these three glorified beings.

While he was yet speaking, behold, a bright cloud overshadowed them.—The brightness described in verse two belongs

he was yet speaking, behold, a bright cloud overshadowed them: and behold, a voice out of the cloud, saying, This is my beloved Son, in whom I am well pleased; hear ye him. 6 And when the disciples heard it, they fell on their face, and were sore afraid. 7 And Jesus came and touched them and said,

to Jesus alone, but this brightness of the cloud overshadowed all of them. While under this cloud they heard the voice of Jehovah which said, "This is my beloved Son, in whom I am well pleased; hear ye him." This voice had announced at the baptism of Jesus that he was God's Son. (Matt. 3: 17.) At this time the voice adds "hear ye him." This confirmed his divine mission. In the presence of Moses the lawgiver and Elijah the head of the prophets, God pointed out Jesus and declared that he was his Son and that he now should be heard. The withdrawal of Moses and Elijah was suggestive; a greater than both of these remained. This was the second time a voice from heaven had proclaimed in the presence of men God's recognition of Jesus as his Son; a third is yet to come. (John 12: 28-30.) In this impressive way God declares the near end of the law and the prophets and gives emphasis to the beginning of the authority of the Lord Jesus Christ on earth. This scene impressed these disciples as is evident from the words of Peter written long afterward. (2 Pet. 1: 16-18.)

6-8 **And when the disciples heard it.**—The brightness of Jesus' appearance had made them happy, but the voice from heaven in its excellent glory filled them with awe and "they fell on their face, and were sore afraid." Daniel did this (Dan. 8: 17) as did John in his vision (Rev. 1: 17). This was not simply fear, but the power of the divine voice subduing the power of soul and body. They were afraid of instant death if they looked on God. The humility of heart and piety of soul are seen in good men who bow themselves in humble fear before the throne of God. Jesus came to them while they were thus prostrated in reverence and awe before God and "touched them and said, Arise and be not afraid." The touch accompanying the address assured them that he was still in the body of flesh and that they need not fear him. (Luke 24: 37-40.) Thus assured of their safety and the continued pres-

Arise, and be not afraid. 8 And lifting up their eyes, they saw no one, save Jesus only.
9 And as they were coming down from the mountain, Jesus commanded them, saying, Tell the vision to no man, until the Son of man be risen from

---

ence of Jesus in the flesh, they looked up but "they saw no one, save Jesus only." Moses and Elijah had disappeared as suddenly as they had appeared; they had withdrawn from the scene and left only Jesus to occupy the field as a lawgiver and prophet.

[Disciples should hear their Master above all others; this is the very essence of true discipleship. He is not a faithful disciple who hears any one else in preference to his Master. In Christianity Christ himself is the great teacher. Any preaching which does not exalt Christ and point the people to the Lamb of God who taketh away the sins of the world is bad. The preacher who seeks to attract the people to himself rather than to Christ is not a faithful servant of God. His work will be for evil rather than for good to the world, in so far as he succeeds in calling after himself a partisan following of personal admirers.]

9 **And as they were coming down from the mountain.**—Jesus had left nine of his apostles at the foot of the mountain, and had taken Peter, James, and John with him upon the mountain, and they had witnessed his transfiguration; now as they came down from the mountain he demanded that they "tell the vision to no man, until the Son of man be risen from the dead." There were evident reasons for this charge to these three disciples. They did not understand the spiritual meaning of what they had seen and heard; three great doctrines were taught in the transfiguration, namely, the divinity of Christ, the end of the Jewish covenant, and the resurrection. These disciples understood neither of these, hence they could not correctly teach them to others. Again their attempt to teach them to others at this time would create envy among the other apostles; the others would think that the vision was meant to entitle Peter, James, and John to special rights in his kingdom; at any rate, Jesus charged them not to repeat what they had seen and heard.

the dead. **10 And his disciples asked him, saying, Why then say the scribes that Elijah must first come? 11 And he answered and said, Elijah indeed cometh, and shall restore all things: 12 but I say unto you, that Elijah is come already, and they knew him not, but did unto him whatsoever they would. Even so shall the Son of man also suffer of them. 13 Then understood the disciples that he spake unto them of John the Baptist.**

10-13 Why then say the scribes that Elijah must first come? —The word "then" implies something previously said; they must have had in mind the conversation that Jesus, Moses, and Elijah had together on the mount of transfiguration. The "scribes" or teachers among the Jews taught that the Messiah would not come until Elijah came; they were correct in this, but they were in error as to John the Baptist being that Elijah that was to come. (Isa. 40: 3; Mal. 4: 5; Matt. 11: 14.) If the disciples understood that John was the Elijah to come, they could not see how the death of Jesus could soon occur; they expected him to establish an earthly kingdom, and as yet he had declined all offers to become such a king. Jesus confirmed the teaching of the scribes and said "that Elijah is come already," but the scribes and others did not recognize in John the Baptist the Elijah of prophecy. They had done "unto him whatsoever they would." The scribes had not put John to death; Herod had done this, but it seems that the religious leaders among the Jews had consented to John's death. Thus Jesus cleared their understanding that the prophets did not mean the Elijah whom they had just seen on the mount, but that he spoke "unto them of John the Baptist." John was the Elijah (Luke 1: 17), but the Jews had without reason rejected John's testimony and baptism (Luke 7: 30). Just as John had been put to death, so "the Son of man" must suffer many things and be set at naught. (Mark 9: 12.)

22. THE EPILEPTIC CURED, POWER OF FAITH, AND TEMPLE TAX
17: 14-27

14 And when they were come to the multitude, there came to him a man, kneeling to him, and saying, 15 Lord, have mercy on my son; for he is epileptic, and suffereth grievously; for oft-times he falleth into the fire, and oft-times into the water. 16 And I brought him to thy disciples, and they could not cure him. 17 And Jesus answered and said, O faithless and perverse generation, how long shall I be with you? how long shall I bear with you?

14-18 And when they were come to the multitude.—A parallel record of this is found in Mark 9: 14-29 and Luke 9: 37-43. Jesus and his three disciples had remained part of a day and night on the top of the mountain, and came down the next day to the place where they had left the other disciples. They found that a multitude had gathered around them with signs of great excitement. The scribes, taking advantage of the absence of Jesus and the three chief disciples, were present and were questioning the nine disciples. They had tried to cast out a demon, but were unable to do so. The exulting scribes, the embarrassed and confused disciples, the amazed people, and the despairing father and afflicted son presented a very pathetic scene. When Jesus came into their midst, all eyes turned to him. The miracle that he is about to work becomes a test of his power. "There came to him a man, kneeling to him, and saying, Lord, have mercy on my son." While the disciples of Jesus were under a fire of questions and taunting by the scribes, this man came to Jesus and saluted him with joyful reverence. Jesus demanded of the scribes why they were thus questioning his disciples, and at that moment the father of the afflicted son came beseeching earnestly that Jesus heal his son. Luke says that this man "cried" in his earnest entreaty for his son as he was an "only child." The scribes rejoiced at the failure of the disciples in healing this son. The son was an "epileptic"; that is, he was possessed with a demon which caused him to suffer "grievously" and caused him to fall "into the fire, and oft-times into the water." The original denotes a "lunatic" or "moon-struck," or ruled by the moon. They thought that such diseases were caused by the influence of the moon. The unfortunate son at times

bring him hither to me. 18 And Jesus rebuked him; and the demon went out of him: and the boy was cured from that hour.

was seized by nervous contractions and spasms which agitated the whole body, deranged the mind, and made him a horror to himself and friends. It seems that the possession of the evil spirit seized him when he was near water or fire, and caused the sudden fits which endangered his life. It is sad to contemplate the weary hours, days, years of that poor father and his only son. We can better understand from this description the depth of his despair and touching appeal when he cried to Jesus, "Have mercy on my son." The man reported that he had brought his son to Jesus' disciples, but they were unable to cure him. Mark tells us that the evil spirit gave a demonstration of its rage as the boy was brought to Jesus and tore him grievously, "and he fell on the ground, and wallowed foaming." (Mark 9: 20.) Jesus permitted this to continue for a few moments while he asked the father how long the son had been afflicted in this way; the father answered ever since he was a child. The father then asked, "If thou canst do anything, have compassion on us, and help us." (Mark 9: 22.) Jesus replied to this request, "If thou canst!" The father may have thought that it was impossible for Jesus to cure his son. Jesus then replied, "All things are possible to him that believeth." The power of Jesus had been questioned, hence this miracle becomes a test of his power. Jesus put the curing of his son on the basis of faith. Jesus virtually said, "It is not if I can do anything, for I can do all things for you; but it is if thou canst believe, all things are possible to him that believeth." The father understood and virtually said with a broken heart "with tears," "Does the cure of my son depend on me?" Jesus had said that it did; he had transferred the condition of healing the unfortunate son to that of the faith of the father and son. When the father understood this he said, "I believe; help thou mine unbelief." (Mark 9: 24.) He prayed Jesus to forgive his weakness and to strengthen his faith. Jesus rebuked the demon and he went out of him, "and the boy was cured from that hour." The

19 Then came the disciples to Jesus apart, and said, Why could not we cast it out? 20 And he saith unto them, Because of your little faith: for

demon did not leave the son without a desperate struggle in which the son was torn and "became as one dead; insomuch that the more part said, He is dead." (Mark 9: 26.) After a great number had pronounced the son dead, Jesus took him by the hand and raised him up, and delivered him to his father in perfect health. How the scribes and critics of Jesus must have felt when they saw what was done! Perhaps even the disciples of Jesus were astonished at the miracle.

19, 20 Then came the disciples to Jesus apart.—The nine disciples who had failed to cast out the demon were ashamed to ask this question before the multitude, but when Jesus had left the multitude and they were alone with him, they asked, "Why could not we cast it out?" They supposed that having been once invested with power over demons, it was not to be limited; they did not understand why this power was limited. The reason was to be found in their lack of spiritual faith and in their desire for human honor. They are to learn the lesson that the power which comes through faith in Jesus and which was transistory during the days of miracles must be maintained through a sustaining and ever-increasing faith in Jesus; the faith which gave power to cast out a demon is needed to cure a deeper-seated disease than even this foul spirit with his train of physical infirmities; all need a faith which purifies the soul.

And he saith unto them, Because of your little faith.—During the absence of Jesus, his disciples had attempted for their own personal honor and glory to exercise power over demons, but it failed for lack of faith. The powers and blessings of God are not to be used for selfish gain or honor; when so used, they put us to shame and become a curse to us. Jesus, after rebuking their "little faith," or lack of faith, said, "If ye have faith as a grain of mustard seed, ye shall say unto this mountain, Remove hence to yonder place." He further states that by such faith the mountain could be removed and that "nothing shall be impossible unto you." Faith as a grain of

verily I say unto you, If ye have faith as a grain of mustard seed, ye shall say unto this mountain, Remove hence to yonder place; and it shall remove; and nothing shall be impossible unto you.[1]

---

[1] Many authorities, some ancient, insert ver. 21 *But this kind goeth not out save by prayer and fasting.* See Mk. 9. 29.

---

mustard seed" means "if ye had the least faith"; it seems that these disciples had some faith, but they had not the degree which they should have had. They believed in Jesus as a powerful prophet, as a king, as one who can do mighty works; but it is doubtful whether they had any idea of the true faith in him as a Savior of sinners, and as sent to save men from sin by the atonement on the cross. Their faith seemed to see no further in his mission than that he would set up an earthly kingdom, and would have power to sustain that kingdom when once established. One grain of the faith shown in Peter's discourse on the day of Pentecost was greater than the faith which these disciples had in Jesus at this time. If God commanded the mountain to be removed, and promised its removal, faith would act on such a promise; but to move a mountain is a useless miracle; faith in removing spiritual mountains in the world may be exercised today.

Verse twenty-one is omitted here. Mark includes it; it is, "And he said unto them, This kind can come out by nothing, save by prayer." (Mark 9: 29.) Some ancient authorities add "and fasting." It is difficult to determine whether Jesus here refers to any peculiar demoniac possession to be cast out only by a certain high degree of faith, or seeks only to convey a sense of the peculiar work of the ministry, as his instruments for destroying the power of the devil in the heart. It is more obvious that he meant that this special kind of evil spirits which infested this son required special faith or special effort to give effect to their faith.

[The kind of faith or power was the gift of God for the special purpose of performing miracles that is not now possessed. But if Christians will cultivate firm and unflinching faith in God and his word, they can do almost anything through Christ except to perform miraculous power. These gifts to perform miracles were given to the church to teach, instruct,

17:22, 23.]   MATTHEW   363

22 And while they ²abode in Galilee, Jesus said unto them, The Son of man shall be ³delivered up into the hands of men; 23 and they shall kill him, and the third day he shall be raised up. And they were exceeding sorry.

²Some ancient authorities read *were gathering themselves together.*
³See ch. 10. 4.

and guide the disciples until the work of revelation was completed or perfected. The perfect knowledge was delivered to the church when revelation was completed. All Christians from that day to this who will follow the word of God faithfully will come to the fullness of the stature of perfect men and women in Christ.]

22, 23 And while they abode in Galilee.—The miracle and conversation of verses fourteen to twenty took place not far from the mount of transfiguration, which was in the vicinity of Caesarea Philippi. Parallel records of this incident are found in Mark 9: 30-33 and Luke 9: 34, 35. According to Mark 9: 30, Jesus and his disciples crossed over the Sea of Galilee into Galilee, where the present scene transpired. It is interesting to note how the instruction concerning the death, burial, and resurrection of Jesus grows clearer each time that Jesus mentions it. There is a gradual unfolding to his disciples his teachings on the great tragic end of his earthly life. At this time Jesus plainly declared that "the Son of man shall be delivered up into the hands of men." This means that someone will deliver him into the hands of his enemies; his disciples knew that the Jews were seeking to destroy him; hence, Jesus tells them that the time is drawing near when his enemies will have him in their possession. He makes plain to them just what they will do to him. He said, "They shall kill him, and the third day he shall be raised up." These things which are now familiar to us, and which all see to have connection with the spirit of the prophecy, were, as yet, hidden from the disciples. Luke is very emphatic on this point; he says, "But they understood not this saying, and it was concealed from them, that they should not perceive it; and they were afraid to ask him about this saying." (Luke 9: 45.) It is well to keep this in mind in order to understand the events which follow. His disciples had not as yet that light of God's

24 And when they were come to Capernaum, they that received the ⁴half-shekel came to Peter, and said, Doth not your teacher pay the ⁴half-shekel? 25 He saith Yea. And when he came into the house; Jesus spake first to him, saying, What thinkest thou, Simon? the kings of the earth, from whom do they receive toll or tribute? from their sons, or from strangers? 26 And when he said, From strangers, Jesus said unto him, Therefore the sons

⁴Gr. *didrachma*. Comp. marginal note on Lk. 15. 8.

spirit which should guide them into all truth; they did not have this until Pentecost; hence they were slow to comprehend the meaning of the doctrine of the cross. While Jesus was with them he was their guide, and saw for them, and defended them from harm; but now he begins to warn them of the facts of his death in order to prepare them for it. We may wonder that they should be so slow to understand, but our wonder should give way to humiliation at the view it opens to us of the blindness of our common humanity. (1 Cor. 2: 14.) His disciples understood enough, however, to be "exceeding sorry." Luke says that Jesus told them to "let these words sink into your ears." (Luke 9: 44.) If they were not to understand them, they were to remember them, and so Luke adds, "but they understood not this saying."

24-27 And when they were come to Capernaum.—From the time that Herod Antipas killed John the Baptist, Capernaum ceased to be the ordinary residence of Jesus; only twice is it recorded that he visited it again. These visits were on his way to the third Passover (John 6: 25) and now as he goes on his way to the Feast of Pentecost. Those who gathered the taxes came to Peter and asked, "Doth not your teacher pay the half-shekel?" These were Jews and not Roman taxgatherers, for they would not have proposed the payment as a matter of question. This "half-shekel" was the tribute money which every Jew, rich or poor, over twenty years of age, was obliged to pay yearly. It was used for purchasing the animals and other matters necessary for the daily service of the temple; it was enjoined by Jehovah through Moses (Ex. 30: 11-16) and amounted (Ex. 38: 26) to half a shekel. It is translated from the Greek "didrachma," and equalled about thirty cents of our money. The payment of it was a mark of subjection to

are free. 27 But, lest we cause them to stumble, go thou to the sea, and cast a hook, and take up the fish that first cometh up; and when thou hast opened his mouth, thou shalt find a ⁵shekel; that take, and give unto them for one and thee.

⁵Gr. *stater.*

Jehovah, as their King, and a symbol of the equal right and responsibility which all his subjects had in his temple. One could volunteer and pay it, but there was no power granted any one to compel its payment. When Peter was asked whether Jesus paid this tribute he answered, "Yea."

When Peter came into the house, Jesus asked him, "What thinkest thou, Simon? the kings of the earth, from whom do they receive toll or tribute? from their sons, or from strangers?" There are three questions propounded to Peter here; it may be that Peter was in doubt, and Jesus removed the doubt by asking these questions. Peter had just heard God declare Jesus to be his Son on the mount of transfiguration. He had declared to the taxgatherers that Jesus paid the half shekel. Instead of coming directly to Jesus the collectors went to Peter, and now Jesus has the occasion to teach his disciples a very needed lesson. It was taught by the "Socratic method," that is, by questions. Peter is asked if the kings of the earth collect taxes "from their sons, or from strangers"? Peter promptly answered "from strangers." "Strangers" does not mean "foreigners," but persons out of their own family and kindred; that is, from the subjects of the kingdom. Jesus promptly answered "therefore the sons are free"; that is, the sons of the king did not have to pay the tax. His point is that the custom of earthly kings is to collect taxes from their own subjects, and not from their immediate family; that the sons of the king are exempt from paying the taxes that other subjects must pay. And now since God is the king and Jesus is his Son, then he is under no obligations to pay the tax; he is exempt. This is another way of declaring himself to be the Son of God.

But lest we cause them to stumble, go thou to the sea, and cast a hook, and take up the fish that first cometh up.—He then instructed Peter to open the mouth of the fish and that he would "find a shekel," and that he should take the shekel and pay the tax for himself and Jesus, as the tax was a half shekel; the shekel would be sufficient to pay for the two. He did not care to offend any one; others would not understand his refusing to pay the tax; Peter would understand his argument and perhaps others of his disciples, but the tax collectors would not. The sonship of Christ was not enough known by the Jews for them to understand the real reason for his refusing to pay it. There is a liberty with which Christ makes us free, but we should use it in imitation of his own example. Peter was by occupation a fisherman; he knew how to use the articles for fishing, and they were probably in the house where Jesus was at this time. The coin that is translated shekel is the Greek "stater" and is equal in value to about sixty cents of our money. It is the duty of Christians to conduct themselves in all matters wherein they may be supposed to have superior knowledge and privilege so as not to offend anyone.

23. WARNINGS AGAINST GIVING OFFENSE
18: 1-14

1 In that hour came the disciples unto Jesus, saying, Who then is

---

1 Who then is greatest in the kingdom of heaven?—Parallel records are found in Mark 9: 33-41 and Luke 9: 46-50. "In that hour," we do not know the exact time; it is not said that Peter went immediately to the sea to catch the fish which should furnish the tribute money. Luke omits the visit to Capernaum, which is incidentally mentioned by Mark and Matthew. His disciples had been greatly troubled at the announcement of the sufferings of Jesus, but their grief soon passed and their thoughts began to turn to the kingdom which he was to set up. They still believed that he would set up a kingdom, and even if he should have to die, someone would have to carry on the kingdom. They thought it would be an earthly kingdom with royal splendor and that the Jews would be supreme over all other nations; furthermore they

18:1-4.]   MATTHEW   367

[a]greatest in the kingdom of heaven? 2 And he called to him a little child, and set him in the midst of them, 3 and said, Verily I say unto you, Except ye turn, and become as little children, ye shall in no wise enter into the king-

[a]Gr. *greater.*

---

thought that there would be distinctions and offices in it; someone must be high treasurer, some governors over provinces, and some prime ministers to stand near the throne. Who would fill these offices? On the way to Capernaum they debated this question. The kinsmen of Jesus naturally supposed that their blood relationship would entitle them to peculiar honors; Peter had not forgotten the distinction with which he had been treated when he confessed Jesus as the Son of God, and James and John were meditating the project for which they afterwards received a rebuke. (Matt. 20: 20-24.) The disciples were occupied with unworthy ambitions and longings for imaginary honors. Jesus asked them about their dispute, and they, ashamed of it, held their peace. (Mark 9: 33.) They were like children or heirs quarreling over an estate before the death of a benefactor.

2-4 And he called to him a little child.—By way of instructing them and rebuking them for their contention, as to who should be the greatest in the kingdom, he called a little child "and set him in the midst of them." Jesus frequently taught and impressed lessons in this way. The symbolic mode of conveying instruction was common in the East at that time. Some have speculated as to whose child this was; there is no ground for any supposition or tradition as to who it was. When the child was placed in their midst Jesus said to them, "Except ye turn, and become as little children, ye shall in no wise enter into the kingdom of heaven." This put the responsibility on them; they had the opportunity and the power to "turn" about and change their life so that they would become fit subjects of his kingdom. Later Peter said to some, "Repent ye therefore, and turn again." (Acts 3: 19.) They were commanded to do this, hence they could do it, and must do it in order to receive the blessings of God. In their turning or change, Jesus tells them what change they should make; they

dom of heaven. 4 Whosoever therefore shall humble himself as this little child, the same is the ⁶greatest in the kingdom of heaven. 5 And whoso shall

are to "become as little children"; children are humble, docile, and free from ambitious designs; Jesus demanded that his disciples trust him and obey him in humility; "for God resisteth the proud, but giveth grace to the humble." (1 Pet. 5: 5.) The condition of their entering the kingdom was thus made clear; if they do not turn and become like the child, *they cannot enter into the kingdom of heaven*. This shows that the disciples at this time were not in the kingdom or church; that the kingdom or church had not been established at this time; for if it had been, these disciples would have been in it.

Whosoever therefore shall humble himself as this little child, the same is the greatest in the kingdom of heaven.—The kingdom of heaven is composed of the meek on earth. The greatest in the sight of God are those who are the most humble and obedient; those who are most like Christ in service to God and to man. Here is a new standard of greatness; it is God's standard of greatness; "the way up is down," down in humility and up in the greatness of God. In the estimation of God, humility is a most sublime virtue. This does not necessarily teach that there are degrees in happiness on earth or in heaven; it was not spoken to teach such. The disciples of Jesus should have been able to understand more of the nature of the kingdom of God. Jesus here answers the questions which had been raised by his disciples (verse one), "Who then is greatest in the kingdom of heaven?" The greatest is the most humble, the least ambitious. (Psalm 131; 1 Cor. 14: 20.)

[The child of God who thus humbles himself like the little child to think the Father knows best, and he knows it is best because his Father says so, will be crowned with the highest honors in the kingdom of heaven. He who thinks he is wise enough to improve on the Father's ways is a fool, and will never find a home in heaven. It is the vital point of a true son to take God's way just as he gave it as the best and only way for a child of God to walk and work.]

receive one such little child in my name receiveth me: 6 but whoso shall cause one of these little ones that believe on me to stumble, it is profitable for him that [7]a great millstone should be hanged about his neck, and *that* he should be sunk in the depth of the sea.

[7]Gr. *a millstone turned by an ass.*

5, 6 And whoso shall receive one such little child.—"Such little child" means not little ones in age, but in disposition and character. To receive such is to have the humility of Christ, to be truly a disciple. (Matt. 10: 40-42.) To encourage his followers Jesus promised to take care of them; he makes common cause with his faithful disciples. (Matt. 25: 35-40; Mark 9: 38-40; Luke 9: 49, 50.) Jesus here passed from the symbol to the things symbolized, from the child by nature to the child by grace. Those who receive the humble unpretending disciples of Jesus receive him, because these disciples belong to him. It is a blessed thought to be so closely identified with Jesus, that the one who receives his disciple receives him.

But whoso shall cause one of these little ones that believe on me to stumble.—This shows that Jesus is talking about his disciples; it is one who believes "on me" and not a child in age. The one who receives such receives Christ and is blessed; but the one who causes one "to stumble" or be offended receives the condemnation. To cause one to fall away from the faith is a fearful sin. (Matt. 5: 29.) To offend in the scriptural use of the word is to cause anyone to fall from the faith, or renounce his belief in Jesus, and upon everyone who causes such a fall the heaviest condemnations of God are pronounced. It is better for "a great millstone" to be "hanged about his neck, and that he should be sunk in the depth of the sea." An ancient mode of punishment for certain crimes was to hang a millstone about the necks of the victim and cast him into the sea to drown; this was practiced by the Syrians, Greeks, and others. The Jews at times had practiced this by casting the victim into the Dead Sea with a stone tied around him. There were two kinds of millstones—those which are used with the hand and turned by women in grinding and then those that were larger and turned by an ass. The term used here in the original means "ass-millstone," which means

7 Woe unto the world because of occasions of stumbling! for it must needs be that the occasions come; but woe to that man through whom the

the heaviest. Such a one should be "sunk in the depth of the sea"; the intensity of the depth is described as the image of the utter ruin which such crimes deserve. This shows that it is a fearful sin to cause even the least of God's children to stumble.

[Jesus speaks of little ones able to believe; the word translated "stumble" means to lead into sin, to cause to offend; the meaning of it is that it is better for him who causes one to stumble to have a millstone hanged about his neck and be cast into the depth of the sea. Jesus speaks here of children who believe, or of the simplest childlike persons who believe.]

7-9 Woe unto the world because of occasions of stumbling!—A woe is pronounced upon those who encourage in sin; "occasions of stumbling" means "stumbling blocks" in the path of the righteous; those things which cause others to sin, the things which cause others to turn from Christ. Condemnation is pronounced upon the world because so many are not only guilty of sin themselves, but encourage others to sin. Jesus says, "For it must needs be that the occasions come." God has not decreed by any secret decree that there shall always be some men in the world who must necessarily work out their own ruin, by the temptation of others into sin, by inventing heresies to corrupt the doctrines of salvation, by making schisms, to lead astray the simple-minded and humble disciple; he only foretells that which will occur. God has allowed men liberty and free will to choose between good and evil. Some will choose evil and cause the ruin of others; the necessity is in the obstinacy of men and not in the decrees of God. The depraved state of society shows the consequences of causing others to sin. The condemnation of God is upon those who ensnare others into sin. God does not slay men, nor deprive them of their free nature, nor limit its natural free action in its allotted range, in order to prevent men from sinning. It is a fundamental law of man's nature that his character shall have full scope freely to develop itself; hence re-

occasion cometh! 8 And if thy hand or thy foot causeth thee to stumble, cut it off, and cast it from thee: it is good for thee to enter into life maimed or halt, rather than having two hands or two feet to be cast into the eternal fire. 9 And if thine eye causeth thee to stumble, pluck it out, and cast it from thee: it is good for thee to enter into life with one eye, rather than having two eyes to be cast into the ⁸hell of fire. 10 See that ye despise not

---
⁸Gr. *Gehenna of fire.*

---

sponsibility can justly exist, penalty can be justified, and rewards can be bestowed.

[It is God's purpose that the servants of God should be tempted to do wrong. Only a bad person could tempt them to go wrong. So though God desired them tempted, to buffet them, the wicked spirit led in the temptation of the unrighteous, woe be to him for it! (Luke 17: 1; 1 Cor. 11: 19; 1 Tim. 4: 1.) The person or thing that tempted to evil was to be cut off or given up, even if as dear as the right eye, the right hand or foot. Causes and occasions of division and strife will come in all the churches. Many will fail to see and know the whole truth, will give trouble and care in their shortsightedness and missteps. They are to be borne with and trained in the law of God.]

And if thy hand or thy foot causeth thee to stumble, cut it off, and cast it from thee.—The same idea is repeated here, almost in the same words, as in the sermon on the mount. (Matt. 5: 29, 30.) It is better for the disciples of Jesus to go into heaven with nothing but his word to plead than to be cast away for the sake of worldly thrones or the gratifications of fleshly ambitions. The words of Jesus here are not to be taken literally, for God does not permit us to injure and maim our bodies in order to avoid temptation, but shows us, by this impressive figure of speech, that we should deny our selfish and proud desires, and "put to death therefore your members which are upon the earth." (Col. 3: 5.) "Enter into life" means life eternal, and "hell of fire" may mean "Gehenna," which is called "eternal fire" (verse eight) as the fire was kept burning in the Valley of Hinnom to consume carcasses and refuse. (Matt. 5: 22.) Mark shows the application of the proverb by saying here "enter into the kingdom of God," which is the same as eternal life with all of its promises.

one of these little ones; for I say unto you, that in heaven their angels do always behold the face of my Father who is in heaven." 12 How think ye?

⁹Many authorities, some ancient, insert ver. 11 *For the Son of man came to save that which was lost.* See Lk. 19. 10.

10, 11 See that ye despise not one of these little ones.—Again "little ones" means disciples of Jesus; to "despise" one of them is to neglect to use the means that will help them in living the Christian life; we are to use all means at our command to help each other; to despise one is to put temptation in their way. Men often despise the poor, or the humble Christian, do them wrong, almost force them, by oppression, into doing evil; sometimes disciples of one race may despise those of another, because the color of the skin does not mark them in their class. God is the avenger of those who so treat his disciples. (1 Thess. 4: 6; James 5: 6.)

The reason assigned by Jesus as a warning to those who would despise his disciples is "that in heaven their angels do always behold the face of my Father who is in heaven." This is a difficult passage; scholars are not agreed as to its meaning. The most general meaning is that each disciple has a "guardian angel" which protects and guides in living the Christian life. They are represented as beholding the "face of my Father who is in heaven." To "behold the face" of God is to be present before his immediate glory, and entrusted with high commissions and power. It has been doubted by some whether there are single angels delegated to minister a special providence to each one of the disciples of Jesus. Many think that there are such special angels to care for each soul. (Psalm 34: 7; Acts 12: 15; Heb. 1: 14.) These scriptures by some are interpreted to mean that each Christian is guarded in his efforts to be holy by his attendant angel.

[This is relied on to prove that each disciple has a "guardian angel," but for this to have any bearing on that subject, it must be first assumed that persons have guardian angels. It may be the spirits of persons after death become angels and those who humble themselves as little children in the future state become angels and stand nearest the throne of God.

This would be more consoling than the other idea. Is there any ground for supposing the redeemed spirits become angels? Jesus said, "In the resurrection they neither marry, nor are given in marriage, but are as angels in heaven." (Matt. 22: 30.) This does not say they become angels, but it does say they become *as* angels—are conformed to their state in important particulars. Acts 12: 15; 23: 8 and Matt. 25: 41 are scriptures that seem to have a bearing on the subject. When properly construed these do not suggest the idea; hence no proof whatever is found of the idea. If Christians or others have guardian angels, what do they for them? Do they suggest thought? When a thought comes into the mind, how can we tell whether it was suggested by an angel or not? Are we not liable to accept evil suggestions as made by the angels? Who is responsible for our actions, ourselves or our "guardian angels"? It seems to be fraught with the same danger that directs spiritual influence; we are liable to attribute our fleshly emotions and desires to the guardian angel. Does the angel make suggestions or exert an influence and give us no rule by which to test when the influence is from the angel or from something else? When man sins, who is responsible —the man or the angel? In the parable of the man who sowed good seed and evil plants grew in the field (Matt. 13: 24-30), the servants, who were the angels, asked, "Shall we gather up the evil plants?" He said, "No; let them grow together until the harvest; then the reapers will separate them." This teaches that there will be no superhuman interference with men until the judgment. The idea of guardian angels is attended with some evil; it is best not to teach it.]

Verse eleven is omitted in the Revised Version because the ancient manuscripts and versions do not have it. Some think that it is quoted from Luke 19: 10, where it is genuine. It states the purpose of the advent of Jesus—"to save that which was lost." Jesus came to save the world; those who accept him will receive the blessings of salvation from past sins, and, if faithful to him, will in the end receive eternal life. (Mark 16: 16; Acts 4: 12; Rom. 3: 23-26.)

if any man have a hundred sheep, and one of them be gone astray, doth he not leave the ninety and nine, and go unto the mountains, and seek that which goeth astray? 13 And if so be that he find it, verily I say unto you, he rejoiceth over it more than over the ninety and nine which have not gone astray. 14 Even so it is not ¹the will of ²your Father who is in heaven, that one of these little ones should perish.

¹Gr. *a thing willed before your Father.*
²Some ancient authorities read *my.*

12-14 If any man have a hundred sheep.—This parable is also found in Luke 15: 4-10. It shows the value that Jesus placed on a human soul. He came to seek and to save the lost; if there is not much value to be placed on a human soul, then Jesus' mission was not worth very much. If we deem his mission to earth very valuable, we must place a very high estimate on the soul. Jesus makes no difference in his estimation of a soul; the least of his disciples is as valuable and precious in his sight as the most renowned. The Pharisees and other religious leaders of that day disregarded the poor, the disgraced, and degraded wretches of human society. They were spoken of as "publicans and sinners" and "publicans and harlots." So Jesus here shows by the parable of the lost sheep the care that should be given to each one. If one has a flock of a hundred sheep and one is lost, the shepherd leaves the ninety-nine and goes to find the one that has gone astray. When it is found, he rejoiceth over it more than the ninety-nine "which have not gone astray." This does not mean that he values the one greater than he does the ninety-nine; but to restore the one to the flock gives him greater joy for the occasion than the remainder of the flock. Jesus makes his own application of this parable when he says, "Even so it is not the will of your Father who is in heaven, that one of these little ones should perish." By implication Jesus teaches that it is possible for those who have become his "little ones" to perish. It is not God's will that any should perish. (Ezek. 33: 11; 2 Pet. 3: 9.) As it is not the will of the shepherd that one of the flock should perish, so it is not the will of our Father that even the least of his disciples perish.

24. HOW OFFENDERS ARE TO BE TREATED
18: 15-35

15 And if thy brother sin ³against thee, go, show him his fault between thee and him alone; if he hear thee, thou hast gained thy brother. 16 But if

³Some ancient authorities omit *against thee.*

15-17 And if thy brother sin against thee.—In addition to what Jesus had already said about causing others to stumble, he now gives instructions how to restore those who do stumble. Certain rules are to be observed and principles followed in dealing with the erring. If any member of the flock commits a fault, that one is to be sought and reclaimed. This teaching is prospective, as the church had not been established at this time. "If thy brother sin." God knew that his people would sin; he knew that they would sin against each other, hence the principle for dealing with those who do sin. The spiritual relationship of the disciples of Christ is compared to a family; hence all dealings with the erring are to bear the marks of love and the salvation of the offender. A sin against an individual Christian is a sin against the law of love; it must be dealt with as such, for it is also a sin against God. Evilspeaking against it and harsh judgments pronounced are not God's way of dealing with the erring. It must be a definite sin, and not an imaginary wrong or grievance that comes under the teachings of Jesus here. Oftentimes members of the body of Christ imagine that they have been sinned against when, in reality, no sin has been committed against them.

Show him his fault between thee and him alone.—Go and in the spirit of meekness (Gal. 6: 1) show him his wrong to that he may be penitent of it. Tell him of his fault in such a prudent manner that he shall feel it and repent. (Lev. 19: 17.) It is better to go to him and show him his wrong than to brood over it and gender hatred toward him. The one who has received the wrong must use all the agencies of righteousness at his command to bring the erring one to a state of repentance so that he may be forgiven. If the one sinned against is unable to bring the erring one to a state of repentance, there is another step to be taken.

he hear *thee* not, take with thee one or two more, that at the mouth of two witnesses or three every word may be established. 17 And if he refuse to hear them, tell it unto the ⁴church; and if he refuse to hear the ⁴church also,

⁴Or, *congregation*

But if he hear thee not, take with thee one or two more.— The erring brother, like the lost sheep, has strayed away, and has been found; if the one who has found him cannot restore him, then he should get others to help him bring the lost back to the flock and safety. The Jews required at least two witnesses to every act of crime and offense against the law. (Deut. 17: 6; 19: 15.) This principle is carried out in the New Testament. (John 8: 17; 2 Cor. 13: 1; Heb. 10: 28.) This was wise or else God would not have commanded it. The design of taking two witnesses may be twofold; first the offending brother may be possibly induced to repent and return, if he has been proud and refractory, when he sees that persons of serious character and candid judgment are condemning his fault; and second, that in administering the discipline, the church later may have certain grounds on which to base its discipline and not upon imaginary or prejudiced ground. These two witnesses may bring to bear all of the influence that they can command upon the erring brother with a view to bringing him to repentance and restoration. But if these fail, there is still another step to be taken.

And if he refuse to hear them, tell it unto the church.— The purpose of all efforts is to save the wrongdoer; hence, when the one who has received the wrong has exhausted all of his means for restoration, but has failed; and then after two or three wise and prudent brethren have exhausted their full resources of spiritual agencies and failed, then the church, the whole body of disciples, is to bring to bear upon him all the good graces and influence to bring him to repentance and full restoration. There is to be a prayerful, sympathetic, and united effort on the part of the church to restore him, but if the church fails, the Lord has given no other means to be used or steps to be taken. What then must be done?

Let him be unto thee as the Gentile and the publican.— He

let him be unto thee as the Gentile and the ⁵publican. 18 Verily I say unto you, What things soever ye shall bind on earth shall be bound in heaven; and what things soever ye shall loose on earth shall be loosed in heaven.

⁵See marginal note on ch. 5. 46.

---

is to be avoided; ye he is entitled to the earnest good will, and all the offices of humanity; the faithful disciples of Christ are to have no religious communion with him until he repents. (1 Cor. 5: 11; 2 Cor. 2: 6, 7; 2 Thess. 3: 14, 15.) The one who will not hear the church has no claim on it for its fellowship and blessings any more than anyone else out of the church.

[When difficulties arise, this scripture teaches how each party is to act to heal the wrong or to obviate its evil influences and to bring good out of it to those who are willing to obey God. All trials and sins bring good to those who obey God. Jesus lays down a principle that applies to all ages and peoples, and is to be practiced wherever there are disciples. It was the way Jesus laid down for his disciples to settle difficulties and troubles that arose among them. Why should such a course be suited to one age or people and not another? If that principle is not applicable now, we would not know how to say one word taught by Jesus is now applicable. When a brother has committed an offense against us, how better to settle it than the way laid down here? Can human wisdom devise a better way than to go and tell him of his trespass and seek to save him from his wrong course? And if he refuse to hear you, then take one or two discreet brethren with you, and try to settle the matter. Can any man do better than that? Then why seek to set it aside?]

18-20 **Verily I say unto you, What things soever ye shall bind on earth.**—Whatsoever the disciples shall order concerning such a man, whether the withdrawal from him or his restoration or repentance, shall be ratified in heaven. This is the same thought as in Matt. 16: 19. This shows that it has a broader application than that of the discipline of an erring brother. The Holy Spirit would guide the apostles in their instruction to the erring brother and the church, hence what would be required by those guided by the Holy Spirit, God

19 Again I say unto you, that if two of you shall agree on earth as touching anything that they shall ask, it ⁶shall be done for them of my Father who is in heaven. 20 For where two or three are gathered together in my name, there am I in the midst of them.

⁶Gr. *shall become.*

---

would require, or should "be bound in heaven." If he repented and was restored, then his sin should "be loosed in heaven." The conditions of restoration should be ratified by our Father who is in heaven. No member of the church should fail to act in the discipline as instructed by the Holy Spirit; to fail to concur with the church would be to fail to agree with God. It would be disastrous to the unity of the church when the offender has been scripturally dealt with for any member to refuse to concur in the discipline. Blood relation or other interests should not prevent one from cooperating with the church in its act of discipline. To do so would be to rebel against God. (John 10: 11; Rom. 16: 17; 1 Cor. 5: 4, 5; Titus 3: 10, 11.)

Again I say unto you, that if two of you shall agree on earth.—The prayers of God's people, when offered in the name of Christ and according to the will of God, will be heard by the Father. Hence, when even "two of you shall agree on earth as touching anything that they shall ask, it shall be done." (Acts 5: 3; 13: 9-11.) God teaches his children to pray, and when they are united in their prayers God hears them. (Matt. 28: 20; John 20: 19; 1 Cor. 4: 1.) It is understood that the scriptural conditions of prayer must be met by the united group as well as by the individual. Jesus has promised to be with those who are thus praying in his name. It is comforting for the disciples to be united in their prayers and to know that Jesus will be with them in their praying. Jesus is with his people by the Holy Spirit and by his divine nature which is omnipresent.

[Churches must be united and act as one body. This passage and others indicate very clearly that God is well pleased when his children meet together and agree as to the subject o prayer. It would be well for Christians to meet and agree as

21 Then came Peter and said to him, Lord, how oft shall my brother sin against me, and I forgive him? until seven times? 22 Jesus saith unto him, I say not unto thee, Until seven times; but, Until ⁷seventy times seven. 23 Therefore is the kingdom of heaven likened unto a certain king, who would make a reckoning with his ⁸servants. 24 And when he had begun to reckon,

⁷Or, *seventy times and seven*
⁸Gr. *bondservants*.

---

to the things desired and then all unite heartily in prayer for the things desired. This would draw them close together and lead to uniformity in prayer. When drawing near to God for his blessings, all would desire to do it in the way most pleasing to him.]

21, 22 Lord, how oft shall my brother sin against me, and I forgive him?—Peter as usual takes the lead and asks; he understood that there should be a free forgiveness of all sin, and his question is appropriate in asking *how often* one should forgive his brother, when the same sin is repeated. Peter did not know how far he should go in extending forgiveness. This gave Jesus the occasion to teach them. "Until seven times," this was a number which Peter thought would go beyond the limit of extending forgiveness. This was a large stretch of charity to forgive one "seven times," as the rabbis taught that three times were sufficient. (Job 33: 29, 30; Amos 1: 3; 2: 6.) The disciples of Christ are to go beyond the righteousness of the Pharisees. Jesus must have astonished his disciples when he said not "Until seven times; but, Until seventy times seven." This denotes an unlimited number; this expression is used in the description of revenge in the case of Lamech. (Gen. 4: 24.) The duty of forgiveness has no limit, save in the want of penitence in the offender. As often as the offender repents, we must forgive. The penitence of the offender should be sincere and the forgiveness of the sin should be sincere. Jesus thus teaches his disciples to exercise forgiveness always, to live in the state or attitude of forgiving wrongs. In no case should a Christian harbor malice or retain resentment toward a sincere penitent offender.

23-35 Therefore is the kingdom of heaven.—Again Matthew uses the phrase "kingdom of heaven." "Therefore"; this shows a conclusion from what has just followed. Since un-

one was brought unto him, that owed him ten thousand ⁹talents. 25 But forasmuch as he had not *wherewith* to pay, his lord commanded him to be sold, and his wife, and children, and all that he had, and payment to be made.

⁹This talent was probably worth about £200, or $1000.

---

limited forgiveness is to be extended to the penitent offender, "the kingdom of heaven" is like "a certain king." Unlimited forgiveness to the penitent is a part of the will of God, and hence belongs to the kingdom of God on earth; this emphasizes the points of this parable. This king "would make a reckoning with his servants." "Servants" here means his public ministers who had to do with financial matters. In an absolute monarchy the king can remove or destroy any of his public officials. This king had a time for reckoning with his officials, and when he began to reckon with them he found one who "owed him ten thousand talents." This was an enormous sum; a round number is used to give us the idea of the hopelessness of payment. "Talent" was not a coin, but represented a value. If the Hebrew talent is here meant, the sum is enormous; the sum in silver would be more than $15,000,000; if reckoned in gold, it was beyond all possibility of payment. We may form some idea of the amount by comparing other sums spoken of in the Bible. In the tabernacle twenty-nine talents of gold were used (Ex. 38:24); for the temple David prepared 3,000 talents of gold, the princess 5,000 (1 Chron. 29:4-7). The queen of Sheba gave Solomon 120 talents (1 Kings 10:10); Hezekiah was taxed thirty talents of gold (2 Kings 18:14); and finally the land was taxed one talent of gold (2 Chron. 36:3). The sum mentioned here that this servant owed his king exceeded all possibility of payment; this huge debt is the likeness of our sins, which no power of ours can ever pay. (Rom. 2:5.) Since the servant "had not wherewith to pay, his lord commanded him to be sold, and his wife, and children, and all that he had, and payment to be made." The Jewish law allowed the selling of insolvent debtors into a mild state of domestic slavery. (Lev. 25:39, 41; 2 Kings 4:1.) The king may have been a Gentile ruler, and this slavery may have been a state of harsh and cruel bondage as such was frequently practiced.

26 The ¹⁰servant therefore fell down, and ¹¹worshipped him, saying, Lord, have patience with me, and I will pay thee all. 27 And the lord of that ¹⁰servant, being moved with compassion, released him, and forgave him the ¹²debt. 28 But that ¹⁰servant went out, and found one of his fellow-servants, who owed him a hundred ¹³shillings: and he laid hold on him, and took *him* by the

¹⁰Gr. *bondservant.*
¹¹See marginal note on ch. 2. 2.
¹²Gr. *loan.*
¹³The word in the Greek denotes a coin worth about eight pence half-penny, or nearly seventeen cents.

The servant therefore fell down, and worshipped him.—In this worship he said, "Lord, have patience with me, and I will pay thee all." This formal act of worship or adoration consisted of prostration on the ground, and kissing the feet and knees of the one worshiped; this servant worshiped the king, for that honor was paid to royal personages. He threw himself on the mercy of the king; probably the king knew that it was impossible for this servant who had involved himself so deeply in debt to pay anything, though he promised to pay it all. The king was "moved with compassion, released him, and forgave him the debt." This was an act of mercy and compassion on his servant who was penitent. The servant who was crushed to earth, about to lose his wife, children, liberty, and all and to become a slave to another was released of all that he owed. Such an act finds a parallel only in the forgiveness of God to sinners. He was set free or "released"; the same word is used of the act of setting Barabbas free. (Matt. 27: 15.)

But that servant went out, and found one of his fellow servants.—This fellow servant owed him only "a hundred shillings." The denarius, or penny, was a Roman coin, worth fifteen cents of our money; the whole sum was about fifteen dollars; or compared with his own debt, in proportion of one million of dollars to one. It was a trifling sum compared to the debt that he owed the king; this small sum may show how little after all we sin against each other compared with our sin against God. He took this servant and severely punished him; he "took him by the throat, saying, Pay what thou owest." His harsh and violent conduct toward his fellow servant is in wide contrast with the conduct of his lord to him.

throat, saying, Pay what thou owest. 29 So his fellow-servant fell down and besought him, saying, Have patience with me, and I will pay thee. 30 And he would not: but went and cast him into prison, till he should pay that which was due. 31 So when his fellow-servants saw what was done, they were exceeding sorry, and came and told unto their lord all that was done. 32 Then his lord called him unto him, and saith to him, Thou wicked [10]servant, I forgave thee all that debt, because thou besoughtest me: 33 shouldest not thou also have had mercy on thy fellow-servant, even as I had mercy on thee? 34 And his lord was wroth, and delivered him to the tormentors, till he should pay all that was due. 35 So shall also my heavenly Father do unto you, if ye forgive not every one his brother from your hearts.

In like manner this fellow servant "fell down and besought him, saying, Have patience with me, and I will pay thee." His attitude and words were similar to those which his fellow servant had used to the king . "And he would not"; he did not exercise the mercy and forgiveness that had been extended to him, but on the contrary he "went and cast him into prison, till he should pay that which was due." Another contrast is brought out in the conduct of the forgiven servant with this fellow servant. When he did this the other servants "saw what was done," and they were "exceeding sorry, and came and told unto their lord all that was done." The conduct of this fellow servant was condemned by the other servants; the cruelty and hardness of heart which he manifested aroused them to righteous indignation, so they reported him to the lord.

Then his lord called him unto him.—There is now to be another reckoning; this offense is worse than the offense of his indebtedness to his lord. His lord pronounced this sentence upon him, "Thou wicked servant, I forgave thee all that debt, because thou besoughtest me: shouldest not thou also have had mercy on thy fellow-servant, even as I had mercy on thee?" The lord did not call him "wicked servant" when he owed him the "ten thousand talents," but he did call him a "wicked servant" for such harsh and cruel treatment toward his fellow servant. His lord "was wroth" with him and "delivered him to the tormentors, till he should pay all that was due." "Tormentors" literally means the "triers" or judges. In the East it was common for men to conceal property and pretend to be very poor in order to escape the rapacity of the powerful; hence the custom was practiced of subjecting them to torture in order to compel them to betray their wealth. These tormentors were jailers and others who were skillful in applying agonies to unwilling prisoners. He was thus to be tormented "till he should pay all that was due," which was during his natural life, for he never could discharge the debt.

Jesus makes his own application of the parable. He says. "So shall also my heavenly Father do unto you, if ye forgive not every one his brother from your hearts." Upon this condition hangs the divine forgiveness of us in this world. (Matt. 5: 7; Luke 6: 37; Eph. 4: 32; Col. 3: 13; James 5: 9.) Some think that this means if we do not forgive our penitent brother God will bring back upon us all the condemnation which belongs to all of our former sins; that is, that God will bring them back upon us, though they have been forgiven, if we do not forgive our brother from the heart. Others think that the condemnation of the sin of refusing to forgive the penitent is severe enough to condemn one to eternal torment. The forgiveness must be "from your hearts"; it must be in deed and in truth. (1 John 3: 18.) In mercy to ourselves we must turn the resentment out from our inmost hearts, that our hearts may be abodes of peace and love. This law of pardon must be supreme, and rule down all rebellious excuses and little lingerings of hatred and revenge.

SECTION FIVE

THE PEREAN MINISTRY
19: 1 to 20: 34

1. FROM GALILEE TO PEREA: TEACHINGS CONCERNING DIVORCE
19: 1-12

1 And it came to pass when Jesus had finished these words, he departed from Galilee, and came into the borders of Judæa beyond the Jordan; 2 and great multitudes followed him; and he healed them there.

The country lying east of the Sea of Galilee and river Jordan was called by Josephus "the Peræa," but it is referred to in the New Testament as "beyond the Jordan." (Matt. 4: 15, 25; 19: 1; Mark 3: 8; John 1: 28; 3: 26; 10: 40.) It is never called Perea in the New Testament. This country seems to have been called in the Old Testament "land of Gilead." It is perhaps the most picturesque and beautiful part of Palestine. In the time of Jesus' personal ministry Perea with Galilee was under the dominion of Herod Antipas. The Jews recognized Perea, the land beyond the Jordan, as a province of the land of Israel, ranking with Judea and Galilee on the west. On the borders of Perea, some think that Jesus was baptized in the Jordan. It was the scene of happy and profitable intercourse with Jesus and his disciples; it furnished the retreat from Jewish enmity, and from whence Jesus was summoned at the death of Lazarus at Bethany. (John 10: 40.)

1, 2 And it came to pass when Jesus had finished these words.—Mark 10: 1-12 gives a parallel record. The interval of time between the last chapter and this is supposed to have been about five months; the events and conversations of the last chapter are thought to have occurred in May, while those recorded here occurred in October and November, only five months before the crucifixion. Jesus left Galilee and crossed the Sea of Galilee and went down on the east side of the river Jordan opposite the country of Judea. So far as we know, Jesus never returned to Galilee till after his resurrection. Matthew passes over many events that occurred on this jour-

3 And there came unto him ¹⁴Pharisees, trying him, and saying, Is it lawful *for a man* to put away his wife for every cause? ⁴And he answered

¹⁴Many authorities, some ancient, insert *the*.

---

ney and at Jerusalem. The records of Matthew, Mark, and Luke have been called the "Galilean gospels" because their scene is mostly in Galilee, and their subject the ministry of Jesus in that section; John's record has been called "the Judean gospel" because its scene is mostly in Judea and in Jerusalem. Great multitudes followed Jesus in Perea and he "healed them there." Apparently a kinder reception was given him here than in Judea and about Jerusalem during the last stage of his public ministry.

3-9 **There came unto him Pharisees, trying him.**—The Pharisees were the bitter enemies of Jesus because much of his teachings contradicted their traditions and practices; also they were the self-appointed leaders of the Jewish religion at this time and they looked upon Jesus as their rival. They sought to injure him in the eyes of the people; hence they came to him with a well-worked-out plan. The Jews were very much divided in opinion as to the law on the marriage and the divorce question. It was impossible to satisfy both parties; he would gain the ill will of those whose opinion he condemned. There were two current opinions among the leaders at this time. The school of Hillel taught that a man might divorce his wife *for any reason,* for any slight offense, or merely for his dislike of her person or manners; they based their opinions on Deut. 24: 1, which says, "If she find no favor in his eyes," then he may "write her a bill of divorcement, and give it in her hand, and send her out of his house." The opposite school of Shammai allowed divorce only for adultery; this school based its decision on the same scripture (Deut. 24: 1) which says, "Because he hath found some unseemly thing in her," which they interpreted as the sin of adultery.

These Pharisees asked Jesus, "Is it lawful for a man to put away his wife for every cause?" They meant for "any cause"; if Jesus answered this question in the negative, he opposed the school of Hillel, and would incur their enmity; but

and said, Have ye not read, [15]that he who [16]made *them* from the beginning made them male and female, 5 and said, [17]For this cause shall a man leave his father and mother, and shall cleave to his wife; and the two shall become one flesh? 6 So that they are no more two, but one flesh. What therefore God hath joined together, let not man put asunder. 7 They say unto him,

---

[15]Gen. i. 27; v. 2.
[16]Some ancient authorities read *created*.
[17]Gen. ii. 24.

---

if he answered it in the affirmative, he would incur the enmity of the school of Shammai. They wanted Jesus to answer this question, knowing that it would injure him with one side or the other. They probably knew his teaching on this question, and were not seeking to know the truth, but desired to arouse against him the worst feelings of men as against one who wished to deprive them of a proper liberty.

And he answered and said, Have ye not read, that he who made them from the beginning made them male and female? —Jesus in his reply avoids the difficulty or occasion of taking sides with either party; he sighted a scripture which went behind the interpretation of both schools of that day, and settled the question by the original design of marriage, as shown by an undisputed text. (Gen. 1: 27; 2: 21, 24.) This would remove the question from the opinions of both Hillel and Shammai and put it on the basis of God's plain word. Neither school could oppose him for basing the question upon an undisputed scripture. In the beginning God "made them male and female"; they were made as one pair, therefore they should be united in pairs; these pairs should remain as God ordained as the basis of the family. Any violation of the union of this pair is fundamentally wrong and contrary to God's original purpose. This act of divine creation has become the symbol of the union between Christ and his church. (Eph. 5: 32, 33.) "For this cause shall a man leave his father and mother, and shall cleave to his wife." The original word here implies a union which nothing can dissolve. The tie of husband and wife is stronger than that of parent and child, as the tie which binds husband and wife maintains its union during life, hence "shall a man leave his father and mother, and shall cleave to his wife." "And the two shall become one flesh."

[19:7, 8.] MATTHEW 387

¹Why then did Moses command to give a bill of divorcement, and to put *her* away? 8 He saith unto them, Moses for your hardness of heart suffered you to put away your wives: but from the beginning it hath not been so. 9 And
¹Dt. xxiv. 1-4.

As in Adam before the creation of Eve the two were *one,* so now, by marriage, the *oneness* is restored; they are two halves of one whole, forming *one person,* "one flesh." As the original woman was by the power of God taken out of the flesh of Adam, so is the wife reminded that she has something of the same relation to her husband; she is wedded to him, the bond between them being altogether of another kind from any human compact or covenant. The only parallels to this relation are the union of the soul and body and Christ and the church. (1 Cor. 6: 15-20; 7: 4, 5; Eph. 5: 28-33.) It matters not what license or privilege may be granted by the laws of the state. "What therefore God hath joined together, let not man put asunder." God's laws by virtue of his creating them male and female take precedence over all human laws. The courts of the land dissolve many unions which God still holds as fundamental and abiding; the laws of the land grant divorces for causes which God does not permit. Man's laws cannot change the mind of God or the fundamental laws of God; hence man's laws cannot annul the marriage bonds which God has sanctioned. Marriage is a solemn oath of union, in which each party vows fidelity till death parts them.

They say unto him, Why then did Moses command to give a bill of divorcement, and put her away?—These shrewd Pharisees saw that they had not entrapped Jesus, but that he had answered their question. Hoping yet to ensnare him, they asked him this question about Moses. A clear and honest desire for truth would have caused them to take another course; it is profitable to note the different ways in which Jesus refutes the cavilling of his enemies, and answers the questions of the simple, earnest seeker of the truth. Moses granted the privilege of giving "a bill of divorcement" when the husband put away his wife. This was a written certificate of her being divorced and the cause of the divorce; this was done so that the woman could be married again, if she so

I say unto you, Whosoever shall put away his wife, ²except for fornication, and shall marry another, committeth adultery: ³and he that marrieth her when she is put away committeth adultery. 10 The disciples say unto him,

²Some ancient authorities read *saving for the cause of fornication, maketh her an adulteress:* as in ch. 5. 32.
³The following words, to the end of the verse, are omitted by some ancient authorities.

minded. Jesus answered this question by saying, "Moses for your hardness of heart suffered you to put away your wives: but from the beginning it hath not been so." If they thought that they would array Jesus against Moses by their question, they were again mistaken. Jesus came to fulfill the law, and in no instance did he violate the law of Moses. The question of these Pharisees simply meant if God did not intend that divorces be granted as they were practiced then, and even now, "why did Moses command a bill of divorcement to be given?" Jesus reminded them that it was not a "command," but a sufferance. God saw fit to grant this latitude through Moses to the Jews, but only to *allow* it. The right and strict law, such as had been in the beginning while Adam and Eve were in the state of innocence, would now be restored in the kingdom which Christ came to establish. The privilege of the law of Moses shows the degeneracy of mankind and that the severest penalities, which human laws can inflict, are necessary to prevent the evils which the wicked passions of men would otherwise produce.

In further teaching this question Jesus said, "Whosoever shall put away his wife, except for fornication, and shall marry another, committeth adultery." Marriage is brought back to its original state and intention, and the sin of adultery is now made evident beyond mistake. Whosoever, then, if married contrary to God's word, that is, in the forbidden degrees, or has put away one wife, not an adulteress, and married another, or vice versa; or whoever has married the woman proved to have been adulterous, such an one is under the curse of God and is in sin so long as he or she remains in this connection. (1 Cor. 5: 5.) All the legislatures, teachings of men, and infidel presses in the world cannot remove the curse; they only number themselves among those who deny

19: 10-12.]　　　　　　　　MATTHEW　　　　　　　　389

If the case of the man is so with his wife, it is not expedient to marry. 11 But he said unto them, Not all men can receive this saying, but they to whom it is given. 12 For there are eunuchs, that were so born from their mother's womb: and there are eunuchs, that were made eunuchs by men: and there are eunuchs, that made themselves eunuchs for the kingdom of heaven's sake. He that is able to receive it, let him receive it.

---

the word of God and call evil good and good evil. Jesus here teaches no new laws; he simply declares what has always been the law of God. Unlawful intercourse with any other person permits the innocent party to break the marriage tie; the guilty party has deserted forever the marriage partner; and has become unfit for further association; the guilty party can never again enter a pure and lawful marriage covenant.

10-12 The disciples say unto him, If the case of the man is so with his wife.—It seems that this was made by his disciples after these Pharisees had departed. His disciples thought the bond too strict which was indissoluble. They saw many cases of weak, quarrelsome, barren women, marriage with whom they thought would be too great an evil to endure, and unless such could be put away, then "it is not expedient to marry." The apostles spoke under the influence of their earlier teachings; they thought it would be better not to marry than to be married and not be able to put away his wife for more causes than that of adultery. Jesus replied to them, "Not all men can receive this saying, but they to whom it is given." "This saying" is not clear; some say that it refers to what his disciples had just said; others to what Jesus had said in reply to the Pharisees. Jesus must refer to his own saying in answer to the questions which the Pharisees had asked; his answer to the Pharisees constitutes one discourse or "saying." Not all can receive this teaching; that is, it is not applicable to those exceptions which Jesus mentions. "For there are eunuchs." "Eunuchs" are those persons who are unable or unwilling to marry. There are three ways in which eunuchs may be made as mentioned by Jesus here. First, those who "were so born from their mother's womb"; those who were born with some physical defect. Second, those eunuchs "made eunuchs by men." That is, by a violent and wicked maiming of the body.

And third, eunuchs who "made themselves eunuchs for the kingdom of heaven's sake"; that is, those who voluntarily subdue the natural inclinations and practice self-denial for the sake of "the kingdom of heaven." To these classes the teaching of Jesus on the subject of marriage and divorce does not apply; it is applicable to those who are "able to receive it, let him receive it."

2. JESUS AND CHILDREN; RICH YOUNG RULER; PERILS OF RICHES; AND REWARDS OF SELF-SACRIFICE
19: 13-30

13 Then were there brought unto him little children, that he should lay his hands on them, and pray: and the disciples rebuked them. 14 But Jesus said, Suffer the little children, and forbid them not, to come unto me: for ⁴to

13-15 Then were there brought unto him little children.—Parallel records of this are found in Mark 10: 13-16 and Luke 18: 15-17. These children were not brought to Jesus to be cured of any disease, but "that he should lay his hands on them, and pray"; that is, they were brought to him for a blessing; they were brought by their parents. It was an ancient custom to lay hands on one in pronouncing the blessing. (Gen. 48: 14; 2 Kings 5: 11; Matt. 9: 18.) The parents believed that since children at the age of eight days were taken into the privileges of covenant with God they could receive a covenant blessing. "The disciples rebuked them"; that is, the disciples rebuked the parents for bringing the children to Jesus. Jesus had just been speaking to the disciples on an important practical topic—the propriety of divorce and the expediency of marriage; the disciples had renewed the subject after leaving the Pharisees (Mark 10: 10) and Jesus had combined his teachings to them in private. These parents came with their children and interrupted the course of instruction; the disciples thought that these parents were interrupting an important subject with trivial affairs. It gave Jesus an opportunity to teach another lesson. He said, "Suffer the little children and forbid them not, to come unto me." This is emphatic and a rebuke to his disciples. Matthew, Mark, and Luke give

such belongeth the kingdom of heaven. 15 And he laid his hands on them, and departed thence.
16 And behold, one came to him and said, ⁵Teacher, what good thing

⁴Or, *of such is*
⁵Some ancient authorities read *Good Teacher.* See Mk. 10. 17; Lk. 18. 18.

---

an account of this with very slight differences. "To come unto me" is a general expression, not necessarily denoting either unaided locomotion or conscious spiritual approach. The disciples rebuked the parents and thus repelled the children they were bringing. Jesus means to say that there must be free access to him by all who would approach him.

For to such belongeth the kingdom of heaven.—"Kingdom of heaven" is a common expression of Matthew; Mark and Luke use "kingdom of God," which means the same. "To such" or "of such" is difficult to interpret. Did Jesus mean to say that "to such," babes physically, "belongeth the kingdom of heaven"? Of did he mean "of such," childlike persons, "belongeth the kingdom of heaven"? He had previously taught the latter in Matt. 18: 3. The only question is whether it also means babes in the flesh. Many who have so interpreted this claim refer to this as authority for "infant baptism" and "infant membership." The connection in Mark's and Luke's records requires the sense of childlike persons as both add, "Whosoever shall not receive the kingdom of God as a little child, he shall in no wise enter therein." This is exactly what Jesus had said on a former occasion (Matt. 18: 3), when, as almost all commentators agree, he was using the little child only as an illustration. Jesus placed his hands upon the children and blessed them; they were the fruits of the union in marriage of which he had been teaching his disciples. No one can tell the effect of Jesus' blessing an infant either remote or direct.

16-22 One came to him and said.—As Jesus had finished blessing the children this young man came to him. In both Mark and Luke this scene follows immediately after that of blessing little children. (Mark 10: 17-22; Luke 18: 18-23.) Mark adds that he came running "and kneeled to him." This

shall I do, that I may have eternal life? 17 And he said unto him, ⁶"Why askest thou me concerning that which is good? One there is who is good: but if thou wouldest enter into life, keep the commandments. 18 He saith unto him, Which? And Jesus said, ⁷Thou shalt not kill, Thou shalt not commit adultery, Thou shalt not steal, Thou shalt not bear false witness, 19 Honor thy father and thy mother; and, ⁸Thou shalt love thy neighbor as

---
⁶Lev. xix. 18.
⁷Ex. xx. 12-16; Dt. v. 16-20.
⁸Some ancient authorities read *Why callest thou me good? None is good save one, even God.* See Mk. 10. 18; Lk. 18. 19.

was the common custom of those who would do honor to a king. It is well to note that he was young and blessed with those things which pertained to youthful life; he was a "ruler," and thus enjoyed honor among his people. He was anxious to know the answer that Jesus would give to the question, "What good thing shall I do, that I may have eternal life." This was an important question, and so far as we are able to determine he was sincere in asking it. He was also in some measure worthy of the blessing for which he asked, as Mark says, "And Jesus looking upon him loved him." This Jesus could not have said had the young man been a hypocrite. This young ruler was self-deceived and self-righteous, but surely he was not a wicked character, a hypocrite. The whole story teaches us that even the very best among us must give up self in order to be saved. It is further noted that this young man understood that there was something for him to do in order to "have eternal life."

Jesus asked him, "Why askest thou me concerning that which is good?" He had asked "what good thing" he should do, and Jesus now tells him, "One there is who is good"; that is, that God was good, and that he should not call him good without either classing him with God or accepting what he taught. This was testing his faith in him. Jesus then told him if he would "enter into life" he should "keep the commandments." Jesus' further instruction showed what commandments he should keep. The young man asked, "Which?" He wanted to know which one of the commandments had greatest weight in inheriting eternal life. It will be noted that Jesus enumerated the ten commandments recorded on the second table of stone, beginning with the second,

thyself. 20 The young man saith unto him, All these things have I observed: what lack I yet? 21 Jesus said unto him, If thou wouldest be perfect, go, sell that which thou hast, and give to the poor, and thou shalt have treasure in heaven: and come, follow me. 22 But when the young man heard the saying, he went away sorrowful; for he was one that had great possessions.

"Thou shalt not kill" (Ex. 20: 13), and recited five of them. He then added, "Thou shalt love thy neighbor as thyself." This was a summary of the rest and was of equal authority with them.

The young man replied that he had done "all these things" and asked, "What lack I yet?" He hoped to receive other instructions that would assure him of his safety and give him peace; or he hoped to receive instructions that he might supply his deficiency. This was also an important question. He has asked Jesus two questions which are of general and practical use today, namely, "What good thing shall I do, that I may have eternal life?" and "What lack I yet?" These two questions may be blended into one. Jesus answered him and said, "if thou wouldest be perfect, go, sell that which thou hast, and give to the poor, and thou shalt have treasure in heaven: and come, follow me." Jesus meant to say, "If thou wilt lack nothing, but have all things necessary to complete thy salvation, give up all for Christ." "If thou wouldest be perfect" as Noah and Job (Gen. 6: 9; Job 1: 1), then you must obey God as did these. He is instructed to sell his possessions and follow him; Jesus did not want one of his disciples to be separated from the others by great wealth. Jesus was poor and his apostles were poor and to have one who was wealthy in the group would separate them. Jesus saw the ruler's claim to merit vanish and the ruler himself saw all of his merits vanish. His heart was enslaved to the riches of this world and he could not follow Jesus with such attitude of soul. There was something hard in this answer, yet nothing peculiar, for God requires every rich or poor one to surrender all to him. Jesus does not require the owners of property today to sell all that they have, but he does require that they use all that they have for his honor and glory. The young man was not willing to make the sacrifice, for when he heard

23 And Jesus said unto his disciples, Verily I say unto you, It is hard for a rich man to enter into the kingdom of heaven. 24 And again I say unto you, It is easier for a camel to go through a needle's eye, than for a rich

what Jesus said "he went away sorrowful." He was not willing to give up his "great possessions" for "eternal life." He saw what he lacked, but was not willing to sacrifice his "great possessions" to supply that which he did lack.

23-26 Verily I say unto you, It is hard for a rich man.—The young man had made no reply; indeed he could not, but he went away sorrowful. This gave Jesus the occasion to teach that "it is hard for a rich man to enter into the kingdom of heaven." Mark explains who this "rich man" is by saying that it is one who trusts in riches. (Mark 10: 24.) This is Jesus' sad application of the lesson taught the rich young ruler. The rich are "hardly" or with difficulty saved because their possessions tempt them to ease and worldly pride. How few rich who do not trust in riches! How few poor who do not trust in riches which they are not able to acquire! Jesus used a proverb to express his thought here, "It is easier for a camel to go through a needle's eye, than for a rich man to enter into the kingdom of God." This proverb is used to express the greatest improbability. If taken literally, it is utterly impossible for a camel to go through a needle's eye. We are to understand proverbs according to the spirit and custom of the language and age in which they are used. This proverb implies that it would be very difficult for the rich to humble themselves to the lowliness of humility in Christ. It was particularly true of those times. (James 2: 6, 7.)

"A camel" was the largest animal known and used by the Jews. The figure used here is very vivid and emphatic; it represents the largest animal trying to go through the smallest eye of the needle; it expresses that which is most difficult or impossible. Some have interpreted this literally by the camels having to kneel down and with great difficulty squeeze through an opening in a ledge of rock, which was called "the needle's eye." Jesus simply means to say that it is exceedingly difficult, if not impossible, for one who trusts in riches

man to enter into the kingdom of God. 25 And when the disciples heard it, they were astonished exceedingly, saying, Who then can be saved? 26 And Jesus looking upon *them* said to them, With men this is impossible; but with God all things are possible. 27 Then answered Peter and said unto him, Lo, we have left all, and followed thee; what then shall we have? 28 And Jesus said unto them, Verily I say unto you, that ye who have followed me, in the regeneration when the Son of man shall sit on the throne of his glory, ye

---

to enter the kingdom of God. The situation of the rich is at best a situation of difficulty and danger; their riches furnish them with so many temptations to intemperance, pride, forgetfulness of God, and contempt of everything serious and sacred.

When Jesus had taught this his disciples were "astonished exceedingly" and asked, "Who then can be saved?" They meant what rich man can receive the gospel and be saved as some think. Others think that they meant to ask, "Who at all can be saved?" If the rich cannot be saved (thought they), who *can* be? They still had the idea of a temporal kingdom, and if Jesus declined the aid and influence of the rich, then how could his kingdom be established? Man's standards and God's have ever differed. The disciples thought that power and wealth gave one a favorable standing with God; they thought that the poor were in some way cursed of God; but now since it is next to impossible for the rich to be saved, then what will become of the poor? With men it was impossible, "but with God all things are possible." They thought that Jesus would call upon all rich men to give up their riches as he had done the rich young ruler; they are now to understand that God has his own standard of righteousness and of admitting people into his kingdom.

27-30 **Then answered Peter and said unto him.**—Peter asked, "We have left all, and followed thee; what then shall we have?" There seems to be something in the expression of this question like that of the rich young ruler. If the young ruler had to give up all and follow Jesus in order to inherit eternal life, the apostles had forsaken all for some time and had been following him about two years or longer, and now what shall they receive in addition to others? Jesus answered

also shall sit upon twelve thrones, judging the twelve tribes of Israel. 29 And every one that hath left houses, or brethren, or sisters, or father, or mother, or children, or lands, for my name's sake, shall receive [10]a hundred-

[9]Many ancient authorities add *or wife:* as in Lk. 18: 29.
[10]Some ancient authorities read *manifold.*

---

by saying, "Ye who have followed me, in the regeneration when the Son of man shall sit on the throne of his glory, ye also shall sit upon twelve thrones, judging the twelve tribes of Israel." The word "regeneration" has given commentators much trouble. It is used only one other time in the New Testament. (Tit. 3: 5.) Here it is "the washing of regeneration," which refers to baptism in conversion. Two interpretations have been given with respect to the meaning of "regeneration." One is that it refers to the times of the future resurrection of all men, or the "new generation," or "regeneration." According to this view the day of judgment and recompense will come at that time. All who have suffered here with Christ will reign with him and receive an exceeding and eternal weight of glory. They refer the time of "regeneration" to a period after Christ comes the second time. The other view is that the "regeneration" belongs to the period of time between Pentecost and the second coming of Christ. It is the time of the church, when the law of the new birth is a law of its increase, when all men shall be in Christ "new creatures," or a new creation, that is, a "re" or "new generation," when old things are passed away, and all things have become new. During this period the Son of man sits on the throne of his glory at the right hand of God. (Mark 16: 19; Heb. 1: 3; 8: 1; Rev. 3: 21.) The apostles are not promised "thrones of glory," but simply "thrones." The idea is that the apostles are the judges, as during their lives they arranged the laws and practices while they were on earth and now, by their inspired writings, they govern the members of the church. This view makes the use of "regeneration" here the same as that used in "the washing of regeneration" in Tit. 3: 5.

And every one that hath left houses, or brethren, or sisters, or father, or mother, or children . . . shall receive a

fold, and shall inherit eternal life. 30 But many shall be last *that are* first; and first *that are* last.

hundredfold, and shall inherit eternal life.—The rich reward promised to those who forsake all and follow Jesus is "eternal life." To inherit is to receive by right from an ancestor, and usually applies to one who has a claim by expectation of something future; to inherit eternal life is to have, not the actual possession, but the expectation of receiving eternal life, as a result of the life which one lives now; it is to be "heirs of God" and "joint-heirs with Christ" by faith and obedience. The term "inherit" and its forms are inheritance, inherit, heirs, etc. These terms are frequently found in the New Testament. "Eternal life" belongs to the "eternal kingdom," to the kingdom above. Jesus, after instructing his disciples about the reward of self-sacrifice and humble service to him, makes this statement, "But many shall be last that are first; and first that are last." Those who are first in the estimation of the world and probably themselves will be the last (if they enter at all) into the kingdom of God; those who are last and lowest in the estimation of the world shall stand the highest in the kingdom of God—they shall be first.

3. LABORERS IN THE VINEYARD; FORETELLS AGAIN HIS
DEATH; REBUKES SELFISH AMBITION OF
JAMES AND JOHN
20: 1-28

1 For the kingdom of heaven is like unto a man that was a householder, who went out early in the morning to hire laborers into his vineyard. 2 And

1-16 For the kingdom of heaven is like.—"For" not only introduces this parable, but connects it to what has just preceded; the parable is an explanation of the last words of the last chapter; it explains one of the principles of "the kingdom of heaven" or church that God would not so much regard the privileges of the Jews, nor the riches of the powerful, as the industry and zeal of his people. The parable has very differently been explained; few commentators are agreed as to the meaning of it. Some see in it the principle that God is no

when he had agreed with the laborers for a ¹shilling a day, he sent them into his vineyard. 3 And he went out about the third hour, and saw others standing in the market-place idle; 4 and to them he said, Go ye also into the vineyard, and whatsoever is right I will give you. And they went their way. 5 Again he went out about the sixth and the ninth hour, and did likewise.

¹See marginal note on ch. 18. 28.

---

respecter of persons in the gifts of honor in his church; that the awards given are not by accidental circumstances as wealth or priority of time. Verse thirty of the last chapter and verse sixteen of this chapter seem to indicate that the parable is an explanation of the thought in these verses. The disciples were expecting great honors in the kingdom of heaven because they were *first* who were called; the Jews were expecting exclusive honors in the kingdom of heaven, but they are to learn that, because they are Abraham's seed, the blessings of the spiritual kingdom of God are distributed even to the Gentiles.

"The kingdom of heaven" or the church, in some particular, "is like unto a man that was a householder." "Householder" is the owner of fields who had need of many laborers. "Vineyard" was a field or plantation of vines, hedged in by walls, ditched, cleared of stones and cultivated. (Matt. 21: 33.) There were many vineyards in Judea; the figure of a vineyard was used by the prophets in which Jehovah had bestowed care upon the Jews as the vinedresser. (Isa. 5: 7; Jer. 12: 10.) The householder went out "to hire laborers" to work in his vineyard; he promised them the usual wage or reward for their services. The amount agreed upon was "a shilling a day." This coin was worth about fifteen to seventeen cents. This seems to us a small sum for a day's work, but when labor and provisions were equally cheap, it may have been a liberal pay for the day's work. At any rate, this was the sum agreed to. He went out "about the third hour, and saw others standing in the market-place idle." The Jews divided the day into twelve equal parts, beginning at sunrise. (John 11: 9.) These parts were longer in summer than in winter, as the days were then nearly four hours and a half longer. Their nights were divided in the same way; both day and night

6 And about the eleventh *hour* he went out, and found others standing; and he saith unto them, Why stand ye here all the day idle? 7 They say unto him, Because no man hath hired us. He saith unto them, Go ye also into the vineyard. 8 And when even was come, the lord of the vineyard saith unto his steward, Call the laborers, and pay them their hire, beginning from the last unto the first. 9 And when they came that *were hired* about the eleventh hour, they received every man a ¹shilling. 10 And when the first came, they supposed that they would receive more; and they likewise received evry man a ¹shilling. 11 And when they received it, they murmured against the householder, 12 saying, These last have spent *but* one hour, and thou hast

---

were then divided into four parts each. (Mark 13: 35.) The days were distinguished by the "third hour" (9:00 o'clock), "the sixth" (noon), "the ninth" (3:00 o'clock in the afternoon), and "sunset." It was customary for laborers to go to the market place and there wait until someone came to employ them; this custom both with the laborers and householders was understood.

And about the eleventh hour he went out, and found others standing.—This was about five o'clock in the afternoon, or one hour before the day ended. At this time he found men standing in the market place, and he asked, "Why stand ye here all the day idle?" They readily answered, "Because no man hath hired us." They seemingly had been ready for work, but had not received an invitation or an opportunity to work. The householder employed them and sent them "into the vineyard." At the close of the day the householder sent his steward to "call the laborers, and pay them their hire, beginning from the last unto the first." He followed the custom of the Jews in obeying the law of Moses. (Lev. 19: 13; Deut. 24: 15.) Jesus is the steward set over the house of God to order all things and give all their wages. (Matt. 11: 27; John 5: 27; Heb. 3: 6.) There may be encouragement for those that have delayed to enter the service of God till late in life, but surely not encouragement to any one to delay entering the service of God; there are numerous scriptures instructing all who are capable of service to enter *now* and not delay.

All received equal amount; each received a shilling. "And when they came that were hired about the eleventh hour, they received every man a shilling." As they began with the last who were hired and approached to the first, the first hired ob-

made them equal unto us, who have borne the burden of the day and the ²scorching heat. 13 But he answered and said to one of them, Friend, I do thee no wrong; didst not thou agree with me for a ¹shilling? 14 Take up that which is thine, and go thy way; it is my will to give unto this last, even as unto thee. 15 Is it not lawful for me to do what I will with mine own?

²Or, *hot wind*

---

served that those who went in the eleventh hour received the same as the earliest hired. When they saw this, they "murmured against the householder" and said, "These last have spent but one hour, and thou hast made them equal unto us, who have borne the burden of the day and the scorching heat." They were not willing for others to receive an equal amount; they thought that it was unfair, as they had worked all day and the others had worked but one hour. The householder kindly answered them, "Friend, I do thee no wrong: didst not thou agree with me for a shilling?" This was the sum that the laborers agreed to work for when they were hired in the early morning; they should now be satisifed with that amount. The householder dismissed them by saying, "It is my will to give unto this last, even as unto thee." If the householder chose to show considerations and liberality with charity to these last, why should the first object to it? They were envious; their eyes were evil. Envy is spoken of as dwelling in the eye and giving to it a malignant power. (Deut. 15: 9; Prov. 28: 22; Mark 7: 22.) Jesus makes his own application of the parable when he says, "So the last shall be first, and the first last." The householder told the steward to begin with the last and end with the first (verse eight). The last were first in a very important sense; they received a reward much greater in proportion to the labor which they had performed. Jesus says "so," that is, as in the parable, so it shall be in the kingdom of heaven. Some versions add "for many be called, but few chosen." Many, in fact all, have the gospel invitation, but not all accept it and live faithful through life.

There are many lessons that may be drawn from this parable. It seems to have been occasioned by Peter's question (Matt. 19: 27), "What then shall we have?" This expresses

or is thine eye evil, because I am good? 16 So the last shall be first, and the first last.

17 And as Jesus was going up to Jerusalem, he took the twelve disciples apart, and on the way he said unto them, 18 Behold, we go up to Jerusalem; and the Son of man shall be ³delivered unto the chief priests and scribes;

³See ch. 10. 4.

---

about the same spirit that those in the parable had who had worked twelve hours. Again those coming in the eleventh hour may be compared to the Gentiles, who came in to the kingdom of God long after the Jews had been the favorite people of God. There is also the lesson of mercy taught; God exercises mercy toward those who have not had advantage equal to those of others. The laborers were all equal in that each was ready to work when called; the eleventh hour men responded at the first opportunity.

17-19 **And as Jesus was going up to Jerusalem.**—Parallel records of this may be found in Mark 10: 32-34 and Luke 18: 31-33. Jesus had now about finished his work in Perea, and it is supposed to be in December, the time of the Feast of Dedication; he has been in Perea about five months teaching and working miracles. The time is at hand in which, by the shedding of blood, there must be the remission of sins. Jerusalem is the place where for ages the typical sacrifices had predicted the real sacrifice which was now to be made once for all. Jesus crosses from the east side to the west side of the Jordan and his disciples follow him. They are afraid; in fact, as Mark states it, they were "amazed" that he would go to Jerusalem at this time. So it becomes necessary for Jesus to explain to them in further detail the death that he was to die.

To quiet them and to remove their fear, "he took the twelve disciples apart" and as they went along the way he explained to them again the death that he must die. Mark tells us that Jesus "was going before them," "and they that followed were afraid." The signs of enmity against him began to thicken and the disciples knew that their Lord was in great danger should he go to Jerusalem. However, Jesus said, "We go up to Jerusalem" and there "the Son of man shall be delivered unto the chief priests and scribes; and they shall condemn

and they shall condemn him to death, 19 and shall deliver him unto the Gentiles to mock, and to scourge, and to crucify; and the third day he shall be raised up.
20 Then came to him the mother of the sons of Zebedee with her sons,

---

him to death." "The chief priests and scribes" represent the Sanhedrin; he was to be betrayed into their hands by Judas. (Matt. 26: 15.) They would condemn him to death, but could not inflict it, hence he should be delivered "unto the Gentiles to mock, and to scourge, and to crucify." This is a graphic description of what the Gentiles or Roman authorities would do to him. This was a strange cruelty that the Jews should give up a prophet to the Gentiles whom they hated; yet they were to deliver Jesus to Pilate and the Roman soldiers. These would "mock," treat with derision, this prophet of the Jews. We are told that the eastern nations have a singular power of this kind and great sensitiveness to such contempt. (Judges 16: 25; Jer. 38: 19.) "To scourge" was a cruel punishment of which whipping is a very mild definition; it was a terrible laceration by the severest thongs that could be devised, and inflicted only upon the lowest criminal; it was done by placing iron spikes or sharp stones in the lashes of whips and applied to the bare back of the victim. "To crucify" was to nail and suspend one to a wooden cross until he died; this was a Roman mode of punishment for slaves and vile criminals. Luke adds "shamefully treated, and spit upon." Jesus hastens to direct the minds of his disciples from this cruel treatment to the fact that "the third day he shall be raised up." As if the picture were too dark for them to look at, Jesus hastens to tell them of his resurrection. This is the third record that Matthew has given of Jesus telling his disciples of his death. (Matt. 16: 21; 17: 22, 23.)

20-28 Then came to him the mother of the sons of Zebedee. —Mark 10: 35-45 gives a parallel record of this. "The mother of the sons of Zebedee," Salome, and her sons were James and John. Salome was in some way connected with other women to the company of the disciples in some of their journeys, as we find her one of those who were last at the cross and earliest at the grave. (Mark 15: 40; 16: 1.) Mark tells us that

⁴worshipping *him,* and asking a certain thing of him. 21. And he said unto her, What wouldest thou? She saith unto him, Command that these my two sons may sit, one on thy right hand, and one on thy left hand, in thy kingdom. 22 But Jesus answered and said, Ye know not what ye ask. Are ye

⁴See marginal note on ch. 2. 2.

James and John joined their mother in the request that she made at this time; they were eager to be first in obtaining a promise. It may be that they regarded the prophecy of Jesus of his death as a crisis and they wished to take advantage of the situation on this visit to Jerusalem. She came "worshipping him" before she made the request of him. "Worshipping," that is, kneeling and doing honor to him as a king. (Matt. 8: 2; 18: 26.) The father, Zebedee, though named, never appears in gospel history after the call of his sons; from this it is inferred that he was either dead or an insignificant character. However faulty the conduct of Salome may appear to be on this occasion, she manifested an undying love for Jesus in the most trying times of his subsequent suffering; she also showed a mother's devotion and consecration to the welfare of her sons. The mother and sons were inspired by a common ambition.

Salome very tactfully approached the subject while kneeling before Jesus by telling him that she wanted to make a certain request of him; we are not to infer that she wanted him to promise to grant it before he knew what request she would make. Jesus asked her what she wanted and she answered, "Command that these my two sons may sit, one on thy right hand, and one on thy left hand, in thy kingdom." She asked Jesus to pass the other disciples by and exalt these two disciples to the highest honor in the palaces of Jerusalem; she wanted one to be prime minister to rule the state, and the other to share the chief favors of all private thoughts. Her request was that James, the Boanerges, or son of thunder, flash like a meteor in splendor over thy kingdom, and the gentler John be thy bosom friend. It seems that the vision of the transfiguration still lingered with James and John and that this request is an explanation of it. Jesus replied, "Ye know

able to drink the cup that I am about to drink? They say unto him, We are able. 23 He saith unto them, My cup indeed ye shall drink: but to sit on my right hand, and on *my* left hand, is not mine to give; but *it is for them* for whom it hath been prepared of my Father. 24 And when the ten heard it,

---

not what ye ask." The question was propounded in ignorance of the real facts. They still misunderstood the nature of his kingdom, and the principle which makes people great in his kingdom. How often the disciples of Jesus today make requests in prayer which they do not understand! Our false conception of things and our worldly ambitions prompt us to make requests which are not pleasing in the sight of God; we should rejoice that Jesus, our High Priest and the Mediator, will not present such prayers to our Father; he understands our weaknesses.

Jesus answered by asking them, "Are ye able to drink the cup that I am about to drink?" They answered him. "We are able." The Jews often described abstract things by images; "to drink the cup" denoted the affliction and punishment by a cup of bitter ingredients, maddening and horrible to drink. (Psalm 11: 6; 75: 8; Isa. 51: 17; Jer. 25: 15.) One of the modes of punishment by death was to cause the victim to drink a cup of poison. Socrates was caused to drink the fatal hemlock. If James and John understood what they answered, they meant to say that they were ready to brave all the bitterness and hardships of Jesus' lot. Jesus often spoke of his passion under this image. (Matt. 26: 39; John 18: 11.) Jesus replied to their answer with a prophetic statement that "my cup indeed ye shall drink: but to sit on my right hand, and on my left hand, is not mine to give." This belonged to the Father to bestow such honors and it had not been committed to him at this time. Mark adds another question, "Are ye able to drink the cup that I drink? or to be baptized with the baptism that I am baptized with?" (Mark 10: 38.) Jesus here paints by another striking word his coming sorrows and sufferings as if a great wave of the sea were burying him, in their confusion and uproar, as if he were to be drowned in a terrible baptism in them. (Psalm 42: 7; 69: 2; Luke 12: 50.) This is a graphic picture of the agonies of the soul of Jesus, yielding to

they were moved with indignation concerning the two brethren. 25 But Jesus called them unto him, and said, Ye know that the rulers of the Gentiles lord it over them, and their great ones exercise authority over them. 26 Not so shall it be among you: but whosover would become great among you shall be ⁵our minister; 27 and whosoever would be first among you shall be

---

⁵Or, *servant*

---

the tremendous tides of human sin, passion, hate, and rage, and sinking alone, out of sight, in the gloomy waves of death. Incidentally we see what is meant by baptism; it is not a mere "sprinkling" of suffering, but an overwhelming of suffering in death; so baptism in water is not a sprinkling, but is a dipping, submersing, or overwhelming, or burial in water.

And when the ten heard it, they were moved with indignation concerning the two brethren.—The other disciples were indignant because they thought that James and John with their mother were taking advantage of them and the situation; they were jealous of each other and angry at these two brothers. However, Jesus called them to him and said, "Ye know that the rulers of the Gentiles lord it over them, and their great ones exercise authority over them." He rebuked the indignation and anger of the ten as he had rebuked the request of James and John; again he taught them the spiritual nature of his kingdom. His kingdom was of a different kind from that of the temporal kingdoms; in the earthly kingdoms the rulers exercised oftentimes tyrannical wills over their subjects, but in his kingdom it should not be that way, for "whosoever would become great among you shall be your minister" or servant. "Gentiles" as here denotes those who are not Jews, or "all nations" other than Jews. Greatness in this kingdom is determined by service and not by official rank. This lesson was taught in Matt. 18: 1. The one who should stand the highest in this kingdom or "would be first among you shall be your servant." Jesus cites himself as an example as "the Son of man came not to be ministered unto, but to minister, and to give his life a ransom for many." It is strange that his disciples could see his examples of service so long and still entertain the notions that his kingdom would be an earthly kingdom. Jesus served the poorest and lowliest of

your ᵃservant: 28 even as the Son of man came not to be ministered unto, but to minister, and to give his life a ransom for many.

ᵃGr. *bondservant.*

---

men; he gave up time, convenience, everything to the sick and poor; he took no reward. What right had his disciples to claim that there was any merit in them that caused him to choose them? If he had intended to establish an earthly kingdom, surely he would have chosen men of wealth and political power instead of some obscure fishermen as they were. Jesus showed himself greatest of all by the greatest service, greatest sufferings, and greatest sacrifices of all. He is the example of greatness to his disciples. Jesus gave his life "a ransom for many."

[How and why the shedding of the blood of Jesus was essential to the salvation of man is, and has been, a trouble to many. The blood is the life. The shedding of the blood is the giving of the life. When we say Jesus shed his blood for the sins of the world, we mean Jesus gave his life for the sins of the world. The blood is the material abiding place of the immaterial principle of life, so that if we take the blood from the body we take the life. Since the blood can be seen by our fleshly senses, and the immaterial principle of life cannot, it is probable that the blood is spoken of to represent the life, the shedding of the blood, the giving up the life. When it is said he shed his blood for the forgiveness of sins, it means he gave up his life to provide for the remission of sins; he became a ransom for many.]

4. TWO BLIND MEN HEALED AT JERICHO
20: 29-34

29 And as they went out from Jericho, a great multitude followed him.

29-30 **And as they went out from Jericho.**—Jesus had left Perea, crossed the Jordan, and was again in Judea. The record by Matthew omits much of the work that Jesus did in Perea. Luke's record is fuller as may be seen from Luke 17 to

30 And behold, two blind men sitting by the way side, when they heard that Jesus was passing by, cried out, saying, Lord, have mercy on us, thou son of

18: 14; John's record is much fuller as perhaps all from John 7 to 11 treats of matters pertaining to his Perean ministry. "As they went out from Jericho." See parallel records in Mark 10: 46-52 and Luke 18: 35 to 19: 1. "Jericho" was the second city in size in Palestine; it was situated on the west banks of the Jordan, about two miles from it and about seventeen miles east-northeast of Jerusalem. It was situated on the road from the "region beyond the Jordan" to Jerusalem. It was famous in Old Testament history. (Josh. 6: 20, 26; 1 Kings 16: 34; 2 Kings 2: 21.) As they departed from Jericho "a great multitude followed him." Luke represents a blind man coming to Jesus "as he drew nigh unto Jericho" (Luke 18: 35), while Matthew states that "two blind men" were sitting by the wayside "when they heard that Jesus was passing by." Some have explained the difficulty of the seeming contradiction between Matthew and Luke by saying that there were two towns, the old and the new; that Jesus passed through one and was entering the other. Others explain it that he healed one blind man when he drew nigh to Jericho and that these two mentioned by Matthew were healed in the city or just as he left the city.

The two blind men who sat by the wayside heard the multitude as Jesus passed by and in the midst of the noise and confusion "cried out, saying, Lord, have mercy on us, thou son of David." One of these was Bartimaeus, a man not so well known in Jericho, as Mark and Luke mention him only; but the mention of him does not exclude another, and Matthew tells us that there was another to share the blessing. It was customary for the poor people to take their station at the gate of the town in order to obtain help from those who passed by. There was an unusual crowd of people passing out the gate at this time and the blind men lifted their voices above the noise of the multitude and "cried out" to Jesus, calling him "thou son of David." This meant that they recognized in him the

David. 31 And the multitude rebuked them, that they should hold their peace: but they cried out the more, saying, Lord, have mercy on us, thou son of David. 32 And Jesus stood still, and called them, and said, What will ye that I should do unto you? 33 They say unto him, Lord, that our eyes may be opened. 34 And Jesus, being moved with compassion, touched their eyes; and straightway they received their sight, and followed him.

Messiah. Frequently Jesus was called "the son of David" since he was a descendant of the house of David.

31-34 **And the multitude rebuked them.**—The multitude "rebuked them" by asking them to "hold their peace." But the rebuke of the multitude did not quiet the blind men, for "they cried out the more" and begged the son of David to have mercy on them. Jesus stopped in the midst of the multitude when he heard the entreaties of the blind men and "stood still"; he then called to them and asked, "What will ye that I should do unto you?" When they understood that Jesus recognized them, Mark, who mentions but one, describes him as flinging off his loose outer garment, which might impede his running, to come up with the Lord before he should depart. They had uttered a general cry for mercy, but Jesus calls for a specific statement of their desire. Not that Jesus was ignorant of their real need, but that he would develop their want into a special prayer or request. They at once replied to his question, "Lord, that our eyes may be opened." We know not how long they had been blind, we know definitely that they wanted to be healed and had faith in Jesus' power to heal them. Jesus was "moved with compassion, touched their eyes." Immediately they received sight "and followed him." It may be that they only followed him up to Jerusalem to the Feast of Dedication; that is, they swelled the multitude which was following him; some think that they became his disciples as they had faith in him as the Messiah, or "son of David." Jesus had bidden them "go thy way," but with an affectionate disobedience "they followed him" as their benefactor. It was their way to follow him, since they were obedient after all. The blessing which they sought in receiving sight may have led them to become his disciples and receive spiritual blessings.

SECTION SIX

LAST DAYS OF JESUS' PUBLIC MINISTRY
21: 1 to 26: 46

1. TRIUMPHAL ENTRY INTO JERUSALEM; SECOND CLEANSING OF THE TEMPLE
21: 1-17

1 And when they drew nigh unto Jerusalem, and came unto Bethphage, unto the mount of Olives, then Jesus sent two disciples, 2 saying unto them,

---

1-5 And when they drew nigh unto Jerusalem.—Parallel records of this incident are found in Mark 11: 1-10; Luke 19: 29-44; and John 12: 12-19. Matthew gives little note to the time, other records give more to the time. We now come to the events of the last week of his earthly ministry and to his last visit to Jerusalem. The events of this last week are of such importance that they are carefully noted. They begin with the first day of the week (our Sunday). Jesus had spent the Sabbath (our Saturday) at Bethany, at the house of Lazarus (John 12: 9), and now approaches Jerusalem; Matthew relates the events of this first day as far as verse seventeen of this chapter. The events to verse twenty with the cursing of the fig tree occurred on the second day, or Monday; from thence to chapter twenty-six Matthew relates what occurred on the third day, or Tuesday. John 10 to 12: 12 records some events which Matthew omits. It was now five days before the Passover, the tenth of the month (Ex. 12: 3), the day on which the Passover lambs were driven into the city to be kept there until Thursday. The true Lamb of God chooses this day for his entrance.

And came unto Bethphage, unto the mount of Olives.—The location of Bethphage is difficult; some place it near Bethany. About one mile east from Jerusalem lay the ridge of the Mount of Olives so called from the great number of olive trees which grew upon it. (Acts 1: 12.) In leaving Jerusalem one must first pass across the valley of Jehoshaphat, called at its lower end the valley of Hinnom or Gehenna. Through it

Go into the village that is over against you, and straightway ye shall find an ass tied, and a colt with her: loose *them,* and bring *them* unto me. 3 And if any one say aught unto you, ye shall say, The Lord hath need of them; and straightway he will send them. 4 Now this is come to pass, that it might be fulfilled which was spoken through the prophet, saying,
5   ¹Tell ye the daughter of Zion,
       Behold, thy King cometh unto thee,
       Meek, and riding upon an ass,
       And upon a colt the foal of an ass.

¹Is. lxii. 11; Zech. ix. 9.

ran the brook Cedron or Kidron. (John 18: 1.) One then passes by the enclosure of Gethsemane (meaning the place of the oil press) which lay along the west side of the hill nearest Jerusalem; ascending the Mount of Olives one could see Jerusalem, and trace the buildings, and especially the temple crowning Mount Moriah. Then passing over the hill or ridge, one first reached Bethphage on the eastern side, and farther still, or two miles from Jerusalem, the village of Bethany, from which Jesus began this day's walk. The Mount of Olives is about a mile in length from north to south and with three peaks. The road to Bethany wound around the middle peak. Palm trees flourish on Mount Olivet, whence the name Bethany, the house of dates and figs, whence the name Bethphage, the house of figs. The oil of the olive was used in the tabernacle and temple worship. (Ex. 30: 24-29.) The people were accustomed to gather the olive branches as also the palm branches in the Feast of Tabernacles. Neh. 18: 15 and Zech. 14: 4 foretold this day's entrance into Jerusalem.

Jesus sent two disciples . . . into the village.—He was now two miles from Jerusalem on the east side of Olivet; the village of Bethphage was between Bethany and Jerusalem; Bethany was behind him and Bethphage was before him; so he sent his two disciples into Bethphage. The roads were doubtless filled with people crowding to the city and driving thither the lambs for the approaching feast. Jesus told them that they would "find an ass tied, and a colt with her"; Mark and Luke mention only the colt, because on it this triumphal procession was made. This colt probably belonged to someone who knew Jesus and freely consented to the use of the animal.

6 And the disciples went, and did even as Jesus appointed them, 7 and brought the ass, and the colt, and put on them their garments; and he sat thereon. 8 And the most part of the multitude spread their garments in the way; and others cut branches from the trees, and spread them in the way. 9 And the multitudes that went before him, and that followed, cried, saying,

---

The Jews were accustomed to riding mules, camels, and asses; the horse was forbidden. (Deut. 17: 16.) Kings and great men rode on the ass; it appears in the sublime vision of Jacob in connection with these very events. (Gen. 49: 11; Isa. 63: 1-3.) Solomon is described as riding on a mule. (1 Kings 1: 38.) Jesus, according to Jewish ideas, appeared in the proper state and dignity of the "Prince of Peace." These two disciples were to tell the owner of the colt that "the Lord hath need of them" and that would be sufficient; he would send them. Jesus at this time assumes the name of "Lord Jehovah," for that is the meaning of the term. (Matt. 22: 44; Heb. 1: 10.) In doing this the prophecy of Isaiah (62: 11) and Zechariah (9: 9) were fulfilled. "The daughters of Zion" means the women of Jerusalem. (Luke 23: 28.) Zion was the southern hill on which the city of Jerusalem was built, containing the royal palace and upper city. David took this city and dwelt in it and it was called "the city of David." (2 Sam. 5: 9.) Solomon caused the ark to be carried there. (1 Kings 8: 1.) It was called Zion from the first. "Meek, and riding upon an ass." Jesus came in peaceable state, not as a conquering monarch, with battle array, on a fiery charger and armed with sword and spear, but as a "prince of peace."

6-11 And the disciples went.—The two disciples promptly obeyed Jesus and found "the ass, and the colt" and brought them to Jesus. They put their clothes upon the colt (Luke 19: 35) as a mark of respect, "and he sat thereon." The crowd understood this action to symbolize that he was their king, as their ancient kings had been so treated; Jehu for instance. (2 Kings 9: 13.) The news spread rapidly and reached the city and by the time that Jesus, riding in this manner, in the midst of the passing travelers, had come to Olivet, the citizens crowded out to meet him. (John 12: 12.) There was a large multitude accompanying him, and now the multitude

Hosanna to the son of David. Blessed *is* he that cometh in the name of the Lord; Hosanna in the highest. 10 And when he was come into Jerusalem, all the city was stirred, saying, Who is this? 11 And the multitudes said, This is the prophet, Jesus, from Nazareth of Galilee.

came out of Jerusalem to meet him and the triumphal procession was thus augmented. It is plain that Jesus could have been made an earthly king at this time, for the vast multitudes were ready to make him their king. (John 12: 19.) The disciples did not understand the spiritual meaning of these events until after Pentecost. (John 12: 16.) "The multitudes that went before him, and that followed, cried, saying, Hosanna to the son of David." They added, "Blessed is he that cometh in the name of the Lord; Hosanna in the highest." At the Feast of Tabernacles the people carried branches in their hands, chanting sentences from the Messianic Psalms. (Psalm 118: 25, 26.) This was their way of expressing their desire for the coming of the Messiah. (Lev. 23: 40.) The multitude now by this act expressed their belief that Jesus was the Messiah. John tells us that the branches of the trees were of the palm trees. (John 12: 13.) The long branches of the palm tree were strictly used during the Feast of Tabernacles. (Lev. 23: 40.) The people dwelt during this feast under booths or tabernacles; there may be a reference to this when John says, "The Word became flesh, and dwelt" or tabernacled "among us." (John 1: 14.) "Hosanna to the son of David" resembles the exclamation raised in the coronation of Solomon, the son of David. (1 Kings 1: 39.) "Hosanna" was a shout of prayerful joy; it is derived from two Hebrew words meaning "be now propitious" and "save us now." (Psalm 118: 25.) "Son of David" is an admission that he is the Messiah. "Blessed is he," that is, the one who comes in the name of the Lord was to come as his ambassador. Mark adds that they cried, "Blessed is the kingdom that cometh, the kingdom of our father David." (Mark 11: 10.) This was praising the kingdom of the Messiah which was promised to the seed of David. Luke adds that they said, "Peace in heaven, and glory in the highest." (Luke 19: 38.) The procession moved slowly into Jerusalem with these acclamations increasing on

12 And Jesus entered into the temple ²of God, and cast out all them that sold and bought in the temple, and overthrew the tables of the money-changers, and the seats of them that sold the doves; 13 and he saith unto them, It is written, ³My house shall be called a house of prayer: ⁴but ye make it a

²Many ancient authorities omit *of God.*
³Is. lvi. 7.
⁴Jer. vii. 11.

---

the way, and "when he was come into Jerusalem, all the city was stirred, saying, Who is this?" The rulers were in great rage and fear; the crowd filled the city with their cries; even children took up the chorus and sang it in the temple; the Pharisees were perplexed and feared for themselves; and said, "Behold how ye prevail nothing; lo, the world is gone after him." (John 12: 19.) In contrast to the sentiment expressed by the Pharisees the multitude said, "This is the prophet, Jesus, from Nazareth of Galilee." This was said in answer to the question, "Who is this?"

12-17 And Jesus entered into the temple of God.—Mark records this event as occurring on the next day, or Monday. (Mark 11: 15-17.) Another parallel record is Luke 19: 45, 46. He may have entered the temple twice, first on the first day and then again the next day. Jesus had entered the temple as a King; he exercised therefore an act of royal power. He came to worship, and after the usual morning prayer, he came out into the part of the temple that is called court of the Gentiles. It was outside the actual temple, though upon Mount Moriah, and surrounded by the temple wall. The temple was the house of prayer for all nations, that is, for the Gentiles as well as the Jews, on condition that they would be circumcised. Jesus was indignant at the unholy practices of the Jews. As he stood and declared his power as the Son of God, a voice, with the sound of thunder, was heard from heaven. (John 12: 28, 29.) Thereupon Jesus proceeded to purify the temple of God. Jesus cast out those who "sold and bought in the temple, and overthrew the tables of the money-changers, and the seats of them that sold the doves." The only coin received in the sacred treasury was the Levitical shekel or half shekel; these money-changers were men who took pains to buy up all

den of robbers. 14 And the blind and the lame came to him in the temple; and he healed them. 15 But when the chief priests and the scribes saw the

the legal coins and sold them again to the Jews, who had come to worship; they charged a high price for the exchange. "Them that sold the doves" were those who kept doves to sell to those who should make a sacrifice. They were used in sacrifice by the poor. (Lev. 14: 22; Luke 2: 21.) All animals for the sacrifices were sought for in the city of Jerusalem by the Jews who came from a distance. Mark adds that Jesus "would not suffer that any man should carry a vessel through the temple." (Mark 11: 16.) These Jews took advantage of their foreign brethren and practiced extortion. Jesus showed his power by cleansing the temple and showed his relation to God when he said, "My house shall be called a house of prayer: but ye make it a den of robbers." Isa. 56: 7 gives this prophecy; Isaiah had spoken thus of the times of the Messiah; the latter part of the quotation seems to refer to Jer. 6: 11. "House of prayer" is a vivid description of the true design of the worship in the temple. God had recorded his name there; it was called holy, and only those who worshiped God according to his law should have entered the temple. It is not strange that Jesus, who had been hounded by his enemies, would now come and take possession of the temple in this fearless way; it is another token to them that he was what he claimed to be, the Son of God. "Den of robbers" is a strong accusation against these Jews for their evil practices. "Den of robbers" is a terrible antithesis to "the house of God," or "house of prayer." This was a serious charge against the Jewish religious leaders.

And the blind and the lame came to him in the temple.—He is still in the court of the temple and the unfortunate come to him, "and he healed them." No one ever came to Jesus humbly seeking help that did not receive it. There was a wide contrast in what Jesus did in the temple and what the Jews were doing; they were practicing extortion on the people for their own selfish gains; he was healing the diseased and

wonderful things that he did, and the children that were crying in the temple and saying, Hosanna to the son of David; they were moved with indignation, 16 and said unto him, Hearest thou what these are saying? And Jesus saith unto them, Yea: did ye never read, ⁵Out of the mouth of babes and sucklings thou hast perfected praise? 17 And he left them, and went forth out of the city to Bethany, and lodged there.

---
⁵Ps. viii. 2.

---

distressed among them; they were working for themselves, he for others. "But when the chief priests and the scribes saw the wonderful things that he did and the children that were crying in the temple and saying, Hosanna to the son of David; they were moved with indignation." The rulers were angry and perplexed; they were angry with the innocent children, who had caught the echo of the praises of their parents. These chief priests and scribes said to Jesus, "Hearest thou what these are saying?" Evidently they wanted him to cause the children to cease; he had exercised his authority in cleansing the temple, now he should rebuke these children for their praises. Evidently they were jealous of Jesus and did not want to hear the children praise him, and they sought to arouse enmity against him from the parents by his rebuking these children. Again he had taken upon himself to cleanse the temple, and he ought not to permit this to continue. Jesus replied to them, "Yea," that is, he heard the praise of the children and quoted the word of God as authority. He said have you never read, "Out of the mouth of babes and sucklings thou hast perfected praise?" This was taken from Psalm 8: 2. These chief priests and scribes seem to be astonished that Jesus, a meek Galilean, should allow them to proclaim his praises as the Messiah. Jesus stood in their midst meek and lowly, only seeking to do good and to heal the diseases of body and soul; he received the praises of the multitude, but showed no signs of any intention of seizing the supreme power and setting the Jews free from the Romans, but now of the perfect praise, praise which came from the purity and innocency of the hearts of the children. Jesus said, in reply to the Pharisees when they rebuked the multitude, "I tell you that, if these shall hold their peace, the stones will cry out." (Luke 19: 40.) Jesus left them to their own evil thoughts and intentions, "and went forth out of the city to Bethany, and lodged there." Bethany was about two miles from Jerusalem. He "lodged there" each night during his last week on earth, except the night of his betrayal.

2. BARREN FIG TREE CURSED; HIS AUTHORITY QUESTIONED, PARABLE OF THE TWO SONS
21: 18-32

18 Now in the morning as he returned to the city, he hungered. 19 And seeing ⁶a fig tree by the way side, he came to it, and found nothing thereon, but leaves only; and he saith unto it, Let there be no fruit from thee henceforward for ever. And immediately the fig tree withered away. 20 And

⁶Or, *a single*

18-22 Now in the morning as he returned to the city.—This was Monday morning, or the second day of the week; he probably left Bethany before breakfast that he might attend the morning service at the temple; at any rate, "he hungered." Our Lord was the bread of life, yet he hungered; he was the water of life, but thirsted. As they went along the way from Bethany to Jerusalem, they saw "a fig tree by the wayside," and when they came to it they "found nothing thereon, but leaves only." He saw this fig tree afar off; it probably stood alone by the roadside, and was in a sense public property. (Deut. 23: 24, 25.) It was in full leaf, but when he came near to it no fruit was found on it. Jesus, of course, knew that there was no fruit there; he came to it to make it a parable of the great truth which was to be impressed on his disciples at that time. In Palestine the fig tree puts out its fruit first, afterward the leaves; by the time that the tree is in full foliage the fruit ought to be ripe. This tree was an exception; a perversion of the laws of its nature; it deceived the eye, was to all appearance fruitful, but only cumbered the ground. Jesus said, "Let there be no fruit from thee henceforward for ever." This is the only miracle that apparently cursed anything. The Jewish nation was like this fig tree; it had apparently luxurious foliage in all the outward forms of holiness, but there was no fruit to the glory of God as was seen in their

when the disciples saw it, they marvelled, saying, How did the fig tree immediately wither away? 21 And Jesus answered and said unto them, Verily I say unto you, If ye have faith, and doubt not, ye shall not only do what is done to the fig tree, but even if ye shall say unto this mountain, Be thou taken up and cast into the sea, it shall be done. 22 And all things, what-

rejection of Jesus. The tree of the Jewish nation had been selected of God, pruned, and kept intact for the coming of the Messiah, the fruit of the nation; they were now rejecting him for whom the nation had existed from the days of Abraham. Jesus pronounced a malediction on the tree, not from any ill will to it for not bearing fruit, since it had no choice in the case, but as a parable acted before the disciples, to impress on their memories, in the most striking manner, the destiny of the city of Jerusalem and the Jewish race. The tree withered, not immediately, but by the next day; it may have begun to wither at once. Some have criticized this act of Jesus in destroying this tree; those who do overlook entirely the lesson that he taught. He caused a tree to die to teach the lesson of the disastrous fall of a nation. It is a rule of human reason that examples may be made for instruction upon worthless objects.

And when the disciples saw it, they marvelled.—It seems that the disciples saw the tree the next morning as they spent the night at Bethany, and were again returning when they discovered that the tree had withered and remarked about its "immediately" withering away. Mark leaves the impression that it was the next day that they saw it, and that Peter called the attention of Jesus to it and expressed wonder. (Mark 11: 19, 20.) This furnished Jesus the occasion to say, "If ye have faith, and doubt not, ye shall not only do what is done to the fig tree, but even if ye shall say unto this mountain, Be thou taken up and cast into the sea, it shall be done." The disciples needed to be strengthened in their faith at this time because great events were to occur within that week. Jesus was preparing them for those momentous events. This verse has puzzled commentators as to whether to take it figuratively or literally. If a literal interpretation is given to it, it would still have its value in teaching them the importance of faith; if a

soever ye shall ask in prayer, believing, ye shall receive.

23 And when he was come into the temple, the chief priests and the elders of the people came unto him as he was teaching, and said, By what authority doest thou these things? and who gave thee this authority? 24 And Jesus

---

spiritual interpretation is given to it, it would still have its value in impressing the importance of faith. Jesus did not explain the symbolical meaning of either the triumphal entry into Jerusalem, the cleansing of the temple, or the withering of the fig tree. This lesson of faith is here impressed from the miracle because Jesus is soon to leave his apostles to their own moral strength, amid the state of surrounding ruin in the destruction of Jerusalem as prefigured by the withered tree. Probably Jesus had reference to the Mount of Olives when he said "this mountain" as they were passing over that mountain to Jerusalem that morning. Jesus then drew the lesson of faith when he said, "All things, whatsoever ye shall ask in prayer, believing, ye shall receive." This promise belonged to his disciples in their ministry; they should have all things which they needed to confirm the Father's will which he had taught them; it also means that God will furnish everything to his people today that they may need to live faithful Christian lives. It is not a promise that God will satisfy all of the wants of people, nor answer every prayer that is made to him. There are conditions of acceptable prayer and these conditions must be met before one has any right to expect an answer. Prayers are offered in the name of Jesus, in faith, and according to the will of God. (1 John 3: 22; 5: 14.) God will not grant blessings to those who are in persistent rebellion to his will, neither to those who do not believe in him, nor to those who will not honor his Son by praying in his name.

23-27 And when he was come into the temple.—On this day as he went into the temple his authority was challenged. "The chief priests and the elders" came to him "as he was teaching, and said, By what authority doest thou these things?" The "chief priests" were the heads of the twenty-four courses or classes of priests. David had divided the priests into twenty-four classes, and had selected one from each class as the head; this one was called a "chief priest."

answered and said unto them, I also will ask you one ⁷question, which if ye tell me, I likewise will tell you by what authority I do these things. 25 The baptism of John, whence was it? from heaven or from men? And they reasoned with themselves, saying, if we shall say, From heaven; he will say unto us, Why then did ye not believe him? 26 But if we shall say, From men; we fear the multitude; for all hold John as a prophet. 27 And they answered Jesus, and said, We know not. He also said unto them, Neither tell I you by what authority I do these things. 28 But what think ye? A

⁷Gr. *word.*

"Elders" were the rulers of the cities. Mark and Luke add "the scribes," who were the authorized teachers and helped to constitute the Sanhedrin. These chief priests, elders, and scribes may have represented the Sanhedrin; they asked for his authority for doing "these things." They wanted to know his authority for entering Jerusalem as he did, his expulsion of the traders and brokers, and his teaching in the temple. They knew by what authority he did "these things," but they were unwilling to acknowledge that authority. To acknowledge God as his authority would have been to acknowledge him as the Son of God and the Messiah; this they were determined not to do. Jesus replied to them by asking them a question, with the proposition that if they would answer him he would answer their question. He then asked them concerning John's baptism whether it was "from heaven or from men." They withdrew aside and began to reason "with themselves" and said, "If we shall say, From heaven; he will say unto us, Why then did ye not believe him? But if we shall say, From men; we fear the multitude." They were in a dilemma; they saw that Jesus had put them in this plight, so they finally decided that they would say, "We know not." This they thought was the easiest way out; they did not want the truth, and would not accept it if presented; so Jesus said, "Neither tell I you by what authority I do these things." These teachers who were the professed guides of the people, and prepared to decide upon all questions, are now put in the ridiculous attitude of saying that they are unable to answer a simple question put to them by this despised man of Galilee. How humiliating it must have been to them! Yet they chose to suffer this humiliation rather than confess the truth which

man had two ¹sons; and he came to the first, and said, ²Son, go work to-day in the vineyard. 29 And he answered and said, I will not: but afterward he repented himself, and went. 30 And he came to the second, and said likewise. And he answered and said, I *go,* sir: and went not. 31 Which of the two did the will of his father? They say, The first. Jesus saith unto them, Verily I say unto you, that the ³publicans and the harlots go into the kingdom of God before you. 32 For John came unto you in the way of righ-

¹Gr. *children.*
²Gr. *Child.*
³See marginal note on ch. 5. 46.

was clear to them. They attempted to evade the dilemma by falsehood. Jesus did not say that he could not answer their question, but that he *would not.*

28-32 But what think ye?—Jesus now exposes the hearts of his enemies by a series of parables; in them he lays bare the evil thoughts which they had against him at this time. They had fully determined to destroy him, and had set themselves in opposition to the common people. (John 7: 49.) These common people, publicans and sinners as they were, would be saved before the scribes and Pharisees. He gives to them the parable of the two sons; these two sons represent two great classes of people today as well as then. The father commanded his first son to go and work in the vineyard and the son rebelled and flatly told his father that he would not go, "but afterward he repented himself, and went." He regretted his lack of respect to his father and returned to his duty. "The second" son was instructed to go and work in the vineyard, and he very politely said that he would go, but "went not." Jesus now put the question directly to them and asked, "Which of the two did the will of his father?" They could not profess inability to answer his question (verse 27); they were obliged to answer, though their answer condemned themselves. Hence they replied, "The first." The first did the will of his father not in his first refusal, but in his subsequent repentance and obedience.

Jesus then replied to them, "Verily I say unto you, that the publicans and the harlots go into the kingdom of God before you." These chief priests, elders, and scribes among the Jews looked upon "publicans and the harlots" as the vilest of

teousness, and ye believed him not; but the ³publicans and the harlots believed him: and ye, when ye saw it, did not even repent yourselves afterward, that ye might believe him.

---

earth and beneath their attention; they would not do anything to help them. What a stinging rebuke Jesus gave them when he said "the publicans and the harlots go into the kingdom of God before you." It is often true that many notorious sinners repent and turn to Christ before a good moral man does. A course of sin in early life is to be regretted and the sinner must suffer the consequences, but when that one realizes his lost condition, he will come to Christ, while the moral character may rely upon early piety and remain away from Christ and be lost. Jesus makes application when he tells them that John came to them "in the way of righteousness, and ye believed him not." Some of them may have accepted John's teachings, but refused to accept the Christ when he came; they were apostate disciples of John. While they did not accept John, yet "the publicans and the harlots believed him." These adversaries of Jesus saw what those who were vile in their own sight were doing, but "did not even repent yourselves afterward, that ye might believe him." They had not only, some of them, rejected John but afterwards, when his preaching bore manifest proof, they would not repent or turn from their evil course, and believe in John nor the Christ whom John represented. John came as a Jew and a prophet of the strictest and purest type; he did the very righteousness which the law demanded, and that for which the Pharisees boasted in their own self-righteous claims; yet they had rejected him. They could not detect in John the slightest departure from the law, still they rejected his message. They could not fail to see Jesus' application.

[This principle is frequently manifested in Bible history. Those favorably situated for knowing and doing the will of God give but little attention to God and his will; those less favorably situated more readily seek for and practice the truth. There are many examples of this given in the scriptures and many illustrations of it in God's dealings with the people in the patriarchal and Jewish dispensation. No clearer example of it is found in the New Testament than in the case of the publicans and sinners and the scribes and Pharisees. There is no sin of which man is more frequently guilty than that of self-righteousness; none is more clearly and frequently condemned of God. Self-righteousness, self-sufficiency, a satisfaction with oneself has never commended men to God. He has placed before us a divine model in Christ Jesus; with much help and many blessings to encourage us in the work, we can never feel we have come up to the model.]

3. PARABLE OF THE WICKED HUSBANDMEN
21 : 33-46

33 Hear another parable. There was a man that was a householder, who planted a vineyard, and set a hedge about it, and digged a winepress in it, and built a tower, and let it out to husbandmen, and went into another coun-

33-41 **Hear another parable.**—A record of this will be found in Mark 12: 1-12 and Luke 20: 9-19. This parable has as its chief point the future act of God in taking from the Jews their privileges and giving them to the Gentiles; this act of God was made necessary by the sins and ingratitude of the Jews. "A householder" is one who had possession or owned a vineyard. (Matt. 21.) "A vineyard" was a plot of ground planted with grapevines which were common in Palestine. (Deut. 32: 32; Isa. 5: 1-7.) The grape was the most important fruit of Judea. A very minute description is given here of the preparation and protection of the vineyard. The householder had planted his vineyard "and set a hedge about it, and digged a winepress in it, and built a tower, and let it out to husbandmen, and went into another country." They built hedges of wild aloe and other thorny shrubs to keep out the foxes and wild hogs and human intruders. The wall which enclosed it guarded it from intruders. (Ex. 23: 22; Num. 23: 9; Eph. 2: 14.) "A winepress" was a vat which was prepared to hold the wine when pressed out; these vats were hollow places dug in the earth and lined with stone, or sometimes cut out of the solid rock. The grapes were placed on an open floor above and trodden by the feet of men, when the juice ran through

try. 34 And when the season of the fruits drew near, he sent his ⁴servants to the husbandmen, to receive ⁵his fruits. 35 And the husbandmen took his

⁴Gr. *bondservants.*
⁵Or, *the fruits of it*

and was collected in the vat. (Judges 9: 27; Neh. 13: 5.) "A tower" was usually built in the middle of the vineyard in which the keepers were to watch the vineyard in the season of vintage. "Husbandmen" were those who leased the vineyard and cultivated it for a certain per cent of its yield. The owner of the vineyard went into a far country, presumably to live there, and "when the season of the fruits drew near, he sent his servants to the husbandmen, to receive his fruits"; that is, he sent to collect his part of the wine and other products of the vine. It was common to let vineyards out in this manner, and after the fruit was ripe or the wine made, the owner sent for his rent which was a part of the products. (Luke 16: 6, 7.) "The servants" here represent those special messengers and prophets who were sent to the Israelites from time to time to recall them to the service of God. (2 Kings 17: 13.) The husbandmen killed the servants and cruelly treated them. The prophets were, many of them, martyrs; Jeremiah was stoned, Isaiah sawn asunder. (1 Kings 19: 10; 2 Chron. 24: 20, 21; 36: 16; Heb. 11: 36, 37.) Stoning was the legal punishment for blasphemy and impiety. (Lev. 20: 2; 24: 16; Deut. 13: 10.) It was sometimes resorted to by a mob without any particular idea of its meaning; it was strange that the crime which the prophets came to prevent should have been falsely laid to their charge. (John 8: 59; Acts 7: 58.)

Finally, after the owner had repeatedly sent his servants to collect the rent from his vineyard, and they had been rejected and some of them killed, the owner sent his son, "a beloved son" and an only son (Mark 12: 6); he said that surely they will "reverence my son." This was his last resource to collect his rent and to see if any gratitude was left. Some have said that no one would act as did these wicked husbandmen, but such evil deeds have been practiced all down through the ages. However when the husbandmen "saw the son," they began to reason among themselves, and said, "This is the

⁴servants, and beat one, and kicked another, and stoned another. 36 Again, he sent other ⁴servants more than the first: and they did unto them in like manner. 37 But afterward he sent unto them his son, saying, They will reverence my son. 38 But the husbandmen, when they saw the son, said among themselves, This is the heir; come, let us kill him, and take his inheritance. 39 And they took him, and cast him forth out of the vineyard, and killed him. 40 When therefore the lord of the vineyard shall come, What will he do unto those husbandmen? 41 They say unto him, He will miserably destroy those miserable men, and will let out the vineyard unto other husbandmen, who shall render him the fruits in their seasons. 42 Jesus saith unto

---

heir"; they decided if they should kill him that they would receive his inheritance. So they took him and cast him out of the vineyard and "killed him." The chief point of the parable is here made; those wicked husbandmen, conspiring against the innocent heir, were a picture of the deep treachery which these, who were standing before Jesus, were at that very time plotting. (John 11: 47-53.) They were at that time desiring his destruction, in order that they might not be disturbed in their own evil ways and doctrines. Mark and Luke are both particular to mention this incident. Jesus "suffered without the gate." (John 19: 17; Heb. 13: 12, 13.) There is an illustration of this feature of the parable of one dying for his vineyard in the case of Naboth. (1 Kings 21: 13.) After relating the parable Jesus then asked another direct question of them, "What will he do unto those husbandmen?" That is, what will the owner of the vineyard do to those wicked husbandmen who killed his servants, and had now reached the climax of wickedness by killing his only and beloved son? Jesus asked this question to make them condemn themselves. The chief priests saw the application of the parable (verse 45) and were angry, but were too shrewd to let the people know their intense anger. So eventually they have answered their own question when they asked Jesus by what authority he did "these things." Jesus appeared before them as the Son of God and the heir of all things, against whom they were seeking a charge, when they asked a question. The parable has a close connection with the events of the succeeding days of the Passion Week. They sought to draw from Jesus a claim to be the Son of God, so that they could condemn him for blasphemy. They condemned themselves when they answered

them, Did ye never read in the scriptures,
⁶The stone which the builders rejected,
The same was made the head of the corner;
This was from the Lord,
And it is marvellous in our eyes?

⁶Ps. cxviii. 22 f.

Jesus' question by saying, "He will miserably destroy those miserable men, and will let out the vineyard unto other husbandmen."

42-46 Jesus saith unto them.—Jesus confused and condemned his adversaries with the scriptures. The parable which he had given them about the wicked husbandmen was so simple and clear that they could not misunderstand his meaning; it pictured their wicked thoughts and plots to them even better than they could have done it themselves. In the parable the son is killed, and cannot punish the husbandmen himself; but, as the Son of God, he is to be raised from the dead and will inflict the punishment. The "rejecting the stone," or "the stone which the builders rejected," was done in casting out the Son and killing him; now the same Son, under the similitude of a stone, becomes the destruction of his enemies. "The stone" in this quotation refers to Christ. (Psalm 118: 22-25.) It is a figure taken from the choosing of stones for a building. (Dan. 2: 45; Acts 4: 11; Eph. 2: 20; 1 Pet. 2: 7.) The husbandmen have become the builders of the spiritual temple; they refuse to lay a foundation on faith in Christ; they reject him, and hope to go on in their work without them. "The head of the corner," the cornerstone, is the principal one in the foundation. It has been supposed by many that it here means the keystone of an arch, which holds up the arch; but it is more simple in the common sense of the chief stone at the angle of the building and is a part of the foundation of the building. Christ is called the foundation because on him rests and in him unites the old and the new covenants. "This was from the Lord"; that is, it was not the wish of the builders; they had no idea that in killing the Son of God they were actually carrying out the divine pattern, and making him by the very cross upon which he suf-

43 Therefore say I unto you, The kingdom of God shall be taken away from you, and shall be given to a nation bringing forth the fruits thereof. 44 [7]And he that falleth on this stone shall be broken to pieces; but on whomsoever it shall fall, it will scatter him as dust. 45 And when the chief priests and the Phrarisees heard his parables, they perceived that he spake of them.

---

[7]Some ancient authorities omit ver. 44.

---

fered the foundation of the kingdom or church. (Acts 2: 22-24; 3: 17, 18.) It was beyond all human expectations and was a mystery which they did not understand.

Therefore say I unto you, The kingdom of God shall be taken away from you.—This is one of the clearest prophecies of the change of covenant to be found in any of the records of the gospel. The kingdom of God, the church, the vineyard, the cornerstone, all these represent the idea of the gospel economy. It should be taken from the Jews, who so persistently rejected Jesus and was to be given to the Gentiles who would bring "forth the fruits thereof." The Jews were God's chosen people; because they had all the advantages and rejected them, these advantages are to be given to the Gentiles. Hence, the Gentiles become the chosen people of God. (1 Pet. 2: 4-10.) There is a double action and solemn warning given here. "And he that falleth on this stone shall be broken to pieces"; this represents one action; those who stumble at this cornerstone, who stumble at the humility of Christ, "shall be broken to pieces," but not utterly destroyed. On the other hand, the second action is that "on whomsoever it shall fall, it will scatter him as dust." This allows no escape. Those who stumble at Christ "shall be broken to pieces," but those upon whom the judgment of Christ shall fall shall be utterly destroyed. His judgment fell on the Jewish nation at the fall of Jerusalem and caused a ruin deplorable beyond all other similar events, and his judgment will ultimately and finally rest upon the wicked at the judgment.

And when the chief priests and the Pharisees heard his parables, they perceived that he spake of them.—They had no trouble in understanding that Jesus referred to them. They were incensed, angry, and revengeful, but "they feared the multitudes, because they took him for a prophet." They saw

46 And when they sought to lay hold on him, they feared the multitudes, because they toook him for a prophet.

the open break and hostility which now lay between them and the Messiah; they must now sin *willfully* against the truth. It seems that they were beyond repentance, but their fury was restrained by fear of the people. The time of his deliverance into their hands was not yet come; during all his quiet teachings in the temple during the Passion Week and under his most terrible rebukes, they are, as it were, spellbound, and unable to lift a hand against him until his work is done, until his hour comes for him to yield himself to their wicked plan. As the common people regarded John the Baptist a prophet, so the multitude now regarded Jesus as a prophet; the immediate task of the scribes and Pharisees now is to turn the multitude against Jesus so that they can carry out their wicked designs.

4. PARABLE OF THE MARRIAGE FEAST; PAYING TRIBUTE TO CAESAR
22:1-22

1. And Jesus answered and spake again in parables unto them, saying, 2 The kingdom of heaven is likened unto a certain king, who made a marriage feast for his son, 3 and sent forth his ⁴servants to call them that were bidden

1-14 And Jesus answered and spake again in parables.—"Jesus answered," not a question which they had asked, but their evil thoughts and intentions. This parable is connected with those of the preceding chapter; it forecasts the fate of the Jews who reject the Son of God, and the doom of all who are at last found faithless. Many think that it is the same as the parable recorded in Luke 14: 16-24; it is similar to it in some points, but is not the same parable. It is the last parable of Jesus in order as given by Matthew; it seems to portray God's dealing with the Jews from the time of the destruction of Jerusalem.

The kingdom of heaven is likened unto a certain king.—The church or the kingdom of heaven is like the following facts related in this parable; it shows how God deals with unfaithful men in it as a certain king did with a contemptuous guest.

to the marriage feast: and they would not come. 4 Again he sent forth other ⁴servants, saying, Tell them that are bidden, Behold, I have made ready my dinner; my oxen and my fatlings are killed, and all things are ready: come to the marriage feast. 5 But they made light of it, and went their ways, one to his own farm, another to his merchandise; 6 and the rest laid hold on his ¹servants, and treated them shamefully, and killed them. 7 But the king was wroth; and he sent his armies, and destroyed those mur-

¹Gr. *bondservants.*

The chief point is that many are called to it, but only they who work out holiness can see the Lord in peace. The Jews boasted of their birthright as making them peculiar favorites of heaven; they are now told that in the act of rejecting Christ that birthright will cease, and individual character alone will determine their final condition. The king made a marriage feast for his son; he sent his servants out to call them that were bidden to the feast, but those bidden refused to come. Again he sent other servants informing them that were bidden that all things were ready. The feast had been prepared; the oxen and fatlings were killed; the meat had been cooked; in fact, everything was prepared and they were ready to sit down to the feast. Those who were bidden "made light of it" and went about their own affairs; some went to their farms, some to their merchandise; and some even laid hold of the servants and "treated them shamefully, and killed them." These servants had gone out and invited those who had previously been invited to attend the feast; the servants did not go out and invite all the neighbors, but only those whom the king had already invited; a refusal to accept the king's invitation meant treason. (Esth. 1: 12.) As the servants only summoned those who had been invited, they announced that all things were ready; hence to treat with contempt these servants was to rebel against the king. Those who were bidden went about their business of buying and selling for gain, and ignored the invitation of the king. Some who were bidden even shamefully treated the messengers and slew them.

When the king learned of this, he was angry and "he sent his armies, and destroyed those murderers, and burned their city." This seems to refer to the time when Jesus was speak-

derers, and burned their city. 8 Then saith he to his ¹servants, The wedding is ready, but they that were bidden were not worthy. 9 Go ye therefore unto the partings of the highways, and as many as ye shall find, bid to the marriage feast. 10 And those ¹servants went out into the highways, and gathered together all as many as they found, both bad and good: and the wedding was filled with guests. 11 But when the king came in to behold the guests, he saw there a man who had not on a wedding-garment: 12 and he saith unto him, Friend, how camest thou in hither not having a wedding-gar-

ing, and it was a warning to his hearers not to proceed in their sinful plots against the Lord of heaven and earth. Those first bidden, but who treated the invitation with contempt, were destroyed, and others were invited. The wedding was ready, "but they that were bidden were not worthy," so the king instructed his servants to go "unto the partings of the highways, and as many as ye shall find, bid to the marriage feast." They were to go into the public streets or at the squares where many streets met, and where a crowd of people might be expected to be found; if we understand it to be in the country, then they were to go to the sections of the highways or at the crossroads, and there bid all to come to the wedding feast. The servants obeyed, "and gathered together all as many as they found, both bad and good: and the wedding was filled with guests." It seems that the first invitation had been extended only to those who were special friends of the king, but now no discrimination was made in extending the second invitation. "Both bad and good" were invited and appreciated the honor, and accepted the invitation. The gospel invitation is to all; no discrimination is made between the rich and poor, moral and vicious, the high and the low, who will repent and reform.

But when the king came in to behold the guests, he saw there a man who had not on a wedding-garment.—The king did not sit at the feast with the guests; those who made great feasts entered the banqueting room to look at those who were invited, after they were arranged at the table; the dignity of the king forbade his entering before and sitting with the guests. Some think that the parabolic history here overleaps vast spaces of time, and at one spring brings us to the judgment day; that this is figured under the image of the king coming in to see the marriage guests. So this marriage lasts

ment? And he was speechless. 13 Then the king said to the ²servants, Bind him hand and foot, and cast him out into the outer darkness; there shall be the weeping and the gnashing of teeth. 14 For many are called, but few chosen.

²Or, *ministers*

---

from the time of the first advent of Jesus to the time of his second coming. However, it may not have such significance. Some think that it was a custom of the king to furnish proper garments for their guests at such feasts. It matters not whether that be true or not; one guest did not have on the wedding garment and had no excuse for not being properly clothed. In viewing the guests as they were arranged at the feast, and on seeing that one was not properly clothed for the feast, the king asked, "Friend, how camest thou in hither not having a wedding-garment?" The man made no excuse, hence "he was speechless"; this shows that he was responsible for his unprepared condition.

Then the king said to the servants, Bind him hand and foot, and cast him out into the outer darkness.—He is cast out from the full blaze and splendor of the feast into the darkness of the street. The word "servants" as used here seems to designate a different class from those who had invited these guests; they were officers. It was customary to bind a criminal for his doom; so this man was bound and thrown from the splendor of the banquet into the horrors of the midnight street. "There shall be the weeping and the gnashing of teeth." This adds vividness to the description of "the outer darkness," and widens the contrast between the splendor of the marriage banquet and the darkness of the street; it may signify the contrast between the glories of heaven and the anguish of hell. Jesus draws from the parable this conclusion. "For many are called, but few chosen." The high and the low, the good and the bad, were called to the marriage feast; all were invited, hence "many are called." Many of the Jews were called, but few accepted the call; many who accepted John's teaching at first failed to accept the Christ when he came. Those who were first called, who slighted the invitation and insulted the king, were the Jews. These were de-

15 Then went the Pharisees, and took counsel how they might ensnare him in *his talk*. 16 And they send to him their disciples, with the Herodians, saying, Teacher, we know that thou art true, and teachest the way of God in truth, and carest not for any one: for thou regardest not the person of men. 17 Tell us therefore, What thinkest thou? Is it lawful to give tribute unto

stroyed and may refer to the destruction of Jerusalem. Those who were called from the highways may represent the Gentiles and some of them prove unworthy of the final blessings of the gospel. There may be other lessons drawn from the parable.

15-22 Then went the Pharisees, and took counsel.—Parallel records of this may be found in Mark 12: 12-17 and Luke 20: 20-26. "Then went the Pharisees"; this is the beginning of a series of councils of the Sanhedrin which resulted in the violent scenes which follow; thy were frightened by the miracle of the raising of Lazarus (John 11: 48-53), and enraged by the parables which Jesus had just pronounced against them. They had listened to three searching parables which put them to a very great disadvantage; they now resort to allies for aid. The first they bring up are the Herodians, who retire from the encounter silenced. The purpose of the Pharisees is to "ensnare him in his talk"; that is, they want to confuse him or entangle him in contradiction. "Ensnare" is a figure drawn from taking wild birds in a snare or net. This first attempt with the Herodians is to involved him in difficulty with the Roman government; they seek to expose, as they thought, his ignorance upon some point of law or religion. The Herodians were a political party rather than a religious sect, as it is not known exactly what their opinions were on religious subjects. It is plain from their name that they were attached to Herod, or rather to his political views; they took their title from Herod the Great. Some think that they taught that it was the safest, most politic wisdom to follow the customs of the Roman law rather than seek to insist upon obedience to the law of God, and especially when those precepts of the law caused any difficulty or danger.

Representatives of the Pharisees and the Herodians came to Jesus and said, "Teacher, we know that thou art true, and

Cæsar, or not? 18 But Jesus perceived their wickedness, and said, Why make ye trial of me, ye hypocrites? 19 Show me the tribute money. And they brought unto him a ³denarius. 20 And he saith unto them, Whose is

---

³See marginal note on ch. 18. 28.

---

teachest the way of God in truth, and carest not for any one: for thou regardest not the person of men." If they had been sincere, they were paying a high tribute to Jesus. In attempting to ensnare him, they begin with flattery and deceit; they seek to inflate him with pride. They make four statements in their attempted flattery. First, "we know that thou art true," that is, that he is genuinely sincere; second, that thou "teachest the way of God in truth," that is, that he taught the truth of God (if they so thought why did they not accept his teaching?); third, that thou "carest not for any one," that is, that he was courageous enough to speak his convictions regardless of whom it might oppose; and fourth, that "thou regardest not the person of men," that is, he was not biased or prejudiced because of any one. What they said of Jesus was true, but they did not believe it as the truth about him. They put on the air of expecting complete independence from him under the hope that he would commit himself to some rebellious statement with respect to Roman law.

Having prepared him now, as they thought, for their question, they propounded it, "What thinkest thou? Is it lawful to give tribute unto Cæsar, or not?" They mean, is it permitted by the law of Moses to pay tribute to Cæsar? The Jews did not like paying tribute to a foreign government. By this question they thought they would put Jesus in a dilemma. If he said that it was *not lawful* to pay tribute to Cæsar, then he would be in bad with the Roman authorities; but if he said that it *was lawful,* then he would lose some of his popularity with the people and would be in bad with them. These Pharisees did not care how he answered the question; they thought that his answer would hang him on one horn of the dilemma. The Jews based their opposition to paying tribute to a foreign government on Deut. 17: 14, 15.

But Jesus perceived their wickedness.—Jesus knew their hearts, he knew their intentions and he asked them, "Why

this image and superscription? 21 They say unto him, Cæsar's. Then saith he unto them, Render therefore unto Cæsar the things that are Cæsar's; and unto God the things that are God's. 22 And when they heard it, they marvelled, and left him, and went away.

make ye trial of me, ye hypocrites?" Jesus was quick to "discern the thoughts and intents of the heart," and knew all that was in man. (John 2: 24, 25.) They were seeking to condemn Jesus by his words, but he reveals to them the thoughts of their hearts. They were asking as though seeking information, but had an evil motive in their question; hence, Jesus called them "hypocrites." This was a severe condemnation. He called for a coin and was given a "denarius"; this coin was worth about seventeen cents in our money. He asked them, "Whose is this image and superscription?" The denarius had on it the image of the Roman emperor and a motto for an inscription. Some claim that it had this inscription: "Cæsar Augustus, Judea being subdued." They answered, "Cæsar's." They did not give the superscription, only the image, while Jesus had asked for both. The inscription was odious to them and they did not wish to repeat it. Jesus then answered, "Render therefore unto Cæsar the things that are Cæsar's; and unto God the things that are God's." Give to Cæsar or human government the things which belong to it; no one could object to this. Neither could any one object to giving to God the things that belong to God; he did not want that which belonged to Cæsar, neither did he want his things given to Cæsar; human laws have no right to infringe upon the laws of God. Christians must as far as possible comply with both, but when human law conflicts with the divine, Christians must obey God and take the consequences. These Pharisees "marvelled" at his wisdom "and left him, and went away." They went away wondering, but not believing; they departed to plot other wickedness, and to accomplish by violence what they could not effect by their skill.

[Tertullian over 1,500 years ago commented on this incident as follows: "The image of Cæsar, which is on the coin, we give to Cæsar. The image of God, which is in man, is to be given to God. Therefore, thou must give the money, indeed,

5. SADDUCEES AND THE RESURRECTION; OPPOSITION OF PHARISEES
22: 23-46

23 On that day there came to him Sadducees, [4]they that say that there is no resurrection: and they asked him, 24 saying, Teacher, Moses said, [5]If a man die, having no children, his brother [6]shall marry his wife, and raise up seed unto his brother. 25 Now there were with us seven brethren: and the

---
[4]Many ancient authorities read *saying*.
[5]Dt. xxv. 5.
[6]Gr. *shall perform the duty of a husband's brother to his wife.*

23-33 On that day there came to him Sadducees.—Parallel records of this are found in Mark 12: 18-27; Luke 20: 27-38. Jesus has been tested already by the Pharisees and the Herodians, and now is subjected to the shrewdness of the Sadducees. The Sadducees were hostile to the Pharisees, and came to Jesus, supposing that he would side with them, as he had just exposed to contempt the treachery of their adversaries. They proceeded on the common fallacy that since Jesus was opposed to their adversaries, he was with them; they did not think that he was able to stand alone, without seeking the favor of some religious party. The Sadducees were opposed to the belief of the separate existence of spirits, and hence opposed to the resurrection. (Acts 23: 7, 8.) They asked Jesus a question which, they thought, was an argument against the resurrection. They referred him to Deut. 25: 5, where Moses said, "If a man die, having no children, his brother shall marry his wife, and raise up seed unto his brother." This law ceased with the close of the Jewish dispensation. The Jews were legally obligated to perpetuate the family, and since the older brother received the birthright and inheritance, together with the family name, if he died without children, this would end that family; hence a brother was required to take the widow of a dead brother and raise children by her in the name of his dead brother.

These Sadducees related this imaginary case to Jesus: "The first married and deceased, and having no seed left his wife

first married and deceased, and having no seed left his wife unto his brother; 26 in like manner the second also, and the third, unto the [7]seventh. 27 And after them all, the woman died. 28 In the resurrection therefore whose wife shall she be of the seven? for they all had her. 29 But Jesus answered and said unto them, Ye do err, not knowing the scriptures, nor the power of God. 30 For in the resurrection they neither marry, nor are given in marriage, but are as angels[8] in heaven. 31 But as touching the resurrection of the dead,

---

[7]Gr. *seven.*

---

unto his brother; in like manner the second also, and the third, unto the seventh." Then after she had had the seven brothers in succession as her husbands, "the woman died." They then asked Jesus, "In the resurrection therefore whose wife shall she be of the seven?" All seven of the brothers had her as a legal wife, now in the resurrection whose wife shall she be? Jesus answered this question by saying, "Ye do err, not knowing the scriptures, nor the power of God." Three things united in their error and the same three things cause people to err in matters of faith today. First, they did not understand the scriptures (Dan. 12: 2; Isa. 26: 19); second, they did not understand that the power of God can do all things; and third, they erred in supposing that the future world would be in all things like the present world. After rebuking for their ignorance Jesus said, "In the resurrection they neither marry, nor are given in marriage, but are as angels in heaven." The objection of the Sadducees is without force, since it was based upon a misunderstanding of conditions. Marriage bears a necessary relation to death, since it was designed by God to perpetuate the human family; but after the resurrection, there is eternal life, and no need for the institution of marriage as there will be no death to destroy the being. Their question was based on the supposition that "in the resurrection" all human relationships on earth would be perpetuated in heaven. There are no males and females in the spirit world, and those who inherit eternal life are as "angels in heaven"; that is, they have all of those qualities of spirit that belong to angels, and have dropped all those human relations and propensities; they are without the passions of the flesh and are pure celestial and immortal beings.

Again Jesus rebuked them for their ignorance concerning

have ye not read that which was spoken unto you by God, saying, 32 ⁹I am the God of Abraham, and the God of Isaac, and the God of Jacob? God is not *the* God of the dead, but of the living. 33 And when the multitudes heard it, they were astonished at his teaching.
34 But the Pharisees, when they heard that he had put the Sadducees to silence, gathered themselves together. 35 And one of them, a lawyer, asked

⁸Many ancient authorities add *of God.*
⁹Ex. iii. 6.

---

the resurrection and asked if they had not read "that which was spoken unto you by God" where he said to Moses, "I am the God of Abraham, and the God of Isaac, and the God of Jacob." (Ex. 3: 6.) He then added that "God is not the God of the dead, but of the living." Jesus answered the Sadducees according to their peculiar theories; they had only the book of Moses from which they had cited the scripture about the brother taking his dead brother's wife. Jesus did not explain the resurrection to them, as they would not have understood it; the resurrection was fully explained after Jesus was raised from the dead. If there had been no resurrection, Jehovah would have said to Moses, "I was the God of Abraham," etc., but "I am the God of Abraham," etc., is what he said to Moses. Jehovah is not "the God of the dead, but of the living," and since he is "the God of Abraham," etc., these patriarchs are living, and if living, there is a life after death; hence a resurrection. Luke records this as follows: "Now he is not the God of the dead, but of the living: for all live unto him." (Luke 20: 38.) Again when the people heard how he had answered the Sadducees, "they were astonished at his teaching." Indeed he taught them, not as their scribes, but as one who could speak with authority. Jesus brought new truths from the Old Testament which the Jews had not seen nor understood.

34-40 **But the Pharisees, when they heard that he had put the Sadducees to silence.**—The Pharisees take another turn in opposing Jews. We are in the midst of the last week of his earthly ministry; Jesus is teaching in the temple. The Pharisees sought first to ensnare him, but he answered and rebuked them; then the Herodians joined the Pharisees in attempting

him a question, trying him: 36 Teacher, which is the great commandment in the law? 37 And he said unto him, [10]Thou shalt love the Lord thy God with all thy heart, and with all thy soul, and with all thy mind. 38 This is the

[10]Dt. vi. 5.

---

to ensnare him; next the Sadducees attacked him; and now the Pharisees seek again to entangle. Parallel records of this are found in Mark 12: 28-34 and Luke 20: 39, 40. The Pharisees were standing near by and heard that Jesus had put to silence the Sadducees. To put "to silence" here comes from the Greek word which strictly means "to muzzle," as one would put a muzzle on a beast. Perhaps the Pharisees enjoyed seeing Jesus thus "muzzle" or put to silence their adversaries, the Sadducees. They are emboldened to make another attack, and this time select one of their number whom they thought would be successful in this attempt to entrap him. They selected "a lawyer," that is, a teacher or doctor of the law; he was not "a lawyer" in our modern use of that term. This question was put to try Jesus. It may be that the lawyer himself asked for information, but he was the tool of the Pharisees. Mark calls this man a "scribe" who asked the question and says that "thou art not far from the kingdom of God." (Mark 12: 34.) This leads us to think that probably the man himself was sincere in asking the question, but being the tool of the Pharisees he was trying to ensnare Jesus. His question was, "Which is the great commandment in the law?" He meant by this which one law must be kept above all others? The teachers among the Pharisees had decided that no man could observe perfectly all the commandments of the law delivered by Moses; they were sticklers for perfect obedience; but they saw in their own lives that no one kept perfectly all the commandments of the law; therefore they had decided that if one man kept perfectly one commandment his obedience to this one would be accepted as obedience to all of the laws. However, the question arose among themselves as to which one was the most important, or which one should be selected to be kept. Some of them exalted one law above the other; some thought the law regulating the Sabbath was the more im-

great and first commandment. 39 ¹¹And a second like *unto it* is this, ¹²Thou shalt love they neighbor as thyself. 40 On these two commandments the whole law hangeth, and the prophets.

¹¹Or, *And a second is like unto it, Thou shalt love &c.*
¹²Lev. xix. 18.

---

portant, others thought that the law regulating conduct with respect to human life the most important.

This lawyer was skilled in the niceties and peculiar phases of the theory of the Pharisees, and perhaps they thought that he was able to argue his point with great ability. Jesus answered him, "Thou shalt love the Lord thy God with all thy heart, and with all thy soul, and with all thy mind." That is, one must love God with his best, highest faculties, with the heart; that is, one must love God with all of his affections and have his desires fixed on him. "With all thy soul" includes all of one's spiritual nature; "with all thy mind" means that all of the intellectual powers must be brought into subjection to the truth of God. It may be that Jesus meant to make no distinction between "heart," "soul," and "mind"; that he meant that one must surrender his entire being to the will of God and use the combined powers and faculties of his being to promote the honor and glory of God. This statement of the law includes the four commandments which were inscribed on the first table of stone, which regulated man's conduct toward God. Man's duties to God come first; they are supreme and must have the right of way in every life that would enjoy God. Jesus did not stop with that commandment, but added that "a second like unto it is this, Thou shalt love thy neighbor as thyself." This is a summary of the six commandments on the second table of stone of the Decalogue, which describe and regulate man's conduct toward his fellow man. In these two summaries Jesus covers the entire law, and said, "On these two commandments the whole law hangeth, and the prophets." All things in the Old Testament dispensation proceed from these two laws; all things that Moses and the prophets wrote were intended to bring men to the supreme principle of love to God and to man. In one sweep Jesus includes the entire will of God as revealed to man, and shows that no one

41 Now while the Pharisees were gathered together, Jesus asked them a question, 42 saying, What think ye of the Christ? whose son is he? They

section or clause of it can be disregarded or exalted above another. They recognized that Jesus had answered "discreetly" and no one of them asked him any more questions. (Luke 20: 40.)

[Love is the fulfilling of the law. The soul that hungers and thirsts to do the will of God loves God. It is deception and folly to talk of loving God while we fail to obey him or do his commandments. This is the love of God, that we keep his commandments. When people do not with the soul desire above all things to do the will of God, they do not love him. To love thy neighbor as thyself is not to feel a magnetic attraction toward him, but it is to have the purpose of heart, soul, and mind to do him good, to work for his happiness and well-being as we labor for our own well-being and happiness. He is a true child of God who is willing to sacrifice every fleshly feeling and impluse and bear all things to do the will of God. He loves his neighbor as himself who can choke back the angry feeling and forget wrongs suffered in order to benefit and help him. We can wisely love self only by loving the neighbor, the enemy.]

41-46 Now while the Pharisees were gathered together.— Parallel records of this are found in Mark 12: 35-37 and Luke 20: 41-44. Before the Pharisees had separated, and while they were still in the temple that day, Jesus asked them a question. He had answered all their questions one by one as they had produced them, and now he proceeds on another line of opposition to them. They have been defeated and stand condemned before the people and in their own sight; so Jesus propounds to them this question, "What think ye of the Christ? whose son is he?" He does not ask them if they think that he is the Messiah, but he calls for their opinion as to whom the Messiah is; that is, "whose son is he" or through whose lineage should he come? They knew the scriptures on this point and answered promptly, "The son of David." They knew that the scriptures taught that he was to be a descend-

say unto him, *The son* of David. 43 He saith unto them, How then doth David in the Spirit call him Lord saying, 44 ¹The Lord said unto my Lord, Sit thou on my right hand, Till I put thine enemies underneath thy feet? 45 If David then calleth him Lord, how is he his son? 46 And no one was able to answer him a word, neither durst any man from that day forth ask him any more questions.

¹Ps. cx. 1.

---

ant of David. (Psalm 132: 11.) When they answered this question, Jesus propounded another, "How then doth David in the Spirit call him Lord?" That is, how could David call one of his descendants Lord? David in speaking was guided by the Holy Spirit. Upon what principle could David call him Lord? Mark states that David did this by the Holy Spirit, and Luke adds that it was "in the book of Psalms" that David called him Lord. (Psalm 110: 1.) Jesus then quotes from Psalm 110: 1 and applies the language to David and says that he spoke by the Holy Spirit and called the Messiah Lord. It seems in order to further confuse these Pharisees that Jesus added another question, "If David then calleth him Lord, how is he his son?" Here was the point for them to explain. They cannot admit it without acknowledging that while he is human as descended from David, so he is divine as the right Messiah sent of God; it shows that his royalty is not on earth, but in heaven. It also shows that the Messiah on earth was to have a twofold nature—fleshly and divine. They were unable to answer him; it is not recorded that they even attempted to answer. They did not ask him any more questions; this closed his debate with them. He had answered and confounded the various sects of the Jews by answering and asking questions. They had failed to catch him in his words; they now resort to violence; next he is brought before their judgment seat; and last they are to be brought before his judgment bar.

6. SCRIBES AND PHARISEES EXPOSED; SEVEN WOES PRONOUNCED
23: 1-39

1 Then spake Jesus to the multitudes and to his disciples, 2 saying, The scribes and the Pharisees sit on Moses' seat: 3 all things therefore whatsoever they bid you, *these* do and observe: but do not ye after their works; for they say, and do not. 4 Yea, they bind heavy burdens ²and grievous to

---
²Many ancient authorities omit *and grievous to be borne.*

1-4 Then spake Jesus to the multitudes and to his disciples. —This entire chapter is an exposition and denouncement of the sin of the scribes and Pharisees; Jesus speaks with unsparing yet with just severity. It is spoken to the people and his disciples; it is his final admonition to the people against the pernicious teachings of the Pharisees and their corrupt lives. Mark tells us that it was spoken to "the common people," and adds that they heard him gladly. (Mark 12: 37.) Luke tells us that he spoke "in the hearing of all the people," and that it was spoken "unto his disciples." (Luke 20: 45.) His address was to his disciples in the presence of the multitude and for the benefit of all who heard. It may be that Matthew did not record this in chronological order; he places it in immediate connection with the events and conversations of the two chapters preceding; that is, during the six days of the Passion Week. Jesus had come to Jerusalem for the last time, never to leave it alive; this condemnation and warning of the scribes and Pharisees has its practical value today.

The scribes and the Pharisees sit on Moses' seat.—They were the transcribers, readers, and teachers of the law of Moses; the "seat" was also used by Grecian philosophers in lecturing, who were thence called "cathedrarii." The synagogue expounders stood while reading the very words of the law, but sat while expounding it. The scribes and the Pharisees were in no way the successors of Moses by ordination or lineal descent; they had no more authority from God than did the Sadducees. "All things therefore whatsoever they bid you, these do and observe." "All things" which they teach according to the law of Moses, Jesus commended and instructed the people to obey, because God was the author of the law. However, the teachers of the law did not practice

be borne, and lay them on men's shoulders; but they themselves will not move them with their finger. 5 But all their works they do to be seen of men: for they make broad their phylacteries, and enlarge the borders *of their*

what they taught; "they say, and do not." They did not practice what they preached. They taught things other than those revealed in the law; their teachings were mingled with the traditions of the rabbis. However, the failure of the scribes and Pharisees to do what the law required, though they preached it, did not excuse the people from obeying the law. This principle holds true today; religious teachers may not practice the word of God as they teach it; it is true that they ought to and are condemned for not doing it; yet that does not excuse anyone else for disobeying the commands of God. Jesus goes further in exposing the practices of these scribes and Pharisees, and charges them with fastening "heavy burdens" which were "grevious to be borne" upon the people; yet "they themselves will not move them with their finger." They placed the heavy burdens of traditional interpretations upon the people, but would not do anything to help the people even bear the burden which these traditions imposed. The figure here is taken from the eastern manner of loading the camels; their burdens are packed in bundles, and put upon their backs. The Pharisees imposed the severest ordinances on the people. Peter called the system a burden which none could bear. (Acts 15: 10). They were not willing to lighten the burden placed on the people even though they saw them fainting under the heavy load; they had no mercy, no justice, no sympathy for the people.

5-7 But all their works they do to be seen of men.—They were not interested in the people obeying God, neither were they anxious to please God themselves; they were more anxious to appear as righteous before men. They did all their works, not for the good or man nor the glory of God, but for the praise of men. Jesus specifies what they did; "for they make broad their phylacteries, and enlarge the borders of their garments." "Phylacteries" mean "preservatives" or "guards." The phylactery was a passage of scripture, written on parchment, folded up, and tied on the forehead, so that it

garments, 6 and love the chief place at feasts, and the chief seats in the synagogues, 7 and the salutations in the marketplaces, and to be called of men, Rabbi. 8 But be not ye called Rabbi; for one is your teacher, and all ye are

should be always in front of their eyes. This was a mechanical observance of Deut. 6: 8. "Enlarge the borders of their garments" means to put a fringe of blue in the borders of their garments to distinguish themselves from heathens. The scribes and Pharisees made "broad" their phylacteries; that is, instead of having one scripture, they had a number of scriptures inscribed and wore on their forehead, and thus appeared to be obedient to many scriptures; they "enlarged" the border of their garments to make it appear that they were righteous above the heathen; then broad phylacteries and enlarged borders could be easily seen, and this was what they desired. They were more interested in being seen of men to appear righteous than they were in being righteous. Another mark of their hypocritical life was that they loved to occupy "the chief place at feasts, and the chief seats in the synagogues." The "chief seats" at the feast were those nearest the master of the feast; they were those prepared for honored guests; they were seats where every one could behold them. "The chief seats in the synagogues" were those seats that were prominent and commanded conspicious attention from others; they occupied these because they loved the applause and admiration of men. Furthermore, they delighted in receiving "the salutations in the market-places," and to be called of men, "Rabbi." Salutations at the street corners and in the assemblies of men were sought by these scribes and Pharisees; they loved to hear their disciples hail them in a crowd as "rabbi," "great teacher." The same inordinate love of human applause is condemned in God's people today. "Rabbi" was an honorary title of the Jewish doctor of the law; it had three degrees, of which the first was "rab," the great or master; the second was "rabbi," my master; the third was "rabboni," my great master.

8-12 **But be not ye called Rabbi.**—"Rabbi" was an honorary title which carried with it pride and arrogance; to call one rabbi implied a degree of obedience to him and his teachings,

brethren. 9 And call no man your father on the earth: for one is your Father, ³*even* he who is in heaven. 10 Neither be ye called masters: for one is your master, *even* the Christ. 11 But he that is ⁴greatest among you shall be your ⁵servant. 12 And whosoever shall exalt himself shall be humbled; and whosoever shall humble himself shall be exalted.

³Gr. *the heavenly.*
⁴Gr. *greater.*
⁵Or, *minister*

which were inconsistent with right judgments; the Jews were content with what the rabbi said, and did not question his authority or judgment. What is here taught is that the disciples of Jesus should not use such titles which would lead them to yield submission to any man's will or judgment. This does not forbid anyone calling another by a professional title; it only denies God's people acknowledging human authority as a guide in following God. "Call no man your father"; this also has the limitations mentioned with respect to "rabbi." Children honor their father by affectionately calling him "father" or some other endearing name; they must call him by some name. No man in the spiritual sense should be called "father," for God is our Father. Paul called Timothy his son in the gospel. (1 Tim. 1: 2, 18; 2 Tim. 1: 2.) In this sense Timothy could speak of Paul as his "father" in the gospel, as Paul could speak of him as his "son" in the gospel. Only God is our Father in a spiritual sense and Jesus with the Bible our teacher; faithful disciples of the Lord recognized no other teacher or father. With like import we should not call anyone our "master," "for one is your master, even the Christ." "Rabbi," "Father," and "Master" should not be used to take the place of God, Christ, or his truth; but such titles of profession as may be used in giving honor to whom honor is due are not forbidden by Jesus here.

But he that is greatest among you shall be your servant.— The title "rabbi" in the sense forbidden by Jesus meant "my great one" and suggested a review of the principle that Jesus had already taught, namely, that the greatest one among his disciples would be the greatest servant among them; that service is the standard of greatness. This principle occurs ten times in the gospels. Jesus honors and blesses true humility

13 But woe unto you, scribes and Pharisees, hypocrites! because ye shut the kingdom of heaven, ⁶against men: for ye enter not in yourselves, neither suffer ye them that are entering in to enter.⁷

⁶Gr. *before.*
⁷Some authorities insert here, or after ver. 12, ver. 14 *Woe unto you, scribes and Pharisees, hypocrites! for ye devour widows' houses, even while for a pretence ye make long prayers: therefore ye shall receive greater condemnation.* See Mk. 12. 40; Lk. 20. 47.

and loving service, but condemns affection and empty pride. God's people are on a level with each other; they occupy the same relation to God and to Christ and should be on the same level with each other. The idea of popes, archbishops, bishops, and ecclesiastical heads in the religion of our Lord is condemned. The one who exalts himself shall be brought low, but the one who is humble God will exalt. Aesop, when asked what Jupiter was doing, replied, "He is humbling the exalted, and exalting the humble."

[One who uses religious services for personal promotion rather than the salvation of souls falls under the curse of God. His duty is to present God and his cause and lose sight of self; if he does this, God will care for him, and he whom God cares for will be blessed and exalted in the next world, if not in this. The young preacher that forgets all else and works for the glory of God is the one that succeeds. In forgetfulness of self he goes where he can do greatest good in saving souls and honoring God. His success in this work gives him character and opens the way for worldly success, and this is the point of danger. When a man looks around for a place where he can get the best support or make for himself the greatest name, he is seeking to exalt himself. If he seeks that which will add to his temporal good, he will not only lose the eternal life, but more often than otherwise he will lose the good of this life. But he who gives up all, forgets his temporal good for the sake of Christ, will save his life, the real good of this life, and all the blessings of the life to come.]

13, 14 But woe unto you, scribes and Pharisees, hypocrites! —Here Jesus begins his pronouncement of "seven woes." "Woe" is a word of solemn denunciation of punishment; it implies that great calamities of the most awful nature are impending over the guilty from the divine justice; it may also imply a retributive destiny for years and ages of sin. The scribes and Pharisees are here called "hypocrites," and upon them Jesus pronounced his most scathing denunciations while on earth. The dark clouds begin now to gather around the great central truth of Jesus' teaching—his crucifixion; he concludes his teaching with these sublime wails over the wickedness of the world as is personified in the scribes and Pharisees. The first woe is pronounced upon them "because ye shut the kingdom of heaven against men." They are represented as not entering themselves, neither permitting others to enter. The kingdom of God was preached in its preparatory stage; it had been presented in promise and prophecy, and now it was presented in its preparatory state, and these scribes and Pharisees, the religious guides of the people, were doing all that they could to contradict the teaching of Jesus and to keep the people from accepting him as the Messiah. They would not accept him themselves, neither would they, by their authority over the people, permit others to accept him. Frequently, people were cast out of the synagogues because they accepted Jesus as the Messiah. In Luke 11:52 the figure is slightly changed and is stated that they "took away the key of knowledge" and would not enter themselves nor permit others to enter, or hinder others who would enter. They shut the kingdom of God by their example (John 7:48); by their doctrine, caviling at all that Jesus said (Matt. 12:24; John 9:13-41; 12:42; 1 Thess. 2:14-16); and by their authority (John 9:22).

Verse fourteen is omitted from the Revised Version. Some authorities insert here or after verse twelve the following: "Woe unto you, scribes and Pharisees, hypocrites! for ye devour widows' houses, even while for a pretence ye make long prayers; therefore ye shall receive greater condemnation." They used long prayers to deceive and gain the ends of avarice; they are said to have remained three hours in prayer, and pretended that their lengthened devotions represented pious character and were worthy of liberal support. Again these leaders plotted with the children of widowed mothers to

15 Woe unto you, scribes and Pharisees, hypocrites! for ye compass sea and land to make one proselyte; and when he is become so, ye make him two fold more a son of ⁸hell than yourselves.

16 Woe unto you, ye blind guides, that say, Whosoever shall swear by the ⁹temple, it is nothing; but whosoever shall swear by the gold of the ⁹temple,

⁸Gr. *Gehenna*.
⁹Or, *sanctuary*: as in ver. 35.

---

gain the estate. The longer they continued their hypocritical prayers, the greater was their condemnation.

15 **Woe unto you, scribes and Pharisees, hypocrites!**—This woe is pronounced upon them because they compassed "sea and land to make one proselyte." They were very zealous to make a proselyte to their cause, but the proselyte was "twofold more a son of hell" than they themselves. They spared no pains to make a convert to their opinions; this new convert from among the Gentiles was called "a proselyte." There were great distinctions allowed among them; there were some who embraced the whole Jewish system and sought earnestly for its rewards; the centurion was probably one of this class (Matt. 8: 5) and possibly Cornelius (Acts 10). These were called "proselytes of righteousness." Others received only certain parts of the system, and were not circumcised, while others received only part of the system and were circumcised. They confused their proselytes and corrupted them by their false doctrines. Often converts from one religion to another simply reject their old supersititions, and seize eagerly all the worst parts of their new faith, and end in becoming infidels; such were these proselytes. "Son of hell" means one worthy of eternal punishment. These religious teachers taught their proselytes their opinions and disregarded the word of God; they exalted the doctrines of men above the word of God; and hence caused their proselytes to despise God, which rendered them worthy of such condemnation.

16-22 **Woe unto you, ye blind guides.**—In pronouncing this woe, Jesus calls the scribes and Pharisees "blind guides." They claimed to be leaders and guides of the people in their service to God. Not only does this condemnation rest upon the blind guides of that age, but upon such guides in religious thought of all. He has now called them "hypocrites," "blind

he is [10]a debtor. 17 Ye fools and blind: for which is greater, the gold, or the temple that hath sanctified the gold? 18 And, Whosoever shall swear by the altar, it is nothing; but whosoever shall swear by the gift that is upon it, he is a [1]debtor. 19 Ye blind: for which is greater, the gift, or the altar that

[10] Or, *bound* by his oath

---

guides," "fools and blind"; it would be difficult to find epithets which signify greater contempt and condemnation. In teaching the people these blind guides said, "Whosoever shall swear by the temple, it is nothing; but whosoever shall swear by the gold of the temple, he is a debtor." If a man swear at all and invoke the condemnation of God, he is bound to keep his oath. In Matt. 5: 33, 37 we have the same principle taught. These "blind guides" said that if one swore by the temple, the oath was not binding; hence they had a loophole to escape from keeping their oath. However, they said if one swears "by the gold of the temple," then one must keep that oath. The "gold of the temple" meant any of the gold with which the temple was ornamented. All this shows a trifling with oaths. A man in a vain conversation would take an oath thoughtlessly by some golden article of the temple; he must keep that oath; but if in all seriousness he swore by the temple, then he need not keep his oath. Some think that the gold here mentioned does not refer to the gilding of the temple, but the offering of gold which was in the treasury. In replying to this doctrine Jesus calls them "fools and blind" and asks "which is greater, the gold, or the temple that hath sanctified the gold?" Which is greater, the gold ornaments of the temple or the temple itself? Or which is greater, the whole or a part of the whole? This reduces their doctrine to an absurdity.

Again they taught with respect to oaths that if one should swear by the altar, then that one would not have to keep his oath; but "whosoever shall swear by the gift that is upon it, he is a debtor." This doctrine was as foolish as that of swearing by the gold upon the temple. The great altar of burnt offerings stood before the porch of the temple. (2 Chron. 5: 1; Matt. 5: 23.) The altar was a place of great veneration, since it was the instrument by which the great idea of sacrifice was

sanctifieth the gift? 20 He therefore that sweareth by the altar, sweareth by it, and by all things thereon. 21 And he that sweareth by the ⁹temple, sweareth by it, and by him that dwelleth therein. 22 And he that sweareth by the heaven, sweareth by the throne of God, and by him that sitteth thereon.

23 Woe unto you, scribes and Pharisees, hypocrites! for ye tithe mint and ¹¹anise and cummin, and have left undone the weightier matters of the law, justice, and mercy, and faith: but these ye ought to have done, and not to

¹¹Or, *dill*

---

preserved. It was the place where men met God to seek pardon. "The gift that is upon it" means the gift that was sacrificed unto God by the people. The law required certain sacrifices to be made. These sacrifices were burned upon the altar. The doctrine of these blind guides was that you could swear by the altar, but not have to keep the oath, but if one swore by the gift that was on the altar, then the oath was binding. This is the same principle involved in the temple and the gold and the temple. Jesus again argues that the altar is greater than the gift, since it is the "altar that sanctifieth the gift." Jesus then adds that when one swears by the altar he swears "by all things thereon." The nice dictinctions which they made proved that they were blind guides and foolish leaders. He adds that those who swear by the temple swear "by him that dwelleth therein"; he swears by the temple and all that belongs to it, and there was no way of escaping the performance of the oath. That it was like those who swear "by the heaven," for one who swears by the heaven swears "by the throne of God, and by him that sitteth thereon." Jesus shows the Pharisaic perversion of the oath and condemns their trivial and foolish way of evading and enjoining oaths upon the people. The law bound every one who made an oath or vow to keep that according to the instructions given in the law.

23, 24 **Woe unto you, scribes and Pharisees, hypocrites!**— The first three woes are passed and the next four are pronounced upon different forms of hypocrisy. This fourth woe is upon an extreme scrupulousness in regard to the slightest ritual performances, with a slight remorse for the grossest immoralities. They abused the law of Moses by exalting inferior precepts to fill the place of the higher commands of mercy

have left the other undone. 24 Ye blind guides, that strain out the gnat, and swallow the camel!

and truth. "Ye tithe mint and anise and cummin, and have left undone the weightier matters of the law, justice, and mercy, and faith." The Jews were required to pay a tenth part or tithe of all their property for the support of the system of worship. The tithe usually went to the priests and Levites. (Num. 18: 20-24.) The tithes were paid in kind, an actual tenth of the year's increase; that is, they paid a tenth of their grain, their vineyards, their cattle, and all that they produced. When a Jew lived at a distance from Jerusalem, he was permitted to change it into money and bring that to the priests. (Deut. 14: 24, 25, 27, 29.) "Mint and anise and cummin" were small vegetable plants, produced by the Jews for seasoning and flavoring their food. "Mint" was the same plant which we know by that name; the Jews scattered it on the floors of their synagogue. "Anise" was what we now call "dill," an herb of strong aromatic flavor; and "cummin" was a plant like our fennel. (Isa. 28: 25-27.) They were all garden herbs of the least value, and specimens of the rigidness of the Pharisees. They were commanded to tithe all the increase of their seed. (Deut. 14: 22.) Jesus did not condemn the tithing of these, but condemned their scrupulousness in tithing these little things, and leaving undone, or disregarding, the weightier matters of "justice, and mercy, and faith." While scrupulously tithing the little things, they were practicing injustice; they disregarded the justice which the law required. (Isa. 1: 17-23.) They showed no mercy in exacting these lesser matters, and were unmerciful toward their fellows. They ignored "faith" which was trust in God. They did not believe their own prophets, for they had testified of Jesus; he was fulfilling the prophecies, but they did not believe him as the Messiah. Again Jesus calls them "blind guides, that strain out the gnat, and swallow the camel!" The gnat was a small insect generated in wine or falling into it; it was considered an unclean animal. (Lev. 11: 4.) For fear of moral contamination they were exceeding careful to strain the liquid

23: 25, 26.]　　　　　　　MATTHEW　　　　　　　451

25 Woe unto you, scribes and Pharisees, hypocrites! for ye cleanse the outside of the cup and of the platter, but within they are full from extortion

---

which they drank. The camel was a huge and unwieldly beast of burden, larger than an ox. This statement of Jesus seems to have been a proverb. The Arabs had this proverb, "He swallowed an elephant, but was strangled by a flea." The meaning of Jesus is that by a verbal exaggeration, which is usual in proverbs, to describe a common but foolish custom. The Pharisee, whose conscience had pricked him and made him sad, if he had by chance swallowed a gnat, could yet go quietly and comfortably under the camel load of such sins as injustice, cruelty, and unfaithfulness; he wept at the shocking accident of failing to tithe a small bundle of herbs, but shouted himself hoarse a little later, "His blood be on us, and on our children" (Matt. 27: 25), at the crucifixion of Jesus.

25, 26 **Woe unto you, scribes and Pharisees, hypocrites!**—The fifth woe is pronounced upon moral hypocrisy, in which men will show a fair exterior of conduct, while they are secretly practicing the most abominable wickedness. Two forms of such hypocrisy are mentioned here by Jesus; they are the secret commercial dishonesties and secret licentiousness. In describing this practice Jesus said, "For ye cleanse the outside of the cup and of the platter, but within they are full from extortion and excess." Their vessels for food and drink are used here to enforce the moral lesson; they cleansed their vessels for food and drink, but did not cleanse themselves; they were like those who cleansed the outside of a cup or dish, while they left the part from which they took their food foul and unsightly. They appeared well to their countrymen, and deceived them as to their real character. They are "full from extortion and excess." The figure is carried out; "they," the dishes, are full of extortion and excess, which the Pharisees swallowed down without scruple. (Prov. 18: 21.) "Extortion" is the unjust wresting away the property or rights of others; "excess" is gluttony or intemperance of all excessive wickedness. They went to the extreme in all of their wicked practices, and at the same time, like cleansed vessels

and excess. 26 Thou blind Pharisee, cleanse first the inside of the cup and of the platter, that the outside thereof may become clean also.

27 Woe unto you, scribes and Pharisees, hypocrites! for ye are like unto whited sepulchres, which outwardly appear beautiful, but inwardly are full of dead men's bones, and of all uncleanness. 28 Even so ye also outwardly appear righteous unto men, but inwardly ye are full of hypocrisy and iniquity.

---

on the outside, were full of wickedness and sin. Again Jesus calls them, "Thou blind Pharisee," and demands that they "cleanse first the inside of the cup and of the platter, that the outside thereof may become clean also." If one will first cleanse the heart, then all the life will soon be pure and pious; the heart has in it the issues of life. (Prov. 4: 23.) The Lord's people should not reverse this law, and hope to reform men by cleansing the outside appearance. This is like the proverb, "Make the tree good, and its fruit good." (Matt. 12: 33.) Cleansing the outside of a literal cup would not necessarily cleanse the inside of it; but the cleansing of the heart of man will result in the purifying of the outward conduct.

27, 28 **Woe unto you, scribes and Pharisees, hypocrites!**—The sixth woe is pronounced upon pious hypocrites or religious insincerity. Jesus enforces this condemnation by a most striking figure taken from a class of objects very similar around Jerusalem. He compares these scribes and Pharisees to "whited sepulchres, which outwardly appear beautiful, but inwardly are full of dead men's bones, and of all uncleanness." It was a custom there to whitewash the sepulchres, which would be noticed by all; it is like our modern custom of keeping flowers or grass on the graves of loved ones. The graves are beautifully kept and adorned with costly monuments, but within they contain the decomposed bodies and foul odors arising from the decomposition. A sepulchre, or a corpse, was considered by the Jews unclean. (Num. 19: 16.) The Pharisees went so far as to mark with lime or chalk the ground under which the sepulchral cave extended. How awful a figure to show the condition of these hypocrites. Jesus makes his own application of the figure and says, "Even so ye also outwardly appear righteous unto men, but inwardly ye are full of hypocrisy and iniquity." This comparison illustrates in

29 Woe unto you, scribes and Pharisees, hypocrites! for ye build the sepulchres of the prophets, and garnish the tombs of the righteous, 30 and say, If we had been in the days of our fathers, we should not have been partakers with them in the blood of the prophets. 31 Wherefore ye witness to yourselves, that ye are sons of them that slew the prophets. 32 Fill ye up then

a striking manner the superficial and deceptive character of the religion of the Pharisees. It may find an application in many of our modern religious practices. Jesus is still looking at their hearts and contrasting their hearts with their profession; he is contrasting what they really are with what they claim to be. Jesus teaches here that an effort to appear to men better than we are is hypocrisy and makes hypocrites of those who attempt it.

29-36 **Woe unto you, scribes and Pharisees, hypocrites!**—This seventh woe pronounced upon these scribes and Pharisees condemns them for building "the sepulchres of the prophets, and garnish the tombs of the righteous." They built domes and columns over the graves of the prophets, and adorned or garnished them. They made it appear that they were honoring the prophets and righteous men of old, yet at the same time they were dishonoring them by rejecting their teachings and examples. The fathers had put to death many of the prophets, and now this generation was honoring these prophets by adorning their graves and saying, "If we had been in the days of our fathers, we should not have been partakers with them in the blood of the prophets." They erected monuments over the prophets who had been slain; they garnished their sepulchres and made them white and beautiful outwardly, that men might believe that they were practicing their virtues. These tombs were in the valley of Jehoshaphat south of Jerusalem. They would like for the present generation to believe that they respected and honored these prophets and would not have consented unto their death, had they lived in the days of the prophets. Jesus brings to their attention that they, in doing this, confessed that they were "sons of them that slew the prophets." They condemned the cruelty of their ancestors; they honored their tombs; but they cherished the hatred that their fathers had toward the prophets

the measure of your fathers. 33 Ye serpents, ye offspring of vipers, how shall ye escape the judgment of ¹hell? 34 Therefore, behold, I send unto you prophets, and wise men, and scribes: some of them shall ye kill and crucify; and some of them shall ye scourge in your synagogues, and persecute from city to city: 35 that upon you may come all the righteous blood shed on the earth, from the blood of Abel the righteous unto the blood of Zachariah son

¹Gr. *Gehenna.*

---

and were seeking to do the same violence against Jesus; in this they condemned themselves. It was easier for them to build and garnish the tombs of the dead prophets than to obey their instruction and accept Jesus as the Messiah.

Jesus tells them to do what he knew they had determined to do; that is, fill to the full measure the iniquity of their fathers. This time he denounces them by saying, "Ye serpents, ye offspring of vipers, how shall ye escape the judgment of hell?" They were called serpents, because they had the subtlety and venom of serpents; as the serpent killed the body, so they destroyed the souls of men; their malice was to destroy even the Savior of the world. It seems that Jesus' denunciation here rises to an appalling climax of woe. They were called "offspring of vipers," which means that they had accumulated so much of the hatred of their fathers that they are fitly called the "offspring of vipers." Jesus asked the question, "How shall ye escape the judgment of hell?" He did not expect an answer to this question; it was another way of saying to them that there was no escape for them. The condemnation of everlasting punishment belongs to such characters. Only by repentance can anyone escape from just condemnation. Some of these may have repented, but the condemnation pronounced by Jesus belongs to such characters as he here described. It is the condemnation of the lost. The question is frequently the strongest mode of affirmation and Jesus here uses it.

In pronouncing this woe Jesus predicts what will be done to other servants of God. Their fathers had killed the prophets, but they were preparing to kill the Messiah who was Prophet, Priest, and King. Jesus said, "I send unto you prophets, and wise men, and scribes: some of them shall ye kill and crucify." The apostles and inspired teachers were sent by Jesus into all the world. These apostles were to be inspired by the Holy

of Barachiah whom ye slew between the sanctuary and the altar. 36 Verily I say unto you, All these things shall come upon this generation.

Spirit and would warn the people of their sins and dangers. (Ex. 7: 1; John 4: 19; 1 Cor. 14: 1, 34.) These were cruelly treated; the Jews stoned Stephen (Acts 7: 59), cut off James' head, or rather caused a cruel king to do it, to please them (Acts 12: 2). They scourged Peter and other apostles (Acts 5: 40), persecuted Paul and Barnabas from city to city, and doubtless many others whose names are written only in the martyrology of the Lamb's book of life. All the apostles, save one, according to tradition, were put to death for the cause of Christ. Frequently they scourged the servants of God. (Acts 22: 19-24; 2 Cor. 11: 24, 25.) To persecute means to oppress wrongfully with a rage. Jesus said that they would do all these things to his faithful servants and would do them and bring upon themselves "all the righteous blood shed on the earth, from the blood of Abel the righteous unto the blood of Zachariah son of Barachiah, whom ye slew between the sanctuary and the altar." There is a measure of guilt which no one can pass by and not condemn without bringing down upon oneself all the accumulated woes of divine vengeance. "Righteous blood" means the blood of innocent persons; righteous Abel was the first martyr for God. (Gen. 4: 8.) "Zachariah son of Barachiah" was slain between the "sanctuary and the altar." We have no divine record of this crime. Some think that he was the prophet "Zechariah," but we have no way of knowing. He was slain on holy ground where they ought to have been worshiping God. What a crime to slay a prophet of God on the very spot where they should be worshiping God. Jesus warns the people by saying that "all these things shall come upon this generation." If this generation had repented and accepted Christ as the Savior, they might have been redeemed; but they rejected him and brought upon themselves the fearful and awful condemnation. These things came upon that generation in the sense that the consummation of earthly punishment for such deeds befell that generation.

37 O Jerusalem, Jerusalem, that killeth the prophets, and stoneth them that are sent unto her! how often would I have gathered thy children together, even as a hen gathereth her chickens under her wings, and ye would not! 38 Behold, your house is left unto you ²desolate. 39 For I say unto you,

²Some ancient authorities omit *desolate.*

37-39 O Jerusalem, Jerusalem, that killeth the prophets.—Here Jesus identifies Jerusalem with the people who inhabited it, those who committed the crime. This is the solemn farewell of the Savior over the city after his last public address. He mourns over the nation and city where Jehovah had shown so much love and mercy for generations. How touching, how pitiful! Jesus sees the dark fate brooding over the city, and his final words are of tenderness, mournfulness, and mercy. He recites the wickedness of the nation and the city. They had killed the prophets and stoned those who had been sent to them; in spite of this Jesus would have gathered them together as a hen "gathereth her chickens under her wings," but they would not let him. This was a simple and dutiful image of tender protection; his wings would have protected them when the storm hovered or the enemy approached. The fearful calamity that should befall Jerusalem and the Jews was brought upon them by themselves; they had opportunity to escape it, but "ye would not."

Your house is left unto you desolate.—It is no longer God's house; it is "your house." God has left it and has no more claim in it; it is "desolate"; that is, God has deserted it. It matters not how much it might be thronged by men or adorned with gifts and sacrifices; after Christ was crucified, all of these availed nothing; the day of its doom began when they crucified the Lord of glory. Jesus then pathetically said to them, "Ye shall not see me henceforth, till ye shall say, Blessed is he that cometh in the name of the Lord." Those of you who were angry at the words of the little children, welcoming the Messiah into the temple, shall see me no more, until my coming in terrific majesty, to avenge these wrongs. Happy will ye be then if ye can echo that chant of welcome to the Son of God. The public ministry of Jesus was finished

Ye shall not see me henceforth, till ye shall say, Blessed is he that cometh in the name of the Lord.

with these words. The plot thickened against him, and he kept aloft from the rulers till Judas betrayed him into their hands. Henceforth, Jesus retires to the bosom of his own disciples to prepare himself for the great sacrifice for the sins of the world.

7. DESTRUCTION OF THE TEMPLE FORETOLD; SIGNS OF HIS SECOND COMING
24: 1-31

1 And Jesus went out from the temple, and was going on his way; and his disciples came to him to show him the buildings of the temple. 2 But he

1, 2 And Jesus went out from the temple.—Parallel records of this are found in Mark 13: 1-37 and Luke 21: 5-36. Jesus had just finished his teachings in the temple with the lamentation over Jerusalem as found in last verses of chapter twenty-three; he went out from the temple to go to Bethany, and as he was leaving the temple and on the way to the Mount of Olives, "his disciples came to him to show him the buildings of the temple." Mark mentions particularly that they showed him the "stones" of the temple, which were very large. It seems that only four of his apostles were with him at this time. Mark says that he "sat on the mount of Olives over against the temple," and that "Peter and James and John and Andrew asked him privately." (Mark 13: 3.) We do not know if the other apostles were present; the Mount of Olives was on the way from Jerusalem to Bethany, probably midway between these two points. He occupied a point on this mount that gave a prominent view of Jerusalem. It may be that just as he left the temple his disciples called his attention to the "stones," and how the temple "was adorned with goodly stones and offerings." The Jews had looked upon the temple as being a permanent structure; Josephus mentions some of the stones of its base as being each in length, twenty-five cubits (37.44 feet); in height, eight cubits (12.14 feet); in breadth, about twelve cubits (18.21 feet). Jerusalem in all her magnif-

answered and said unto them, See ye not all these things? verily I say unto you, There shall not be left here one stone upon another, that shall not be thrown down.

icence was like "a bride adorned for her husband," "a city of palaces and right royally enthroned as none other." Alone and isolated in its grandeur stood the temple mount; terrace upon terrace its courts rose, till, high above the city, within the enclosure of marble cloisters, cedar-roofed and richly ornamented, the temple itself stood out a mass of snowy marble and of gold, glittering in the sunlight against the half encircling green background of Olivet. In all his wanderings the Jew had not seen a city like his own Jerusalem. It is claimed that the building occupied an area of about nineteen acres. "The temple of Jerusalem was one of the wonders of the world." The Talmud says, "He that never saw the temple of Herod never saw a fine building."

When the disciples called Jesus' attention to the temple, that gave him an occasion to say that "there shall not be left here one stone upon another, that shall not be thrown down." Here Jesus predicted the destruction of the temple. Jesus said, "See ye not all these things?" Attention is called to the seeming permanence and security of the temple with its massive stones and ornaments. Nothing could seem more improbable to them than this prediction; the world was at peace; the Jewish nation was subject to the Roman Empire, and under its protection; thus it was protected by the greatest earthly power. It was astonishing to his disciples when he uttered the prediction that not one stone would be left upon another. Within forty years from the time of this prophecy it was fulfilled. History records that Vespasian and his son Titus besieged Jerusalem for three years, and it was taken and destroyed 70 A.D. The expression used by Jesus means that it would be utterly destroyed; "there shall not be left here one stone upon another, that shall not be thrown down." How completely this prediction has been fulfilled. Not a vestige of the temple remained; even its location is doubtful today. Titus made every effort possible to preserve the temple from

3 And as he sat on the mount of Olives, the disciples came unto him privately, saying, Tell us, when shall these things be? and what *shall be* the sign of thy ³coming, and of ⁴the end of the world? 4 And Jesus answered and said unto them, Take heed that no man lead you astray. 5 For many

³Gr. *presence.*
⁴Or, *the consummation of the age*

---

destruction, and only when it was found to be impossible did he order the work of destruction to be completed.

3 Tell us, when shall these things be?—As Jesus sat "on the mount of Olives" and predicted the destruction of Jerusalem and the temple, in their great astonishment and confusion, his disciples asked two or three questions. Some interpret them as *three* questions, while others analyze them into two questions. The questions seem to be as follows: "When shall these things be?" And "What shall be the sign of thy coming, and of the end of the world?" Those who see three questions analyze them as follows: "When shall these things be?" "What shall be the sign of thy coming?" and "What shall be the sign of the end of the world?" It seems correct to combine two of these questions into one, and make the inquiry of the sign of his coming and of the end of the world the same. The first question is simple and the second is a compound one. There are three points of inquiry, namely, When shall these things be? What is the sign of thy coming? What is the sign of the end of the world? The three points then are "these things," "thy coming," and "the end of the world." The remainder of chapter twenty-four and chapter twenty-five give Jesus' answer to these questions. We are now to investigate his answer to the questions: When shall the temple be destroyed? What will be the sign of thy coming in glory and the end of the world? It is well to keep these questions in mind and apply the answer of Jesus to each question in order; otherwise confusion will arise and distorted interpretations be given.

4-8 Take heed that no man lead you astray.—Jesus here gives a solemn warning to call attention to what follows; his disciples should have an intense interest in it; they should lay it to heart, as the first question would be answered during

shall come in my name, saying, I am the Christ; and shall lead many astray. 6 And ye shall hear of wars and rumors of wars; see that ye be not troubled: for *these things* must needs come to pass; but the end is not yet. 7 For nation shall rise against nation, and kingdom against kingdom; and there shall be famines and earthquakes in divers places. 8 But all these

their life; they should know when it is fulfilled that Jesus had predicted so minutely the destruction of the temple. Some think that the disciples thought that when Jerusalem would be destroyed would be the end of the world; yet it seems that they had some doubt about this. Jesus' first care was to set them right on this point; hence he warns them that no future false Christ should tempt them to believe that his second advent had arrived. "For many shall come in my name" and claim to be the Christ and "lead many astray." Some have reckoned that there have been fifteen false Messiahs among the Jews from the first to the seventeenth century; hence that prediction has been fulfilled.

And ye shall hear of wars and rumors of wars.—The Roman Empire was composed of many provinces and petty kingdoms; they all composed a discordant government like "iron mixed with miry clay." (Dan. 2: 43.) There were wars and rumors of wars all the time; ambitious men seized the imperial throne one after another and in less than two years four had seized the throne—Nero, Otho, Galba, and Vitellius. The whole empire was continually convulsed before the destruction of Jerusalem. Jesus predicted these troublous times and then added that "these things must needs come to pass; but the end is not yet." The end of the city would not come as a result of these distant wars; trouble must come nearer and more fearful punishments must follow; hence, Jesus proceeds to describe these times by saying, "Nation shall rise against nation, and kingdom against kingdom." Internal strife in the Roman Empire where province, kingdom, and nation shall rise up against each other and cause unrest and disturbance in all parts of the empire. These are the last days of the stable government of Rome. Not only will these wars harass and disturb civilization, but "there shall be famines and earthquakes in divers places." The punishment of God should intervene

things are the beginning of travail. 9 Then shall they deliver you up into tribulation, and shall kill you: and ye shall be hated of all the nations for my name's sake. 10 And then shall many stumble, and shall [5]deliver up one another, and shall hate one another. 11 And many false prophets shall arise,

[5]See ch. 10. 4.

and the heaven should refuse to rain and the parched earth should not yield its increase. In addition to the wars the multiplied horrors which result from famine should come upon them; four famines are mentioned in history during the reign of Claudius; want, starvation, and pestilence came upon the people and made the nation desperate. There were many earthquakes which occurred in the reigns of Claudius and Nero; these earthquakes affected Judea, but the end is not yet, for "all these things are the beginning of travail." The first pangs which foretell the more fearful troubles are here mentioned. Wars and rumors of wars, nations and kingdoms arrayed against each other, famines and earthquakes, are all "the beginning of travail."

9-13 **Then shall they deliver you up.**—Jesus frequently warned his disciples about the persecution which they would be called upon to endure; they are now warned of physical sufferings; they would be called upon to suffer in the propagation of the gospel previous to the downfall of the Jewish nation. And then they would be subjected to all sorts of evil punishment; they would be delivered "up unto tribulation" and evn killed. They were to be "hated of all the nations for my name's sake." The early Christians suffered all of these cruel persecutions. Possibly no people have ever had to suffer more than the Lord's people have suffered for him; he was persecuted and even crucified; his disciples have been persecuted from city to city and have suffered death for the cause of Christ. Jesus foretold his disciples that they would be called upon to thus suffer for him. The calamities predicted by Jesus fell upon the people and Christians were cruelly treated because they were accused of being responsible for calamities which befell the nations. (Matt. 10: 17-19; Acts 3: 4; 7: 59; 12: 2; 16: 23; 18: 12; 24: 26.) Many would be caused to stumble after they were delivered up for persecution; some

and shall lead many astray. 12 And because iniquity shall be multiplied, the love of the many shall wax cold. 13 But he that endureth to the end, the same shall be saved. 14 And ⁶this gospel of the kingdom shall be preached in the ⁷whole world for a testimony unto all the nations; and then shall the end come.

⁶Or, *these good tidings*
⁷Gr. *inhabited earth.*

---

would apostatize in order to escape the bitter persecutions that were heaped upon them; even some of the disciples would betray other disciples and deliver them up to the tormentors. In this way they would "hate one another." (2 Tim. 1: 15; 4: 16.)

And many false prophets shall arise, and shall lead many astray.—There may have been false apostles and teachers. (Acts 8: 9-11; 2 Cor. 11: 13; Gal. 1: 7; 2 Tim. 2: 17, 18; 1 John 4: 1.) There have always been false teachers and pretenders in the church. Not only were there pretenders to knowledge of the future, but also heretical teachers who would arise and deceive the simple. Apostasies and scandals have ever cursed the church; weak and unfaithful members have proved to be enemies of the church. Possibly the worst enemies of the church today are those within the ranks of professed disciples of Jesus. "And because iniquity shall be multiplied, the love of the many shall wax cold." The love of many grows cold when iniquity abounds; the church is in the world and feels the deflective force and influence of the world; the weak ones will yield and apostatize. The blessing is pronounced upon those "that endureth to the end, the same shall be saved." Only those who are faithful to the end will receive the blessings. Christians cannot give up nor become weary in well-doing; they must endure the hardships, suffer the persecutions, and be faithful until death in order to receive the crown of life. (Rev. 2: 10.) Those who endure "shall be saved"—not from the destruction of Jerusalem, but from the condemnation at the judgment.

14 **And this gospel of the kingdom.**—"This gospel," or good tidings of the kingdom, has reference to the kingdom of Dan. 2: 44; the spiritual kingdom of God which was to take the place of the Jewish nation. Before the temporal kingdom

15 When therefore ye see the abomination of desolation, which was

passed away forever the spiritual kingdom must be announced and the tidings of it spread abroad and rooted in the minds of men everywhere. It must "be preached in the whole world for a testimony unto all the nations." The Jewish race was the old stock of Judaism which must be cut off and become the foundation for the spiritual kingdom of God. The gospel was first preached to the Jews, and then to the Gentiles. There was a fulfillment of this as the apostles testified that the good news of Christ had been sent to almost every known country. (Rom. 1: 8; 15: 19, 24-28; Gal. 1: 17; Col. 1: 6, 23.) The kingdom was set up on the day of Pentecost and began to spread until it was permanently established within thirty years after the ascension of Christ. The gospel had been published throughout the Roman world as then known, and every nation had received its testimony before the destruction of Jerusalem. All had an opportunity to know of Christ and his kingdom. After the nations should know of it, "then shall the end come." By Nero's time the Christians had become so numerous at Rome as to raise the jealousy of the government and to elicit a bloody persecution. Clement, the fellow laborer of Paul, says "that that apostle was a preacher both in the east and west—that he taught the whole world righteousness, and went as far as the utmost bounds of the west." How unlikely was the fulfillment of this prediction when it was uttered! How short a time before its fulfillment!

15 **When therefore ye see the abomination.**—Parallel records are found in Mark 13: 14-20 and Luke 21: 20-24. The destruction of Jerusalem is made a type of the destruction of the world, or the wickedness of the world; "abomination of desolation" may be the same as "abominable desolations." The word "abominable" implies in the Hebrew use the sins of idolatry. It may mean here the wickedness of the Roman government in the destruction of Jerusalem and the temple; the Roman army which was an abomination as being pagan, and desolating as being conquering and devastating. Luke describes this desolation and gives the time of it as follows:

spoken of through Daniel the prophet, standing in ⁹the holy place (let him that readeth understand), 16 then let them that are in Judaea flee unto the mountains: 17 let him that is on the housetop not go down to take out the things that are in his house: 18 and let him that is in the field not return

⁸Dan. ix 27; xi. 31; xii. 11.
⁹Or, *a holy place*

"But when ye see Jerusalem compassed with armies, then know that her desolation is at hand." (Luke 21: 20.) The armies referred to are the Roman armies which besieged and destroyed Jerusalem. It is the desolation of which Daniel the prophet predicted. (Dan. 9: 26, 27; 11: 31; 12: 11.) Jerusalem was considered holy and the temple sacred; when the disciples of Jesus should see the Roman eagles about to enter the city, they were to leave it. Those who read the prophecy of Daniel should give careful thought to it and understand that the times and events of the future which had been prophesied were about to be fulfilled in the destruction of the city.

16-22 Then let them that are in Judaea flee.—Those who were in Judea and Jerusalem were to flee when the Roman army invaded that country. Jesus instructed his disciples to flee so that they might escape the terrible punishment that would come upon the Jewish nation. They are told to flee to the mountains. The angels told Lot to flee from Sodom. (Gen. 19: 17.) Armies at that time avoided a rough mountainous country; in the mountains were also natural hiding places; David found such places in his times of peril. (1 Sam. 13: 6; 22: 1; Psalm 11: 1.) The disciples warned by Jesus could flee and escape the destruction that would come upon the Jews. "Let him that is on the housetop not go down." He should not go down to "take out the things that are in his house." Those on the housetop should flee quickly, as they who neglected everything, so that they may save their lives. The houses of Palestine were built with flat roofs, and with a staircase running down into the chief entrance, so that they could leave them without passing into any of the rooms. The roofs were often used for prayer, or in the warm months for sleeping. There was to be no lingering when the announcement was made that the Roman army approached. Those

back to take his cloak. 19 But woe unto them that are with child and to them that give suck in those days! 20 And pray ye that your flight be not in the winter, neither on a sabbath: 21 for then shall be great tribulation, such as hath not been from the beginning of the world until now, no, nor ever shall

---

who were "in the field" should not "return back to take his cloak." Those who were in the field had left off certain garments when they went out to work; they were not to take time to return to the house and get their extra clothing. The Jews laid aside the upper robe when they engaged in labor; but in journeys they always wore it, girding it around their loins. The disciples of Jesus were not to stop to make preparations for the journey, nor linger to take care of property, but must leave all and flee.

But woe unto them that are with child.—This may include both the Jewish and the Christian women; the Jewish women would find their suffering redoubled in their offspring; Christian women would find it difficult to escape and flee in such condition, and would be overtaken in the flight. Mothers with children would find it difficult to escape; both mother and children would likely fall into the hands of the enemy, hence the woe expressed by Jesus at this time. They were to pray that their "flight be not in the winter, neither on a sabbath." The event was certain, yet the circumstances might be mitigated; nothing would now put off the destruction of the city, for the Jewish nation would not repent; hence Christians should pray that the time might be most favorable for them to escape. The winter months were cold and dangerous to such a party of fugitives, made up in part of weak women, invalids, and children. If the flight should have to be made on the Sabbath, the gates of the city would be closed and would hinder their progress in flight. (Neh. 13: 19-22.) Even the Jews might hinder the Christians from escaping as they might wish to impose the law with respect to travel on the Sabbath. A Sabbath day's journey was about five or six furlongs or a little more than half a mile. If this law was enforced, they would not escape the destruction that would be brought upon Jerusalem. Jesus minutely describes the suffering which would come upon the city, "for then shall be great tribulation, such

be. 22 And except those days had been shortened, no flesh would have been saved: for for the elect's sake those days shall be shortened. 23 Then if any

as hath not been from the beginning of the world until now, no, nor ever shall be." These words of Jesus were literally true. Nothing in history parallels the description given by historians in describing the fall of Jerusalem. No misery equaled in degree that which was visited upon the Jew. The famine, pestilence, discord, and madness of their leaders, the loss of faith in everything, the despair of help the fighting and bloodshed within the city and without, the iron crushings of the great serpentlike army which contracted its coils in slow but merciless destruction; the superstitious horrors occasioned by mad prophets and terrified priests—all these and many other things form truly "the bloodiest picture in the book of time." Josephus says, "Our city, of all those subjected to the Romans, was raised to the highest felicity, and was thrust down again to the lowest depth of misery; for if the misfortunes of all from the beginning of the world were compared with those of the Jews, they would appear much inferior on comparison." Only *two events* can be compared with it by the Christian, for only two were acts of divine wrath—the deluge and the overthrow of the cities of the plain. The destruction of Jerusalem was the most dreadful prototype which God has yet laid before the eyes of men of that "certain fearful expectation of judgment, and a fierceness of fire which shall devour the adversaries" at the last day. (Heb. 10: 27.) Hence, when Jesus predicted the destruction of Jerusalem, he blended his description of it with that of his last coming to judge the world.

And except those days had been shortened, no flesh would have been saved.—History records that Titus determined to reduce Jerusalem by famine, a long and destructive mode of conquest, and for this purpose he surrounded it with a wall and ditch. After completing his preparation for this attack on the city, he received news from Rome which urged him to hasten to Rome. He changed his plan and pressed the city by assault, that he might return to Rome, where his presence was

man shall say unto you, Lo, here is the Christ, or, Here; believe ¹*it* not. 24 For there shall arise false Christs, and false prophets, and shall show great signs and wonders; so as to lead astray, if possible, even the elect. 25 Be-

¹Or, him

---

greatly needed; hence, "those days had been shortened." The overruling providence of God shortened these days "for the elect's sake." "The elect" has reference to the Christians who were among the Jews at that time. This elect group were to be preserved in order that the gospel might be handed down to future ages.

23-28 Then if any man shall say unto you.—Again the disciples are warned against false teachers. Some expected the end of the world to follow the destruction of the holy city; they would be looking for Christ to come as soon as the city was destroyed. In this state of expectancy they would be easily deceived. It was necessary to give them this caution that they might not be led away by deceivers; again they needed this caution to keep them from confusing the prophecy of the typical and real end of the world. Jesus would have his disciples possess in patience their souls and wait the issue of events. During such trying times some would say, "Lo, here is the Christ, or, Here; believe it not." Jesus warns them that "false Christs, and false prophets" should arise and seek to deceive them by "great signs and wonders." Jesus frequently warned his disciples against impostors, and especially against those who would arise before and during the siege of Jerusalem. These deceivers would promise great things and would base their pretensions upon the very words of Christ and would make a show or pretense of miracles. The false prophets would be known by pretending that Christ was here or there, that is, not openly showing himself, as Jesus had done, but seeking seclusion and darkness. Their pretended miracles would also be done in the dark and they would lead astray "if possible, even the elect." The disciples who were faithful and true to their profession and practice would not be deceived, because the soundness of mind, of a true creed, and a sincere piety, would save them from deception. (1 Tim. 3: 9.)

hold, I have told you beforehand. 26 If therefore they shall say unto you, Behold, he is in the wilderness; go not forth: Behold, he is in the inner chambers; believe [2]*it not*. 27 For as the lightning cometh forth from the east, and is seen even unto the west; so shall be the [3]coming of the Son of man. 28 Wheresoever the carcase is, there will the [4]eagles be gathered together.

[2]Or, them
[3]Gr. *presence*.
[4]Or, *vultures*

Heresy, pride of opinion, and error of practice render people liable to be blown about by every wind of false doctrine. (Eph. 4: 14 .) When the destruction of the temple should come, "false Christs" would appear and claim with great energy that they were the promised Messiahs. Every genuine has its counterfeit. There are false gods, false Christs, false spirits, false apostles, false prophets, false teachers, false doctrines, and false churches; God's people must be on the alert and not be deceived by any of them.

Jesus points out the arts of deceivers in advance; Josephus tells us "that many impostors and magicians persuaded the people to follow them to the desert, where they promised to show them signs and wonders done of God." These deceivers would pretend that Christ had come, but that he had concealed himself in some place for caution against the Romans until the moment of deliverance come. During the siege of the city a false prophet persuaded the people to the number of six thousand to go the temple and behold signs of deliverance; they all perished. Jesus adds that "as the lightning cometh forth from the east, and is seen even unto the west; so shall be the coming of the Son of man." The lightning needs no one to herald it, but is in an instant of time visible throughout the whole world, even to those who are sitting in their chambers, so the coming of Christ shall be seen everywhere at once, because of the brightness of his glory. The rapidity and destruction of the Roman armies were types of his final coming. As the people would know the presence of the Roman army at the destruction of Jerusalem, so they would know the appearance of Christ when he comes; it will be sudden and momentary, but certain, and those false prophets would be rebuked for their deception. "Wheresoever the carcase is, there

29 But immediately after the tribulation of those days the sun shall be darkened, and the moon shall not give her light, and the stars shall fall from

will the eagles be gathered together." Probably this is an allusion to Deut. 28: 49. Where the body of an animal falls, however secret the spot or desert the place, there were the eagles to be found scenting it from afar. It is claimed that eagles do not feed on dead bodies; this is true, but the Jews and Greeks made no distinction between the word "eagle" which included the entire species of birds of prey, which included vultures. Some think that the griffon vulture is meant which surpasses the eagle in size and power. Aristotle notes how this bird scents its prey from afar, and congregates in the wake of an army. This seems to refer to the false Christs and false prophets, as there is nothing in the three verses next preceding this which can be represented by a carcass or by vultures flocking to it. Some think that the carcass is the decaying Jewish nation, and the eagles or vultures are the false Christs and false prophets who would flock together and prey upon the sufferings and fears of the people.

[Many persons, impostors and self-deceived, aspire to fill the places of persons of honor. Many did come claiming to be Christ. There is still a constant stream of men claiming to be God's chosen servants leading multitudes into sin and infidelity with pretended claims.]

29-31 **But immediately after the tribulation.**—Immediately after the terrible events just described as accompanying the destruction of Jerusalem certain things should follow. This verse and those immediately following it have given commentators much trouble. The great questions are (1) whether they can be legitimately applied to the first coming of Jesus in the destruction of Jerusalem, or (2) whether they refer to his second coming and final judgment. The inquiry is simply whether these catastrophes should immediately follow the destruction of Jerusalem or should follow the second coming of Jesus at the end of the Christian dispensation. To prove the first is to disprove the second, at least in the sense of a primary and exclusive reference. The figures and symbols used

heaven, and the powers of the heavens shall be shaken: 30 and then shall appear the sign of the Son of man in heaven: and then shall all the tribes of the earth mourn, and they shall see the Son of man coming on the clouds of heaven with power and great glory. 31 And he shall send forth his angels [5]with [6]a great sound of a trumpet, and they shall gather together his elect

[5]Many ancient authorities read *with a great trumpet, and they shall gather &c.*
[6]Or, *a trumpet of great sound*

---

here are put more strongly by Matthew than by Mark (13: 24-27) and Luke (21: 25-27). If Matthew and Mark had said only what Luke has and nothing more difficult of reference to the coming of the destruction of Jerusalem, little difficulty would be had in referring the whole passage to the destruction of Jerusalem. However, Luke clearly seems to refer the whole scene to "the Son of man coming in a cloud with power and great glory." (Luke 21: 27.) This would refer the scene to the final and personal return of Jesus. Obviously then Jesus describes the visible phenomena of the heaven as the visible appearance of Christ at the judgment. These verses form a part of the scene recorded in Matt. 25: 31-46. There seem to be at least six particular events embraced here. The visible firmamental convulsions, the sign of Christ's coming, the visible Judge, the consequent wailing of the tribes of earth, the angels with the trumpet sound, and the gathering of the elect. None of these things took place at the destruction of Jerusalem. In the first class Jesus mentions that the "sun shall be darkened," "the moon shall not give her light," "stars shall fall from heaven," and "the powers of the heavens shall be shaken." After these catastrophes "the sign of the Son of man in heaven" shall be seen, and then "the tribes of the earth mourn." The angels will appear "with a great sound of a trumpet" and shall call together "his elect from the four winds, from one end of heaven to the other." The Old Testament frequently spoke of the sun, moon, and stars being darkened and used them as symbols. (Isa. 13: 10; Joel 2: 10.) Peter gives a vivid description of these things. (2 Pet. 3: 10. See also Heb. 1: 12 and Rev. 20: 11.) The disappearance of the visible heavens and earth shall occur so that something entirely different may appear. "The sign of the Son of man" is not the sign of something preceding the coming of Christ,

from the four winds, from one end of heaven to the other.

but is the appearing of Christ. In the great harvest at the last day the angels will gather first the saints of God together. (Matt. 13: 39; 2 Thess. 1: 7.) The summons for the saints to come together will be made "with the voice of the archangel, and with the trump of God." (1 Thess. 4: 16.) It was the custom to assemble the children of Israel by the trumpet sound. (Ex. 19: 16; Num. 10: 10.) The beginning of the new year among the Jews was celebrated with a great convocation which was assembled by the sound of the trumpet. (Lev. 23: 24, 25.) "From the four winds" means from every quarter of the globe. (Isa. 43: 5, 6; Ezek. 27: 9.) This was an ancient mode of describing the entire globe, which was held to consist of four quarters, corresponding to the four points of the compass, from which the four winds were called.

8. LESSON FROM THE FIG TREE; FAITHFUL AND UNFAITHFUL SERVANTS
24: 32-51

32 Now from the fig tree learn her parable: when her branch is now become tender, and putteth forth its leaves, ye know that the summer is

32-35 **Now from the fig tree learn her parable.**—There is an analogy which Jesus teaches from the fig tree; the disciples were to learn a truth from the fig tree which would help them understand his teaching. The fig tree is a native product of Palestine; in a warm climate fruit forms a very large portion of the customary food, and hence the fruit tree is a favorite source of illustrations. Jesus spoke this on the Mount of Olives where fig trees were growing all around him; he was near Bethphage, which means house of figs. They knew that summer was nigh by the putting forth of the leaves of the fig tree, as we say that "robins are the harbingers of spring." "Even so ye also, when ye see all these things, know ye that he is nigh, even at the doors." As the swelling buds and leaves of the fig tree indicate the near approach of summer, so when Je-

nigh; 33 even so ye also, when ye see all these things, know ye that ⁷he is nigh, *even* at the doors. 34 Verily I say unto you, This generation shall not pass away, till all these things be accomplished. 35 Heaven and earth shall pass away, but my words shall not pass away. 36 But of that day and hour knoweth no one, not even the angels of heaven, ⁸neither the Son, but the

---
⁷Or, *it*
⁸Many authorities, some ancient, omit *neither the Son*.

---

rusalem is destroyed you may know that God's judgment is sure and swift and will be as certain in the last day. This destruction would come upon Jerusalem during the lifetime of some who were present before that generation passes away. This means that there would be some people living who would see the awful destruction pronounced against Jerusalem; this destruction is a type of the destruction of the final incorrigible wicked. Often prophetic language has a double significance. Jehovah told Adam that he would die in the day that he ate the forbidden fruit (Gen. 2: 7); yet Adam lived 930 years. There was a primary fulfillment of this when Adam was separated from the Garden of Eden, and a secondary fulfillment of it in his death (Rom. 5: 12), Isaiah foretold the birth of Jesus from a virgin, yet added a prophecy which confines it to his own generation. (Isa. 7: 14-17.) The prophet combined type and antitype in the same words. David spoke of the Messiah under the type of Solomon. Words and events, new kingdoms and dynasties, are the prophetic alphabet for spelling out the divine plan; so the destruction of Jerusalem becomes the type of the final judgment and destruction. Sometimes it is difficult to take the language of Jesus and apply it to both the type and antitype. God's word is sure and those things which seem to be changeless and eternal will fail, but not one word of what Jesus told would fail of accomplishment.

36 But of that day and hour knoweth no one.—Mark 13: 32 denies the knowledge of that day and hour to any man—to the angels in heaven, and to the Son; he restricts a knowledge of it to the Father. It seems clear that Jesus here speaks of his second coming. Of the exact season and year of this, it is not a part of the divine plan that any man should be informed; certainty as to the date would nullify the whole effect of the

Father only. 37 And as *were* the days of Noah, so shall be the ³coming of the Son of man. 38 For as in those days which were before the flood they were eating and drinking, marrying and giving in marriage, until the day that Noah entered into the ark, 39 and they knew not until the flood came, and took them all away; so shall be the ³coming of the Son of man.

prophecy, since the great lesson drawn from it was "watch and pray." If Jesus had told them that forty years from that time on such a day he would come, they would have been inclined to be indolent and unfaithful and unwatchful. The uncertainty of the time leads us to watch and pray. All schemes which attempt to fix the exact date of the coming of Christ are foolish and deceptive. (2 Thess. 2: 2.) Jesus did not want his disciples to misunderstand him, hence he has stated that no one knows of the time when he will return, hence no one has any right to fix a time for his coming. It is certain that he will return, but no one can go further with respect to his coming than to declare that he will return.

37-41 **And as were the days of Noah.**—Jesus here gives another caution; the world would go on in all its business, sins, pleasures, even as in the days of Noah. Noah warned the people before the flood, but they continued in all of the commerces of their civilization—socially, morally, and economically; they gave no heed to his warnings; they were eating and drinking and marrying up to the very time "that Noah entered into the ark" and the destruction of the flood came upon them "and took them all away" while they were still engaged in the common affairs of their wicked lives. Jesus makes his own comparison; he says "so shall be the coming of the Son of man." The people of Noah's day ridiculed the idea of a flood; those of Jerusalem ridiculed the idea of the destruction of their holy city; in like manner sinful people will be filled with cares and pleasures of the world at the time that Jesus comes. The archangels' trump strangely in the revelry of the bridal feast, the crash and conflict of the battle in war, the hum and whir of the factory, the confusing noises of the city life, and the ceaseless roar of the restless seas will sound strange to the unbeliever.

40 Then shall two men be in the field; one is taken, and one is left; 41 two women *shall be* grinding at the mill; one is taken, and one is left. 42 Watch therefore: for ye know not on what day your Lord cometh. 43 ⁹But know this, that if the master of the house had known in what watch the thief was

⁹Or, *But this ye know*

Then shall two men be in the field; one is taken, and one is left.—Companions in the field and in the affairs of life will be separated; the angels that gather the redeemed will take one and leave the other. Here Jesus emphasizes the unexpected and sudden return to earth; this comparison enforces the one about Noah. Again "two women shall be grinding at the mill; one is taken, and one is left." The grinding was done then by hand mills, and was usually done by women as they prepared the food or baked the bread. It is not very laborious to grind the meal and was an indoor work. The mills were made of two circular stones which turn on a fixed center; the lower one is stationary, the upper revolves upon it, crushing the grain between the rough surfaces. Two women at one mill are very near to each other, and grasp the handle of the millstone together. The closest ties and occupations of two friends walking together, two of a family preparing the daily meal, shall be broken suddenly and forever. Again Jesus emphasizes the suddenness of the destruction of Jerusalem and of his second coming and the judgment.

42-44 **Watch therefore.**—Here Jesus gives his own conclusion; these words are the moral or practical inference of the entire discourse. The disciple who would be saved, in view of all these facts which must come to pass, must "watch"; Christians must act the part of sentinels in a night guard, or be stewards who get all things ready for the Master's coming; or must be as the bride who desires not to be be made ashamed at the coming of the bridegroom. Christians must not be like the world in the time of the flood, slumbering and revelling; they must watch, for they know not the hour when Jesus will return. Jesus gives the illustration of the master of the house. "If the master of the house had known in what watch the thief was coming, he would have watched" and would have been ready for the thief and saved his household

coming, he would have watched, and would not have suffered his house to be [10]broken through. 44 Therefore be ye also ready; for in an hour that ye think not the Son of man cometh. 45 Who then is the faithful and wise [11]servant, which his lord hath set over his household, to give them their food in due season? 46 Blessed is

[10]Gr. *digged through.*
[11]Gr. *bondservant.*

affairs. The thief comes without warning, in the dead hours of the night, silently, fearful, and dangerous; the Christ will come in an instant, to wake the soul to the tremendous truths of an eternal world. This figure is used frequently in the New Testament. (1 Thess. 5: 2; 2 Pet. 3: 10; Rev. 3: 3; 16: 15.) Only those who take the same care of their souls, which a master of a family would take for his household goods, will be prepared for the coming of Christ. "In what watch" means in what division of the night; the night was divided into four quarters. Oftentimes thieves would dig through the walls of the house and carry away their loot. Again Jesus draws his own conclusion and makes application to his disciples; they are to be ready when he comes, and since they do not know when he is coming, they are to live in a state of readiness or watchfulness. The comparison between the coming of Christ and that of a thief is the more impressive from the dissimilarity between the two characters.

45-51 Who then is the faithful and wise servant?—Again Jesus uses another illustration or parable. The master of a household and servants are frequently used by Jesus. In this instance Jesus changes the image from a householder watching for a thief to a servant waiting for his master. Servants had specific duties assigned to them; it was the duty of certain servants to provide the food and have it ready at mealtime or "in due season." The servant that is faithful and has all things ready for the master when he comes receives the commendation and blessings of his master. The Bible speaks of a number of faithful servants. There was Eliezer, Abraham's faithful slave (Gen. 15: 2; 24: 2); also Joseph in Potiphar's house as a slave; Daniel in Babylonian captivity; and Onesimus. The faithful servant is honored and blessed by his master. In like manner he will be rewarded for his faithful-

that ¹¹servant, whom his lord when he cometh shall find so doing. 47 Verily I say unto you, that he will set him over all that he hath. 48 But if that evil ¹¹servant shall say in his heart, My lord tarrieth; 49 and shall begin to beat his fellow-servants, and shall eat and drink with the drunken; 50 the lord of that ¹servant shall come in a day when he expecteth not, and in an hour when he knoweth not, 51 and shall ²cut him asunder, and appoint his portion with the hypocrites: there shall be the weeping and the gnashing of teeth.

¹Gr. *bondservant.*
²O , *severely scourge him*

ness when the master comes, but the unfaithful and evil servant will be punished. The wicked servant seeks to take advantage of the absence of his master. He not only neglected the tasks assigned to him in the absence of his master, but he abused his fellow servants and lived a riotous drunken life. Such a one deserves the severest punishment of the master. His master will come at a time that he is least expecting him and will know of his wickedness. He will "cut him asunder, and appoint his portion with the hypocrites." "Cut asunder" is a common mode of punishment in that country. (1 Sam. 15: 33; 2 Sam. 12: 31; Dan. 2: 5; 3: 28; Heb. 11: 37.) His portion will be among the hypocrites and there shall be "weeping and the gnashing of teeth." His portion belongs with the hypocrites as he belongs to that class. The entire description throughout these verses applies most fitly to the suddenness and to all the results that follow the destruction of Jerusalem and the coming of Christ. "Weeping and the gnashing of teeth" is a phrase often used to denote the bitterest agony and convulsions of pain and rage; the bitterest sting of the punishment is that he brought it upon himself.

9. THE TEN VIRGINS; PARABLE OF THE TALENTS; THE JUDGMENT
25: 1-46

1 Then shall the kingdom of heaven be likened unto ten virgins, who took their ³lamps, and went forth to meet the bridegroom. 2 And five of them

³Or, *torches*

1-13 Then shall the kingdom of heaven be likened.—Jesus is still on the Mount of Olives on the way to Bethany; this is a continuation of the discourse to his disciples recorded in chap-

were foolish, and five were wise. 3 For the foolish, when they took their ³lamps, took no oil with them: 4 but the wise took oil in their vessels with their ³lamps. 5 Now while the bridegroom tarried, they all slumbered and slept. 6 But at midnight there is a cry, Behold, the bridegroom! Come ye

---

ter twenty-four; we are still in the last week of his earthly ministry. "Then" is a significant word in this connection; it has reference to the time of Jesus' sudden coming; he no further predicts the destruction of Jerusalem, but directs attention far beyond to his second coming and the final judgment. In that solemn, decisive hour, there will be a scene in the earthly life and destiny of all the disciples of Jesus, which is well illustrated by the parable of the ten virgins. These scenes pertain to "the kingdom of heaven," a phrase frequently used by Matthew; they point to the rewards of that kingdom. The disciples had asked Jesus about his coming and now in some particular it will be like virgins waiting at night for the coming of the bridegroom to receive the bride.

Ten virgins.—There is no significance in the number "ten"; some have thought that this number is taken to represent the five senses, in which one class of five is prepared, and the other class of five unprepared; again some have conjectured that the number ten is taken because ten were required as the least number to form a synagogue. There are two classes of virgins represented in the parable. The Jewish marriages and feasts which followed them were celebrated at night; the newly married couple went from the house of the bride in procession after nightfall accompanied by attendants bearing torches to light the way; another party went forth to meet them with torches and accompanied them to the house of the bridegroom where a feast was prepared. "Lamps" were made then like torches; they were made by wrapping up a roll of linen and inserting it in a mould of copper or earthenware fixed to a handle of wood. It contained very little oil, and the linen from time to time had to be supplied with fresh oil from another vessel which was carried in the other hand. In this parable the bridegroom, accompanied by his friends ("the sons of the bridechamber"), went at night to the residence of his bride and brought her with pomp and gladness to his own

forth to meet him. 7 Then all those virgins arose, and trimmed their ³lamps. 8 And the foolish said unto the wise, Give us of your oil; for our ³lamps are going out. 9 But the wise answered, saying, Peradventure there will not be enough for us and you: go ye rather to them that sell, and buy for yourselves. 10 And while they went away to buy, the bridegroom came; and they that were ready went in with him to the marriage feast: and the door was shut. 11 Afterward came also the other virgins, saying, Lord, Lord,

---

home. She was accompanied by her young companions; at some point on the way another group of virgins were waiting to join the procession and to share in the joyous festivities. This waiting involved the watching and the preparation with their burning lamps. They all took their lamps, but five took an extra supply of oil, and the other five took no extra supply. While the bridegroom tarried, "they all slumbered and slept"; that is, all nodded and slept; they did not retire for sleep. At midnight it was announced that the bridegroom approached, and no one expected him then, for "all" were sleeping; the five wise virgins were ready to join the procession, but the foolish ones were in no way ready; they slept while their hour of preparation was passing.

Then all those virgins arose, and trimmed their lamps.—The lamps were trimmed by removing the incrustations of the wicks and supplying fresh oil. The foolish virgins asked the others to supply them with oil as their lamps were "going out"; but the wise ones refused because they did not have a sufficient supply for themselves and others, and suggested that they go and purchase sufficient oil for their lamps. The foolish virgins went away to buy, and the procession of the bridegroom came and passed on before the five foolish returned with a supply of oil. The bridegroom went into his house, and those who were prepared and present went in with him, "and the door was shut." A little later the five foolish virgins came and asked to be admitted, but received the answer, "I know you not." They were not admitted. There was no more admission after the doors were shut. "I know you not" is an emphatic manner of sealing the condemnation of the foolish virgins. They had not cared enough for the feast to make the customary preparation, and now the bridegroom expressed his ignorance of them. They had lost the

open to us. 12 But he answered and said, Verily I say unto you, I know you not. 13 Watch therefore, for ye know not the day nor the hour.
14 For *it is as when* a man, going into another country, called his own

happiness of his feast. Those who do not know Christ here he will not know hereafter; to be unknown by him is to be cast away from him. There are abundant opportunities and pressing invitations to enter the kingdom, but there comes a time when it is too late to enter. We shut the door against ourselves by neglecting to be prepared to enter. Jesus draws his own conclusion and says, "Watch therefore, for ye know not the day nor the hour." Christians are like the virgins waiting for Christ's return in a long night of uncertainty; of the hour of that event they can know nothing, therefore they must be ready for it at all times. We watch by serving the Lord as faithfully as if he were looking upon us; we watch by being on our guard against every temptation and danger. Watchfulness is a state of readiness. The warning to watch bids us to imitate the five wise virgins and to take warning from the fate of the five foolish ones.

[There are always one or two points in a parable that illustrate the truth to be taught. When more than is intended to be illustrated by it is brought out, falsehood and not truth is taught. The concluding exhortation of this parable shows clearly the lesson is that those professing to be his disciples should be watchful, waiting, ready to receive him when he comes, not to wait till his coming to make ready. While they are making ready to enter into his eternal kingdom with those prepared and ready and enjoy the rich blessings prepared for them, the others who have waited till his coming will be refused an entrance. "I know you not"—never approved you. If a man teaches anything else than this, it only shows how men will twist and torture and pervert the word of God to support a theory of their own. It shows they are much more zealous in maintaining their theories than they are of the integrity of the word of God and his teaching.]

14-30 **For it is as when a man.**—The parable of the ten virgins emphasizes the importance of watchfulness for the com-

⁴servants, and delivered unto them his goods. 15 And unto one he gave five talents, to another two, to another one; to each according to his several ability; and he went on his journey. 16 Straightway he that received the five talents went and traded with them, and made other five talents. 17 In like manner he also that *received* the two gained other two. 18 But he that re-

⁴Gr. *bondservants.*

---

ing of Christ and preparation for the judgment; the parable of the talents teaches the duty of working during the time of watchfulness. "For the kingdom of heaven is as when a man, going into another country"; the phrase "kingdom of heaven" is omitted as it is not in the original. The obvious meaning is that "the kingdom of heaven" is like this man who went into another country and committed his goods unto his servants. The parable of the ten virgins was introduced with the comparison of "the kingdom of heaven," and this parable institutes a comparison between this man and the kingdom of heaven. The future history of the church is sketched in the similitude here presented. A certain master going into another country to be gone for some time called three of his servants to him and divided his goods into certain portions and committed them to the servants according to their several abilities. He gave to them different trusts called "talents" according to their abilities; he dealt righteously with them in that he did not impose upon one that which he was unable to do. These servants were "his own servants," not "hired servants"; hence, he had the right to impose upon them certain responsibilities, and knowing their ability, he gave to each that which could be handled. To one was committed "five talents," and to the second "two talents," and to the third only "one talent." A talent in silver was valued at about $1,500. The value of these talents is not known. The word "talent" has acquired in our language the meaning of abilities; it may now mean the powers of mind or degree of intelligence but did not have such meaning in the days of our Savior; some think that it has acquired its modern meaning from this parable.

After delivering to each servant these talents, the master left them in full possession of the trusts which had been com-

ceived the one went away and digged in the earth, and hid his lord's money. 19 Now after a long time the lord of those ⁴servants cometh, and maketh a reckoning with them. 20 And he that received the five talents came and brought other five talents, saying, Lord, thou deliveredst unto me five talents: lo, I have gained other five talents. 21 His lord said unto him, Well done, good and faithful ¹servant: thou hast been faithful over a few things, I will set thee over many things; enter thou into the joy of thy lord. 22 And he also that *received* the two talents came and said, Lord, thou deliveredst unto me two talents: lo, I have gained other two talents. 23 His lord said

mitted to them. The first servant to whom was instrusted five talents began active service and used the talents in such a way as to bring great gain to his master. The "goods" which were placed in their hands represented his property and was of such a nature that could be traded and gain be had. Likewise the servant who was intrusted with "two talents" used them and gained two other talents. The first and second servants doubled their capital. The third servant who received only one talent did not use his talent; he did not exercise the ability that he had, did not take advantage of his opportunity, and failed to gain anything. He "digged in the earth, and hid his lord's money." He was honest in that he did not squander his master's goods and desired to restore to his master that which was committed to him.

Now after a long time the lord of these servants cometh.— The master returned and the day of reckoning was at hand "after a long time" indicates the uncertainty of the time of our Lord's coming; the master had been away for a long time and the servants had ceased to think of his coming as they did at first, and had settled down into their usual habits. The disposition that we made of the talents by each servant reveals the kind of character each was. The one with the greatest ability came first and rendered an account of his stewardship. He reminded his lord that he had been intrusted with five talents and that he had "gained other five talents." His lord pronounced a blessing upon him, called him "good and faithful servant," and promised to appoint him over many things; he had showed a disposition to work for the interest of his master; he had displayed good judgment and had brought great gain to his master, and henceforth he could occupy a higher position with larger opportunities for service, and at the same time he

unto him, Well done, good and faithful ¹servant: thou hast been faithful over a few things, I will set thee over many things; enter thou into the joy of thy lord. 24 And he also that had received the one talent came and said, Lord, I knew thee that thou art a hard man, reaping where thou didst not sow, and gathering where thou didst not scatter; 25 and I was afraid, and went away and hid thy talent in the earth: lo, thou hast thine own. 26 But his lord answered and said unto him, Thou wicked and slothful ¹servant, thou knew-

could come into fuller joys with his master. It was customary with eastern monarchies to have some of their satraps and other officers of provinces to reside at the courts of the kings; it was a great honor to be invited to live with the king. David bestowed such honor upon Jonathan's son.

The servant to whom had been intrusted two talents came and rendered an account of his stewardship; he had used the two talents and had doubled his capital. He reported the gain that he had made. The master was pleased with his services and pronounced upon him the same blessing that he had upon the first, and extended to him the same privileges that he had to the first one. Each servant was intrusted with that which he had ability to use, and each had used to his full ability the talents for the gain of the master; each had done his best, and the master made no distinction between the honors bestowed upon them. The third servant came to render an account of his stewardship. It seems that he had lingered until the last; the one who had gained so much was ready to give an account with joy; the one with less ability who had been faithful also came with joy and rendered his account; but the one who had done nothing for his master waited until the last. He had despised the small trust committed to him, and now comes the answer for his neglect. He began to make excuse, but his excuses were in vain. The master had a right to look for as much faithfulness in this servant with one talent as he did in the one who had five. God looks for as much fidelity in his children today who have but little talent as he does in those who have much.

The third servant, in rendering his account, began to accuse and abuse his master. He said, "I know thee that thou art a hard man, reaping where thou didst not sow, and gathering

est that I reap where I sowed not, and gather where I did not scatter; 27 thou oughtest therefore to have put my money to the bankers, and at my coming I should have received back mine own with interest. 28. Take ye away therefore the talent from him, and give it unto him that hath the ten talents. 29 For unto every one that hath shall be given, and he shall have abundance:

---

where thou didst not scatter." He knew his master to be severe and a man who rigidly exacted all that was his own. He uses the figure of a threshing floor; the grain and chaff, after the oxen had trodden them into a confused mass, were winnowed by a wooden shovel called a fan. This servant said that his master was one who expected the grain where he had not taken the trouble of the harvesting and the threshing floor. He further stated that he was afraid "and went away and hid" the talent in the earth; he then presented to his master that which had been committed to his trust. We note here the self-flattering excuse which this servant made; he appears to be overhonest in his effort to appear honest. He was selfish; he would do no labor except on conditions; again his faults insulting reflection on the character of his master, did not justify his failure to work to the interest of his master. This type of humanity is all too common; the churl thinks his master is churlish. We attribute to others what we find in ourselves. Very few people excuse their own sin without blaming God or someone else for it. He gave back all that he had received; he had done no harm, but he had done no good with that which was intrusted to him. He had been in possession of his master's money for "a long time"; if he had been a free man, he would have owed interest on it; but he had been to slothful to use the talent to any gain for his master. His master had really lost by the indolence of this servant.

After the account rendered by this slothful servant, his master began to reckon with him. The reckoning day always comes. He calls him a "wicked and slothful servant"; he was wicked as the insult and churlishness of his excuse showed; he was slothful and stupid with respect to the use of that which belongs to others. "Wicked and slothful" is the opposite of "good and faithful." The master echoes the language

but from him that hath not, even that which he hath shall be taken away. 30 And cast ye out the unprofitable ¹servant into the outer darkness: there shall be the weeping and the gnashing of teeth.

of the servant in order to condemn him on his own grounds; he did not admit that he was the kind of a master that the servant accused him of being; but since the servant accused him of being such a master, he would deal with him as he had accused him of being. He then tells the servant what he should have done with the talent, even if he believed his master to be what he had accused him of being; that he should have put the money to the bankers so that he would have received some interest. It was not lawful to loan money to a fellow Israelite on interest, but could be done to Gentiles. There was a way in which he could have used his master's money to an advantage. (Ex. 22: 25; Lev. 15: 36; Deut. 23: 19, 20.) After reprimanding the "wicked and slothful servant," the master pronounced the sentence upon him. As he had pronounced blessings upon the other two and had bestowed honor upon them for their faithfulness, so now he pronounces a curse upon this servant and assigns him to a place of dishonor. He said, "Take ye away therefore the talent from him, and give it unto him that hath the ten talents." The master then teaches that "unto every one that hath shall be given, and he shall have abundance: but from him that hath not, even that which he hath shall be taken away." The meaning is that to those who have for their labor and fidelity a profit shall have an increase of gifts; more shall be given; but from such as have not, because they have not used what they had, shall be taken away. The opportunity of using the talent and even the talent itself shall be taken from him. This is a general truth; the more one has and uses faithfully, the more that one will receive; and that which one has, if not used faithfully, shall be taken from him. This is illustrated with the men of five talents and two talents and also the man with the one buried talent. The unprofitable servant was cast out "into the outer darkness"; Jesus then adds again the statement, "there shall be the weeping and the gnashing of teeth." "The outer darkness" into which this unprofitable servant was cast is put in contrast with "the joy of thy lord" into which the faithful servants entered.

The meaning of the parable is clear and emphatic; the lord of the servants is Christ whose coming is the subject under consideration. The servants are his own disciples to whom he has intrusted his gospel, his church, and the worship of the church. The conduct of the two faithful servants emphasizes the way in which we are to "watch" as commanded in verse thirteen; the conduct of the slothful servant points out the way that many do in failing to watch. The reckoning with the servants is like the final judgment which takes place when Christ comes again.

[The talents bestowed on the servant by God are his mental ability, his money, his bodily strength, his time, and any opportunity he possesses. The demand is any or all of these shall be used in the service of God. The servants with the five and two talents are those who with differing ability faithfully used their means, time, and opportunities in the service of God. The slothful servant is he who devotes his time, talent, and opportunities to forwarding his own selfish ends and purposes, and fails to work to serve God. All these classes are of those claiming to be servants of God. The rewards of the faithful servants and the punishment of the wicked servant foretoken the fate of those different classes of the professed servants of God. Now with these plain statements of God's dealing with the different classes of his servants, how can any man who spends his time, his talent, his capabilities, and his means for the advancement of his own ends and purposes, and does almost nothing for the service of God, hope for his blessing? He who does not honor God with his time, his ability, and means must be cast "into the outer darkness" where there is "weeping and the gnashing of teeth." It must be thus, or Jesus bore false testimony.

Jesus delivers his truths to men according to their several abilities. All men do not have the same capacity to understand and use the truths God has revealed to men. According

31 But when the Son of man shall come in his glory, and all the angels with him, then shall he sit on the throne of his glory: 32 and before him

to their capacity to understand and use, he holds them accountable for returns to them. In appropriating these truths to our own hearts we fit ourselves to use them for the good of others.]

31-33 But when the Son of man shall come in his glory.— Here we have a picture of the final judgment. In chapter 24: 19-31, an introduction is given of the judgment day; other teachings have intervened and now Jesus continued the description which had already been introduced. We do not call this description "a parable"; in the preceding parables the likeness or parabolic similarity is expressly declared, but here the context shows that Jesus is simply giving a vivid description of the final judgment. This judgment is to take place "when the Son of man shall come in his glory." The Judge of all is "the Son of man"; this Son of man is also the Son of God. "The Judge of all the earth" is Jehovah. (Gen. 18: 25; Acts 10: 42; 2 Tim. 4: 1.) "In his glory" means in all the majesty of his nature as the Son of God. He laid aside the glory of heaven when he came to earth and took upon himself the form of man. (Phil. 2: 6, 7.) He delivered the law of God to man and established his kingdom and will come with that glory which befits his regal authority and splendor. "The angels with him"; that is, the angels that belong to him and which attended him while on earth. "The throne of his glory" simply means "his glorious throne." The scenery of the judgment will be of such a kind as to fill the minds of men with an awful sense of divine power. A great white throne will be in the midst of the assembled nations and the Judge will sit upon this throne. (2 Pet. 3: 10-12; Rev. 20: 11-15.) Jesus will be clothed with both judicial and regal authorities. The throne is the seat and source of sovereign power. It is called "white throne" as it is immaculately pure in its government and decision. So terrible will that day be that from the Judge's face the earth and the heavens will flee away. (Rev. 20: 11.)

shall be gathered all the nations: and he shall separate them one from another, as the shepherd separateth the sheep from the goats; 33 and he shall set the sheep on his right hand, but the goats on the left. 34 Then shall the King say unto them on his right hand, Come, ye blessed of my Father, in-

And before him shall be gathered all the nations.—"All the nations" is equivalent to "the whole human race"; not only those who shall be alive at his coming, but all who have ever lived are embraced within the scope of the term "all the nations." No one will escape the judgment of God.

He shall separate them one from another, as the shepherd separateth the sheep from the goats.—The figure of the shepherd is introduced here to make the scene impressive and clear; in the language of the East, sheep were emblems of good men, because of their gentle and innocent ways; the goats of bad men, from their wildness and repulsive habits. (Psalm 100: 3; Zech. 10: 3.) "On his right hand, on the left hand," means places of honor and condemnation. It was the custom of the Sanhedrin, the Jewish high court, to place the guilty person on the left hand of the judges, and the innocent on the right. The right hand was considered the place of honor. (Psalm 45: 9.) The two classes are represented here by sheep and goats; it is the same classification as that of the just and of the unjust (Acts 24: 15), and the same as those that enter into life and into damnation (John 5: 29). The only point emphasized here is the similarity of the separation of the sheep and goats by the shepherd and the separation of the righteous and wicked by the great Judge.

34-40 **Then shall the King say.**—The Christ is the King, and he will say to those who are on "his right hand, Come, ye blessed of my Father." Heaven is a free gift, bestowed by the Father on those who have been faithful to his Son. They are to "inherit the kingdom prepared" for them "from the foundation of the world." There is running through the entire Bible the thought that God will save his faithful people, those who have obeyed him; they are promised remission of sins, salvation, and if faithful unto death, a crown of righteousness, or eternal salvation. (Rev. 2: 10.) At the judgment Jesus will show his triumph and royal power by rewarding to his faith-

herit the kingdom prepared for you from the foundation of the world: 35 for I was hungry, and ye gave me to eat; I was thirsty, and ye gave me drink; I was a stranger, and ye took me in; 36 naked, and ye clothed me; I was sick, and ye visited me; I was in prison, and ye came unto me. 37 Then shall the righteous answer him, saying, Lord, when saw we thee hungry,

ful disciples the eternal blessings of his kingdom, which may be summed up in the term, "heaven." This kingdom was "prepared" "from the foundation of the world." It had been prepared for just such faithful servants of God as are represented here by the sheep. It was no new plan, no secret decree, no arbitrary election, but the one constant covenant condition of mercy that had extended from the creation of man to the judgment of God at the last day.

Next Jesus assigns the reason for extending these eternal blessings. He says that he had been hungry, thirsty, a stranger, naked, sick, and a prisoner, and that they had fed him, given him drink, taken him in, clothed him, visited him, and came unto him in prison. These six conditions represent all of the conditions in which God's people may be today, that is, the total number of physical conditions. Ministering to them are acts of mercy; they do not represent single acts, but the habits or customary life of those who ministered and who continued such lives unto death; they imply a life of charity, the "faith working through love." (1 Cor. 13: 1-13; Gal. 5: 6.) They had lived by a faith that worked. (James 2: 14.) These acts were done in the name of Christ. "A stranger" was one who was a foreigner and needed hospitality; "naked" was to be destitute of raiment. (Luke 10: 30.) Those who had lived such lives asked the question when they had seen Christ in such conditions and had ministered unto him. They did not ask the question because they distrusted Christ's words, but they were in amazement at so great exultation at the greatness of their own glory for what little they had done while on earth. "For I reckon that the sufferings of this present time are not worthy to be compared with the glory which shall be revealed to us-ward." (Rom. 8: 18.) The great Judge and King then will answer by saying, "Inasmuch as ye did it unto one of these my brethren, even these least, ye did it unto me."

and fed thee? or athirst, and gave thee drink? 38 And when saw we thee a stranger, and took thee in? or naked, and clothed thee? 39 And when saw we thee sick, or in prison, and came unto thee? 40 And the King shall answer and say unto them, Verily I say unto you, Inasmuch as ye did it unto one of these my brethren, *even* these least, ye did it unto me. 41 Then shall he say also unto them on the left hand, ¹Depart from me, ye cursed, into the eternal fire which is prepared for the devil and his angels: 42 for I was

¹Or, *Depart from me under a curse*

Christ is identified with the church; members of the church are members of the body of Christ; hence to minister unto a member of the church is to minister unto a member of his body, to minister unto him. He is the head of the body (Eph. 5: 32) and controls the members of the body. Christians sustain a vital union with Christ. (John 15: 4, 5; 1 Cor. 10: 17; Eph. 1: 22, 23; 4: 15, 16; Col. 1: 18-28.) Jesus here assigns their ministration to his disciples as the reason for their inheriting the kingdom and the blessings of heaven. There seems to be a climax in the enumeration of the ministrations mentioned here; they are food, drink, shelter, and then clothing the naked, visiting the sick, and comforting the prisoner. These are voluntary acts of self-forgetting love and reveal the type of character that may enjoy the bliss of heaven.

41-46 **Then shall he say also unto them on the left hand.**—There is a wide contrast between that which was said and done to those on the right hand and those on the left hand; first there was a separation of the two, and as the judgment proceeds the separation widens until they are as far apart as heaven and hell. "Depart from me, ye cursed, into the eternal fire which is prepared for the devil and his angels." The curse is only the announcement and sealing of the woes which are the due returns of their sins. There is no middle ground between it and the reward of the holy life. "Eternal fire" is the term used to express the fearful doom of the wicked. As the wicked will be raised from the dead, they must suffer the horrors of mind and soul; they shall suffer an increase of punishment from that which they suffered on earth. Fire now gives the severest possible pain; it is used to express the greatest degree of anguish of soul; this anguish continues through eternity. Hell was "prepared for the devil and his

hungry, and ye did not give me to eat; I was thirsty, and ye gave me no drink; 43 I was a stranger, and ye took me not in; naked, and ye clothed me not; sick, and in prison, and ye visited me not. 44 Then shall they also answer, saying, Lord, when saw we thee hungry, or athirst, or a stranger, or naked, or sick, or in prison, and did not minister unto thee? 45 Then shall he answer them, saying, Verily I say unto you, Inasmuch as ye did it not unto one of these least, ye did it not unto me. 46 And these shall go away into eternal punishment: but the righteous into eternal life.

---

angels," not for man. Heaven was prepared for man, and hell prepared for the devil and his angels; but some men fit themselves for the companionship of "the devil and his angels," and must be assigned to their destiny. Eternal punishment is one of the subjects of which the mind can form but feeble conceptions; the language of man cannot describe accurately such punishment. The punishment of the wicked as given by Jesus in this scene was because they had neglected to do the righteous deeds that the other class had done. Nothing is said about their wickedness otherwise; they are not accused of being notorious murderers and outlaws, but simply had neglected to do that which they had opportunity to do. They had failed to feed the hungry and give drink to the thirsty and lodge strangers, clothe the naked and minister to the sick and encourage those in prison in the name of Christ. They are represented as asking when they failed to do this, and received the same reply, "Inasmuch as ye did it not unto one of these least, ye did it not unto me." A failure to meet the needs and distresses of the Lord's people was a failure to minister unto him. Their primal and all-comprehensive sin is the rejection of Christ through the ministration to his disciples. From this cause, whatever sins they have committed stand unforgiven; they stand without a cover in all their life's guilt, in complete exposure to the full unrestrained measure of justice without mercy. It is not probable that such a conversation will take place at the judgment, but Jesus represents this teaching in the form of a conversation to impress it upon all.

And these shall go away into eternal punishment: but the righteous into eternal life.—Verse forty-six is a repetition of the final award of the righteous as in verse thirty-four, and of the wicked as in verse forty-one. They are brought together here side by side and repeated for the purpose of showing the contrast in the strongest light. Nothing is added here to the reward of the righteous as given in verse thirty-four, and nothing is added to the doom of the wicked as given in verse forty-one; but these opposite destinies are set here, the one over against the other in order to heighten the moral impression of each by the force of contrast. It is worthy of note to observe that "eternal" is from the Greek "aionios" and belongs with equal force to the punishment and to life. Both the punishment for the wicked and life for the righteous are "eternal." One state is coequal with the other and both are endless. God has interwoven the two, so that the man who will attempt to deny the flames of hell must deny the joys of heaven. The pains of hell are repeatedly declared as ceaseless. "Everlasting burnings" (Isa. 33: 14); "shame and everlasting contempt" (Dan. 12: 2); "eternal fire" (Matt. 18: 8); "eternal judgment" (Heb. 6: 2); "eternal sin" (Mark 3: 29); "the blackness of darkness hath been reserved for ever" (Jude 13). We are assured here that the state and condition of all men will be eternal.

There are some who hold that the righteous are raised from the dead at a first resurrection one thousand years before the resurrection of the wicked at a second resurrection; such a position is out of harmony with the entire scene of the judgment as described here by Jesus. At the second coming of Christ, at an unknown time, stand the righteous and the wicked at once before the judgment bar of God, and listen in common to each other's trial and sentence before either passes to his final doom. The punishment of the wicked is without end and without remedy; there is no desire on the part of God to injure in the divine punishment; all is done that can be done in righteousness to reform the sinner before that great day; and when there is no hope of his becoming righteous, there is nothing left but punishment and exclusion from heaven. This is the best that can be done for him; it is the necessary result of his character; it is necessary for the protection of righteousness; it is necessary as a warning, and means of persuading others to become righteous, hence it should be preached as Jesus taught it.

[This shows that Jesus was better pleased when they helped the needy, not knowing they were doing it to Jesus and expecting no reward, than if they had done it to him, and so expecting a reward. Then those who failed to do it to the humble brethren of Jesus because they did not know they were doing it to Jesus and thought they would receive no reward, were turned aside to the place prepared for the devil and his angels. This shows that the spirit that does things only as one understands good will come to him for it is not the spirit most pleasing to God. He makes known to man the blessings that will come through obedience, because man in his weakness and perversity needs the spur that fear gives to lead him to obedience; but God prefers the obedience that comes from the love that casts out fear. This was the obedience that Jesus rendered.]

10. PREDICTION OF HIS CRUCIFIXION; FEAST IN SIMON'S HOUSE
26: 1-13

1 And it came to pass, when Jesus had finished all these words, he said unto his disciples, 2 Ye know that after two days the passover cometh, and

---

1-5 When Jesus had finished all these words.—"When Jesus had finished all these words," those recorded in chapters twenty-four and twenty-five; they were spoken toward evening on the Mount of Olives overlooking Jerusalem, while on the way from Jerusalem to Bethany. This was "two days" before "the passover"; it was near the close of the last week of Jesus' earthly ministry. Jesus announced again the very near approach of his crucifixion; it was so near that he expressed it in the present tense, "the Son of man is delivered up to be crucified." The Passover was the greatest annual feast of the Jews. (See Ex. 12.) It was celebrated on the fourteenth day of the month Nisan, the first month of the Jewish year. The Passover, properly speaking, lasted one day, but it was followed with the feast of unleavened bread which lasted seven days; because of the close connection of these two feasts, they were given the one name; the Passover

the Son of man is ²delivered up to be crucified. 3 Then were gathered together the chief priests, and the elders of the people, unto the court of the high priest, who was called Caiaphas; 4 and they took counsel together that they might take Jesus by subtlety, and kill him. 5 But they said, Not during the feast, lest a tumult arise among the people.

²See ch. 10. 4.

was sometimes spoken of as the feast of unleavened bread. (Num. 28: 16-25.) The public teaching of Jesus has now been completed; he tells plainly the time of his crucifixion, and Matthew now records the events which belong to the crucifixion.

Then were gathered together the chief priests, and the elders of the people.—"The chief priests" were the heads of the twenty-four courses of priests who served in the temple by turn, but who would be likely to be present at the great Passover Feast. The Sanhedrin alone had the power to try offenders against religion. The raising of Lazarus in Bethany (John 11: 47, 48) and the rebukes which Jesus had given them in the presence of the people (Matt. 21: 45) caused this session. They assembled in "the court of the high priest." "The high priest" began with Aaron in the priesthood and had gone on by succession with great regularity until some outrages had changed the order. The high priest was judge of all the cases of offense against religion, and exercised great power in the political history of the people. The Roman government had interfered with the succession of high priests because they exercised such political influence over the people. The high priest was president of the Sanhedrin. "The court" of the high priest corresponded to the palace of the king; sometimes an inner court was covered and seats placed around three sides, while the fourth side could be separated from the first court; the reception room where the Sanhedrin usually met before going into official session was termed a court, but it was as private as any place, for no one was privileged to meet there except those who belonged to the Sanhedrin. At this time Caiaphas was serving as high priest. The assembly was called to take "counsel together that they might take Jesus by subtlety, and kill him." Here is where the plot was

6 Now when Jesus was in Bethany, in the house of Simon the leper, 7 there came unto him a woman having ³an alabaster cruse of exceeding pre-

---

³Or, *a flask*

---

laid and developed for the crucifixion of Jesus. They sought by stratagem, by guile, by some snare, to accomplish their end secretly, without any public arrest of Jesus. Caiaphas, who was serving as high priest, was son-in-law of Annas; he was made high priest A.D. 26 and held the office till A.D. 35. Annas had been deposed by Roman authority and his son-in-law Caiaphas had been exalted to the position. It was the decision of the Sanhedrin in this formal assembly that they would not destroy Jesus "during the feast, lest a tumult arise among the people." People had come to the feast from every nation where the Jews had been scattered; many of the people regarded Jesus as a prophet and some as the Messiah. The Sanhedrin had seen that the people were on the side of Jesus, hence they did not wish to excite further prejudice in his favor; so their decision was to wait until after the Feast of the Passover and the people had dispersed from Jerusalem before they would put Jesus to death. God overruled and the hour arrived and Jesus was crucified at the Passover. It was customary with the Roman rulers to select the Passover as the best occasion of the execution of criminals when the large multitude was present. The sight was calculated to impress the public mind and thus show the authority of the Roman government. The Jewish leaders did not want to be responsible for "a tumult" among the people, but they were willing to crucify their Messiah. How inconsistent!

6-13 Now when Jesus was in Bethany.—The time of this feast is not definitely known; some think that it should come in chronological order between chapters twenty and twenty-one. (Mark 14: 3-9; John 12: 1-11.) Matthew and Mark go back, as is frequently done by historians, so what occurred three days before, because it explains in part the treason of Judas, which culminates at this time in his offering to betray Jesus for thirty pieces of silver. This helps the Jewish rulers to decide on what plan to take for gaining possession of Jesus

cious ointment, and she poured it upon his head, as ⁴he sat at meat. 8 But when the disciples saw it, they had indignation, saying, To what purpose is

⁴Or, *reclined at table*

and bringing him to trial; hence, the supper at Simon's house in Bethany is placed by Matthew between verses five and fourteen of this chapter as the logical connection between the two.

Simon the leper.—He had been a leper and had been cured; the law forbade a leper to mingle with the people (Lev. 13: 45, 46); for this reason we conclude that Simon had been cured. Lazarus, whom Jesus had raised from the dead, was at the supper; the woman who came with "an alabaster cruse of exceeding precious ointment" was Mary, the sister of Lazarus; Martha, the other sister of Lazarus, served; this proves that they were neighbors to Simon, and may have been kinspeople. "Alabaster" was a very valuable marble or gypsum and was sometimes called onyx. It was filled with "precious ointment" which Mary poured "upon his head, as he sat at meat." The ointment was of spikenard and was very costly; sometimes it is called "nard" and is said to have been extracted from the root or bark of the "spikenard." It had an exquisiteness of fragrance and softness. Mary disregarded the cost in her great love for Jesus. It was usual with the Jews to anoint the head and other parts of the body with perfumed oils to render the skin pliable and soft. (Matt. 6: 17, 18.) Some have estimated the cost of this to have been $300 to $400. It was poured not only upon his head, but also upon his feet. No common deed could tell him how deep was her gratitude, how strong her desire to honor him, how loving her sympathy, how great was her faith in him, as the Messiah, the Redeemer of the world.

But when the disciples saw it, they had indignation.—John tells us that Judas Iscariot was the leader and the mouthpiece of the indignation against Mary. It will be noted that Matthew does not hesitate to record this fault and complaint which the apostles made against so honoring Jesus. Their

this waste? 9 For this *ointment* might have been sold for much, and given to the poor. 10 But Jesus perceiving it said unto them, Why trouble ye the woman? for she hath wrought a good work upon me. 11 For ye have the poor always with you; but me ye have not always. 12 For in that she ⁵poured this ointment upon my body, she did it to prepare me for burial. 13

⁵Gr. *cast*.

---

complaint was registered by their saying, "To what purpose is this waste?" They could see no use in wasting so much as the price of this box of ointment; to them it was a useless squandering of what could have been used to a better purpose. Judas wanted it sold and the price put in the treasury so he could steal it. (John 12: 6.) Judas was insincere in his complaint, but very likely the other apostles who joined him in the "indignation" were sincere. It was suggested that it could have been sold "for three hundred shillings, and given to the poor"; its value was two and a half times greater than the thirty pieces of silver that Judas received for betraying his Lord. Again we see portrayed in Judas an inconsistency; he is arguing for the poor, but plotting to betray the Son of God!

When Jesus heard what was said he asked, "Why trouble ye the woman? for she hath wrought a good work upon me." Mary may have been troubled by the murmur against her among Jesus' own disciples; she stood in silence attempting no defense; but the voice of Jesus, whom she loved, was raised in her defense and rebuked those who had become indignant. Jesus praised her work. "Good work" here implies more than what is ordinarily expressed by "good"; it means noble or honorable work. It was the act of a noble soul expressing a noble deed. It was a work of love which was done, pure desire to honor Jesus. Jesus in rebuking his disciples said, "Ye have the poor always with you; but me ye have not always." Mark adds, "Whensoever ye will ye can do them good." (Mark 14: 7.) Jesus would not remain long with them; in fact, only two or three days would he be with them. His disciples would have plenty of time and opportunities to aid the poor; the more that they helped the poor in the name of Christ the greater blessings they would receive. The opportunity of making such expressions of love directly to Jesus

Verily I say unto you, Wheresoever ⁶this gospel shall be preached in the whole world, that also which this woman hath done shall be spoken of for a memorial of her.

⁶Or, *these good tidings*

would not occur again; hereafter they could through all generations express it in gifts only to his poor. Jesus added that Mary had done this "to prepare me for burial." We do not know whether Mary had this in mind when she anointed Jesus, but Jesus gave to her act this interpretation. In ancient times it was usual to embalm bodies with costly spices and perfumes. (John 19: 39, 40.) So Mary's act anticipated this usage. Jesus then pronounced this, "Wheresoever this gospel shall be preached in the whole world, that also which this woman hath done shall be spoken of for a memorial of her." "This gospel" is an abridged form of "the gospel of the kingdom"; it is the gospel which later he commanded to be preached in all the world. (Mark 16: 15.) Frequently people do things with not the slightest intention of their deeds becoming memorial; this was true with Mary at this time, but Jesus has memorialized this act and wherever the full gospel of Jesus has been preached, reference to what this good woman did for Jesus has been made. The very thing which caused indignation among his disciples has become a memorial of love and service to him; the disciples condemned the act, but Jesus has honored and blessed it. This story of Mary's good work has been told in every known tongue, and is now being related in more than 350 languages to every great nation on earth. Mary, like Abel, though "being dead yet speaketh." (Heb. 11: 4.)

11. BARGAIN OF JUDAS; THE LAST SUPPER
26: 14-25

14 Then one of the twelve, who was called Judas Iscariot, went unto the chief priests, 15 and said, What are ye willing to give me, and I will ⁷deliver

14-16 Then one of the twelve.—Parallel records of this are found in Mark 14: 10, 11 and Luke 22: 1-5. Probably the record of John 13: 1-30 should come before this act of Judas.

him unto you? And they weighed unto him thirty pieces of silver. 16 And from that time he sought opportunity to ⁷deliver him *unto them.*

---

⁷See ch. 10. 4.

"Then one of the twelve," Judas Iscariot; he was angry at the rebuke that Jesus had given for objecting to Mary's using the precious ointment; his hate, avarice, and fears urged him to immediate action. Luke says that "Satan entered into Judas." Matthew does not record any epithet or accusation against Judas for the crime that he committed. He "went unto the chief priests" and offered to make a bargain with them; he went with those who were conspiring against Jesus. Luke adds "captains"; these were the leaders of a guard of priests and Levites whose duty was to protect the temple and the sacred rites from being interrupted by riotous persons; they were at the command of the chief priests for such a work as this. Judas left the company of the disciples on the evening of the first day of unleavened bread, when it was usual for pious Jews to put away all leaven from out of their houses. In his heart was "the leaven of malice and wickedness." (1 Cor. 5: 8.)

Judas made the proposition to the chief priests and captains to deliver Jesus to them; they did not first tempt him, but the evil originated in his own heart. "What are ye willing to give me, and I will deliver him unto you?" Luke tells us that "they were glad, and covenanted to give him money." (Luke 22: 5.) They made an agreement with him that he should inform them of the place where Jesus spent his evenings, that they might take him secretly; otherwise they would have searched for him in vain in the crowded city. The word "covenanted" has the force of putting forth money; they promptly "weighed unto him thirty pieces of silver." Probably thirty shekels, or about fifteen dollars of our money; this was the price of a common slave. (Ex. 21: 32.) This comported well with their hypocrisy and hatred, to fix the price of the Son of God as the price of a slave! The price fulfilled a prophecy. (Zech. 11: 12.) Judas now driven by the fire of hasty resentment, and led by the attractions of gain to seek a bribe for

17 Now on the first *day* of unleavened bread the disciples came to Jesus, saying, Where wilt thou that we make ready for thee to eat the passover? 18 And he said, Go into the city to such a man, and say unto him, The Teacher saith, My time is at hand; I keep the passover at thy house with my

---

treason, "sought opportunity to deliver him unto them." The opportunity that he sought was the absence of the multitude; the people were so strongly on the side of Jesus that the authorities were afraid to tak him openly; their method was to take him secretly, charge him with some crime, and thus gain the multitude against him. The convenient season for the treachery of Judas was soon to come. The very men who took advantage of the treachery of Judas despised him, and spoke the most cutting words to him, as one having in his hands "the price of blood." After Judas had left the disciples, Jesus continued his converation with them as is recorded in John 13: 31 to John 15.

17-19 **Now on the first day of unleavened bread.**—Parallel records are found in Mark 14: 12-16 and Luke 22: 7-13. "The first day of unleavened bread" was the day of preparation for the Passover Feast. There were eight days of unleavened bread. The first was the fourteenth of the month Nisan, which, on this occasion, we are told, came on March 25. The Jews were not required to remove all leaven, which with them was simply sour dough, used in baking bread, from their houses, until evening, when the lamb was killed; but to avoid all danger of offense, they began to purge their houses from attic to cellar, by the light of day, with care and precaution somewhat akin to superstition. We have no record of what Jesus and nine of his disciples did during this day, Thursday. Peter and John were sent into the city to make preparation for the Passover, and Judas was conniving with the enemies of Jesus; probably Jesus remained in Bethany with the nine disciples until time to eat the passover Thursday evening. They had asked Jesus, "Where wilt thou that we make ready for thee to eat the passover?" Jesus commanded Peter and John to "go into the city," which was Jerusalem. The paschal lamb could be eaten nowhere else. Peter and John had asked the question where, that is, at what place in Jerusalem, would

disciples. 19 And the disciples did as Jesus appointed them; and they made ready the passover.

they eat the passover. This was asked early that morning. It required two to convey the lamb to the temple and to witness to the priest the number who were to eat it. Jesus sent Peter and John to find the particular man, "bearing a pitcher," who was probably a disciple. This caution may have been used to prevent Judas molesting the company. He could not, if he were present, determine just what place Jesus would eat the passover with his disciples. They were to address this man and tell him that "the Teacher" or Master requested that he "keep the passover at thy house with my disciples." It was usual for the people of Jerusalem during this great feast to open their houses to strangers who came to the city to keep the feast.

The day was spent by Peter and John in executing this command. After finding the man, and seeing the rooms, they had to buy the lamb, carry it to the temple, and have it killed there, and the blood sprinkled in the name of a paschal lamb or a passover for thirteen people. Judas was necessarily included, because if he had offered to withdraw, it must have been done before Peter and John left, and that would excite suspicion; or if he had already left the company, before Peter and John, he would likely return and eat the passover with Jesus and the other apostles. After killing the lamb they would carry it to the place where it was to be eaten, get the bread and wine ready, and the bitter herbs, and any other things necessary for the feast. According to Josephus, the lamb could not have been slain until after the evening sacrifice at 3:00 P.M., so that they would be occupied until evening; Josephus also informs us that no paschal lamb could be killed for any company fewer than ten nor more than twenty. "My time is at hand"; the time of his betrayal to the Jews had arrived; his disciples did not comprehend this statement. It seems that Jesus and his disciples ate the passover on Thursday evening, while the priests delayed their supper till the following day. (John 18:28.)

20 Now when even was come, he was ¹sitting at meat with the twelve ²disciples; 21 and as they were eating, he said, Verily I say unto you, that

---

¹Or, *reclining at table*
²Many authorities, some ancient, omit *disciples*.

There was a latitude of time allowed by the Jews for the eating of the passover. The lamb was to be slain at the temple, with certain words and rites; it was slain before the setting of the sun on setting of the sun on Thursday and might be eaten at any time after dark and before the next morning. (Ex. 12: 8-10.) One might postpone eating it until a late hour; but much was to be done that night, and Jesus chose the earliest hour which the law required. The Jews fixed the time of the new moon by its appearance; but between the apparent and real age of the moon, as the latter would be marked by astronomical calculations, there was the difference of a day. Matthew, Mark, and Luke made it clear that Thursday was a proper day for the Passover, while John as clearly shows that the Pharisees kept this feast on the following day. (John 19: 14-31.) Peter and John were faithful in carrying out the command and made ready the passover. They procured, examined, killed, and roasted the lamb, searched for leaven in order for its removal, procured water and wine, and prepared all things necessary for the paschal supper.

20-25 **Now when even was come.**—The Passover evening had arrived, and Jesus and his disciples went from Bethany to Jerusalem; the lamb was killed between "the evenings," that is, between 3:00 P.M. and sunset. (Ex. 12: 6.) It could be eaten at any hour of that night. (Ex. 12: 8.) The first passover was eaten while standing, with loins girded, feet shod, ready to go on a journey. (Ex. 12: 11.) But Jesus and his disciples were "sitting at meat," or reclined, as no journey was to be made at this time. After the children of Israel had settled in the promised land, they adopted the custom of reclining while eating the passover. If Jesus and his disciples that night followed the customs of the Jews, they were reclined on their meal couches, took a cup of wine in the right hand, and uttered the prayer of consecration, saying, "Blessed be thy name, O Lord our God, King of the universe, who hast

one of you shall ³betray me. 22 And they were exceeding sorrowful, and began to say unto him every one, Is it I, Lord? 23 And he answered and said, He that dipped his hand with me in the dish, the same shall ³betray me. 24 The Son of man goeth, even as it is written of him: but woe unto that man through whom the Son of man is ³betrayed! good were it ⁴for that man

---

³See marginal note on ch. 10. 4.

---

created the fruit of the vine." "And as they were eating," John says that Jesus "was troubled in the spirit, and testified." His human nature began to be overwhelmed with the increasing weight of the awful suffering which he was to endure; the first part of his sorrow was the sin of Judas, whom he now convicts openly of his crime. His disciples could not understand his suffering and did not suspect that he would be delivered up by one of their number. It was a surprise to them when Jesus announced "that one of you shall betray me." The record is clear that Jesus sat at meat "with the twelve disciples"; this included Judas. Judas could not be absent, as it was impossible for him after the lamb was killed at the temple to transfer his name to another company; he was obliged, therefore, to violate every obligation, human and divine, to achieve his guilty purpose. Judas went from this sacred feast to the enemies of Christ. (Psalm 41: 9; John 13: 18.)

When Jesus announced that one of the twelve would betray him, they were exceedingly sorrowful and began "to say unto him every one, Is it I, Lord?" They were amazed, grieved, and doubtful; they did not understand his statement, neither could they understand why he should so mar or disturb the Passover Feast with such an accusation against them; so they anxiously inquired, each for himself, "Is it I?" Jesus gave an answer by saying, "He that dipped his hand with me in the dish, the same shall betray me." Jesus saw the disciples grieved and agitated by his announcement and gave indication as to who would be the traitor; he makes a sign by which the traitor shall be known to all by fulfilling to the letter a prophecy. (Psalm 41: 9.) It was customary then in the East, and still is, to place food before guests in a large dish and each one may dip his hand in the dish and take such portion of the food as

if he had not been born. 25 And Judas, who ³betrayed him, answered and said, Is it I, Rabbi? He saith unto him, Thou hast said.

⁴Gr. *for him if that man.*

he may desire. At the Passover supper the Jews provided a particular dish made of bitter herbs, palm branches, and raisins seasoned with vinegar; the whole mixture serving to remind them of the hard bondage of their ancestors in Egypt. It may be that Judas dipped his hand with Jesus into this dish. Jesus then quoted a prophecy to be fulfilled and uttered a "woe unto that man through whom the Son of man is betrayed!" He then added that "good were it for that man if he had not been born." After all the others had inquired if they would betray him, Judas then asked, "Is it I, Rabbi?" Judas is bold and wily to the last; the innocent disciples say "Lord," but the guilty one said "Rabbi." By this change Judas denied the claim that Jesus was his "Lord." Jesus answered mildly the insulting hypocritical question and said, "Thou hast said." This was the very mildest form of affirmation; how gently Jesus thus deals with the bold insult of the hardened wretch that should betray him.

12. LORD'S SUPPER; PETER'S DENIAL FORETOLD; GETHSEMANE
26: 26-46

26 And as they were eating, Jesus took ⁵bread, and blessed, and brake it; and he gave to the disciples, and said, Take, eat; this is my body. 27 And he took ⁶a cup, and gave thanks, and gave to them, saying, Drink ye all of

⁵Or, *a loaf*
⁶Some ancient authorities read *the cup.*

26-30 And as they were eating, Jesus took bread.—Parallel records are found in Mark 14: 22-25; Luke 22: 19, 20; John 15: 1-27; and 1 Cor. 11: 23-25. At the close of the meal or Passover, the final cup of wine, called the "cup of blessing," was drunk. There were as many as "five cups" passed during the Passover Feast; the wine was kept in a large container and was passed around, and each filled his own cup with such

it; 28 for this is my blood of the ⁷covenant, which is poured out for many

⁷Many ancient authorities insert *new*.

---

portion as was desired; scriptures were recited and a pause made in the feast as the cups were replenished. Luke tells us that Jesus said, "With desire I have desired to eat this passover with you before I suffer." (Luke 22: 15.) Jesus would leave his disciples with this most sacred memorial. He took bread, the bread and wine which were before him and which had been prepared for the Passover. He "blessed" it or gave thanks for it; some think that the word "blessed" means more than giving of thanks; that it signified a prayer for all the blessings which may properly be desired for the object which is blessed. Jesus blessed the loaves and fishes, which thereby became capable of the miraculous increase. (Matt. 14: 19; Mark 8: 7; Luke 9: 16.) After blessing and breaking it, he distributed it to his disciples; he gave to the disciples, and said, "Take, eat; this is my body." "This represents my body" was the meaning that Jesus gave to this bread. This was a common expression among the Jews. (Gen. 40: 12; 41: 26; Dan. 7: 23; 8: 21; 1 Cor. 10: 4; Gal. 4: 24.) Jesus did not mean that this bread was to be "transubstantiated," that is, changed into his literal flesh. While his disciples were wondering what he meant, he took "a cup, and gave thanks, and gave to them, saying, Drink ye all of it." That is, let all of you drink of it. He then added, "For this is my blood of the covenant, which is poured out for many unto remission of sins." He took of the "fruit of the vine" which was being used in the Passover Feast and give to it a new significance. As the bread represented his body, so the fruit of the vine represented his blood. The secret mystery of life was in the blood of animals and men. (Gen. 9: 4; Lev. 7: 26, 27; Acts 15: 20.) Jesus here declares that his life was offered as the great means and way of salvation for men. His blood represents his life. (John 6: 54-56; Col. 1: 20; Heb. 9: 12, 14, 22; 1 Pet. 1: 2; 1 John 1: 7.) This blood was shed for the remission of sins; it was "poured out for many unto remission of

unto remission of sins. 29 But I say unto you, I shall not drink henceforth of this fruit of the vine, until that day when I drink it new with you in my Father's kingdom.
30 And when they had sung a hymn, they went out into the mount of Olives.

---

sins." This expression is similar to Acts 2: 38, "unto the remission of your sins."

I shall not drink henceforth of this fruit of the vine, until that day when I drink it new with you in my Father's kingdom.—This is the last time that the Passover would be celebrated by his disciples with its old signification; after the death and resurrection of Jesus, an entirely new meaning would be given to the Passover; Jesus now has become the Passover for Christians. (1 Cor. 5: 7.) "The fruit of the vine" stands for the whole supper as used here; it is an example of the part used for the whole. "Until that day," that is, not until after the resurrection and the descent of the Holy Spirit. We have no record that Jesus ate the Lord's Supper with his disciples before his ascension. "In my Father's kingdom" means the kingdom of God or the church which was established on the day of Pentecost when the Holy Spirit came. Jesus did not literally drink wine with his disciples in the kingdom as it now is, nor will he do so in the eternal kingdom of heaven. The term "drink" is used figuratively to express that communion which Jesus has with his disciples while they are eating the Lord's Supper. "I drink it new" means a new method of using the wine. It is taken from its significance in the Passover Feast and given a new meaning in the Lord's Supper. At the Passover the Jews were accustomed to chant the Psalms (112 to 119). It is probable that the Lord's Supper was concluded with this portion of the Psalms as "they had sung a hymn" and afterwards "went out into the mount of Olives." This was the place to which Jesus led his disciples and was about a quarter of a mile from the city. It is thought that it was about eight o'clock in the evening when the supper was concluded. Judas had left the company, and Jesus then, after the supper, continued his talk and his prayer with his disciples until much later that night.

31 Then saith Jesus unto them, All ye shall be offended in me this night: for it is written, ⁸I will smite the shepherd, and the sheep of the flock shall be scattered abroad. 32 But after I am raised up, I will go before you into Galilee. 33 But Peter answered and said unto him, If all shall be ⁹offended

⁸Zech. xiii. 7.

31-35 All ye shall be offended in me this night.—Jesus now again warned his disciples, and Peter in particular, of the very near approach of the time of his betrayal. "All ye shall be offended in me this night"; it means that all will be ashamed to own me in the disgrace of the arrest and trial. Again Jesus quoted from one of the prophets and said, "I will smite the shepherd, and the sheep of the flock shall be scattered abroad." This quotation is from Zech. 13: 7; Jesus refers them to this prophecy to prevent them from despair at seeing him fall before his enemies. "I will smite" is an expression used to denote what God permitted to be done; he suffered evil and compels it to work out his purposes of good. He does not compel any man to sin, but when they do evil, he orders that evil to work out his own glory. (Psalm 76: 10.) He permitted the death of Christ in order to save the world. "The shepherd" is used of the Messiah very early in the scriptures. (Gen. 49: 24; Psalm 23: 1; Isa. 40: 11.) The word "sheep" is used to signify his disciples. "Shall be scattered" means that his disciples should flee in the darkness of night at his betrayal as sheep flee at the invasion of wild beasts and the loss of their shepherd; he means that his disciples will be as timid in their flight at his arrest as sheep are when the shepherd has been smitten.

But after I am raised up, I will go before you into Galilee.—In his deep distress and in the foreboding evils that await him, Jesus thinks tenderly of his disciples; he desires to comfort and console them; but how slow they are to believe him; they understood him not, though he had told them time and again of his death and resurrection. "I will go before you into Galilee"; Galilee had been the chief scene of his ministry among them, and there he would again appear to them afar from his enemies. (Matt. 27: 16; Mark 16: 7.) Peter in his impetuosity said, "If all shall be offered in thee, I will

in thee, I will never be ⁰offended. 34 Jesus said unto him, Verily I say unto thee, that this night, before the cock crow, thou shalt deny me thrice. 35 Peter saith unto him, Even if I must die with thee, *yet* will I not deny thee. Likewise also said all the disciples.

⁰Gr. *caused to stumble.*

never be offended." Peter was not boasting; he thought he knew his own heart, but he did not; he meant to say that all the others might forsake him, but he would not. He thought that he would remain faithful unto the end. Very likely they had before them the example of Judas leaving his Master, and now Jesus declares that all of them would be offended in him that night; that is, the others would forsake him, but Peter boldly declares that it matters not what others may do, he would remain faithful to Jesus.

Jesus knew Peter's heart and said, "Verily I say unto thee, that this night, before the cock crow, thou shalt deny me thrice." This was hardly four hours before Peter did deny his Lord; Peter's natural courage was not the kind that he needed at this time. "Before the cock crow" means before a certain time that night; Mark and Luke add the word "twice"; Matthew omits it simply because the second was technically called "the cock crow." The habit of this fowl is to crow at three periods of the night—at midnight, halfway between midnight and dawn, and an hour before the dawn of day. The crowing at three o'clock is properly called "the cock crow." (Mark 13: 35.) John means the same thing, that is, it shall not be the time for the cock to crow before Peter would deny his Lord. When the others saw and heard Peter's bold declaration of fidelity to his Lord, they "likewise" declared themselves. Peter had said, "Even if I must die with thee, yet will I not deny thee." None of them except John kept the promise; they were kept from the gross sin of Peter only by lacking the courage to follow Jesus afar off; John alone remained with him to the last, and heard his last words; and John alone of them all is thought to have died a "natural death"; tradition says that all the others suffered death for Christ. We are to think of Jesus as arising with his disciples about nine or ten o'clock in the evening from the Passover Feast and walking,

36 Then cometh Jesus with them unto [10]a place called Gethsemane, and saith unto his disciples, Sit ye here, while I go yonder and pray. 37 And he took with him Peter and the two sons of Zebedee, and began to be sorrowful and sore troubled. 38 Then saith he unto them, My soul is exceeding sorrowful, even unto death: abide ye here, and watch with me. 39 And he went

[10]Gr. *an enclosed piece of ground.*

---

followed by his accustomed disciples, with the exception of Judas, down to the gorge, and across the brook Kidron, until he came into a wood or grove called Gethsemane.

36-46 Then cometh Jesus with them unto a place called Gethsemane.—"Gethsemane" means the place of oil presses; it was a field or plot of ground surrounded by a wall, containing several olive trees, and probably some buildings. There is still at the foot of Mount of Olives a square enclosure, surrounded by an ordinary stone wall to mark the spot; no one knows definitely the exact spot. Luke tells us that Jesus was accustomed to retiring to this place for prayer; hence, Judas knew that he would find him in this enclosure at this hour. As they came to Gethsemane Jesus said to his disciples, that is, to eight of them. "Sit ye here, while I go yonder and pray." Probably he went into a more retired part of the garden in the shade of the olive trees; but he "took with him Peter and the two sons of Zebedee" further into the garden; and then he, leaving Peter, James and John there, went about a stone's throw further into the garden and there prostrated himself in prayer. There are three scenes presented here; the first is the group of eight disciples near the entrance of the garden; the second, a group of three, Peter, James, and John, further in the garden; the third is Jesus still further in on his face in prayer. He is overwhelmed in sorrow "and sore troubled." These words are a climax, the last being the more emphatic. He was sorrowful and baptized in mental anguish. Upon him God had put the sorrow and burden of all; he bore our griefs, carried our sorrows, and the chastisement of our peace was upon him. (Isa. 53.) The sea of human sin and woe was then surging about his soul and he said, "My soul is exceeding sorrowful." His mind and spirit were filled with

forward a little, and fell on his face, and prayed, saying, My Father, if it be possible, let this cup pass away from me: nevertheless, not as I will, but as thou wilt. 40 And he cometh unto the disciples, and findeth them sleeping, and saith unto Peter, What, could ye not watch with me one hour? 41 [11]Watch and pray, that ye enter not into temptation: the spirit indeed is willing, but the flesh is weak. 42 Again a second time he went away, and

---

[11]Or, *Watch ye, and pray that ye enter not*

---

intense grief; it bore on him inwardly and from the spiritual world, not so much from the fears of danger at things in this scene of suffering.

And he went forward a little, and fell on his face.—In this prostrate and agonized position he prayed, "My Father, if it be possible, let this cup pass away from me: nevertheless, not as I will, but as thou wilt." "This cup" has reference to his sorrow; it was likened to a cup filled with horribly bitter and poison potion. His sorrow as "evil unto death"; not sorrowful in anticipation of death, but a sorrow pressed so heavily upon him that it would drown and quench the spark of life, but for the divine aid impregnating and strengthening his humanity. He came to do his Father's will; even in his prayer it is the Father's will that must be done; even in his death God's will is to be done. In the face of the sufferings and under the shadow of the cross, he is perfectly resigned to the Father's will. He prayed this prayer three times. Each time that he prayed he went to his disciples for human sympathy and encouragement, but he found them sleeping each time. With a kind rebuke he said to Peter, "What, could ye not watch with me one hour?" Luke adds that he found them asleep "for sorrow." They had been with him all the day and now it was late at night and sleep had overcome them; again some think that after deep sorrow and grief, sleep comes upon one and it is exceedingly difficult to stay awake. Jesus knew the weakness of the flesh and said, "The spirit indeed is willing, but the flesh is weak." No one knew better the weakness of the flesh than did Jesus. How kind was this reproof, how gentle and self-forgetting this excuse for them, and how profound a warning of his words, "Watch and pray, that ye enter not into temptation."

prayed, saying, My Father, if this cannot pass away, except I drink it, thy will be done. 43 And he came again and found them sleeping, for their eyes were heavy. 44 And he left them again, and went away, and prayed a third time, saying again the same words. 45 Then cometh he to the disciples, and saith unto them, ¹²Sleep on now, and take your rest: behold, the hour is at hand, and the Son of man is ³betrayed into the hands of sinners. 46 Arise, let us be going: behold, he is at hand that ¹betrayeth me.

¹²Or, *Do ye sleep on, then, and take your rest?*
¹See marginal note on ch. 10. 4.

Again a second time he went away, and prayed.—This time he prayed that if the cup could not pass away "except I drink it, thy will be done." He came again to his disciples and found them sleeping. Again he went away "and prayed a third time, saying again the same words." It is estimated that he spent about one hour in the solitude of prayer in the garden; and he had actually no witnesses but the celestial guards who came to strengthen him after his moments of agony. The writers of the gospel describe in brief terms his sufferings and agony in Gethsemane; they show us only the outline of his sufferings. His humanity quailed beneath the suffering and he sought strength in earnest prayer. Luke tells us that "his sweat became as it were great drops of blood falling down upon the ground." This was a degree of mental anguish of which we may speak in words, but can only form a feeble conception. The last time that he came to his disciples and found them sleeping he said, "Sleep on now, and take your rest: behold, the hour is at hand, and the Son of man is betrayed into the hands of sinners. Arise, let us be going: behold, he is at hand that betrayeth me." It was no longer possible for his disciples to be of any service to him; the hour for watching and praying had passed; the enemy was at hand. "The hour is at hand," that is, the hour for the betrayal was at hand; it was the hour so often predicted. (John 2: 4; 12: 23.) An hour was used for any short space of time. The Son of man "is betrayed into the hands of sinners." He is now ready, to give himself into the hands of wicked men such as Judas, Caiaphas, Pilate, Herod, and others.

SECTION SEVEN

ARREST, TRIAL, CRUCIFIXION, BURIAL, AND RESURRECTION OF JESUS; THE COMMISSION
26: 47 to 28: 20

1. BETRAYAL AND ARREST
26: 47-56

47 And while he yet spake, lo, Judas, one of the twelve, came, and with him a great multitude with swords and staves, from the chief priests and elders of the people. 48 Now he that ¹betrayed him gave them a sign, say-

---

47-56 And while he yet spake.—Jesus had just finished his prayers in Gethsemane and had comforted his disciples; even before he had finished speaking to them, "Judas, one of the twelve, came, and with him a great multitude." Other records are found in Mark 14: 43-52; Luke 22: 47-53; and John 18: 3-12. The Judas who led the company is designated as "one of the twelve"; he knew the place as John informs us because Jesus was in the habit of going to it for prayer. He had left Jesus and the other disciples after the supper and had gone to the temple guard and informed them that he was ready to betray Jesus into their hands. John says that Judas had received "the band of soldiers, and officers" from the chief priests and that they came with lanterns and torches. They needed these lanterns and torches to search out the dark nooks of the garden and explore the secret places of it. The temple guard was set to preserve order in the temple during the time of the great feasts and was at the command of the chief priests. (Matt. 27: 65.) Other citizens accompanied them and so there was "a great multitude with swords and staves, from the chief priests and elders of the people." They were armed with such weapons as were at their command; it was a perilous adventure, if Jesus had chosen to resist. They were armed with sticks or clubs as though they were taking some violent criminal. All of the company was acting by the authority of the Sanhedrin.

Now he that betrayed him gave them a sign.—Judas led the company; his part was to lead the company to Jesus and point

ing, Whomsoever I shall kiss, that is he: take him. 49 And straightway he came to Jesus, and said, Hail, Rabbi; and ²kissed him. 50 And Jesus said unto him, Friend, *do* that for which thou art come. Then they came and laid

²Gr. *kissed him much.*

---

him out or designate him from the others who might be in the garden. He had it understood with them that he would use the kiss as the sign, and said that they should take the one that he would kiss. The kiss as a common mode of salutation implied intimacy and affection; it showed how base was the disposition of the traitor who dared, by such a style of address, to point out his familiar friend and Master to his enemies. They may have feared that Jesus would escape; they did not know what to expect. John informs us that Jesus awed the multitude with words, so that both his disciples and his enemies would know that he was yielding himself into their hands and that they were unable to do anything except by his willingness. The multitude fell back and fell to the ground in confusion; Jesus then made provisions for the safety of his disciples before yielding himself into their hands. (John 18: 12.) When Judas approached Jesus he said, "Hail, Rabbi." He then kissed him. There was hypocrisy in the salutation; it means rejoice, be happy. The Hebrew word "Rabbi" was a term of salutation from a disciple to his teacher. Judas put himself on this plane with cunning art; he denied by his salutation any higher confidence in Jesus than one might have in any learned scribe, and yet he appeared to show Jesus great respect. Judas showed himself here as a master of the arts of deception; he is smooth-tongued, pious-seeming, crafty, self-seeking, and able to deceive the mind of the people; he was known only by him whom he was betraying. He "kissed him"! We do not know whether to wonder at his boldness or to be shocked at the shamelessness of such hypocrisy. Either he was a man of singular confidence to dare this act, or was in a grievous strait from fear of the multitude, lest they should remember that he too had been till then a disciple of Jesus.

Jesus simply said, "Friend, do that for which thou art come." "Friend" means companion, or fellow; it means one

hands on Jesus, and took him. 51 And behold, one of them that were were Jesus stretched out his hand, and drew his sword, and smote the ³servant of the high priest, and struck off his ear. 52 Then saith Jesus unto him, Put up again thy sword into its place: for all they that take the sword shall perish with the sword. 53 Or thinkest thou that I cannot beseech my Father, and he shall even now send me more than twelve legions of angels? 54 How then should the scriptures be fulfilled, that thus it must be? 55 In that hour

---

³Gr. *broadservant.*

who has followed or kept company with another, for the sincere Savior could hardly call him "friend" in the sense that he was in sympathy with him. The band rushed forward and took hold of Jesus and bound him. John tells us that Peter drew his sword and "smote the servant of the high priest, and struck off his ear." There were two swords among the disciples. (Luke 22: 38.) The name of this servant was Malchus; Jesus rebuked Peter for this rash act and touched the ear and healed it. This rash act of Peter was partly the cause of his second denial, as some relative of Malchus was among those who questioned him. (John 18: 26.)

In rebuking Peter for this rash act Jesus said, "All they that take the sword shall perish with the sword." Jesus did not resist force by force, nor take the sword to conquer earthly kingdoms. Those who use the sword shall perish by the sword; the sword will be the source of their destruction. Individuals, communities, states, or nations that rely upon force, physical force, for maintenance and existence shall perish. The kingdom of God is not supported by physical force. Jesus would not let his disciples defend him and his cause with physical force, surely he will not permit his disciples to go to war to maintain other causes by force. He informed them that if his cause should be defended by physical force he could beseech the Father and that he would send "more than twelve legions of angels." This was a rebuke to those who had come out to take him with physical force as well as a rebuke to Peter for attempting to defend him with a sword. It emphasized that Jesus was giving himself into their hands and not that they were simply taking him contrary to his will by force. "Twelve legions" means a great number; a legion was a division of the Roman army containing six thousand

said Jesus to the multitudes, Are ye come out as against a robber with swords and staves to seize me? I sat daily in the temple teaching, and ye took me not. 56 But all this is come to pass, that the scriptures of the prophets might be fulfilled. Then all the disciples left him, and fled.

---

men; twelve legions would mean that there was a legion for each of his disciples and himself. This was a legion for each of his disciples and himself. This was said, not as if Jesus needed the help of angels, but to convince Peter and others that if it were the Father's will he could summon the heavenly hosts to help him and that he did not need the help of any man bearing a sword. (2 Kings 6:17; Dan. 7:19; Matt. 4:11.)

All that Jesus did was a fulfillment of the prophecies; it was the plan of God foretold by the prophets that the Messiah should be treated in this way, and that if Peter and others should attempt to defend him with physical weapons, they would defeat the purpose of God as foretold by the prophets. Jesus then addressed the multitude and said, "Are ye come out as against a robber with swords and staves to seize me?" This implied that they could do nothing against him unless he permitted it. It was ridiculous; why did they come out against Jesus and his little company of eleven men with such armed band? Why such a force against a harmless and defenseless group? Why should they with a multitude of armed men come out in the silence of the night against this defenseless one? Jesus had not avoided them during this week; he had "sat daily in the temple teaching" and they had not taken him. His question put them to shame and emphasized again that they could do nothing with him without his permission. Jesus pointed out that their conduct was a fulfillment of prophecies. "Then all the disciples left him, and fled." If Matthew and the other writers of the gospel had been impostors, they would never have forged such a report as this! They would not have represented themselves as fleeing. Matthew was one of the apostles and he records that he with the others forsook Jesus and fled. We are not told where they went and what they did for the next twenty-four hours; two of them recovered courage enough to return and witness the scenes

26: 57, 58.]   MATTHEW   515

which followed. (John 18: 15.) These two were Peter and John. Mark records that a young man aroused probably out of sleep was seen for a moment and efforts were made to seize him but that he escaped out of their hands.

2. TRIAL BEFORE CAIAPHAS AND SANHEDRIN
26: 57-68

57 And they that had taken Jesus led him away to *the house of* Caiaphas the high priest, where the scribes and the elders were gathered together. 58

57-62 And they that had taken Jesus.—The company had been sent out by the authority of the high priest, so when Jesus was arrested they "led him away to the house of Caiaphas the high priest." They carried Jesus away first to the house of Annas, the father-in-law of Caiaphas, where he was followed by Peter and John. (Luke 22: 54-57; John 18: 13-17.) The first denial of Peter occurred at this time as he stood in the lower hall warming himself. (Matt. 26: 69, 70; Mark 14: 66-68; Luke 22: 55-57; John 18: 18.) After this denial a cock was heard to crow for midnight; meanwhile Annas inquired of Jesus concerning his doctrine; but as Annas was no longer high priest, Jesus refused to answer him. (John 18: 22-24.) Then Annas sent him to Caiaphas who was the actual high priest. Peter followed him and entered with the crowd. It is thought that with this event Thursday closed according to Roman time. According to Jewish time it had been Friday since sunset. Annas was a man of great energy and influence and was called high priest through courtesy; some think that he had been high priest, but had been deposed by Roman authorities and his son-in-law, Caiaphas, had been honored with the office. Jesus' presence before Annas formed no part of the trial which is recorded by Matthew. The Sanhedrin had been assembled and was ready when they arrived with Jesus. The Sanhedrin constituted the Supreme Court of all matters touching their religion. The first question, on the arrest of Jesus, was, had he violated the law in any particular that was worthy of death?

But Peter followed him afar off, unto the court of the high priest, and entered in, and sat with the officers, to see the end. 59 Now the chief priests and the whole council sought false witness against Jesus, that they might put him to death; 60 and they found it not, though many false witnesses came. But afterward came two, 61 and said, This man said, I am able to destroy

But Peter followed him afar off.—The two events, the trial of Jesus and the denial of Peter occurred at the same time. It was left to the choice of the writer as to which would be recorded first. Matthew records the trial of Jesus first and finishes his record of the trial, and then gives the denials of Peter all at once; Mark, who wrote under the direction of Peter, has given the words which passed, and John has followed the order of time. Peter followed afar off, but even this manifested his love for Jesus. By following at all, he manifests love for Jesus; by following *afar off* he showed fear. He compromised with his fears and his love; Satan made it impossible for him to remain mutual. He occupied the dubious ground of compromise with sin. He came "unto the court of the high priest, and entered in, and sat with the officers, to see the end." Peter remained among the servants in the vestibule as if he were a mere spectator; this was the first compromise, and while Jesus was before Annas, the first denial occurred. He sat with the servants around a fire of coals; it was cold enough that night for a fire. He is found among the enemies of Jesus and it is exceedingly difficult to remain loyal to Jesus while he is consorting with his enemies.

The Sanhedrin now has Jesus before it; he is its prisoner; but it has no charges against him. "Now the chief priests and the whole council sought false witness against Jesus, that they might put him to death." They sought for some testimony which would convict him of death; there was no difficulty in finding witnesses who testified with vague accusations of hatred and bigotry, but for a long time they could not find any two whose testimony was consistent. They sought to examine Jesus by questions about his teachings and his disciples, that they might find some inconsistencies in his teaching or some false doctrine; then they sought to convict his disciples of some violations of the law so that they might

the ⁴temple of God, and to build it in three days. 62 And the high priest stood up, and said unto him, Answerest thou nothing? what is it which these

⁴Or, *sanctuary:* as in ch. 23. 35; 27. 5.

blame Jesus with the mistakes of his disciples. But Jesus refused to answer their questions; he was there to *suffer* rather than to *teach*. He had lately spoken their doom in the woes of chapter twenty-three; he left them to proceed for themselves and to make out a charge of impiety to a capital degree, in their own way. They were sorely pressed for materials to aid their malice and to make out their charge. Finally, after examining "many false witnesses," two were found who said, "This man said, I am able to destroy the temple of God, and to build it in three days." This was a perversion of the truth; Jesus had not said this, but two witnesses testified that he had said this. The law required two witnesses. (Deut. 17: 6, 7; Heb. 10: 28.) The falsehood of these two witnesses lay, not in their affirming an untruth, but in perverting the truth and wresting an innocent speech into a crime. "This man said," literally "this fellow said"; "this one," pointing at Jesus. Jesus had said, "Destroy this temple, and in three days I will raise it up." (John 2: 19.) Jesus did not say that he would destroy the temple; but in these words by telling them to destroy it, he avoided the only charge which they sought to make out against him. (Acts 6: 14.) Jesus had reference to his body and spoke of it as the temple; he meant that should they destroy his body or put him to death in three days he would be raised from the dead. Now these witnesses quote him as saying, "I will destroy this temple that is made with hands, and in three days I will build another made without hands." (Mark 14: 58.) This was an ingenious and wicked perversion of his words. Their words contained two distinct accusations: (1) a conspiracy to destroy the temple; (2) a claim to the power of doing a miracle against their holy place. The first they knew was false; the second they thought best to say nothing about. The high priest attempted to get Jesus to make some reply to this accusation, "but he held his peace, and answered nothing." It was useless for Jesus to make

witness against thee? 63 But Jesus held his peace. And the high priest said unto him, I adjure thee by the living God, that thou tell us whether thou art the Christ, the Son of God. 64 Jesus saith unto him, Thou hast said: nevertheless I say unto you, Henceforth ye shall see the Son of man sitting at the right hand of Power, and coming on the clouds of heaven. 65 Then the

reply to the testimony of these witnesses; they were not seeking the truth and they would pervert his words.

63-68 And the high priest said unto him.—After attempting to extort something from Jesus in reply to the testimony that had been given, and failing in this, Caiaphas then attempted to put Jesus under oath and either make him testify or violate the law of Moses. He said, "I adjure thee by the living God, that thou tell us whether thou art the Christ, the Son of God." The high priest, angered by the failure to get Jesus to speak, and eager to arouse the passion of the assembly against him, changed his ground and compelled Jesus to speak. "I adjure thee" was the usual form of putting a man under oath. (Lev. 5: 1.) When thus adjured by any one having authority, it was wrong for any pious Jew to keep silence or conceal the truth. Jesus, notwithstanding the improper rage of the high priest, obediently and meekly replied to "the ruler of his people." Jesus answered, "Thou hast said." This was equivalent to an affirmative answer; it meant yes I am "the Christ, the Son of the living God." "The Christ" means the same as "the Messiah"; the first is Greek and the latter Hebrew, and both mean "anointed." This was equivalent to "the Son of God." The two words are used to express the same thing. (Matt. 16: 16; Luke 22: 67, 70.) Jesus meant to say that "I affirm in this solemn hour that I am the Christ the Son of God, though I must die for the claim." Jesus knew that he would be charged with blasphemy when he made the answer; he then added, "Henceforth ye shall see the Son of man sitting at the right hand of Power, and coming on the clouds of heaven." This means his second coming; notwithstanding his present humiliation and crucifixion as a criminal before them, yet he would appear in his true dignity as their terrible judge when he comes again.

high priest rent his garments, saying, He hath spoken blasphemy: what further need have we of witnesses? behold, now ye have heard the blasphemy: 66 what think ye? They answered and said, He is [5]worthy of death. 67

---
[5]Gr. *liable to.*

Then the high priest rent his garments, saying, He hath spoken blasphemy.—Rending his garments was a sign of his horror and indignation at a blasphemer. The Jews expressed great grief or mourning by such significant gestures; the high priest was strictly forbidden to do this from fear of God, whose servant he was. (Lev. 10: 6; 21: 10.) "He hath spoken blasphemy." He thought that he had put Jesus under oath and that now he claimed under oath to be the Son of God. If the claim of Jesus was not true, then he was guilty of blasphemy; but if his claim be the truth, then he was not guilty of this serious charge. Caiaphas and the chief priests and elders disbelieved him, not from want of evidence, but from want of *will;* they did not want to believe him. They condemned him as an impostor, without a pretense of examining his claims and life, whether he had taught the truth or done miracles of mercy. Caiaphas then said to the other members of the Sanhedrin, "What further need have we of witnesses? behold, now ye have heard the blasphemy: what think ye?" In his rage he now put the matter before the Sanhedrin for a decision. They are to vote "guilty" or "innocent." The charge against Jesus is blasphemy. Caiaphas had already voted, and the other members of the Sanhedrin had already prejudged Jesus and a formal sentence is pronounced against him. "He is worthy of death." He has done that for which the law of Moses adjudges the punishment of death. (Lev. 24: 10-16.) Stoning was the punishment for this crime. (Acts 7: 58; 14: 19.) The Sanhedrin could not enforce their own sentence for fear of the Roman government. They either feared the Roman governor or the people; they thought it safer to resort to the Roman governor to carry out their plans. In doing this they fulfilled the purposes of God as expressed by the prophets. It was now the morning watch, between three and six A.M. of Friday. (Luke 22: 63-70.) Luke says "as soon as it was day," that is, when the day was dawning.

Then did they spit in his face and buffet him: and some smote him [6]with the palms of their hands, 68 saying, Prophesy unto us, thou Christ: who is he that struck thee?

[6]Or, *with rods*

The denials of Peter, which had now taken place, marked the time as after three o'clock in the morning.

Then did they spit in his face and buffet him.—Spitting in the face was a mark of the highest contempt; their rage had carried them to this point; the members of the Sanhedrin lost all the dignity and mercy which they had and degraded themselves by heaping upon Jesus such abuse. They struck him on the head with their fists; this treatment was intended to show their hatred of him as a blasphemer; this was an impotent substitute for stoning to death. They "smote him with the palms of their hands"; they struck him on the face or mouth; this was to mark their horror of what he had spoken. At the same time that they were abusing him they asked him to "prophesy unto us, thou Christ: who is he that struck thee?" Mark says that they had blindfolded him before they struck him and requested that he use his power as a prophet to tell them who had smitten him. These cruel mockeries were as disgraceful to the Sanhedrin as they intended them to be to Jesus. They became guilty of blasphemy themselves as they were so abusing the Son of God. Because Jesus was silent, they imagined themselves to be just and triumphant; they misunderstood his silence. They had passed their sentence before daylight and had decided to take Jesus before Pilate; they had some hours to wait before Pilate's court opened. They put in the time while waiting for Pilate abusing Jesus. Jesus could have with one look or word smitten them dead, but he endured all their indignities in silence; he suffered them all that we might learn to suffer in silence as did he. (Heb. 12: 1, 2.)

3. PETER'S THREE DENIALS; JESUS BEFORE PILATE; THE DEATH OF JUDAS
26: 69 to 27: 10

69 Now Peter was sitting without in the court: and a maid came unto him, saying, Thou also wast with Jesus the Galilæan. 70 But he denied before them all, saying, I know not what thou sayest. 71 And when he was gone out into the porch, another *maid* saw him, and saith unto them that

---

69-75 Now Peter was sitting without in the court.—Parallel records are found in Mark 14: 66-68; Luke 22: 55-57; John 18: 18 of Peter's denials. These denials were made during the trials of Jesus before Annas and the Sanhedrin. The first denial was made in the apartment of Annas; John was acquainted with the high priest and had passed in, but afterwards returned and brought Peter into the vestibule by requesting the maidservant who kept the door to let Peter through. She noticed Peter at that time with John, and then seeing him remaining behind in the room where the servants were, asked him if he was not one of the friends of Jesus. It is probable that she had no design of injuring him, but simply wondered at his remaining there while John had passed in. She said, "Thou also wast with Jesus the Galilæan." Thou "also" or as well as John was with him, then why do you shrink or refuse to go in with him? It does not seem that Peter was at any time this night in any particular danger. "But he denied before them all." In his denial he said, "I know not what thou sayest." He denied that he was a disciple of Jesus; this was a bold and shameful act; he denied that he understood what was said. Perhaps he was permitted to waver that he might see that none should dare to trust in his own strength.

And when he was gone out into the porch, another maid saw him.—Parallels of this are found in Mark 14: 69-72; Luke 22: 58-62; and John 18: 25-27. Peter went out into the porch, that is, the small room btween the doorway and the larger rooms; he was in a fearful state; he could not bear the looks of those around the fire and he went away to hide his confusion. The cock crowed for midnight. Another maid saw him, and Luke records that a man spoke to him at the same mo-

were there, This man also was with Jesus of Nazareth. 72 And again he denied with an oath, I know not the man. 73 And after a little while they that stood by came and said to Peter, Of a truth thou also art *one* of them; for thy speech maketh thee known. 74 Then began he to curse and to swear, I know not the man. And straightway the cock crew. 75 And Peter remembered the word which Jesus had said, Before the cock crow, thou shalt deny me thrice. And he went out, and wept bitterly.

---

ment; this occurred between one and two o'clock in the morning. The scene of the trial had gone on. Peter was engaged in watching its progress. We may suppose that his mind was confused by the strange meekness and submission of Jesus. This maiden said, "This man also was with Jesus of Nazareth." "And again he denied with an oath, I know not the man." These were the very words in which Jesus had predicted his denial. (Luke 22:34.) Peter denied all knowledge of Jesus, whether as the Christ or as Jesus; he cut himself loose from him for a time by his denial. It appears that two maidens and a man at the same place recognized him at once and accused him of being one of the disciples of Jesus; to them all Peter denied with an oath, a very convincing proof that he was not a disciple of Jesus as he thought.

And after a little while they that stood by came and said to Peter, Of a truth thou also art one of them.—This was about an hour after, or between two and three o'clock in the morning. Peter was now desperate, angry, and filled with evil passions and returned to the room where the fire was burning, resolved to stick to his denial. (John 18:25.) The repetition of sin never leaves a man as it found him; he changed rapidly; Peter lost his shame; his Master was condemned, and he had lost something of his love, and in the consequences of ruin to all his earthly hopes he denied knowing Jesus and emphasized his denial by cursing and swearing. Proof was given that he was one of the disciples of Jesus as "thy speech maketh thee known." The dialect of the Galileans was recognized and distinguished them from others. A kinsman of Malchus observed him, and, with others, urged on him this peculiarity, as a reason for supposing him to be a follower of Jesus. Peter was in great fear and also in bitter anger. He began to ana-

1 Now, when morning was come, all the chief priests and the elders of the people took counsel against Jesus to put him to death: 2 and they bound

thematize himself, and to swear with oaths that he had no acquaintance with Jesus. Peter does not seem to have been in any danger; the Pharisees showed no desire to injure him or the other disciples of Jesus; the matter does not seem to have been urged in anger against him. Peter, like the wicked, was in fear where no fear was. (Psalm 53: 5.) Perhaps Peter never forgot this dreadful night. It was now three o'clock in the morning. Luke records that Jesus turned and "looked" upon Peter; the cocks at the same moment crew. Won by the look of tender compassion, and reminded of the prophecy of his fall, the mysterious foreknowledge of Jesus flashed again upon him. The spell of evil was broken, "and he went out, and wept bitterly."

Neither of the four writers of the gospel manifests the least desire to suppress the sad fall of Peter. Mark says, "And when he thought thereon, he wept" (Mark 14: 72), while Matthew records that he "wept bitterly." Luke records that "he went out, and wept bitterly." (Luke 22: 62.) It is remarkable that John, who records the denial, omits any record of his repentance. However, we know that he did repent. Peter might well shed bitter tears even though his denial was only a sin of infirmity. The frankness and honesty of the historians are to be observed; not one of them attempts to suppress this shameful act of Peter; he was committed with the "keys of the kingdom of heaven," but with fairness and integrity the writers record his denial. When Matthew, Mark, and Luke wrote, Peter was still alive; in fact, Mark probably wrote under the direction of Peter. No impostors would have recorded this event.

27: 1, 2 **Now when morning was come.**—This was early Friday morning, between three and six o'clock, called the morning watch. Parallel records are found in Mark 15: 1; Luke 23: 1, 2 ; and John 18: 28-32. Jesus has been subjected to the trials before the Sanhedrin. "The chief priests and the elders

him, and led him away, and delivered him up to Pilate the governor.

of the people," which composed the Sanhedrin, "took counsel against Jesus to put him to death." This was a matter of no little importance and difficulty to them, and it required shrewd management of their part to get the consent of the stern and obstinate Pilate to put Jesus to death. Pilate, the Roman governor, was an idolater and would disregard the charge of "blasphemy," as he cared nothing for the God or religion of the Jews. They must therefore prepare their charges beforehand, and offer to Pilate some charges against Jesus which he would regard as contrary to Roman law, and at the same time excite his prejudice against Jesus and enlist his sympathy for them. It was no small task to prepare such charges; they had to manufacture them, as there were no real charges to be made against Jesus. In their council they planned to prefer the charges that Jesus had perverted the nation of the Jews, forbidding to give tribute to Caesar and making himself a king. (Luke 23: 2.) The Sanhedrin had to deal with the affections of the people as well as the obstinate Pilate. They were shrewd enough to have their charges and plans well formed before they delivered Jesus to Pilate.

They bound him, and led him away, and delivered him up to Pilate the governor.—Jesus had been bound in the garden of Gethsemane when he was first arrested; he had probably been loosed, and had to be bound again. It was their custom to send prisoners bound to the Roman governor as a sign that they had already condemned them. "Pilate the governor" had been appointed "procurator" of Judea by the Roman emperor Tiberius, about six years before this event; he continued in the office for four years afterward, in all ten years. Pilate was described by King Agrippa who knew him well as a man naturally inflexible and obstinately self-willed. He frequently defied the Jewish people until the clamor against him succeeded in effecting his disgrace with the emperor Caligula. He was banished to Vienne in Gaul, where he is said to have died by his own hand. His usual residence was Caesarea, but

3 Then Judas, who ¹betrayed him, when he saw that he was condemned, repented himself, and brought back the thirty pieces of silver to the chief

¹See marginal note on ch. 10. 4.

he came to Jerusalem on certain occasions, and especially on the great feast days of the Jews.

3-10 Then Judas, who betrayed him.—The remorse of Judas, which Matthew relates in this place, as if to dispose of it, may be supposed to have occurred after the final condemnation of Jesus. Matthew does not mean by placing his record of the event at this place to say that it occurred *just at this time,* but as a consequence of the condemnation. It is not likely that any of the chief priests and elders would have been found in the temple until after the sentence of Pilate. When Judas saw that Jesus had been condemned, he "repented himself." It is impossible to analyze and follow the mazes of his dark mind in its terrible progress of crime and despair. Many have speculated about the motives of Judas in betraying Jesus. They may be summed up as follows: (1) Anger at the public rebuke given him by Jesus in the house of Simon the Leper (Matt. 26: 6-14); (2) avarice, covetousness, the price of thirty pieces of silver (John 12: 6); (3) a much larger covetousness, an ambition to be the treasurer, not merely of a few poor disciples, but of a great and splendid temporal kingdom of the Messiah; he would hasten on the coming of that kingdom by compelling Jesus to defend himself; he began to fear that unless he did something desperate there was to be no kingdom after all; (4) perhaps he abandoned what seemed to him a failing cause, and hoped by his treachery to gain a position of honor and influence in the Pharisaic party; (5) and finally, anger and spite at the goodness which continually condemned him awakened his conscience, and called him to a life he was determined not to live. In the New Testament he is termed a thief (John 12: 6) and a devil (John 6: 70), meaning that his prevailing passions were avarice and malice. Also Satan entered into him, and gave a supernatural keenness to these passions. His repentance was only horror and remorse

priests and elders, 4 saying, I have sinned in that I have ¹betrayed ²innocent blood. But they said, What is that to us? see thou *to it*. 5 And he cast down the pieces of silver into the sanctuary and departed; and he went away

²Many ancient authorities read *righteous*.

---

at the effect of his anger and covetousness; it was not that deep repentance which seeks God's mercy and forgiveness.

He confessed, "I have sinned in that I have betrayed innocent blood." He had broken the law of God. (Ex. 23: 7.) Humble confession and restitution, though necessary to true repentance, do not always prove that one is penitent. He had betrayed "innocent blood" in that he had given the life of an innocent person into the hands of those who would put him to death; he became an agent or factor in the crucifixion of Jesus. Judas is an unwilling, yet a very valuable, witness to the innocence of Jesus; he had been his disciple and had known him in all situations for about three years; he had heard all his teachings, public and private; surely, if it were possible to have found a fault with Jesus, Judas would have urged it now as an excuse for his betrayal.

[The sin of Judas was from a lack of moral principle, a true regard for truth and justice. From this sin there seemed to be no recovery. Under a sense of shame and disgrace, he confessed his sin, returned the bribe, hanged himself, and went to "his own place." (Acts 1: 25.)]

What is that to us? see thou to it.—Judas had brought the thirty pieces of silver back to "the chief priests and elders" and had confessed that he had betrayed "innocent blood"; but these men refused to give Judas any encouragement in correcting the wrong that he had done. They did not care for his feelings; Judas had done what they wished and they had paid him for it; as to the rest they did not care what became of Judas. This reply to Judas was in harmony with their conduct all along. They should have paused and examined the cause of Judas' conduct, or, at least, they should have tried to satisfy him that they had done right in condemning Jesus. It is to be observed that Judas "repented" only when his sin was completed. When the chief priests and elders refused to take the

and hanged himself. 6 And the chief priests took the pieces of silver and said, It is not lawful to put them into the ³treasury, since it is the price of blood. 7 And they took counsel, and bought with them the potter's field, to

³Gr. *corbanas,* that is, *sacred treasury.* Comp. Mk. 7. 11.

---

thirty pieces of silver back, Judas "cast down the pieces of silver into the sanctuary and departed." This was the end of all his dreams of avarice; the thirty pieces of silver which he had received burned into his soul with a guilt of remorse that he could not drive away; it was the price of blood and his ingratitude to Jesus rose up before him until his whole soul was in agony which he could not endure, "and he went away and hanged himself." He seems to have done this in such haste and confusion of mind that the rope gave way and he was precipitated down a steep place, and disemboweled on the sharp rocks. (Acts 1 : 18.) Everyone who was hanged on a tree was pronounced accursed by the law of Moses. (Deut. 21 : 22, 23.) [There is no conflict between Matt. 27 : 5 and Acts 1 : 18. In Acts it is said, "And falling headlong, he burst asunder in the midst, and all his bowels gushed out." He hanged himself, the rope broke, he fell, his belly burst, and his bowels gushed out. Instead of there being a contradiction between the statement in Matthew and in Acts, the two accounts supplement each other and harmonize.]

And the chief priests took the pieces of silver.—They gathered up the silver and said that "it is not lawful to put them into the treasury, since it is the price of blood." Money which had been made abominable by certain crimes was in no case to be offered to Jehovah. (Deut. 23 : 18.) The treasury here meant the "alms chest" which was kept in the court of the women, and all that was placed in it was solemnly devoted to the service of Jehovah. Judas confessed to having betrayed "innocent blood," and the priests to having bought it; they thus condemned themselves. They took "counsel" as to what they would do with the money and finally decided to buy "the potter's field, to bury strangers in." This was evidently after the death of Jesus. The "potter's field" was a field which the potters had used; it is said in Acts 1 : 18 of Judas that he pur-

bury strangers in. 8 Wherefore the field was called, The field of blood, unto this day. 9 Then was fulfilled that which was spoken through Jeremiah the prophet, saying, ⁴And ⁵they took the thirty pieces of silver, the price of him that was priced, ⁶whom *certain* of the children of Israel did price; 10 and ⁷they gave them for the potter's field, as the Lord appointed me.

⁴Zech. xi. 12, 13.
⁵Or, *I took*
⁶Or, *whom they priced on the part of the sons of Israel*
⁷Some ancient authorities read *I gave.*

---

chased a field with the reward of iniquity, and was the first to mark it as a field of blood by his own death. Judas did not make this purchase only in the sense of furnishing the means to purchase it; perhaps the priests also put his name prominent in the purchase. It is usual for a writer to represent one as doing that which he causes another to do. They wanted this field to bury the Jews who came to Jerusalem from foreign places and died while there attending the feasts. The field bought by the money perpetuated the memory of the foul bargain both of Judas and the Sanhedrin. This field "was called, The field of blood, unto this day." It was called in the native tongue "Akeldama" (Acts 1:19), which means the field of blood. The facts of this account of the death of Jesus were perpetuated by the existence of this field as a burying place. Matthew in referring to it shows that he challenges investigation into the truth of his record. At the time that Matthew wrote it was still familiar to the Jews; it was some years after the crucifixion before Matthew wrote this record. Matthew was not afraid for anyone to check his record with the facts; this is a proof of his sincerity and accuracy. "Then was fulfilled that which was spoken through Jeremiah the prophet." We meet here a difficulty. No such passage occurs in the writings of Jeremiah. There is something like it in Zech. 11: 12, 13. There are four explanations why the name "Jeremiah" is used here instead of "Zechariah." (1) The names may have been mistaken in transcribing as they are sometimes written in a contracted form—"Iriou" for Jeremiah, and "Zriou" for Zechariah; in this form it would be only the mistake of one letter and could easily be made by one in transcribing. (2) Jeremiah may be used here for the book of the prophets, as being the first in rank on the list; that is, Jeremiah and Zechariah and some of the other prophets grouped together and the name "Jeremiah" given to the group, when the actual quotation was from Zechariah. (3) That the word "Jeremiah" was not writen by Matthew but was added by some unlearned transcriber. (4) That Matthew referred to some action and words of Jeremiah not recorded by him in his prophecies, but handed down in some traditional form, and recorded in substance by the prophet Zechariah. Our ignorance must bear the blame of difficulty that arises here; we believe firmly in the inspiration of Matthew and the accuracy of his record. These minor difficulties are left in our path as a trial of our faith. The price of the thirty pieces of silver was the price of a common slave; hence they rated Jesus at the price of a slave.

4. JESUS BEFORE PILATE
27: 11-26

11 Now Jesus stood before the governor: and the governor asked him, saying, Art thou the King of the Jews? And Jesus said unto him, Thou

11-14 Now Jesus stood before the governor.—Parallel records are found in Mark 15: 2-5; Luke 23: 3, 4; and John 18: 33-38. It was now probably between 6:30 and 8:30 Friday morning. By the law (Num. 19: 22) whoever touched any unclean person, among whom the later Jews reckoned Gentiles, was unclean, and unable to celebrate the Passover. (Acts 10: 28.) The Jews on this account would not go into the castle of Antonia, which was occupied by Pilate; to accommodate them, a sort of court of judgment seat had been prepared outside the walls of the castle, called in Hebrew "Gabbatha," or the pavement (John 19: 13), probably a raised space, paved with stones. The seat for Pilate was fixed here and a door leading into the inner hall; Jesus was carried within, and arraigned before the Romans; Pilate came to hear the accusations against Jesus, and after hearing them he went in and examined Jesus. He asked him, "Art thou the King of the Jews?" This qustion Pilate asked after hearing the accu-

sayest. 12 And when he was accused by the chief priests and elders, he answered nothing. 13 Then saith Pilate unto him, Hearest thou not how many things they witness against thee? 14 And he gave him no answer, not even to one word; insomuch that the governor marvelled greatly. 15 Now at ⁸the

⁸Or, *a feast*

---

sation of the Jews. (John 18: 28, 40.) As the Messiah, Jesus claimed to be King; but his kingdom could not in any way disturb the lawful temporal authorities of the Roman government. The charge made against him rested on this claim, which the priests knew he would not deny. The Jews also falsely added that Jesus had forbidden to pay tribute to Caesar. (Luke 23: 2.) Jesus answered Pilate, "Thou sayest." This meant "thou sayest what I am"; it meant yea, it is so. Jesus then explained to him that his kingdom was "not of this world." (John 18: 36.) Pilate seems thereupon to have taken something like a right view of the case, thinking Jesus a teacher of truth, and fond of using royal titles to enhance the dignity of his teaching. Pilate was fully satisfied of the innocency of Jesus. (John 18: 38.)

And when he was accused by the chief priests and elders, he answered nothing.—He made no reply to idle clamors against him; there was true wisdom in the course he pursued. Jesus answered Pilate when questioned and satisfied him of his innocence; but he did not plead for his life against the accusations of the Jews; he saw that there was no use to answer the Jews who were determined to have him put to death. Pilate asked him why he did not reply to the Jews when "they witnessed" against him. Pilate marveled at his manner, so gentle, firm, suffering, meek, so devoid of impatience, anger, haste, or any human infirmity. Pilate could not understand why he did not make reply to the accusations that his own people made against him. Jesus' silence and lack of fear, his open, ready confession of their main charge that he was a King in the realm of truth were a full and entire refutation. He submitted, as to the will of God, with a truly royal patience. Jesus ignored the many charges that they brought against him. (Mark 15: 3.) Jesus knew that Pilate did not believe the charges that the Jews brought against him, hence

feast the governor was wont to release unto the multitude one prisoner,

he was silent. We are not to understand that Jesus appeared in any degree sullen, but that he did not pretend to refute the charges brought against him; he replied readily to all proper questions.

15-18 Now at the feast the governor was wont to release unto the multitude one prisoner.—Parallels of this event are found in Mark 15: 6-14; Luke 23: 13-19; and John 18: 39, 40. Pilate did not understand the silence of Jesus; he was perplexed and at this juncture he learned that Jesus had lived in Galilee which was under the jurisdiction of Herod Antipas. Herod was at Jerusalem at this time; hence, Pilate in order to escape from a difficulty, and at the same time pay a mark of respect to Herod, sent Jesus to Herod. (Luke 23: 5-12.) This was the first step to Pilate's fall—a compromise with conscience. After Herod had returned him it was more difficult for Pilate to make his decision. Jesus was silent before Herod, and Herod sent him back to Pilate. Pleased with the mutual compliment, these rulers made a peace contract.

"Now at the feast," which was the Passover Feast. It was the custom to release some prisoner on the petition of the Jews; this was done during the feast in order to secure popularity and give importance to the visit which Pilate made to Jerusalem. In a conquered country there would always be political prisoners and others who were held in high esteem by the conquered people. To release one of these would be an act of grace especially pleasing to the people. There was "a notable prisoner, called Barabbas." He was well known for his bold, seditious spirit, and rendered notorious for a particular act of rebellion; his crimes were popular. (Luke 23: 19.) He had led a rebellion against the Romans, and in the confusion resulting, had committed murder. He is stamped by inspiration as a "robber." If the Jews had written Barabbas' biography, perhaps they would have pronounced a eulogy upon him; but inspiration calls him a robber. Pilate put the question directly to the Jews, "Whom will ye that I release

whom they would. 16 And they had then a notable prisoner, called Barabbas. 17 When therefore they were gathered together, Pilate said unto them, Whom will ye that I release unto you? Barabbas, or Jesus who is called Christ? 18 For he knew that for envy they had delivered him up. 19 And while he was sitting on the judgment-seat, his wife sent unto him, saying, Have thou nothing to do with that righteous man; for I have suffered many

---

unto you? Barabbas, or Jesus who is called Christ?" Pilate saw clearly that every accusation against Jesus was groundless. His first experiment of sending Jesus to Herod had failed; he now proposes a new plan. This was his second compromise with his conscience. He ought at once to have given him his freedom and rebuked the Jews for their false charges against him. The priests went among the people and persuaded the people to vote for Barabbas' release. "Jesus who is called Christ" is the mildest title that he could use without exciting further prejudice against Jesus. Afterwards to annoy the priest, he gave Jesus the royal title of King of the Jews. Pilate's error lay in not foreseeing that in giving the choice to the multitude he in a measure lost it himself. "For he knew that for envy they had delivered him up." The word "envy" in ancient writings implies somewhat more than it does now. It signified all those hostile feelings which are included under the general term "unpopularity." Fear of his power with the people, jealousy at his purity, his wisdom and miracles, a mean desire to crush a good and great man, with all the wicked, malicious feelings of a fickle multitude are ranked under the word "envy" as used here. John explains what their envy was when he says, "Behold how ye prevail nothing; lo, the world is gone after him." (John 12: 19.) Again they said, "If we let him thus alone, all men will believe on him." (John 11: 48.) We find here that the subjects dictate to their conqueror; the people prefer a murderer to the Son of God. In their blind rage and determination to put Jesus to death the Jews work out the plan of salvation for others—of ruin to themselves.

19-23 And while he was sitting on the judgment-seat.—The seat or throne erected in the open court for judgment is here meant. Pilate had thus far passed in and out before the peo-

things this day in a dream because of him. 20 Now the chief priests and the elders persuaded the multitudes that they should ask for Barabbas, and destroy Jesus. 21 But the governor answered and said unto them, Which of the two will ye that I release unto you? And they said, Barabbas. 22 Pilate saith unto them, What then shall I do unto Jesus who is called Christ? They all say, Let him be crucified. 23 And he said, Why what evil hath he

ple in an informal and friendly manner; he now assumes the seat of power, and by the act shows that he proceeds to a regular trial. At this juncture he received word from his wife telling him to "have thou nothing to do with that righteous man." Pilate's wife was named Procula; tradition relates that she was led by her dream to become a Christian. She warns her husband, Pilate, the governor, to have nothing to do with the condemnation of Jesus as he is a righteous man. It is probable that Pilate would have heeded this warning had he not already compromised with the enemies of Jesus. His wife added the reason for sending the warning as she had "suffered many things this day in a dream because of him." Dreams were considered by all the ancient nations as indications of the divine pleasure in difficult cases. Among the Jews it was one mode of revelation. (1 Sam. 28: 6, 15; Dan. 2: 1, 2.) In the New Testament, the angel of the Lord is said to have appeared in dreams to Joseph. (Matt. 1: 20; 2: 12.) This dream of Pilate's wife was correct, and Pilate believed it to be a true admonition.

Now the chief priests and the elders persuaded the multitudes that they should ask for Barabbas, and destroy Jesus.— The Jewish rulers understood the intention of Pilate; they saw that he was seeking to release Jesus; they were as determined that he should not do this; therefore they persuaded the multitude to cry for the release of Barabbas. It seems that Pilate had not taken into consideration that he had yielded his right to decide when he put the matter to the Jews as to which they desired him to release. He gave the multitude the right to decide and bound himself to abide by their judgment. Pilate now saw this and was terrified by the consequence of his own compromise, by the admonition of his wife, by the innocence of Jesus, and threatened by the mob with present se-

done? But they cried out exceedingly, saying, Let him be crucified. 24 So when Pilate saw that he prevailed nothing, but rather that a tumult was arising, he took water, and washed his hands before the multitude, saying, I am innocent [9]of the blood of this righteous man; see ye *to it*. 25 And all the

[9]Some ancient authorities read *of this blood: see ye &c.*

---

dition, and future complaint to the arbitrary tyrant Tiberius, Pilate wavered and yielded. The multitude through the influence of the leader was now ready, and when Pilate asked the question which he should release, they answered at once "Barabbas." Next, Pilate asked what should be done with "Jesus who is called Christ?" The leaders and multitude were ready and made reply, "Let him be crucified."

Why, what evil hath he done?—This question was asked of them three times; Pilate was so anxious for the escape of Jesus, yet so intimidated by the dilemma in which he had placed himself that he was ill at ease. He offered another compromise with them, that he would scourge Jesus and let him go; but the passions of the crowd gained impetus by Pilate's indulgence. "Let him be crucified" was the shout which went up from the multitude which had a few days before shouted Hosanna. Crucifixion was perhaps the punishment due to Barabbas, and the offer of his name may have suggested it. At least the leaders had led the multitude to demand the release of Barabbas and the crucifixion of Jesus.

24-26 So when Pilate saw that he prevailed nothing.—Pilate now makes another appeal to the feelings of the Jews; what follows is not so much a trial of Jesus as it is a battle between Pilate and the Jews. Pilate tried several expedients by which he hoped to avoid the responsibility of doing the right thing, namely, that of releasing Jesus. His expedients were as follows: (1) Sending Jesus to Herod to avoid making a decision himself; (2) summoned not only the rulers, but the people to hear the report from the court of Herod; he declared that Herod agreed with his former declaration that Jesus was innocent (Luke 23: 13-15); (3) he proposed to scourge Jesus in the hope that the Jews would accept that punishment as a substitution for the penalty of death; (4) to follow his custom of releasing a prisoner at their feast with the hope of releasing

people answered and said, His blood *be* on us, and on our children. 26 Then released he unto them Barabbas; but Jesus he scourged and delivered to be crucified.

Jesus; (5) by attempting to throw all the responsibility on the Jews after pronouncing him innocent; (6) finally after scourging him by bringing him before them while he was still suffering and bleeding from the scourging calculated to excite their pity for him and saying, "Behold, the man!" (John 19: 5, 6.) Pilate called for a basin of water, and in the presence of the crowd he washed his hands, saying that he was not responsible for the death of Jesus, and placing the responsibility on the Jews. Pilate did everything that he could do to release Jesus but the right thing, which was to declare him innocent and by the authority by which he had enforced his verdict. He was too weak to do this. The Jews washed their hands with water in case of suspected murder to declare their innocence. (Deut. 21:6.) Pilate was the judge and was bound either to condemn or pardon Jesus; he attempted to do neither. Certain responsibilities cannot be put away. The Jews replied, "His blood be on us, and on our children." They said that they would take the responsibility and the penalty; it was an awful imprecation, and was fearfully answered. Jesus had said that on that generation should come all the righteous blood shed on the earth. (Matt. 23: 35.) The Jews blinded by prejudice called down the curse upon themselves. Barabbas was released, "but Jesus he scourged and delivered to be crucified." He ordered Jesus to be scourged. Scourging increased the pains of that mode of death; it was termed "the horrible scourge" from its severity. The scourge was made of several thongs with a handle; the thongs were made rough with bits of iron or bone, for tearing the flesh, and has been called "a scorpion." The last argument that Pilate had was given; he had left the choice with the people and there was nothing further that he could do but deliver Jesus into the hands of the executioners. This he did. In doing this he gave the sentence that he had tried so hard to avoid giving. We now behold Pilate as a judge who condemned a man whom he knew to be innocent.

In the providence of God we see Jesus condemned to death, while at the same time he is declared by Pilate, Herod, Procula, Judas, the Roman centurion, and one of the thieves on the cross as innocent.

5. ROMAN SOLDIERS MOCK JESUS; THE CRUCIFIXION
27: 27-44

27 Then the soldiers of the governor took Jesus into the [10]Prætorium, and gathered unto him the whole [11]band. 28 And they [12]stripped him, and

---

[10]Or, *palace* See Mk. 15, 16.
[11]Or, *cohort*
[12]Some ancient authorities read *clothed*.

27-31 Then the soldiers of the governor took Jesus.—Jesus was taken from the presence of the governor and Jews "into the Prætorium" which was the common hall; the sentence had been given in the open air; the soldiers took Jesus into the hall adjoining their own quarters in order to make preparations for his execution. "The whole band" was gathered; "band" here means cohort and was the tenth part of a legion; it varied in number from three hundred to one thousand men according to the size of a legion. This "band" stripped him, and put on him "a scarlet robe." Probably they stripped him of his outer robe in order to carry on their brutal treatment. "A scarlet robe" was put on him; it was probably some wornout garment of royalty; this robe mentioned was a military cloak of purple worn by the Roman emperors and chief men. It was put on Jesus to ridicule his title of royalty; the insult in their mind was probably meant as a mark of contempt toward the whole Jewish nation. "They platted a crown of thorns and put it upon his head"; this crown of thorns was woven by a few turns of the flexible branches of a thorny bush which grew near Jerusalem. They crowned Jesus with this mock wreath in ridicule and put "a reed in his right hand"; this was in imitation of the sceptre carried by kings. (Esth. 4: 11.) These reeds grew in Palestine in marshy places, especially along the banks of the Jordan. In their mockery these soldiers now had Jesus with an old worn and faded robe, a crown of thorns on his head, and a reed as a sceptre in his hand. They further mocked him by kneeling "down before

put on him a scarlet robe. 29 And they platted a crown of thorns and put it upon his head, and a reed in his right hand; and they kneeled down before him, and mocked him, saying, Hail, King of the Jews! 30 And they spat upon him and took the reed and smote him on the head. 31 And when they had mocked him, they took off from him the robe, and put on him his garments, and led him away to crucify him.

32 And as they came out, they found a man of Cyrene, Simon by name: him they ¹compelled to go *with them,* that he might bear his cross.

¹Gr. *impressed.*

---

him" and said, "Hail, King of the Jews!" This was the usual salutation that they gave to their emperors. It was notorious that the sceptre had departed from Judah and the priests had for almost the first time declared, "We have no king but Cæsar." The Roman soldiers mock at the Jewish nation in the person of Jesus.

They further mocked him by spitting upon him, "and took the reed and smote him on the head." We do not wish to linger over this scene of insolence and outrage which they heaped upon Jesus; it is difficult to believe that one human being can be so depraved as to so treat another one, to say nothing of so treating the Son of God. They smote him on the head to drive the sharp thorns into the living flesh, thus mercilessly adding to their horrid cruelty. "These cruelties were doubtless perpetrated while a part of the band was engaged in preparation for the execution. After mocking him with heartless and cruel mockery for some time, "they took off from him the robe and put on him his garments, and led him away to crucify him." The time of day was probably about eight o'clock in the morning. He was led to a spot without the city gates. (Heb. 13: 11, 12.) We do not know the exact spot as none of the writers of the gospel tell us the direction in which he was led from the city. While Jesus was led forth, a multitude, mostly women, followed him weeping, and Jesus addressed them with a prophecy of the sorrows which the sins of their countrymen were bringing upon them. (Luke 23: 27-31.)

32 And as they came out, they found a man of Cyrene.— Many think that they went out of the city by the Damascus gate, but we do not know. They found a man of Cyrene by

33 And when they were come unto a place called Golgotha, that is to say, The place of a skull, 34 they gave him wine to drink mingled with gall: and when he had tasted it, he would not drink. 35 And when they had crucified

the name of Simon; he was a Jew dwelling in that part of Libya called Pentapolis Cyrenaica, in which was a large colony of Jews. He had come to Jerusalem to attend the feast. "They compelled" him "to go with them, that he might bear his cross." It was customary for the victim to bear his own cross to the place of execution; this was a part of the punishment inflicted on the victim. Simon was "compelled" to bear the cross of Jesus; he did it unwillingly; it was an ignominious office. A great company of people and women followed, bewailing and lamenting his fate. It is thought that Jesus was weary from his long vigils and sufferings, and was staggering under the weight of his cross. It is not known whether Simon carried the full load of the cross or whether he carried only one end of it, while Jesus continued to carry the other end. It was customary for a soldier to go in advance of the victim and carry a white wooden board on which was written the nature of the crime; next came four soldiers, under a centurion, with the hammer and nails, guarding the victim, who bore the cross on which he was to suffer.

33-37 And when they were come unto a place called Golgotha.—This is the Hebrew name for the place and John tells us that it means "The place of a skull." (John 19: 17.) It is not known why it was so called; some think that it was a hill in the place of a skull; others think that it was a common place of execution of criminals and skulls could be around there. It has been given the name of "Calvary" from a Latin derivation. Matthew omits in his detail the horrible work of nailing him to the cross, and describes some of the scenes which took place while he was on the cross. They "gave him wine to drink mingled with gall"; Mark says that they "offered him wine mingled with myrrh: but he received it not." (Mark 15: 23.) The wine of the Roman soldiers hardly deserved the name as it soon fermented and became sour to the taste. "Gall" and "myrrh" are words meaning in this case the same

him, they parted his garments among them, casting lots; 36 and they sat and watched him there. 37 And they set up over his head his accusation written,

thing, a bitter infusion. This had the effect of stupefying the mind and nerves and shortened the life. It was offered by some pitying person to shorten the agonies of Jesus.

And when they had crucified him, they parted his garments among them.—They nailed him to the cross. The cross was made of two pieces of wood, placed one across the other, in the shape familiar to every one. The hands of the victim was nailed or tied to the transverse beam, and the feet crossed on each other and nailed to their place. Sometimes the victim was nailed to the cross before it was erected; then another mode was that of erecting the cross first and nailing the victim to it. We do not know which method was used in the crucifixion of Jesus. It is generally believed that Jesus was first nailed to the cross and that then it was fixed in an upright position in the earth and then was left under the charge of a guard until death slowly came to relieve the indescribable agonies of the sufferer. Sometimes the agonies continued for days, and again they were of short duration. The Jewish law prohibited leaving a body hanging on a tree longer than one day. (Deut. 21: 22, 23.) Crucifixion was a Roman method of putting to death; it was a horrible, lingering death, combining horrors of mind and body which words failed to describe; it was an ignominious punishment, reserved for slaves or the basest criminals; but to the mind of a Jew, it carried also the terrors of a religious curse. We cannot analyze the sufferings one by one; the agonies, the shame, the horror and anguish of our Savior's death no tongue can tell and no pen can describe.

They parted his garments among them, casting lots.—They divided his garments into four parts, to every soldier a part. (John 19: 23.) The clothes belonged to the executioners; the coat or upper garment of Jesus was without seam, woven throughout. The four soldiers were unwilling to tear it, and therefore cast lots for it, which fulfilled a prophecy. (Psalm 22: 18.) It was now the third hour, that is, nine o'clock in the

THIS IS JESUS THE KING OF THE JEWS. 38 Then are there crucified with him two robbers, one on the right hand and one on the left. 39 And they that passed by railed on him, wagging their heads, 40 and saying,

morning. (Mark 15: 35.) It was the hour of offering up the lamb in the daily sacrifice of the temple; this lamb, which since the time of Moses had never ceased to be offered daily while the Jews had a temple or a city, was a type of Christ the true lamb of God. (1 Cor. 5: 6, 7.) The soldiers sat down and watched him there; the soldiers who had crucified Jesus were made responsible for him until his death. They watched to prevent his friends from coming to steal away his body. It was the custom to place a placard above the head of the victim describing the crime that had been committed. This was done with respect to Jesus and the accusation was written in three languages—Hebrew, Greek, and Latin. The accusation was: "THIS IS JESUS THE KING OF THE JEWS." It was painted or engraved in black letters on a white ground, and put over his head; this was done by order of Pilate. To make it well known, and to insult as many Jews as possible, Pilate caused it to be written in these three languages so that none could fail to read it. John gives the full sentence: "JESUS OF NAZARETH, THE KING OF THE JEWS." (John 19: 19.) The place of execution was a public place and the inscription was read by "many of the Jews." John was an eyewitness to the crucifixion and has given accurately the inscription, while the other writers have given the meaning of it. It was on this accusation that Jesus had been condemned by the Roman authorities; no other crime had been brought against him. It seems that Pilate wished to vindicate himself for the part he had in the crucifixion and wanted it to appear that Jesus was a political aspirant for the throne as King of the Jews.

38-44 Then are there crucified with him two robbers.—Judea at that time abounded in robbers. Pilate did not reside in Jerusalem, but took advantage of his occasional visits there to pass judgment on criminals whom he found condemned. We do not know who these two robbers were; some have thought

Thou that destroyest the [2]temple, and buildest it in three days, save thyself: if thou art the Son of God, come down from the cross. 41 In like manner also the chief priests mocking *him,* with the scribes and elders, said, 42 He saved others; [3]himself he cannot save. He is the King of Israel; let him

[2]Or, *sanctuary*
[3]Or, *can he not save himself?*

---

that they were companions of Barabbas. The design was to insult Jesus and the Jewish nation by making it appear that Jesus was a companion of such wretches. In doing this they fulfilled a prophecy of Isaiah which says, "He poured out his soul unto death, and was numbered with the transgressors." (Isa. 53: 12.) Jesus was crucified between these two robbers. Those who passed by "railed on him, wagging their heads, and saying, Thou that destroyest the temple, and buildest it in three days, save thyself." This meant that Jesus had made the pretense of being able to destroy the temple and rebuild it in so short a time; he was now asked to show his power by rescuing himself from the cross. They further derided him by saying that he could not save himself therefore he could not save others. They thought that the certain death of Jesus was positive proof that he was an impostor. Many who passed by and reviled him were evil men; some may have been good men who did not believe that he was the Son of God.

In like manner also the chief priests mocking him, with the scribes and elders.—These religious people and leaders and teachers of the people left their work and joined the revilers of the Son of God; they had haunted him, contradicting him, and persecuting him all through his personal ministry, and now they would not let him have a peaceable hour in which to die. They tormented him up to his last moments. They said, "He saved others; himself he cannot save." This was evidence to them that he was a pretender and impostor. They further reviled him by saying, "He is the King of Israel"; they added that if he would "now come down from the cross" they would "believe on him." We are caused to wonder at this savage joy in the Jewish rulers; however it is easily explained if we remember that they were afraid of Jesus even

now come down from the cross, and we will believe on him. 43 He trusteth on God; let him deliver him now, if he desireth him: for he said, I am the Son of God. 44 And the robbers also that were crucified with him cast upon him the same reproach.

unto this hour. They asked him to perform a miracle in rescuing himself from the cross. Jesus did no miracle in his course on such a motive as this. This was the same proposition that Satan made to him at his temptation soon after his baptism. (Matt. 4: 3, 6.) It is to be noted that even at this time they had no evil to charge against him. If they could have found anything wrong in his life or teaching, they would have thrown it in his face at this time. They become unwilling witnesses to the goodness and purity of his life. They would not have believed on him had he come down from the cross; he had done miracles as great as that and they had not believed on him. They said that he trusted in God and that he claimed to be the Son of God, and now let God deliver him. How sadly they misunderstood him! They thought that because God permitted him to be crucified he was not the Son of God. How faulty was their reasoning!

And the robbers also that were crucified with him cast upon him the same reproach.—At first both robbers did this, but one of them afterward repented; there is no contradiction in the accounts given by Matthew and Luke. Either both of the robbers did this at first, and then one changed; or with much greater probability, some think, the expression is simply a general one. The record is clear that both robbers joined in the ridicule. (Luke 23: 39-43.) Jesus had had the robber Barabbas preferred before him; he has been placed in his crucifixion between two robbers; he has been reviled by the soldiers who executed him, by the people who passed by, by the religious teachers who came out of the city to help upon him their cruelty, and now even by those who were suffering on the cross by his side.

6. DEATH AND BURIAL OF JESUS
27: 45-61

45. Now from the sixth hour there was darkness over all the [4]land until the ninth hour. 46 And about the ninth hour Jesus cried with a loud voice, saying, [5]Eli, Eli, lama sabachthani? that is, My God, my God, [6]why hast thou forsaken me? 47 And some of them that stood there, when they heard it,

[4]Or, *earth*
[5]Ps. xxii. 1.
[6]Or, *why didst thou forsake me?*

45-50 Now from the sixth hour there was darkness.—The supernatural darkness continued three hours, from noon until three o'clock in the afternoon. The Jews divided the daylight into twelve parts. This darkness is mentioned also by Mark and Luke, but is omitted in John's record. The Passover always occurred at the full moon, when an eclipse of the sun is physically impossible, as the course of the moon is in the opposite part of the heaven. We do not know any physical cause for this darkness; we only know it to be a fact, whether or not we ever can determine the physical causes for this darkness. How widely this darkness extended is not told except it was "over all the land until the ninth hour"; certainly it was over the country around Jerusalem. Darkness was typical of the powers of darkness which seemed to be prevailing; it was also typical of the great sufferings of the atoning for sin and the dark hour of sin and depravity that could crucify God's beloved Son; it could also typify the darkness of sin over all the earth, which was to be dispelled by the cross of Jesus and by his resurrection from the dead, when he brought light and life by his resurrection.

About the ninth hour Jesus cried with a loud voice.—This was three o'clock in the afternoon at the time when the lamb for the daily evening offering was sacrificed. (Mark 15: 34-41; Luke 23: 45-49; John 19: 28-37.) At this time Jesus cried with a loud voice and said, "Eli, Eli, lama sabachthani? that is, My God, my God, why hast thou forsaken me?" This is part of the twenty-second Psalm. This cry classes itself with the agonies of Gethsemane in the point that both involve the deep mysteries of the atonement—those which pertain to the mutual relations of the Father and the Son in those sufferings

said, This man calleth Elijah. 48 And straightway one of them ran, and took a sponge, and filled it with vinegar, and put it on a reed, and gave him to drink. 49 And the rest said, Let be; let us see whether Elijah cometh to save him.⁷ 50 And Jesus cried again with a loud voice, and yielded up his

⁷Many ancient authorities add *And another took a spear and pierced his side, and there came out water and blood.* See Jn. 19. 34.

and that death under which his blood was shed for the "remission of sins." We cannot fathom the depth of the wisdom of God in thus giving his Son as a sacrifice for the sins of the world. Jesus here applied Psalm 22: 1 to himself as prophetic; it is uttered by him to show that he is enduring an intolerable agony, deeper than any external affliction. We have seven recorded statements that Jesus made while on the cross. We cannot determine the exact chronological order of these seven utterances. Some think that this one was the fourth in order. Those who stood by and heard did not understand the language and thought that he called for Elijah. The mistake may easily have been made by some one sitting near, as the words resembled the sound of the name of Elias in Hebrew. The boldness which had prompted them to taunt Jesus had vanished, and hearing him cry out at this time, they may have expected in terror that the fiery prophet would descend in the chariot of fire to carry him away; hence, "one of them ran, and took a sponge, and filled it with vinegar, and put it on a reed, and gave him to drink." This was done in kindness, and seems to show that his enemies had quailed before the darkness. He had also said, "I thirst," and some one ran to relieve it. Some one filled the sponge with sour wine or vinegar, such as the soldiers used, and putting it upon a reed of hyssop, so as to reach his lips, as he hung on the cross, gave it to him to quench the dreadful feverish thirst which he endured. John says, "There was set there a vessel full of vinegar." (John 19: 29.) It did not have the qualities that stupefy and shorten life; hence when it was presented to him, he drank it. Some of them said, "Let us see whether Elijah cometh to save him." Their attitude toward Jesus is now changed and they begin to fear. "Jesus cried again with a loud voice, and yielded up his spirit." Jesus uttered the words, "It is fin-

spirit. 51 And behold, the veil of the ²temple was rent in two from the top to the bottom; and the earth did quake; and the rocks were rent; 52 and the tombs were opened; and many bodies of the saints that had fallen asleep were raised; 53 and coming forth out of the tombs after his resurrection they entered into the holy city and appeared unto many. 54 Now the centurion,

ished" (John 19: 30), and then, "Father, into thy hands I commend my spirit" (Luke 23: 46). His work, his agony, his sacrifice, were finished. His humiliation, the work of redemption, the types and prophecies, the imperfect covenant of the Mosaic law, the faith and patience of the saints, the great power of sin and Satan, the curse lifted—all were finished. The soul of Jesus was not taken from him by necessity as our lives are (John 10: 18); he died for the sins of the world; he gave his life a ransom for many.

51-56 **And behold, the veil of the temple was rent.**—We have a description of the veil of the tabernacle in Ex. 26: 31-33. This veil divided the tabernacle into two parts as the veil of the temple divided it into two parts, the holy place and the most holy. This veil was rent by the tempest and concussion of the earthquake. This signified the breaking down of the partition wall between Jew and Gentile, and the opening of the way for all men into the innermost recesses of the true temple, which is the church of God. It also signified the opening of those heavenly regions that the Holy Spirit should come down to bless men; and finally, it showed the desertion of the temple by Jehovah and the end of the Jewish covenant. It was divided into two pieces. About this time of day the priest was burning incense before the holy of holies, and must have witnessed it. "The earth did quake"; an earthquake is a violent quaking or concussion of the earth, accompanied by fearful rending of it in various places, and tempestuous winds in the air. The rending of the rocks by this earthquake opened the tombs of certain saints, "and many bodies of the saints that had fallen asleep were raised." The opening of graves occurred at the moment that Jesus died, while the resurrection and visible appearance in the city of the bodies of the saints occurred "after his resurrection." Matthew mentions the last event here because it is associated

and they that were with him watching Jesus, when they saw the earthquake, and the things that were done, feared exceedingly, saying, Truly this was ⁸the Son of God. 55 And many women were there beholding from afar, who had followed Jesus from Galilee, ministering unto him: 56 among whom was Mary Magdalene, and Mary the mother of ⁹James and Joses, and the mother of the sons of Zebedee.

⁸Or, *a son of God.*
⁹Or, *Jacob*

---

with the rending of the rocks, which opened the rock-hewn sepulchres in which the bodies of the saints had been placed. No one knows what became of the saints that were raised. Some think that they lived again in the flesh as did Lazarus and others who had been raised from the dead, while others think that they ascended to heaven. Matthew is the only historian that records this event. The scripture frequently speaks of death as asleep. (Deut. 31: 16; John 11: 11.)

Now the centurion, and they that were with him watching Jesus, when they saw the earthquake, and the things that were done, feared exceedingly.—It is not stated that the centurion knew anything about what had occurred to the tombs. The "centurion" was a Roman officer over a hundred soldiers; his duty on this occasion was to watch the bodies of the crucified until they were entirely dead. Not only the centurion, but those "that were with him" were awe-stricken and said, "Truly this was the Son of God." There were many of them and many exclamations. Luke records that the centurion glorified God and said, "Certainly this was a righteous man." (Luke 23: 47.) This language seems to intimate that he had some knowledge of the true God; we have in him a disinterested witness to the divine character of our Lord which is invaluable. He was a plain man, a soldier and a heathen, he had no prejudices to mislead him or bias him even in favor of Jesus; he gave his unsolicited testimony to the divinity of Jesus from what he saw at the crucifixion.

And many women were there beholding from afar.—These women had followed him from Galilee and had ministered unto him. This company of women, of which frequent mention is made, were relatives of some of his disciples. (Luke

57 And when even was come, there came a rich man from Arimathæa, named Joseph, who also himself was Jesus' disciple: 58 this man went to

22:49; John 19:25.) Their sex protected them from the dangers to which men might have been exposed; a few of them stood with the mother of Jesus near the cross. They remained "last at the cross" with John. It was fitting that this sex which had originally led the way to our common misery away from God should follow to the last Jesus who had taken flesh of them to expiate our common sin. Woman was the first to sin and to lead man to sin, but she was the last at the cross and the first at the empty tomb, and the first to bear the good news that Jesus had been raised from the dead. Among these women were "Mary Magdalene, and Mary the mother of James and Joses, and the mother of the sons of Zebedee." Jesus had cast seven demons out of Mary Magdalene; this Mary was probably the wife of Cleophas, or Clopas (John 19: 25). There is much division of opinion as to the identity of some of these persons. The mother of Zebedee's children was Salome, and the mother of the apostles James and John. Mary, the mother of Jesus, was with them; they were "faithful unto death."

57-61 And when even was come.—At about five o'clock in the afternoon before sunset "a rich man from Arimathæa, named Joseph" went to Pilate and asked for the body of Jesus to bury it; he came to the cross and found that Jesus was dead, and then went in to the city to Pilate. "Arimathæa" was the same as the Old Testament town "Ramathaim-zophim," which was the birthplace of Samuel. (1 Sam. 1: 19.) Joseph was a pious man and highly spoken of by the writers of the gospel. He was "a councillor of honorable estate" (Mark 15: 43), and "himself was looking for the kingdom of God"; he went boldly to Pilate and asked for the body. He was a good man and opposed the wickedness of his fellow councillors (Luke 23: 51), and was, with an allowed prudence, a disciple of Jesus. (John 19: 38.) He dared not remove the body of Jesus without permission; he knew the feeling of all parties and was probably a man entitled to the respect of Gov-

Pilate, and asked for the body of Jesus. Then Pilate commanded it to be given up. 59 And Joseph took the body, and wrapped it in a clean linen cloth, 60 and laid it in his own new tomb, which he had hewn out in the rock: and he rolled a great stone to the door of the tomb, and departed. 61 And Mary Magdalene was there, and the other Mary, sitting over against the sepulchre.

ernor Pilate. It was usual to leave the bodies of those who were crucified to decay in the places where they died. Pilate granted him the permission to take the body from the cross and make such disposition of it as he wished.

And Joseph took the body, and wrapped it in a clean linen cloth.—The body of a dead person was rolled in swaths of linen; Nicodemus joined him and brought with him servants bearing "a mixture of myrrh and aloes, about a hundred pounds." (John 19: 39.) There was so little time left before the Sabbath—Saturday—that thy hastily disposed of the body, intending to supply the other necessary things on the first day of the week; so they returned from the sepulchre and made preparations to that effect. (Luke 23: 56, 24: 1.) The body was placed in Joseph's "own new tomb, which he had hewn out in the rock." This tomb stood in a garden or enclosed place and was very near the place of crucifixion. It was a new tomb, and judging by the size of it, there was room for only a single body. It had two portions, an outer chamber or vault, and an inner one which was narrow and smaller, where the body was placed. There could be no mistake as to the resurrection; it was a solid rock, a new tomb without other bodies, and sealed and guarded by soldiers. It was impossible to remove the body by force or deception. In this burial a prophecy was fulfilled, which seemed strange that it should be spoken of one "numbered with the transgressors" (Isa. 53: 12), that he should make his grave with the rich. A "great stone" was rolled against the door or entrance of the tomb.

This act of Joseph is remembered for his thoughtfulness and love for the Master. He was "a good and righteous man" (Luke 23: 50); he was "looking for the kingdom of God" (Mark 15: 43; Luke 23: 51); he became a disciple of Jesus, but secretly for fear of the Jews he did not openly follow him (John 19: 38). The scenes around the cross seem to have kindled in him new life and he summoned courage to perform this public act of service. "And Mary Magdalene was there, and the other Mary, sitting over against the sepulchre." These women were present to note the place of the burial and to give expression to their grief; they probably remained till sunset or the close of the day. They simply watched the tomb for a while and then went home to prepare spices and ointment for the completion of the embalming, and then rested over the Sabbath day, when they could perform their own service of love to the body.

7. GUARD PLACED AROUND THE TOMB; RESURRECTION OF JESUS
27: 62 to 28: 10

62 Now on the morrow, which is *the day* after the Preparation, the chief priests and the Pharisees were gathered together unto Pilate, 63 saying, Sir, we remember that that deceiver said while he was yet alive, After three days

62-66 **Now on the morrow.**—This was the next day, "which is the day after the Preparation." Friday, the sixth day of the week, was called the day of Preparation, as all labor for the seventh day was to be done then. (Ex. 16: 22.) This year it was the Passover; the next day after it was the Sabbath and called by John "a high day." (John 19: 31.) Some think that the term "Preparation" became, before Matthew wrote, the solemn designation among the Christians to distinguish the Friday of crucifixion. The "chief priests and the Pharisees" conferred with each other as to what should be done; hence, they went to Pilate sometime during the day to make their request; their principles forbade their doing any labor on the Sabbath. We may suppose that they obtained consent either before the Sabbath began or immediately after it closed. They probably had examined the tomb and saw that the body was safe and the tomb sealed. Matthew is the only one that records these circumstances. The chief priests and Pharisees were aware that Jesus had predicted his own resurrection. Hence, they said to Pilate, "We remember that that deceiver

I will rise again. 64 Command therefore that the sepulchre be made sure until the third day, lest haply his disciples come and steal him away, and say

said while he was yet alive, After three days I will rise again." They were afraid that he would rise, hence they thought to forestall the possibility of it by a powerful Roman guard around the tomb. However they did not express that fear to Pilate; they deceived Pilate as to their fear and cast aspersion on the disciples of Jesus. They approached Pilate as though it had just occurred to them that something might take place with respect to the body. Jesus had repeatedly said to his disciples that he would be raised on the third day and the public had learned of this. (Matt. 12:40; John 2:19; 10:15-18.)

Command therefore that the sepulchre be made sure until the third day.—They spoke of Jesus as "that deceiver," and that his disciples would attempt to practice deception with respect to his resurrection. They asked for the power and authority of the Roman government to prevent his disciples from attempting to practice any deception. They thought him to be a pretender as to the Messiahship. They were shrewd in their malice; they said that if the sepulchre was not guarded his disciples might "come and steal him away, and say unto the people, He is risen from the dead." If this should be done, they knew that his disciples could point to the empty tomb as evidence that he had been raised from the dead. Their shrewdness and precaution in making it sure that no one would molest the tomb are commended to all. If the tomb should be found empty, it would give the disciples of Jesus an advantage over them, and they thought that this "last error will be worse than the first." Here they acknowledge that they had made an error. That which they called an error was beyond their control after the resurrection; they could no longer conspire against Jesus, nor stop the spread of the faith in him. In their attempt to put an end to the influence of Jesus, they did exactly what was needed to make it more sure that he was the Messiah and that he actually rose from the dead. It was taken for granted that he was dead, but they feared deception on the part of his disciples. It may

unto the people, He is risen from the dead: and the last error will be worse than the first. 65 Pilate said unto them, ¹Ye have a guard: go ²make it *as sure as ye can.* 66 So they went, and made the sepulchre sure, sealing the stone, the guard being with them.

¹Or, *Take a guard*
²Gr. *make it sure, as ye know.*

be that "the last error" has reference to the people in thinking that Jesus was the Messiah because he had risen from the dead. It would be worse for the people to think that he was the Messiah *because he had risen from the dead* than it would be to believe him to be the Messiah *because of his teaching.* They could more easily pervert, contradict, and refute his *teachings,* so they thought, than to *deny his resurrection.* Note that these chief priests and Pharisees said to Pilate "after three days" that Jesus had said he would rise again; hence they asked for a guard "until the third day," that is, until the third day had passed; again they understood "after three days" and "until the third day" to mean the same and that they would need the guard no longer.

Pilate said unto them, Ye have a guard.—That is, Pilate said take a guard and do as you wish. Some have understood this to mean that Pilate refused to give permission to use a guard; that he refused to have anything further to do with them and that if they wanted the tomb guarded they should guard it with the temple officers or their own officials. However, it seems clear that Pilate gave permission for them to use the Roman guard as the imperative construction of the Greek verb bears this out. Pilate gave them permission to detail a Roman guard for this purpose and commanded them to "make it as sure as ye can." They had permission to take all the armed men that they needed, and to make the sepulchre sure to their satisfaction. "So they went, and made the sepulchre sure, sealing the stone, the guard being with them." The stone was rolled over the door of the tomb and sealed; the Roman guard was stationed around it whose duty was to watch with unsleeping vigilance on pain of death. In sealing the tomb one or more cords were stretched across the stone rolled before the opening into the tomb and sealed at each end to the rock by wax or sealing clay. The guard of

1 Now late on the sabbath day, as it began to dawn toward the first day of the week, came Mary Magdalene and the other Mary to see the sepulchre.

Roman soldiers was placed at the entrance of the tomb as a double means of preventing fraud. The sepulchre was watched so no fraud could have been practiced. We may infer that the Jews saw to it that the tomb was sealed and the guard placed around it, for had the soldiers alone sealed it, the Jews might have said that the soldiers had suffered the disciples to steal the body; they could not say this since they sealed the tomb and placed the guard around it. It is probable that Pilate's seal was used as the Roman guard was held responsible for it.

28: 1-4 **Now late on the sabbath day.**—"Late on the sabbath" or after the Sabbath was ended, Saturday evening, Mary Magdalene and two others provided sweet spices, that they might be ready to go early next morning and embalm the body of Jesus. (Mark 16: 1.) Matthew takes up his narrative of the events with the coming of these women to the sepulchre. It was "very early on the first day of the week" (Mark 16: 2); or "at early dawn" (Luke 24: 1); or on the first day of the week "early, while it was yet dark" (John 20: 1); somewhere between three and four o'clock in the morning these women left their homes and started for the sepulchre. It is well to note how the four writers of the gospel express the time of their coming to the tomb. Matthew and John begin their record at the same time; all of the four writers describe such events as they were guided by the Holy Spirit to do; none of them propose to give the exact chronological order, and none of them contradict each other, but all harmonize. This "first day of the week" is what we call "Sunday" or "the Lord's day." On this day Jesus rose from the dead "the firstfruits" of them that slept, the earnest and surety of the resurrection of all who sleep in him. (Rom. 11: 16; 1 Cor. 15: 20, 23.) Jesus was buried between four and six o'clock on Friday afternoon, and rose early on Sunday morning, so he was in the tomb part of three days. Each part of a day was reckoned as a day, just as in computing the reigns of the Jew-

2 And behold, there was a great earthquake; for an angel of the Lord descended from heaven, and came and rolled away the stone, and sat upon it. 3 His appearance was as lightning, and his raiment white as snow: 4 and for fear of him the watchers did quake, and became as dead men. 5 And the

ish kings each part of a year is reckoned as a year. Mary Magdalene and the other Mary came "to see the sepulchre." It was their intention also to embalm the body. They may have had a vague idea or expectation of the resurrection; they surely knew something about what he had said about his resurrection, whether they understood it or not. However, we may regard it as affection mourning over the dead rather than faith in a living Savior, which brought them so early to the sepulchre.

And behold, there was a great earthquake.—This earthquake seems to have occurred while they were on the way and they saw the effects of it when they arrived at the sepulchure. This earthquake was a fitting sign to accompany the rising of the Lord; he came forth a mighty conqueror. Jesus did not suffer profane eyes to look upon him after he was raised from the dead. The earthquake occurred at the time the angel "of the Lord descended from heaven" and rolled the stone away, thus breaking the seal. This divine messenger overawed the guards and rolled away the stone, not to let Jesus out of the tomb, but to let others in to see that he had risen. The angel was there to confirm the evidence borne by the empty tomb. Jesus arose with tremendous power and angelic witnesses. When the women arrived the stone had been rolled away and the angel "sat upon it." Sitting was a significant sign of majesty. The angel sat, terrible to the keepers. (Matt. 26: 64; Acts 7: 55.) The angel rose and was standing to comfort the women as they came. When Mary drew near, she saw what had been unnoticed, a second angel within the tomb.

His appearance was as lightning.—In vivid and intense brightness there was a surpassingly dazzling light which flashed with terrible beauty in the eyes of the keepers, like the vividness and blaze of lightning. Angelic appearances seem to be assumed at will or as necessity demanded for the im-

angel answered and said unto the women, Fear not ye; for I know that ye seek Jesus, who hath been crucified. 6 He is not here; for he is risen, even

pression to be made, otherwise the women would have been terrified; but when they drew near, they saw them only in mild, comforting, subdued light as "a young man sitting on the right side, arrayed in a white robe." (Mark 16: 5.) Luke says that they beheld "two men" who "stood by them in dazzling apparel." (Luke 24: 4.) John says that Mary beheld "two angels in white sitting, one at the head, and one at the feet, where the body of Jesus had lain." (John 20: 12.) "His raiment white as snow" is the description given by Matthew. White is naturally associated in our mind with purity, innocence, and joy; it is a fit emblem of the angels. Angels assume the form of people and dress as men. This angel confounded the wicked and comforted the righteous; "for fear of him the watchers did quake, and became as dead men." This appearance of the angel might well have terrified the heathen soldiers. Our Lord therefore arose unseen, while they were lying prostrate around the garden in front of the tomb. After a time they recovered and fled into the city to relate the news of this miracle. They had been placed there to keep a few men from theft; they now report a portentous deliverance against which they had no power to contend. They were helpless and powerless, since God's power wrought the miracle of the resurrection.

5-8 And the angel answered and said unto the women.—We learn from Mark and Luke that the angel first spake to the women after they went into the sepulchre. (Mark 16: 5, 6; Luke 24: 2-5.) There seems to be a pause between the fourth and fifth verses; for from some cause unknown, the women did not reach the sepulchre until about six o'clock when the sun was rising. (Mark 16: 2.) If they had remained in the city whither they had gone to get spices, some on Friday (Luke 23: 54-56), some on Saturday evening (Mark 16: 1) they may not have been able to pass the gates until they were opened later. They saw, as they came in sight of the garden, that the stone was rolled away. They had discussed the roll-

as he said. Come, see the place ³where the Lord lay. 7 And go quickly,

³Many ancient authorities read *where he lay*.

ing away of the stone as they went along the way and asked one another, "Who shall roll us away the stone from the door of the tomb?" (Mark 16: 3.) So they were amazed when they saw the stone had been rolled away. Mary Magdalene thought that the Lord's body had been treated with some indignity and returned in grief to inform Peter and John. (Mark 16:3, 4.) After she was gone, the other two women entered the outer chamber of the tomb, and saw the angel sitting on the right of the entrance into the inner chamber, where the body had been placed. This second angel spoke to them. It seems that the vision of two angels described by Luke (24: 1-9) was seen by the second company of women, who had left the cross on Friday evening and returned to the city, intending to come back to the tomb after the Sabbath had passed. The women had infinitely more reason to rejoice than to fear; hence the angel said, "Fear not ye; for I know that ye seek Jesus, who hath been crucified." The angel understood them and had come to help them; he knew that love had brought them to the tomb. "Fear not ye" is a usual salutation of celestial beings, even from the days of Abraham (Gen. 15: 1; Judges 6: 23). The human heart instinctively trembles at any sudden manifestation of spiritual beings. (Job 4: 13-16; Matt. 14: 26.) The keepers and the enemies of Jesus had reason to fear, but not these disciples; the purpose of the angel was not to shed terror and stupefaction upon the guards, but to speak peace and courage to the mourning friends of Jesus.

He is not here.—They had come to embalm his body, and now they are not informed that his body was not there. None of the disciples of Jesus had fully understood what rising from the dead meant (Mark 9: 10), and therefore they did not expect the event. The angel speaks of Jesus in terms of his majestic title. "For he is risen, even as he said. Come, see the place where the Lord lay." This put at ease the mind of the women, for they supposed that his body had been taken

and tell his disciples, He is risen from the dead; and lo, he goeth before you into Galilee; there shall ye see him: lo, I have told you. 8 And they departed quickly from the tomb with fear and great joy, and ran to bring his

from the tomb and placed somewhere else; the angel gives the reason for the empty tomb—"he is risen." The angel refers them to the language of Jesus—he had done just what he said he would do. They are requested to view the place where the body lay. They are to see for themselves that the tomb is empty. The spot where Jesus was laid is affectionately pointed out by the angel to the women. They are commissioned to "go quickly, and tell his disciples, He is risen from the dead." The good news is to be heralded at once to his disciples; no delay should be had in bearing this news to the disturbed, sorrowful, and despondent disciples. These women are made the first messengers of the glad news of the resurrection. They are to tell his disciples and Mark adds "Peter." (Mark 16: 7.) This was a mark of forgiveness to the penitent Peter who was then sorrowing for his sin of denying Jesus. The disciples were in despair, and so as a woman had led man to sin, so women now bring them the good news of salvation. The second part of the message was that "lo, he goeth before you into Galilee; there shall ye see him." The sorrow of the disciples may now end; their doubts are to be removed; their night is turned into day. It seems fitting that the resurrection should occur at the dawning of the day; it was the dawning of the world's day of redemption. Jesus had promised his disciples before his death that he would be raised and would go before them into Galilee. (Matt. 26: 32.) The angel now repeats the promise that Jesus had made. The women "departed quickly from the tomb with fear and great joy." There is a fear which is easily and naturally felt with love and joy; it prepares the mind and heart for richer blessings. The women departed "quickly" and "ran" to bring the message to his disciples. They knew the joy which their message would convey, and urged by some fear of the angel they made no delay. After their departure, Peter and John came running to the tomb, followed by Mary Magdalene.

[28:9, 10.] MATTHEW 557

disciples word. 9 And behold, Jesus met them, saying, All hail. And they came and took hold of his feet, and ⁴worshipped him. 10 Then saith Jesus unto them, Fear not: go tell my brethren that they depart into Galilee, and there shall they see me.

⁴See marginal note on ch. 2. 2.

They examined the graveclothes, but saw no vision, and soon left the sepulchre in utter amazement. (Luke 24: 12; John 20: 3-10.) Mary remained weeping, and as she stooped to look into the sepulchre saw two angels who comforted her. As she turned the Lord appeared to her, revealed himself to her, and sent her on a message to his brethren. (Mark 16: 9; John 20: 11-17.) She seems to have met or overtaken the other women, Mary, wife of Cleophas, and Salome, and our Lord appeared to the three.

9, 10 **And behold, Jesus met them.**—The order of events seems to have been this: Mary Magdalene, after notifying Peter and the apostles, returned to the sepulchre, which she reached after the others had left, and Jesus appeared to her near the tomb. This was his first appearance after the resurrection. Then as they "ran to bring his disciples word," by some other route than Mary Magdalene took, "behold, Jesus met them," his second appearance, and made himself known by saying, "All hail." The Greek means simply, "hail, rejoice"; they knew him by this salutation and worshipped him. "They came and took hold of his feet, and worshipped him." This was a common mode of showing reverence. (2 Kings 4: 37.) They embraced his feet in their hands or arms, to manifest their affection and joy at seeing him again as well as to express reverence of his supernatural appearance. On this and other occasions Jesus permitted persons to worship him; he would not have done this had he been only man. Peter refused it. (Acts 10: 25.) Supreme worship is due to God; Christ is the Son of God, whom we worship, since to worship any other creature is idolatry. Jesus then comforted them and said, "Fear not: go tell my brethren that they depart into Galilee, and there shall they see me." Jesus comforted them and gave them this message which the angel had given and which he had before his death promised them. He calls them "my brethren"; he was not ashamed to call them brethren. (Heb. 2: 11.) His disciples were to go into Galilee. There he met with them by the Sea of Galilee. (John 21: 1-14.) Afterward he appeared to "above five hundred brethren at once" (1 Cor. 15: 6); and a third time in Galilee to James and all the apostles (1 Cor. 15: 7). The following tabulated list of his appearances, together with the time and place recorded, is here submitted:

OUR LORD'S APPEARANCES AFTER HIS RESURRECTION

Order	Time	To Whom	Where	Record
1	Early Sunday morning	Mary Magdalene	Near the tomb at Jerusalem	Mark 16: 9; John 20: 11-18
2	Sunday morning	Women returning from the tomb	Near Jerusalem	Matt. 28: 9, 10
3	Sunday	Simon Peter alone	Near Jerusalem	Luke 24: 34
4	Sunday afternoon	Two disciples going to Emmaus	Between Jerusalem and Emmaus, and at Emmaus	Luke 24: 13-31
5	Sunday evening	Apostles, except Thomas	Jerusalem	John 20: 19-25
6	Sunday evening of the next week	Apostles, Thomas being present	Jerusalem	John 20: 26-29
7	Unknown	Seven disciples fishing	Sea of Galilee	John 21: 1-13
8	Unknown	Eleven disciples on a mountain	Galilee	Matt. 28: 16-20
9	Unknown	Above 500 brethren at once	Galilee	1 Cor. 15: 6
10	Unknown	James only	Jerusalem, probably	1 Cor. 15: 7
11	Unknown	All the apostles at ascension	Mount of Olives near Bethany	Luke 24: 50, 51; Acts 1: 6-12

8. SANHEDRIN'S FALSEHOOD; THE COMMISSION
28: 11-20

11 Now while they were going, behold, some of the guard came into the city, and told unto the chief priests all the things that were come to pass. 12 And when they were assembled with the elders, and had taken counsel, they

11-15 Now while they were going.—As the women left to bear the message the guards had a message to deliver to the chief priests; it may be that the guards left the tomb immediately after the earthquake and the resurrection of Jesus, and before the women arrived at the sepulchre. The words of the women seemed like idle dreams. (Mark 16: 10, 11; Luke 24: 10, 11; John 20: 18.) So while the women were relating what they had seen and heard to the disciples, the soldiers returned to the city and some of them related to the Jewish rulers what they had seen and heard. These soldiers being heathen men were more ready to admit the resurrection and perhaps carried their report to Pilate. For though it was death to a Roman soldier to be unfaithful on duty, when only men were opposed to him, it is altogether probable that the signs of the earthquake confirmed the soldiers' testimony and that Pilate was willing to believe them and excuse them. The chief priests believed them, or they would have searched for the body at once and denounced the guard to the governor.

And when they were assembled with the elders.—The Sanhedrin took counsel as to what should be done. It seems that the whole Sanhedrin was convened to consult on what should be done to meet the embarrassing situation. The report of the soldiers must be contradicted and silenced. The Sanhedrin was desperate in its efforts to determine what should be done. They had said before, "If we let him thus alone, all men will believe on him." (John 11: 48.) When they had asked Pilate for a guard to prevent the disciples from stealing the body, and pretend that it was risen from the dead, they said, "The last error will be worse than the first" (Matt. 27: 64), but now the body was gone—the tomb was empty; the evidences of divine interposition remained and everything corresponded with the report of the soldiers. Why did they not first search the spot and endeavor to trace the perpetrators of the deed?

gave much money unto the soldiers, 13 saying, Say ye, His disciples came by night, and stole him away while we slept. 14 And if this ⁵come to the governor's ears, we will persuade him, and rid you of care. 15 So they took the money, and did as they were taught: and this saying was spread abroad among the Jews, *and continueth* until this day.

⁵Or, *come to a hearing before the governor*

They evidently believed the soldiers; they believed that it had come true, in some supernatural manner, that Jesus had broken out from the grave as he had before raised Lazarus.

The Sanhedrin finally decided, after taking counsel, to bribe the soldiers with money and persuade them to say, "His disciples came by night, and stole him away while we slept." "They gave much money unto the soldiers"; that is, they gave a large amount of money. They were obliged to offer a very liberal bribe, for it was a dangerous situation for the soldiers to bear testimony that they had been asleep on duty. It was absurd for them to bear such testimony; the testimony of sleeping men to an event which occurred while they were asleep is ridiculous; yet that is just what these Jews persuaded the soldiers to testify. Not only did they give them a large sum of money, but they promised that "if this come to the governor's ears, we will persuade him, and rid you of care." If Pilate already knew what had occurred, or if some of the soldiers had already reported to him, while others reported to the chief priests, these Jews did not know of it. The soldiers would probably take the money anyway. The Jews thought that Pilate would soon leave Jerusalem for Caesarea and that he would forget anything about the guard unless some of the Jews should complain to Pilate against the soldiers. If Pilate had thought that some of his soldiers slept while on duty, he would not have excused them; he would, according to Roman law, have had them put to death.

So they took the money, and did as they were taught.—The soldiers were guilty of receiving a bribe, and the Sanhedrin was guilty of paying a bribe; we cannot estimate the magnitude of the crime; however, it seems that the Sanhedrin was more culpable as it was more eager for the crime to be committed. The Jews were religious leaders, while the soldiers

16 But the eleven disciples went into Galilee, unto the mountain where Jesus had appointed them. 17 And when they saw him, they ⁴worshipped *him;* but some doubted. 18 And Jesus came to them and spake unto them,

were ignorant heathen men. "This saying was spread abroad among the Jews, and continueth until this day." This story that the Sanhedrin hired the soldiers to tell became known among the Jews and was current at the time that Matthew wrote this record, which was eight or ten years after the deed was perpetrated. Their story was so extraordinary that it lived a long time; it was an unheard-of thing for Roman soldiers to sleep while on duty. If they were asleep, how did they know what took place; or if they only supposed as to what took place, how could the disciples have rolled away the stone without awakening them? This bribe would have made any soldier under such circumstances remain silent. The "Jews" and the Christians at the time Matthew wrote had different interests and this report was common among the Jews.

The women were the first witnesses of the resurrection of Christ; they were glad witnesses. The Roman soldiers were the second witnesses; they were unwilling witnesses of the resurrection. Their false testimony was not original with them; the Jewish Sanhedrin must bear the responsibility for it; hence the Sanhedrin also becomes a witness of the resurrection, because none of them attempted to refute the testimony of the soldiers that Jesus had been raised from the dead. It is not probable that the body of Jesus was stolen, neither was it possible for the disciples to steal his body. We now take leave of the enemies of Jesus as recorded by Matthew; they are hypocrites to the last; they are bribers of falsehoods, slanderers of the apostles, and blasphemers of Jesus. We are glad to depart from them and leave them to their own sin and to the mercy of a just God.

16, 17 But the eleven disciples went into Galilee.—Jesus had told his disciples before his death that he would be raised and would meet them in Galilee; the angel told the women to bear the message to the disciples that Jesus would meet his disciples in Galilee; and then Jesus, when he appeared to the women, told them to "go tell my brethren that they depart into

Galilee, and there shall they see me." Matthew now records that meeting. "The eleven disciples" met him at the appointed place. Judas was dead, and was no more numbered with them. We cannot determine the exact time when this meeting took place evidently Jesus had appeared to his disciples time and again before he met them in Galilee. He appeared to two disciples on the road to Emmaus, a village about seven and a half miles from Jerusalem. (Mark 16: 12, 13; Luke 24: 13-32.) They immediately returned to Jerusalem, and all the disciples being assembled except Thomas, Jesus appeared and convinced them of his resurrection. (Luke 24: 33-34.) This ended the first Sunday or first day of the week. On the following first day of the week Jesus appeared to the eleven (Mark 16: 14; John 20: 26-32), again at the Sea of Galilee, and then as Matthew here relates; this seems to be the order of his appearances to this time. They met on "the mountain where Jesus had appointed them." No writer of the gospel informs us which mountain was appointed; hence, it is impossible for us to know. Tradition points out that it was Mount Tabor. "And when they saw him, they worshipped him; but some doubted." Thomas may have been one of the doubters; at this time all doubts had not been removed. The disciples were slow in comprehending the full significance of his resurrection. He had repeatedly told them that he would be raised from the dead, and now with incontestable proof he shows them that he has been raised from the dead; yet "some doubted." The disciples, at the arrest of Jesus in Gehsemane, had scattered; only Peter and John followed him to his trials; only John witnessed the crucifixion. The other disciples believed that he had been crucified; they had no doubt about this, and yet they had stronger proof of his resurrection than they had of his crucifixion. They had seen him after his resurrection and now even worshipped him. The fact of the resurrection was a strange one; there was no other like it. The daughter of Jairus, the widow's son, and Lazarus were only revivified or raised from the dead and recalled to this life; but Jesus rose to the incorruption, glory and power of an endless life. Hence, the disciples were slow to believe. However, they were finally convinced. The slowness of the disciples to

saying, All authority hath been given unto me in heaven and on earth. 19 Go

believe furnished an occasion for the strongest cumulative evidence to be gathered, so that the resurrection of Christ rests upon the most simple and incontestable evidence. If Jesus was not raised from the dead, then he was an impostor, his disciples were deceivers or deluded, and the church was built upon a falsehood. Jesus arose from the dead; there is no other explanation of the empty tomb.

18-20 And Jesus came to them and spake.—At this time Jesus gave to them "the world-wide, time-lasting commission." All doubts had now been removed; all evidence was now before them, and they are now ready to receive this all-important commission. They are to see that the death of Jesus did not end all, but that his death, burial, and resurrection constituted the essential facts of the gospel which they are to proclaim to the world; their work, instead of ending, is just now beginning; their despair at the death of Jesus is turned into the glorious hope of the gospel.

All authority hath been given unto me in heaven and on earth.—Our Lord has power to do all the work of mediation and grace between God and man; he was the Son of God in his divine nature, and had from eternity almighty power. (John 1: 3; Col. 1: 16; Heb. 1: 8.) All power, in an absolute sense, cannot be attributed to him in his human nature, for it cannot be possessed and used by any creature. Since he has been raised from the dead, he now can claim all power in his person as Christ, both God and man. After his obedience unto death, and his sacrifice on the cross, he became the "mediator," the one authorized to stand between God and man. To our Lord was "all authority" now committed, that he should be Prophet, Priest, King, Mediator, Intercessor, and Savior of his people, and Judge over all created beings. (John 5: 22, 23; 1 Cor. 15: 25-27; Eph. 1: 20-23; Phil. 2: 9-11.) "As the Father hath sent me, even so send I you." (John 20: 21.) Thus does he give them a commission founded upon his own, to do the work in its application to men in every age, which he began and made possible by his death and resurrection.

ye therefore, and make disciples of all the nations, baptizing them into the name of the Father and of the Son and of the Holy Spirit: 20 teaching them

Go ye therefore, and make disciples of all the nations.—"Therefore" gives authority to what he is commanding; because he has all power and authority, he has a right to say to them "go." He has the power to make their going successful; therefore "go," be aggressive; they are to have "all authority" behind them in doing what he now commands them to do. He has all authority, all power, all wisdom, and he now gives to his disciples an aggressiveness in evangelizing the world for him. They are to "make disciples of all the nations"; that is, they are to "disciple" "all the nations"; that is, they are to preach the gospel and teach the people. To disciple a person to Christ is to lead that one to become a follower of Christ, to be a learner in his school, to be obedient to his commands, to become a Christian. To "make disciples" means to give all kinds of instruction for entrance into the church of our Lord.

Baptizing them into the name of the Father and of the Son and of the Holy Spirit.—Those who are "discipled" are to be baptized; they were not to baptize "all the nations," but those of "all nations" who were "discipled." "Baptizing them" means those who receive the teachings. "Them," in the Greek, is in the masculine gender "autous," and cannot have for its antecedent "nations," "ethna," because "nations" is in the neuter gender; hence, only those of the nations who are made disciples by preaching the gospel are to be baptized. The baptism is to be done "into the name of the Father and of the Son and of the Holy Spirit." The name of the Father and of the Son and of the Holy Spirit means the combined authority of the Godhead. To be baptized into this is to be brought by baptism into actual subjection to the combined authority of heaven. To be baptized into the name of these three brings one into covenant relation with the Godhead. Baptism is, therefore, not only a sacred act of obedience, but it brings one into the fullness of the blessings of the Father, Son, and Holy Spirit. Christ is a universal Savior and his gospel is a universal gospel; obedience to him brings one into all the blessings which God has to give to man.

to observe all things whatsoever I commanded you: and lo, I am with you ⁶always, even unto ⁷the end of the world.

⁶Gr. *all the days.*
⁷Or, *the consummation of the age.*

Teaching them to observe all things whatsoever I commanded you.—Those who are "discipled" to Jesus, and who have then baptized into the name of the Father, the Son, and the Holy Spirit are to be taught "to observe all things" which train and develop a child of God. Three things are commanded in the commission to be done, namely: (1) make disciples; (2) baptize those who are discipled; (3) then teach them to be obedient to all the commands of God. These three things are enjoined upon the disciples; they are joined and none of them should be omitted or neglected. A promise is given to them in this charge, "and lo, I am with you always, even unto the end of the world." This promise carries with it the cooperation of divine agencies; it is limited in time only by "the end of the world." That is, the end of the gospel dispensation. This promise extends his spiritual presence and blessings to all who serve under this commission.

Jesus remained on earth affer his resurrection "by the space of forty days, and speaking the things concerning the kingdom of God." (Acts 1: 3.) He ascended to the Father about ten days before Pentecost His disciples were to wait in Jerusalem "until ye be clothed with power from on high." (Luke 24: 49.) They were to wait until Jesus ascended to the Father and sent the Holy Spirit here to guide them. "But the Comforter, even the Holy Spirit, whom the Father will send in my name, he shall teach you all things, and bring to your remembrance all that I said unto you." (John 14: 26.) When the Holy Spirit came on Pentecost, he filled the apostles and they began with renewed efforts the great task of evangelizing the world. Jesus was not willing to leave such an important work to his disciples without divine guidance. Although he had kept them in training for about three years, the work was so imperative and the salvation of souls so important that the Holy Spirit was dispatched from heaven to guide the apostles in carrying out this commission. God's plan of salvation has been completed; salvation is offered unto all. The commission sets forth the conditions of salvation. The commission expresses the terms of salvation; no one is commissioned to preach any other gospel. The four writers of the gospel have left on record this commission; it has been expressed in different ways. A summary of the commission is here submitted.

THE COMMISSION

Matt. 28: 18-20	Make disciples			Baptism	
Mark 16: 15, 16	Preach	Faith		Baptism	Salvation
Luke 24: 46, 47	Preach		Repentance		Salvation
John 20: 21-23	Preach				Salvation
ALL combined	Preach	Faith	Repentance	Baptism	Salvation

BIBLIOGRAPHY

Abbot, Lyman: *The New Testament, with Notes and Comments* (Matthew).
Allen, Willoughby C.: *International Critical Commentary* (Matthew).
Bengal, John Albert: *Gnomon of the New Testament* (Matthew).
Boles, H. Leo: *Elam's Notes,* 1929-1931.
Boles, H. Leo: *International Sunday School Lesson, Adult Quarterly, 1932-1936.*
Broadus, John A.: *An American Commentary on the New Testament* (Matthew).
Broughton, Len G.: *Kingdom Parables and Their Teaching.*
Brown, David: *A Commentary, Critical, Experimental, and Practical* (Matthew).
Bruce, Alexander B.: *The Humiliation of Christ.*
Bruce, William: *Commentary on the Gospel According to Matthew.*
Burkitt, William: *Expository Notes on the New Testament* (Matthew).
Buttrick, George A.: *The Parables of Jesus.*
Cadoux, A. T.: *The Parables of Jesus.*
Campbell, George: *The Four Gospels* (Matthew).
Clarke, Adam: *Commentary and Critical Notes.*
Clark, George W.: *Brief Notes on the New Testament* (Matthew).
Cowles, Henry: *Matthew and Mark with Notes.*
Dale, R. W.: *The Living Christ and the Four Gospels.*
Dods, Marcus: *The Parables of Our Lord.*
Elam, E. A.: *Elam's Notes,* 1922-1928.
Erdman, Charles R.: *The Gospel of Matthew.*
Gibson, John Monro: *The Expositor's Bible* (Matthew).
Habershon, Ada R.: *The Study of the Parables.*
Hall, C. H.: *Notes, Practical and Expository, on the Gospels* (Matthew).
Hammond, C. E.: *Outline of Textual Criticism of the New Testament.*
Hastings, James: *Dictionary of the Bible.*
Henry, Matthew: *An Exposition of the Old and New Testament* (Matthew).
Jacobus, Melancthon W.: *Notes on the Gospels, Critical and Explanatory* (Matthew).
Jacobus, Nourse, and Zenos: *A New Standard Bible Dictionary.*
Jameson, Fausset, and Brown: *A Commentary on the Old and New Testaments.*
Johnson, B. W.: *The People's New Testament* (Matthew).
Laidlow, John: *The Miracles of Our Lord.*
Lange, John Peter: *The Gospel According to Matthew.*

Lipscomb, David: *Gospel Advocate*, 1855-1915.
Macknight, James: *A Harmony of the Four Gospels* (Matthew).
Maclaren, Alexander: *The Gospel of Matthew*.
McGarvey, J. W.: *The New Testament Commentary* (Matthew and Mark).
Meyer, H. A. W.: *Critical and Exegetical Handbook, Gospel of Matthew*.
Morgan, G. Campbell: *The Parables of the Kingdom*.
Oxford Edition, *A Plain Commentary on the Four Holy Gospels* (Matthew).
Peloubet, F. N.: *The Teachers' Commentary on Matthew*.
Peloubet, F. N.: *Select Notes on International Lessons*, 1880-1935.
Robertson, A. T.: *A Short Grammar of the Greek New Testament*.
Robertson, A. T.: *Epochs in the Life of Jesus*.
Robertson, A. T.: *Studies in the New Testament*.
Robertson, A. T.: *The Pharisees and Jesus*.
Robinson, Theodore H.: *The Gospel of Matthew*.
Ryle, J. C.: *Expository Thoughts on the Gospels* (Matthew).
Scott, Thomas: *The Holy Bible with Explanatory Notes* (Matthew).
Smith, William: *Dictionary of the Bible*.
Stalker, James: *The Life of Jesus Christ*.
Stier, Rudolph: *The Words of the Lord Jesus* (Matthew).
Streeter, Burnett Hillman: *The Four Gospels, a Study of Origins* (Matthew).
Summers, Thos. O.: *Commentary on the Gospels* (Matthew).
Thayer, J. H.: *Greek-English Lexicon of the New Testament*.
Trench, Richard Chenevix: *Notes on the Miracles of our Lord*.
Trench, Richard Chenevix: *Notes on the Parables of Our Lord*.
Vincent, Marvin R.: *Word Studies in the New Testament* (Matthew).
Weiss, Bernhard: *A Commentary on the New Testament* (Matthew).
Weston, Henry G.: *Matthew the Genesis of the New Testament*.
Whedon, D. D.: *Commentary on the Gospels* (Matthew).
Young, Robert: *Analytical Concordance to the Bible*.

TRANSLATIONS OF THE NEW TESTAMENT

The Twentieth Century New Testament.
The New Testament in Modern Speech, Weymouth.
New Testament, A. T. Anderson.
New Testament, Goodspeed.
Douay Version.
The Riverside New Testament, Ballantine.
New Testament Critically Emphasized, Rotherham.

BIBLIOGRAPHY

Greek-English New Testament.
New Testament, Latin Vulgate.
The Holy Bible, Young.
Emphatic Diaglott.
The New Testament, American Bible Union.
Modern Readers' Bible, Moulton.
The Holy Bible, Moffatt.
Centenary Translation of New Testament, Montgomery.
The New Testament in Modern Speech, Fenton.
Translation of the New Testament, Godbey.
The Authorized Version (King James).
Revised Version (Standard Edition).

INDEX TO SUBJECTS

A

	Page
Abraham	16
Abomination of Desolation	463
A Caution	175
All Authority Given unto Him	563
A Little Child	367
Angel Answered the Woman	554
Answered Scribes and Pharisees	274
Apostles Chosen	220
Apostles Commissioned	220
Apostles Sent Forth	220
Appearances After His Resurrection	558
Arrest of Jesus	511

B

Baptism and Temptation	64
Baptism of Jesus	88
Baptism of Holy Spirit	84
Bargain of Judas	497
Barabbas	533
Barren Fig Tree	416
Beatitudes	119
Beelzebub	267
Beginning of Galilean Ministry	108
Bethlehem of Judea	43
Bethany	494
Bethphage	409
Betrayal and Arrest	511
Bibliography	567
Birth of Jesus	34
Binding on Earth	377
Bill of Divorcement	387
Blasphemy	269
Blind and Lame Come to Him	414
Burial of Jesus	511

C

Call of Peter and Andrew	112
Call of James and John	112
Call of Matthew	205
Called Rabbi	443
Cast Lots	539
Canaanitish Woman	331
Capernaum	251
Causing One to Stumble	368
Centurion	188
Certain Cities Condemned	248
Chief Priest and Pharisees	426
Chief Priest and Elders	493
Chief Priest Took the Silver	527
Confession	75
Confession at Caesarea	341

	Page
Cost of Discipleship	334
Contents	5
Come to Capernaum	364
Commission Given	564
Cross Bearing	237
Crucifixion of Jesus	511

D

David	256
Days Shortened	466
Days of Noah	473
Day of Unleavened Bread	499
Death and Burial of Jesus	543
Despising One of These Little Ones	372
Destruction of Temple	457
Disciples of John	208
Disciples Went into Galilee	561
Disciple and Teacher	230
Dumb Man Healed	216

E

Elijah Must First Come	358
Explanation of Parable of Sower	286

F

Faithful and Unfaithful Servants	471
False Prophets	462
Feast of Matthew	206
Feast in Simon's House	492
Feeding Five Thousand	314
Feeding Four Thousand	335
Fellow Servants	381
First Day of Week	552
Flight into Egypt	50
Following Jesus	350
Food of John the Baptist	71
Forgiveness	162
Foretells His Death	397
For and Against Jesus	268
From Galilee to Perea	384

G

Gadarenes	199
Gates of Hades	346
Genealogy of Jesus	16
Gentiles and the Publicans	377
Gethsemane	503, 508
Go Before into Galilee	506
Going up to Jerusalem	401
Golgotha	538

	Page
Golden Rule	175
Gospel of the Kingdom	462
Gospel of God	116
Great Faith	334
Great Invitation	253
Greatest Among You	444
Group of Miracles	186
Group of Parables	284
Guard Around the Tomb	549

H

Hated of All Men	229
Hard for Rich Man	394
Hear Another Parable	422
Hearing and Doing	183
Hearing and Not Doing	184
Herod	35
Herod Seeks to Destroy Jesus	52
Herod Destroying the Children	57
Herod Laid Hold of John	310
Herod's Birthday	311
Herd of Swine	201
His Authority Questioned	416
Hours of Darkness	543
How Offenders to Be Treated	375
Hypocrites	326

I

Idle Words	273
I Will Build My Church	345
If Thy Brother Sin against Thee	375
Introduction	9
Inscription Over the Cross	540

J

Jesus Retires to Galilee	108
Jesus Rejected at Nazareth	305
Jesus in Gennesaret	322
Jesus Rebuked Peter	349
Jesus and the Children	390
Jesus Sent Two Disciples	410
Jesus Entered into the Temple	413
Jesus Went Out from Temple	457
Jesus Before Pilate	521, 529
Jesus' Estimate of John	240
Jesus' Relation to the Law	130
Jews Offended in Him	307
John the Baptist	64
John the Baptist Beheaded	308
Joseph Took the Body	548
Judas Iscariot	525

K

Keys of the Kingdom	346
Kingdom of Heaven	68, 297, 379
Kingdom of Their Father	301
Killeth the Prophets	456

L

	Page
Laborers in the Vineyard	397
Last Days of the Public Ministry	409
Leaven of the Pharisees	340
Leaven of the Sadducees	340
Leper Cured	186
Lessons from Fig Tree	471
Light of the World	128
Limited Commission	223
Lord of the Sabbath	259
Lord's Supper	503
Losing and Saving Life	351

M

Man of Cyrene	537
Man Sick of Palsy	202
Massacre of the Innocents	55
Mary and Joseph	23
Men of Nineveh	277
Messengers from John the Baptist	240
Mission and Work of John	64
"Model Prayer"	159
Moses and Elijah	354
Multitude Rebuked Them	408

N

Names of the Apostles	221
No One Knoweth the Day	472

O

Occasions of Stumbling	370
Offering of Thy Gift	137
Offspring of Viper	272
One Possessed with Demon	265
Opposition Developed	255
Opposition of Scribes	223
Opposition of Pharisees	434
Outline of Matthew	14

P

Parable of the Sower	285
Parable of the Tares	288
Parable of the Mustard Seed	296
Parable of the Leaven	297
Parable of the Hidden Treasure	302
Parable of the Precious Pearl	302
Parable of the Net	381
Parable of the Unmerciful Servant	381
Parable of the Laborers in the Vineyard	397
Parable of the Two Sons	416
Parable of the Wicked Husbandmen	422

INDEX 573

	Page
Parable of the Marriage Feast	427
Parable of the Ten Virgins	477
Parable of the Talents	486
Parable of the Sheep and the Goats	486
Parables Declared	329
Paying Tribute to Caesar	427
Parted His Garments	539
Peter's Wife's Mother	187, 193
Peter Rebuked Jesus	349
Peter's Proposition	355
Peter's Denial	521
Peter's Denial Foretold	503
Peter Followed Afar	516
Perils of Riches	390
Pharisees	75
Pharisees Come to Jesus	385
Pharisees and Sadducees Unite against Jesus	337
Pharisees Counsel	431
Pharisees Gathered Together	439
Pilate Prevailed Nothing	534
Power of Faith	359
Prediction of Crucifixion	492
Preface	3
Praying in Gethsemane	509
Principles of Kingdom	108
Principles of Love	150
Praying	156
Prayer Encouraged	175
Prayer of Thanksgiving	248
Prophets and Law until John	245
Prophecy of Isaiah	263
Putting New Wine in Old Bottles	209

Q
| Queen of the South | 277 |

R
Reason for Parables	285
Rebukes James and John	397
Receiving Christ	238
Repentance	66
Resurrection	511
Resurrection of Jesus	549
Return to Nazareth	58
Reward of Discipleship	234
Reward of Self-Sacrifice	390
Rich Young Ruler	390
Robbers Crucified with Him	542
Roman Soldiers Mocked Jesus	536
Rulers of the House	212
Rumors of War	460

S
	Page
Sadducees	75
Sadducees and the Resurrection	434
Sadducees Silenced	436
Salt of the Earth	127
Sanhedrin's Bribe	560
Second Cleansing of the Temple	409
Seeking the Kingdom	170
Serving Two Masters	166
Seven Woes	447
Scribes	195
Scribes and Pharisees on Moses' Seat	441
Signs of His Second Coming	457
Simon the Leper	495
Solemn Warnings	179
Sons of the Kingdom	191
Son of Man Coming	352
Spit in His Face	520
Spiritual Relationship	281
Stilled the Tempest	197

T
Take My Yoke	254
Teachings Against Murder	134
Teachings against Adultery	139
Teachings against Divorce	139
Teachings against Oaths	144
Teachings against Retaliation	144
Teachings against Hypocrisy	154
Teachings against Riches	164
Teachings against Judging	172
Teaching Them All Things	565
Teaching Concerning Divorce	384
Tell It to the Church	376
Temple Tax	359
Temptation of Jesus	95
Tertullian	433
Theme of His Preaching	116
The Two Ways	175
The Galilean Ministry	186
The Two Blind Men	213
The Need of More Laborers	217
The Temple	258
The Tithe	14
The Cross Foretold	348
The Transfiguration	353
The Epileptic Cured	359
The Perean Ministry	384
The Tribulation	469
The Ten Virgins	476
The Judgment	476
The Separation	487
The Last Supper	497
The Trial of Jesus	511
The Crucifixion of Jesus	536
The Commission	511

	Page
The Trial before Caiaphas	515
The Trial before the Sanhedrin	515
The Death of Judas	521
Triumphal Entry into Jerusalem	409
Two Blind Men Healed at Jericho	406
Two Agreeing	378

U

Unclean Spirit	278
Upon This Rock	345

V

Various Estimates of Jesus	342
Veil of the Temple	545
Virgin Birth	30
Voice Out of Heaven	92

W

	Page
Walking on the Water	314
Warning against Giving Offense	366
What Shall We Receive	395
What Think Ye	420
When the Son of Man Comes	486
Who Is My Mother	282
Wise Men	37
Woe unto Scribes	445
Women Present	547
Woman with Issue of Blood	211

Y

Yoke of Christ	254

Z

Zebedee's Sons	402